TRANSCARCERATION: ESSAYS IN THE SOCIOLOGY OF SOCIAL CONTROL

CAMBRIDGE STUDIES IN CRIMINOLOGY

XX. *Borstal Reassessed*, R. Hood
XXI. *Murder Followed by Suicide*, D. J. West
XXII. *Crime in England and Wales*, F. H. McClintock and N. H. Avison
XXIII. *Delinquency in Girls*, J. Cowie, V. Cowie and E. Slater
XXIV. *The Police: A Study in Manpower*, J. Martin and Gail Wilson
XXV. *Present Conduct and Future Delinquency*, D. J. West
XXVI. *Crime, Law and the Scholars*, G. O. Mueller
XXVII. *Principles of Sentencing*, D. A. Thomas
XXVIII. *The Social Consequences of Conviction*, J. Martin and D. Webster
XXIX. *Suspended Sentence*, M. Ancel
XXX. *Local Prisons: The Crisis in the English Penal System*, R. F. Sparks
XXXI. *Sentencing the Motoring Offender*, R. Hood
XXXII. *Criminals Coming of Age*, A. E. Bottoms and F. H. McClintock
XXXIII. *Drivers After Sentence*, T. C. Willett
XXXIV. *Who Becomes Delinquent?* D. J. West and D. P. Farrington
XXV. *The Delinquent Way of Life*, D.J. West and D.P. Farrington
XXXVII. *The Social Organization of Juvenile Justice*, Aaron Cicourel
XXXVIII. *Alibi*, R. N. Gooderson
XXXIX. *Juvenile Justice?* A. Morris and M. McIsaac
XL. *Understanding Sexual Attacks*, D. J. West, C. Roy, F. L. Nichols
XLI. *Prisons Past and Future*, John Freeman (ed.)
XLII. *Community Service Orders*, Warren Young
XLIII. *Solicitors and the Wider Community*, David Podmore
XLIV. *The Phantom Capitalists: The Organization and Control of Long-Term Fraud*, Michael Levi
XLV. *The Control of Commercial Fraud*, L. H. Leigh
XLVI. *Crime, Justice and Underdevelopment*, Colin Sumner (ed.)
XLVII. *Dangerousness and Criminal Justice*, Jean Floud and Warren Young
XLVIII. *The Home Office 1848–1914: From Clerks to Bureaucrats*, Jill Pellew
XLIX. *Burglary in a Dwelling*, Mike Maguire and Trevor Bennett
L. *Delinquency: Its Roots, Careers and Prospects*, D. J. West
LI. *Consumerist Criminology*, Leslie T. Wilkins
LIII. *Victims in the Criminal Justice System*, Joanna Shapland, Jon Willmore and Peter Duff
LIV. *A Guide to United Nations Criminal Policy* Manuel López-Rey
LV. *Transcarceration: Essays in the Sociology of Social Control* John Lowman, Robert J. Menzies and T.S. Palys (eds)

Transcarceration: Essays in the Sociology of Social Control

John Lowman
Robert J. Menzies
T.S. Palys

Series Editor: A.E. Bottoms

Gower

Aldershot · Brookfield USA · Hong Kong · Singapore · Sydney

Published by
Gower Publishing Company Limited
Gower House
Croft Road
Aldershot
Hants GU11 3HR
England

Gower Publishing Company
Old Post Road
Brookfield
Vermont 05036
USA

British Library Cataloguing in Publication Data

Transcarceration: essays in the sociology
of social control. — (Cambridge studies
in criminology; 55).
1. Social control 2. Deviant behaviour
I. Lowman, John II. Menzies, Robert J.
III. Palys, T.S. IV. Series
302.5'42 HM73

Library of Congress Cataloging-in-Publication Data

Transcarceration: essays in the sociology of social
control.

(Cambridge studies in criminology; 55)
Bibliography: p.
Includes index.
1. Social control — Congresses. 2. Corrections — Congresses. 3. Criminal justice, Administration of — Congresses. I. Lowman, John, 1950- . II. Menzies Robert J., 1951- . III. Palys, T.S., 1951-
IV. Series.
HM291.T69 1987 303.3'3 87-7523

ISBN 0 566 05106 0

Printed in Great Britain at the University Press, Cambridge

Contents

PART III: TRANSINSTITUTIONALIZATION AND THE CARCERAL NETWORK

PART IV: DECARCERATION, DECENTRALIZATION, AND THE FUTURE OF CONTROL SYSTEMS

Tables

Figures

Acknowledgments

This book emerged from a symposium held by the School of Criminology, Simon Fraser University in April 1984. As is typical of such a production, there have been many players, both onstage and behind the scenes. We would like to thank the Social Sciences and Humanities Research Council of Canada (and especially Josée Bellehumeur, Programme Officer), and the Symposium and Publications Grants Committees at Simon Fraser University for providing grants in support of both the original symposium and the current anthology. Simon N. Verdun-Jones, Director of the School of Criminology, merits special mention for providing the kind of environment in which a project of this size could be comfortably brought to completion. We also thank the members of the Criminology Research Centre at SFU, and in particular William Glackman for his wise counsel and cybernetic know-how, Alison Hatch for her technical advice along the way, and Joyce Palmer for putting together most of our tables at such short notice. Our colleagues in the School of Criminology, too numerous to list by name here, have been of immeasurable help in countless ways. Alice Dykstra devoted endless hours to tracking down obscure references. The Simon Fraser University Instructional Media Centre was responsible for drawing the figures reproduced in this book. We especially want to thank Laura Fraser for her editorial skills, and for her tenacity and indulgence in typing some 600 pages of manuscript onto computer disk. In addition, Gloria Baker-Brown compiled the subject index, and Donna Robertson assisted in the construction of the name index. Anthony E. Bottoms of the Institute of Criminology at the University of Cambridge, John Irwin, Jane Anthony and Jeanette Gilbert of Gower Press have been central figures in the production of this book. We are particularly grateful for the talents and patience that they displayed in marshalling the volume through to completion. Finally, we acknowledge the kind co-operation of Christina E. Blake of Rutgers University Press, Stella Welford of basil Blackwell, and Nina Stettner of Sage Publications, Inc. in furnishing us with permission to reprint materials originally published elsewhere.

About the editors and contributors

Susan M. Addario is a Research Associate in the Centre of Criminology, University of Toronto. She has written primarily in the area of dangerous offender legislation and private policing. Among her publications is *Constructing Dangerousness: Scientific, Legal and Policy Implications* (with Christopher D. Webster and Bernard Dickens). She is currently working on a study of self regulation within a North American stock exchange, with Clifford Shearing and Philip Stenning.

Thomas G. Blomberg received his doctorate in Criminology from the University of California at Berkeley, and is currently Professor of Criminology at Florida State University. His research interests include the development and control of coercive justice institutions. In addition to articles in professional journals and chapters contributed, he is co-editor or author of *Courts and Diversion* (1979), and *Juvenile Court and Community Corrections* (1984). His current research involves a study of the implementation and outcomes of various home confinement practices across the United States.

Stanley Cohen has been Professor of Criminology at the Hebrew University, Jerusalem since 1980. Previously he taught in the Departments of Sociology at the Universities of Durham and Essex, England. Among his books are: *Folk Devils and Moral Panics* (1972), *Psychological Survival* (with L. Taylor) (1972), and *The Manufacture of News* (1973). Most recently he has edited (with Andrew Scull) *Social Control and the State* (1984) and written *Visions of Social Control: Crime, Punishment and Classification* (1985).

Nanette J. Davis is a Professor of Sociology at Portland State University, Portland, Oregon. She has published in the area of deviance and social control, including *Sociological Constructions of Deviance, Women and Deviance; Social Control: The Production of Deviance in the Modern State* (with Bo Anderson); and *From Crime to Choice: The Transformation of Abortion in America*. She is currently working on *Social Control of Deviance: A Critical Perspective* (Random House). Other publications include journal articles and book chapters that explore the changing nature of social control over women.

Karlene Faith received degrees from the University of California in Anthropology and History of Consciousness, with a focus on minority groups and criminal justice. She has developed curricula and taught in a number of disciplines on California campuses, and also administered women's studies and prison education programmes. Among her publications is *Soledad Prison: University of the Poor* (1975) of which she was editor. Since 1982 Dr Faith has been the Distance Education Co-ordinator for the School of Criminology at Simon Fraser University.

Stuart Henry is a Visiting Associate Professor in the Department of Sociology at Eastern Michigan University. He undertook his doctoral work at the University of Kent at Canterbury before joining London University's Addiction Research Unit to study self-help and mutual aid groups. While teaching at Middlesex and Trent Polytechnics, and at Old Dominion University he undertook research into a range of non-state social control institutions. Dr Henry co-authored *Self-help and Health* (1977), edited *Informal Institutions* (1981), and authored *The Hidden Economy* (1978) and *Private Justice* (1983).

John Lowman is an Associate Professor of Criminology in the School of Criminology at Simon Fraser University. He received a BA from the University of Sheffield, an MA from York University (Ontario), and a PhD from the University of British Columbia. He has published articles on prisons, prostitution, prostitution law, and the geography of social control. He is co-editor (with M.A. Jackson, T.S. Palys and S.A.M. Gavigan) of *Regulating Sex: An Anthology of Commentaries on the Findings and Recommendations of the Badgley and Fraser Reports* (1986), and is writing a book on prostitution.

Gary T. Marx is a Professor of Sociology in the Urban Studies and Political Science Departments at the Massachusetts Institute of Technology. He received his PhD from the University of California at Berkeley. Dr Marx is the author of *Protest and Prejudice* and *Undercover Police: The Paradoxes and Problems of a Necessary Evil*, and editor of *Racial Conflict*, *Muckraking Society* and other books. He is currently engaged in research on types of interdependence between rule-breakers and rule-enforcers, and is collaborating in research with Nancy Reichman on new forms of surveillance.

Thomas Mathiesen was born in 1933. He holds a BA in Sociology from the University of Wisconsin (1955), an MA in Sociology from the University of Oslo (1958), and a PhD from the University of Oslo (1965). Dr Mathiesen has been a Professor of Sociology of Law at the University of Oslo since 1972. He has written four books in the English language, among them *The Defences of the Weak* (1965), *The Politics of Abolition* (1974), and *Law, Society and Political Action* (1980).

Roger Matthews is a Senior Lecturer in Criminology at Middlesex Polytechnic. He received his doctorate from Essex University in 1984 and is currently engaged in research on penal policy and the regulation of prostitution. He is the co-editor (with Jock Young) of *Confronting Crime* (Sage Publications, 1986).

John L. McMullan is an Associate Professor of Sociology, Saint

Mary's University and Honorary Associate Professor of Sociology, Dalhousie University, Halifax, Canada. He received his doctorate from the London School of Economics. Dr McMullan has published widely on the history of organized crime, and on the political economy of crime and legal control. Among his publications are *The Canting Crew* (Rutgers University Press, 1984), and with R.S. Ratner, *State Control: Criminal Justice Politics in Canada* (University of British Columbia Press, 1987).

Dario Melossi earned a degree in Law from the University of Bologna in 1972 and a PhD in Sociology from the University of California, Santa Barbara in 1986. He is currently Assistant Professor of Sociology at the University of California, Davis, and Researcher on leave from the School of Law at the University of Bologna. He has published widely on critical criminology and the relationship of punishment to political and economic conditions. Dr Melossi, together with Massimo Pavarini, is the author of *The Prison and the Factory* (1977; English edition 1981). Most recently, he has been working on a study in social, political and legal theory entitled *The State of Social Control* (forthcoming, for Polity Press, Cambridge).

Robert J. Menzies received his MA in Criminology and his PhD in Sociology from the University of Toronto. He is currently an Associate Professor of Criminology at Simon Fraser University. He has published widely on the subject of predicting dangerousness, and on the role of clinical professionals in the criminal courts. He is co-author of *Clinical Assessment Before Trial* (Butterworths 1982), and is currently completing a book on the social construction of psychiatric decisions in forensic clinics, entitled *The Survival of the Sanest: Order and Disorder in a Pretrial Forensic Clinic.*

Raymond J Michalowski received his undergraduate degree from Fordham University, and his doctoral degree from Ohio State University. He is currently Professor of Sociology at the University of North Carolina at Charlotte. His research and writing include the areas of criminological theory, social control, vehicular homicide and corporate crime. His most recent works are *Order, Law and Crime* (Random House), and *Radikale Kriminologie* (AJZ Press) edited with Helmut Janssen. He is currently working (with Ronald Kramer) on a book about corporate crime by transnationals.

Joseph P. Morrissey is Director of the Evaluation Research Unit, New York State Office of Mental Health, and Adjunct Professor of Sociology with the State University of New York at Albany. He holds degrees from Holy Cross College (BA), Clark University (MA), and the University of North Carolina at Chapel Hill (PhD). He has published widely on the sociology of mental hospitalization and mental health service delivery, including: *The Enduring Asylum* (1981); *Interorganisa-*

tional Relations: A Sourcebook for Mental Health Programmes (1982); and *Network Analysis Methods for Mental Health Service System Research* (1985).

Ted Palys received his PhD (1979) in Social Psychology from Carleton University in Ottawa, Canada. After a year at the University of British Columbia as a Visiting Professor, he moved across the city to Simon Fraser University, where he is an Associate Professor in the School of Criminology. His academic interests and prior publications are in the areas of epistemology, decision-making, social impacts of computer technology, and pornography. He is co-editor (with J. Lowman, M.A. Jackson and S.A.M. Gavigan) of *Regulating Sex: An Anthology of Commentaries on the Findings and Recommendations of the Badgley and Fraser Reports*, and is currently completing a textbook on research methodology that is tentatively titled *Research Decisions*.

Michael A. Pearson received his graduate and undergraduate training at Florida State University. He is currently Assistant Professor of Sociology at the University of North Carolina at Charlotte. His research interests include the areas of social control, social movements, and race relations. He is co-author with William Gay of *The Nuclear Arms Race* (American Library Association, 1986).

Harold E. Pepinsky is Associate Professor of Forensic Studies and East Asian Languages and Cultures at Indiana University, Bloomington. He holds an AB from the University of Michigan, a JD from Harvard Law School, and a PhD from the University of Pennsylvania. He is the editor of *Rethinking Criminology* (Sage, 1982), author of *Crime and Conflict: A Study of Law and Society* (Academic Press, 1976) and *Crime Control Strategies: An Introduction to the Study of Crime* (Oxford University Press, 1980), and, with Paul Jesilow, co-author of *Myths That Cause Crime* (Seven Locks Press, 1984).

R.S. Ratner is an Associate Professor in the Department of Anthropology and Sociology, University of British Columbia. He holds a BA from Columbia University and a PhD from Yale University. Dr Ratner is the author of numerous articles in the 'critical criminology' genre, and he is co-editor (with John L. McMullan) of the forthcoming *State Control: Criminal Justice Politics in Canada*, University of British Columbia Press. He chairs the Prisoners' Rights Committee of the British Columbia Civil Liberties Association.

Nancy Reichman is an Assistant Professor of Sociology at the University of Denver. She has written several articles on fraud in the insurance industry. Currently she is engaged in research on the interaction among risk, crime, and social control and is collaborating in research with Gary T. Marx on new forms of surveillance.

Andrew Scull, Professor of Sociology at the University of California, San Diego, was educated at Balliol College, Oxford and at Princeton

University. At various times during the past decade, he has held fellowships from the Guggenheim Foundation, the American Council of Learned Societies, and the Shelby Cullon Davis Center for Historical Studies at Princeton University. His books include *Decarceration; Museums of Madness*; *Madhouses, Mad-doctors and Madmen*; *Social Control and the State*; and *Durkheim and the Law*. In addition he has contributed numerous articles and review essays to leading journals in sociology, history, psychiatry, and law.

Clifford D. Shearing is an Associate Professor of Criminology and Sociology at the University of Toronto. He has published widely on the subjects of policing and sociological theory. Among his many publications are *Organizational Police Deviance, Dial-A-Cop: A Study of Police Mobilization*, and (with P.C. Stenning and M.B. Farnell) *Contract Security in Ontario*. Dr Shearing is currently doing a study of self-regulation within a North American Stock Exchange, with Susan Addario and Philip Stenning.

Nigel South is a Research Associate at the Centre for Criminology, Middlesex Polytechnic and Research Sociologist, Institute for the Study of Drug Dependence, London. He has taught in London and New York and has previously written on aspects of private justice, the informal economies, cultural studies and drug-related problems and services, Dr South is the author of a forthcoming study on *Private Security*, and is co-author of *Message in a Bottle* (1983) and *Helping Drug Users* (1985).

Steven Spitzer is Professor and Chairperson of the Department of Sociology at Suffolk University. He received his BA (1965) and MA (1967) from the University of Maryland, and his PhD (1971) from Indiana University. Dr Spitzer has published widely on the subjects of Marxist criminology, the sociology of law, the political economy of policing and control, and historical perspectives on responses to crime. He has been continuing editor and co-editor of *Research in Law, Deviance and Social Control* (formerly *Research in Law and Sociology*), published by Jai Press.

Henry J. Steadman is Director of the Bureau of Planning and Evaluation Research of the New York State Office of Mental Health, and Adjunct Professor of Sociology at the State University of New York (SUNY), Albany. He has published widely on the interface of mental health and criminal justice. His books include: *Beating A Rap? Defendants Found Incompetent to Stand Trial* (1979); *Careers of the Criminally Insane* with Joseph J. Cocozza (1974); and most recently *Mentally Disordered Offenders: Perspectives From Law and Social Science* (1983), co-edited with John Monahan.

Philip C. Stenning is Senior Research Associate and Special Lecturer at the Centre of Criminology, University of Toronto. He has published primarily on policing, prosecution, firearms control, and criminal law topics. Among his many publications are *Police Commissions and Boards in Canada*, *Legal Status of the Police*, *Appearing for the Crown*, and (with C.D. Shearing and M.B. Farnell) *Contract Security in Ontario*. Dr Stenning is currently doing a study of self-regulation within a North American Stock Exchange, with Susan Addario and Clifford Shearing.

Robert P. Weiss, Associate Professor of Sociology at the State University of New York at Plattsburgh, has also served on the faculties of the University of Minnesota, Twin Cities, and the University of Houston-Clear Lake. His research interests have centred on criminal behaviours and their control, especially as these relate to social structural change. He has published on the topics of radical criminology, community crime prevention, the development of the private detective agency in the United States, and on the theoretical literature relating to the development of the penal sanction.

Foreword

Eavesdrop on any conference of mental health professionals: the chances are that you will hear much talk of 'community mental health services' and the like. Eavesdrop on any conference of probation officers, or social workers involved with juvenile justice: the chances are that you will hear much talk of 'alternatives to custody', 'diversion strategies' and the like.

These — and related ideas — seem to be some of the major themes of the social control systems of Western industrialized states in the second half of the twentieth century. But how are we to understand them properly? And are we to welcome them, or not? Scholars from varying disciplines, and with different primary interests, have struggled in recent years to answer these questions — and to clarify the many prior questions that have to be confronted before these major questions can be properly addressed. *Transcarceration* includes essays from some of the major contributors to these debates; but it is certainly not just a re-heating of an old and tired dish. The editors have sought contributions which will take the debates forward, and have set them in an organizing framework designed to enhance clarity in what can often be a very confusing field. The volume as a whole is also, and rightly, committed to trying to make sense of the issues it addresses within an overall social framework, rather than from narrow or technicist perspectives. I am confident that *Transcarceration* will become compulsory reading for all who are concerned to understand the nature of the social control exercised over 'problem' populations in modern societies.

It is gratifying that with this volume the *Cambridge Studies in Criminology* series is able to continue the tradition, begun by Sir Leon Radzinowicz, of being international in its scope; and I am particularly pleased that we have been able to forge a link, through the editors, with one of the major centres of Canadian criminological scholarship.

Anthony E. Bottoms

Introduction: transcarceration and the modern state of penality

John Lowman
Robert J. Menzies
T. S. Palys

> Imagine that the entrance to the deviancy control system is something like a gigantic fishing net. Strange and complex in its appearance and movements, the net is cast by an army of different fishermen and fisherwomen working all day and even into the night according to more or less known rules and routines, subject to more or less authority and control from above, knowing more or less what the other is doing. Society is the ocean — vast, troubled and full of uncharted currents, rocks and other hazards. Deviants are the fish.
>
> Stanley Cohen. *Visions of Social Control* 1985a

Each year the School of Criminology at Simon Fraser University sponsors a symposium on Contemporary Issues in Criminology. The two day symposium held in April 1984 focused on theoretical perspectives regarding the proliferation of non-segregative methods of controlling the 'mad and the bad', and other 'problem' populations in contemporary capitalist societies. Our main concern was with the 'decentralization of social control' taking shape through diversion, decarceration, delegalization and deinstitutionalization — the principal signifiers of the 'control talk' (cf. Cohen 1983, 1985a) of neoprogressivism — and through the accelerating privatization of control institutions accompanying these changes. It was from the 1984 symposium that this current anthology emerged.

In collecting essays for the book our main concern was with 'revisionist' perspectives on social control — that is, those which resist analysis of treatment, punishment and reform in their own terms, preferring instead to situate them in a wider social analysis. In what follows we bring together some of the diverse theoretical perspectives and substantive interests characteristic of the revisionist literature.

Before describing the contents of the book, its main terms of reference require some clarification.

Revisionist perspectives on social control

Historically, the study of 'social control' has been trapped within disciplinary boundaries. Isolated systems of discourse (such as psychiatry and penology) have developed around what have been treated as closed or effectively discrete systems of control. This hypostatization of control institutions, while consolidating the relationship between power and knowledge within each component (both in theory and practice) has stifled the development of a critical perspective on control as a holistic phenomenon. As systems have become increasingly intertwined, merging in complex patterns of power allocation, resource deployment and mutual accommodation, the inadequacy of traditional analytic categories has become all the more obvious. The recognition of these problems has resulted in a series of fundamental reformulations of theory about social control and reform practices. This in turn has led to a synthesis of the analytic objects of what were formerly disparate enterprises. Thinking about control, like control itself, is undergoing a process of organizational realignment, a deinstitutionalization of another kind. Liberated from the confines of traditional analyses there is a sense of a new unity — and a new terrain of debate. A number of dominant themes have emerged that reflexively lend a sense of commonality to the revisionist literature, as they dissolve traditional categories, demarcate new disputes, construct new boundaries and forge new alliances. The essays in this book reflect efforts to locate, clarify, qualify, and evaluate the impact of these trends.

In the comments that follow we elaborate several issues that are particularly germane to the contemporary sociology of control. We begin by looking briefly at the evolution of the social control concept itself. The shifting conceptual frontiers between social control and coercive control are discussed, along with varying perspectives on control patterns as depicted in the prevailing literature. We then note the difficulties involved in formulating a distinction between public and private realms, given the blurring of system boundaries associated with what we subsequently term 'transcarceration'. Next, we invoke the work of Foucault and Cohen to counter the tendency to view recent carceral trends as singular or unidimensional phenomena. Specifically, we argue that what has been described recently as 'decarceration' is but a moment of the oscillation between inclusive and exclusive modes of social control; a transcarceral model of control is powered by an alternating rather than a direct current. Finally, we articulate this model of transcarceration, a perspective which captures the holistic and diffused character of state power over dependants and deviants, and its permeation through the regulatory systems of civil society.

The spectral qualities of 'social control'

Traditionally, a distinction has been wrought in sociological theory between 'social control' and 'coercive control' (Janowitz 1975; Meier

1982; Melossi this volume). This distinction, although heuristically attractive, has tended to ossify theory, making it difficult to transcend institutional and temporal boundaries. Consequently, the social component of coercive control has been minimized, just as the coercive component of social control has been largely extinguished from the analysis. More generally, the compartmentalization of the control concept has perpetrated an array of dualisms, conjuring up problematic dichotomies between control mechanisms that are formal and informal, institutionalized and non-institutionalized, non-familial and familial, state and civil, public and private. In its turn, the revisionist literature has also resorted to dualistic conceptual formations. Either its focus on social structures and institutional control mechanisms thoroughly diminishes the power of human agency, or that power is inflated to a point where it floats clear of structural constraint.

In its earliest incarnations (Bentley 1908; Mead 1925, 1934; Park and Burgess 1969; originally 1921; Ross 1901; Thomas and Znaniecki 1927) social control was virtually synonymous with socialization; it was conceptualized as operating at the level of face-to-face interaction (or, less frequently, between individuals and formal institutions). The objectives of control were not problematized. Conflict over norms was not recognized, and political and economic factors were largely ignored. The consummate desirability and benevolence of 'social' control were rarely questioned. The state hardly entered the analysis at all.

In its modern rendition, the coercive element of the control concept has come to predominate. The micro-level of analysis has developed primarily in the sociology of deviance, the macro-level in the sociology of law. The analysis of coercive control, confined to a legalistic discourse and method, has converged around the operation of the state. Sociologists of legal (coercive) control have concentrated on grand theories involving political economy, ideology, formal doctrine, and the impact of over-arching power structures that are variously defined by gender and race (see Davis and Faith, this volume; Michalowski and Pearson, this volume). The emergent processes of dispute settlement, interaction between rule-breakers and rule-enforcers, and informal and localized control processes were left to labelling-theorists, ethnographers, and others rooted in an intersubjective rather than structural level of analysis. The study of non-state regulatory systems, particularly what Henry (1983; see also this volume) has termed 'private justice', are only recently being conceived as authentic objects of a social control analysis.

Given this cacophony of meaning, we are left with what Cohen (1985a) has aptly characterized as a 'Mickey Mouse' concept. Social control has indeed become a 'key that unlocks many doors' (Ross, in Janowitz 1975, p. 89), although not in the sense envisioned by its early exponents. Now it is a skeleton key, opening so many doors that its analytic power has been drained. We are left with a spectral category, which eludes integration, and like Foucault's analysis of power, becomes all things to all theorists.

In adopting the constantly shifting concept of 'social control' as our main reference point, it is to its most recent sociological incarnation that we turn. Cohen's (1985a) definition succinctly describes the sense in which we use the term, in contrast to earlier meanings anchored to an amorphous concept of socialization and social order (cf. Janowitz 1975; Meier 1982). Noting the move away from both the classic definition of social control as the central problem of sociology and from the much more restricted terrain of crime control in institutional criminology, Cohen defines his object as those:

> ... organized responses to crime, deviance and allied forms of deviant and/or socially problematic behaviour which are actually conceived of as such, whether in the reactive sense (after the putative act has taken place or the actor been identified) or in the proactive sense (to prevent the act). These responses may be sponsored directly by the state or by more autonomous professional agents in, say, social work and psychiatry. Their goals may be as specific as individual punishment and treatment or as diffuse as 'crime prevention', 'public safety' and 'community mental health'. (1985, p. 3)

We explicitly include under the ambit of social control what Henry (1983; see also this volume) has designated as 'private justice' — the non-state institutions for dispensing justice that arise in a variety of organizations and contexts, particularly the workplace, and operate semi-autonomously from the state.

Our particular use of the social control concept in this anthology is strategic. Noting the irreconcilable nature of competing claims about the meaning of social control, we have chosen to circumvent arguments that defy resolution because they concern matters of convention as much as they do understanding. The revisionist conceptualization of social control is ushered in to serve the development of an anti-criminology that recognizes the interrelatedness of different formal control institutions, and their links to informal control systems both within and outside the state. This approach denies the exclusivity of the traditional subject matter of criminology, namely crime and its control. It also incorporates an anti-penology by locating the transformation and operation of control institutions in the mode of production and/or in the 'mode of information' (cf. Poster's (1984) discussion of Marx and Foucault) prevailing in contemporary capitalist societies, rather than in the inner workings of the penal system itself. In following the logic of a socioanalysis of penality (cf. Garland 1985; Garland and Young 1983) we have organized this collection of essays around the problematics of the various revisionist histories and theories of social control that were stimulated by Rothman's (1971) *Discovery of the Asylum* and by the rediscovery of Rusche and Kirchheimer's (1939) seminal work on *Punishment and Social Structure*.

Six main explanatory themes have been developed (singularly or in combination) in revisionist accounts of changes in institutional modes of social control. These can be categorized roughly as follows:

1. The tendency for institutional imperatives and contingencies (convenience) to overpower the immediate benevolent intentions (conscience) of reformers (Rothman 1971, 1980);
2. The role of economic contingencies in determining the reform activities of the state (Scull 1977);
3. The reproduction of class relations through systems of penality (Ignatieff 1978; Melossi and Pavarini 1981);
4. The microphysics of power generated by the ascendancy of discipline and surveillance as the primary 'economy' of power (Foucault 1977);
5. The role of language and classification as they mediate political, economic and institutional theories and practices (Cohen 1979, 1983, 1985a; Foucault 1973, 1977, 1981);
6. Strategies of control in the 'penal-welfare' complex (Garland 1985).

These different accounts of reform are manifested in a variety of combinations and permutations in the contributions to this book.

State and civil society: the blurring of boundaries

It is obvious that a theory of the state must be central to any analysis of social control in twentieth century capitalist societies (cf. Cohen and Scull 1983), since the state has assumed direct responsibility for supporting the institutions of control (both in facilitating direct control of 'dangerous populations', and in helping to reconstruct the legitimacy of the system). A substantial component of the revisionist social control literature has been concerned with the mechanisms by which the state appears to be divesting itself of this responsibility.

A fiscal crisis of the state has been said to arise because of the increased socialization of the costs of reproducing capital to the point where the state has to spend more money than it can accrue in order to maintain the status quo (O'Connor 1973). Scull (1977) has selectively adapted this analysis (cf. Lowman and Menzies 1986) to suggest that decontrol (in the form of decarceration of mental patients and, perhaps, criminals) ultimately took hold in response to financial exigency — not for the humanitarian reasons that apparently fuelled reform. For Scull decarceration is tantamount to destatization.

Although the need for an analysis of the state seems clear, the developing literature on decentralization highlights many of the theoretical difficulties in formulating definitions of the state. The public and private sectors of control are recurrently treated as discrete mechanisms with independent dynamics and insulated structures. The traditional dichotomy between state and civil society is problematic, particularly in reference to the manufacture, management and manipulation of deviance. Criminologists have been especially prone to the characterization of the state as a unidimensional Leviathan which is either:

1. Unreflexively under the ambit of the political economy and its agents (the 'instrumentalist' tendency); or
2. Invulnerable, immutable and impervious to the efforts (good or bad) of human agency and intention.

In either case there is no allowance for flexible boundaries, historical specificity or dialectical relationships among institutions within and outside the state. More to the point, the demarcation of 'within' and 'outside' — given the complex structure of the modern state — is increasingly problematic.

These definitional issues have wide-ranging implications for students of social control. For example, writings on 'privatization' may falsely imply that a line can be sketched out on an institutional map, across which deviants are being transferred from 'state-run' to 'privately-run' organizations. This ignores the probability that the 'private' agents of control are either directly or indirectly supported by the public sector. It is theoretically fruitless for theories of control to attempt a rigid demarcation of these two domains of authority. In the concrete, everyday reality of law and control, the state can be located and monitored only through its association with civil society, and vice versa. The sociologically interesting problem is to investigate the dialectics, as well as the dichotomies, of this relationship, a theme taken up by several authors in this volume (see, particularly, Addario, Stenning and Shearing; Henry; Spitzer;[1] and Weiss).

Another perspective on this issue would be to consider how, during periods of adjustment in the exercise and legitimation of control, institutional agents mutually align themselves to maximize power. How do we transcend simplistic distinctions between 'public' and 'private' to isolate factors more directly associated with the expansion and contraction of social control? How can we come to grips with this dialectical notion of a reflexive 'civil state' without succumbing to equally facile interpretations of an omnipresent, omniscient 'total state' that has no limits and no vulnerability to reform or change?

Inclusion and exclusion

In retrospect, the concept of decentralization which we used to define the theme of the 1984 symposium missed the contradictory relationship between political economy and institutions of care and control. As Cohen (1984) suggests, just as inclusionary and exclusionary modes of social control develop simultaneously, the decentralization of control from one sector of the state may be accompanied by centralization in another. With the emergence of strong 'law and order' ideologies, centralized control institutions have in fact been revitalized during the past five to ten years. Images of deviants being dispersed into the community by the centrifugal forces of deinstitutionalization may have been appropriate for describing criminal justice and mental health trends in the 1960s, but inaccurate when it comes to the situation in the 1980s.

Contemporary observers of penology, welfare and mental health need to contend with countervailing forces that pull delinquents, dependants and dollars towards the segregative nuclei of these institutions. Mechanistic analysis might have had some relevance for the initial development of community mental health policies almost three decades ago. But within the present domain of public and private talk about retribution, 'response-ability', public safety and fear of crime, it is increasingly apparent that 'total institutions' complement the economic policies adopted by conservative governments of the 1980s. In this respect it is informative to see the kind of reformulation and respecification of the fiscal crisis thesis by Scull — in the second edition of *Decarceration* (the Afterword of which is reprinted in this volume) — which takes into account exactly these kinds of concerns. Ultimately, he concedes that criminal justice and mental health cannot be treated as unitary phenomena. It now seems clear, particularly in jurisdictions governed by neo-conservative parties, that moral conservatism (arguing for increased containment and surveillance of deviant populations) will take precedence over fiscal conservatism (stressing the transfer of control responsibility into private and quasi-private hands), although both trends are likely to occur simultaneously (depending on the kind of deviant population with which one is concerned). Two interesting possibilities flow from this observation.

First, it has been argued (Austin and Krisberg 1981; Blomberg 1977a; Cohen 1979, 1985a; Lerman 1982; Matthews 1979) that fiscal crisis, against the historically specific context of parallel 'community' institutions of corrections, health and welfare, has paradoxically contributed to the expansion of the state control apparatus. That is, economic recession will be experienced most acutely in the domain of private justice, local agencies, community programmes, liaison groups, half-way houses and so on. To accommodate these depletions in the external over-arching institutions, the original nucleus of the system (hospitals and prisons) may undergo a period of re-growth, resulting in even higher populations of prisons (and eventually hospitals), more prison construction, and increases in selective state funding. The rapid acceleration of incarceration has already been well documented in North America, a theme taken up in this volume by Ratner in his paper on the use of 'Mandatory Supervision' (a form of parole) in Canada, and by Michalowski and Pearson in their chapter on correctional trends at the state level in the United States.

Second, as centripetal forces occur within and across systems, agencies of community corrections, community welfare and community mental health might very well wither away during the coming decade. The tension, competition and contradiction between the total institution and desegregative policy never disappeared, even during the liberal reformist periods of the sixties and seventies (when advocates of diversion, decarceration and community treatment were committed to individualized response and predictive restraint). Today we are cynical enough to reject claims that those deviants on the outside are any more or less threatening or 'treatable' or vulnerable than those on the inside. The left and the right have semi-consciously embarked on the road to a similar crusade against community treatment and corrections. Critical criminologists have recognized that 'privatized' and 'decarcerated' agencies have simply extended the power and scope of state vigilance, and relaxed the requirements of operating according to a model of due process. Neo-conservatives have responded to deinstitutionalized populations as a 'colony of welfare bums' who should either be cut loose to prey on each other, or returned to prisons *en masse* (through stricter sentencing policies) and hospitals (via deregulation of commitment procedures).

We are left, then, with a paradox that permeates analysis of these developments. First, be it through unanticipated (and unintended) consequences, the inviolability of pre-existing structures, the 'dark conspiracies of malevolent state puppeteers', or the ineptness of 'benevolent reformist puppets', liberal policies of decentralization, privatization and decarceration have ironically contributed to the power of state control in the past two decades. Second, the response to this outward expansion, coupled with the 'new' fiscal crisis of the 1980s, results in a consolidation and intensive (rather than extensive) proliferation of the state control apparatus. Even as health/education/welfare spending is evaporating on a variety of fronts, right-wing law-and-order ideology has guaranteed that prisons will be insulated, to a certain extent, from these fiscal assaults (although fiscal considerations are already producing extreme prison overcrowding in the US and Canada). While the metaphors for growth in the 1960s and

1970s were 'thinner meshes and wider nets', the current decade is witnessing a return to dense, crude, confining modes of control and prevention. Community programmes will be tolerated by fiscal gate-keepers only to the extent that they contribute in overt ways to the defusing of 'social dynamite' and to the dispersal of 'social junk' (cf. Spitzer 1975). The prison is still the centrepiece around which the punitive system is tightly arranged.

A transcarceral model of control

One of the main themes of the literature emerging out of revisionist histories of 'total institutions', particularly in describing neoprogressive reform (such as 'community corrections'), has built on Foucault's argument that discipline and surveillance create a more extensive form of power (a 'carceral archipelago') in which the power to punish is inserted more deeply and more certainly into the social fabric. The advent of community corrections and other non-segregative techniques of control has resulted in more control, not less, as the control net is widened and its mesh thinned (Cohen 1979, 1985a).

Our interest is in the development of a transcarceral model of social control (Lowman and Menzies 1986; Menzies 1985). We are dealing with a peno-juridical, mental health, welfare and tutelage complex (cf. Donzelot 1979), in which power structures can be examined only by appreciating cross-institutional arrangements and dynamics. Thus 'privatization', 'decontrol', 'deinstitutionalization', 'decentralization' and so on, have consequences for security, courts, corrections, probation, parole, welfare and mental health. For delinquents, deviants and dependants, this means that their careers are likely to be characterized by institutional mobility, as they are pushed from one section of the help-control complex to another. For control agents, this means that 'control' will essentially have no locus and the control mandate will increasingly entail the 'fitting together' of subsystems rather than the consolidation of one agency in isolation from its alternatives.

It is not simply in institutional terms that the impact of changing control strategies must be conceptualized. While the circulation of clients among institutions has led to an interest in the phenomenon of 'transinstitutionalization', such a characterization can only offer a partial understanding of the modern education-health-welfare-criminal-justice complex. It confines the understanding of control strategies to their institutional expression. It fails to acknowledge the versatility of control as its objects and points of application proliferate. In contrast, a transcarceral model captures the many realities of control as experienced by its practitioners and targets, throughout the various domains of its exercise. Within such a conceptual schema, control comprises and infiltrates many levels of discourse, and many arenas of action. It defies simple encapsulation in the rigid dichotomies of traditional analysis. As a fully reflexive social force it simultaneously serves and constitutes many interests. It is both coercive and benevolent, an instrument of the state and a weapon of resistance, an ideological medium and a counter-hegemonic force. And it is often an end in itself.

At a pragmatic level one of the most significant problems confronting research on the transcarceral system involves tracing the paths of 'conscript clienteles' (cf. Friedenberg 1977) across institutional boundaries (cf. Steadman and Morrissey, this volume), and beyond them. In addition to the institutional careers of deviants, we need to trace the impact of control strategies on the fabric of community life. The emergence of the transcarceral system has been augmented by the consolidation of ghettos of neglect. Often decarceration has amounted to little more than benign abandonment through the dumping of politically powerless people out of the system (but only those not perceived as threatening), as in the case of the decarcerated mental hospital patients described by Scull (1977), so that it is merely the 'packaging of their misery' that is transformed.

The irony of control through what appears to be the 'natural' process of urban development is the mutual energization of permissiveness and control in certain segregated areas (cf. Greenwood and Young 1980). The immediate convenience of this strategy, especially when fiscal crisis and law-and-order politics coincide, lies in the channelling of visible deviance into reservoirs of permissiveness lying outside traditional state institutions. Their existence allows the regulation of deviant populations both within and without the state. The tragedy of this strategy is that deviance is turned upon itself. At the periphery of the transcarceral system 'deviants' are left with few options other than mutual predation such that predation and victimization become interchangeable.

There is a double contradiction in this strategy. First, its promise of divestment, redistribution and decontrol has actually led to the *extension* of state power and the *over*production of deviance. Second, the abrogation of state responsibility, through the transfer of jurisdiction over problem populations into civil society, promises to accentuate the very problems that it was designed to resolve. Instead of providing resolution, civil institutions respond according to their own exigencies and alternative justifications for action, and ultimately these entail the replacement of subject populations back into the state apparatus. When state programmes and civil alternatives are seen to fail by all participants, there emerges an altogether different control strategy based upon classification and containment instead of detection and suppression. The transcarceral system takes hold. Momentum increases as cycles of control accelerate. Original objectives are lost. The soft machine is in perpetual motion.

In other cases it may be the packaging of social control practices that changes as new professions find their vocational *raison d'être* (and private or personal profit) in 'servicing' the mad, the bad and the disabled. In any event, it is not sufficient to restrict one's inquiry to criminal justice, or juvenile justice, or to mental health or to social welfare. Increasingly, the analysis of deviance and control must take into account the flexibility and fluidity of deviant designations, and the tendency of institutions to undergo constant realignment according to the particular social physics and exigencies of the moment.

The essays presented in this anthology represent the many perspectives brought to bear on the institutions, practices and experiences of transcarceral control. Six interrelated themes appear in various guises throughout the book. In concert, they provide the theoretical framework around which the anthology and, to a greater or lesser degree, the individual chapters are organized. These comprise:

1. The nature of the social control concept itself;
2. The relations between what Cohen (1985a) has termed *inclusive* and *exclusive* forms of control and punishment, and their varying manifestations in different social formations;
3. Investigations into the principles and operation of panoptic power, as manifested in the proliferation of information, surveillance and security systems;
4. Understanding the power of language and the language of power in practical and theoretical social control discourses;
5. Theoretical perspectives on neoprogressivism which attempt to explain why reforms ostensibly designed to reduce control had the diametrically opposite effect, namely the extension of control systems;
6. The singular nature of, and the relations among, the different institutions — police, judiciary, corrections, juvenile justice, psychiatry, welfare, the family, private justice, and other agencies in state and civil society — that together constitute the transcarceral system.

Organization of the anthology

The anthology is organized into four sections, although they should not be construed as mutually exclusive in either their theoretical orientation or their substantive focus. What follows is a brief outline of the book (detailed synopses of each chapter are provided in the introductions to the four sections).

Part I, 'Social control, social justice and the state', includes five essays examining issues in the definition and application of the social control concept. Melossi examines the history of the construct and proposes a theory of law and social control based on an analysis of collective action as articulated through specific vocabularies of motives. Spitzer discusses the commodification of security in contemporary capitalist societies. By examining various political, economic and ideological factors, he explores the utility of Marx's analysis of the fetishism of commodities for understanding the commodification of security, and suggests a number of other more productive directions for analysing security in capitalist social formations, particularly in terms of the consumption of security as a commodity. This leads to a general critique of the tendency of the revisionist literature to locate social control mainly, or only, in the institutions of the state, a development, Spitzer concludes, which tends to underestimate the role of the market in the operation of social control in most capitalist societies.

Mathiesen's essay also problematizes certain aspects of the revisionist literature, in this case Foucault's claim that a fundamental transformation of society occurred in the nineteenth century as a result of the ascendance of panoptic power. Arguing that the surveillance principle is an ancient form of power, Mathiesen challenges Foucault's reading of history. He also examines the importance of linking the analysis of power with an analysis of mass media, arguing that the political struggle against modern surveillance systems must be directed toward the creation of alternative communication networks. Pepinsky takes up a similar theme by redefining social justice as 'information sharing' and sketches out the dimensions of a model of social control designed to radically democratize decision-making processes.

Henry's paper takes up altogether different issues by examining the relations between state law and what he defines as 'private justice' (that is, institutions of social control in organizations and groups located outside the state). The main purpose of the paper is to show how private justice exists in a semi-autonomous relationship to the state.

Part II, 'Security, surveillance, and the expansion of state power', comprises five essays which discuss various manifestations and techniques of social control in both past and present Western societies.

McMullan's paper deals with state power and the decentralized character of social control mechanisms in sixteenth- and seventeenth-century London. This excerpt from his book, *The Canting Crew* (1984), serves as an important palliative to the tendency to perceive the decentralization of control as a modern phenomenon. South's chapter, on the security and surveillance of the physical environment, serves as an important reminder that manipulation of the environment has always served as an important medium of social control. Crime prevention through environmental design is merely a new name for a very old strategy.

The essays by Addario, Shearing and Stenning, and Davis and Faith, share a common interest in problematizing instrumentalist interpretations of the state's regulatory activity, showing instead that the state is an important site of struggle. Addario, Shearing and Stenning examine the state's role in setting evidentiary boundaries in the resolution of disputes between employers and unions. Davis and Faith, in examining recent transformations in gender control, document the persistence of patriarchal power throughout the neoprogressive period. But again they reassert the importance of the law as a site of resistance to, as well as a medium of, oppression.

Marx and Reichman (in a paper reprinted from the *American Behavioral Scientist*) discuss one of the most significant aspects of the modern technology of panoptic power, the routinization of the 'discovery of secrets' made possible by the use of computerized information search procedures. Freeing control personnel from their reliance on complainants or informants for information, the computer promises to open up previously inaccessible terrains of surveillance and, in so doing, to consolidate the foundation of power in 'knowledge'.

In Part III of the book, 'Transinstitutionalization and the carceral network', attention turns specifically to the transcarceral system in a series of papers which consider the phenomenon of trans-institutionalization, and various developments in the centrepiece of the control system, the prison itself. Blomberg leads this section off with a discussion of community corrections, diversion programmes and kindred developments that were ostensibly designed to reduce control but actually served to supplement it. His discussion of recent correctional trends, particularly the development of 'home confinement' (that is, domestic imprisonment), leads to a characterization of the US as a 'minimum security society'. Steadman and Morrissey's analysis examines the impact of *de*institutionalization of mental patients on the American criminal justice system. They indicate that *trans*institutionalization is most likely to occur at the 'bottom end' of the correctional system as the marginal mental patient, having committed relatively minor predatory crimes, circulates through county jails and various community programmes. Michalowski and Pearson's analysis focuses on a different aspect of the deinstitutionalization process in America by examining decarceration at the state level. They depict considerable variations in correctional expenditures among states. And although prison populations have risen dramatically in the past fifteen years, they conclude that a *relative* decarceration has occurred. Nevertheless, they find the unilinear fiscal crisis thesis proposed by Scull (1977) difficult to apply to decarceration patterns at the state level. Weiss examines a different trend in American corrections — although again one seemingly prompted by a combination of fiscal and ideological considerations — the privatization of prison industry. He examines the implications of private prison industry for class and labour relations, and discusses the likely ascendancy of the profit motive over the rehabilitative ideal. In the final chapter in this section, Ratner examines the Canadian parole system, particularly the functioning of 'Mandatory Supervision' provisions, and proposals currently under consideration for a legislative overhaul of the system. He indicates that, of its various functions, the most important is the capacity of parole supervision to act as a managerial tool for controlling the size of prison populations in a system that is rapidly surpassing its holding capacity.

Part IV, 'Decarceration, decentralization and the future of control systems', includes three essays reflecting on recent developments in the social control literature. The first, reprinted from the second edition of Scull's book *Decarceration*, is both an autocritique and reassertion of various components of his explanation of decarceration first published in 1977. By way of autocritique he suggests that recent dramatic increases in prison populations indicate that mental hospitals and prisons cannot be treated as an analytically unitary phenomenon. Nevertheless, he maintains that recent patterns of deinstitutionalization of mental patients reassert the integrity of the fiscal crisis explanation proposed in the first edition of *Decarceration*. Matthews, building on an earlier critique of Scull's work (Matthews 1979), offers a general critique of the literature that has developed around the decarceration theme. In particular, he criticizes any attempt to directly 'read off' social control strategies from underlying economic conditions. His ensuing critique is directed at three problematic features of the contemporary social control literature: its globalism, its empiricism, and its impossibilism.

The final paper in the book represents what Cohen refers to as a 'Pilgrim's Progress' through the *destructuring* movements that provided the rationale for the 'decentralization of social control', the central theme of the symposium from which this book originated. Cohen reflects on the development of radical and critical criminologies ('the literature that does not even like to call itself criminology'), and on the growing disenchantment with their idealism and utopianism. Reforms based on the ideal of destructuration did not turn out as they were supposed to — they seemed to feed into the very problems they were intended to address. This disillusionment has spawned a 'new realism' of the left. Cohen's paper provides a discussion of this new realism and outlines what he sees as the price it has to pay in charting a course 'between visionary politics and *realpolitik*'.

More detailed synoposes of essays are provided at the beginning of each of the four Parts of the book.

PART I
SOCIAL CONTROL, SOCIAL JUSTICE AND THE STATE

Introduction

The five essays in Part I generally explore the concepts of social control and social justice as they are imparted through the disciplinary mechanisms of state and civil society. This section is intended to introduce many of the conceptual and pragmatic issues that recurrently surface throughout the book. These chapters provide a framework for describing the current dilemmas confronting sociologists on the subject of social control and justice, as these constructs emerge in the discourse of sociology and in public and private practices of surveillance and containment.

Chapters 1 to 5 raise, and respond to, a number of questions that are intrinsic to revisionist formulations of social control. What is the essence of social control, and how has the concept evolved throughout the changing currents of twentieth century social thought? How can it be incorporated into theorization about contemporary trends in penality and justice? What is its relation to the contemporary 'trade' in security and safety, and what are the implications of widely circulated themes of 'insecurity' for the control culture and market-place? What are the origins of control strategies based on inclusion and exclusion, and how are these connected to mechanisms of panoptic surveillance (where the few watch over the many), and celebrations of power (where the many watch over the few)? Are there alternative prospects for understanding and allocating 'just' forms of control, for example through the reconceptualization of justice as a form of shared knowledge about prospects and potentialities? Finally, what alternative modalities of dispute settlement and control can be secured in private arenas, and what is their impact on, and relation to, the centralized repositories of public law and state justice?

This section begins with an article by Dario Melossi entitled 'The law and the state as practical rhetorics of motives: the case of "decarceration"'. This chapter explores the development of the 'social control' concept throughout the course of this century. Melossi reviews the emergence of a new paradigm for comprehending social control with the advent of American Pragmatism and the Chicago School at the turn of this century. As a framework for understanding the Hobbesian problem of order, legal formalism and individualism had set the individual against society and had placed the state and its legislative products at the centre of theoretical accounts. In contrast, members of the Chicago School, and others in the same tradition, came to 'decentralize' control theory, by applying the idea that state law could not singularly account for conformity or deviance, and that social order was deeply rooted in the fabric of modern society.

Melossi discusses the contributions of Park, Burgess, Mead, Bentley, Dewey and others, as social control developed into a master concept in American social theory. Park and the Chicagoans recognized the discursive character of control, the potential to secure order through refinement of communication, and through the expansion and ventilation of linguistic systems. Mead concentrates on the ability of members to assume the attitudes of others, to commune with the 'generalized other', and to establish a common linguistic competence out of which threads of mutual and self-control would emerge. In this developing paradigm, the Austinian view of state order was replaced by a vision of social control that was unremittingly human, dynamic, interactive, emerging out of discourse and communication, and out of the human web of mutual socialization and self control.

As Melossi recounts, the rise of the Harvard School, and the prominent figure of Parsons, represented something of a throwback to the externalism and formalism of earlier times. In the Parsonian concept of a 'social system', social control and law (moral and legal orders) were galvanized within a single normative structure. Social control was not a matter of linguistic competence or intersubjectivity or common human motive, but simply a hydraulic mechanism, invoked after the fact of deviance to restore the 'One Big Order' (informal and formal) to its natural state of harmony.

However, with the writings of C. Wright Mills and the advent of labelling theory (the 'neo-Chicago School') came a solidification of social control within the nucleus of modern social theory. Mills considered the impact of 'vocabularies of motives' on both deviance and control. Such vocabularies could be seen as a source of 'deviance' (when human thought and action are engaged in a crossfire of competing vocabularies), and as a resource for the exercise of social control (through the activation of accounts that organize, structure and legitimate conduct designed to secure order). With labelling theory and ethnomethodology came an increasing emphasis on the account–ability of controllers, and especially of those who *used* (not simply 'applied') the law against criminals and other subjects of legal ordering practices. Increasingly, rules-in-use, law-in-action, and mediation of conduct and rhetoric in official control strategies became important concepts for understanding the dynamics and impact of legal control.

Melossi's brief history of ideas leads to his argument for a 'sociological theory of law as a vocabulary of motives'. The author suggests, following from the Pragmatists, Chicagoans, Mills and the neo-Chicago School, that 'the law' is just one of many energizers that provide motive force for the exercise of social control. Accordingly, the law is not an entity to be applied by enforcers, but rather a rhetorical resource for account–ability, a pool of motives through which the character and very essence of social control can be understood. Melossi applies this understanding of law to the relationship between the business cycle and imprisonment rates, and in the process explains why their inverse correlation is not mediated by changes in crime rates. Melossi, instead, attributes the expansion of prison populations during economic decline to 'vocabularies of punitive motives', that shape legal control practices and policies, and that are seemingly independent of (and clearly *not* a response to) official crimes rates.

Finally, Melossi maintains that such a perspective on legal ordering can be used to account for the deinstitutionalization/decarceration phenomenon. He views the patterns of institutional and non-institutional control of deviants and dependants during the 1960s and 1970s to represent the confluence and contradictions among a number of competing rhetorics and 'vocabularies of motives', including the pressure to 'decentre' control systems, the construction of 'fiscal crisis' scenarios, motives of non-intervention, less eligibility, social contract and so on — all of which were involved in the discourse of decarceration, and through which the strategies and policies of dealing with convicts and mental patients evolved. Melossi is not attempting here to articulate a total theory of decarceration. Rather, he is presenting a potential line of theorization, incorporating his perspective on the state, law and control as 'practical rhetorics of motives'. His review of social control theory has provided a useful entrée to the following chapters, all of which deal in some fashion with this omnipresent concept. His preliminary application of this theory to decarceration sets the tone of subsequent discussion on the origins, dynamics and impact of inclusive and exclusive strategies for controlling legal subjects in contemporary society.

In the second chapter of the book Steven Spitzer also discusses issues concerning the use of the social control concept. By examining the 'commodification of security' in capitalist societies he lays the foundation for a critique of the state-centred orientation of revisionist conceptualizations of social control. Towards this end he begins with Marx's analysis of security and the fetishism of commodities as a basis for a new perspective which problematizes the notion that control is to be understood simply or only in terms of state power.

Although Spitzer finds Marx's analysis of the fetishism of commodities useful for beginning an analysis of the commodification of security, he argues that it is deficient by virtue of failing to analyse consumption as well as production. For Spitzer, Marx's productivist orientation is ill-equipped to analyse use-values which are created non-materially. Further, Spitzer argues that the non-material component of use value must become far more central to the analysis of value in modern capitalist social formations. Unlike the commodities described by Marx in *Capital* (where, for example, the tangible material 'wood' becomes a 'table'), security is defined in abstract terms. It is a commodity which requires conceptualization in subjective as well as objective terms, since it is created symbolically as well as tangibly. Security has a meaning beyond that invested in it at the time of its production.

In examining recent analyses of security, Spitzer finds that they either create a straw consumer who makes security choices on the basis of rational calculation, or ignore human agency by focusing solely on analysis of aggregate political and economic structures.

In extending this critique to the broader social control literature he problematizes the functionalism of traditional socialization perspectives (as earlier described by Melossi in Chapter 1), and the state-centred orientation of the revisionist schools. In describing the transition to state-oriented theories, Spitzer argues that 'in throwing out that "bathwater" of older and one-sided "socialization" models, we must be careful not to abandon the "baby" that links social organization and social control. . .'.

Spitzer's argument powerfully demonstrates the utility of proceeding beyond state-centred conceptualizations in order to rethink the relationships among power, material conditions and objective states. Specifically Spitzer argues that we must move beyond an analysis of social control that is content with scrutinizing the contexts of constraint and deprivation as highlighted by state-centred theories. In its stead he focuses his analysis on consumption patterns, especially in terms of the contexts of choice and gratification as they are constructed and manipulated in capitalist societies. In this sense, Spitzer's construal of 'social control' is much less Orwell's *1984*, and much more Terry Gilliam's *Brazil*: that is, a view of society which sees social control processes as involving not only the social organization of 'fear and terror' (that is, a political process), but also (and perhaps more importantly) the social organization of 'need and gratification' (that is, an economic process).

In Chapter 3, 'The eagle and the sun: on panoptical systems and mass media in modern society', Thomas Mathiesen presents a critique of Foucault's interpretation of the history of panopticism. The discussion begins with a review of Foucault's concept of panoptic surveillance. In *Discipline and Punish*, Foucault argued that during the eighteenth and nineteenth centuries a profound transformation of control systems occurred, from a modality of 'spectacle', of 'the eagle and the sun' (where the many see the few), to one of panopticism (where the few watch over the many). Mathiesen writes that such an interpretation represents a serious misreading of the history of power. He submits that the symbols and arrangements of spectacle have not been discarded with the development of panopticism, but instead have dialectically grown with, and supported, expanding technologies, discourses and structures of surveillance in modern society. Such 'viewing of the few' is embodied in the prominence of state and corporate architecture, in the celebration of royalty and other elites, and most critically in the development of the mass media, a parallel system enabling the many to 'see and contemplate' the few.

According to Mathiesen, the 'spectacle' has survived in the form of media representations of power. It allows the knowledge, agendas, models and discourses of the powerful (the 'foreground figures') to wash over audiences (the recipients of symbols, images and interpretations produced by and for the elite). Modern versions of the 'eagle and the sun' provide a second tier of power, equally as enhancing and expansive as the rise of panopticism, and mutually engaged with surveillance strategies in a reflexive configuration of state power.

In his analysis of their origins and modern manifestations, Mathiesen finds many points of comparison between panoptical surveillance structures and media structures. First, he maintains that both have archaic origins. In contradistinction to Foucault, Mathiesen locates the roots of panopticism *not* in the writings of Bentham, but instead in the very origin of state domination. He cites the registration practices of the Roman State, the confessional knowledge system adopted by the Catholic Church, and the pyramidal structure of the military as forms of panopticism that clearly antedated the eighteenth and nineteenth century panopticons described by Foucault. Similarly, Mathiesen discovers ancient forms of media structures that differ from modern forms not so much in their dynamics or function, but more in the increasing isolation of 'receivers' from 'senders' and from each other. Although he does not embellish upon this idea to any great extent, Mathiesen offers an important insight into the relationship between these two modalities of power. He speculates that, whereas there may be historical evidence supporting the historical separation of media and panoptical power, there is every indication that they are once again merging into a single reflex of domination, particularly as they assume common technologies towards the conclusion of the present century.

Second, Mathiesen notes the fan-shaped form of both control structures, manifested:

1. In the diffused power, emanating from the centre to the periphery, in panoptical churches, armies, factories, inquisitorial courts, and prisons; and

2. In the delivery of knowledge through the media from a central location outwards to a theoretically boundless constellation of audiences.

Still, these fans are not static, but instead are numerous, layered and interrelated in complex patterns. They assume many different configurations according to the historical and sociopolitical context. As the author writes, '. . . many people, if not all, are subject to one form of fan-shaped panoptical system or another — the prison, crime prevention systems in the community, the police, the various security agencies or companies, political surveillance, the taxation authorities, and so on'.

Third, such fan-shaped power structures are one-way rather than reciprocal. In the panopticon there is little opportunity for the watched to meet, interrogate or even identify their monitors. In the modern media the flow of information is also typically unidirectional. Although there may be an apparent technological break with such one-way systems, arising from the development of information utilities and two-way cable vision, in real terms such apparent exchange networks function to intensify the power of the senders, who remain free to control the selection, storage and dissemination of information, as well as the very terms and conditions of its conveyance. As Mathiesen insists, such interactive media do not redistribute power, but instead they radically limit the choices available to receivers, while expanding the scope of knowledge designed to legitimate and entrench the authority of the senders.

In his concluding section, Mathiesen adopts an important trajectory of analysis, by insisting that the modern media structure provides an empowering *belief system*, supplanting the traditional church in supporting the exercise of *panoptical control*. Foucault notwithstanding, the former has not been supplanted by the latter, but instead has survived and spread through the instruments of mass media to parallel and enhance modern structures of surveillance. Their relationship is not mutually exclusive, but rather dialectical. Any modern analysis of power, and of state control, must take both structures into account, and must map the contours of their reflexive relation. Moreover, by 'reuniting the bifurcation' between panoptical and media structures, new strategies of resistance may emerge. These must be grounded in the development of alternative communication networks. Anti-control strategies need to confront not just the panoptical systems of surveillance that have proliferated in the 'viewer society', but also the networks and technologies of knowledge distribution that have allowed the few to relay symbols and signals to the many who are being watched — messages that both legitimize the activities and motives of controllers, and resonate the knowledge/power system that constitutes the modern panopticon.

Reacting to the implicit acceptance of the idea that social control (even in its revisionist incarnation) represents the social response to a perceived state of 'deviance', Harold E. Pepinsky suggests in Chapter 4 ('Justice as information sharing') that social control really has nothing to do with 'deviance' at all. Rather than being provoked by 'deviance', social control is a system for responding to, managing and deflecting the problems created by information blockage. The social reaction to deviance emerges in Pepinsky's perspective as a kind of catharsis, a displacement of the fear and resentment created by systematic blockages of information.

Pepinsky reformulates the object of social control as the information systems that underlie joint human action and that generate particular systems of material distribution. In these terms 'justice' can be defined as the free sharing of information, with injustice arising from the blockage of information flows. In this model of justice and deviance, distributive justice makes little sense if the prior requirements of information sharing are not achieved.

Pepinsky argues that the propensity to share information is a fundamental human trait. The prolonged existence of the human species, its adaptability to almost any geographic environment, and the development it has undergone, cannot be explained without acknowledging the human capacity to share information.

The problem with the definition of justice proposed here, Pepinsky notes, is that its requirements can only be met in limited networks of no more than a few hundred people. The question becomes what kind of organizations facilitate justice, and how can their size be controlled. In taking up these issues, he discusses the experience of the Mondragon community of worker co-operatives in Spain, a context for testing the preliminary propositions of a theory of peace and justice based on information sharing.

Generally Pepinsky rejects any definition of justice as material equality, arguing instead that equality must be understood as the democratization of decision-making. From this perspective, the mutual accountability of all individuals and groups is the fundamental precondition of social justice.

Chapter 5, contributed by Stuart Henry and entitled 'The construction and deconstruction of social control: thoughts on the discursive production of state law and private justice', begins with a discussion of the social control construct. Henry agrees with Cohen's (1983) disdain for its use as an umbrella concept covering everything from infant socialization to all governmental policy. And like Cohen, he also argues that the limitation of the term to organized state-initiated responses to crime is unduly myopic. But at this juncture Henry departs somewhat from the main thrust of Cohen's (1985a) analysis by suggesting that non-state systems of 'private justice' — that is, 'institutions of social control that maintain the normative order of groups and organizations' — also warrant inclusion.

Henry's argument begins with qualified support of legal pluralism, criticizing the tendency to view state law as the hub around which all other forms of control revolve, with the connecting spokes conceived as unidirectional pathways of influence *from* state *to* other forms of justice. Associated with this perspective is a reified perception of state law, and hence an implicit reaffirmation, rather than a questioning, of the legal status quo. Consequently, Henry's objective is to contribute to a theory of social control which emphasizes the role of human agency, and which thereby recognizes the dynamic and active way in which notions of law and social control are constructed and affirmed. It is only in this way that one can appreciate how it might be *de*constructed and changed.

It becomes readily apparent that Henry's arguments for the inclusion of 'private justice' under the rubric of social control are much more than a qualification regarding comprehensiveness. Instead, his discussion of private justice provides an effective vehicle for demonstrating the *interdependence* and *mutual penetration* among various forms of justice, and the ways in which each shapes and reaffirms, and is shaped and reaffirmed by, the others. Standing on the shoulders of Giddens (for example, 1984) and Fowler (for example 1985), Henry presents examples of discourse from his research on industrial disciplinary boards which illustrate how individuals' discursive practices reaffirm the existence and legitimacy of both private *and* state law. They demonstrate his point that even rejection of, and contrast with, the existing legal order, express implicit acceptance of the status quo.

The arguments that Henry presents are inherently reflexive, and should encourage theorists of social control to reconsider the ways in which their own critical constructions may serve to preserve and entrench rather than to challenge and change the existing legal order.

1 The law and the state as practical rhetorics of motives: the case of 'decarceration'[1]

Dario Melossi

For centuries after the collapse of a social order that was held together by a complex political-religious belief, European order was centred on what Kelsen once called the 'god of the law, the state' (1961, p. 191; originally 1945). Between the end of the nineteenth and the beginning of the twentieth centuries, this new 'political theology' entered a deep crisis (Melossi, 1983).

This chapter sketches an outline of the creation of a new paradigm of social order based on 'social control', a creation that happened to a large extent in the 'new world' in the intellectual milieu of Pragmatism and Chicago social science.[2] A sociological theory of the law, based in this Chicagoan concept of social control, is developed. Some uses of the theory for analysing recent events affecting the management of 'social problems' will also be discussed.

Pragmatism, the state and social control

In the United States, the heritage of the British common law system, together with the federalist slant of the American Constitution, from the beginning worked against any conceptualization of the state as a central feature of the American polity. In the young American society, effectiveness of government could not rely on traditional restraints. As James Madison noted (1787), adequate control of 'factions' would not come from moral or religious considerations alone. During the nineteenth century, law in a 'weak state' society (Hamilton and Sutton 1984) would be the answer to the problem of control. From the time of American independence until the Progressive Era, a 'formalist' interpretation of common law and of the Constitution powerfully limited the disruptiveness of increasing social differentiation and complexity.

Especially toward the end of the nineteenth century and on into the Progressive Era, the Supreme Court systematically used its power of judicial review to protect the 'weak' state from unions and their progressive allies, who demanded that the judiciary take an evolutionary interpretation of the constitutional charter, in keeping with the new era of industrialization and massive social transformation. During the years when these progressive forces were slowly coming to the fore, it became clear that social order could no longer be secured by enforcement of the legal-political order. Rather, social order had to be grounded deeper in the fabric of society. Yet it could not be based on traditional values. It was at this juncture — to solve this riddle — that the question, and the concept, of *social control* became of paramount importance in the development of American social science.

Although 'Pragmatism' came to designate a specific philosophical position, associated primarily with the names of Pierce, James, Dewey and Mead, some of the basic attitudes and concerns which were typical of it, were shared by a much broader intellectual movement, especially in the social sciences. Whether as 'realism' in jurisprudence, political science or history, as 'institutionalism' in political economy or the law, as 'anti-formalism' in all disciplines (White 1947), such authors as Veblen, Bentley, Commons, Holmes, Pound and Beard were pursuing a common goal — that of putting the social institutions and sciences of America in line with times which they saw as in need of being described and tackled 'realistically'.

The decline of an idea of social order based on 'the state', together with the emergence of a concept of 'social control', was part and parcel of this broader movement. The *processual* and realist slant of his thinking brought the political scientist Bentley, in 1908, to reject the concept of state and to adopt instead that of 'government'. Although Herbert Spencer used the term 'control' (Janowitz 1975, p. 89), Edward Alsworth Ross (1901) was the one who introduced the term 'social control' into the American sociological vocabulary. By developing this concept, the Chicago School of sociology constructed an intellectual instrument which captured the dominant vocabulary of motives prevailing in the twentieth century capitalist society *par excellence*. The social and cultural reality of the Chicago 'laboratory' between the Progressive Era and the 1920s provided the Chicago intelligentsia with the spectacle of such a degree of conflict among different cultures, classes and subcultures that it became necessary for them to question the traditional European view that the basic conflict was somehow 'outside society' — between 'nature' and 'society', between 'man' and 'civilization'.

This social-contractualist view of the relationship between individual and society — which had dominated European thinking from the Classical age to the then-contemporary Freudian period — was overcome by turning the question of the social order upside down. Rather than a conception of a 'state' or 'civilization' which imposes its coercive, external 'law' on 'human nature', the new conceptualization was that of an order which stems from social interaction.

Probably the most exemplary work to illustrate the 'horizontal' character of the American concept of conflict, as opposed to the 'vertical' European one, was by Robert E. Park. In his German dissertation, *The Crowd and the Public*, Park (1972, originally 1904) tackled a topic that was hotly contested in Europe at the time — so-called 'crowd' or 'group' psychology, *Massempsychologie*. In Europe, this kind of psychology seemed to be an answer to rising political and social unrest. The crowd was often seen as a dark, cataclysmic force. Nested in the big cities, and the prey of demagogery, the crowd was seen, within the Darwinian perspective of social sciences at the time, as easily regressing toward atavistic forms (Sighele 1894), and capable of sudden, undignified, violent behaviour (Le Bon 1892).

This elitist rhetoric, soon to become the ideological currency of rising Fascist movements, was not popular with Park or with Chicago sociology in general. They could not entertain this aristocratic nostalgia, characteristic of the 'petty bourgeois European philistines', as Gramsci (1975, p. 723; originally 1929–1935) called them. In fact, the crowd was seen as the salt of the earth in a land like America, characterized by 'rational demographic composition' — where, in other words, no parasitical strata could couch their elitist privilege as the cultural superiority of the European 'civilization' (Gramsci, 1975, p. 2141; originally 1929–1935). The 'tradition' that had made it so difficult for democracy to grow in Europe was not present in America, where the question of order and control had become, by the time Park was writing, one of finding social control processes that could furnish the democratic system with solid foundations. This question dominated Chicago intellectual life and the best American minds in social sciences until, at least, the post-Roosevelt change of mood, coinciding with the discovery of a world-wide imperial destiny for America.

It was the formation of a 'public' which fascinated Park. To him, the main problem of society was identified in the constitution of a sphere of public opinion which would sort out the conflicts of democracy. How would this common discourse be created? It was the main conviction of the Chicagoans that *communication* is the key to the social fabric, and that the necessary condition for conflict negotiation is to assure the possibility of communication among individuals, social groups, ethnic communities and organizations. Immigration and successful integration of immigrants in the American metropolis furnished Park and associates with the central metaphor for their work. The four 'social processes' — competition, conflict, accommodation and assimilation — which figure predominantly in Park and Burgess' *Introduction to the Science of Sociology* (1921), were derived from analysis of the immigration process. Other fundamental works from Chicago had the same inspiration, as, for example, Thomas and Znaniecki's (1927) analysis of Polish peasantry. Also, the influence on John Dewey and George Herbert Mead on Jane Adams and her Hull House social settlement for the Chicago immigrants should not be forgotten (Mills 1966, pp. 307–24; originally 1942; Smith 1931).

Implicit in this thinking was a fundamental optimism that was typical of the Progressive Era: the idea, that is, that establishing a broader discourse would lead to the discovery of the most rational way of solving conflicts. In Park's (1970; originally 1922) book on the control of the immigrant press, as in the Chicagoans' works dealing with radical forms of politics (for example, Nels Anderson's (1923) *The Hobo* and parts of Park and Burgess' book (1969, pp. 425–431; originally 1921)), the way to deal with national or political dissent was to break down any linguistic barriers which did not allow the parties to share a common definition, a common universe of discourse. This was the proper terrain of *social control.* The competition among different vocabularies was at the centre of their interest. The different native language of the immigrant, or the different vernacular of the International Workers of the World member (two differences which were often one) were to be analysed (and controlled) by treating such differences as instances of limited worlds, that could be overcome by the practical and linguistic entrance into the larger universe of American society.

This was the reason why, in their introduction, Park and Burgess called social control 'the central problem of sociology' (1969, p. 42; originally 1921). The polemical target was the 'European' position that social problems could be solved 'by the authority of the law'. This legalist position was ridiculed again and again. As Thomas and Znaniecki (1927) had observed in the introduction to their book on Polish peasants, what Chicago sociologists were trying to do was to deny the possibility of operating with the 'magic' of the law, with government 'by decree'. 'Real' control could only be based on knowledge (Thomas and Znaniecki 1927, p.3). Park and Burgess observed the same when they recalled Comte and the idea that the very foundation of sociology was based on the failure of attempts at political and legal regulation. Without knowledge of regularities in human behaviour, they thought, governments are completely powerless, unable to cope with an age of social movements and organizations (1969, p. 1; originally 1921).

According to this view the very ground of democracy was therefore constituted by processes of social control, because these processes account for the possibility of concerted action, or *consensus* — a consensus, however, that is strictly cognitive and reliant on 'co-orientation' towards an identical meaning (Sapir 1933; Scheff 1967). It is a concept of consensus as participation in the same universe of discourse (Park 1939).

This same kind of conceptualization was more thoroughly developed by George Herbert Mead, who defined social control as depending 'upon the degree to which the individuals in society are able to assume the attitudes of the others who are involved with them in common endeavour' (1964c, p. 291; originally 1925). To him, there was coincidence between social control and self-control. Mead's position thus represented a decisive break with the Western tradition of opposing the individual to the world, in epistemology as well as in social-contractual theories. Both were seen as being built around 'an adequate social object', the problem of which:

> ... is not that of becoming acquainted with the indefinite number of acts that are involved in social behaviour, but that of so overcoming the distances in space and time, and the barriers of language and convention and social status, that we can converse with ourselves in the role of those who are involved with us in the common undertaking of life ... Any self is a social self, but it is restricted to the group whose roles it assumes, and it will never abandon this self until it finds itself entering into the larger society and maintaining itself there. (Mead 1964c, p. 292; originally 1925)

In order to enter into the 'larger society', and in order to grasp the set of 'social objects' which make up a person's universe, the person must take the role of a 'generalized other', in a process which takes place by means of vocal gestures: that is, *language* (Mead 1934). Social integration was not to be sought, according to Mead, in some 'superindividual' entity or in 'moral education' or in a 'psychic bond'. Social integration was seen as based in the mastering of a common linguistic competence. The process of language learning and language practicing, namely, the process of communication, is 'a principle of social organization' (1934, p. 260) which makes any type of 'co-operative activity' possible: 'The process of communication is one which is more universal than that of the universal religion or universal economic process in that it is one that serves them both' (1934, p. 259). But this is true only because religion or the economy are specific instances of co-operative activity. 'Co-operative activity', in general, 'must lie back of the process of discourse' (1934, p. 259). In so far as the self is 'controlled' by plural and possibly conflicting 'audiences', social control is also the process that is at the root of innovation and individuality. Hans Joas, in his very perceptive reconstruction of Meadian ethics (1980, pp. 121–44), quotes Mead as saying that he was involved in constructing his own 'Phenomenology of Mind' (p. 232). This was so because the possibility of entering larger and larger 'audiences', or 'universes of discourse', constituted, at the same time, the possibility for criticizing the narrower circles of praxis and language which the self had inhabited until then.

When such a fundamental social-psychological construction is transported into the realm of political affairs and into a theory of democracy, Mead's statement that democracy is in fact 'an institutionalization of revolution' (1915, p. 150) makes good sense. The reformulation of the basic issue of social order that had been so produced was possible only when the claims of an external 'god', the state, which 'gives' the law, were negated, and claims of self-government of a society speaking many different vernaculars had come to the fore. In the political thinking of the Pragmatists and the Chicago sociologists, there was confidence that a Babel of vernaculars would not destroy American democracy but that, on the contrary, democracy would contribute to social control by providing a broader and more elevated language for interaction of the sundry social circles making up society.

As I have already noted, it was Bentley who rejected the state concept and the related concept of sovereignty, and who also developed the processualist perspective:

> The 'state' itself is, to the best of my knowledge and belief, no factor in our investigation. It is like the 'social whole': we are not interested in it as such, but exclusively in the processes within it. The 'idea of the state' has been very prominent, no doubt, among the intellectual amusements of the past, and at particular places and times it has served to help give coherent and pretentious expression to some particular group's activity. But in either case it is too minute a factor to deserve space in a work covering as broad a range as this. Nor need the state, as 'the tyranny of the minority over the majority', concern us . . . I may add here that 'sovereignty' is of no more interest to us than the state. Sovereignty has its very important place in arguments in defense of an existing government, or in verbal assaults on a government in the name of the populace or of some other pretender, or in fine-spun legal expositions of what is about to be done. But as soon as it gets out of the pages of the lawbook or the political pamphlet, it is a piteous, threadbare joke. So long as there is plenty of firm earth under foot there is no advantage in trying to sail the clouds in a cartoonist's airship. (Bentley 1908, pp. 263–4)

No more 'American' put-down of a state-concept could be imagined, especially the reference to a *cartoonist's* airship! The problem with such a radical denial of the state concept was of course that it failed to account for the ways in which 'state' and 'sovereignty' had 'amused' and legitimated individuals, peoples, and groups.

Close to Bentley, but differing from him at least on this very point, was Dewey, whose *The Public and Its Problems* (1927) gave us probably the most accomplished account of the question of relationships between the social and the political order from the perspective heretofore discussed. To a certain extent Dewey followed Bentley's outright rejection of traditional discussions about the state-concept. However, he gave his analysis a twist which propelled it far beyond the limitations of Bentley's discussion.

The nexus between the public and control, already present in Park's writing, was further elaborated by Dewey. 'The state' was not denied in Dewey's work, even if he was apparently incensed about what he called the idea of the state 'as authorship'. But the term was given secondary importance as a working concept *vis-à-vis* the idea of the public. Dewey's theory of the public was based on the fundamental idea that matters resulting from 'private' transactions which are of consequence to a third party become, for this very reason, *public*. As such, they are to be regulated in the interest of the affected third parties. Those matters that do not have effects on third parties remain in the realm of 'the private'. On this ground, the state, if it is anything, is the 'sum' of 'the public' plus those individuals and offices which *serve* the public on the matters to be regulated.

Who decides which matters should be regulated? There is no meta-rule to answer the question, as would be the case for theories of the state as authorship. The state is, according to Dewey, a function of what the public *de facto* constitutes itself about. Such constitution has social control as its aim. The one body of rights which is private and individual, from this perspective, is that which the public recognizes as not having consequences for itself. This was a fundamental issue at the time that Dewey was writing *The Public and Its Problems*. The possible limitations on a right which had traditionally been described by legal doctrine as 'absolute', like the right of 'private property', was very much in public discussion, especially with reference to labour legislation.

It is quite obvious that tensions anticipating the coming upheaval of the New Deal run through Dewey's work. In a few years, Adolf A. Berle and Gardiner C. Means would observe, in *The Modern Corporation and Private Property* (1933), that the separation of management control and ownership in private corporations had, *de facto*, abolished private property under conditions of capitalism (something that Marx had noticed, too), and would demand some degree of public regulation of economic life based on such recognition. Earlier than that, the institutionalist economist John M. Clark had published his book *Social Control of Business* (1926), where the policy conclusions in the last chapter were presented from the perspective of a 'dictator' — even if 'a frankly imaginary picture of a dictator' as he put it more prudently in the second edition of his book (1939, p. 520).

This new meaning of the words 'social control' — that was to become the standard meaning in a macro-sociological sense — was consistent with the contemporaneous elaboration by Mead in social psychology. Dewey's 'public' was in fact nothing but another word for Mead's 'audience'. In fact, social control was still, at the political level elaborated by Dewey, a specific definition of the situation which now became entrusted to a 'specialized staff' (in Weber's terms). It was still a question of 'generalized others', whether these were the individual's primary relations, the press, or Roosevelt's officers entrusted by (a certain) 'public' with enforcing the Wagner Act, for example. Dewey's polemical target was the kind of 'individualism' that in the Western philosophical tradition had made the individual an intuitive starting point (Joas 1980, p. 152). There is more than a passing relationship, Dewey observed, between the idea of the legal subject and that of the knowing ego, between Locke and Descartes (Dewey 1927, p. 88). This is one reason why Richard Rorty keeps telling us that 'James and Dewey ... are waiting at the end of the road which, for example, Foucault and Deleuze are currently travelling' (1982, p. xviii).

Dewey's and Mead's 'political' positions were the result of thirty to forty years of intellectual work in all disciplines of the social sciences. The old order of individualism and formalism had been consistently and methodically shattered and a new one, based on different principles, was being erected. In the new order, the idea of 'social control', as opposed to that of 'state', loomed large.

Social control as response to deviance

The Chicago School's criticism of individualist and social contractualist views was neither the first, nor the only one. Besides the concern of conservative idealists and romantics about the corruption brought about by unchecked 'modern' individualism, there had developed during the nineteenth century, especially in France, a holistic tendency from which 'sociology' proper emerged. This tendency stamped its imprint on the work of Emile Durkheim, and it was Durkheim's positions on social order and social control that Parsons claimed to have elaborated a few decades later. There are reasons, as we shall see, to maintain that neither Durkheim nor Parsons broke decisively with the social-contractualist perspective, as Mead and other Pragmatists had done.

Parsons' very theory and, in general, the atmosphere of the 'Pareto circle' at Harvard in the 1930s, constituted, indeed, a 'return' to Europe for American sociology. The Australian psychologist Mayo went to the Harvard Business School influenced by the idea of *anomie* and by recent developments in Europe, and most particularly by the writings of Durkheim, Freud and Piaget (Mayo 1960, p. 142; originally 1933). At the same time, and in not casual coincidence with Mayo's interests in the employee's anomie in work organization (an interest which led him to the Hawthorne studies), Rockefeller's funds started to divert from Chicago to Harvard and to the East Coast in general (Lengermann 1979). Another important figure at Harvard, in the Department of Industrial Relations, was Henderson, who liked the 'systemic' character of Pareto's economy and around whom the so-called Pareto circle was formed. Within the circle, Parsons developed the ideas that he eventually presented in *The Structure of Social Action* (1937).

In this book, Parsons noted, and commented favourably on, what he described as Durkheim's shift, over time, from a concept of 'constraint' as 'external', characterized by legal sanctions, to a view that constraint is 'internal'. According to this 'later' Durkheim, such internalization would be the product of an order of moral or religious nature, different from the legal order. Still, because Durkheim's concept of collective consciousness was not based on mechanisms internal to social interaction, moral constraint was shaped after the model of the law. Durkheim's concept of order, be it legal, moral, or religious, was always somehow a concept of order coming from sources *external* to the individual. Also in Parsons' structural-functionalism, the hypostatization of socialization and social control processes as attributes of *one* social system governed by *one* normative structure, was not so different from the concept of legal order given by the great Leviathan to save men from the war of all against all. The oneness of Parsons' normative system is very much like the oneness of the legal order in jurisprudence (Lamo 1980).

Parsons' concept of social control was therefore very different from the one based on the pluralist assumptions of the Pragmatists and the Chicago School. There, social controls were viewed as corresponding to social circles or groupings — in accordance with a Simmelian view which had been popular at Chicago. Furthermore, Parsons viewed social control not as a fundamental process of interaction but as a re-equilibrating mechanism of social stability, occurring after the putative normative order had been breached by deviance. This view made it difficult for Parsons to explain deviance in wholly cultural terms because the presupposition of a plural normative world had been dropped. That is why one of the most significant additions to Parsons' thought between *The Structure of Social Action* (1937) and *The Social System* (1951) was psychoanalysis (Parsons 1977, pp. 34–9; originally 1970). Parsons' theorizing therefore did not move very far from the starting point: namely what he had defined as 'Hobbes' problem of order' (Lamo 1980). As with Freud, the social-contractual solution was essentially extended from the voluntary, conscious faculties of individuals to their unconscious 'in the degree to which (such a pact) is internalized during the process of socialization' (Lamo 1980, p. 65).

In this theoretical model, the processes of socialization, deviance and social control, the latter redefined as a response to deviance, are the result of interaction between the individual and a unitary, comprehensive, normative structure. This implicitly posits a fusion of the concepts of deviance and crime, and of social control and law, because if there is but one normative structure, it naturally comprehends both moral and legal orders.

This was to become the standard view of the American sociology of deviance and criminology for years — despite the scientific authority of the 'competing' differential association theory of Chicagoan origin (Gibbs 1982; Meier 1982; Sutherland and Cressey 1960). This might be explained by noting that sociological theory which unified law and morality was consistent with the general climate of American society during the period between the New Deal and the 1950s, a period characterized by an increasing tendency toward stabilization and integration. The Babelian Chicago model had been temporarily resolved by promoting one language to the status of dominant language. It would take a new and different Babel to make American sociologists doubt the adequacy of such a solution.

Developments in the Chicagoan tradition

The Pragmatist tradition deriving from Dewey, Mead and the Chicago School never gave up the basic premise of a working relation between discourse (that is, the higher and more articulate conversation which is made possible by using significant symbols) and those practical sets of collective action which bound the conditions of discourse. This relation is founded on a philosophical concept which shifts the locus of discourse from the traditional introspective mode of the Western Cartesian tradition to an interactive mode. In other words, as we have already seen for both Mead and Dewey, for the Pragmatists the discourse was no longer a product of the reflection of the 'I' on its relation to the 'world', but the product instead of the conversation which takes place between the 'I' and 'the other' (Joas 1980, 1983, p. 9). It is this basic philosophical difference which dictates the two alternative ways of conceptualizing social control. In the first case — what I have called the social-contractualist model — social control is constituted by the relation of an original, 'Cartesian', 'I' to external natural and social conditions which pressure the 'I' from every side. This 'I' was appropriately called 'poor Ego' by Freud (1933, p. 77). In the second case, the process of social control presides over the very formation of a self concept, and self-control and social control are two names for the same process.

These Meadian fundamentals were developed by the young C. Wright Mills, who advanced the idea that 'vocabularies of motives' control the behaviour of participants in specific 'sets of collective action' by orientating it toward the repertoire of motives available in a vocabulary (Mills 1963a; originally 1939; 1963b, originally 1940). Mills' important addition was his emphasis on the concept of a plurality of 'audiences' which compete for a successful definition of meanings: 'The control of others is not usually direct but rather through manipulations of a field of objects' (Mills 1963b, p. 445; originally 1940). Besides Pragmatism, which had been the subject of his dissertation (1966, originally 1942), Mills was influenced by Karl Mannheim's and Max Scheler's *Wissensoziologie* (with Max Weber in the background) and by the linguistic interests of authors like Kenneth Burke and Edward Sapir.

A given vocabulary of motives refers to an historically given audience which is effective in controlling, to a certain extent, 'I's' behaviour (Shibutani 1962). Conflict, and thus 'deviance', result from the way in which contradictory vocabularies of motives, established in relation to different audiences, cross each other. Mills insisted on the inescapable relation of vocabularies of motives to situated action, which developed Mead's idea of an embedded relation of communication and co-operation. There was no place, in this view, for an idea of structure independent of the way in which individual agents continuously both reproduce and alter the established features of their interaction.

In the early 1960s, this pluralist, conflictual, change-orientated view of social relationships could be developed further. By then, the explosion of North American society into an increasing myriad of diverse identities claiming entitlement to social and legal recognition of their political and moral autonomy, brought about the re-emergence of this paradigm of social control. A concept of 'active' social control, alternative to the homeostatic concept of social control developed by Parsons but very much in line with Mead's idea of social control, had been identified by Lemert (1951) as actually producing deviance instead of eliminating it. It was this conception which, in the early 1960s, was developed into what came to be called the labelling perspective on deviance. The neo-Chicagoans expressed a new situation of normative pluralism and a vision of democracy as conflict and competition among unevenly powerful groups.

In this direction of research, a whole new perspective on the sociology of deviance and of social control has more recently developed, that has tried to bypass the traditional jurisprudential debate between the formalists' emphasis on 'the law in the books', and the realists' focus on 'the law in action'. In the works of authors like Bittner (1967), Sudnow (1965), and Maynard (1984), the question asked is not whether the law is 'in the books' or 'in action', but rather to what extent a vocabulary based on positive law is furnished as a successful account of action. It seems, in other words, that rule use (or 'law in action') can be conceived of as the dependent variable in a process which involves competition of different vocabularies of motives within a system of situated action. One of these vocabularies of motives is the one described in the formalist view of the law, namely 'law in the books'.

There are reasons, that is, why the specific linguistic constructs which are articulated in the law, and in jurisprudential discourse around the law, are or are not (or are only to a certain extent) motives for action. These reasons have to do with the competition that a specific vocabulary of motives must endure from concurrent vocabularies of motives of a different nature and coming from different sources within the set of collective action. Study of this competitive process — and of its spatial and temporal context — is open to the generalizing process typical of sociology. It therefore lays the ground for a sociological theory of law as a vocabulary of motives.

A theory of law as a vocabulary of motives: the case of decarceration

Considering the law 'in the books' as a specific vocabulary of motives, a theory of the relationships of society to the law can be developed, on the ground of Mead's and Mills' concept of social control discussed above. 'Law in the books', the strict concept of law as 'positive' law, coming either from the formalist tradition of the common law or from the 'positivist' one of continental jurisprudence — as in Kelsen's pure theory of law — is viewed, in the theory I am proposing, as a specific vocabulary of motives constituted by the positive law and the apparatus of interpretation furnished by legal theory and jurisprudence. Law is, therefore, at least in the books, the specific vocabulary that is socially and formally selected as a guide to behaviour in opposition to other potentially conflicting vocabularies. The chosen constructs are provided with a specific 'sanction', a legal sanction. It is important to stress that such sanction is nothing but a motive, the strength of which, in its relationship to other motives, socially provided with different (that is, non-legal) sanctions, is an empirical fact. There is no reason whatsoever for endowing (legal) coercion with the mystical qualities with which it is often adorned in the most subtle 'airships' of political philosophy. Legal coercion is nothing but the process by means of which that part of the public which backs a certain legal proposition tries to furnish other sectors of the public with a motive (or an additional motive) to conform to the behaviour prescribed in that proposition.

'Law in action', on the other hand, is seen in this theoretical perspective as the actual behaviour of those officials who, in a given legal order, are supposed to make and 'enforce' the positive law. It is suggested that such agencies actually 'use' the law instead of 'enforcing' it, and that such 'usage' is the outcome of a situation determined by the input of vocabularies of motives other than the law in the books. As long as the main rules of the game are respected — that is, as long as the whole legal order, or a part of it, are not rejected outright — such an outcome is likely to be expressed in the highly predetermined and formalized language of the law in the books, on which the agencies of control rely as a resource to be used. The process of law in action feeds back in turn on the broader societal process, in ways that have been studied, for instance, in Turk's (1976) paper on the law as a weapon of social conflict, or by those who have described the very strong surge in the Congress of Industrial Organizations membership following the 1937 United States Supreme Court decision upholding the Wagner Act (Klare 1978).

The explanatory value of the theory could be shown by applying it, for instance, to such diverse research topics as the transformation of private property rights in the evolution of labour law and corporation law from an 'individualist' to an 'institutionalist' vocabulary; or, as I have recently done (Melossi 1985a), to research the relationship between the political business cycle and punishment. It is the latter that I would like to consider briefly as an example of the application of my theory.

By designing and testing a structural model of Italian time-series data of the political business cycle, and of the imprisonment, conviction and crime rates, for the period 1896–1965, I showed that, at least in Italy and for the period indicated, the statistically significant negative association between business cycle and imprisonment rate does not seem to have been mediated via the crime rate, in opposition to what a common-sense interpretation would generally expect (Melossi 1985a). In fact, analogous results have been shown before in the literature, for other penal systems, such as the American federal and state prison systems (Jankovic 1977), and for Canada (Greenberg, 1977c), and England and Wales (Box and Hale 1986). Once criminal activity is to be discarded as the intervening variable between the business cycle and imprisonment, the nature of the association is open to question. Rather vague formulations, such as 'the need for social control', 'the needs of capitalism', and other similarly unsatisfactory accounts of a functionalist nature, have been advanced.

I proposed instead (Melossi 1985a) that the observed statistical association between change in imprisonment rates and change in economic indicators — an association which is not mediated by change in crime rates — depends on an intervening variable that I have called 'vocabularies of punitive motive'. These are specifications, for the public interested in punishment, of pendulum-like movements in the 'moral climate' of the general public, movements which accompany the alternation of economic periods of expansion and recession. These oscillations are in turn the product of interactions among classes, groups and organizations — interactions which influence the production of what we consider 'economic' indicators. Within the (empirically determinate) boundaries designed by the vocabulary of the 'law in the books', the actual behaviour of those 'officials of the public' who are in charge of law 'enforcement', is determined by a changing definition of the situation. This change is not related only to horizontal variables such as social class. It is also related to longitudinal variables such as the political business cycle; in another paper (Melossi 1985b) I have described a 'longitudinally-grounded labelling theory' in accordance with this argument.

In the specific case of punishment, law in action, therefore, is the result of changing motivational constructs. These are expressed, 'in the last instance', in the language supplied by legal tradition, but the regularities in the way in which (and in the degree to which) such tradition is actually *used* seem to depend, in part, on a roughly cyclical unfolding of the political climate.[3]

This theoretical framework may be used, more specifically, for analysis of what has been defined as a process of 'deinstitutionalization' or 'decarceration' of criminals and the mentally ill. Phenomena of deinstitutionalization seem indeed to be better explained by short- and long-term changes in societal vocabularies of motives about crime and mental health than by fiscal considerations alone (Scull 1977). There is no doubt that cultural orientations may assume the guise of fiscal considerations but the crucial point is that periods of economic recession are characterized by both a restriction on governmental expenditures and a more severe policy toward perceived deviance — whereas periods of prosperity are associated with higher governmental expenditures, less severity and more policy experimentation.

Governmental expenditures in such areas as imprisonment and mental health care, in other words, are not associated with a *specific* policy of intervention but with the overall quality of such intervention (measured for instance by per capita expense). Therefore, situations of 'fiscal crisis' during periods when there is strong societal commitment to practices of institutionalization, will result, not in deinstitutionalization, but in a decline in standards of living within more crowded institutions.

In fact, a period of unprecedented economic prosperity in 1955–1965 joined the culmination of a long-term societal trend of hostility to institutionalization. The 'decentring' of social control theories — as in the labelling theorists' work — fed back an intellectual hostility for centralized control, especially of a legal, governmental kind, into the social system and more specifically into the management of 'total institutions' (Goffman 1959). This overall situation ushered in a phase of intense experimentation and declining incarceration in both mental and penal settings in almost all of the advanced Western industrial societies. At the same time, the related pressure of a radically pluralist society on the structures of government — which was at the roots of the surge in the ideology and, less often, in the implementation of 'community treatment' between the 1960s and early 1970s led to a backlash among more traditional and privileged social groups.

This backlash contributed to production of the ensuing double crisis, a juxtaposition of the crisis in legitimation (Habermas 1975) with the 'fiscal crisis' (O'Connor 1973). But also, the rhetoric on decentralizing social control, as this had filtered into public opinion, became part of a more general mood of denial of governmental intervention *tout court*. A new integrative paradigm started to emerge that was based on a *laissez-faire*, individualist vocabulary steeped in classical social-contractual themes (Friedman 1962; Nozick 1974). Such a vocabulary inspired a neo-Malthusian policy of non-intervention in social issues that was quick to adopt the previous emphasis on 'community treatment' for the mentally sick and other non-criminal types of social deviants. But, at the same time, the classic 'less eligibility' position connected to a *laissez-faire* vocabulary (Rusche and Kirchheimer 1939) encouraged an unprecedented return to penal severity and outmoded penal theories for the 'internal enemy' (Mead 1915), the criminal.

This produced, during the following period of serious recession, a dramatic inversion of the previous tendency for penal decarceration but not for mental deinstitutionalization. In both areas there was a sharp reduction in the standard of living due to restrictions on fiscal expenditures, a decline that has concerned *both* a rising population in penal institutions, *and* a rising number of mental patients released into the community. Such a differential treatment of criminal and mental deviants during the recession of the 1970s should be attributed to a shifting social appreciation of 'what ought to be done' about social problems such as crime and mental illness. Since decarceration had been presented as a progressive, humane policy, purportedly more benign than life in institutions, the new climate of severity and repression which increasingly accompanied the 1970s reverted back to incarceration for those bearing the stronger negative stigma which is socially attached to criminal behaviour. In contrast, deinstitutionalization was retained for those who were labelled under the medical-social characterization of mentally ill.

In conclusion, by developing a theory of the law based on a Chicagoan-informed concept of social control, I have tried to show that concepts such as the law, the state and even the economy are beliefs shared by participants in temporary crystallizations of forms of action ('structures'). These concepts are better understood as beliefs which make our participation in such forms of action possible, than as atom-like 'things' out of which our social world is constituted and by which our destinies are led.

2 Security and control in capitalist societies: the fetishism of security and the secret thereof

Steven Spitzer

And you all know security is mortals' chiefest enemy.

Hecate to the three witches in *Macbeth* (Shakespeare 1954: Act III, Scene 5, p. 59)

Security is the supreme social concept of civil society, the concept of the *police*, the concept that the whole society exists only to guarantee to each of its members the preservation of his person, his rights, and his property ... Civil society does not raise itself above its egoism through the concept of security. Rather, security is the *guarantee* of the egoism.

Karl Marx (1843) commenting on the French constitution of 1793 (1967, p. 236)

In ... the religious world ... the productions of the human brain appear as independent beings endowed with life, and entering into relation both with one another and the human race. So it is in the world of commodities with the products of men's hands. This I call the Fetishism which attaches itself to the products of labour, so soon as they are produced as commodities, and which is therefore inseparable from the production of commodities.

Karl Marx, *Capital*, Vol. 1, (1974, p. 77)

This chapter seeks to unravel some of the threads in the process through which security is transformed into a commodity and then bought and sold through a market system. A number of economic, political and ideological developments are explored in order to better understand the commodification of security and its fetishistic character in capitalist societies. But the commodification and fetishism of security are not taken as significant simply because they are associated with the rise of 'private justice' or institutions of 'private policing' in these societies — developments which are discussed elsewhere in this volume and which are clearly real and dramatic enough in their own right. Even more important, it is argued, are the links between these transformations and a broader and deeper set of changes in the ordering and disordering of modern life. Thus, while this analysis is very much concerned with the sources and consequences of the 'privatization' of policing and other control arrangements, this concern is rooted in a more general effort to critique and improve upon existing accounts of how modern systems of social control under capitalism have come into existence, how they operate, and what they might become in the years ahead.

The chapter begins by exploring the way in which security is a commodity, how security is related to the commodity system, and some of the definitional problems associated with the study of security markets. The utility of Marx's analysis of the fetishism of commodities is then explored as a framework for the study of security in capitalist societies. The framework is criticized in an effort to move beyond the conceptual and historical limitations of Marx's model, and to delineate a number of more productive directions in interpretation and research. To more effectively investigate these directions, a new perspective on security and social control is developed. Through this perspective it becomes possible to reassess the commodification of social control practices and products in capitalist societies, and to critique the existing range of state-centred theories of social control. Following a specific discussion of why 'commodity control' is both underestimated and misunderstood by many control theorists, a number of specific connections between security and modern capitalism are explored. These connections are investigated with special attention to the current mechanisms and strategies of 'private' control, and provide a framework for moving beyond forms of control which remain tied to either a decentralized and fragmented commerce in security on the one hand (the tyranny of the market), or a remote and interest-serving political apparatus (the tyranny of the state) on the other.

Security and the commodity system

The *Oxford English Dictionary* defines the condition of 'security' in terms of protection from danger; safety; and freedom from doubt, care, anxiety or apprehension. To be secure is to be assured, confident and safe. The central question that faces us is: how can this condition and the feelings that surround it be turned into a commodity that can be purchased in the market-place?

At first blush, the boundaries around security services and products appear to be clear. The security commodity is something that is produced and consumed to make people feel safe, free from doubt, care, anxiety or apprehension. Yet upon closer examination a problem appears: since efforts to achieve safety, freedom from danger, assurance and confidence are essential features of everyday life under capitalist (as well as many other kinds of social) arrangements, it is necessary to distinguish between those aspects of the 'security market' which have emerged to address directly the safety of persons and property, and those whose connection to security is less tangible and direct. While this distinction between direct and indirect security effects need not detain us for long, it is clear that the boundary between the two may be difficult to draw.

As we will see in the discussion below, the perceived dangerousness and uncertainty of social existence, and the many forms and forces of 'insecurity' and 'risk' are an important ingredient in many decisions to enter the market-place, irrespective of the commodity sought. The attractiveness and market value of a broad range of commodities is enhanced precisely because they promise a greater degree of safety and freedom from anxiety than their alternatives. Because safety (like love, happiness, prosperity, and fulfilment) is a social need which can be activated in a wide range of decisions to consume, virtually all commodities can be invested with the 'aura' of security — that is, presented, promoted, and ultimately consumed because of their ostensible ability to free the consumer from worry, trouble, and harm.

This interpenetration between specialized security products and services, and other products and services which are more attractive because they make us feel more secure, can be seen most vividly on the boundary between private goods and public miseries — a boundary which is relevant to the relationship between the 'privatization of profit' and the 'socialization of costs' (Birnbaum 1969; O'Connor 1973) in capitalist societies. Consumers buy private houses in 'good neighbourhoods' rather than suffer the ravages of public housing, use 'safe' private automobiles rather than 'risky' public transportation, enrol their children in 'wholesome' private rather than 'dangerous' public schools, and patronize expensive and highly trained (read trustworthy) medical specialists rather than rely upon either the overextended and primitive facilities of public clinics or the ministrations of lay healers.

Whatever the security value of commodities such as these, the decision to purchase them does not depend exclusively on their status as security products. This is also true of the security features of many products (for example, tamper-proof caps on over-the-counter drugs, anti-theft devices as standard equipment on automobiles, hotels with safes for valuables) which may enhance the attractiveness of the product without transforming it into a security device. In this sense, it is defensible to distinguish commodities which are purchased on the assumption that their primary function is to protect consumers from dangers to property and persons (for example, guard dogs, karate lessons, burglar alarms and 'risk' analyses) from those whose relationship to the reduction of anxiety and uncertainty is less direct. While we are more concerned with the former category in my subsequent analysis, it is also clear that specific markets in security arise in conjunction with, and are deeply embedded in, broader preoccupations with making micro- and macro-environments more secure. This pattern, tied as it is to a generalized paranoia and malaise in capitalist societies, means that security commodities can never be completely differentiated from commodities which are invested with 'security' attributes or generate 'security' effects. Indeed, it is this very confusion that lies, as we shall see, at the heart of the system of what we will call 'commodity control'.

Once we acknowledge the fact that the commodification of security is intimately related to our individual and collective feelings of insecurity, it is clear that any analysis of this process must investigate the subjectivity of the consumer and understand the forces shaping his or her 'security needs'. This is no less true for the corporation that undertakes an extensive programme of 'access control', 'loss prevention' and 'risk analysis' than for the individual who purchases an inexpensive security device. That these 'needs' may be redefined, expanded or contracted under many different conditions of social and political organization is obvious. What seems to be less obvious, at least to those who have studied security in capitalist societies, is that the study of security needs cannot be undertaken wholly from without. We must also be willing to enter the mist-enveloped regions of fear and desire (Ewen and Ewen 1982), and place emotion at the centre of the analysis.

Very few students of the security industry — 'critical', 'apologetic', or otherwise — have felt comfortable in analysing security in this way. It is far easier to remain in the realm of rational calculation, assuming that both the producers and the consumers of security services and devices are motivated by nothing more than that standard ingredient of bourgeois psychology — self-interest. And even though some critics have pointed out the ways in which security protects the interests of some at the expense of others (see Klare 1975; Shearing and Stenning 1981, 1983, 1985), these inquiries have, for the most part, remained wedded to the rationalistic discourse of 'rights' and 'interests', identifying the central dangers of the security industry as its encroachment on the civil liberties of the population. The problem with this approach is not only, as I will argue below, that it focuses too single-mindedly on the relationship between the controllers and the controlled, but also that it assumes that security can be understood without examining the hopes and fears of those who are willing, in ever increasing numbers, to purchase it in the market-place.[1]

The rise of structural explanations of the emergence and transformation of the security industry (see Shearing and Stenning 1985; Spitzer and Scull 1977, 1980) have not solved this problem. Rather, they have diverted attention from it by concentrating on the linkages between security activities and the patterning of political and economic life. And in so far as it is easier to impute rationality, if not omniscience, to corporate actors (both corporate producers and corporate consumers of the security commodity), those accounts which focus on the rationalization of security under corporate capitalism

(Shearing and Stenning 1981, 1983, 1985) also tend to ignore the subjective side of the security problem. The point here is not simply that this inattention leads to an assumption of rationality where there is really 'irrationality' or 'pseudo-rationality' at best, but that we must be much more sensitive to the relationship between the subjective dimensions of security and insecurity and the objective dimensions of social control.

A final point about the problems surrounding the analysis of security as a commodity: security is especially difficult to study in so far as it is primarily defined in negative terms. In other words, security is said to exist when something *does not* occur rather than when it does. Security in the more restricted sense in which it is used here exists when stores are not robbed, pedestrians are not molested, computer codes not broken, and executives and their family members are able to enjoy life free from threats, assassinations or kidnapping. In more general terms, we are secure when we can negotiate our daily existence without encountering the pitfalls and catastrophes which might conceivably befall us. Because security depends upon the *absence* of a certain range of foreseeable and unforeseeable events, conditions and activities, it is extremely difficult to specify what contributes or fails to contribute to security in any given case. Two contradictions are exposed through this realization. On the one hand, while security is presented as a sound, 'calculated', and 'rational' investment, it is an investment which is based on 'faith' — faith in the possibility, or (in the case of more sophisticated analyses) the probability, of achieving control over an unpredictable, risky and ultimately unknowable world. On the other hand, while the growth of capitalism depends, as Marx and Engels (1967, p.83) observed, on a 'constant revolutionizing of production, uninterrupted disturbance of all social relations, everlasting uncertainty and agitation', so that 'all that is solid melts into air' (see Berman 1982), the security market seems to have emerged as a profoundly conservative and defensive epicycle within this more general process. To be secure is to be safe, but to be safe is to be moribund — at least within the general logic of the capitalist system.

The first contradiction leads us in the direction of analysing security as a new form of 'magic' within a system that eschews the invisible and the unknowable. As we will see in the discussion below, because the full significance of this paradox remains poorly understood, there is a tendency to take the security complex too much on its own terms and, in consequence, fail to understand the inherent limits on the growth and effectiveness of security markets. The second contradiction forces us to confront, in a somewhat different way, the tensions between capitalist development and the security fetish. The security fetish may not only lead to restrictions on the forces which threaten to undermine the capitalist order (this is the thrust of much of the Marxist critique of security: see Klare 1975; South 1984; Weiss 1978), it may also lead to restrictions on the development of capital itself. Security remains a conservative force which, like freedom, must — at least in bourgeois society (see Marx 1967; Neumann 1957, Ch. 6) — define itself in terms of freedom *from* some unwelcome intrusion, usurpation, or limitation. In this sense, it can become a fetter on, as well as condition for, capitalist growth. Security, as Gorz has indicated, always implies the preservation of 'an established order against whatever seems to threaten, disturb or endanger it from without or from within' (1984, p. 158). Viewed in this way, it is clear that security, even when it is being provided by and sold to capitalists, may paralyse as well as protect the forces of capitalist innovation. And if capitalism requires uncertainty for its development *as a system*, but individual actors and organizations need to reduce uncertainty to operate and profit, then security clearly stands in a complex and contradictory relationship to capitalist vitality and growth.

The security hieroglyph: Marx's method and beyond

In Section 4 of the first volume of *Capital*, Marx (1974) discusses 'The fetishism of commodities and the secret thereof'. He begins by suggesting that while commodities are actually nothing mysterious, within capitalist society they are changed into something transcendental and mystical. The essence of this transformation involves, according to Marx, the same kind of alienation that is found in the religious world (see the opening quote from *Capital* vol. I, p. 77).

The key for Marx is the separation of a commodity from its maker and its objectification — a process through which the social character of (wo)man's labour takes on what Lukacs (1971, pp. 83–222) has called a 'phantom objectivity' and confronts him/her as if it had a life of its own. Marx's purpose in attempting to decipher the hieroglyphic of the commodity is to reveal the secret behind the power that our social products seem to have over our lives — a power which both sanctifies the commodity and obscures the real relationship between the process of labour and its results. He is especially concerned with this second feature of the fetishism of commodities since he hopes to use this line of argument not only to demystify the capitalist system, but also to demonstrate the validity of his labour theory of value. Thus, for Marx, the essence of the commodity system resides in the fact that the commodities we worship are no more magical than the idols worshipped by primitive tribes; they are artifacts and images which are, in the final analysis, neither more nor less than the product of human minds and hands.

Applying this line of reasoning to the study of the security commodity it is clear that we have much to learn from Marx's insights. First, and perhaps most important, are the questions that Marx forces us to confront about the origins of security. Where does security come from? Who and what really makes us secure (both objectively and subjectively)? Why and how has security been separated from its true social context in human association and turned into something which seems to be beyond our control? These questions not only focus our attention on the contrasts between security under commodified and non-commodified conditions, they also lead us to ask further questions about the historical process through which those living under pre-capitalist social arrangements gradually lost touch with the real sources of security as a social process. Why is it that for most of human history and in many different social and cultural contexts, day-to-day security was provided through systems of self-help (Black 1980) — what Marx would call 'natural production units' — in which the participants were both the providers and the recipients of the security 'service'? How did the producers of security emerge as a specialized and distinctive class and why have the non-producers become so dependent on the goods and services they provide? Finally, what explains the emergence of security systems that are both alienated from those who really produce them *and* controlled through non-market forms of administration and allocation?

The last question in this interrogatory leads us to ponder why the reification and objectification of security takes place within the arena of the market-place rather than through the 'public' institutions of the state. This issue, of course, has been at the heart of those studies that have focused on the relationship between public and private policing (Hallcrest 1985; Scott and McPherson 1971; Shearing and Stenning 1981). A full understanding of the fetishism of security necessarily leads us into an analysis of the 'publicization' (cf. Spitzer 1975b, 1983a; Spitzer and Scull 1977; Unger 1976) as well as the 'privatization' (Spitzer and Scull 1980) of security, a path that would take us too far afield. At this juncture we may simply note that the commodification of security is not the only way in which the objective and subjective control of safety and protection have been wrested from, or relinquished by, those who need it; it is, however, a form of usurpation which is difficult, although not impossible, to imagine outside of a commodity system.[2]

Returning to the question of whether Marx's general approach to the fetishism of commodities can be fruitfully applied to the investigation of the peculiar commodity of security, it is apparent that there are many directions which we might want to pursue. Basic to all of these, however, is the examination of the 'dehumanized and dehumanizing function of the commodity relation' (Lukacs 1971, p. 92). Following the thrust of Marx's argument, the commodification of security means not only that security is alienated from our control and understanding, but also that the search for security through commodities — like the search for other forms of fulfillment within the commodity system — becomes a fundamentally 'alienating' experience in its own right. Instead of bringing us closer together and strengthening the bonds of community and society, the security commodity becomes a means of setting us apart. This is not only true in so far as we literally build walls around ourselves, but also in the sense that the search for market-based security makes the possibilities of genuine co-operation more remote. Paradoxically, the more we enter into relationships to obtain the security commodity, the more insecure we feel; the more we depend upon the commodity rather than each other to keep us safe and confident, the less safe and confident we feel; the more we divide the world into those who are able to enhance our security and those who threaten it, the less we are able to provide it for ourselves.

The 'quest for security'[3] through the market thus not only sets us apart from each other and leads us to see those beyond the commodity relationship as threats rather than resources, it may also directly contribute to a sense of insecurity as well. As Slater has observed, possessions may actually generate scarcity because 'the more emotion one invests in them the more chances for significant gratification are lost — the more committed to them one becomes the more deprived one feels, like a thirsty man drinking salt water' (1970, pp. 108–9). In the present context this means that one of the consequences of the commodification of security may be a growing inability to return to or re-invent a variety of non-commodified relationships within which 'true' security might be achieved. Or, as Gorz (1984) has argued, the striving for security, when it is removed from real human needs and possibilities, may become one of the most important barriers to both *feeling* and *being* secure — especially in a world where, as Orwell might have put it, 'war is peace'.

But however suggestive observations of this sort might be, a preoccupation with the alienated and alienating character of security may also lead us astray. If we become too obsessed with the relationship between commodities and their producers it is difficult to attend to other dimensions of the commodification process. Despite the tendency of many Marxists to treat the study of consumption as epiphenomenal, we might learn more about security in contemporary capitalist societies by exploring its relationship to the sphere of consumption than to the sphere of production.

Starting from the premise that both the capitalist system and its security 'needs' have been revolutionized in the years since Marx's breakthrough, and recognizing that the commodification of security has had as much to do with the changing forms of capitalist organization as with the unchanging characteristics of the commodity form,[4] we can begin to fashion a perspective that builds upon, but is not limited to, Marx's model of commodification.

As has already been pointed out, although security has become a commodity in modern capitalist societies, it is a peculiar one indeed since security is a derivative rather than a primary commodity form. Unlike the table which is transformed directly from wood in Marx's (1974, p. 77) example in *Capital*, security is a commodity which is neither directly available to the senses nor defined exclusively in physical terms. At bottom, security remains a quality which is derived from rather than constituted within the physical commodity itself. This becomes obvious when we recognize that security 'uses' are in no sense the only uses to which 'security commodities' may be put: consider the gun that wounds its owner, the dog who licks the burglar, or the alarm that goes off for no apparent reason.

Moreover, there is a second step in the creation of the security commodity that is not present in the types of transformations with which Marx was concerned. Not only must the commodity be created physically (as in the manufacture of a fence from wood), but for security to assume a marketable form it must be created symbolically as well. This symbolic work defines the actual 'uses' to which security is put, since the relationship between the physical product and its uses (that is, its 'use value') is in no sense as straightforward or transparent as Marx's discussion would lead us to believe. And once we realize that use value is not simply a functionally specific, 'natural' and 'real' standard against which we can measure the objectified and 'artificial' character of 'exchange value', then it becomes increasingly difficult to claim that we have demystified the commodity form. If commodities such as security actually have fluctuating and variable 'use values' (see Baudrillard 1975), as well as fluctuating and variable 'exchange values', then a large part of the analysis of these commodities must move beyond the study of commodity production as a physical process. This is especially true to the extent that a commodity, such as security, is constituted primarily through a process of symbolic production — through the transformation of images and expectations as much as, if not more than, alterations of the material world.

From this perspective, security is one of those commodities which possesses a virtually limitless ability to absorb signifiers. Security attributes of various products and services are presented as an unqualified good in so far as they promise us freedom from fear, doubt, uncertainty, predation, and so forth. Like many other commodities, security takes on what Buxton (1983) has called 'enhanced use value'.

In contrast to the conception of 'use value' developed by Marx — a conception based on an assumption of direct functional use — enhanced use value does *not* inhere within the commodity itself; it is created, rather, through a loading of the commodity with special symbolic value. This value is not established in a vacuum or through the practical 'uses' to which the commodity is put; it is created, rather, through the organization of life around specific 'lifestyles' or modes of consumption. Clothing, music and food, as well as forms of transportation, housing, and recreation are not simply alternative means of consumption in capitalist (and perhaps many socialist) societies; they are symbolic arenas within which the meaning and significance of social objects and practices are defined. Viewed in this way, commodities clearly perform a number of important functions. Among these are the abilities to:

1. Identify consumers with specific values, customs and activities;
2. Differentiate and socially order consumers according to shifting assessments of social worth; and
3. Provide forms of transient bonding within what Boorstin (1973) has called 'consumption communities'.

Whether we choose to focus on the signalling, separating, or bonding functions of the modern commodity system, one thing is clear: any analysis of security as a commodity must involve a study of the social roots and consequences of the 'loading' that all commodities undergo in the 'culture of consumption' (Fox and Lears 1983).

The new commodity system is thus fetishistic in a double sense. Not only does the commodity take on meanings which are divorced from the process of production out of which it has been created, but those meanings are themselves socially organized and imputed through another kind of production — the production of claims, promises and representations by the modern industries of advertising and marketing (Ewen 1975; Ewen and Ewen 1982; Williams 1958). This second layer of production, a process of which Marx could have been only dimly aware, requires a fundamental rethinking of what it is that is actually being bought and sold in the operation of the commodity system. Rather than arguing that commodities can be meaningfully measured against, and defined in terms of, some utilitarian standard of 'needs' and 'uses', it is far more desirable to see the products of these two 'layers' of production as composed of 'bundles of attributes' (Leiss 1976). And it is within these attributes and their social construction that we find the secret of the security fetish. Even where the security industry justifies its social contribution in terms of specific technological devices and tangible security products, it is clear that the meaning of these products is based on the very 'bundles of attributes' of which Leiss speaks — attributes which become 'progressively more unstable, temporary collections of objective and imputed characteristics — that is, highly complex material-symbolic entities' (Leiss 1976, p. 89). Under these conditions the commodity becomes 'infinitely divisible and divorced from any cognitively stable context' (Agnew 1983, p. 71). It becomes, in other words, increasingly difficult to know what one has actually bought. In the case of security this problem is especially striking since, as has already been noted, the relationship between what makes us secure and insecure is always problematic.

It can be seen, therefore, that the process of commodification comes to be increasingly embedded in, and dependent upon, the social organization of consumption. And further, this process comes to reflect the more general transformations that have taken place in the movement of capitalism from a system based on accumulation and expansion of the means of production to one based upon disaccumulation (Sklare 1969) and the creation of a system of mass distribution and consumption (Ewen 1975; Lears 1981). While the complexities of this revolution *within* capitalism cannot be developed here, it is clear that it has profoundly altered the 'laws of motion' of the capitalist system and placed 'symbolic' commodities like security at the heart, rather than the periphery, of its organization.

The analysis of security is further complicated by the fact that much of the market in security commodities consists in the purchase and sale of services — activities which are defined as successful when they leave no visible alteration of the status quo, much less bring into being a physical product. The development of the 'service economy' (Singlemann 1978) and its increasing significance for the survival of capitalist arrangements were never fully appreciated by Marx, who viewed services primarily as the work of the 'unproductive classes' (Marx 1969, vol. I, pp. 401–7; 1973, pp. 468–9) and defined the market in services as extraneous to, and derivative from, capital accumulation. Treating the income derived from services as mere 'money' or 'revenue' rather than 'capital', Marx (1969, vol. I, p. 402) would have had a difficult time incorporating 'service industries', such as today's security corporations, within his analytical model. His materialism and 'productivist' orientation enabled Marx to penetrate the 'mist-enveloped' region of the physical commodity, yet it left him ill-equipped to investigate commodities whose 'use value' was realized through their non-material or extra-material effects. While it is possible to argue that services purchased by individuals, groups and organizations are ultimately justified in terms of, and become profitable through, their support for the system of material production, it is far more difficult — at least within the confines of an orthodox Marxist approach — to explain why these services have assumed such a central position in the expansion and transformation of modern capitalist arrangements. For this reason, we must look beyond Marx's analysis of the commodity to grasp the full meaning and implications of the new 'trade in security'.

Taken together, the enhanced use value and service aspects of the security commodity lead us to a rethinking of the relationship between security and the capitalist system. This rethinking encourages us to explore the consumption side of the production-consumption link as well as the specific changes in the economic organization of capitalism that have taken place over the last seventy-five years. Perhaps the most visible symptom of these changes has been the rise of the 'culture of consumption'.

Described by a growing number of critical historians concerned with the significance of consumption within modern capitalist societies (Agnew 1983; Ewen and Ewen 1982; Fox and Lears 1983; Leiss 1976; Williams 1958), the culture of consumption has been traced to 'the maturation of the national market-place, including the establishment of national advertising; the emergence of a new stratum of professionals and managers, rooted in a web of complex new organizations (corporations, government, universities, professional associations, media, foundations, and others); and the rise of a new gospel of therapeutic release preached by a host of writers, publishers, ministers, social scientists, doctors, and the advertisers themselves' (Fox and Lears 1983, p. xi). The implications of these developments can be no more than sketched here, but their significance for our purposes is the way in which they have contributed to a hegemonic 'way of seeing' in contemporary capitalist societies.

This way of seeing is connected, on the one hand, with the rise of a social world where 'it increasingly *makes sense* that if solutions are to be had, they can be bought' (Ewen and Ewen 1982, p. 42), and, on the other hand, with the cultivation and shaping of polyvalent cultural symbols and their investment in the consuming act — an investment wherein the '*commodity* increasingly invades the realm of satisfaction' (Ewen and Ewen 1982, p. 262).

But this invasion is never launched in a vacuum; it is based, as one marketing specialist has observed, on striking the 'responsive chord' (Schwartz 1974, p. 65) in the consumer. Since all potential consumers have stored within them a 'lifetime of experiences', it is up to the advertising specialist to 'provide the stimuli to regenerate those experiences, bring them into the foreground, and associate them with the product' (Schwartz 1974, p. 65). The problem thus becomes one of tapping into a *self* which is the 'haunted repository of sensitivity, vulnerability, and emotion, or need and desire' (Ewen and Ewen 1982, p. 262). There are two directions in which this process has moved in contemporary capitalist societies:

1. Toward a stimulation and channelling of desires; and
2. Toward a stimulation and channelling of fears.

For the security commodity, and those who promote and sell it, it is the second of these processes which is decisive. To be more specific, the hegemony of the security commodity is complete when the ravages of insecurity (anxiety, doubt, uncertainty, and a whole range of concrete and generalized fears) are 'only a reminder to those who have not yet bought the right product' (Ewen and Ewen 1982, p. 74).

Towards a new conception of security and control

Over the last several years, a number of important contributions have been made to the analysis of social control (Black 1984a,b; Cohen 1985a; Cohen and Scull 1983; Davis and Anderson 1983; Garland and Young 1983). In contrast to the functionalist approach to theorizing about social control (cf. Janowitz 1975), each of these works has placed the state and public coercion at the centre of the drama surrounding the investigation of rules and rule-breaking. While this shift toward state-centred explanations has been valuable in many respects, it has also created a new problem: the tendency to overestimate the role of the state and underestimate the role of the market in interpreting how social control actually operates in capitalist societies. To the extent that advanced capitalist societies, with a few exceptions such as South Africa, are less likely to depend on the state and public institutions to achieve social control and more likely to resort to the market and 'private' mechanisms to effect the ordering of social life (Lindblom 1977), this tendency has distorted and truncated the analysis of social control. The consequences of this preoccupation with what might be described as an Orwellian/panoptic vision of state-centred control are significant — not only because this view misrepresents the dynamics of coercion in most Western societies, but also because it lessens our ability to work toward a better understanding of how politics and markets are related in the orchestration of coercive control across societies and over time. Such an understanding is indispensable in assessing the role of security in modern states.

Whether we begin with Weber's 'bureaucratization of the world' (Bendix 1960, pp. 421–2), Foucault's (1977) 'technologies of power', Bentham's (1843) 'panoptic vision', or Orwell's (1949) 'Big Brother', it is clear that much of modern theorizing about social control and the 'revisionist' history that has grown up along with it (Cohen 1985a, p. 13) seeks to develop a link between the purposes and 'functions' of social control on the one hand and the development of public bureaucracies on the other. While some explanations focus more on the institutions of public power themselves and others on those who gain access to them, all are agreed that it is within the state's power to manipulate, dominate and constrain that we are to discover the secrets of social control in the modern age. Tracing the causes and effects of social control back to the operations of a reified 'state' and the elites who control it means that even in those instances when it appears that social control has become *less* repressive — through what Cohen (1985a, p. 31) calls the 'destructuring impulse' — it is still the state and its agenda of repression that are both the engine and beneficiary of social control. While there is little doubt that states have expanded their ability to regulate populations through the growth and legitimation of political institutions (Giddens 1985; Poggi 1978; Spitzer 1975a, 1983a) it is also true that the ways in which obedience is orchestrated in specific nation states will differ significantly over space and time (Spitzer 1983a). To the extent that the state-centred model overlooks the operation of informal and privatized systems of social control within 'totalitarian' societies (cf. Abel 1982a; Gross 1984), it is seriously flawed. But even more serious problems become apparent when we try to apply this model to understand how social control operates in 'weak states' (Hamilton and Sutton 1984; Skowronek 1982) — those Western capitalist societies in which 'free enterprise' has penetrated everyday life far more effectively and thoroughly than the state.

The paradox surrounding revisionist theories of social control is thus that they seek to link social control to political organization in those very societies in which the link is least developed, while ignoring the role played by economic organization in regulating social life. Focusing exclusively on political institutions, these theorists have failed to appreciate two important facts:

1. Capitalist societies are structurally different from non-capitalist societies in the sense that economic institutions are explicitly separated from political institutions; and
2. There is often a reciprocal relationship between political and economic control — political controls are most needed when economic controls break down, but most likely to prove counter-productive when economic institutions are operating smoothly (Wolfe 1977).

To clarify the relationship between economic and political organization under capitalism, it is important to remember that 'Capitalism is the first mode of production in history in which the means whereby surplus is pumped out of the direct producer is "purely" economic in form — the wage contract: the equal exchange between free agents which reproduces, hourly and daily, inequality and oppression. All other ... modes of exploitation operate through *extra-economic* sanctions — kin, customary, religious, legal or political'

(Anderson 1974, p.403). In other words, capitalism operates most effectively when social control is exercised *outside* of the economic system, while all other modes of production (including slavery, feudalism and arguably state-socialist command economies) depend upon an explicit and direct connection among economic, political and 'social' controls. What this means in practice is that we are most likely to see social regulation equated with political regulation in societies *without* 'official' markets in labour and other commodities. It also means that advanced capitalist societies, in contrast to the type of society envisioned by Orwell, must rely to a far greater extent on the social organization of need and gratification (an economic process) than the social organization of fear and terror (a political process).

To talk about the social organization of needs is to enter a terrain upon which very few social control theorists have been willing to tread. One reason for this is that most attempts to develop a critical perspective on social control (see Cohen and Scull 1983) have tried to break with the habit of examining the subjective states of the controlled. The motives, expectations and orientations of rule-breakers were a favourite topic of those (for example, Mead, Park and Burgess, Parsons, Ross) who equated the study of social control with the problem of internalizing social expectations. But in throwing out the 'bathwater' of older and one-sided 'socialization' models, we must be careful not to abandon the 'baby' that links social organization and social control — a link that is mediated as much by the consciousness, desires and goals of those who are to be controlled as the interests and agendas of the controllers.

To seriously consider the role played by needs in the organization of social control, attention must be focused on the ways in which fears and desires are channelled through social institutions. The market is one such institution, and an important one in the sense that it presents itself as an arena of free choice. When the market mediates human relationships it is the process of 'choice' rather than 'constraint' that governs associations. And in so far as people 'choose' the solutions to their problems and the methods of their own personal fulfilment, we need a model which goes beyond the concept of control as constraint. Control and constraint are often used synonymously; yet it is clear that in capitalist societies choice may be far more basic to the ordering of social life. From this perspective, any theory of social control must not only understand the ways in which control is exercised through what is prevented or punished, but also through what is allowed (D'Amico 1978, p.89). It is in this second sense that social control comes to be defined as 'the very mechanism which ties the individual to his society' — a mechanism which 'is anchored in the new needs which it has produced' (Marcuse 1964, p.9).

Shifting the study of social control from the context of constraint and deprivation to the context of choice and gratification requires a rethinking of the relationship among power, material conditions and subjective states. The central ingredients in the psychology of control under Fascism — material deprivation, identification with a powerful political leader and aggression toward internal and external enemies (Reich 1970) — are remote from the workings of modern capitalist systems. Most striking in this regard are the ways in which indulgence has replaced denial, and patterns of inclusion/exclusion are far more orientated toward 'consumption communities' and 'lifestyles' than races and nation states. While security and power may certainly be provided by identification with the state, it is the micro-environment of everyday consumption that most strongly addresses the anxieties of the masses. In this context, security becomes a personal and immediate concern, a problem which is much more likely to be solved by purchasing the right product or service than by either persecuting an objectionable minority or conquering the world.

In refining our view of security and control in modern capitalist states, it is important to remember that punishment and coercion have by no means ceased to perform a number of key political functions. The growth of private security has in no sense signalled the end of public coercion. What it has done, however, is to help establish a two-tiered and interdependent system of social control.[5] For those on the top tier, the market promises an escape (albeit largely illusionary) from the dangers, discomforts, and depredations of existence under capitalism; for the rest of society it is the state or 'community' that must be called upon to provide relief. Much like the other areas within which public and private sectors intertwine (that is, education, health care, transportation, and so on), each successive failure of the state provides yet another opportunity for the expansion of the market. In a society in which the collective responsibilities are taken seriously, the failure of public organizations and agencies to provide basic security would be the basis for a legitimacy crisis. But when individuals confront the social environment as consumers rather than citizens, the purchase of security represents a far more reliable and profitable choice. It is perhaps the ultimate irony that this choice, despite its short-run virtues, continues to undermine the possibilities for equality and community — two of the most important ingredients in any society which is to be both 'social' and 'secure'.

3 The eagle and the sun: on panoptical systems and mass media in modern society[1]

Thomas Mathiesen

Panopticism

In 1975 Michel Foucault published his now widely acclaimed and controversial book *Surveiller et Punir* — on surveillance and punishment in modern society. The book appeared in English in 1977, under the title of *Discipline and Punish* (Foucault 1977/1979).

In this book, Foucault reintroduced the concept of 'panoptical' surveillance. The new disciplinary prisons which developed between 1750 and 1850 were 'panoptical': they were organized so that a few could supervise or survey a large number. Foucault discussed Jeremy Bentham's so-called 'panopticon' — a prison structure proposed by Bentham towards the end of the eighteenth century, which may have influenced the form of the new prisons. Bentham's 'panopticon' was (at least in one version) circular with a ring of cells on each floor, and with open barred doors towards the centre, so that all prisoners could be supervised simultaneously from a tower in the middle.

Prisons built during the nineteenth century bore the mark of the panopticon model, as indeed contemporary prisons also do, although concrete arrangements vary. A main point for Foucault, however, was the new kind of society which was implied by the transformation. 'In appearance', he said, panopticism 'is merely the solution of a technical problem, but, through it, a whole type of society emerges' (1977, p.216). To Foucault, panopticism represented a fundamental movement or transformation *from the situation where the many see the few to the situation where the few see the many*.

He let the German prison reformer M.H. Julius describe the transformation. Antiquity had been a civilization of spectacle. 'To render accessible to a multitude of men the inspection of a small number of objects': this was the problem to which the architecture of temples, theatres and circuses responded. This was the age of public life, intensive feasts, sensual proximity. The modern age poses the opposite problem: 'To procure for a small number, or even for a single individual, the instantaneous view of a great multitude' (Julius 1831, in Foucault 1979, p.216). Foucault formulated it this way: 'Our society is one not of spectacle, but of surveillance ... We are much less Greeks than we believe. We are neither in the amphitheatre, nor on the stage, but in the panoptic machine, invested by its effects of power, which we bring to ourselves since we are part of its mechanism' (1979, p.217).

'At the moment of its full blossoming', Foucault continued, the new society 'still assumes with the Emperor the old aspect of the power of spectacle'. The old monarch may be kept in the new state. But the tendency is that 'the pomp of sovereignty, the necessarily spectacular manifestations of power', gradually yield to 'the daily exercise of surveillance, in a panopticism in which the vigilance of intersecting gazes was soon to render useless both the eagle and the sun' (1979, p.217). There is, in other words, a definite transformation.

On this background Foucault sketched how panopticism has been transported 'from the penal institution to the entire social body' (1979, p.298). A carceral surveillance society has developed, in which the principle of panopticism gradually and imperceptibly has invaded large segments. And, as an observer of the development of modern control systems in Norway and other Western countries, I find the panoptical principle, where the few see the many, to be a pronounced aspect of various systems and parts of society. While Foucault's analysis raises a number of issues (such as that of the closer relationship among surveillance, effective control and actual discipline: see for example, Bottoms 1983), this particular development of the structure of surveillance is a striking feature of modern society.

Yet, even if it is a striking feature, the question remains: is it true, as Foucault emphasized, that our society has witnessed a development *from* a situation where the many see the few *to* a situation where the few see the many? Is it true, as he so vividly described, that 'the eagle and the sun', the symbols of unique power, have been rendered useless and superfluous?

The eagle and the sun

This crucial question, which is a question of our societal form, remains quite open. Even if society's surveillance policy has developed in the direction suggested above, it does not follow that a departure has taken place from the centralizing symbols of power, or from the corollary arrangements of spectacle where the many see the few vested with such symbols.

In fact, informal impressions suggest that such symbols and such arrangements have not really been discarded. Some countries still have their royal families, and some royal families still rely on the most extensive symbolism. The British royal family is a case in point. And if the country does not have a royal family, it usually has a president. The French president is not unfamiliar with pomp and circumstance. On given occasions the British royal family, as well as the French president, manage to gather large crowds. The streets may still be filled with enthusiasts.

Now, it may be said that the British king or queen, and the French president, are not today's bearers of actual power. Those who own the means of production, broadly speaking the capitalist class, and those who develop and issue the general rules governing such ownership, broadly speaking the representatives of the state, come closer to power. And these bearers of power are no doubt more withdrawn than their predecessors. The owners of the means of production have moved to the outskirts of the cities, in order to live anonymously, and they prefer to undertake their transactions outside the public eye. To a considerable extent, the same is the case for the representatives of the state.

Nevertheless, even these bearers of power to some extent stand out, so that the many may see them, or at least see their substitutes. A walk through the streets of postwar Frankfurt reveals the colossal, towering dimensions of the bank palaces. Any demonstration against enlargement of the airport, or against atomic weapons, through the streets of Frankfurt will in this way be constantly reminded of an important seat of power. In Oslo things are smaller-sized, but the Oslo Credit Bank's building at Stortorvet, and Norwegian Hydro's building of glass and concrete in Bygdøy Allé, are enormous by Norwegian standards.

A walk through Oslo also convinces one of the outstanding and noticeable format of the Government Building — the state's material location. And still larger, and more central, are the state's buildings in other countries. To be sure, it is not always easy to determine whether it is in fact the state which is housed in these buildings. In an interesting article on the very topic of 'the state's buildings', the Norwegian architect Dag Myklebust has pointed out that in recent history state buildings have become much more anonymous and much more like other large edifices: 'There is nothing about the Government buildings which tells you that it is precisely that. The Prime Minister's office on the 15th floor might just as well have housed the managers of a saltpetre factory' (Myklebust 1984). But both types of buildings do in fact stand out *in bold relief*, and Myklebust has an interesting comment on the anonymity of modern state buildings that '[m]any will perhaps find it quite natural that the architectural expression of capitalism coincides with that of government power. As a matter of fact, lately the State's ownership in Hydro has increased' (1984, p. 12). Hydro is, in fact, a company engaged in saltpetre production.

This, however, is not the most important point. Still more important is the development, as a parallel to the panoptical process, of a unique and enormously extensive system enabling the many to see and contemplate the few, so that the tendency for the few to see and supervise the many is contextualized by a highly significant counterpart.

I am thinking of the development of the total system of the modern mass media. Corresponding to panopticism, imbued with certain basic parallels in structure, probably vested with certain reciprocal supplementary functions, and — during the past few years — merged with panopticism through a common technology, the system of modern mass media has been going through a most significant and accelerating development. The total time-span of this development — the past 150 years — coincides most remarkably with the period of modern growth of panopticism. Increasingly a few have been enabled to see the many, but also increasingly, the many have been enabled to see a few — to see the VIPs, the reporters, the stars, almost a new class in the public sphere.

A number of media and communications researchers have analysed the development in detail. The Americans Melvin DeFleur and Sandra Ball-Rokeach (1982) are among them. They have analysed the interesting and complex background and trends in the development of the modern newspapers, the film, radio and television. This is not the place to present this development in detail. Two conclusions to be drawn from their work may, however, be pointed out.

In the first place, the various mass media in the nineteenth and the twentieth centuries have followed each other and to some extent taken each other's place. The development of a new medium has, in some measure (and with variations) been followed by stagnation in older media.

But, in the second place, the media have by no means supplanted each other completely. To a considerable extent they accumulate and thus supplement each other. In fact several of them may actually interact and support each other rather than compete. For example, the popularity of the radio in the United States continued to increase after television, because the radio found new forms and new areas to cover. In Norway today, the modern tabloid newspapers increase their circulation as the modern television media develop.

In short, through the extraordinary development of the modern mass media, and as a highly significant parallel to the panoptical development, the many have also increasingly been enabled to see the few. It is surprising that students of panopticism have overlooked this for so long. Together with the development of panopticism, the organization of the spectacle has not been abandoned, the eagle and the sun have not been superfluous. In fact, the opposite is the case.

This may be made more concrete, in connection with the two main tendencies in media development summarized above: the tendency for the more modern media to partially supplant the older ones, and the tendency towards greater total exposure to media presentations.

In the first place, the foreground figures in the modern media have, in a very literal sense, become continually more visible. First came the newspapers without pictures. What the foreground figures had to say could be read, but only that. Then, after a while, the newspapers came with pictures, illustrating what the foreground figures had to say. Then came the film, which brought in a whole new area of real stars, whom people could now see, first without hearing them, but after a while also in sound. As a parallel the radio made it possible to hear still other special reporters, prominent men and women. And finally, in came television, after some time with large screens and wonderful colours, on which the foreground figures became more visible than ever, moving right into peoples' daily lives. At the same time, and in order to compete, the newspapers as well as the motion pictures changed. The newspapers changed in the direction of a continually greater emphasis on the cultivation of individual personalities, and in the direction of short articles, large pictures, and outstanding prominence of the individuals on whom they focused. The motion pictures changed towards large epics of various kinds — films about enormous catastrophes, future visions and star wars — spectacles in which the visible appearance of specific individuals is extremely pronounced.

Second, the greater visibility, in a literal as well as a symbolic sense, of foreground figures has at the same time been extended to a continually greater number of viewers. A continually larger number — and this development has been explosive — has been able to see the continually more visible few. In this way the visibility aspect and the quantity aspect merge into a common tendency contradicting the Foucaultian thesis that the many no longer see the few, the thesis that the spectacle has receded into the background and has had to give way.

So far, I have to some extent taken for granted that those who stand out and are seen are actually *few*. The point needs an elaboration. Of course, the newspapers are full of material from various sources. So are the motion picture, the radio and television. Nevertheless, the presentations are first of all characterized by material from, or about, the *relatively* few. This is probably especially the case in the most visual media such as television. Here specific news reporters, eminent media VIPs and interpreters are continually presenting themselves and are continually being seen. And, most significantly, the sources of the media are the societal elites. This fact has been corroborated in a number of media studies (for two Norwegian examples, see Olsen and Sætren 1980; Vaage 1985). Although the media present a tremendous amount of 'fluff' (or, to retain Foucault's language, 'feathers and rays'), the serious core information is *elite information*, presented within elite paradigms. Thus, although power is highly ramified and diversified in modern society, it is indeed people invested with power who are increasingly seen by the few.

Let us now look in more detail at some important *parallels in structure* between the panoptical surveillance systems and the modern mass media. By way of conclusion, I shall also briefly refer to some of the reciprocally supplementary functions of the two systems. Due to limitations of space, the analysis will be general — important variations, nuances and reservations are discussed elsewhere (Mathiesen 1984/85).

Parallels in structure

There are three parallels between the surveillance systems and the mass media which I wish to emphasize. Strictly speaking, the first one is not a parallel in structure, but rather a parallel in the history of the structures, but it is natural to discuss it here.

The 'archaic' form of the structures

In the first place, the panoptical surveillance structure and the media structure are archaic, or 'ancient', as means or potential means of power in society.

Clearly it was Foucault's view that the history of the panoptical control structure as a main model commenced in the late eighteenth and the early nineteenth centuries, though he also mentioned historical lines going further back (especially to the control structures created in plague-stricken towns: see Foucault 1979, pp. 195–200), and he did mention that the panoptical techniques taken 'one by one' have 'a long history behind them' (1979, p. 224). This historical understanding is expressed through the dramatic *break* which Foucault emphasized so strongly from the control policy of the mid-eighteenth century to that of the mid-nineteenth century, and the parallel transformation of discipline.

As far as I can comprehend, this historical understanding must be erroneous. It seems closer to the facts that a panoptical surveillance system, though strongly developed towards the end of the eighteenth century and especially in the nineteenth century, has ancient historical roots; that not only individual surveillance techniques, but *the very model* of the panoptical surveillance system, which in modern times has accelerated as a form, goes back to the beginning of the Christian era or before. In the Gospel of Luke (Luke 2:1) it is stated: 'And it came to pass in those days that there went out a decree from Caesar Augustus that all the world shall be taxed. And this taxing was first made when Cirenius was governor of Syria. And all went to be taxed, everyone into his own city.' In other words, the Roman State undertook such a large task as to tax, and thereby register, what was at that time 'all the world' in the archives of the state. The registration no doubt had several purposes in addition to that of taxation, and there is little reason to doubt that one of those purposes was surveillance of the large masses under Roman rule. Their surveillance was hardly always successful as a control measure — we need only remind ourselves that, during the first great registration, Herod failed in his search for at least one first-born male child. But this does not make the purpose of surveillance less important, and the intended consequences probably functioned to some extent. This was precisely the kind of surveillance which strongly emphasized that a few in centrally located positions were to see (at least important features of) the many. Probably all great state structures in history have had (at least the beginnings of) such systems. In our own historical past, two institutions have probably been particularly important: the *church* and the *military*. Especially the Catholic Church, with the confession, where the isolated individual confides his or her secrets to the unseen representative of the church who in turn observes the individual, has functioned as a setting in which the few have seen the many — undoubtedly with surveillance as part of the goal and function. The military has not only had a strict and disciplinary hierarchy, but also a hierarchy which has provided great possibilities for hidden surveillance from the upper echelons of the system. The church and the military may be seen as settings in which rather extensive construction and testing of panoptical surveillance have taken place — long before the eighteenth and nineteenth centuries.

There is probably less disagreement on the understanding that the structure of the modern media, with emphasis on maximum diffusion from a few leading figures of visual impressions, sound impressions, and other impressions, is also ancient in terms of basic form. Foucault emphasizes the ancient nature of this structure, though he does not relate it to the modern media — his point is that this *is* the old form. The older institutions of spectacle differ in several important respects from the modern ones. In the older context, people were gathered together; in the modern media context, the 'audience' has increasingly become delocalized so that people have become isolated from each other. In the older context, 'sender' and 'receiver' were in each other's proximity; in the modern media context, distance between the two has increased. Such differences, and especially the general fragmentation which is alluded to here, may have consequences for persuasion as well as protest. Yet, the similarity and continuity is also striking, and since the Roman State was mentioned above, we may refer to it again in the present context: the Colosseum, with the emperor present in extensive pomp and circumstance, provides a good example here. The church and the military also provide good examples — the Pope when he speaks from the Vatican at St Peter's, or the magnificent ceremonial entry of the military leader after his victory. We see, then, that the same concrete institutions have contained panoptical surveillance systems as well as mediation of the greatness of rulers. This overlap is important.

It is probably correct to say that the accelerating development of both models in the nineteenth and twentieth centuries involved their separation and specialization, in contrast to the archaic forms which more often coincided. It may be argued that towards the beginning of the twenty-first century the two models are perhaps merging once more, due to the common modern technology, so that the historical development may have followed a kind of U-shaped curve, from a state where the models were interwoven to a separation of them followed by renewed interweaving.

The main point here, however, is that the models of both systems go back far beyond the nineteenth century, and that they have historical roots in central social institutions. What has happened in the nineteenth and especially in the twentieth century, is that organizational and technological changes have advanced the use of both models by leaps and bounds. Organizationally, the perfecting of modern bureaucratic administrative systems and the transition to industrial production have probably been particularly important. The classical bureaucratic administrative system has formed the basis of a pyramidal structure emphasizing surveillance. The industrial factory has formed a similar base, not least through the foreman and other intermediary roles as modern supervisors. From a technological point of view, the development of media technology has of course been particularly important. The changes in organization and technology are in turn related to extensive and profound societal changes in our own time.

The fan-shaped form of the structures

Second, the panoptical control structure and the media structure have the fan-shaped form as a common property.

Going back once more to the nineteenth century prison, we see the fan-shaped form of the panoptical control system quite clearly. As is well known, the nineteenth century prison was constructed in a star form, as large wings converging in a centre from whence the wings could be supervised. But the fan-shaped form did not only characterize the nineteenth century prison, it characterized, and characterizes, the panoptical control structure in general — of course with modifications and variations. The panopticism of the church was star-shaped — people came (and are coming) to the centrally located church to listen and to confess, and from the church as a centre, surveillance could take place. In his analysis of the Spanish Inquisition, the Danish historian Gunnar Henningsen has given an insightful picture of the fan-shaped form of one of the most important panoptical church institutions in historical times:

As a spider it sat there on guard, watching so that catholicism was not exposed to harmful influences from abroad or from corrupted souls within the country itself. It had its own intelligence service, its own secret police, its own court, its own gaol (the 'secret prison'), its own penitentiary ('the penitence house'), its own doctor, but no executioner. He was borrowed from the town's secular authorities when he was needed. There were 18 similar tribunals distributed throughout the enormous Spanish Empire, and from each of them there were links to the super-spider in Madrid, *La Suprema*, called the Inquisition Council.

> ... If the inquisitors managed to agree, they governed the tribunal quite independently of Madrid, but if they could not agree, the tribunal was in constant correspondence with the Inquisition Council. (Henningsen 1981, p. 28, translated from the Danish by the present author)

We should note that this description of the Inquisition only pictures the 'internal' fan-shaped form of the organization, that is, the lines between the peripheral and central parts of the internal professional system. The main feature of the fan-shaped form, however, is that it stretches out to 'the clients', who also are related to the core system in a fan-shaped form. Such was the organization of church confession, the organization of the nineteenth century prison, of the Inquisition — and such is the organization of the most advanced surveillance systems in our own society.

As indicated already, the fan-shaped form is also a basic property of the media structure. The Norwegian historian and journalist Hans Fredrik Dahl has formulated the point as follows:

> Many communication media — the telegraph, the telephone — create connections between one point and another. The characteristic of mass communication is the fan: transmission from one transmittor point to many receiver points at the same time. (Dahl 1973, pp. 18–19, translated from the Norwegian by the present author)

In the development of each medium, the leap from the point-to-point form to the fan-shaped form constitutes a set of well-defined historical processes. The use of the art of printing — to distribute periodicals, pamphlets and newspapers to many at the same time — was related to the special political conditions of eighteenth century England. The transition from wireless technology, used in point-to-point communication in shipping and the military, to 'broadcasting' or 'round-radio-telephony', was based on specific historical conditions during the years immediately following World War I. Technologically speaking, then, the modern mass media have their historical background in simpler point-to-point communication.

It should be mentioned that the dimensions of the fan show great variations among various mass media (Dahl 1973). State television and radio in Norway are today just about 'total' in the sense of distribution of sets — they reach almost the whole Norwegian population from one centre. The newspapers are considerably less 'total' if we look at the individual papers; for example, some are local newspapers addressing themselves to people within a specific geographical area. However, if we look at the newspapers in general, their fan is also close to 'total' — a large majority of people in the country read at least one newspaper. The same point can be made as well for the weekly magazines. In other words, the way the fan is characterized depends on the level of analysis.

The same holds, however, for the panoptical surveillance structure. Surveillance performed by the state is particularly important. Such surveillance may also be seen as divided into a number of different subsystems, with different — often consciously delimited — fans. But on a different level of analysis it may be said that very many people, if not all, are subject to one form of fan-shaped panoptical supervision or another — the prison, crime prevention systems in the community, the police, the various security agencies or companies, political surveillance, the taxation authorities, and so on.

People are not constantly under surveillance. Often surveillance is inactivated and only potentially present, but the same may of course be said of mediation through the modern media. A number of media studies suggest important variations in the use of different media throughout the population.

The one-way direction of the structures

Third, the panoptic surveillance structure and the media structure have a one-way direction in common as a basic property.

The one-way direction of panopticism is obvious, and is based on the fan-shaped form. We see it quite clearly in the nineteenth century prison — there the few in the centre one-sidedly supervise the many in the various wings; there is no reciprocal supervision. An exchange may take place, for example when the guard from a security company walks his round, but it is still the guard who is doing the supervising; at least he is supervising many different individuals on his round while those who see him do so individually. Important parts of police supervision, as well as political surveillance, take place with a minimum of exchange even on this individual level. Recent technological developments within the modern control structures probably enhance this tendency.

The one-way direction of the modern mass media is also very noticeable. Today the information, the message, the language symbols, or whatever the 'content of information' is called, goes from a central point to a number of other points. The newspapers, the film, the radio and television are cases in point. Today the tendency is greatly enhanced by the modern development of broadcasting and communication satellites. Powerful corporations control transmissions through them, they own the adjoining cable networks, and so on. A multiplication and diversification of transmission occurs, but the one-way direction is still fundamental on the national, international, and indeed the global level. As it is stated in the slogan of 'Sky Channel', a network which transmits soap operas, entertainment films and similar materials via satellite to a number of European countries, including Norway: 'Sky Channel REACHES OUT TO YOU!'

Yet, this parallel to panopticism must be looked at more closely. Mass communication technology is presently developing extremely fast; new techniques quickly make the technology of a few years ago obsolete. The growth of computer technology, minicomputer networks, cable television and communication satellites has led a number of communication analysts to predict the development of fundamentally new types of mass communication in the more or less near future (cf. DeFleur and Ball-Rokeach 1983, p. 104; Parker 1973). One main emphasis has been a far more active participation by the receivers. Parker for example gives this presentation of the situation at an imagined breakfast table in the future:

> A fantasy trip into the future may give a feeling for such a communication medium. Sitting at the breakfast table, you might cause the latest headlines to appear on a small display screen simply by touching a key. These headlines might have been rewritten five minutes before. Pointing at a headline might get the story displayed. If it is a continuing story about, say, the Middle East or an election campaign, you might want to get either a report of the latest incident or background information or interpretation. For someone with a special interest — for example, in some legislation pending in Congress — it could be possible to retrieve the latest story whether or not it received a headline, or even appeared in the latest edition.
>
> With a slightly more expensive computer terminal, your news summary can be printed out for you while you are shaving or getting dressed. A wide variety of background information might be made available by an information utility, on demand by the receiver. Suppose you encounter a name of a person you would like to know more about: ask for a biographical sketch. Suppose you do not completely understand the economic reasoning behind an action by the International Monetary Fund: there might be available a short tutorial program on some aspect of international economics, or you may just seek a brief explanation of some technical term.... (Parker 1973, p. 622)

In this picture the old morning paper, on the doorstep, is quite out of date. If there is anything in such a picture, we should not be surprised that the old-fashioned newspapers of today wish to move into the new media.

To repeat, a main point is here the active participation of the receivers. The one-way fan-shaped structure, through which standardized information is spread in a large circle, is apparently broken, and substituted by a two-way communication system in which the receiver gains access to specialized information, against the background of his own active input. According to this view, the break with the one-way fan, the active participation of the receivers, has two technical versions.

In the first place there is *the information utility*, of which we have already given a hypothetical example. Today we find this type of information utility, in which the receiver through active input may get the specialized information he or she wants, in the travel bureaux, in the banks, in the libraries, and so on. These are places where people themselves see how the information utility may be used, but it is also used in a number of other places, such as in the police, in the large oil companies, and in a number of other large economic organizations. The latter organizations received the information utilities first. The time-shared computer, which makes instant service to a large number of receivers possible, is the basic technological tool.

The second version is *two-way cable vision*, especially based on fibre-optic cable technology. The idea is that the one-way cable system of today will be modified so that the receivers may send as well as receive messages. When introduced on a large scale, this will presumably break the conventional monologue television form. We already find this beginning in television discussion programmes where the participants are brought into the discussion from several distant points. An attempt at a kind of 'electronic city council' has been established in Tulsa, Oklahoma, where 26 cable stations are connected so that people in each station may enter a dialogue with people operating from the other stations (DeFleur and Ball-Rokeach 1982, p. 107).

On this general basis, the future may be described in highly imaginative terms, as when the Norwegian lawyer and author Jon Bing describes a new type of novel: 'The computers make a new type of novel possible, the "interactive" or "reciprocal" novel. The author enters a dialogue with his computer, and carves out the action according to a proposal from the computer program through an advanced game.... The reader becomes the central person, and through the reader's choices the author discloses what consequences the choices have' (Dagbladet, 8 April 1983, translated by the present author; see also Bing 1984).

It is difficult to predict the future. Let us, however, assume that a certain, relatively high, level of interactive activity will be present in the mass media in the first part of the next century. The central question is whether such interactive activity in fact means that the media systems are met by terms set by the receivers.

It is my thesis that this will not be the case, other than in a very limited way. I have two arguments. First, there seems to be general empirical grounds for saying that information and communication systems in a society are first of all modelled and used in such a way that they maintain or support the power of groups which are already in power (cf. Innis 1950). I do not find good sociological reasons for maintaining that the future will be radically different in this way. Second, and more concretely, with the technological possibilities and sociological probabilities as we can foresee them today, the sender side will — even with a high degree of interactive activity — still define the criteria or frames of reference for the information which is to be stored, which is to be available, and which subsequently may be selected, combined and recombined. We can see it today: when the librarian helps us by providing a list of books which we need, the point of departure is databases built on criteria defined by others. The content is also defined by others. When the travel agency helps us to plan a vacation, the point of departure is defined by the possibilities of choice which the various airlines and companies have to offer. These possibilities are created on the basis of various considerations, especially considerations of profit. There is a reason to believe that the highly sophisticated future extensions of these systems, complex information utilities and multi-way cable television, will be based on similar definitions of criteria and terms.

From time to time the technological level of society is described as being characterized by 'inertia' (Østerberg 1971, p. 63). With the speed, changeability and pace of development of data technology, this description does not seem immediately appropriate: the technology may seem very elastic. In connection with the complex systems we are discussing here it may also seem as if the people who participate are the creators of terms or premises — just as the automobile driver may experience him- or herself as such a creator behind the wheel. And in a limited sense it is of course true that terms are established: the media participant acts so that specific new effects are introduced in the information utility, just as the driver drives in such a way that specific consequences are activated in the environment. But in a somewhat broader perspective this is not a question of creating terms or premises but of choosing among possibilities provided by terms set by others. In a somewhat broader perspective, then, the human actor in these contexts is *a chooser and not a creator*. The Norwegian sociologist Tom Johansen has formulated it as follows, and this formulation is relevant to the complex media future:

> When I have now demonstrated that the actions of daily life increasingly constitute choices among given alternatives, and that *the choice* as action is

> becoming predominant, it is implied that action life is dislocated: Homo Creator yields to Homo Elector. It is a question of choice actions: not to manufacture things yourself or produce, but to select, to choose among the most handy utility articles, such is our time. (Johansen 1981, p.112, translated from the Norwegian by the present author)

The choice among possibilities based on terms set by others, which will be the situation of the media participant, may also be formulated as a question of what Stein Bråten has called *model power* (Bråten 1983). Bråten distinguishes between participants who are strong in terms of models, that is, rich in conceptions and concepts within a given area, and participants who are weak in terms of models, that is, deficient in relevant conceptions. Bråten summarizes his theory of model power as follows:

> 1. For an actor A to control x, a model of x is presupposed, developed on A's terms (that is, as seen from A's standpoint).
>
> 2. For 2 actors, A and B, to enter a dialogue, it is presupposed that they have access to models of the issues to which they are referring, and of each other.
>
> From the latter point follows, for an interaction situation between an A who is strong in models and a B who is weak in models, that:
>
> 3. The B who is weak in models will try to acquire the models of the A who is strong in models.
>
> From 1 and 2 it follows that:
>
> 4. The more B 'succeeds' in acquiring A's models, which are developed on A's terms, *the more B comes under A's control.*
>
> (Bråten 1983, p.25, translated from the Norwegian by the present author)

Bråten points out that 'it is easy to find situations in which such mechanisms of model power are activated, regardless of how strong the will is for dialogue and communication: at the company board meeting which is based on a particular agenda, in the classroom situation which is based on issues specified in the curriculum, in the computer context with planning on the terms of experts. Insight may be offered, but not always self-insight as a precondition for autonomy and independence and for capacity to go beyond the current situation on one's own terms' (1983, pp.25–6). Others have made the same point in a different terminology, as when media researchers have described the 'agenda function' of the media, and when phenomenologists raise the question of who 'defines the situation'. What Bråten's presentation particularly sensitizes us to, is how those 'weak in models' come under the control of those who are strong in models by in fact 'succeeding' in acquiring the models of the strong.

This analysis seems well suited for understanding the probable outcome of the interactive media of the future. In other words, the sender side in the future will still be strong in models, and will be defining the terms and the situation whereby the receiver side (precisely through this interactive participation) will acquire the models and come under the control of the senders. Perhaps the receiver side will, by its interactive participation, come even *more* under sender control than is the case in today's simpler media situation. When those who are weak in models enter actual and extensive interaction with those who are strong, the former are easily 'sucked up'. This is well known in the industrial context, the context of the school, and so on. It is 'co-optation' over again. There is reason to believe that co-optation will also take place in the media, even if the initial intention may be quite different.

In short, the term-setting from below will be *apparent*. As apparent, it will mask the fact that the one-way fan is maintained as far as the basic terms or premises go. It will make the one-way fan more diffuse and less visible, and hence all the more easily overlooked. The many will continue to see the few, and due to the interactive processes they will perhaps do so more extensively than before, but at the same time more often without knowing it.

Conclusions

Some threads may be tied together.

A number of analysts have emphasized the possible control function of the panoptical surveillance system. By 'control' is here simply meant actual behavioural influence in the direction of discipline. It has also been emphasized that as panopticism is decentralized, social control follows suit.

But a panoptical surveillance system, whether that of the Spanish Inquisition, the Catholic Church, the military machine or that of political surveillance of the modern state, presupposes a *context of beliefs* if it is to step up from mere surveillance to actual control. Although sanctions that are imposed may lead to control, these sanctions are usually invoked only in extreme cases. The very point of surveillance is essentially to avoid the expenses, efforts and illegitimacy of constant sanctioning. Yet in modern society surveillance is sufficiently imprecise and inefficient to require the frequent utilization of overt sanctions.

The Spanish Inquisition could rely on deep-seated and complex beliefs in the danger of witches and heretics. The Catholic Church could (and can) rely on deep-seated religious beliefs. And so on. Without the belief systems, the surveillance systems would, to a large extent, have been ineffective. Witches and heretics would no longer have been given up to the authorities; people would no longer come to confession (the very seat of panoptical surveillance). The relationship between panoptical control and beliefs is complex. Suffice it here to say that it is dialectical. The present point is that without the belief system, the panoptical structure would crumble.

I contend that today *the modern mass media provide the most important belief context for the panoptical surveillance system.* The mass media are a functional equivalent to the medieval church in inculcating the necessary belief context of obedience and subservience. Curran has put the matter very succinctly:

> The mass media have now assumed the role of the Church, in a more secular age, of interpreting and making sense of the world to the mass public. Like their priestly predecessors, professional communicators amplify systems of representation that legitimise the social system. The priesthood told their congregations that the power structure was divinely sanctioned; their successors inform their audiences that the power structure is democratically sanctioned through the ballot box. Dissidents were frequently de-legitimised by churchmen as 'infidels' intent upon resisting God's will; dissidents in contemporary Britain are frequently stigmatised as 'extremists' who reject democracy ... The medieval Church taught that the only legitimate way of securing redress for injustice was to appeal to the oppressor's conscience and, failing that, to a higher secular authority; the modern mass media similarly sanction only constitutional and lawful procedures as legitimate methods of protest ... The medieval Church masked the sources of inequality by ascribing social injustice to the sin of the individual; the modern mass media tend, in more complex and sophisticated ways, to misdirect their audiences by the ways in which they define and explain structural inequalities ... By stressing the randomness of God's unseen hand, the medieval Church encouraged passive acceptance of a subordinate status in society; the randomness of fate is a recurrent theme in much modern media entertainment ... The Church none the less offered the chiliastic consolation of eternal salvation to 'the meek [who] shall inherit the earth'; the media similarly give prominence to show-business personalities and football stars who, as 'a powerless élite', afford easily identifiable symbols for vicarious fulfillment... (Curran 1982, pp.227–228)

Though there are exceptions (Cohen 1971, 1972; Cohen and Young 1973; Hall *et al.* 1978), the study of panoptical surveillance systems, and of media systems, constitute two expanding but largely separate fields of research and inquiry. The Foucaultian thesis of a great historical development from the many who see the few to the few who see the many, from the eagle and the sun to panopticism, is perhaps a reflection of this bifurcation, and has at least promoted it. The bifurcation is unfortunate, first because it is historically incorrect: panopticism and its opposite number have significant reciprocally supplementary functions. Second, and more important, the greatly expanding mass media system provides the necessary belief context, the obedient, disciplined, subservient set of beliefs necessary for the surveillance systems to be functional. Concretely, surveillance in a broad sense, and certainly the policing of society, is given general legitimacy. The view that there are good grounds for combatting 'external and internal enemies of the state' is subtly inculcated. The belief that surveillance is in fact efficient, both as surveillance and as control, is disseminated, and this definition of the situation becomes real in its consequences. The belief that surveillance is *not* efficient, that we need *more* of it, is simultaneously disseminated, and this definition of the situation also becomes real in its consequence. Both definitions of the situation are important for panopticism to thrive.

If this analysis is correct, it also has consequences for political action. The political struggle against the development of modern surveillance systems must be strongly directed towards creating alternative communication networks for disseminating information about surveillance and political control in society. Space forbids detailed analysis of such alternative networks (for details see Mathiesen 1984/85), suffice it to say that communication must be as direct and as much characterized by dialogue as possible, in contrast to the indirect communication through a technology implying distance between 'sender' and 'receiver'. The latter technology stands a great chance of being co-opted by powerful forces and of becoming a one-way support of panopticism. A great deal of imagination must and may be put into the effort of creating such politically viable alternatives.

Lest panopticism is to continue to survive...

4 Justice as information sharing[1]

Harold E. Pepinsky

The concept of 'social control' has recently been defined as 'those organised responses to crime, delinquency and allied forms of deviant and/or socially problematic behaviour which are actually conceived as such' (Cohen 1985a, p. 3). But suppose that 'responses to deviance' are responses to frustration that has nothing to do with deviance at all. And what if responses to the false definition of a problem compound that problem? Should that be the case, 'social control' would be an inherently self-defeating endeavour. As such, the achievement of social control would require that the very object of control be redefined. That is the premise of this chapter.

The chapter begins by reformulating the object of social control in general, and crime control in particular. It is not a prescription that behaviour conform to a certain standard, nor that material wealth be distributed in any predetermined way, but that the human interaction which generates certain material distributions and social relations take a certain form — one in which participants freely share information about their various circumstances.

Having redefined the kind of wrong or 'injustice' that spawns the need for social control, the essay proceeds to illustrate the various injustices that lead people to fear 'crime'. Finally the essay outlines what forms of social control might genuinely free people from fear of crime and the underlying injustice that it represents.

The problem

The meanings of the prime objects of study in criminology — 'crime' and 'justice' — have remained elusive. Is 'crime' a violation of penal law (see Sutherland 1940, 1945; Tappan 1947), and 'justice' the legal remedy? This traditional premise has become untenable to a growing number of criminologists, who observe that penal law is itself unjust, and that many violations of human rights which properly rank among our worst crimes are not covered by criminal law (for example, Schwendinger and Schwendinger 1970). 'Crime' and 'justice' have to be defined in extra-legal terms. To signify this broad purview, many criminologists have suggested that we study not merely crime and legal punishment, but 'social control' (as in this volume; see also Streib 1977), 'pain' (Christie 1981), or 'justice' (see Myren 1980).

But if law is an arbitrary standard for distinguishing right conduct from wrong, so are the more encompassing standards, such as 'human rights', that we try to substitute for it. Rawls (1971) has made the most elaborate recent attempt to formulate a transcendant standard of justice, concluding that:

> All social primary goods — liberty and opportunity, income and wealth, and the bases of self-respect — are to be distributed equally unless an unequal distribution of any or all of these goods is to the advantage of the least favoured. (Rawls 1971, p. 303)

By extension, it can be said that withholding or taking more than one's just share from others is basically what we ought to call 'crime', and that criminals deserve to have such illicit gains taken from them and redistributed as justice requires. Or, if what has been taken cannot be recovered, justice at least requires hurting the offender as much as the offender's injustice hurt others. Recent retributivists taking this position include Van den Haag (1975) and Von Hirsch (1976), although it is important to recognize that the logic of retribution remains the same as one moves from the political right toward advocacy of revolution on the political left (Pepinsky 1980). Rather than the issue of retribution, it is the equality of various kinds of material distribution that separates right and left.

I wish to suggest here, however, that it is the logic of material equality which is fundamentally flawed. As long as notions of right and wrong rest on questions of material distribution, we are always bound to reach a point at which no principle can distinguish one person's justice from another's crime. 'Goods' or material resources are inherently scarce. One person's possession or use of material resources ultimately becomes another's deprivation. Even when supplies of commodities or services expand, people's 'need' to have them keeps pace. No amount of technological advance or expansion of wealth or bounty seems to satiate the appetite of those who have been contending for bigger pieces of material pies.

As long as people contend for a 'fair' share of scarce resources, practically anyone at anytime can claim to be 'less favoured', hence more deserving than others. The rich can argue that wealth is a burden and a handicap which makes the owner 'less favoured'. Those who continue to gain more than others often argue that they do so because they work harder, and that poorer people remain poor because they fail to capitalize on opportunities available to them. Watching 'haves' argue that they are 'have-nots' angers many observers (including me) but the point is that defining justice and crime in terms of material distribution invites this kind of argument, and provides no transcendant principle for settling the priority of different types of claims.

Materially defined justice is ambiguous not only as a label, but as a predictor of violence and peace. Justice is commonly supposed to be a means to an end. As such, people who live in a just world should have no occasion for violence. If injustice is the cause of violence, and if injustice is defined as inequality of material resources, then obviously affluent people ought to be more peaceful. And yet, the more affluent people, corporations and nations become, the greater their apparent propensity for violence (cf. Zinn 1980). Criminologists have repeatedly discovered a strong positive correlation between wealth and power on the one hand, and the propensity for violence and predation on the other (Pepinsky and Jesilow 1985; Reiman 1984). On the victim's side, the anger and fear people feel bear no manifest relation to the amount of physical loss they suffer as in, for example, the seemingly enigmatic finding that elderly people report less victimization than others, but fear crime more (Merry 1981). Similarly punishment often seems more severe than the offence should warrant (Pepinsky 1982; Reiman 1984). Drastic material redistribution does not seem to reduce the propensities of groups of people — even of the beneficiaries — to further acts of violence against foreign and domestic 'enemies'. Galtung (1969) observes that when we respond to injustice and violence with counter-violence, we rarely achieve peace. To get beyond violence we must respond to structural conditions with some form of 'positive peace' that transcends the attempt to get even with those who offend us.

In sum, a workable definition of justice needs to focus on distribution of something that is not material, that is not subject to scarcity, and that determines whether people become either fearful or secure, violent or peaceful.

This essay explores the possibility that 'information sharing' can be used as one such working definition of justice. If, as proposed here, justice requires free flow of information among people, then justice can only be arranged on a small scale, in limited networks of no more than several hundred people at a time.

Information cannot be used up

The more information is used, the more it grows. Consider, for instance, what happens if a trade secret such as a manufacturing process is revealed. The manufacturer who reveals the secret can still use the process. If someone else uses the information to copy the process, and if the information flow remains open, the original manufacturer can learn from problems and successes that the copier encounters in refining or changing the process. No one loses information as long as the flow continues.

As information is shared, human energy resonates. This resonance is manifested in surges of power which are greater than the sum of their individual human constituents. It can be seen, and indeed its power felt, in filmed events like Felix Greene's 'Inside North Vietnam', where seemingly leaderless waves of people reconstruct bombed-out railway track with simple tools at incredible speed, or more recently, in 'The Witness', with the lightning-like barn-raising by a group of Amish men. Sometimes the power is felt more than seen, as when disputants in mediation (Witty 1980) or reconciliation (Immarigeon 1984) sessions first exchange anger and recrimination, then negotiate ways to build beyond the dispute, and occasionally close by embracing in a surge of warmth and relief.

Whatever the form, however serious or irrelevant any material product of information sharing, the resonance has these qualities:

1. The energy coming out of the interaction is greater than the simple sum of energy contributed by each individual participant. If thirty Amish men build a large barn in a single day, one of them working thirty days would not be able to complete the same amount of work. While purely material consumption is entropic (that is, less usable energy comes out of a machine than goes in), reciprocal giving and taking of information among people is synergistic (that is, it creates more energy than is input; on 'synergy' see Fuller 1975, 1979).
2. No single person or set of information produces the resonance. One person's action always presupposes information provided by others. One person's mistake may be the key to another person's understanding how the mistake could have been avoided. We can see manifestations of the resonance of information sharing, but not the source. This is characteristic of all synergism which, unlike entropic processes in the material world, cannot be directly observed or located in time or space (Fuller 1975, 1979).
3. The independent contribution of any person or information set to resonance is likewise nil. Resonance lies in the blending of information; you cannot pick pieces of the resonance off and attribute them to various 'inputs'. Thus, in so far as empirical analyses dwell on identifying independent variables, they are unable to describe the emergent qualities of resonance.

Unlike acquisition of material goods, the acquisition of information is not a zero-sum game: in theory, an infinite number of people could possess any item of information simultaneously. Sharing information is not even a mixed-sum game, since pooling information has the potential of increasing sums beyond *a priori* limits. In material games, people are forced to divide their winnings; in the game of information sharing, the simple act of playing together multiplies everyone's winnings. The only way to become 'less favoured' by information sharing is to fail to play the game. The failure is lost power and opportunity for everyone involved, and since one cannot foresee precisely where the power and opportunity will strike until the information is shared, any participant's loss is potentially as great as any other's. Hence, persons of material wealth and power have as great a stake as the poor in sharing information across class lines. The more information each side gives, and the more closely it listens to the information the other side offers, the more it learns. If we define the resonance of information sharing as 'justice', everyone becomes a winner, and we avoid the problem of any one person or group's justice having to be another's crime.

The human propensity to share information

Unlike most life forms, people require prolonged care after birth, go for years without being able to bear offspring, gestate for extended periods, and bear exceptionally few offspring. Meanwhile, the environment often shifts capriciously and radically. The odds of human survival are at least partly determined by our ability to survive and thrive in different environments. The extraordinary capacity of humans to tolerate a wider range of environments than other complex species reflects, among other things, our superior ability in gathering and disseminating information.

Since the human reproductive cycle is so long, the survival of each offspring is relatively crucial to the survival of the species. Since human tolerance of climatic or dietary variation is limited biologically, survival of each member of the species rests primarily on individual humans manipulating methods of food production and shelter as environments shift. Human adaptability relies not on each person's living and dying by his or her own successes and mistakes alone, but on a continuous pooling and reassessment of information in the company of other human beings.

This propensity to share information would manifest itself most in situations eliciting feelings of alarm. The perception that other people react the same way, with the same objective, regardless of one's input, would cause alarm. Similarly, alarm should result if one's own objectives or actions remain unchanged in the face of information inputs from other people, even from subordinates. Satisfaction should occur with the perception that each person's information input affected every other person's actions. Under these ideal circumstances information from each person or faction would appear necessary for justice to be achieved, but *insufficient* by itself. This is the dialogue Freire (1972) describes as 'life affirming', a situation where each party to an action is a subject helping to create a new environment rather than an object of unilateral control.

The fact that our species has survived so long indicates that people largely succeed in achieving satisfying and life affirming interaction. The strength of the propensity to share information should make people hypersensitive to its failure to occur. A determination to impose order could stem from the ensuing alarm. In that case unilateral attempts to impose order would be understandable, but inherently self-defeating.

Although human survival presupposes that people share information to a remarkable degree, destructive human practices suggest that human beings fail to share information to a noticeable degree, and that human sensitivity to the failure to share information is considerable. In a perverse way, the establishment of destructive human institutions is a measure of the strength of our suffering once we notice any failure to share information.

Nevertheless, our survival and proliferation indicate that we possess a basic propensity to keep each other alive by continuously pooling information. The prolonged existence of humanity cannot be explained in the absence of this trait.

Small wonder, then, that information sharing is a basic theme of so many human religions. In the Old Testament we are told that people who fail to attend to the plight of their less fortunate neighbours are themselves ultimately doomed. New Testament teachings portray eternal life as being dependent on love for one's neighbour. The central premise of Buddhism is that survival rests on compassion — one's ability to hear someone else's plight and be guided accordingly. As a corollary of these injunctions many religions prohibit pride, and especially the belief that one's understanding of the world is so superior to that of other people that one can afford to stop listening and learning from their ongoing experience.

There is no reason to suppose that human beings are born with a sense of how many resources are sufficient to satiate a material appetite. Beyond extremes of hunger and physical discomfort, people can live in material simplicity — in what we richer folk might call poverty — and yet consider themselves 'prosperous' (as did Eastern Native American tribes, for instance: see Heckewelder 1819/1971). On the other hand, like John D. Rockefeller, materially wealthy people can pronounce that it still takes 'just a little bit more' money to make oneself happy. Regardless of material circumstances, the question remains whether one considers other people an asset or a threat to one's own future well being. Given that humans are social beings, they look to each other to help overcome material adversity. Since no amount of material success seems to reassure people that they have enough to stop taking from others, a concern for keeping channels of information flow open seems logically prior to the acquisition of material wealth. Only after one feels that others have severed communication channels is one likely to resent or envy their material well being.

Human consumption provokes hostility and violence only when it signifies that the consumer does not care either to reveal information about his or her circumstances or intentions, or to listen to other people. This blockage of information makes human beings mutually threatening. It does not matter who does the blocking, or who derives material gain. When, for instance, John D. Rockefeller declines to account for his actions to his workers, or to listen to their plight, he too must feel threatened. Human regard for others is first and foremost a matter of how well we listen to one another.

In summary, the following observations about the human propensity to share information can be noted:

1. This propensity must be very strong for human beings to be able to survive in almost any ecosystem.
2. If the propensity is so strong, failure to share information should arouse primal fear when humans encounter information blockage. Given limits on human attention span and information processing capacity, failure to listen to other people or to make oneself accountable occurs regularly. Presumably, given that humanity is survival-prone, human beings appear to 'lump' together and repress sporadic failures to communicate with people around them (Felstiner 1974), and limit their primal alarm to systematic failures of accountability.
3. Unpredictable as our environment is, the restriction of information to channels within classes appears to arouse primal fear equally among rich and poor. Aggrandizing and hoarding material wealth — 'the spirit of capitalism' (Weber 1904/1985) — can be understood as an attempt to negate the threat that the material wealth of today may be the poverty of tomorrow. Conversely, in societies where information flows freely among groups, people may feel socially and economically secure despite living in material simplicity. These are enigmas to someone who defines justice in material terms: they make sense if one posits an underlying propensity to share information, and recognizes the power that the sharing represents.

Injuries of injustice

Although Western urban elderly persons report less victimization than younger persons, they report greater fear of crime. Similarly, street crime produces greater fear than white-collar or organizational crime (Balvig 1979; Merry 1981; Pepinsky and Jesilow 1985; Reiman 1984). If one looks at the risk of predation and violence in strictly material or conventional legal terms these enigmas of fear appear to be distorted and exaggerated. If, however, one defines the threat as a blockage in information flow, the elderly persons' fear of crime becomes real and rational.

On the whole, the elderly are isolated. They can scarcely resist being knocked down by young thieves on city streets. If they fall down and break a hip at home they may not be discovered for days or weeks. If they need food or shelter or medicine they risk being ignored. The overwhelming 'injustice' for persons in this condition is that people are unaccountable to them or disinclined to listen to them. It may be a misplaced projection of the injustice they suffer that causes elderly persons to ascribe their danger to neighbourhood youths (Merry 1981), but the threat of being used or ignored or abandoned is quite real. The young people could be obliterated or contained, but the threat and level of victimization would remain essentially unaddressed. Crime against the elderly cannot meaningfully be measured in amounts of money snatched from purses: its seriousness instead lies in the social isolation of these elderly victims.

Redefining injustice as blocked information flow helps explain widespread alarm in recent years over street crime. On the one hand, in strictly material legal terms, it cannot be established, for example, that Americans risk street crime more today than a hundred years ago (Pepinsky and Jesilow 1985, pp. 21–34). Yet strangers on contemporary Western streets are probably 'stranger' than their counterparts of yesteryear, so that when property disappears, or physical injury is suffered, we feel more threatened by the social distance of the 'perpetrator'. And more disturbing than the offender who strikes in anger is the one who strikes out of apparent indifference. If indeed information does flow less freely in the modern world, it is easier to understand why comparable physical losses signify more crime and arouse more outrage now than they did formerly (a recurrent theme of Christie's work (1981, 1982)). And the fear is 'rational', in that physical loss among people who fail to share information is harder to overcome than among those who communicate freely.

Predation can be seen as a failure of information flow, from the personal to the multinational level. At the personal level, blockages of information may facilitate predation in two ways. First, they allow people to take from or hurt others without sensing the pain they cause. Those who conduct victim–offender reconciliation sessions commonly report that offenders are surprised to learn of the pain and fear they have caused (Immarigeon 1984). It is now common to refer to rape as a crime of violence rather than a sex crime. Large department stores are said to be most vulnerable to shoplifting because customers do not personally know their owners. Milgram (1965) found that as experimental subjects inflicted what they thought were increasingly powerful electric shocks on victims, they came to ignore victim responses, and turned their attention instead to interaction with the experimenter who was telling them what to do. Christie (1981) writes that the principal factor distinguishing people inclined to violence and punishment from those who inflict less pain on one another, is the level of intimacy in their respective social relations.

Blockage of information flow may also stimulate people to predation and violence against convenient victims. Kuperstock's (1985, pp. 20–3) description of subjects she typically encounters in an offender rehabilitation programme serves to illustrates this point. 'Dale', having been given a bicycle by his father, was told to pay five dollars toward the price every Friday, with the proviso that the first week he was late with the payment, the bike would be returned to the store. Dale made the payments out of money he collected on his newspaper route. When summer came, customers left on vacation without notice. Dale was unable to collect enough money to make the payment. His father seemed to have made it clear that the repayment clause of the arrangement was not negotiable. Given the boy's inability to discuss ways to keep the bicycle, Dale simply passed the unilateral action along: he went into the homes of vacationing customers and took the money from them. An inability to share in the decision-making process (that is, to share information) led Dale to victimize someone else.

Alternatively, the public identification of offenders may, as Durkheim (1895/1982) and Coser (1956) suggest, represent a bid to gain solidarity with others. Brogden (1982) suggests that the remarkable degree of consensus across classes in nineteenth-century Britain, concerning the central role of chronically unemployed young men in perpetrating the 'crime problem', represents just such a case. One might then suppose that agreement on what constituted appropriate targets of law enforcement produced justice, by giving people a common problem about which to share information. Scapegoating, however, is likely to create more violence than it prevents because:

1. Any injustice, including the severing of communication channels to one's scapegoats, arouses fear in those who prevail as well as in those who are scapegoated. From this perspective one can see that it was John D. Rockefeller's isolation that led to his wealth becoming an abiding source of his own anxiety.
2. The issues which led to the scapegoating in the first place remain unaddressed.
3. A vital part of the propensity to share information is the ability to raise unforeseen issues and problems as environmental circumstances change. The ability to reset agendas to include new issues is a major part of what Christie (1977) means by 'owning' a dispute.

> Scapegoating prevents the reconstruction of disputes as conditions change. It is perhaps for this reason that strikes and riots by blacks occurred in record numbers in the United States during World War II, when the fight against foreign enemies left industrial managers and politicians too busy to be bothered listening to complaints about domestic working conditions (Zinn 1980, pp.398–434). For the same reason wars on crime and foreign wars have been found to build upon one another, with casualty and incarceration rates continually rising (Pepinsky and Jesilow 1985, pp.158–60; Zinn 1980), so that now one in twelve American black men in their twenties is spending the day in jail or prison (Pepinsky and Jesilow 1985, pp.11, 161–2).

If the hunger for sharing information does exist, the reduction of violence, including the threat of crime, depends as heavily on what information is produced as it does on the fact that it is shared at all. Joining with some people in order to exclude others undoes the good of joining. For production to be peaceful, the products must be peaceful (a central premise for people advocating conversion from military production: cf. *Changing Work*, 1985, pp.20–48). Political revolutions are as ill-equipped to permanently reduce violence as are wars, including wars on crime (Pepinsky 1982). In Galtung's (1969) terms, effective peace-making must be 'positive' rather than 'negative' or violent. The question remains: how, if ever, is truly positive peace-making or justice to be accomplished?

Doing justice

Von Hirsch (1976) and Newman (1984) describe systems for 'doing justice' to offenders in material ways.[2] If the primary objective of 'justice' is to release information from closed systems, the issue becomes not what to do to whom, but how to extend participation in decision-making. This is precisely the shift that Wilkins (1984) asks criminologists to make — away from the classification of offenders, toward the opening or 'democratization' of information flow. Justice as information sharing concerns the expansion of accountability among groups of people. It concerns the extension of power in decision-making rather than the preordination of that power. The primary issue is not who gets what, but *who decides* who gets what.

For justice not to become exclusive and deteriorate into violence, accountability must not be systematically closed to anyone concerned. There is obviously a threshold size of group in which justice can be achieved. The experience of the Mondragon community of worker co-operatives in Basque Spain seems to indicate that justice cannot be planned for more than several hundred people at a time, in slowly expanding networks of limited numbers of groups (Gutierezz-Johnson 1984; Henk and Logan 1982; Oakeshott 1978).

In a broad international survey of industrial reorganization, Oakeshott (1978) praises Mondragon for several reasons. First, this 25-year-old network, which now contains 150 enterprises, is an unparalleled economic success; none of the enterprises has failed, and the assets of the co-operative bank at the centre of the network have risen dramatically over the years (for recent figures, see Gutierrez-Johnson 1984). Second, years of forethought and attention to minute constitutional detail preceded the formation of the earliest enterprises. Third, membership in the enterprise is open to all residents in the community, with financial assistance and training provided by the network, so that employment and inclusion remain available to the outside community and to succeeding generations of potential participants. Fourth, the array of enterprises is numerous and varied enough to permit comparative evaluation. Fifth, the enterprises have welcomed outside observation and study.

On the whole, worker satisfaction and productivity in the enterprises are high, while absenteeism and disciplinary problems are comparatively infrequent (Henk and Logan 1982). Oakeshott (1978) lists as the key factors in Mondragon's success:

1. Painstaking, written and formalized records that ensure mutual accountability among successive groups of people;
2. A meticulously graded and adjustable balance between private and collective shares of worker ownership that remains open to new members;
3. An interlocking web of mutual accountability and standing to act between worker-owners and hired professional management;
4. Financial and managerial accountability; and
5. A blend of bank ownership of community enterprises combined with ownership and partial directorship of the bank.

The complexity of the interweaving of ownership and managerial rights and obligations which the bank requires of each enterprise (and to which the bank itself is bound by the individuals and enterprises which in turn own it) is far greater than that found in national constitutions or standard articles of incorporation.

Although unrest and dissatisfaction are remarkably subdued, problems do, however, arise. Observers and Mondragon members generally agree that workers have trouble participating in management, and managers have trouble gaining full worker trust. Two more substantial problems have arisen.

One of the problems is with labour relations at the largest enterprise, one of Spain's biggest heavy appliance manufacturers, with several thousand worker-owners rather than several hundred as is the case with most of the other enterprises. The one strike in Mondragon's history (in 1974) involved this company. Worker-owners are forbidden to strike on penalty of being expelled. Although the strike soon ended with the expulsion of several worker leaders, labour relations in this enterprise are still reported to be relatively troubled.

The other problem is that the bank has become very wealthy as a result of the community's expansion. The bank's investments have extended from Mondragon enterprises into the outside world. As the Mondragon membership has grown, the markets of the community's companies have also extended into the international economy. This growth has meant that the bank has become increasingly bureaucratized, and that community members are less insulated from wider economic forces.

Generally, conflict increases when the community becomes too large for workers and managers to remain sensitive to each others' perceptions of appropriate business strategy; communication channels begin to close.[3] The reasons for this breakdown are situated in the relationship between the extraordinary economic success of Mondragon enterprises and the relative intricacy of their constitutions. It is difficult enough to arrange free flow of information among several hundred people at a time. It is impossible to imagine how to organize such information flows among nation states and multinational corporations without excluding large groups of people. To this extent human organizations must be limited in scale and radically decentralized if justice is to be achieved.

As in Mondragon, networks of small communities can, perhaps, be built. Information and interaction among small-scale communities can certainly take place so long as neither the communities nor the networks allow the larger-scale agglomerations produced by such interaction to define what the smaller communities do. People need to retain a sense of being encapsulated within smaller groups (Jacobsen 1978, pp. 184–93) in order to preserve a sense of justice — a sense that the information that they and their associates provide continually reshapes their destiny. Whatever plans are laid, a sense of justice requires that responsibility for planning goals rests with people organized in small units.

New forms of industrial organization like those in Mondragon are a good place to test alternative ways to achieve justice. The experience of Mondragon can more readily be generalized to 'the real world' than the early organization of Israeli kibbutzim (Schwartz 1954) or life among the Hutterites (Bennett 1967). It may be that the 'tightness' of these communities (Christie 1982) permits members to live peaceably. But such communities are also more isolated than could normally be achieved in a shrinking world.

Preliminary propositions for a theory of peace and justice based on information sharing can be summarized as follows:

1. Justice requires intricate rules facilitating ownership rights among *all* members of a community.
2. Rules must specify who makes decisions instead of focusing on the substance of those decisions (for example, on who gets to manage a dispute (Christie 1977) rather than on which penalties go with which crimes (Von Hirsch 1976)).
3. Just systems are necessarily limited in scale involving no more than a few hundred people at a time.

Conclusions

This has been a preliminary exploration of a new way of thinking about justice as information sharing rather than justice as material equality. This definition of justice enables resolution of paradoxes inherent in material definitions of justice and crime. A focus on failures to share information seems to explain otherwise enigmatic connections between fear and violence on the one hand, and material circumstances on the other. Several propositions begin to emerge about what peace through justice might require. In particular, the size of social control systems must be limited.

Many people would argue that human beings have an innate propensity for violence rather than a propensity for peace or information sharing. Rather than providing proof that peace can or will be accomplished, this chapter provides a perspective on how to proceed *as if* peace can be achieved through justice. Here's hoping...

5 The construction and deconstruction of social control: thoughts on the discursive production of state law and private justice[1]

Stuart Henry

Introduction

In his recent writing, Cohen has rightly described social control as a 'Mickey Mouse concept, used to include all social processes ranging from infant socialization to public education, all social policies whether called health, education or welfare' (1983, pp. 101–2; see also Cohen 1985a). Instead he opts for a more focused definition which includes '...all organised responses to crime, delinquency and allied forms of deviance — whether sponsored directly by the state or by institutions such as social work and psychiatry, and whether designated as treatment, prevention, punishment or whatever' (1983, p.102). Such a definition, however, excludes the whole range of non-state institutions for dispensing justice and sanctions that emerge within groups and organizations for controlling their membership. Elsewhere (Henry 1983, 1986) I have defined such non-state systems as 'private justice' and suggested that they include the practices of such institutions as the disciplinary bodies, boards and councils of industrial and commercial organizations, professional and trade associations and unions, down to the peer sanctioning of relatively amorphous voluntary associations such as local self-help and mutual aid groups. Private justice, then, comprises those institutions of social control that maintain the normative order of groups and organizations. But such justice does not exist in isolation, and this chapter is about the ways in which it interrelates with the more formalized state legal order. Before proceeding, however, a little more clarification is necessary.

Private justice should not be confused with informal and community-based alternatives to justice which have emerged as part of what Cohen describes as the 'destructuring' of state control, such as decentralization, deformalization, decriminalization, delegalization, diversion, deprofessionalization, deinstitutionalization and decarceration. As Cohen and others have convincingly argued, these developments have merely been ways of dispersing social control and simultaneously widening the state net in times of fiscal and legitimation crises (Abel 1981, 1982b; Brady 1981; Cohen 1979, 1985a; Santos 1980; Scull 1977).

Private justice also needs to be distinguished from 'privatization' whereby 'the state ceases to supply a particular service and it is then supplied by private enterprises which are directly paid by the public as customers' (Cohen 1985a, p. 64). Nor are the forms of privatization in which the state contracts out certain services to private enterprise (but retains overall control) a part of what I take to be private justice. Private policing by commercial security companies, however, forms a special case that straddles the boundary between privatized state control and private justice. When a private security company is contracted by the state to police public arenas or by a private corporation to protect their property from the threat of external crime, then it is part of Cohen's concept of destructured social control. But where the private security company is contracted by groups of organizations to perform a policing function on its own membership, then it becomes part of what I call private justice. It will then be a component of an administrative chain in which deviants from the rules or principles of the organization are processed through a private judicial machinery concerned with considering their offence and dispensing sanctions to those found guilty.

That private justice can also exist as a reserve arsenal of social control, relied on by the state system, is of no little importance even if it has been little studied. But unlike much state control, whether direct or indirect, private justice can, and often does, oppose the state's law in the exercise of its control. The concept of social control is too indiscriminating to capture this duality of support and opposition. But private justice itself is somewhat overdiscriminating, implying that its control is isolated and autonomous, unaffected by the wider structural setting in which it is set. A concept is needed which captures the simultaneous separateness and connectedness of private justice and state control. For this purpose I have adopted the concept of 'legal pluralism' as best suited to acknowledge what I have described elsewhere as the semi-autonomous quality of private justice (Henry 1983). Legal pluralism, as we shall see in more detail shortly, holds that every society contains a plurality of legal orders and legal subsystems (or fragments of these). Each exercises controls over the membership of the social forms in which they are rooted, and does so in ways that are sometimes concurrent with, and sometimes contradictory to, wider state law and ancillary components of social control.

The aim of this chapter is to demonstrate firstly that state law and the state's system of justice and control exist in a mutually interdependent relationship with a plurality of institutions of private justice, and secondly that a principal medium for sustaining this relationship is the discursive construction practice of human agency. After first outlining some of the seminal ideas of legal pluralist theory, I will turn to the view that recent developments in legal pluralism have advanced thinking about social control by incorporating the Hegelian/Marxian concept of dialectic into conceptions about the relations between state law and non-state control forms. I proceed with a critique of the most sophisticated of these approaches, Peter Fitzpatrick's theory of integral plurality, arguing that ultimately this fails to radically change the existing grip of control since, by reifying human agency, it denies a major means of deconstructing the very forms whereby humans connive in their own oppression. I then argue that a genuinely radical critique needs to reconsider state law and the plurality of non-state control institutions as manifestations of socially constructed agency-based control forms. I argue that control forms, and the social forms in which they are rooted and designed to police, are no more than the recursively generated constitutive representations whose relationship to each other stems from human agents' discursive practices. Drawing on examples of discourse taken from my study of industrial discipline (Henry 1983), I show how human agents' discursive practices recursively constitute the control forms on which institutions of state social control and private justice are founded. Finally, I illustrate how human agents can begin to deconstruct existing control forms by ceasing to invest in their discursive production, while simultaneously investing in the production of alternatives.

Legal pluralism and the dialectical relations between law and social control

The suggestion that state law and its institutions of justice are but one form of social control has been a central feature of legal pluralism from Gierke (1900), Ross (1901) and Ehrlich (1912) through Gurvitch (1947) to the more recent anthropologically influenced works of Pospisil (1971), Abel (1982), Griffiths (1981), Fitzpatrick (1983a, 1983b, 1984) and Marxists like Santos (1984) and Spitzer (1982). The central idea is well expressed by Pospisil who argues that '... any human society ... does not possess a single legal system but as many such systems as there are functioning groups' (1971, p.98). The multiplicity of these systems forms a mosaic of contradictory controls which simultaneously bear on any person.

The pluralist tradition has been concerned with both the character of non-state controls and their relationship to state law. Gierke (1958, originally 1900) saw society as an organic whole composed of numerous institutions, each being the source of its own autonomous legal order that was ultimately subordinate to state law. But the state did not create these institutional legal orders, even if it could control them. For

Ehrlich (1912), state law was a diffuse series of layers of law-like rules and controls reaching down to the spontaneous 'living law' of various human associations; state law would only be an effective control if it did not lag behind its own source, living law. From this perspective, living law was the source of all law.

But, contrary to the impression created by these early writers, the state has no more of a monopoly on formality and control than the non-state forms have on spontaneity, informality and legitimation. Rather, as Gurvitch (1947) was to point out, there are numerous sources of law, each having supporting systems and techniques of control. Each of these legal orders can also be found to operate at various levels or depths of formality, from a fixed, written law down to a spontaneous, informal set of controls.

In its various guises, then, legal pluralism acknowledges:

1. The simultaneous existence of numerous non-state forms of law and justice;
2. The rooting of each in a diffuse set of institutions;
3. The operation of each at different levels of formality/informality; and
4. The hierarchical relationship among the different forms of non-state control and state law which reflects the location of power in the parent organization wherein the controls are situated.

Recent contributions to this debate have disabused the assumption of earlier theories that non-state forms of law, justice and control are either the spontaneous informal source of state law, or are independent though ultimately subordinate to it. Similarly, any notion of directly coercive subordination and domination is rejected in favour of a model of ideological domination through a dialectical and mutually interpenetrating relationship. In this model, non-state control forms are both manifestations of the internal contradictions of the totality, and semi-autonomously constituted through their mutual dependence on local and wider structures which they variously oppose and support.

Some theorists, notably Abel (1981, 1982) and Spitzer (1982), consider the state's subordination of non-state forms a matter of ideological manipulation and co-optation, exploiting the human tendency to produce informal institutions involving *gemeinschaft*-like, face-to-face relations and community. Abel posits an endless cyclical relationship between formal and informal law, in which first formality and then informality is expansive, with the movement between the two serving to legitimate the wider structure of capitalist relations. Galanter (1981) argues that formal justice moves outwards, influencing indigenous orders of justice that exist in a variety of groups and organizational settings where disputes are actually resolved; simultaneously this 'legal shadow' provides 'many rooms' of justice to handle the overflow from the formal state system. Cohen (1979, 1985a) and Brady (1981) have shown how informality is a non-threatening way for state law to expand its sphere of influence and widen its net of control. In all these analyses there is an assumption that if mutual interpenetration is present, one side of it only serves dominant interests, interests that are allowed rather than claimed. It is argued that penetration by the state of non-state forms is greater than the penetration of the state by those forms; state law shapes private justice more than private justice shapes state law.

Fitzpatrick's (1983a, 1983b, 1984) dialectical concept of 'integral plurality' appears to offer a considerable break with this tradition. The break is, however, not complete. As Fitzpatrick states from the outset, his position is at odds with a genuine pluralism for 'it does not seek to deny over-arching and integrating structures' (1984, p. 118). In spite of this, Fitzpatrick claims, and I have illustrated (Henry 1983, 1985, 1986), that integral plurality offers the promise of a genuine mutuality of penetration. Thus, Fitzpatrick says that state law is, in part, shaped by the plurality of other social forms, while these forms are simultaneously being shaped by it. He argues that this is because '...elements of law *are* elements of other forms and vice versa' (1984, p. 122). Further, while law may incorporate other forms, transforming those that it appropriates into its own image and likeness, the process is not unilateral but mutual, such that 'law in turn supports the other social forms but becomes in the process part of the other forms' (Fitzpatrick 1984, p. 118). I argue below that without a human-agency-based theory of how such social forms are constructed, the integral relations of state law with other forms tend toward affirmation rather than destructuration.

After elaborating the contradictory relations of opposition and support whereby law is constituted by its convergence with, separation from, support for, opposition to and distance maintained from other forms, Fitzpatrick is led to the surprising conclusion that 'law is the unsettled product of relations with a plurality of social forms. As such, law's identity is constantly and inherently subject to challenge and change' (Fitzpatrick 1984, p. 138). Unfortunately, this conclusion is not demonstrated by the bulk of Fitzpatrick's analysis. It is only with fleeting ambivalence that he acknowledges that law is shaped by the social forms with which it is dialectically related. For the most part, the reverse position is demonstrated, namely, that law is constituted through all of its relations with other social forms, even when these forms are in opposition to it. If this is true, and I share Fitzpatrick's view that it is, then it is difficult to see how law is constantly subject to challenge and change. A more plausible conclusion to Fitzpatrick's analysis would be that law and the plurality of forms with which it is interrelated are continually being reinforced and their identities reaffirmed, such that law is the settled product of stable and stagnating recursive practices.

Fitzpatrick's conclusion is unconvincing, in part because he omits a consideration of human agency, and in so doing reifies the conception of state law and social form. As Berger and Pullberg (1966) long ago reminded us, reification is the outcome of the process whereby the human agent forgets that he/she has produced the surrounding social world. More recently, Giddens has pointed out that 'reification is a discursive notion'. He says, 'reified discourse refers to the "facticity" with which social phenomena confront individual actors in such a way as to ignore how they are produced and reproduced through human agency' (Giddens 1984, p. 180). To deny human agents their own authorship of the structures which appear to oppress them is the ultimate connivance at oppression, one that Fitzpatrick does not challenge. For example, in discussing the dialectical relations between law and social forms, he talks of law incorporating, law transforming those it appropriates, law maintaining an identity, law having an autonomy, and law accepting integrity. But *law* does not do these things, human agents do. It is *how* they do so that must be articulated if we are to genuinely challenge the outgoing generation of existing social productions, rather than merely contribute to their reproduction.

As I shall argue below, it is only through human agents' discursive production and reproduction that law and private justice institutions are constituted. It is in the conceptual separation of different social forms, and of control forms associated with them, that each is constituted with a distinctive identity. By omitting a consideration of agency-based discursive production of social forms and control forms, Fitzpatrick invests in the same reified notion of structure that is employed by the human participants themselves. Consequently he fails to see that relations of opposition and support are always constitutive of existing forms in so far as they respond to existing definitions of those forms; law is never undermined by opposition to it, even where marginal transformations tinker with ongoing discursive production.

In order to explain how it is that law and social forms are constantly being constructed in ways that are mutually reaffirmative and constitutive, we need to revise the reified conception of social forms and control forms characteristic of recent versions of legal pluralism, by reintroducing the notion of human agency as the source of discursive production.

Human agency and the discursive production of social forms and control forms

According to Giddens' theory of structuration, human agency and social forms are not separable, but instead must be treated simultaneously as 'social practices ordered across time and space'. He argues that '[h]uman social activities ... are recursive. That is to say they are not brought into being by social actors but continually recreated by them via the very means whereby they express themselves as actors' (1984, p. 2). In this sense, what are taken to be the structural properties of societies, such as law and social control, are both the medium and the ongoing outcome of the practices that constitute them. This perspective leads us to the possibility of a non-reified conception of social form. Guided by this perspective, I define social form as the set of relations among members of a network, as undertaken by those members, in terms of summary representations recursively generated through discourse and routine construction practices. Cicourel (1964, 1968, 1981) and Knorr-Cetina (1981a, 1981b) have shown how such representations result from the structuring practices of human agents:

> The outcome of these practices are representations which thrive upon the alleged correspondence to that which they represent, but at the same time can be seen as highly situated constructions which involve several layers of interpretation and selection ... agents routinely transform situated micro-events into summary representations by relying on practices through which they convince themselves of having achieved appropriate representation.... Not only are summary representations actively constructed and pursued in everyday social interaction, the equivalence between these constructions and that which they represent must also be seen as actively negotiated, interpreted and constructed ... representations as understood here are not imaginary pictures of the world which belong to the realm of free floating ideas. Summary representations are not only routinely and actively constructed in everyday life, they are also routinely invested with faith and interest, they are fought over and manipulated. (Knorr-Cetina 1981b, pp. 33–4, 36)

Social forms, then, are the recurrent outcome of human agents' constitutive discursive construction practices.[2] As representations of relations, social forms are constituted through language use and the conceptual distinctions made by human agents. Indeed, as Fowler and his colleagues argue, 'language is a reality-creating social practice' whose use 'continuously constitutes the statuses and roles on which people base their claims to exercise power' (Fowler 1985, p. 62). Such constructions preserve hierarchies of power, 'guarding the exploitative opportunities of the ruling classes and keeping the lower orders in voluntary or involuntary subservience' (Fowler 1985, p. 64). Language use is constitutive. Its role, says Fowler, is:

> ... to continuously articulate ideology, to insist on systems of beliefs that legitimate the institutions of power ... possessing the terms crystalizes the relevant concepts for their users; using them in discourse keeps the ideas current in the community's consciousness, helps transmit them from group to group and generation to generation. In this way ideology is reproduced and disseminated within society — ideology in the neutral sense of a worldview, a largely unconscious theory of the way the world works accepted as commonsense. (1985, pp. 64–5)

In the course of making conceptual distinctions we may constitute social forms as very broad macro-representations of the whole society or as micro-representations of one aspect of that totality. It is clear, for example, that what one takes to be a social whole (or the widest possible macro-representation of social form) can vary. It may be captured by the representation 'society', or, for other purposes and on other occasions, by a broader representation such as 'world system' or 'global village'. To take one characterization of the starting point is not only to invest in further construction of that particular representation, but also to engage in the constitution of other social forms, since our construction of a totality reflects on and colours the parts which we take to be constituent of the totality. Abstraction from the social whole is itself a further constituting practice which reaffirms the original construction, reflecting back on it while investing in its elaboration.

Parts of a whole are not only coloured by agents' conception of the whole from which they are abstracted, but are themselves always subdivisible into their own constituent parts. When this occurs we may choose to describe the original part as a whole. An obvious example is the representation 'capitalist society' which may be constituted as both a part, say of the world system, and also as a whole containing numerous sub-forms that at once can be taken to both reflect and constitute its character. Similarly, at a different level of abstraction we may speak of a part of capitalist society, say the family, as itself divisible into constituent social forms which, as parts, constitute the family as a social whole. In this vein Swingewood has said, 'the bourgeoisie as an abstraction is also a totality; the various social strata within it are parts of this whole; but within these exist other subdivisions, groups and committees. The point is that totality is always part of something larger and the part is simultaneously a totality' (1975, p. 57).

Of crucial importance, too, is the nature of the relationship between social forms as parts and the totality or social whole. This relationship should not be misunderstood as hierarchical, in which macro-representations, such as society, are either more complex or more controlling than the parts which are taken to make up the whole. For Knorr-Cetina;

> The assumption that higher order levels of social life must also be more complex seems to be derived from the assumption that they somehow subsume levels of smaller scale, which in turn seems to be related to the idea that macro-structures effectively *control* micro-events. However, we may remind ourselves that the degree, desirability and effectivity of such control is a continual matter of controversy and struggle in social life. Indeed, we might just as plausibly assume that micro-social interactions evolve parallel to and partially independent of activities qualified as belonging to a higher hierarchical level. (1981b, pp. 38–9)

This is so because the nature of social forms as either macro- or micro-representations is constituted by human agents' constructive practices. It is only when human agents lose sight of their own authorship of social forms, by reifying them as having an objective existence outside of the practices employed in their ongoing generation, that it is possible to conceive of forms as separate from each other and in relations of subordination and domination.

In so far as reification is one of the characteristics of discursive practice, then we can expect relationships among social forms, as socially constructed representations, to be dialectical.[3] To refer to the relationship between social forms as dialectical is to say that parts of a totality cannot be permanently separated from the totality for they are integral to it, such that some of their relations *are* some of the relations of the totality and vice versa. But the constructive practices of constituting social forms as parts, by creating distinctions between them and the wider whole, and the reificatory process of burying the practices of construction, produce a constant movement and tension among component parts, and between these parts and the whole which they constitute. As both parts and a whole change with changes in the other, they have been described as 'co-determining'. As Lewontin, Rose and Kamin express it:

> According to the dialectical view the properties of parts and wholes co-determine each other.... Dialectical explanations attempt to provide a coherent, unitary but non-reductionist account of the material universe. For dialectics the universe is unitary but always in change; the phenomena we see at any instant are parts of the processes, processes with their histories and futures whose paths are not uniquely determined by their constituent units. (1984, pp. 11–12)

To this we might add that whereas the paths of phenomena are not uniquely determined by their constituent units, nor are they uniquely determined by the whole of which they are taken to be a part. One of the best illustrations I have yet found of the co-determining nature of part–whole dialectics, which simultaneously demonstrates their generation through discursive practices, is the following account of whale songs:

> It has been observed by marine biologists, that whale songs have a characteristic form for each school of whales; that if whale songs are recorded on one day and then another, the same school has the same song. However, when biologists return to record that school's song say one year later, the song is completely different. The explanation for this change is that the characteristic song is the result of individual whales hearing and sharing in singing each other's song; each rendition is shaped by the total structure that is the whale song. But at the same time each individual has enough autonomy to add small variations and innovations to the main theme; the continuously produced whale song is a resource d medium through which each individual and unique whale can creativeiy reproduce the song. This creative interpretation and selection is not enough to completely transform the song, that is and remains the total medium, but it is enough to change the song just a little. Other whales in the school pick up the general song, incorporating as it now does, the slight modifications of those whales who have been singing. They too go through the same creative process in their reproduction. The result is that after a period of time the micro-contributions of the individual whales transform the very totality of the whale song which has given and continues to give shape and general direction to their individual action. (paraphrased from David Attenborough, *Animal Language*, BBC 1982)

As I have said above, one of the major ways in which social forms, as representations, are constructed is through the conceptual distinction from other forms. It is in this sense that I conceive of 'control forms', which are the relations among human agents acting to police the conceptual distinctions among discursively constructed social forms. This is not to say that control forms are separate from social forms. They cannot be, since the relations of one are some of the relations of the other and vice versa. The one contains the other and defies analytical surgery. Control forms, then, are rooted in, and are a part of, the particular social forms whose boundaries they police. They are manifest in the relations through which agents' investment of faith and interests in social forms are fought over and manipulated.

Moreover, control forms are dialectically interrelated to other social forms and other control forms with which they are connected. This is because agents aligning themselves with one set of constructions of social form are thereby constituting the boundary as much as those aligning themselves with another form. To defend a construction is to invest in that to which it is opposed. As such, that which is opposed is made stronger, the stronger the defence (Morrissey 1985). It is for this reason that we can talk of the dialectical relations among control forms of different social forms existing simultaneously in mutual relations of opposition and support.

It is in this context of control forms that I conceive of law and institutions of private justice as the organized acting out of discursively constructed control forms. They are the manifestation of human agents reifying representations into objectively existing social forms without regard to the discursive practices used to constitute them. For law, we have the familiar institutions of police, courts, prisons, and so on; for private justice, we have localized non-state systems of administering and sanctioning individuals accused of rule-breaking or disputing within a particular setting. The range of institutions of private justice is as varied as their sources of generation. These can include:

1. Sub-administrative units *within* the wider control form of state law, which manifest their own controls, as with police discretion, plea bargaining and informal prison discipline;
2. Public and private industrial and commercial organizations with their ostensibly self-contained disciplinary bodies, boards and panels; and
3. The relatively amorphous voluntary associations such as self-help and mutual aid groups, whose members may impose ostracism, shaming and expulsion of those of their fellows seen to be threatening or challenging the group spirit.

Private justice institutions can be formally constituted, as occurs when the control form becomes a written representation containing rules and procedures for action. Or they can be informally constituted, being generated spontaneously by members sharing tacit assumptions about how to proceed in acting out a control form.

In short, the revised conception of social form, incorporating the related concept of control form, maintains that both are socially constructed agency-based discursive representations toward which human agents organize their behaviour across time and space while continuing to produce them discursively. From an analysis of discourse, it is possible to see how the two manifestations of control form — law and private justice — are constituted as representations through the contrasts and similarities that agents draw between them. It is also apparent that the dialectical relations between law and private justice are traceable to the failure of human agents to see these resultant forms as the outcome of their own agency. It should be no surprise that representations such as social forms and control forms are sometimes convergent since they are socially constructed by the same agency; but they are simultaneously divergent, since routine reificatory practices cut representations from the source of their production, and the distinctions through which agents constitute them become the qualities of separation and divergence between them.

In what follows, I shall briefly illustrate some aspects of mutual constitution through discursive production. The examples I use will be drawn from a study of discipline in industry (Henry 1983). As in my previous analyses from this perspective (Henry 1985, 1986), I shall not consider separately the issues of convergence and divergence; since each passage illustrates aspects of each, they will be considered together.

The discursive production of law and industrial discipline

In the first example below it can be seen how, in describing the intertwining of law (the Code of Practice and industrial tribunal) and discipline in industry, the manager constitutes each control form by juxtaposing one with the other. The two control forms, although presented as similar, are not conceptualized as the same. The law is said to have been based on industrial disciplinary practice, but it is, once constituted, viewed as being different from the forms from which it was derived.

In constructing the Code, elements of disciplinary practice were selected and abstracted from the particular contexts in which they were operative. This was done first by managers who, in their consultations with members of the advisory bodies ACAS (Advisory Conciliation and Arbitration Service) and NJAC (National Joint Advisory Council) (see Henry 1983), gave summary representations of what were taken to be the important aspects of their discipline, and second by the members of the advisory bodies, who produced summary representations of the managers' representations, which were then generalized into the Code. The resultant discursive separation (of what was originally seen as a part of disciplinary practice) was illustrated by one manager in his claims about 'our discipline' and 'our agreements', marking these off as separate from *the* Code which itself is seen as external to that which it now controls and influences. The conceptual separation and externality of the Code is revealed in that it is seen to reflect, but no longer *is* the practice of industry. Ultimately, having been constructed by members of ACAS and NJAC (who 'consult with', 'find out', 'bring agreements, practices and customs together' and 'recommend'), the members' constructive practices disappear, leaving the reified 'Code' that somehow autonomously 'raised questions which we had to consider' and forced the company 'to adopt similar provisions'. In the words of one manager:

> The form our discipline takes is that adopted in the Code of Practice (1977) ... since going about these things in a different way might lead towards an industrial tribunal.... The Code of Practice does in fact reflect the practices of industry. In drawing up the Code, ACAS, and the NJAC (advisory bodies to government) before them, did consult extensively with industry to find out what the practice was for discipline. They have to some extent brought all these agreements, practices and customs together and said this appears to be what industry does and finds acceptable and therefore this is what we will recommend in the Code of Practice. We had disciplinary procedures for

some years which predated the Code, but the Code certainly raised questions which we had to consider and we had to adopt similar provisions in our agreements.

Consider the depiction of law (the industrial tribunal) and the representation of a workplace disciplinary tribunal (in which trade union members sit in judgement of fellow employees) given in the discourse from the industrial relations manager in the following quote:

> The chairman of the industrial tribunal rules that if a trade union mutually agreed to a system of tribunal and one in which the man's trade union can say 'We don't agree' and therefore you've got a hung jury — you have to adjourn it and let the man go back to work, then it was fair. He said ours was clearly written up in an agreement which everybody had put their signature to . . . He said, 'I would like to point out that I think you should inform your employee of the offence he has committed in writing. You should spell out his rights under the law and his rights to appeal. He should have his shop steward with him.' So we accepted all that. 'And having done that I think your system is very good.'

As in the previous example the manager clearly presents the company's discipline as different from the law by describing it as 'ours' and he cites the chairman of the legally constituted industrial tribunal as talking of 'your system'. In deferring to the ruling of the chairman of the industrial tribunal the manager invests in the greater power being represented by the chairman. He affirms the chairman's prerogative to rule on what is right or wrong, and he accepts that the chairman's judgements are the legitimate source of 'fairness' and consensus. In doing so, he also denies the power of his own system to operate with its own definitions of fairness. His reliance on law to provide legitimation and support for the company's system simultaneously subordinates that control form to law, which reinforces law's distance and superiority while claiming the control form's right to operate in law's shadow. Moreover, in citing the chairman's recommendations, the manager invokes and affirms some of law's abstract propositions such as formal written procedure, rights to appeal, and to be informed and represented. He then shares in the celebration of such invocations as 'very good'.

The next two examples of discourse show how, in both opposition to and support of law, the state control form is affirmed as the arbiter of fairness, with the power to control the disciplinary form which is drawn on by managers as an external resource:

> I think we are better with the Code. . . . It enables the manager to manage more effectively in the secure knowledge that he is behaving in a way which is regarded as reasonable. I constantly argue with managers who say 'Oh the tribunals (labour courts) mean we can't sack anybody', and I say 'on the

> contrary what the legislation has given us is the means by which we can dismiss someone fairly as a result of his own misconduct'.

> Dismissal is the ultimate power that we've got and even that is, of course, very very much restricted by the legislation in recent years — the Employment Protection Act. Everything is now dealt with, with the view that it might go to one of these tribunals. . . . To be fair, I understand that if this is dealt with properly through our own procedures, a tribunal will not throw it out.

In the following examples we can see how prevailing legal abstractions, such as 'defence', 'witnesses', 'appeals' and so on, are emphasized in order to point to the similarity between the disciplinary system and the courts. In descriptions such as these, not only does legitimacy accrue to the disciplinary form, but in the process there is an affirmation that concepts and abstractions attributed to law are the proper way to handle control problems:

> They can conduct their own *defence* . . . They are allowed to bring *witnesses* at the *appeals* stage. At the first stage they are entitled to *call witnesses*. They can call who they like to be *advocate* — a fellow employee. Some of the men have much more faith in a *barrack room lawyer type* . . . So the system attempts to apply *justice* and *justice is seen to be done*. We take a very serious view of discipline, that it should be applied with *justice*.

> Our disciplinary procedure in fact is almost comparable to the *court procedure*. The individual will be taken through the *alleged offence*. If the manager feels satisfied that there is a *serious misdemeanour* committed he will issue *formal charges* as we call them . . . at a formal interview he gives his *defence*. The formal interview, then, takes the appearance, as it were, of a *Magistrate's Court* in that the man will come before the manager on an appointed date to *answer the charges*. The group manager will act *as the prosecution* and the person has the facilities for bringing with him a trade union appointed person as a spokesperson or *advocate*. . . . Usually the group manager will have a *note-taker*, taking down the *exchange of evidence*. . . . The group manager will have to *weigh up the evidence* on both sides, whether or not he'll find the person *guilty or not guilty* and then *decide on the punishment*. The individual has the *right to lodge an appeal*.

Even where differences are being highlighted and law is being opposed, as in the following examples of discourse taken from employees, law is still being affirmed and constituted as external, powerful, more wide-ranging in its effects, more distant and objective in its handling and judging of cases, and more bureaucratic. Simultaneously, the disciplinary control form is being constituted in relation to this as substantive, particularistic, understanding and personal. The discursive production of these differences does not undermine law or challenge its conceptions, but is part of its elaboration:

> If they hadn't got the tribunal they'd have outside police in, wouldn't they? And then your name and everything's gone. Here you might get two or three days' suspension ... which is surely better than having it plastered in all the papers.
>
> The tribunal's better than the courts — it keeps it in the family. If a person's done some pilfering, at court they don't take anything else into consideration. It's just another case. Also it's a big waste of time.... One of the main advantages here is that it's over and done with in a short time.
>
> If you go to a court they've never been here and they don't know the run of the place. They don't know how things work, the layout, this sort of thing.
>
> Outside people deal with different crimes everyday and it's just one in a line. They don't understand the nature of the offence really. Whereas here they know the details exactly: what crimes are, what's going on, where it took place — they've experienced it themselves and they judge the crime on what they know.
>
> When the law becomes involved it's different because the judiciary is involved in something they don't really understand: the feelings on the shop floor, what motivates people. But that chairman, those three union fellows, that manager who had come up through the shop floor himself, knew what it was like out there, what could have aggravated the situation. You need someone who's in tune with the shop floor, the way people feel, or what aggravates them.

In the final illustrations, this time from unionists and a manager, we see again how prevailing legal conceptions penetrate the disciplinary control form when members are contrasting that form to their own practices. Although the representations of this disciplinary control are at variance with those of the law or courts, nonetheless the same concepts are the medium for discussing issues of control. Thus, violation of private property is theft and grounds for intervention by the disciplinary control form. The descriptions and elaborations of differences are therefore only elaborations of the prevailing distinctions and, as with previous illustrations, do not undermine or challenge those conceptions but further invest in them:

> There's a difference in someone intentionally going to steal and succumbing to temptation. No way would I ever defend anybody that's walking out with half a dozen packets of it.
>
> The question is the volume and the value of the goods stolen. If it's say minor, one packet, we very often say to the management, 'Give him a good ticking off and tell him not to do it again', because it's not worthy of anything more. Then as the volume increases ... you will go from say a day's suspension up, depending on the value of the goods stolen, to as much as two weeks suspension, if the offence is very grave.

> Our understanding of what is a 'fair cop' as opposed to what the outside courts might say, is totally different. We would understand that it is relatively easy to pilfer but that someone would have to go out of their way to amass a large bedwrapper full of different sorts of them. Whereas to the courts a bag full of one sort would be indistinguishable from a bag full of another sort ... I think you do actually temper what goes on by your knowledge of the site and ... of the working condition.

The last quote brings us back to the individual whale singing the school song. The manager says 'our understanding' is totally different from what the 'outside courts' might say. But the prevailing conceptions are all that is available as a medium through which to sing. He must sing their song, and in his struggle to contrast his own system to the courts his assertions serve as much to entrench, affirm and reproduce the school song which heralds the separateness of state law, as they do to establish his system's individual identity.

If affirmation and mutual consideration of existing control forms occur through discourse, irrespective of whether this is produced as supportive or oppositional, how is it possible for human agents to free themselves from existing structures of control? It would appear that the only route to freedom is by human agents' disinvestment in existing discursive productions, and their investment in alternative ones. In a society where human agents are imbued with common language and concepts, and shared representations of social forms and control forms, this is extremely difficult, and requires considerable and continuous self-reflexive efforts. There are, however, some who, in constructing alternative social forms such as cooperatives, communes and collectives, make available to themselves a different representation of control form. By disinvestment in the existing social order and by replacement discourse rather than oppositional discourse, human agents can begin to transcend the available discursive medium and thereby release themselves from their own participation in its control. In the final section I briefly consider examples of such replacement discourse, and of the alternative control forms that are revealed and made available through it.

Replacement discourse in the deconstruction of prevailing control forms

When co-op members are asked how they maintain control over their fellow members, a recurring response is that they do not. Instead of celebrating formal disciplinary rules and procedures, co-op members see control in terms of everyday ongoing relations which are their own discipline. As one member expressed it, 'The co-operative spirit is actually doing the right thing without the formality'. The form of control was described, not in relation to formal courts and law, but on its own terms:

> I think to a large extent we seem to have evolved mechanisms of preventing disciplinary problems ... All the time I'm asking them what they think about the standard of what I'm doing. There's a group feeling that we should do this.

This investment in an alternative control form, without simultaneously constituting prevailing conceptions of law, can be seen clearly in the following member's account:

> We have no supervision as such and find that the best form of control is by our fellow work-mates in the same group and through open discussion, with criticisms of each other in as constructive a way as possible.

Unlike the accounts described in the previous section on industrial discipline, the examples of discourse from members of co-operatives present a representational form in which members are described as holding and exercising responsibility for discipline in relation to their own actions. No third-party parallel with courts is drawn. In fact, no mention is made of courts, law or policing. Rather, action deemed controllable is described in relation to the practices of the co-operative rather than in relation to any outside measure:

> I can think of three people who left, and in each case it was because they had trouble fitting in with the way the rest of us worked. They didn't take enough responsibility for the work they did and didn't have the feeling of needing to present it all the time so that we could see how good it was. What happened was that as often as they failed to present their work they were told in the normal course of the way the rest of us are always criticising each other. This hurt their pride too much and they left.

The phrase depicting deviance is constituting this, not as rule-breaking, but as failing to take enough responsibility; and the sanction is expressed not as punishment (as was the case in industrial discipline), but on its own terms as they were 'told in the normal course of the way the rest of us are always criticising each other'. In the following example, deviance, described here in terms of forgetting responsibility, is not talked of as being met by sanctions and punishment as conventional responses, nor is there any mention of such concepts. Instead, response is described in ways which constitute the emerging control form without investing in existing forms:

> People who would normally act in a very responsible co-operative way sometimes forget what the co-op system is and don't use it properly.... If you can remind people of their duties, talk to them on a friendly basis, then they think 'Of course' and they'll sort of act in a co-operative way. It's no more complicated than that.

The following examples of co-op members' discourse demonstrate that in the co-operative social form, control is presented as the reversal of how it is conventionally understood. Indeed, conventional control is itself constituted as the object of control. Although the form of control discussed and employed is the negation of conventional control, the established form is not reproduced and it is not addressed in conventional terms. Hence:

> You get some very strange people wanting to do certain things and if there is a power vacuum they will jump in and fill it. It's as if you're stepping back and saying 'We the workers don't control. There's nothing here. Here it is.' Well you just get one or two powerful characters and they can have a field day.... The members actually booted out one or two people who had really caused a lot of difficulty. There was a fairly vigorous sort of warfare. These people came to committee meetings particularly when they wanted to control something.... Then they decided, right, you know, we'll come and get what we want. But they didn't get it. People had just about enough of them because they were obnoxious sort of dominant figures ... and people decided to give them the boot by no other way than making them feel unwelcome at committee meetings. First of all this person was replaced in office so they got a reduction in control there. Then they came less often to committee. So it didn't happen at once. It was a gradual process over quite a long time.

As I argue elsewhere (Henry 1983, 1985), this is not to imply that members of co-ops in capitalist societies never invest in conventional control structures, or partake in the reproduction of existing control forms. The following example of discourse shows not only that they do, but how they do:

> You see the problem when you're trying to use discipline or just logic, is that people get in the way, because people aren't disciplined and they aren't logical, right? To run an efficient rent system you've got to get the human element out as much as possible because that's what messes the whole thing up — people's emotions and whatever. I know it sounds daft trying to get the human element out, but a system where you don't have to go and explain why you haven't paid and involve yourself in totally irrelevant problems ... I don't see why anybody has to be intimidated, humiliated. As far as I'm concerned it's cut and dried.... So that's why we introduced the new system.... Now if they are four weeks behind with their rent they get a Notice to Quit, and when that expires we take court proceedings. Of course the main objection we have from people is ... 'Oh that's a bit heavy isn't it?' or if it's a possession order 'Getting the law involved.' But ... if the law wasn't involved people wouldn't be secure in their short-life housing. They'd be in squats, because all short-life housing is official squats.... I'd much rather not get the law involved.... I think it's a drag giving credibility to the law in this sense because the law doesn't particularly like co-ops or the people who are in them.... We are allowing the police to harass our members, more or less, which is very heavy but there's no option. You see

> you can't do evictions yourself because that's illegal. But that's what I'd like to see; co-op members doing their own evictions.... See the people who come to meetings ... don't want to be disliked. But if you're going to lay on someone you're not going to be liked. So people won't go.

However, this ambivalence by co-op members towards control forms, as Rothschild-Whitt (1979) says, 'is a feature of people in collectivist organisations having to "constantly shift gears ... they learn to act one way inside their collectives and another way outside"'. This is said to derive from the fact that 'alternative work organisations are as yet isolated examples of collectivism in an otherwise capitalistic-bureaucratic context.' (1979, p.522). The position is not one of which co-operative members are themselves unaware, as the final example of discourse demonstrates:

> We are trying to glimpse possible relationships in the present outside world. Unless you know what it would be like to have a society where people co-operate, unless you've got some glimpse of it, I don't see what you're doing trying to get it. Or even if you manage to get it what you are going to do with it.... The only way things change, in my experience — all the things I'm referring to are a very intricate set of relationships ranging from personal ones to huge ones involving organisations — is in an imaginative, co-operative way, where someone offers a possibility with a degree of energy, forethought and conviction about how that possibility will be organised, so that it becomes evident to other people that that is what happens.... Now no more do I believe we operate as perfectly as a collective could operate. Obviously it's contradicted by lots of things in the outside world. We are on one level a cooperative experimenting with new ways of doing things and on another level we are a small company.... If you want to eat ... it's necessary to earn money and that means making endless concessions and of course they are real concessions.... I don't believe that the job we do operates as it could in a better world, but it's developing a kind of tool and learning how to use it and it's very clumsy. What happens is a lot of people's emotions and ideas and paths of behaviour aren't tuned to it.... It's like we're being sucked forwards. People groan at their incapacity to fit but they don't hesitate at the direction they are going.

Conclusion

The foregoing analysis has demonstrated that law and various forms of private justice are dialectically related, as a result of their being the socially organized actions of discursively produced and reproduced control forms, which themselves are representations contained within similarly constituted social forms. The analysis suggests that it is not enough to conceive only of dialectical relations if we are to help in freeing human agents from investment in the discursive productions that oppress them, and thereby from their own oppression of themselves. To go further we must expose the conceptual links and divisions through which control forms are constituted. Having begun this process it becomes apparent that oppositional discourse is no more liberating than supportive discourse. That which denies also affirms. Both opposition and support invest in constructions that reaffirm existing relations of power, power which flows from the very agents over whom it *appears* to be exercised by others. Release from this self-administered subordination can only come from disinvestment, from ceasing to construct that which is.

But disinvestment, in and of itself, is lacking because, as we have seen, it is vulnerable to agents' invocation of available forms from conventional discourse. What is necessary, then, is self-reflexive replacement discourse: investment in an alternative set of constructions while simultaneously ceasing to invest in existing forms and structures. It is rather like asking someone to learn a new language that is still being created, and to talk only in terms of what is imminent or becoming. This is neither easy, quick nor simple; it is struggle. Such is the price of liberation from coercive control forms.

PART II
SECURITY, SURVEILLANCE, AND THE EXPANSION OF STATE POWER

Introduction

The five essays comprising Part II of the book discuss the various manifestations of social control, exploring respectively historical trends in the deployment of control personnel, the gender dimensions of the objects and the application of control, the impact of information technology on control styles, the manipulation of physical environments in facilitating control, and the modern state's role in delimiting realms of control.

The section begins with John McMullan's chapter entitled 'Policing the criminal underworld: state power and decentralized social control in London 1550–1700'. This contribution comprises material originally published in the author's book *The Canting Crew* (Rutgers University Press). McMullan conducts an historical analysis of crime and control in London during the period in question. The chapter provides an important contextual framework for this anthology, as it demonstrates that the 'decentralization' control has an extremely lengthy pedigree. McMullan argues that state control was considerably undermined, during the sixteenth and seventeenth centuries, by the fragmentation of the state policing apparatus, and by the survival of traditional feudal territories and protectorates in the city of London. State control during the historical period was hindered by a complex network of legal administration that was riddled with corruption and patronage, and by the ability of 'masterless men and women' to resist the control efforts of loosely co-ordinated police organizations.

McMullan provides an account of the evolution and dynamics of policing institutions in the 1500s and 1600s. He demonstrates the reflexive patterns of accommodation through which individual officials were able to circumvent efforts to centralize state authority, and through which criminals, racketeers and rogues of all varieties were able to manipulate control practices and mediate between the worlds of crime and crime control. The feudal 'liberties' in outcast London, geographical survivors of a medieval social structure, provided the urban criminal protectorates that offered 'sanctuary' to the targets of policing endeavours, that deflected and diffused the coercive overtures of the English state. It was virtually impossible for the nascent and inefficient representatives of centralized authority to penetrate the dense barriers thrown up around these isolated, fractionalized, decentralized city rookeries.

For their part, 'anomalies and gaps' in the state's policing apparatus made life relatively easy for the criminal underworld. Traditional systems of patronage, nepotism, negotiation, favouritism and speculation on offices largely subverted attempts to rationalize the exercise of central authority through the law. The various extant police organizations represented the remnants of this feudal legacy. First, watch and ward policing, from the beginning, held very limited legal power over the citizenry, it lacked a central command structure, and over time it collapsed into a corrupt system of office speculation, where brokers farmed out positions to incompetent and poorly-equipped 'Charlies' for low wages. Second, the Privy Council police organization lacked the numbers or resources for the routine management of criminal problems; as well it was seen as a particularly coercive and capricious instrument of state domination, and hence it received little co-operation from either its own members or the citizens of London. Third, the city marshalry was too weak in number to effect consistent crime control. Given these limitations, representatives of the state were induced to negotiate with known criminals in an effort to extract information about the London underworld, and to develop a state-citizen network of intelligence that was probably far more effective than the corrupt and patronage-ridden marshalry itself. Finally, the army and militias in Stuart and Tudor England were typically *ad hoc* institutions that assembled in war and dispersed in peace. As McMullan notes, the state had little monopoly over these forces, since members of the propertied classes were able to fashion their own fighting units to serve private and regional interests, and since in any event neither the army nor the militias were routinely used to quell domestic strife or deal with criminality.

Lastly, in the final section of the chapter McMullan points to the strategies of accommodation by which individuals and groups emerged to mediate between state power and the activity of underworld criminality. Given the weak structure of official control agencies, a system of pardons, rewards and impeachments emerged through which undercover agents were able to disperse and dispense control into the criminal community. 'Thief-takers' and 'underkeepers' were often both agents of the state and organizational leaders of the criminal underground. Crime and its control became a complex network of exchange and negotiation, as entrepreneurs filled the gap left by a weak infrastructure of state policing. McMullan's chapter thus demonstrates a system that developed three to four centuries in the past, in which control over crime was not experienced as an absolute or holistic phenomenon, but rather as a fragmented, fragile and mobile web of accommodation, buffeted by centripetal and centrifugal forces. The English state's authority to police its citizens was dependent on its compatibility with implicit and traditional organizational norms, and on the compliance of mediators among the citizenry, who emerged to extend state control into the urban community, and hence shaped the limits and the very essence of domination.

As the title of Chapter 7 suggests, Nigel South focuses on the securing of the 'environment' (a term he uses primarily to designate the built environment). He begins by reminding us that contemporary concerns and procedures regarding the provision of physical security are not as new as many contemporary authors have implied. Manipulation of the physical environment has always served as an important medium of social control.

South eschews the myopic focus on effectiveness characterizing 'environmental criminology' and much of the literature on 'situational crime prevention'. His concern is with the broader social issues that lie behind contemporary initiatives such as the Crime Prevention Through Environmental Design movement, and private policing. South's concerns lie with the *priority* we attach to thicker doors and stronger locks, and with the narrow perspective that such a view of 'security' presupposes. This traditional approach is seen as an overly technicist one that merely reaffirms status quo interests, focuses our attention on the symptoms rather than causes of crime, and ultimately inhibits rather than enhances our quality of life. He argues, for example, that situational crime prevention activities (for example, target hardening, increasing surveillance opportunities) not only do little more than displace criminal activity, but also have debilitating psychological and social effects on the defended community itself.

South also describes the 'language' of control encapsulated in architectural forms and other aspects of the built environment. The infusion of such architectural symbolism into the routines of social life helps to consolidate visions of a 'well-policed' city where, for example, spatially routinized behaviour patterns emerge which serve to define and contain 'deviant' enclaves, thereby subjecting persons defined as deviant to increased surveillance and scrutiny.

South concludes by noting that although we clearly would wish to create a comfortable and safe environment for ourselves, our commitment should be to an *overall improvement* in the environment rather than merely equating 'comfort and safety' with 'security and surveillance'.

Susan M. Addario, Clifford D. Shearing and Philip C. Stenning begin Chapter 8 ('Behind union lines: the setting of evidentiary boundaries') by asserting that the state wields a powerful instrument in its ability to set evidentiary boundaries. The rules embodied in law, and the procedures by which they are implemented, each influence the course and discourse of any given dispute resolution. Thus, boundary regulation is seen as a significant strategy enabling state personnel to stack the deck to benefit favoured constituencies.

The authors' choice of research site — a case study of labour-management dispute resolution — is appropriate for several reasons. First, the authors note that while evidentiary issues in criminal proceedings have received a great deal of attention, there is little research on the civil domain where, instead of being a party to the action (in the role of prosecution), the state occupies an ostensibly more neutral role. Second, the particular case they observed involved a company hiring a private security firm which subsequently placed an undercover informant in a workers' union to gain intelligence on union activity. This breached the rules of 'fair play' established in the *Labour Relations Act*, which led the union to charge its adversary with a violation of the Act so as to force a hearing before the Labour Relations Board.

In their analysis of the dispute and its resolution at the hearing, the authors first show that the state's and company's common concern with property encourage a close liaison between the police and the company. Further they argue that similar vocational objectives and a regulatory process that requires close contact between the state's police and private security firms, combine to encourage an alliance between the police and the security agency. Collectively, these factors create a situation where one sees the police, the company, and the private security firm on one side (in terms of information flow), with the union left in isolation on the other side as the perceived threat.

Taken alone, these findings lend support for the notion that the state is a Leviathan which implicitly controls legal outcomes through the creation of evidentiary boundaries. But Addario, Shearing and Stenning go beyond this unidimensional view to discuss the efforts of groups to circumvent evidentiary boundaries (for example, the company in this case study, by planting an informant), and show how the state is a site of struggle between adversarial groups. Thus, the union's decision to pursue charges against the security company provided an opportunity not only to make a point with respect to their immediate situation, but also, via precedent, to obtain a victory which had implications for all union–management disputes. In this sense, the authors make a case for *not* viewing the state as a static entity which imposes its will by framing the rules of the game, but rather as a malleable entity where questions of evidentiary boundaries provide strategic opportunities for struggle (a point also made in the following chapter by Davis and Faith).

In Chapter 9 ('Women and the state: changing models of social control'), Nanette J. Davis and Karlene Faith focus on social transformations of gender control, starting from the observation that women are generally much more subject to social control (as variously defined) than are their male counterparts. Indeed, part of the very impetus of the women's movement has been to throw off the shackles of social control that would normally not even apply to men; for women social control represents a double domination. The struggle for women's rights has met with varying degrees of success. And in the process of this struggle the perception of the progressive woman appears to have changed from an image of 'social deviant' to one of 'political opponent'. Davis and Faith examine the implications of this changing perception for interpreting changes in the social control of women.

Noting a dawning recognition over recent decades of the pervasiveness of patriarchy in all segments of society, the authors describe the way in which many methods and models that were originally presented as objective and value free actually embody a patriarchal perspective in their delineation and interpretation of gender-related data. Indeed, one could argue that the subsequent shift in interpretive emphasis from 'sex differences' to 'gender differences' was accompanied by increased sensitization to the status of 'sex roles' as a social construction rather than biological given. It is a similarly profound cognitive shift that the authors seek to mobilize in civil society, particularly through state-sponsored initiatives, in order to secure women's rights. The authors document the persistence of patriarchal relations in the social expression of pornography, rape, and prostitution, and the sexualization of female crime more generally.

Much of the hostility toward women still in evidence today (even in what are considered to be progressive social circles) is attributed to the lack of a *fundamental* shift in the 'scripts' of gender relations, that is, changes *have* occurred, but they deal with the appearances of patriarchy rather than its essential nature.

If such fundamental change is to occur, one must deal with the question of 'how?', and it is here that the authors' distinction between 'woman as deviant' and 'woman as political threat' is shown to be associated with a shift in social control tactics. With the woman as deviant perception, changes can be achieved because there is a broad base of tolerance for (non-threatening) deviation. But when the object of women's resistance to power is patriarchy itself, 'woman' is recast as a political threat and the foundation of tolerance begins to crumble.

The *current* crisis in control that the authors discuss is based on the view that we are no longer talking about deviant women looking to be allowed unescorted into a public bar, but rather that we are witnessing the *political threat* associated with half of our society seeking full rights, access and participation. The state is seen as balking at so fundamental a change, however, and hence the 'state as woman's ally' versus 'state as woman's opponent' balance can be seen as tipping more towards the latter pole.

Nonetheless, the authors remind us that although the law *has* served as an instrument of oppression, it has more recently been shown to be a potential instrument for securing freedom. This suggests that the law has *been* patriarchal, but is not *inherently* so, leading Davis and Faith to place greater emphasis on the prospective legal battles which might be fought in defining a more egalitarian society. In this sense, the authors reveal considerable reservation about the practical utility of notions of 'private' and 'informal' justice. Although such modes of resolution may offer conciliation and localized peace, the authors assert that they are inherently limiting in so far as each concerns only one person in one situation in a society rife with inequality. In contrast, the magic of law and formal legal resolution emerges from the power of *precedent*, through which a victory by one woman in one situation can become a victory for all. Thus, with the perception of woman as political threat, and with women being encouraged to utilize the formal legal apparatus, we are led seemingly inevitably to the authors' prophetic conclusion that 'whatever the future', it promises *not* to be serene'.

The final chapter in Part II, by Gary T. Marx and Nancy Reichman, is entitled 'Routinizing the discovery of secrets: computers as informants'. This article, reprinted from the *American Behavioral Scientist*, is concerned with the development of information technologies that expand the state's ambit of knowledge over its citizenry. As the authors indicate in their introduction, a computer-based system of discovery holds considerable advantage over one based on citizen co-operation, since the latter is limited to offences actually known to human informants, and since citizens tend to exercise discretionary control over the information they are willing to send on to authorities. Systematic data-searching provides a new tool for integrating information and for uncovering patterns of criminality that are vulnerable to detection.

The expansion of computer technology has permitted authorities to enter terrains previously inaccessible to official scrutiny. Through the use of such techniques as data aggregation, cross-referencing, matching and profiling, computerized data-searching has facilitated the location of offenders amid the haystack of law-abiding populations. Computer matching has been especially successful in the discovery of impersonation and false representation, where fraudulent recipients of welfare or medical benefits, tax evaders and other such miscreants have been identified during the exercise of technological 'surveillance waves'. Profiling involves the correlation of data items to establish 'red flags' that may locate an individual in a potential criminal category. The identification of configurations of personal characteristics that are compatible with those of 'typical' hijackers, drug couriers, tax evaders, fraudulent insurance claimants, cheaters on university entrance exams, and so on may provide what Marx and Reichman term an 'early warning system' that can initiate a more intensive and individualized response. A particularly insidious variant of this process is the application of profiling to identify drug users, through aggregate analysis of computerized work records to detect high rates of absenteeism, lateness, sick leave, accidents, and Workers' Compensation claims.

Marx and Reichman are describing an Orwellian system that has seemingly unlimited potential for the exercise of control through the acquisition and circulation of knowledge about the citizenry. Moreover, there are systematic errors built into computer detection processes, that appear to load in the direction of false positives (Type I errors), meaning that vast numbers of innocent citizens will be fingered by overinclusive computer programs and overzealous computer programmers. Yet interestingly, the authors argue that such weaknesses and inconsistencies in the computerized information network hinder (at least in the short term) the impact of coercive control overtures: '... the sources of error we have noted clearly call into question limits on the efficiency and accuracy of computer control technology and illustrate the high cost of mistakes'.

Routine use of computer networks to uncover the dark (and not-so-dark) secrets of citizens clearly demonstrates the extraordinary dissemination of control into broadening terrains of public and private life. Rights to privacy, to presumption of innocence, to face one's accusers (a pile of nuts, bolts and silicon chips?), to voluntary and informed consent, may be permanently subverted as these machines reach farther and farther into what were formerly private domains. While the authors are somewhat reserved in their discussion of policy implications and the impact on civil liberties, and while they back away from painting the 'worst-case scenario', they are nonetheless keenly alert to the nightmare possibilities of such information empires in the unopposed hands of state officials.

And finally, there are critical theoretical issues that have special relevance for an understanding of modern state control. Marx and Reichman agree with Spitzer that such trends are entirely consistent with the 'rationalization' of crime control in capitalist society, with the concentration on broad-brush control strategies that minimize the individuality of offenders and other deviants, and focus instead on the furtherance of 'effectiveness, efficiency, certainty and predictability' at the aggregate, the systems level. As catalysts to this process, computers release authorities from dependency on the population for knowledge about offending, and hence amplify their autonomy and power. While the authors assert that such power is currently circumscribed by the infancy of such control practices, there is clearly a need to interpret such developments as a sinister representation of the 'precise panoptic vision', of a modern control wave aimed at the unification of knowledge and power.

6 Policing the criminal underworld: state power and decentralized social control in London 1550–1700

John L. McMullan

Introduction

This chapter examines the coercive capacity of the Absolutist State in England with particular reference to crime control in sixteenth and seventeenth century London. Three basic tasks are undertaken. First, I investigate the penetration of capitalist relations in the London market-place, showing how the transition from feudalism to commercial capitalism gave rise to a widened set of criminal opportunities, institutions and networks which developed parallel to feudal-like relations of administration, but which escaped their effective control. Second, I demonstrate that the reconstitution and extension (in *de facto* yet not *de jure* terms) of traditional feudal/ecclesiastical jurisdictions, and the weak, decentralized and patronage-ridden nature of formal state control combined to form a hardened feudal administrative complex which was reluctant and organizationally incapable of systematically monitoring the twin problems of 'masterless men and women' and criminal 'roguery' in London. Finally, I examine the state's attempt to exact formal control through an informal system of pardons, office speculation and patronage, and show how the exercise of state power through such arrangements led to a peculiar and uneven translation of law into practice, a major effect of which was to enhance the centralization of power within the criminal underworld.

Capitalism, crime and feudal jurisdictions

The emergence and formation of population settlements in England contributed to a disparate system of social control. Topographical boundaries and poor transport afforded many areas a virtual autonomy from state supervision, and afforded haven for radicals, religious dissenters and criminals (Hill 1972, Ch.5). The onus for law enforcement often rested on local settlements or parish villages. Coastal

---

This chapter comprises selected material, in somewhat revised and abridged form, from *The Canting Crew: London's Criminal Underground, 1550–1700* by John. McMullan. The author thanks Dr. Paul Rock for his guidance and assistance.

districts possessed their own vigilante groups to guard their shores from pirates and wandering mariners (Parkes 1925, pp.49–51). Even in large towns, communal policing was a decentralized and volunteer affair with local ward officials in command (Salisbury-Jones 1938, pp. 126–66).

These control patterns reflected the political and economic fragmentation of the country into 'independent shire-states, each with its own distinct ethos and loyalty' (Everitt 1966, p.59). Traditions of oral communication and face-to-face relations were central. The village parish and town ward were the basic living units, and supra-parochial institutions were generally weak. Communities were self-supporting, visited only by small numbers of itinerant peddlars, carters, badgers, and merchant middlemen. While England was not entirely a static society (Cornwall 1967, p.152), population migration was still mostly confined to the neighbouring parish or county (French 1969, pp.39–52; Slack 1972, 1974).

London was the exception. The city was a 'demographic monster', and by most accounts it was a highly mobile and, in parts, an unsettled area. London's population multiplied by eightfold to approximately 350 000 inhabitants between 1500 and 1650 (Hill 1972, p. 40; Jordan 1960, pp.15–16), and by the late Stuart period, the city was absorbing 8000 or so new migrants every year (Clark and Slack 1978, p.64). At the beginning of the sixteenth century, London was five times the size of the largest provincial town, but by the mid-seventeenth century, it was between ten and fifteen times as large (Fisher 1976, p.205). It has been estimated that one-sixth of England's total population spent at least part of their lives in the metropolis (Wrigley 1967, pp.48–50).

Economic changes impacted profoundly on London's growth. Throughout much of the sixteenth and seventeenth centuries serfdom was in decline. New sets of class relations asserted themselves around agrarian capitalism in the countryside. A gradual transition from 'feudalism to capitalism' and accompanying class changes and conflicts were buttressed by the spectacular extension of overseas trade and the widespread seizure of colonial markets. Emerging overseas trading cartels restructured the English economy, undermined the prominence of provincial towns and made London *the* economic centre of the country. As Hobsbawm noted, 'London for the first time was the pivot of a national market, for "middling" goods, unlike the city in continental states' (1967, pp.50–1).

The growth of London as the 'economic engine' of the country also meant that it furthered capitalist expansion into the countryside. But the consequences of capitalization in the countryside were felt in London. A cyclical movement was occurring between the increase in capital accumulation and the growth in a landless population. The first was possible in part because of seizures of overseas markets, changes in the organization of production and rising food and consumer prices resulting from the expanding populations of towns and cities (Hill 1969). But in turn, the populations of towns were being pulled from the growing numbers of dispossessed people forced to sell their labour power. Peasants were being enclosed from the land and, increasingly, arable land was being converted from tillage to pasture (James 1967, p. 241; Tawney 1912).

London was then the focal region for capital-labour conflict, attracting great numbers of 'masterless men and women'. It was a preferred centre of labour migration for a number of reasons. First, the fringes and suburbs of the city provided havens for the expanding domestic and exporting industries, and hence provided more opportunities for seasonal employment than were available elsewhere. Second, the size of London as a home market and its access to foreign markets favoured it as a centre of commerce. Third, London afforded greater social support facilities. Inns and alehouses were plentiful and lodgings and food were easily obtained. The metropolis, by its size and anonymity, provided the opportunities for those pushed out of one place to start afresh. Finally, the multiplicity of better organized charity foundations attracted and held the unemployed in the capital (Pound 1971, p.59).

Despite, or perhaps because of its amenities, London was particularly well suited as a centre for crime. The expansion of the city as a centre of consumer goods made available a considerable volume of inexpensive portable commodities that offered widened opportunities for crime. Shoplifters, for example, were attracted to the burgeoning networks of open mercers, goldsmiths, haberdasheries, stalls and shops. The penetration of cheap consumer items down the social scale meant that large populations carried accessible objects of market value. A steady dishonest wage was earned from the petty opportunistic pilferage of scarves, linen, cheap jewellery, silks, and metal artifacts (Cockburn 1977, pp.62–6). Moreover, the proliferating numbers of nobility, gentry and skilled professionals in the city were attractive targets for cheats, pickpockets and swindlers (Fisher 1962, p.200).

The growing possibilities for crime, engendered by the changing economic importance of London to the emerging commercial capitalist economy, were accompanied by feudal territorial customs. Ancient boundaries marked off various living spaces, and the city was a myriad of diverse social worlds. An eccentric geometry segregated wealthy and poor, professions and lesser trades, workshops and living quarters (Lupton 1632). Aside from the anonymity that the city afforded by virtue of its size, social density and heterogeneity, crime was further enhanced by traditions of territoriality that offered social protection in unregulated areas.

By the mid-sixteenth century the city was ringed by a number of these wayward districts, many of which possessed the character of medieval 'liberties' (Brett-James 1935). The name referred to the special privileges granted certain regions of the city by virtue of their having been ecclesiastical franchises which, by charter or proscription, were independent of any city or state control. Some regions were exempt from specific taxes; others were private municipalities for certain crafts; still others were free zones immune from city policing and authority. The 'liberties' of Fleet Prison and of St Martin-le-Grand Chapel, for example, were guaranteed by statute (Thornley 1924, pp. 182–207), and frequently harboured law-breakers, debtors and felons under feudal rights to sanctuary (Kempe 1825).

In the feudal era, any wanted person who took refuge in consecrated settings had the right to claim sanctuary. This right to protection was guarded by custom and law, and residents could not usually be arrested. Sanctuary was initially of two types: temporary and permanent (Kempe 1825). The former was afforded for a period of forty days, provided fugitives accepted the discipline of the area and agreed to 'abjure the realm'. Such a practice was *de jure* abolished by the sixteenth century. Permanent forms of sanctuary, however, continued despite such abolition until the eighteenth century. This was a more entrenched protectorate and represented a guaranteed full-time franchise, segregated from traditional forms of authority with new allegiances and customary rules (Thornley 1924, p.184).

The power and autonomy of sanctuary were most pronounced during the feudal period. Although many of the feudal rights and obligations of territory were eroded throughout the sixteenth and seventeenth centuries (Thornley 1924), *de facto* practices continued and the Elizabethan and Stuart state lacked the means to eradicate many of the territorial principalities. Differentiated regions, resistant to city and state control, were maintained by a combination of customary feudal right and outright defiance. 'Bastard' sanctuaries took root in the shadow of ecclesiastical territorial privilege. Church yards, hospital grounds, bedlams and welfare principalities became, in part, the foci of criminal asylum in London (Brett-James 1935; Dugdale 1658, pp.16–18). Enforcement agencies found it difficult to penetrate the maze-like architecture of these dense urban wards. Indeed throughout the Elizabethan and Stuart period such areas extended their borders, absorbed wider sections of the city suburbs, and expanded into an archipelago of crime sanctuaries displaying considerable stability and organization (Rock 1977).

The boundaries of these 'crime areas' were ecologically reinforced by existing urban divisions, with parochialism an entrenched feature of London social organization. Communities were local, contained and discrete social universes. Road names such as Bread and Milk streets, and Goldsmiths Row indicated respective trades, and occupational frontiers were not easily crossed (Stow 1958). Contacts and co-operation among ward sectors were weak. Aliens, for example, were quartered in enclosed territories. 'Middle-class professions' were geographically separated from the lower types of occupations (Cressey 1970, pp.53–60). London resembled a mosaic of distinct yet interlocked social worlds.

State coercive apparatus and crime control

Patronage and formal social control

Opportunities for crime were further buttressed by the internal anomalies and gaps in the coercive capacity of the Absolutist State. As MacCaffrey noted, 'the absence of either a professional army or a paid bureaucracy left it without the final arbiters of forceful compulsion' (1969, p. 97). Instead, formal state control was an elaborate, negotiated and tenuous artifice. Patronage was especially pervasive as a system of government. Political order was effectively mediated by elaborate webs of affiliation and parochial hierarchies which developed around semi-autonomous centres of influence (MacCaffrey 1969, p. 98). These networks were seldom institutionalized and state control was a matter of shifting diplomacy and favouritism. Court, central administration, regional government, military and naval service, land administration, and the judiciary were all tied to elaborate networks of office speculation and influence peddling (Prestwich 1966). Policing was frequently defined as a private domain and exploited as such (Stone 1961). What emerged from this rudimentary political structure, created by inadequate fiscal policy and a weak bureaucratic apparatus, was a fluid system of patron-client power blocks themselves capable, at times, of formidable competition to central government (Williams 1963, pp. 1–17).

The mandate of law, in particular, was defined by the moral status of the well patronized. Membership in a powerful family or place in a patrimonial bureaucracy guaranteed privileges of justice. The private manipulation of the law, its uncontrolled arbitrariness, its calculated loopholes and its unequal distribution of punishment, provided segments of the population with an effective immunity (Samaha 1974). The concentrations of power at certain privileged points meant that law functioned according to modalities that were irregular, ineffective, inconstant and uncertain in their effects. Law was open to purchase and direct favouritism (Samaha 1974, Chs.2, 3).

The distribution of patronage often fell outside supervision. Seldom could the central Crown government enforce official scrutiny

(Hurstfield 1973, pp.304–5). The sale of offices and their associated gratuities, *douceurs* and reciprocal favours lacked safeguards (MacCaffrey 1969, p.125). Patrimonial bureaucracy was liable to considerable abuse. As MacCaffrey noted:

> The nature of the prizes ... were first of all too small; too few offices provided adequate salaries, and the incumbent was driven to increase his income by any means open to him. Second, the terms of appointments were in many cases ill defined; the fees and profits attached to an office were all too often only hazily known, either to Crown or to patentie, and this encouraged the office-holder to 'exploit his opportunities, often to the detriment of both Crown and subject'. Third, the private exploitation of political advantage created a vast 'black market' in which political influence and favour were increasingly bought and sold ... Lastly, the poverty of the Crown drove it to make unwise concessions to suitors for favour or place.... But grants of this speculative type encouraged the recipient to more and more unabashed exploitation of its possibilities. (1969, p.125)

The obtrusive speculation upon office was a feature of most levels of the social control structure. Justices of the peace, prison administrators and city marshals, for example, frequently acquired their posts through sponsorship, and a system of tutelage linked underkeepers to keepers and to prison overseers (Dobb 1953). Office holders came to possess discretionary powers, and could arrange legal outcomes. In one year alone, out of a total of 1651 prisoners discharged, 285 were released by direct bribery (Salgado 1977, p.71). Law-breaking within the legal machinery acquired a level of protection and legitimacy, through a complicated method of subtle alliances and betrayals, that made collusion with criminals a possibility.

Watch and ward policing

Policing was similarly subject to elaborate negotiation. By the mid-sixteenth century, the hue and cry was unable to manage a sustained policing response. Urbanization, commercial growth and demographic changes rendered the *posse* anachronistic. Precinct watches and the citizens' constabulary were in decline. These essentially unpaid and volunteer offices were not being adequately serviced. The already heavy workloads of watchmen and constables were further compounded by the medley of contradictory charters, passports, edicts, orders and privileges issued under the Elizabethan state (Leem 1901, p. 99).

Despite their numerous and cumbersome duties, constables were surprisingly restricted in their powers of arrest. In some precincts of their wards they had no jurisdiction, and could not enter, pursue or arrest. In other places they needed official clearance, and seldom could leave the boundaries of their ward division except by agreement of the neighbouring constabulary. Occupational hazards further restricted their activities. Constables were liable for wrongful arrests and for loss of prisoners in their custody, and could be penalized by having their property repossessed or by having their business forfeited to pay off court debts. They had to patrol unknown and hostile territories, and cope with more numerous gangs of thieves and robbers, investigate the multitudes of base tenements, patrol the hidden and concealed lanes, alleys and courtyards, and manage the severances of growing numbers of vagrants. Such duties placed the volunteer constables and watchmen at considerable physical risk, particularly in policing the criminal precincts where walled sanctuaries and traditions of defiance and force challenged the jurisdiction of watch and constable, and where the physical terrain made detection and apprehension highly problematic. Amateur police personnel were easily outmanoeuvred in the twisting lanes of the sanctuaries and in the interstices between ward jurisdictions (Brindenbaugh 1968, pp. 390–2).

Their onerous workload was further complicated by the quagmire of ambiguous jurisdictions, privileged territories, expanding and contradictory regulations and laws, and responsibility to more than one authority. They were at the disposal not only of their aldermen but also of the Privy Council, and were further obliged to obey the orders of Provost Marshals and later still the city marshalry (Rumbelow 1971, Ch.3). This overlap of authorities produced considerable conflict and hostility.

Policing then lacked a central command. Twenty-six local ward policing units were responsible for law, order and crime control. Centralizing programmes which took power away from local wards and institutions were met with opposition. Thus, policing was an amalgam of disjointed bodies with an array of heterogeneous rules. The separate parochial units policed boundaries which did not coincide with the mobility of the criminal, and lacked the communication and organizational scope to pursue criminals from ward to ward. At best, policing functions were organized around periodic forays and purges of crime doers (Brindenbaugh 1968).

Economic considerations also acted against holding office and serving watch. Occupational and commercial commitments cut across public office. The compulsory tasks of serving as constables or even watchmen were unprofitable in themselves and directed valuable energy and time away from profit-making and income-earning ventures. Commitment waned and the recruitment and organization of policing were subject to decline and corruption.

The responsibilities associated with communal ward policing encouraged financially able citizens to find methods of exempting themselves from watch and constabulary functions. Increasingly, elected ward officials deputized their apprentices or domestics as replacements, or hired substitute labour. A market in the speculation of policing offices and duties emerged. Gradually, a body of regular full-time constables and watchmen, with widened discretionary powers, interposed themselves in the position of middlemen. They were paid money to act as proxies or to hire alternative watchmen. Since there were no controls over wages to be paid, constables acquired considerable bargaining power. They negotiated fees for hiring substitutes and set the wages for hired watchmen. The two rates did not need to coincide and hence ward officials were able to procure a secret income (Rumbelow 1971). In time the volunteer unpaid watch acquired within it a full-time wage paid element, recruited from the older and 'baser' sort of London society. These 'Charlies', as they were called, were frequently unfit for watch service. They were old, in poor health, inadequately armed, non-uniformed, and lax in their duties (Samaha 1974, pp.86–7). Constables pocketed 'dead pay', understaffed the watch, neglected their stations, seldom enforced curfews, and failed to police from ward to ward (*Journal of Court of Common Council*, 1663; Watch and Ward Misc. Mss., Box 245). Surveillance was irregular and reluctant. Criminals could guard against the patrols and regulate their crimes accordingly. Moreover, since officials refused to hire alternative labour, policing came to lack sufficient numbers. Whereas the 1663 Act of Common Council set the number of watchmen in the city of London (21 of 26 wards) at 747, less than one-half were actually hired (Rumbelow 1971, Appendix I).

The Privy Council as a policing force

The inadequacies of watch and ward policing in London forced the state to bolster its social control forces more directly and formally through the offices of the Privy Council and through the creation of a specific city marshalry.

Privy Council policing represented an array of *ad hoc* temporary projects, but was not itself a policing organization. The Privy Council lacked the numbers and institutional know-how to manage various problems of law enforcement. It was a political council concerned among other things with problems of government, social unrest and rebellion. It functioned more as a 'summoner' of social control forces than as an actual agent. Thus it was instrumental in raising fighting troops, dispensing coercive forces to 'trouble spots', and co-ordinating militias against foreign invasions. However, it did concern itself with domestic problems, and in London and elsewhere it evolved a series of 'special' social control practices aimed at crime detection and repression.

The system of swearing in para-police constables and the use of secret, organized searches and round-ups were tactics devised to increase accessibility to, and information about, disreputable populations. They were concerned to achieve, 'from above', what ward policing could not effect at a local level.

The appointment of extra policemen or Provost Marshals with widened powers of search and arrest was a relatively common practice throughout Elizabeth I's reign. Typically, Provost Marshals were paid appointees of the Privy Council or the Corporation of London. Their mandates were temporary and usually included an entitlement to hire armed assistants, with powers to apprehend and punish. Their sphere of action was wide, and was frequently supported by systematic territorial searches of adjoining counties.

Yet the office of the Provost Marshal was organizationally ill-equipped to perform work other than the suppression of periodic unrest, and even that work created friction. In the monitoring of mobile vagrants and the casual poor, or in detecting crime, it had a most indirect impact. It represented little more than a temporary force that was dependent on co-ordination with the local ward forces. With uncanny regularity, extra constables were reappointed, but they were incapable of engaging in the commonplace business of surveilling and deterring crime. The Privy Council itself assessed the Provost Marshals and concluded that they had failed in their objectives (*Acts of the Privy Council* 1595, p.330). Masterless men, we are told, 'stealthily return[ed] to the alehouses' from outside the city gates 'in the night season' (Ibid, p.438; cf. Brindenbaugh 1968).

In conjunction with extra policing officials, the Privy Council evolved a 'system' of mass searches and arrests. Round-ups were prearranged and timed to last for a limited duration (*Acts of the Privy Council*, 1596–1597, p.23; 1597–1598, pp.56, 88, 92, 97; 1598, pp. 128,140). Some 'privy searches' lasted for twenty-four hours, others went on for weeks. Frequently they were undertaken under cover of darkness, and were usually co-ordinated to take place throughout the entire city and the surrounding counties so as to prevent fleeing over borders and escaping arrest. William Fleetwood, the City Recorder, provides an apt description of the privy search:

> I did the same night send warrants out into the said quarters and into Westminster and the Duchy; and in the morning I went abroad myself and I took that day seventy-four rogues, and the same day toward night ... took all the names of the rogues and sent them from the sessions house into Bridewell. ... Upon the twelfth day in the forenoon, the Master of the Rolls, myself and others received a charge before my Lords of the Council as touching rogues and masterless men and to have a privy search. The same day ... I met the governors of Bridewell ... we examined all the said rogues and gave them substantial punishment.... Upon Sunday ... I conferred

> order for Southwark, Lambeth, and Newington from whence I received a school of forty rogues, men and women, and above. I bestowed them in Bridewell. I did the same afternoon peruse Paul's where I took about twenty cloaked rogues . . . I placed them also in Bridewell. . . . Upon Friday morning at the Justice Hall there brought in above a hundred lewd people taken in the privy search. . . . Upon Friday last we sat at the Justice Hall from 7 in the morning until 7 at night, where were condemned certain horse-stealers, cutpurses and such like to the number of ten whereof nine were executed. (as quoted in Judges 1930, p. xxxix)

A characteristic feature of these mass round-ups was that they were designed to counteract the sluggishness of the watch and of the legal process. 'Normal' policing institutions were short-circuited in favour of special investigations with authority to apprehend and execute the law without delay. Such direct state manipulation of the enforcement process may have had some limited symbolic effect in bolstering its coercive capacities, but it also betrayed its fragility. The state came to rely progressively on such crude extraordinary implements, but these coercive control measures were essentially *ad hoc* and short-term in their impact. They temporarily alleviated street disorders, closed down some of the haunts and institutions, apprehended and punished a number of the outcasts and dispersed the rest. Yet their battle was by and large a losing one, for the pattern was one of return and reoccurrence (Brindenbaugh 1968; Kamen 1976). Privy Council policing proved capable of suppressing particular crises, but it was ineffective in the commonplace business of routinely keeping the peace and detecting crime.

The evidence suggests that ward constables had little liking for these man-hunts. They were required to take custody of responsibility for the mass of prisoners, and were expected to inflict the harsh punishments of pilloring and whipping. They had to assist in dangerous pursuit and arrest campaigns and were liable to the authority of overseers in their own territories. Frequently, the constables developed covert tactics of non-cooperation. They minimized appearances in public, evaded recognition by removing identifiable clothing and badges, and concealed their station and residence by removing their white staff of office from their doorways (*Repertories of Court of Aldermen*, vol. 23, folio 548; Rumbelow 1971).

Supervision over policing, then, was problematic even though civil government initiatives were now being fashioned. There were directives and a flow of reports required, but the bureaucratic process did not penetrate to the foundations of police organization. It proved incapable of systematically standardizing and directing policing. There was little familiarity with local ward affairs, and that unfamiliarity prevented routine peace-keeping and crime detection and control from taking root. Their numbers and organizational features were insufficient to function adequately as a crime control institution.

The city marshalry

The third tier of practical policing was the city marshalry. In response to lax and inappropriate watch performance and supervision, the Court of Aldermen established their own force to regulate all aspects of city policing. The model for this city position was the office of Provost Marshal. The Court of Aldermen regularized these duties and powers into a permanent office, and in 1603 appointed a Provost Marshal for the City of London. Initially, the city marshalry was composed of a marshal and two assistants. These offices were originally appointed or elected, but towards the latter part of the seventeenth century were contracted out to cover mounting city debts (Rumbelow 1971).

The marshalry was the City of London's response to the need for a centrally directed police force, and was charged with five major tasks. The Provost Marshal had to:

1. Carry off rogues and vagrants to Bridewell;
2. See that due punishments were inflicted acccording to the law;
3. Supervise the constables and the watch;
4. Maintain supervision over ward officials to see that plague regulations were adhered to; and
5. Attend to miscellaneous street activities such as licensing traders, fruiterers, hucksters and other unlicensed itinerants (*Repertories of Court of Aldermen*, vol. 26, folios 1979).

The Marshal and his officers were paid officials, were uniformed, and carried firearms. Their numbers increased from two in 1603 to four in 1617 and to six by 1626 (*Repertories of Court Aldermen*, vol. 34, folios 125, 183).

Almost from their inception, the city marshalry faced serious difficulties. Numerically, they were too weak to be effective in crime control, and were easily overpowered by sizeable groupings. Policing was inadequate at the crucial level of detection and apprehension of crime. Not only were constables and watchmen neglectful, reluctant and poorly organized, but communal support, and co-operation were also absent. Fear, lack of crime-reporting skills, the threat of counter prosecutions, the practical economic difficulties of framing and carrying out arrest indictments, and a lack of confidence in the judicial system distanced the citizen from the police and the courts (Samaha 1974, Ch. 3).

Proclamations and orders from all levels of government point to an indifferent citizenry. A proclamation by the Lord Mayor in 1603 noted the 'remissences and negligence' of enforcement personnel (*Lord Mayor's Proclamations*, 1603). A King's Proclamation in 1616 observed that many 'robberies and felonies, burglaries, pilferies and other horrible crimes' were committed because of 'want of good execution' of the law. A Royal Proclamation five years later stated that policing in London was poor and corruption widespread, and further admonitions in 1628, 1630, 1634, and 1642 confirmed the same themes of street disorder, crime, and lax reporting and punishment of such abuses (Rumbelow 1971, Ch. 3). So defective was policing and so unco-operative the citizenry that Parliament ordered 'extra' precautions and personnel to be deployed to open up the relatively enclosed worlds of crime. The watch was given more arms and the city was supplied with 'expert guides capable of leading a hue and cry' and knowledgeable in the ways and locales of the 'speedy flight of thieves and robbers'. Stricter surveillance and security schemes were advocated to keep crime *outside* city boundaries and local hosteliers were required to monitor and report on travellers (Corporation of City of London, *Misc. Proclamations*, 1649).

Increasingly the state relied upon private self-interest groups. Citizens were exhorted and paid to transform themselves into agents of control. The management of deviance and crime was organized around a personal profit-making business. State rewards — albeit unsystematic — were offered for successful presentation of certain offences. Proclamations and orders from King and Parliament offered sums of money or commodities in kind to enterprising searchers. Neighbours and fellow tradesmen were encouraged to spy and turn evidence on each other.

Arrested suspects were similarly urged to inform on their accomplices in order to gain their own reprieve. Impeachment was designed to give the criminal informer a limited immunity from legal prosecution and to create internal tensions within the world of crime. Forgers and counterfeiters were set against each other. A person in custody or escaping the law because of trading in false silver or gold objects could earn a pardon for all similar crimes which he may have committed if he impeached his mates. He was entitled:

> to such part of the (seized) forfeiture of the said other party to the same offence, as amply as any other informer or relator, not having offended, might have done. . . . (*King's Proclamations* 1627)

He thus could receive a reprieve and a share of the discovered goods, incentives which engendered a climate of suspicion. The threat of competitive impeachments was designed to undermine working partnerships and trust, and it also made the boundaries between crime and legality unclear. Law and enforcement became negotiable. Indeed, the constant use of reprieves may have been an impetus to commit crime (Spitzer and Scull 1980, pp.265–80). The thief who was not in custody could earn a free pardon for all similar crimes if he impeached his colleagues. Thus, he could continue in his illegal practices knowing that he could barter for an impeachment (Hutton, in Judges 1930, pp. 265–91; Rock 1977).

Offices in the formal state control apparatus were not shielded from such trading and selling. Prison administrators and officials, constables, beadles, and watchmen farmed their positions for private profit and advantage. Many office holders routinely bought positions and sought personal returns on their investment. Incumbents tacitly expected to reimburse themselves by means of influence peddling, bribery, and extortion (Hurstfield 1967, pp.16–34; Swart 1949). The private exploitation of political office created a vast black market in which opportunism and outright corruption flourished.

This was particularly so for the city marshalry. From 1627 to 1637 the city was effectively without its appointed official. The office holder, Davis, had 'farmed out' his position for profit. He continued to draw the marshal's salary, however, and paid his hireling a percentage of his wage. Attempts to replace Davis met with failure when the Crown intervened on his behalf. In 1632, the nominee marshal and the under-marshal were subjected to an investigation. Prisoners, common thieves and felons were allegedly being released without due cause. For this and other unspecified misdemeanours, the deputy was dismissed from office and imprisoned, and Davis was enjoined to resume his office. He refused and again deputized a replacement who, from 1632 to 1637, served as deputized city marshal. Davis again fixed the rate as a percentage of his salary and successfully evaded attempts to cut his salary and have him turned out. Eventually, after ten years' non-performance of office, Davis was coerced into being reinstated. He served six years until finally being dismissed for abuse of powers and incompetence (Rumbelow 1971, pp. 50–1).

Succeeding marshals appear to have been more stable in holding office, although their supervision over constables, beadles and the watch was problematic. A proclamation in 1655 criticized justices of the peace, constables and 'other officers' for 'want of zeal, care and diligence' in executing the law, and a proclamation by the Lord Mayor six months later complained of poor policing supervision, crime detection and co-operation. Constables were enjoined to make themselves 'better known and more readily found', and were further ordered to have their signs of office 'set or fixed at their street doors' so all may 'detect their dwelling place' (Corporation of the City of London, *Misc. Proclamations*, 1655; *Lord Mayor's Proclamations*, 1656).

As a regular full-time paid police force, the city marshalry could not act as an authoritative agent of control. They lacked the strength, co-ordination and institutional competence to co-ordinate ward policing and manage specific problems of crime control. They faced resentment from local officials and non-co-operation from the citizenry. Their presence generated friction, and they were poorly equipped to handle specific episodes of social unrest. As mobile surveyors of crime they may have been able to increase the aegis of police authority, but their ability to serve as effective enforcers was hampered by a weak decentralized organizational base.

The army and the militias

The fragility of city policing was paralleled by equally inadequate military forces. Since the army and militia were primarily involved in fighting foreign campaigns and in serving as reserve units against alien invasions (Boynton 1967), the routine surveillance of vagrancy and crime fell outside their range. Crime control was thus an irregular part of their mandate and only sporadically undertaken.

England possessed little in the way of a centralized national citizen's army. Because of its natural frontiers and the absence of land borders with the continent, there was no need for a full-time standing army. The military system was quasi-feudal in character. There was little organizational unity. Loyalties seldom flowed to a central core but were instead tied to local patrons who had enlisted the bands of fighting men (Hale 1962, pp. 19–33; Roberts 1956). The English army was an *ad hoc* and loose agglomeration of professional mercenaries, and of locally sponsored and trained retainers, that was formed in time of war and disbanded in peace time (Stone 1965, pp.199–270). Moreover, the state possessed no monopoly over the means of violence, since men of property could command resources and technical knowledge that could be fashioned into fighting units. Indeed, the distribution of violence was further decentralized during this period, as the use of firearms percolated down to all sectors of society (Cockburn 1977, pp.58–9).

For all of these reasons the organization of violence did not cohere into a rational state controlled institution. As a domestic police force the army lacked administrative competence. While it was an effective repressive weapon in curbing territorial revolts, and while it could disperse and defeat 'riotous' crowds, it was virtually incapable of monitoring the everyday world of crime.

At the same time the rise, during this period, of trained bands and militias contributed little to the centralization of crime control, since these were essentially the regional forces of the landed gentry. Whereas the state exerted a measure of control over the militias by scrutinizing appointments and making them dependent on court favours, militias remained a part of a decentralized system of social control in which recruitment was local and voluntary (Cruickshank 1966).

In sum, the means of violence were diffuse and fragmented, and the state was unable to accumulate sufficient power to gain control over its exercise. The result was an uneven and hesitant domestic surveillance. The shire-state nature of coercive institutions circumscribed their role organizationally and the volunteer nature of membership limited them temporally. Their primary strength lay in their ability to control renegade populations. However, mundane criminal pursuits, in London and elsewhere, were outside their scope of action (Western 1965, pp.70–73). Rarely were the army or militias deployed in patrolling crime. The services of the military were directed primarily at the treasonable and the politically suspect. The army, the militias and the trained bands were a regionalized back-up force. Their involvement and impact on crime control were oblique.

The mediation of state power and criminal organization

As the above discussion demonstrates, the English state lacked the coercive capacity to exact a uniform compliance through its policing apparatus. Crime control in London comprised welters of competing jurisdictions, authorities and agencies. The major tiers of city policing organization — watch and ward, privy council messengers, and city marshalmen — overlapped uncertainly, and often pulled in contrary directions. The regulation of crime was irregular, reluctant, and distorted by ecological factors, population pressures, centrifugal power relations, numerical shortages, internal irregularities, and organizational incompleteness and strains.

Rudimentary government structures and weak policing led to a complicated and subterranean process of crime mediation and management. Coercion was applied by a strategy of intrigue and subversion. Spying, informing for profit, impeachment, and the use of pardons were the machinations of state control. As Hill observed, ‘informers were encouraged to inform against informers until it became a national profession’ (1969, p.97). The actual enforcement of law, then, was reliant upon private intermediaries, ‘seeking rather to nourish than to abolish offences’ (Hill 1969, pp.96–97), and who often ‘dissolved into first class members of the criminal classes’ (Beresford 1957–1958, p.231).

Clandestine agents were drawn from a number of sources. Some were members of crafts who informed on a part-time basis, while others were licensed agents of the state enjoined to form working groups of inspectors on a career basis. Some acquired ‘policing’ monopolies in specific territories or in set businesses (Elton 1958, pp. 79–113). Still other informers worked alone or in small working teams and without specialization (Davies 1956, p.47), and were frequently recruited from the world they were to supervise (Beresford 1957–1958; Davies 1956, p.40). Most were people who possessed inside knowledge. However, informers were sometimes mobile, handling cases in adjoining regions. Some possessed permanent networks with agents spread across the country (Elton 1958). Their scope of action was generally limited to cases of non-indictable offences or misdemeanours. However, informers could capitalize on personal rewards as well as state benefits.

Since crime victims and related private agencies were in the market for the retrieval of information and stolen property, informers were led to develop a system of pardons, money rewards and impeachments. As Beresford noted, such undercover agents played both sides against the middle and were often 'an army of contact men, informers, and other parasites who batten on the innocent — and the avaricious' (1957–1958, p.231). As Davies observed:

> ... the prolonged expenses of taking prosecution through to trial, and the risk of costly upset thereafter, strongly tempted informers to make illegal use of the first entry of an information and the writ issued thereupon. (1956, p.58)

Illegal charges took several forms:

1. Licensed compositions but at inflated rates;
2. Unlicensed charges on actual evidence;
3. Monies extorted by forged or pretended informations; and
4. Fees from defendants for false information to prevent the entering of valid prosecutions (Davies, 1956 pp.58–76).

The regulation of criminal worlds mirrored the pattern of commerce and trade enforcement. An array of blackmailers, false accusers and framers of evidence emerged around the world of crime. In policing terms, informers and thief-catchers were recruited from criminal worlds and sent back to survey them.

Thief-taking was particularly aided with the introduction of the warrants as a means for checking theft. Warrants were secured by injured parties from justices of the peace and members of the Privy Council in order that thieves might, through imprisonment, be forced to make good the loss suffered. The warrant authorized arrest on suspicion of crime, and served initially to force apprehended criminals to confess, inform, return stolen articles or face a far more expensive and unpleasant stay in prison (Greene, in Judges 1930, pp.165–166; Pringle 1955, Chs. 1,2). Receivers of stolen property, in particular, were in a position to benefit as power brokers. At the centre of crime mechandising and information, they could easily serve as police agents.

Intimately acquainted with criminal structures, they were in a position to husband, protect or betray specific groups of criminals (McIntosh 1976; Rock 1977).

Prison underkeepers also doubled as receivers and thief-takers, although they rarely had to take possession of stolen property. As prison officials, they were largely unpaid employees and, like many city officials, relied on fees, bribery and illegal charges to earn a wage. Theirs was a dangerous undertaking, watching over felons, and pursuing armed and violent men. No stock of knowledge or code of control procedures guided their enforcement of the law. Since the keepers of the prison appointed, maintained and dismissed the underkeepers themselves, the controlling authorities seldom intervened in their activities, and prison keepers and their associates interposed themselves on the interface between the reputable and the criminal (Dobb 1953, p.161). Their legitimate calling was a convenient cover for dealing in stolen property. Such thief-takers challenged the traditional role of the fence. As their stake became more promising financially, they found it in their interest to manipulate and dominate thieves (*A Brief Collection of Some Part of Executions . . .*, 1620).

Thief-takers established an elaborate system of checks and balances over crime. They had scouts and spies who haunted the criminal areas and institutions, and thereby obtained information on what crimes were committed and by whom. Similar to other receivers, they operated a system that distributed stolen property back to the rightful owners (Howson 1970; Hutton, in Judges 1930, pp. 265–29; Rock 1977). Once a target had been set, they used their legal calling and their knowledge of criminal contacts to track down a thief. They were well stocked with warrants — some forged, some genuine — with which to intimidate thieves and pickpockets.

Cliques of thief-catchers, with an intimate knowledge of deviant worlds, thus trafficked in crime. They nurtured as well as betrayed, and gained increasing influence over the organization of thieving. Compensations were received from prison keepers for arresting malefactors, and profits were reaped from blackmail, and from receiving and returning stolen property (Fennor, in Judges 1930, pp. 423–487). It was thus often in their interest to encourage and cultivate crime. Fennor, in his exposé of prison conditions, reports that prison sergeants routinely extorted money from wanted criminals. For a price they would warn thieves of imminent arrest. Hutton (in Judges 1930, pp.289–290) relates how thief-takers, after having criminals arrested, would then arrange for their release by either buying them out of prison or arranging that witnesses did not appear.

Thief-takers merged easily with the world they regulated, handling informers and spies, encouraging betrayals, and manipulating the economy of pardons and rewards. Most importantly, within the organization of crime, they exerted a tendency toward centralization. The growth of this form of criminal entrepreneurship strengthened a likelihood toward market dominance. Enjoying a practical immunity, and strengthened by the cloak of officialdom, thief-taker-fences increased their organizational prominence. The combination of the market merchandiser role, and the legitimate state-endorsed enforcement role, provided these intermediaries with considerable power. In particular, they rearranged criminal relationships into a more integrated and co-ordinated underworld. This occurred in three major ways.

First, as a result of their acquaintance with criminal structures and their involvement in police work, they acquired influence over the fate of criminals. Certain forms of crime and groups of criminals could thus be defended and protected, particularly those who accepted their supervisory role. Political immunity was afforded the favoured (Pringle 1955). Their official role in routine enforcement operations provided middlemen with a powerful leverage over segmented sectors of London crime. Private entrepreneurship in crime control led thief-takers and fences to direct as well as protect and counsel criminal projects. They constituted an active agency of social control and a criminal overseer at the same time (Armitage 1932).

Second, the power of informers and thief-takers merged with that of the fence and represented the major locus of exchange between criminal, victim, and weak state control. On the border between legality and illegality, they cultivated a public role around which considerable influence was exercised. The thief-taker-fence arrangement was designed to return stolen property while at the same time herding and protecting the thieves who initially robbed (*The Life and Death of Mary Frith* ..., 1612; Raynor and Crook 1926, pp.169–179). They thus sponsored forms of crime and enhanced the stability, routinization and continuity of criminal practices. The growth of these intermediaries tightened the patterning of relations within the criminal underworld.

Third, thief-taking fuelled a tendency towards centralization within the organization of crime. Small-scale thieving establishments were put at risk. The role of the receiver became inundated with political prominence which affected the internal design of the London underworld. Simply said, centripetal patterns started to emerge. The new discipline of the criminal go-betweens strengthened, and even regularized and extended, the organization of crime. The thief-taker's authority was recognized by the state. Justices of the peace encouraged victims to seek out intermediaries to recover their rightful property. The state's trade in warrants and pardons linked the judiciary to private thief-taking enterprises. The state, in encouraging a trade in crime-farming, fashioned a more coherent design for the underworld. Working teams of pickpockets, cheats and thieves evolved ancillary organizational roles to buy protection from pursuit, arrest and impeachment. Some formed wider alliances of companionship and security. Many attached themselves more closely as clients to receiver patrons in order to be afforded a limited protection. The legitimacy accorded criminal middlemen forged more cohesive alliances between theft rings and receivers (McIntosh 1976, pp.257–261).

However, the authority of these crime brokers was never complete, and the centripetal patterns should not be exaggerated. There did not exist a conspiracy of power or leadership; rather a tightening of segmented associations occurred. For such entrepreneurs as Moll Cutpurse (who had gained some control over the organization of thieving in the 1620s and 1630s), it was possible to corner specific provinces of theft activities, but not to translate this partial market dominance into administrative control (Raynor and Crook 1926). Criminal competitors, other fences, informers and prison officials ran parallel rackets. Since these intermediaries seldom had advance knowledge of crimes, there is little to support the view of a criminal conspiracy with a master mind exercising central control (McIntosh 1976, pp.259–261). Through a system of advance credit, counselling, provision of shelter, and purchase of stolen loot, thief-taker-fences could protect their thieves against their own informing and betrayals but they could not guarantee immunity from others.

According to Howson, for seventeenth and eighteenth century entrepreneurs of crime like Moll Cutpurse, the real problem was to 'keep the underworld divided for easier control without permitting it to fall apart' (1970, p.145). They managed this by dominating market relations with thieves, by providing assistance to reliable thieves, and by the threat of informing on those who took business to competitors. However this did not lead to centralized administrative authority over thievery. Indeed, as late as the 1680s 'there were hundreds of warehouses and repositories where thieves could sell their booty, within minutes of stealing it, at a price not far below its full value' (Howson 1970, p.36). It was only with the eighteenth century that the monopolization of thievery was achieved and theft gangs made completely subordinate. So one can see, in the period from 1550 to 1700, a confederation of theft networks tending towards the more administratively-centred system of the eighteenth century, in which thief-takers were to monopolize not only market circumstances, but also police work and the entire fate of thieves who worked for them.

Conclusion

In sum, the growing opportunities for crime, and the social importance of territoriality and custom, were further bolstered by the precarious nature of the administration of justice. Decentralized state power, geographical jurisdictions, and political patronage mutually reinforced each other, encouraging diverse possibilities for crime. Gaps in law enforcement abounded, central authority was lacking, and the dubious and sometimes corrupt effects of patronage were woven into the fabric of communal and state social control institutions. Populations of masterless men and women, some resorting to crime, lived in the interstices of the changing social relations brought on by transformations in the underlying organization of production, and the relatively weak decentralized policing apparatus. Here they established as never before their work teams, networks, institutions and techniques for crime.

7 The security and surveillance of the environment

Nigel South

Introduction

In 1984 the British Home Office issued a circular on crime prevention. Significantly, it produced this document in conjunction with the Government Departments of the Environment, Health and Social Security, Education and Science, and the Welsh Office. This reflects an exercise in centralized co-ordination around the very broad area of crime prevention at both Departmental policy level and, through the canvassing of opinions from senior officials, at the level of implementing delivery of a range of public services — police, probation, housing, social services, education and others. The declared aim is the initiation of multi-agency co-ordination (or at least co-operation) among those who 'have a contribution to make in developing local prevention strategies' (Home Office 1984). In this chapter I am not so much concerned with the broad significance and ramifications of such a multi-agency strategy as with one key feature of such a proposed approach.

My particular focus here concerns the securing of the environment, through both public and private sector initiatives, following from the principle of reducing crime by reducing the opportunity to commit it. At a practical level this means a strategy based partly on the manipulation, design and social management of the environment to strengthen it, and partly on supporting values like community spirit, neighbourliness and respect for order, to combat property and street crimes such as burglary, vandalism, theft, sexual attack, mugging and so on. Such ideas are neither new within the context of recent policy proposals or recommendations, nor are they by any means new when considered in terms of the history of physical security as designed to protect, detect and deter.

It should indeed be emphasized at the outset that a broad concern with the restoration of community-based social control and stabilization of local order is, of course, not solely a preoccupation of the technicist, conservative criminology which is currently its most powerful sponsor. Such a goal has an honourable liberal history, notably exemplified for example in the social reformism of the Chicago School (cf. Cohen 1985a, p.211). As Cohen notes, the legacy of the latter, in the 'ideal of the urban village', has today come together 'with the conscious planning of the physical environment in order to reduce crime and vandalism'. This convergence is most clearly discernible in Oscar Newman's work on the concept of defensible space (Cohen 1985a, p.215; Newman 1972).[1]

I do not intend to go through this particular history here. However, as a starting point to this project, my purpose is to offer just a few historical reminders about the familiarity of certain crime prevention strategies before seeking to broaden consideration of 'new' approaches to environmental security. I believe that this needs to be done both at a theoretical level and at the level of practical policy, even if this leaves us (as usual) with no simple and immediate answers. At a theoretical level I shall briefly refer to work on the symbolic significance of the social spaces (public and private) that we inhabit. At the policy level I shall try to explore how such crime prevention initiatives relate to other developments in social control and to the ambiguities in policy and practice of which we should be wary.

'... The horizon of scarecrows has broadened'

The principles of physical security or the securing of the environment are age-old. The fortifications of ancient castles provide interesting parallels with today's prisons and with the design of modern strong rooms. Physical security, it should be remembered, has historically addressed the twin problems of keeping people in and keeping people out!

In medieval times the classic architecture of protection and containment, and hence control, was a series of barriers or walls in a system of concentric circles (or other shapes) protecting the ultimate sanctuary of the keep, with a fortified drawbridge which could be raised or lowered (across a moat for example) with a portcullis gate at the point of control of access to the castle (cf. Hayter 1968, p. xix). The early watchman or look-out, as the name implies, maintained a vigil looking beyond the city or castle walls and moat. This was a well-planned and sophisticated defence *and* detection system. Indeed the popular idea of the moat itself as simply a form of physical defence or barrier is less accurate than seeing its main significance as an intrusion early-warning device, to alert guards in the darkness. As Hayter delicately puts it, 'It is very difficult to cross still and stagnant water without making a noise' (1968, p. xix).

The essentials of these and other ideas and practices are familiar and recurrent. They are key features of strategies for security, surveillance and crime prevention/control in history and the present day. The sentiments of discourses on these themes are also apparently timeless, especially in their mixed tones of optimism and pessimism. Some slight mix of the two is found, for example, in the comments of John Wade, in his *Treatise on the Police and Crimes of the Metropolis*:

> But something we are persuaded, might be invented for rendering both houses and warehouses more secure, and it is really a reproach to this mechanical age that nothing in the construction of locks, doors and windows, and even in the protection of walls, and in the mode of giving alarms, can be devised, that shall frustrate any nocturnal efforts of the midnight plunderer. (Wade 1829, p. 193)

More recently, in a well known modern text on private security, Lipson (a former US Secret Service agent and head of the American Express security division) is keen to point to improvements in modern security and its efficiency as related to the use of modern technology, but he is also aware that in many cases such developments reflect the application of new electronic and building systems to old ploys for the detection and surveillance of intruders and employees alike. For example:

> ... the hidden passages and listening posts of ancient castles were models for the observation posts built into ... [for example] ... many large post offices. Specially constructed slits permitted postal inspectors to spy on working employees. Gambling casinos ... use one-way mirrors for the same purpose. (Lipson 1975, p.141)

Modern technologies take up old ideas and instead of simply spying and reporting on what goes on in shadowy corners, now 'infra-red sensitised film [is used] for surreptitious photography in darkened places' (Lipson 1975, p.141). Where in the past military defensive strategy 'borrowed' from the farmer's defence of the land and seed, and set scarecrow, dummy guards to augment visible forces, so today:

> ... surreptitious may no longer be a proper description for CCTV (closed circuit television) ... [which] ... has become so commonplace. As a result dummy cameras ... are hung in very obvious places to act as deterrents ... It can be said that the horizon of scarecrows has broadened. (Lipson 1975, p.141)

The point here is that in considering the nature of current developments in crime prevention and the securing of the environment (and indeed 'social control' broadly), concern over, or applause for, the movements of the times should remember their long lineage. This is particularly true with the idea of designing or manipulating the environment to aid crime prevention/control and ensure the security of the public and private spheres. It is not that such aims may not be well-intentioned or intrinsically 'good things' (although in some respects they can carry with them an odd sense of benign malevolence), rather that their enthusiastic embrace should be tempered by a note of realism informed by precedent and by the contemporary developments with which they are linked. As Stan Cohen puts it, the influential 'dreadful realization' behind the CPTED (Crime Prevention Through Environmental Design) movements of the late 1960s and the 1970s was that 'while the medieval fortress town had been a place of safe retreat against the external enemy, the enemy was now within the gates' (1985, p.215).

Some trends, themes and problems in current approaches to crime prevention

At this stage I must briefly outline some of the trends and themes in the approaches to crime prevention which tend to predominate in the literature and in practice. These are the principal models or strategies which underlie my concerns in this paper, but here I will only summarize some of their positive and negative implications.[2]

First, *situational crime prevention* focuses on the management, design and manipulation of the built physical environment, in order to reduce the opportunity to commit crime and increase the risk of detection if deterrence fails. Critically speaking, this approach can be construed as either naively shortsighted or cynically selfish in so far as it explicitly aims to keep crime out of a particular place (home, neighbourhood, and so on). It rarely involves very much in the way of active community participation, or of positive rather than negative reactive motivation. Generally deterrence is sought through the creation of 'defensible space' and, where active participation follows, it is usually in the form of defensive responses such as citizen patrols, vigilantism or the employment of security patrols.

There seems to be little evidence of any great success with this approach, and my characterization of it as either shortsighted or selfish is highlighted by its noted tendency to simply displace the incidence of crime to more vulnerable situations. Given the problems of implementation and the significant economic cost of environmental design programmes, a displacement effect would be unsurprising (Lowman 1982, p.327). Indeed, Reppetto (1976) has identified five different types of such displacement effect.

The approach can also have negative consequences for the 'defended' community itself. Accompanying attitudes and demands for conformity can promote a climate of fear of crime which works against positive community participation as people adopt a siege mentality or seek adherence to self-imposed curfews. Alternatively residents may come to feel that it is safer to simply move away from the area if they are able. Whatever the kind of community, this flight means a loss of economic involvement and input into the area which can only exacerbate problems further. At a broader level still, situational strategies have the potential to intensify social divisions and inequalities of living environment and access and movement, related to the 'us' versus 'them' erection of boundaries.

Second, *broader community-orientated approaches* have also been developed. These can stress the roles to be played by networks that are formal and institutional and/or informal and communal. As Weiss puts it, 'both of these approaches seek compliance to norms by self-policing, and stress greater direct involvement of the family, the school and various community agencies in prevention' (forthcoming 1987).

In the United Kingdom the trend in community-orientated crime prevention strategies, frequently articulated by the Commissioner of the Metropolitan Police, Sir Kenneth Newman, is towards multi-agency co-operation. This is envisaged as including agencies like police, probation, social services and housing departments, as suggested in the 1984 Home Office Circular. It also embraces private security services and voluntary neighbourhood crime-watch schemes (Metropolitan Police 1985). This over-arching approach would seem to contain some strong and some rather naive and worrying points. Additionally, with regard to matters of funding and national housing construction problems, it is in places either cynical or downright ignorant.

That there has been something of a 're-discovery' of crime prevention as a project to be taken seriously by both public and private sector commentators, policy-makers and agencies seems beyond doubt. By this I do not mean that the police, policy-makers, the public or commentators on crime problems have not generally remembered that the prevention of crime is fairly desirable (although, of course, other interests might have militated against this at various times and in various ways). It remains odd, however, that such an apparently obvious social goal needed to be rediscovered and reasserted at all, whether — politically speaking — by the right, left or middle-ground.

In practice it is, of course, the case that *private* security services, which owe their allegiance to employers concerned about profit margins and which operate outside the agenda of public policing priorities, have long placed strong emphasis on 'loss-prevention' work. While this emphasis has meant the adoption of a narrower purview than the crime prevention obligations of the public police, their approach to 'preventive policing' has been more generally reliant on technological aids (cf. Stenning and Shearing 1980, p.232). There are signs that such distinctions are now being blurred (as are other distinctions between public and private sector policing/security: cf. South 1985). Private sector agencies increasingly seek involvement in wider crime prevention services and strategies. Public sector policing is initiating programmes to help it keep in touch with the community 'on the ground', but at the same time it increasingly adopts a technicist approach to combatting crime and, operationally, becomes more technologically orientated. The fact that these are recent and current developments allows some scope for fairly confident speculation that they will continue for the near future.

What I seek to explore in the rest of this paper are some aspects of the ideas, practices and social relations, past and present, which can be traced back from, and teased out of, this renaissance of concern to take crime prevention seriously, and in particular to ensure the security and surveillance of the social environment.

Securing the social environment

Given its significance as the concrete context in which people negotiate everyday life, it is surprising that relatively little critical work in criminology seems to have addressed the shaping of the physical and spatial dimensions of social control. Recent work has generally focused on how architecture might be enlisted to reduce delinquency, mugging, vandalism, graffiti, and more serious crime through effective security and surveillance procedures. The concept of 'defensible space' developed by Newman and others has been particularly influential here (Newman 1972, 1973).

Studies exploring the hypotheses of defensible space theory have tended to seek data and measures of the relationship between characteristics of built environments and their residents (or users) and levels of crime victimization, fear of crime and 'residential instability' (for example, Newman and Franck 1980). To nobody's great surprise such studies have generally confirmed principal defensible space hypotheses; for example, there is a positive connection between the physical features of a built environment and levels of victimization, fear and residential instability. The size of a building is also found to be related to actual victimization and to fear of crime.

Such research leads to conclusions which call for the improvement of physical design features, particularly in public housing projects and developments, including measures to reduce accessibility to non-residents and to restrict the number of residents living in each building. Other studies concerned with the link between crime and the built environment (cf. Murray *et al.* 1980), find strong evidence for the effectiveness of measures aimed at controlling or monitoring movement (for example locks, alarms, surveillance cameras, guard posts and so on). Efforts to increase visibility and to enhance the influence of physical design over social behaviour, with a view to reducing crime and fear, have also become favoured suggestions — although evaluations of available evidence hardly confirm any of these measures as overwhelming successes (Murray 1983).

Clearly, though, there is much that is commendable in such research and practical recommendations. However, notions of monitoring movement, controlling access and influencing behaviour through the design of our built environment also invite thoughts of caution. It is not that such measures are not already, in many respects, routine. On the contrary they have a long history. Nor is it wrong to suggest that they are properly *supposed* to make people 'think cautiously', thereby deterring burglars, muggers, vandals, and so on. Without lapsing into paranoia, the issue is how far to take the implications of a view of society and crime which;

1. Has a tendency to eschew consideration of the deeper *causes* of crime;
2. Wilfully or neglectfully forgets the complexities, inequalities and competing interests of modern society; and,
3. Instead suggests that we can more usefully (in a sense which smacks of behaviourism) bend our energies to 'designing out crime'.

There is clearly of course, a dimension of social control to how architectural intention can influence and direct options of behaviour, access and freedom of use. Such subtle (and sometimes less-than-subtle) intentions have been discerned in a number of recent historical studies. The evolution of penal architecture, for example, is now quite well documented, most notably by Foucault (1977; but cf. Cohen 1985a; Cohen and Scull 1983). In his 'excavation' of the architecture of power Foucault provides a now classic discussion of the contribution of spatial dimensions, control over their boundaries and the exercise of discipline and training within them, to the permeation and integration of discipline throughout the 'micro-relations' of society (cf. Shearing and Stenning 1985, p.337). Corrigan and Gillespie (1978) briefly refer to what they term 'social architecture', that is '. . . the reinforcement of notions of society by the use of architecture'. They find such significant supports of social values and social order oddly neglected. Thus they suggest that it is rare, for example:

> to find more than passing comment on the one concrete result of the 1834 Poor Law: the construction of very large buildings for the use of the Union — work-houses, pauper schools and hospitals. But we must now fit this burst of activity into a more general range of Public (social) architecture: the erection of a range of buildings identified with certain notions of 'correctness' and reinforcing certain definitions of 'proper' social activity. [The provision] of 'proper' educational and reading facilities . . . [rendered] curious, makeshift, old-fashioned and fundamentally *improper* any alternative provision by groups of working men. (Corrigan and Gillespie 1978, p.12).

As these authors remark, ' "Architecture" and "intentions" define the nature of the desired "Public"' (Corrigan and Gillespie 1978, p. 29, note p.79). It is this idea of how the design of the environment can enhance distinctions between the desirable and undesirable in the population that should be one source of concern.

The growth of what I refer to here as environmental security (the term is not solely mine but is also used by security consultants and architects) seems one of the most disturbing aspects of the ways in which public and governmental concerns over 'crime control' have been identified as offering key opportunities for the growth and further expansion of non-accountable private security services. To take, as one example, the most recent endorsement of this prospect, the Hallcrest Systems 1985 *Report on Private Security and Police in America* suggests the involvement of security consultants in city and county planning and zoning, integrating security and police services in Planned Urban Developments (PUD) (Cunningham and Taylor 1985, p.3). Perhaps an even more disturbing (though wholly unsurprising) interest in developing the theories and techniques for the security and surveillance of the environment has come from the military. Although this could lead into a somewhat different area of discussion it is important to at least note that, whether they be in the private or the public sector, strategists of security implementation have much in common. It should be remembered that while there is a soft side to Crime Prevention Through Environmental Design, there is also a hard edge to accompanying concerns to ensure that the environment can be effectively policed.

A very brief illustration of this 'hard edge' can be given by reference to the work of the British Army security theorist, Frank Kitson. In his book *Low Intensity Operations: Subversion, Insurgency and Peace-keeping* (1971) Kitson argues that a society which is well policed in a 'low key' but effective manner in the first place will have fewer 'problems'. Kitson served as a commanding officer in Belfast for two years in the early 1970s and, bringing such philosophies with him, was able to put into practice ideas for developing the 'well policed city'. One element of the strategy that follows is the aim of making the actual physical 'bricks and mortar' structure of the community or area accessible to those engaged in policing and control. As McGuffin writes, 'in-depth planning is taken seriously by the Army — even down to their insistence on being involved in the planning of new housing estates, such as Twinbrook in Belfast, where there are only two entrances and two exits to the entire estate' (1974, p.145).

In the most pessimistic scenario, environmental security is a harbinger of the routinization of systems of minimally- or non-accountable surveillance over ordinary citizens and their movements within commercial and public spaces. Importantly, the increasingly explicit development of the systems and technology of environmental security and surveillance is in line with both the 'liberal' policy of crime prevention to which policing agencies are often urged to return, as well as with more aggressive and active styles of policing which are often adopted in more specialized areas of operation (such as 'the fight' against organized crime, drugs and so on).

The idea of effective environmental security is far from the accomplishment of, but is perhaps an uncomfortable step toward, achieving that 'perfection of power' which Foucault (1977) observes 'should render its operation unnecessary'. There is, unhappily, nothing particularly fanciful in such a suggestion. The development of surveillance systems as a mode of control is based on quite pragmatic principles, including the objective that subjects should come to bear the burden of controlling themselves and their associates.

Space and social order

In *Discipline and Punish*, Foucault (1977) illuminates the importance of control over the spatial dimensions of a segmentalized society for the achievement of a 'disciplined' social order. As Hussein observes:

> Discipline proceeds from the distribution of individuals in space. Thus spatial distribution is accomplished by means of several techniques. It may involve an enclosure. The spread of disciplinary techniques is coupled with the institution of enclosed spaces to confine ... Side by side with these spaces there also developed manufacturing spaces in the form of factories. Order and inspection on which the exercise of discipline is premised required in a number of cases a well delineated and controlled space. (1978, p. 935)

But the importance of delineating, controlling and thereby defining spaces is not an exercise upon which some past epoch alone founded aspects of its subtler prerequisites for the exercise of discipline and maintenance of social control. Rather, the symbolic defining of space (and the enforcement of definition) is clearly a major and extremely significant (if neglected) feature of the modern maintenance of social control and social order. In this regard the work of Edelman (1978) is also highly illuminating.

As Edelman observes, 'like the linguistic terms that serve as symbols, spaces can ... take on quite different meanings for different people and for different social situations' (1978, p.2). For Edelman, architectural symbolism is based on both non-obvious dialectical meanings held by elites and non-elites helping to perpetuate domination and submission, as well as 'purely symbolic', commonly-held dialectical meanings. Offices of state and authority come to be viewed as 'symbols of government by the people, equality before the law', and so on. They are held to be arenas of legitimate power where grace and favour, 'luck and arbitrary power' play no part. There is, then, the co-existence of those meanings which *re*produce aspects of inequality and domination alongside those which 'reassure' and comfort, evoking the legitimacy of order and the security found in the status quo.

In the context of such an analysis, the implications of the manipulation of the environment to promote environmental security can be seen as a development to enhance and emphasize the subtleties of social inequality, rather than rendering all citizens more equally protected. As Edelman suggests of the world of work:

> Spaces reaffirm a dialectic of hierarchical distinctions. ... Work spaces in bureaucratic settings illustrate a similar point. Interior spaces can be constant reminders to workers and to onlookers of hierarchical distinctions: who wield authority to reward or punish, who are competent and independent and who, by contrast, are under surveillance, in need of regulation to avoid nonconformity or incompetence. Architectural features create fine distinctions in these respects through symbols everyone learns to recognise ... It is, of course, the architectural *contrasts* that exalt or degrade occupants in such hierarchical settings. (1978, pp.4–5)

Thus, according to this argument, social roles assigned and defined, unrelated to merit and competence, and perhaps biased by discrimination and prejudice, can be strengthened and solidified by the symbolic power of the spaces in which they are given meaning. 'The space as symbol encourages people to act out the generalized expectation' (1978, p.5). 'Spaces' themselves, then, have the power to subtly direct and discipline the population — from prison to workplace to shopping precinct or housing estate.

Urban planners, architects of complex building construction and environmental security consultants all make decisions about physical layout and public and private areas based, for example, upon a notion of the 'pedestrian line of desire'. As Cohen notes, 'urban planners use the term "line of desire" to indicate the direction of maximum pedestrian flow between fixed points, for example from tube station to office, or from home to shops' (1979, p.185). Deviation from such expected, routine routes of travel is seen in policing practice as tinged in some way with a 'guilt by association'. Only certain troublesome categories of people tend to deviate from such routine avenues, breaking with norms which impose a 'system of unofficial curfew, informal out-of-bounds' defining who are the 'wrong people, wrong age, wrong sex, in the wrong place and the wrong time' (Cohen 1979, p. 131). Both the police and private security services, being concerned with the protection of private property and 'on the look-out for trouble', develop a strong awareness of the potentially deviant and suspicious character of those who stray — whether there is the possibility of trespass or not.

In itself, this latter issue of trespass and 'access' to certain physical spaces and property raises an important point to note with regard to the security and surveillance of the environment. The 'justice' of old ideas about trespass in ambivalently defined, privately owned but publicly accessible spaces has been confused more than ever in the post-World War II period with the expansive development of what Shearing and Stenning (1981) refer to as 'mass private property'. As these authors eloquently put the case:

> Historically, the notions of 'private property' and 'private place' have never been recognized as entirely congruent by any legal system. Yet most of the powers and authority of those who own or possess private property, have been premised on the assumption that they usually are. The modern development of mass private property, however, has resulted in more and more areas of the urban environment which, although they are privately owned and controlled, are quite clearly not 'private places' in any meaningful sense. (Shearing and Stenning 1981, p. 238)

Environmental security and the idea of crime prevention through physical design of our living space relate to broad socioeconomic trends rather than just the theory of defensible space or the fiscal attraction of technology over labour-intensive control strategies. Our physical environment, and in particular the urban space which the majority of people inhabit today, has been reconstituted throughout the twentieth century on a material level of awesome proportions. Whole cities have grown, others have declined slowly, still others have lost their hearts in war or economic recession, their shells hanging on, bitterly empty. But still the story has been one of urban growth, and with the reconstitution of the physical property base of society (and the attendant accumulation of mass private property) have come changes in the patterns of ownership and access.

In the process of replacing single-storey dwellings and rows of single unit commercial buildings with multi-storey towers and complexes, what might previously have been:

> a single public street ... patrolled by the public police, is developed into a mass of private 'streets' (the corridors in an apartment building, or the walkways in a townhouse project) which in all probability will become the domain of private security. (Shearing and Stenning 1981, p. 229)

Similarly, new and integrated commercial facilities are likely to be patrolled:

> by private security personnel hired by the corporate owner of the new complex. While the public police will not be barred from such places, the very nature and design of such places ensure that they will no longer form part of the regular patrol beat of the public police. (Shearing and Stenning 1981, p.229)

Whilst Shearing and Stenning are writing here principally with reference to Canada and the United States, very similar developments have taken place in the United Kingdom, elsewhere in Europe, and in Australia and New Zealand.

It is clear therefore that 'new' initiatives in crime prevention, based on the management and manipulation of the physical environment (and 'social' use of it), have a long history, aspects of which make cautious and critical thinking advisable. Further, they connect with a broad range of contemporary developments in relation to the problems of the inner cities, deteriorating public housing stock, changes in ownership and the use of private property, and the post-World War II shifts in the division of policing labour in society, in which the expansive, international growth of private security has played a key role (South 1984).

Conclusion: a design for living?

It is not fanciful but accurate to characterize Crime Prevention Through Environmental Design as 'social engineering' (Lowman 1982, p.330). This is true no less today, in its application with respect to 'problem' housing estates or the defence of the vulnerable against the predatory or the 'haves' against the 'have-nots' than it was in the nineteenth or earlier centuries. As Lowman argues:

> crime prevention through environmental design has been hailed by its practitioners as a product of the 20th century; its pedigree is usually traced back through Newman (1972) and Jeffrey (1971) to Jane Jacobs (1961). But environmental design is, in a sense, a child of the 19th century (if not earlier) redressed for 20th century consumption. (1982, p. 330)

The physical reconstruction and literal illumination of the city in the nineteenth century, the attempts to marshal, reform or displace and disperse sections of the population as light was thrown on the dark places of the urban heart, is a process that is being re-wrought in the cities of the late twentieth century. It is thus with some sense of historical *déjà vu* that we note the promotion, among contemporary 'futurists' of crime control, of a 'forward-looking' shift from 'law and order responses directed at the individual offender, to dealing with systems, opportunities, and environments' (Cohen 1985a, p.214).

The rhetoric and technology of primary prevention has obvious appeal to a variety of constituencies. Sitting well with the original goals of the public policing institution, the concept resonates with a wide range of political opinions and social concerns. It is attractive in its ambitions to prevent crime, allow social intervention to assist the vulnerable (yet in a cost-effective manner), whilst supposedly strengthening participation in and attachment to the invoked notion of community.

The task for a more critical but realistic criminology is to shift the emphasis of theory, policy and practice from a preoccupation with the security and surveillance of the lived environment, towards a commitment to the *overall improvement* of that environment. In addressing crime problems from this different perspective we must be concerned not only with 'public safety', but also with the assistance and social and material comfort that can be given to *victims* of crime and of racial and sexual harassment. This is a task for a criminological agenda which is policy orientated, socially responsible and humane. Such a criminology must itself displace the positivistic and bureaucratic criminological tones and techniques which currently claim the attention of policy-makers in the United Kingdom and North America (cf. Young 1987).

At the policy level we must recognize and point out ambiguity, good intentions and cynical rationalizations. One case in point would be nationally initiated or recommended programmes for security through environmental design and management. Briefly, were such programmes to be the responsibility and preserve of a central government department, then criticism and concern might follow on the grounds of the familiar remoteness of executive offices from elected representatives, leading to an absence of direct accountability and of effective arenas for airing the voice of the communities affected. In such a case the decentralization of such bureaucratic functions devolved to the level of local communities might be a progressive demand. On the other hand, decentralized responsibility for crime prevention and local security is more probably likely to be favoured partly on grounds related to familiar 'fiscal crisis' arguments. For example, in Britain, the Department of the Environment has commendably suggested to a number of local authorities that are receiving central funding for a variety of urban programmes, that they consider the inclusion of crime prevention initiatives in their future projects (Home Office 1984, p.6). However, the prevailing mood is quite clearly one in which additional expenditure from central government sources is to be discouraged where possible. Instead, attention has been drawn to the roles that might be played by private charities, commercial organizations and others in funding local initiatives, whilst projects requiring resources in the form of human input might usefully turn to local voluntary groups (cf. Home Office 1984, p.6).

The problem is that in the short term it is cheaper and quicker to physically and socially construct an environment which is more suggestive of a fortress than a comfortable, safe and secure environment. Currently in the United Kingdom, the limits set on central government funding in a wide range of areas of social policy seem to incline toward the palliative rather than curative or positively transformative. The drawing in of local voluntary groups and sources of finance to help to implement local projects might, in many circumstances, be a very positive community development — despite the absence of alternative resources. But there are clearly shortcomings and dangers here unless there is *genuine* involvement, not simply in providing resources, but also in the planning and control of projects.

Crime prevention packages obviously require more than just the improvement of the physical environment. Social resources and the human input to provide assistance, low-key patrol and high-efficiency response to calls are also necessary. In the changing division of policing labour (cf. South 1985), there is immense scope for the increased but differentiated involvement of both public policing and private security services. Yet perhaps tenants groups and voluntary associations in housing developments, organized in genuinely *accountable* forms, have a stronger role to play than has yet emerged or been envisaged.[3] Local residents — the people affected and who desire a secure but *human* environment — in coalition with *accountable* local police and social services, might provide scope for a democratic, legitimate and realistic form of multi-agency/multi-representative co-ordination of efforts directed at crime prevention and control and the improvement of the environment. If we are at all concerned about the human quality and diversity of life and of how and where we live, then this proposal is surely preferable to a perspective which largely equates crime prevention and control with the development of better behavioural 'designs for living'.

8 Behind union lines: the setting of evidentiary boundaries

Susan M. Addario
Clifford D. Shearing
Philip C. Stenning

Introduction

Limitation of access to information is a fundamental feature of social order. Evidentiary boundaries create a shifting network of backstage and frontstage regions that shape interaction (Goffman 1959). The location of such boundaries is a subject of constant negotiation and conflict (Giddens 1984, pp.122–129). Boundaries may have a physical form or may be expressed in rules that limit what may be seen and heard (Stinchcombe 1963). Some rules merely have the force of custom (for example, rules about where one may look in a public washroom) while others may be enforced by a corporate entity, such as the state (Reiss 1986).

By limiting access to information, evidentiary boundaries serve to control interaction by structuring the rules by which that interaction occurs. This is particularly relevant in conflicts where information, or its absence, can influence outcomes. By lending its support to one particular configuration of boundaries, the state becomes a critical influence in conflict resolution. Parties involved in conflict seek to strengthen their position both by lobbying the state to define evidentiary boundaries in ways that they hope will assist them, and by calling on the state in the midst of conflict to enforce rules that endorse boundaries that are favourable to them.

While the role of the state with respect to evidentiary boundaries has been well studied with respect to criminal law, this has *not* been the case with respect to civil law. This distinction is important because in criminal law the state becomes a party to conflict, while in civil law it acts primarily as a referee that may be called upon to ensure that evidentiary boundaries are not breached.

In this chapter we examine the interaction between the state and conflicting parties in the civil sphere by examining a management–labour dispute involving a strike. The case that forms the basis for the analysis provides an opportunity to study two primary issues:

1. The use of undercover agents to breach evidentiary boundaries; and
2. The use of a surrogate to minimize the consequences of disruptive tactics for longer term relationships.

Before we present the case on which the analysis is based, a brief discussion of the importance of evidentiary boundaries to labour–management conflict, as well as the relevance of each of the above issues, is necessary to provide a context for the discussion to follow.

In labour–management conflicts, information is a key resource for two primary reasons. First, as the conflict generally focuses on the way in which the economic pie, generated by labour and capital, is to be divided, information and misinformation about the size of the pie is important. Second, each side requires knowledge of the other's strengths, weaknesses[1] and planning in order to react effectively.

This is particularly true in a strike or lockout. Not only do such situations lead each party to be more reticent about sharing information which it might otherwise share, but physical access to places in which relevant information would normally be available is also typically curtailed substantially or eliminated altogether. In addition, routine relationships (for example, between workers and their supervisors), which normally provide significant channels for the exchange of information, are disrupted or suspended. Under these circumstances, innovative forms of intelligence gathering, which normally would not be contemplated, will often be pursued. One of these is spying through covert infiltration. On the union side, this may involve the cultivation of informants within management (for example, the boss' secretary or some relatively inconspicuous junior manager). On the management side, it will typically involve either cultivating 'loyal' workers as informants, or 'planting' an informant within the workforce in general, or within the bargaining unit in particular. In addition to intelligence gathering activities, such an informant may be given other tactical responsibilities, which may range from the circulation of 'disinformation' to more active disruptive tactics or provocation.

The risks of covert intelligence in a strike situation are very substantial. Detection of such activity by the other side can bring general discredit to the party resorting to it, so that even legitimate bargaining positions and strategies lose credibility and effectiveness. One way to reduce such risks is to employ surrogates or agents to undertake intelligence work. In this way, it is hoped, if 'things go wrong', the antagonism which would otherwise be directed at the main party to the dispute can be deflected onto the agent through a concerted (and perhaps even prearranged) posture of disassociation. The principal will claim that in doing whatever was considered to be wrong, the agent was acting outside, or in contravention of, the principal's instructions and/or that the principal was kept unaware of such activities. Specific strategies (such as the adoption of a 'need to know' basis for the communication of information between the agent and the principal, a 'nothing in writing' policy and the so-called 'principle of deniability' (French and Beliveau 1979, p.35)) can be implemented to lend subsequent plausibility to such claims of disassociation.[2]

As we shall see from the case we are about to discuss, this kind of distancing through surrogacy can also be exploited to advantage by the victim of covert infiltration once it has been 'exposed'. Where both sides in a dispute have a strong vested interest in preserving an ongoing relationship after the dispute has been resolved, this can have great importance, since it allows the battle to be waged vicariously, with the agent as the 'sacrificial lamb'. In this way, effective attacks can be made on the opposing party while still allowing for 'face-saving' when the time for settlement and reconciliation arrives. The scapegoat status of the agent thus provides the occasion for a ritual of symbolic blaming and punishment from which both parties can derive advantage. The case we shall be describing in this chapter provides a particularly good illustration of the efficacy of such distancing through surrogacy.

In the course of the strike, to be outlined below, a complaint was laid by the Union about the use of an undercover agent. This resulted in a public hearing before the Ontario Labour Relations Board of the Ontario Ministry of Labour ('the Board'). One of the authors attended the hearing and made notes on the testimony presented before the Board. In addition, informal discussions were held with participants during breaks in the proceedings. These observations, together with the decision handed down by the Board, provide the basis for the analysis to follow. All citations are either from the observer's notes or the Board's decision.

We begin our discussion with a brief presentation of the facts of the case. The law with respect to the use of undercover agents as spies in labour–management disputes in Ontario is then outlined. This legal frame provides a context for the subsequent discussion of how the Union and the Company sought to shape the evidentiary boundaries that structured their relationship through their interaction with two state institutions, namely, the police and the Board.

The case

In September of 1981, 357 members of the local branch of a major North American union began what was eventually to become a seven-month strike at a manufacturer of automotive parts in Ontario. The Company and the Union had enjoyed a sixteen-year collective bargaining relationship without incident. The major strike issues in the autumn of

1981 were the Union's demand for changes in contract language which would guarantee common seniority among the three production units covered by the collective agreement, improvements in the pension plan, and a new method of work measurement.

It became obvious to both sides, following meetings held throughout the summer of 1981, that negotiation of the collective agreement was going to be a difficult task, and that a strike was distinctly possible. The Company had been involved in a strike which resulted in extensive damage at another one of its operations in 1980. The workers at that facility had, however, been represented by a different union.

Once the Company concluded that a strike was likely, it began to take steps to develop an intelligence strategy that would take it behind the Union's lines. One aspect of this, according to Company testimony, was the utilization of existing labour–management contacts:

> We had our own intelligence networks, from the foreman and the employees. People don't stop talking to each other, just because they are on strike. We were in day-to-day contact with people on the line through the foremen.

At the beginning of September 1981, some twenty-five days before the strike began, the Company supplemented this existing intelligence network, which the Union claimed provided little or no information, by retaining the services of a contract security agency ('the Security Company'). An arrangement was made for a private investigator employed by the Security Company to be hired as a bargaining unit employee at one of the Company's production units. This new intelligence strategy was adopted by the Company well before the strike actually began.

The Security Company that was selected had already conducted business with the Company, having been used previously to gather information about an employee drawing Worker's Compensation benefits. As a senior executive of the Company noted, however, this was no Hobson's choice. Strike-related services are well advertised, and stiff competition exists:

> When it gets around that you are facing a strike, they come out of the woodwork. You can bring in dogs, truckers, bikers, whatever. Whenever we get a strike, the mailings are incredible. You can have your pick.

The undercover agent ('the Investigator') was hired as a cleaner and coffee server. He immediately began writing daily reports detailing Union activity and continued until he was removed from the assignment by the Security Company in mid-February 1982.

The Investigator's reports were wide ranging. In describing the scope of these reports the Union's lawyer commented:

> [The Investigator] tells us that there was no restriction of his function, so the reports were as expansive and exhaustive as he could make them. They included observation regarding union morale and attitudes, the legal tactics of the union, bargaining positions and support for them, and the extent of support amongst the strikers for the union leadership and the strike.

The Board accepted this description, and categorized the Investigator's reports under three major headings:

1. Interference by the Investigator in Union activities;
2. Intelligence regarding bargaining issues and strategies; and
3. Reporting on internal union dissension.

They outlined the activities of the Investigator as follows:

> that [the Security Company], and its employee [the Investigator], while acting on behalf of [the Company],
> (a) attempted to compromise the local union president ... by suggesting that he sell his company-supplied earmuffs to [the Investigator] and later that he pilfer from the company two cases of coffee cups for use during the strike ...
> (c) actively challenged the union leadership and fostered dissent within the union through the statements of [the Investigator] to members of the bargaining unit, his activities in support of the dissident group within the union, and his comments and challenges to the union executive at meetings and at other times throughout the strike; and
> (d) committed a number of acts, including the throwing of tomatoes and eggs at a management employee, the throwing of rocks at other management employees, the placing of nails under the tires of cars attempting to enter the company's premises and the counselling of union members to trespass on company property, which ran counter to the direction of the union leadership to refrain from such activity. (OLRB Decision, pp.46,47)

In commenting on the Investigator's activities, the Board observed that his reports dealt at length with the differing responses to Company offers within union ranks. In addition, it drew attention to the manner in which the Investigator sought to assist the Company in responding to the Union.

> [The Investigator] reported to the company on the efforts of the union to stop the flow of goods from its plant and to locate the warehouse from which it believed the company was shipping products during the strike. [The Investigator] contacted [his supervisor at the Security Company] at his home on November 20th to advise him there would be no one on the picket line or at the strike office between 3:00 and 6:00 a.m. He suggested that [his supervisor] contact the company in case it wished to move goods or equipment in or out of the plant during this period. Furthermore, [the Investigator] reported to the company on such matters as where striking employees were working and who was supplying wood and food to the picket line. (CLRB Decision, p. 26)

This evidence gives substance to the suggestive wording frequently found in security agencies' advertising, wording which invites one to 'read between the lines'. To cite one example:

> The purpose of our company in today's society is to fill the void where public service and protection stop and the needs of private enterprise still exist ... Senior management and their legal counsel realise that in order to protect corporate assets they must have access to information unobtainable without specialised skills and techniques. Our organisation specialises in providing that information with the utmost emphasis on confidentiality and discretion. ... [U]ndercover operatives ensure management valuable insight into plant morale, labour relations, safety, productivity and loss control.

This indirect evidence was confirmed during the Hearing by an officer of the branch of the Provincial Police responsible for licensing contract security agents. During the course of testimony he was asked to estimate the number of licensed contract security agencies involved in activities similar to those described at the Hearing. His answer was 'Just about all of them'. Asked to identify the number of agencies whose central service was labour espionage and other strike-related services, he answered that somewhere between six and twelve agencies were heavily involved at any one time. In a subsequent conversation with one of the authors, he characterized these firms as 'the black shirt ones'.

In February 1982, the Union began to suspect that the Investigator was an undercover agent 'planted' by the Company. At the Hearing, one of the members of the Union's negotiating team described how the Union acted on this suspicion:

> There was always something smelly about him but we couldn't actually believe that the company would put a spy on the line. Then [the Investigator] mentioned to me in mid-February that when the company got a [Section 40 vote], 80 per cent of the people on the line would vote to go back to work. I thought, how does this guy know about the Section 40 vote? ... So I asked someone to call [the Metropolitan Police liaison officers] and they gave us [an officer's] number at the [Provincial Police] to call. He asked me to come down to headquarters ... When I got there he confirmed our suspicions about [the Investigator] and he also asked for an assurance that nothing would happen to him. He didn't need that, because while I was going there, they called [the Security Company] and told them that we were on to [him], that his cover was gone. By the time I got back to strike headquarters, [the Investigator] had picked up his pay and left.

Following confirmation of its suspicions and the overwhelming rejection by the Union rank and file of the Company's last offer, in a Labour Board-ordered vote, the Union added to an existing complaint at the Ontario Labour Relations Board of bad faith bargaining, the further charges of interference and intimidation by the employer.

Subsequently, the Security Company was added as a respondent to the complaints of interference and intimidation. As part of its settlement of the labour dispute with its employer in April 1982, however, the Union withdrew its complaints against the Company, leaving the Security Company as the sole respondent.

The legal frame

The law provides a framework of rules and discourse within which labour–management relations are conducted. The cornerstone of this legal frame in Ontario is the province's *Labour Relations Act*. In addition, there is a substantial body of 'labour jurisprudence' encompassing a wide range of matters which arise in labour–management relations. Contributing to this body of jurisprudence are the decisions of the courts, the provincial Labour Relations Board, and labour arbitrators in individual disputes. These sources of case law vary in their levels of 'authoritativeness', that is, in the extent to which the principles and interpretations which are manifest in their decisions subsequently condition or determine the conduct of third parties.

This body of law provides a legal framework within which intelligence and counter-intelligence activities during labour–management conflicts may be placed. The strike stage of the dispute is structured by the legal rights guaranteed by legislation to each party to protect their property, and to move goods and people in and out of their facilities. Unions have the right to withhold the labour of their members and to picket company facilities.

Most significant to the dispute examined in this chapter are three provisions (Sections 64, 66(c) and 70) of the Ontario *Labour Relations Act*. These sections of the Act contain prohibitions designed to protect the exclusivity of the union's bargaining rights and to ensure an arm's length relationship between employer and union. They prohibit an employer, or anyone acting on behalf of an employer, from interfering with the administration of a trade union or with the representation of employees by a trade union during the course of a lawful strike. This prohibition, however, is expressly stated to be without prejudice to an employer's right to express his or her views, provided this is done without threats, coercion, intimidation or promises. The statute thus seeks to strike a balance during a strike between the right of an employer to protect his or her property, and the right of a union to conduct itself without interference or intimidation by the employer.

As might be expected, it has been left largely to the Labour Relations Board to provide detailed interpretations of how these provisions are to be applied, and to establish the appropriate balances in different kinds of situations. This pattern has characterized the legal history of disputes concerning the infiltration of trade unions by employers or by third parties acting on behalf of employers. In a series of cases heard by the Board during the late 1970s and early 1980s,[3] it was established that any such infiltration, the intention or effect of which was to interfere with the administration of its affairs by a union, was to be considered *per se* a violation of the Ontario Labour Relations Act. These cases, however, also seemed to establish that union infiltration would be considered lawful and proper if its purpose was confined to providing an employer with information necessary to protect his or her property.

At the time of the case being discussed in this chapter, therefore, the most recent rulings of the Labour Relations Board appeared to countenance the legality of union infiltration by employers, provided it was for the sole purpose of protecting the employer's property, and did not have the intention or effect of interfering with the administration of its affairs by the union. The onus of proving that such infiltration was unlawful, of course, would typically lie on a complainant union. As a result, the evidentiary boundaries which the law (as expounded by the Board) had declared to be proper in labour–management relations were somewhat blurred and seemed presumptively to favour the employer, procedurally if not substantially.

Labour laws are not, however, the only legal boundaries which hedge disputes such as the one under consideration. In Ontario, organized labour has also been affected by the application of criminal law provisions and sanctions. Relevant here are provisions of the *Criminal Code* detailing the offences of intimidation (s.381), mischief (s.387) and assault (s.244 and s.245). In addition, Section 382 of the Code provides that various forms of anti-union activity by employers constitute criminal offences. Finally, the Criminal Code offence of conspiracy (s.423) can be applied against employers or workers who conspire together to contravene some other law.

In June 1981, just three months before the strike in the present case began, a fine of $25000 was levied against an employer who had been convicted of conspiring with the principals of a private security firm to interfere with the formation of a trade union and the representation of its employees by such union. In March of the following year, a month before the Company and Union in the present case reached a settlement of their dispute, the Ontario Court of Appeal, on an appeal against sentence by the Crown, raised this fine to $100000 (*R. v. K-Mart Canada Ltd.* (1982) 66 Canadian Criminal Cases (2d)329).

Police connections

One of the institutions of the state which plays a significant role in defining the boundaries of legitimate intelligence and counter-intelligence activities in disputes such as the one we have been examining, is of course the public police.

The police, as state agents, have a duty to protect persons and property. As it is management's property and management personnel that are most typically at risk in a strike situation, this legal requirement serves to create a *de facto* alliance between the police and management. Where a security agency is employed by management to protect its interests this alliance is extended to include the agency as well. As one officer during his evidence noted:

> From our point of view, if they do the job right, why shouldn't they be there, and undercover? If they can prevent damage to property or violence, or if they can identify the people who are doing the damage, then I'm all for them being there.

This alliance with private security is facilitated by the occupational linkages that relate the police and private security persons to one another (Shearing, Stenning and Farnell 1980), as the remark below by one of the Union witnesses suggests:

> These guys [the police] are soft on the security industry because that's where they are headed. They are just waiting for an offer with a big salary. Now why should I talk to this guy today when tomorrow he might be working for a security outfit?

What the hearing evidence suggests, and what was confirmed by our interviews with the various participants about similar situations, is that in strike situations a close relationship develops among contract security, the police and management over the conduct of the strike. In contrast, the union operates in comparative isolation. In the police/security-agency/company relationship, the two levels of police involved played slightly different, but co-ordinated, roles.

Two officers from the Metropolitan Police's strike liaison team visited both the picket line and strike headquarters regularly. Their purpose was primarily information gathering. In addition, they used these visits to inform the Union of the legal context in which they were operating.[4] Although they knew of the Investigator's presence on the picket line, this information was never shared with the Union. When a Provincial Police member attending the Hearing was asked by one of the authors to comment on this — given the existence of legislation requiring private investigators to show identification when asked to do so — he replied:

> That wasn't meant to cover this situation. That was meant for when you have a security guard who is making an arrest. Besides, they didn't ask him the right question. And anyway, do you think that an undercover agent is going to admit being undercover? He wouldn't last very long if he did that, would he?

In contrast, the testimony of Company executives indicated that the strike liaison officers and the Company had kept in close touch regarding the decision to place a man undercover. This contact included the sharing of legal constraints with the Company. For instance, a senior executive with the Company testified that:

> Early in the strike, one of the local liaison officers came into the plant and showed me an article about K-Mart.[5] He asked me if we had an investigator on the line, and I said yes. He told me he thought we should remove him for our own good. I told him I didn't want to remove him and I wouldn't. I also talked to the Provincial Police.

While the liaison officers apparently had never discussed matters in a similar way with the Union, they nonetheless publicly adopted a neutral stance during the strike and refrained from taking any overt action that would appear to favour the Company at the expense of the Union.

The Provincial Police situation was similar. Their focus was primarily on the undercover agent. They maintained an information-sharing relationship with the Security Company and the Company but not the Union, both because there was little reason for them to deal with the Union and because any involvement by them may well have jeopardized the Investigator's case.

The isolation of the Union and the corresponding alliance among the Company, the Security Company and the Police was recognized by the Union and was the source of considerable animosity towards the police. As one Union witness noted:

> [The police] have a history of being management tools; why should we tell them anything? We know it would get back to the company. Besides, our witnesses were afraid that if they said anything about [the Investigator] to the police, he and a few of his buddies would take care of them. They saw what [the Security Company] goons did to the women on the ... strike.

The conclusion these findings suggest is that unions find themselves isolated during strike situations. Their isolation is shaped by law and structured through occupational linkages. The police, employer and security agency are bound to each other through their mutual interest in the protection of property. The police and the security agency are bound through the regulatory relationship provided for by legislation,[6] through the police interest in career advancement within private security, and through participation in a shared occupation, namely, policing. These bonds structure the dynamics of the strike situation.

Arguments before the board

As part of its settlement with the Company, the Union withdrew the complaint it had launched against the Company with the Ontario

Labour Relations Board. This move paved the way for the re-establishment of harmonious working relations between the Company and the Union. Nevertheless, the Union had other longer term goals which could be served by pursuing its complaint against the Security Company. Specifically, the Union sought to draw on the authority of the state to clarify the legitimate evidentiary boundaries in strike situations, and to send a clear message both to employers and to the private security companies which provide them with intelligence services. It was hoped that some enduring benefits could thereby be yielded to both this Union and the labour movement generally, and that this goal could be achieved without seriously threatening the ongoing relationship between the Union and the Company. Furthermore, the Union was in this way able to adopt, to its own advantage, a strategy of distancing through surrogacy, similar to that adopted by the Company in hiring the Security Company in the first place.

The central issue at the Hearing was whether the activities of the Investigator were legal and reasonable in light of both the Company's legal right to protect its property and non-striking employees' interests and the bargaining unit's legal right to be free from interference by the Company. The Security Company took the position that its activities, and those of its Investigator, had been quite proper and lawful. Its counsel stressed the earlier strike-related property damage which the client Company had experienced, and insisted that the prime motive for hiring the Investigator in this case had been the protection of property. It even argued that proceeding in this manner, rather than by hiring uniformed guards, may have had a beneficial effect by keeping the 'temperature of the strike' down. Counsel for the Security Company added that had the motive for its actions been 'union busting', it 'would have done a lot more'. Officials of the automotive Company testified at the Hearing that they had verbally instructed the Security Company (there were apparently no written instructions):

> ... to blend in, to find out whether or not sabotage was planned, to find out who the troublemakers were so we could watch them and lay charges if need be.

The Union argued that the Investigator's activities had gone far beyond the Company's stated objectives of property protection and prevention of violence, and that he had focused his attention primarily on the legitimate strike activity of the Union. The Union argued:

1. That the Investigator had attempted to compromise the integrity of the Union leadership by suggesting ways they could steal supplies from the Company;

2. That he had actively fostered dissent within the bargaining unit;
3. That he had participated centrally in the activities of dissident groups; and
4. That he had committed acts of aggression against management employees and had counselled unlawful activity against Company property.

All this, the Union pointed out, was contrary to the instructions of the Union leadership to refrain from such activities. In short, they maintained that he was not merely as undercover agent, but an *agent provocateur* intent on encouraging actions that would discredit the Union.

Further, the Union argued, the Investigator's role as *agent provocateur* was double-edged, since his reports served to exacerbate conflict between the Union and the Company. Because he reported verbal threats and plans for violence, none of which were executed, the Union submitted that his 'fabrications' inflamed Company officials, particularly the Company President, and made them more determined than ever to 'break the union'.

In addition, it was argued that his reports of low morale within the Union encouraged the Company officials to believe that, if they could hold out long enough, the strike would fall apart, and they would never have to bargain on the Union's major strike issues.

The Investigator did not challenge the substance of the Union's evidence. Indeed, he could not easily do so, as much of it was directly supported by entries in his daily reports to the Company's Vice President of Operations and distributed to the President and the Company's bargaining team, that the Union had presented as evidence. He offered a different interpretation, however. His picket line activity was, he argued, designed to protect his cover as an enthusiastic supporter of the Union and the strike. Information on Union bargaining strategy and the depth of dissent within the bargaining unit was merely 'background' to the more important issues of possible violence, sabotage and property damage. Further, he noted that his presence and his activity on the picket line were known and condoned by the licensing authority, by the Provincial Police, and by the local Metropolitan Police strike liaison officers. His undercover work, it was contended, was in the realm of legitimate property protection and acceptable undercover activity.

The Board's decision

The Labour Board found for the Union. After reviewing the relevant case law detailing the legitimate application of surveillance in the workplace and management rights to take adequate steps to secure and protect company premises, the Board found that the Security Company's activities were not primarily directed at either of those strategies. The Board commented that it regarded the Investigator's activities with 'deep concern' because, in its experience, strike situations were 'volatile enough without the introduction of this type of outside influence'. 'It is one thing', the Board said, 'to report upon disorder on the picket line, it is quite another to be part of it' (OLRB Decision, p.50).

The Board concluded from its view of the evidence that, despite the Company's claims to the contrary, the Investigator played a vital role in assisting the Company to frustrate Union tactics. The Board held that the Investigator's activities constituted an unlawful interference with the administration of the Union and with its representation of employees in the bargaining unit. This, said the Board, was 'not only a flagrant undermining of the arm's length relationship established under the Act between employer and trade union, but an attempt on behalf of the employer to circumvent the bargaining agent in order to deal directly with its employees.'

The Board sought to explain, in the following terms, why the evidentiary boundaries of intelligence gathering should be applied to establish the illegitimacy of the Security Company's actions in this case:

> A trade union, as the representative of all the employees in the bargaining unit, adopts bargaining stances which it considers to be in the best interest of, and in line with the bargaining objectives of, the membership as a whole and need not reveal to the employer information pertaining to the sentiments of individual members or about when or under what circumstances it might be prepared to alter its bargaining position. Any attempt by the employer, or anyone acting on behalf of the employer, to obtain this kind of information by going directly to the employees in the bargaining unit, undermines the exclusivity of the union's bargaining rights and, therefore, is in breach of section 64 of the Act. (OLRB Decision, p. 48)

In drawing the appropriate legal boundaries for covert intelligence gathering in such circumstances, the Board went considerably further in holding that 'the infiltration of a trade union by an employer or anyone acting on behalf of an employer during a strike or lockout is, *per se*, a violation of the Act; that is, it is unlawful regardless of the stated purpose for which the infiltration is undertaken of its effect' (OLRB Decision, p. 51). In reaching this conclusion,[7] the Board expressly noted the structural problems which would be generated by any less stringent legal rule on this matter:

> [A]n employer knows full well that when he takes it upon himself to infiltrate a trade union in anticipation of or during a strike or lockout, the person infiltrating the trade union will inevitably become privy to

information ... which, although unrelated to the protection of the employer's property, is directly related to the furtherance of his collective bargaining objectives. Even if an undercover agent could distinguish one from the other and restrict himself to property-related matters, which is problematic, the fact remains that the employer has secured for himself an unfair advantage in his collective bargaining confrontation with the union; an unfair advantage which we would have no hestitation in finding to be in breach of the duty to bargain in good faith ... (OLRB Decision, pp.51–52)

The Board referred to the actual reporting on collective bargaining matters by the employer's agent as an 'almost inevitable consequence of this type of employer action' (OLRB, p.52) and noted the damaging effect which a rule permitting such infiltration could have on labour relations generally:

Given the covert nature of the activity complained of, there is no way for an employee to know if an employer-paid undercover investigator is in place. Where the door for this type of activity during a strike or lockout is left open, therefore, employes will have good reason to fear the worst, with no real means at their disposal to detect the worst. In these circumstances, it can reasonably be said that if employers are permitted to infiltrate trade unions during or in anticipation of a strike or lockout for any reason, employees generally will be inhibited in the exercise of their rights under the Act. (OLRB Decision, p.53)

As a result of its conclusions, the Board made a number of orders against the Security Company. It ordered the Security Company to cease and desist from infiltrating unions on behalf of employers during or in anticipation of any strike or lockout. It ordered the Security Company to compensate the Union for half[8] of the monies its members had lost as a result of the Investigator's unnecessary prolongation of the strike, and to reimburse the Union for half of the strike pay which had been paid to the Investigator whilst posing as a worker. Finally, the Board ordered that, for a period of two years from the date of the Board's order, the Security Company was to give written notice (in a form drafted by the Board and appended to its order) to any trade union which represented the employees of any employer by whom it was retained in relation to, or in anticipation of, any strike or lockout. The required form contained notice that the Security Company had been retained, a brief summary of the circumstances and findings of the Board in the present case, an acknowledgement of the legal rights of unions under strike and lockout situations, and an undertaking to respect and not contravene these rights.

The immediate result of the Board's decision in this case appeared to have been to drive the Security Company concerned out of business. The significance of this particular outcome is somewhat unclear, however, since the licensing authority for such security companies in the jurisdiction concerned is apparently unable to give firm assurances that the principals have not simply regrouped and obtained new licenses under new business names, using other associates as the official license holders.

Conclusion

We have examined this case in order to illustrate the role played by the state in establishing the boundaries of legitimate intelligence and counter-intelligence activities in strike situations, and in mediating disputes which arise from allegations that such boundaries have been overstepped. In addition, the case provides interesting evidence of the way in which contract security can be employed, as part of the collective bargaining process, to effectively take management behind union lines.

As this case clearly illustrates, the law, as interpreted by courts and labour relations boards, plays an important role in structuring the course and discourse of such disputes. While the law is often thought of principally as a medium of state control over private conduct, the present case illustrates how in some situations it may more usefully be viewed as a resource available to the disputants, than as a controlling device as such (Turk 1976). The jurisdiction of the Ontario Labour Relations Board over this kind of dispute, for instance, is dependent upon the consent of at least one of the parties to the dispute. As the Union's withdrawal of its complaint against the Company (leaving the Security Company as the sole respondent) demonstrates, the resource of the law will typically be invoked strategically by the parties so as to maximize their advantage. Thus, recourse to the Board by the Union, via a complaint under the Labour Relations Act, is but one of many resources for which the law provides in the conduct of its relations with management and management's agents. As the Board itself pointed out, it is by no means the only source of such state assistance to a union:

> ... those affected, and indeed the public at large, in assessing our response to the unlawful conduct of [the Security Company] in this matter, should understand that the Ontario Labour Relations Board is but a single agency in a comprehensive web of administrative, regulatory and policing agencies designed to oversee the actions and activities of all persons in our society with a view to ensuring order, protecting freedoms and enforcing the laws that have been enacted by our legislatures. For example there are strict licensing requirements for security companies under the *Private Investigators and Security Guard Act*. ... Furthermore, the *Criminal Code* makes it an offence to conspire to effect an unlawful purpose. (OLRB Decision, p.63)

These observations, of course, suggest that the role of the state in these situations is rather more controlling than the facts of this case would seem to suggest. Viewed from the perspective of the parties to the dispute, it is certainly arguable, when one looks at outcomes, that the role of the state in such situations is facilitative rather than controlling. In this case, the fact that the law allows such disputes to be withdrawn from the state's jurisdiction on the consent of the parties meant that both union and management, through the technique of distancing through surrogacy, could strategically invoke the law and the state, while still remaining relatively immune from its control. The law itself, at least prior to the dispute, was couched in sufficiently vague and general terms to allow the Company to act on the edge of legality with relative impunity. This was strikingly evident from the remarkably candid responses of one of the Company's senior executives when he was asked if he would 'do it the same way again':

> Yes. I would hire [the Security Company] again. They did a good job in the area they were hired for. I sure as hell wouldn't ask for written reports, though.

The Union was able to maximize its gains from the discovery of an undercover agent within its ranks while minimizing the negative consequences of this for its continuing relationship with management. Further, by directly attacking the Security Company, rather than the employer, the Union was able to express its dissatisfaction with the Company's tactics and vindicate itself, while minimizing harm to its ongoing relationship with the Company. In addition, it was able to draw on the considerable authority of the state, via the Labour Relations Board, to effect a significant redefinition of the evidentiary boundaries to be considered legitimate in strike and lockout situations. The net result was that the Union was able to strengthen its bargaining position by revitalizing worker morale, which had been badly eroded by a strike that was in its sixth month when the Investigator's cover was 'blown'. This enabled the Union to survive easily a Labour Board-ordered vote on the Company's most recent offer. The complaint filed with the Board also served as an additional bargaining tool for the Union which it used as a lever in agreeing to drop charges against the Company. By leaving the Security Company as the sole respondent the Union was able to 'have its cake and eat it'. The Security Company argued unsuccessfully[9] before the Board that even if it were found to have been at fault it should not be penalized by the Board because 'the Union, in resolving the collective bargaining impasse, negotiated what it thought it should get from [the Company] in compensation for the activities of [the Investigator]'. It was by no means clear at the conclusion of the case, however, that this was not at least a partly accurate assessment of what had occurred.

Indeed, the only party to the dispute whose conduct may have been significantly controlled by the state's involvement was the Security Company. Even here, the extent of real control is difficult to assess. To some extent, the costs to the Security Company of the Hearing and its outcome may have been viewed by the Security Company simply as part of the routine costs of doing this kind of business. Although the Security Company as such went out of business after the Hearing, the notorious inadequacies of governmental regulation of this industry (cf. Stenning and Cornish 1975) raise serious questions as to whether this was not simply another strategy to avoid paying the compensation ordered by the Board. Certainly, the Company's attitude after the Hearing, to the effect that it would do things the same way again, only more carefully in future, suggests that the impact of the Board's decision on the security industry as a whole may be somewhat less than hoped for.

As Mnookin and Kornhauser (1979) have so perceptively noted, such disputes as the one we have been considering here are often conducted 'in the shadow of the law'. The law does not control them in the accepted sense, but still it exerts an unmistakeable influence (cf. Galanter 1981) by establishing (sometimes by more than mere suggestion) a context, a discourse, and the evidentiary boundaries within which they are conducted. The parties carry their dispute out into the full light of the law when, and to the extent that, it suits them. Their behaviour at other times, while certainly more than mere shadow boxing, is aptly captured by Edgar Wallace's evocative description of another kind of contest:

''E missed me with a fair amount of skill.'

9 Women and the state: changing models of social control

Nanette J. Davis
Karlene Faith

Introduction

Deviance is a social construction, a pejorative category used to control those who defy the political status quo. It represents a socially constructed commitment to apartness, a concept referring to any activity that fails to serve the interests of those who define and control the parameters of conventionality.

Nonetheless, individualistic modes of non-conformity, even eccentricity, are tolerated as long as they remain *individualistic*; allowing non-conformity preserves the myth, common to democracies, that individual freedom is honoured. But when sufficient numbers of people identify with a particular form of 'deviance', that group is perceived as a political challenge. The process of creating formal and informal sanctions to combat deviance is channelled from the base of political hegemony through the conduits of the law, social institutions, the media and the family. Deviations from the norm are met with responses ranging from derision and ridicule to treatment and punishment. It is only when deviants begin to develop a power base in the political arena that the label is rendered inoperable, and the group is redefined as a political minority and challenger. Whereas deviants are perceived as vulnerable and expendable, political opponents represent a threat. Women are now challenging the assumptions that have classified female aspirations as deviance and that have prevented women's full participation in the political process.

This chapter examines the historical role of women as deviants and, more recently, as political opponents.

Social transformations in gender control

Feminist research on gender roles took the lead in exposing the institutional routines and everyday practices that kept women 'in their place' (Davis 1977; Stockard and Johnson 1980; Weitz 1977). The sexual stereotypes of women as emotional, not very bright, passive and dependent, and made for motherhood, have been reinforced in sociological studies of deviance that reflect conventional prejudices. A new generation of scholars have argued that theories, methods, and 'models' of the social order, once believed to be ideologically 'pure', embody male perspectives or are used in male-emphasizing ways that reproduce negative stereotypes about women (Bernard 1981; Davis and Anderson 1982; Schur 1984).

In addressing the sociology of deviance, feminists have charged that these beliefs and practices distort and devalue women's experiences, and they have urged the use of the *gender* concept to explore inequality. Schur defines gender as 'a normative system, and a pervasive network of interrelated norms and sanctions through which female (and male) behaviour is evaluated and controlled' (1984, p. 11). This perspective enables us to focus on how sociological studies contribute to the prevailing patterns of deviance definition (Davis and Anderson 1982; Klein 1973; Millman 1975; Schur 1984; Smart 1977).

1. When social scientists explain female deviance, it is usually in terms of sex role stereotypes that have been grounded in myths about biological sex differences and women's 'innate' psychological qualities. Women are frequently depicted as totally governed by their sexuality, family roles or relationships with men. These assumptions are embedded in philosophical and theological underpinnings that stress the 'natural' inequality of the sexes (Bernard 1981; Coward 1983).
2. The most common interpretation of female deviance in this model is 'maladjustment', or 'pathology' (Schur 1984). Female deviance is rarely considered in positive ways, as in active rebellion, simple unwillingness to conform, coping mechanisms, or as therapy (Chesler 1972).
3. An alternative to the 'pathology' argument is the notion of the 'functions' of female deviance, which is said to maintain the social order. For example, Kingsley Davis (1937) believed that prostitutes served the 'army of strangers and perverts' which otherwise would overwhelm the conventional order. At the same time, little account was taken of the exploitative character of this arrangement or of the institutional evasion of protection for prostitutes, inasmuch as it is primarily 'functional' for men.
4. By focusing on offenders, deviance studies have neglected their victims. Women who have suffered from physical violence, degradation, unfair treatment, and legal and economic discrimination because of male power, become 'deserving' victims (Ryan 1972). As 'all-purpose deviants' (Schur 1984, p. 7) women have also been blamed for male deviance. Throughout history, women have been patronized, cajoled, threatened, and suffered through the burden of playing the universal 'idol-scapegoat' (Dinnerstein 1977).
5. The label 'deviance' is too narrow and stigmatizing to account for

the full range of normalized modes of social control that occur in interpersonal behaviour and everyday interactions that subordinate and devalue women. Instead, a macro-conception — including the role of the state — is required to understand women's place in history and the social order. For example, Boulding's (1976) critique of history involves the recognition that women, forcibly excluded from public life, have dwelt in 'underlife' structures (home, family, convent) where their experiences have been rendered invisible by male-dominated interpretations of the world.

6. The sociocultural context of deviance has been presumed, rather than investigated as an important entity in its own right. Types of deviance, motivations for deviance and adaptations to control occur in an historical context. At the same time, some forms of deviance represent continuities in response to control. Infanticide in the middle ages and abortion today both occur in situations where women receive inadequate recognition and material support for managing a central life role (Oakley 1976).
7. Sanctions for female deviance have been described as 'lenient' or as employing the 'chivalry' principle. This neglects the normal coercion that characterizes female socialization and gender role practices. Daly (1978) argues that normal female role enactment is invariably linked to violence, citing the stoning of female (but not male) adulterers in the Bible, suttee (widow burning) in India, footbinding in old China, witch-hunts in medieval Europe and colonial America, genital mutilations under the guise of medical 'treatment' in the nineteenth century, and the pornographic and random physical violence against women that is so prevalent in contemporary society.

Women and social control

Major transformations in social control have occurred over the course of this century. These include first a shift from the dual institutional solution (that is, domesticity or total institutions in the nineteenth century) to the twentieth century phenomenon of 'transinstitutionalization' (Steadman and Morrissey, chapter 12 of this volume). This involves the state at different levels of involvement in the full range of institutional structures, including the family, economy, law, education, therapy, criminal justice, welfare, medical services and so forth. Through its fiscal control and police power, the state has the capacity to move individuals from one regulatory institution to another. Particular groups of women are far more vulnerable to commitment than their male counterparts. Disobedient or runaway adolescent females, those who are sexually active or pregnant in violation of husband's or father's wishes, and the 'unfit' mother are far more likely to be candidates for intervention than disobedient, runaway, sexually promiscuous, or domestically-abusive males (Roth and Lerner 1982).

Because women are currently neither fully traditional (that is, dependent) nor modern (that is, autonomous and financially independent), contemporary modes of control tend to be erratic and arbitrary (see Travis and Wade 1984). For example, a leniency principle may be applied to a relatively serious offence, whereas the same system may punish the female offender for fairly trivial infractions (Chesney-Lind 1977; Edwards 1984). Certainly, women continue to be penalized for violating traditional sex roles, but the means available tend to be more varied, less visible, and more diffuse in this period, compared with earlier ones (for example, when execution was commonplace, even for offences now classified as misdemeanours).

In this century, there has been a shift from the state's over-reliance on total institutions to increased use of decentralized, community-based structures (Davis and Anderson 1983). This includes welfare, community mental health, food stamp programmes, social security, Medicaid, and other government-sponsored social programmes. Despite bureaucratic obstacles that eliminate many needy recipients, women find themselves disproportionately in the means-tested public assistance system. In 1977, the overwhelming majority of single parent families in the United States[1] were headed by females, and two-thirds of these families were dependent on social welfare. Women at all stages of the life cycle comprised 60 per cent of public assistance recipients (Danzinger, Haveman and Plotnick 1980).

A significant factor in shifting control strategies has been changing ideologies of control. Total institutions were attacked during the 1960s and early 1970s because they violated people's sense of liberty, their integrity, and their human rights (Beck 1977; Davis 1980). Critics from both within and outside the system urged deinstitutionalization — the return of deviant persons from total institutions to the community (Davis 1980; Schur 1973; Szasz 1970). Under the community-based system, the scope of control can be much broader. Social control can also be less visible, and more effective.

Decentralization of control mechanisms

Feminists and radical critics have led the most recent charge against the overreach of the corporate state with its class-race bifurcation of control. They point to the two-tiered system wherein middle- and upper-class women receive decentralized, privatized services (where there is some limited choice based on ability to pay), while poor and third world women endure a centralized repressive form of control, as in welfare, coercive mental health treatments, and incarceration (Hutter and Williams 1981). Others argue that women have been especially abused by the psychiatric profession, which has translated 'problems of living' into full-blown psychiatric indicators for intervention (see Chesler 1972; Smith and David 1975).

Contradictions in control are not so much a recent phenomenon as they are exacerbated by modern urban life. As urban, female and family-related problems continue to increase and/or come to public attention (for example divorce, child abuse, wife battering, teenage suicide, and single parenting) women are often blamed as the 'cause' of widespread social malaise (Davis and Keith 1984). Furthermore, the state has had relatively little impact in preventing violent crimes against women, or in ameliorating their suffering once victimized. Rape, domestic violence, street crimes against prostitutes and poor women, and other physical abuses against females are often ignored by officials — viewed as part of the nature of things — or they are treated in ineffective and often inappropriate ways (cf. Dobash and Dobash 1979, 1981). In rape trials the victim may become the defendant, for it is her sexual history and lifestyle that become the issue for the court (Clark and Lewis 1977). The recent, highly-publicized case of the woman testifying that, as a teenager, she had falsely accused a man of rape, after he had already served time in prison, has fuelled the already existing biases against females as credible witnesses (see Brozan 1985).

In adopting a hard line toward females labelled deviant, as in the use of prison for relatively petty offences or in the denial of welfare and other state benefits, the state creates a permanent pool of dependent women (Carlen 1983). Bureaucratic intervention has succeeded in isolating women in their needs, and has hastened the loss of special gender privileges. The 'mother' and the 'lady' could be advantageous roles for nineteenth century women. Under bureaucratic control, there are no analogous protective devices for the anomic modern woman.

In sum, the decentralization of social control has actually widened the control net for women. The state now uses a complex of institutional systems to maintain social order, including ideology (for example, the feminine mystique), the family, education, welfare, criminal justice, mental health, medicine, employment and the market-place (for example, consumerism). At the same time, the social status of millions of women and their children has actually declined (Hartmann 1976).

The feminization of poverty

The 1980 United States census shows that women's incomes compare unfavourably with men's regardless of marital status, age, race, or occupation. The most disadvantaged women in income terms are married, late middle-aged, black, and those working in sales (where they earn less than half that of men similarly employed (Belle 1982)).

Looking at all categories of workers, women bring home, on the average, 40 per cent less than men in their annual pay cheque. Women college graduates earn less than men high school graduates and about as much as high school drop-outs. A female PhD makes as much as a male high school graduate (Barrett 1979).

In 1980 black women continued to experience the greatest income disparity, earning an overall average of $8258 less than white men per year; but black women were only slightly behind white women with a difference of $788 on a yearly basis (Hacker 1983, p.146). Income inequality is a pervasive condition of life for women.

Women's earnings, relative to those of men, have actually declined in recent years; and over half of the occupations women typically enter will not support a family above the poverty line (Fox and Hesse-Biber 1984). Kahn-Hut, Daniels and Colvard (1982) identify structural obstacles that impede women's commitment to work. The logic of occupational hierarchy resists more equitable treatment of women because inequality reduces profits, raises the costs of public services and alters customary relations between men and women, and between superordinates and subordinates. Lack of support structures for childcare and housework (or their scarcity and lack of affordability) imply that most women confront almost insurmountable problems in their efforts for occupational equality. And sexual harassment, a pervasive problem for women workers, is a more obvious form of systematic sex discrimination that deters many women from seeking the better positions in the labour-force.

With the escalating rate of marital separation and divorce, particularly among families with dependent children, many women have been pushed into poverty (Ross and Sawhill 1975). And because few families receive regular child support payments from the non-custodial father over the years after a divorce, women are obliged to turn to welfare payments to support their families. Today there are over four million families and ten million children living in poverty in the United States, and 65 per cent of poverty families are headed by women.

The spectre of welfare combined with the lesser earning power of women, and the limited social acceptability of single mothers, reduce a woman's autonomy *vis-à-vis* the family and limit her ability to make choices about her own life. A social policy of keeping women economically dependent has ramifications far beyond low wage-scales. In a society where adult status is linked so intricately to paid work, any job is better than no job, even if low wages demean workers, and make them more compliant. For women this has the additional consequence of reinforcing the status quo, regardless of the injuries of sexism. Patriarchal relations survive, not only because traditional laws and customs dictate women's inferiority, but also because economic dependency in capitalist societies plays such a crucial role in limiting social, educational and political opportunities (Turner and Starnes 1976).

The survival of patriarchal relations in the twentieth century: pornography, rape, sexualization of female crime, and prostitution

In this section our inquiry centres on patriarchal relations that serve as a basis for defining women's 'deviant' identity in sexually demeaning and dependent ways: pornography, rape, the sexualization of female crime, and prostitution.

Pornography

Pornography has not always been recognized as hazardous to women's lives and mental health. In the eighteenth century, a French nobleman of leisure, the Marquis de Sade, created a new genre of fiction that featured men as relentless sex machines and women as their passive instruments (Seaver and Wainhouse 1966). De Sade wrote during the first flush of industrialization, which involved intense cultural preoccupation with machines. In this literature, men became human sex machines performing extreme and abnormal feats with their slave-like female victims. Female bondage, degeneration, mutilation and death were frequent themes. Although both church and state were outraged at this sado-masochistic material, de Sade's popularized version of sexual horrors has continued to punish, humiliate and terrify women through language and visual documentation for 200 years (Griffin 1981, p.85).

Feminist critics began speaking out against pornography using the theme of 'take back the night' (Lederer 1980). The *what* of pornography, they argued, is not sex, but power and violence. The *who* of concern are no longer male writers, artists and consumers, but women. Feminist scholars stress that pornography is a reaffirmation of male control, especially for men (at all levels of society) who lack control over their lives within the capitalist system (Diamond 1980, pp.686–701).

One of the most contentious issues in the debate surrounding pornography is whether, in addition to reflecting male violence against women, it is also a catalyst for aggression against women (Donnerstein 1980; Schur 1984; Snitow, Stansell and Thompson 1983). The general conclusion of feminist scholars is that the escalation of misogynist violence in the mass media reinforces the acceptability of violence against women. The 'snuff' films, where publicists declare that women are being actually killed on film, are simply the extreme version of this strong anti-woman sentiment. Misogyny, in the media context, is a profitable component of a capitalist economy. Supply and demand are mutually rewarding.

The politics of rape

Rape is a common form of male violence, and has no class or age barriers. It has been reported that females below the age of six months have been raped, as have women in their eighties. Research is now slowly appearing that depicts rape as an outcome of the 'normal' fabric of society, rather than the 'abnormal' personality of rapists (Mahoney 1983, p.428) or the 'deviant' character of victims. Holmstrom and Burgess (1983) argue that rape is an aspect of the aggressiveness and coercion in male-female relationships. Erving Goffman (1978) has called rape 'a model for interpersonal contamination in our society'. And Gibbons (1984) contends that forcible rape is probably better regarded as conduct on the extreme end of a behavioural continuum rather than as a markedly aberrant or deviant form of activity.

Generalized attitudes which emphasize male power and domination over women provide the ideological and social-structural support for rape, and for practices of 'blaming the victim' that characterize this crime. Rape is a highly patterned behaviour, often planned and repetitive. These features confirm its social origin, and oppose the traditional view of rape as an unfettered biological impulse.

Stranger–stranger rape occurs in about half of all reported cases (McDermott 1979), and they are more apt to capture media and police attention (Rabkin 1979). Public areas — streets, parks, playgrounds — are the most frequent locations for stranger-stranger rapes, involving 47 per cent of reported cases, followed by the victim's home (18 per cent). Weapons are used in approximately 40 per cent of these cases with knives and guns employed most frequently. The presence of a gun increases the likelihood that an attempted rape will be completed (McDermott 1979).

In a study of incarcerated rapists in Virginia prisons, Scully and Marolla (1984) identify the vocabularies of motive, or common cultural stereotypes, that convicted rapists employ to justify their crime of rape:[2]

1. *Women as seductresses.* In addition to common cultural stereotypes, the fields of psychiatry and criminology have traditionally provided justifications for rape, often by portraying raped women as the victims of their own seduction. In rape accounts, it is the woman who is the aggressor, a seductress who lures the unsuspecting innocent man into sexual action. Victims are reported to have made the sexual advance, offered to exchange sex for money or drugs, or been a 'pick-up' and hence fair game.

2. *Women say 'no' when they mean 'yes'*. Rapists often describe their victim as initially resisting, but claim that they had believed that she didn't really mean it. Resistance becomes defined as 'teasing' or as a 'semi-struggle', which the male believes he must subdue. Denial of rape, the victim and the circumstances is common among convicted rapists. Or the rapist views sexual aggression as a man's prerogative at the time of the rape. From this perspective, as long as the victim survived without major physical injury, rape had not occurred.
3. *Most women eventually relax and enjoy it*. Rapists testify both to the court and to researchers that not only was the victim willing, but also that she enjoyed herself. 'From her actions, she was enjoying it', one convicted rapist said. Those who deny the rape are most likely to extoll their sexual prowess and personal attractiveness. By contrast, men who acknowledge their rape conduct use terms such as 'dirty', 'humiliated' and 'disgusted' to describe how they thought rape made women feel (feelings consistent with the rapist's desire to degrade women).
4. *Nice girls don't get raped*. The victim's reputation as well as characteristics or behaviour which violate normative sex role expectations are perceived as contributing to the commission of a crime. The stereotype that 'nice girls don't get raped' justifies the claim that the victim was disreputable: a prostitute, a 'loose' woman, one who has had many affairs, or is divorced, or who had a child out of wedlock, or was hitchhiking. Such situations are said to create the 'legitimate' victim. One convict said about his victim that: 'If you wanted drugs or a quick piece of ass, she would do it'. Another said: 'In court she said she was a virgin, but I could tell during sex (rape) that she was very experienced'. Excuses and justifications also clustered around what the woman wore (for example, short skirts), her demeanour, her occupation (for example, a waitress was reputed to have 'low' morals), or around claims that they were wrongly accused by 'dirty sluts'. Discrediting and blaming the victim while excusing their own actions as justified, because of the ill-repute of the victim, imply that the victim got what she deserved.
5. *Only a minor wrongdoing*. Many of the convicted rapists pleaded guilty to a lesser charge. They conceded being 'over-sexed', showing poor judgement or trickery, being guilty of adultery and/or violence, or contributing to the delinquency of a minor, but refuted the idea that their behaviour was equivalent to rape. Scully and Marolla (1984, p.537) report the case of a rapist who, when the victim resisted his advances, beat her and stated:

   > I did something stupid. I pulled a knife on her and I hit her as hard as I would hit a man. But I shouldn't be in prison for what I did. I shouldn't have all this time for going to bed with a broad.

Among these convicts, 'normality' prevailed. They disavowed deviance by citing abuse of alcohol and drugs, having emotional problems (for example, feeling depressed) and promoting a 'nice guy' image. 'When sex is viewed as a male entitlement, rape is no longer seen as criminal', Scully and Marolla conclude.[3]

Feminist perspectives on rape

From a feminist perspective, rape is neither an 'alternative' sexuality, nor a 'victimless' crime. Women do not desire or seek rape; instead they are assaulted 'against their will'.

Brownmiller's (1975) attack on rape ideology within Western society entails three major points:

1. Rape is exclusively a male invention (and not a female-precipitated crime), that both expresses inequality and prevents equality of the sexes. The hidden currents of male-female relationships are based ultimately upon male power and coercion. In turn, these rest upon the concept of women as property.
2. Male dominance is a male-on-male strategy. This is expressed most dramatically in war situations, wherein rape of women of a conquered nation becomes symbolic of the total power of the conquerers over a now subdued population. For women of a defeated nation, the ultimate indignity, of course, is that they have become stigmatized by rape, rejected both by the conquerers and by their own husbands and kin groups.
3. Rape is not a sexual act, but a crime of violence which, like the frequent lynching of blacks following emancipation, preserves a status order of inequality from challenge. Nor is it necessary that all men rape in order to achieve male control. In the social context of power relations, the pervasive threat of rape may be perceived as a '*process of intimidation by which all men keep all women in a state of fear*' (Brownmiller 1975, p.5; also see Schur 1984).

Sanday (1981, pp.5–27) has examined 156 tribal societies, some of which showed a high incidence of rape while others were characterized by little or no rape. She concluded that 'rape is part of a cultural configuration which includes interpersonal violence, male dominance, and sexual separation'. What conditions, then, lead to a cultural emphasis on male domination and sexual separation? Sanday points out that such cultural features most often emerge in societies that are facing depleted food resources, migration, and other factors which promote dependence on male destructive capacities as opposed to gender equality. As for rape in American society, Sanday speculates that males who perceive that they do not have mastery over their own destiny are most likely to have been involved in rape (cf. Bart 1985).

Taking a Marxist perspective, Schwendinger and Schwendinger (1981) emphasize the role played by capitalism in shaping personality and violence patterns:

> Capitalist conditions produce the personality developments that link masculinity with violence and femininity with non-violence. For instance, the allocation of women to social production for use within the family is consequential for character formation. Under these conditions women undergo early childhood experiences that greatly restrict their engagement in violence and in many other forms of conduct. They act far less violently than men, whose character structures are more closely aligned with the exploitative requirements of the capitalist mode of production and the instrumental norms of its competitive market. Furthermore, men retain a monopoly over weapons and training for war. (1981, p. 17)

From this perspective capitalist conditions promote the distinctive gender inequality that contributes to violence against women both by strangers and within the home.

The male view of women as private property reflects traditional beliefs about privacy (one's life is one's own business) and property (one's value is measured by what one owns, including women, and how one protects/controls it). The privacy doctrine that pervades (Western) law '...preserves, protects, strengthens, masks, hides, distorts and reflects women's sexual abuse. Its central role — [the] control of women's sexuality, of intimate, sensitive spheres of interaction — has gone unrecognised' (Colker 1983, p.199).

When men exercise power in the private sphere they are exercising a power bequeathed to them by the public sphere. The idea that one half of the population will take care of (and control) the other half, is a romantic view of domestic safety (Burton 1985). The privacy doctrine, when enacted by law, virtually ensures women's subordination and victimization in 'the privacy of the home'.

Stang Dahl and Snare (1978, p. 22) point to the failure of the state to intervene in violence within the family:

> ...the kind of primary control which affects women in the private sector has a distinctly coercive trait. Linked to the close supervision women experience is the legal conception of the sacred character of private life and the nonintervention practice of social agencies in cases of family violence and conflicts. Additionally, the powerless situation of women is ideologically reinforced by academic disciplines which continue to rely only on a consensus model in their approach to the marriage contract and the household realm. (1978, p.22)

In addition to gender inequality, other factors may be operating to maintain female vulnerability to violence. Even in cities where the greatest progress has been made toward equalizing average earnings, education levels, employment and occupational prestige between the sexes, rape rates failed to show a decline, and in some instances they actually rose, due in part, it is speculated, to reporting increases (Ellis, Atkeson and Calhoun 1981). In the larger context of gender stratification, where most women continue to work at low-paid, low-status positions, and where there is virtually a male monopoly of social resources and control, rape will continue to express and symbolize the gender separation. Where measurable progress for women has occurred, it may actually create a greater threat among males (Russell 1975). According to Schur, 'anti-feminist backlash could produce — or currently could be producing — short term *increases* in rape' (1984, p.156).

Recent efforts to apply harsh punishments such as surgical castration or hormone treatments, in the belief that maiming criminals will correct the rape problem, reflect wishful thinking. Clearly, rape and the toleration of rape will not decline significantly unless major transformations in gender norms and relations occur. Schur warns us that piecemeal reform distorts the underlying problem: the necessity for fundamental changes in gender 'scripts'.

> Given its close ties to socially approved scripts, nothing less than a basic alteration in those scripts can 'solve' the rape problem. And until females are more highly valued so that their rights are deemed worth upholding, the implicit denial of the problem's seriousness may well persist. (1984, p.156)

The sexualization of female crime

The expression 'wayward girls' — referring to juvenile females involved in status offences[4] such as truancy, incorrigibility and sexual misconduct — has an old-fashioned ring to it. Yet the 'wayward' category has served as the major channel for recruiting females into the criminal justice system. In fact, as late as the mid-1960s, 88.5 per cent of the offences leading to commitment of juvenile females in the United States were of this nature, compared with only 22 per cent for boys (Datesman and Scarpitti 1980, p.40). Officially delinquent girls were thus labelled and incarcerated largely for behaviours that would not be considered criminal in an adult.

The 'sexualization' of female crime implies that the court punishes females for socially 'inappropriate' sexuality, while males receive punishments commensurate with their more serious crimes. The juvenile justice system's phrase 'for their own protection' is used to justify stricter supervision of young women than it is for men. Running away, incorrigibility, promiscuity and prostitution are equated as 'moral offences' requiring the 'protection' of the courts (Chesney-Lind 1977).

According to Steffensmeier (1980) three factors account for an increase in female arrests over the past decade. One is the heightened tendency to prosecute for shoplifting and fraud. Second is the increased willingness of citizens to report crimes by women. And finally, the policy shift in the criminal justice system, encouraging arrest, prosecution and conviction of females, has fundamentally altered crime rate profiles. Overall, women still represent less than 15 per cent of persons arrested, and the relative gap between the sexes in the commission of violent and white-collar crimes is basically unchanged (Steffensmeier 1980, pp.1080–1108). Conversely, recent sex role research underscores the idea that, despite the increased flexibility of female roles and the legal changes that have occurred, the traditional roles of wife-mother and sex object persist (Blake 1974, pp.137–47; Steffensmeier 1980, p.1099; Weitz 1977). Nowhere is this finding better demonstrated than in research on prostitution.

Prostitutes: symbolic offenders

Prostitution is now recognized as 'an extreme case of sex stratification' (Heyl 1979) in which the commodification of female sexuality contributes to the woman's devaluation and objectification. Ownership and exchange of female sexuality serve as the core element of our entire gender system (Collins 1971; Laws 1979; Levi-Strauss 1949). The prostitute as 'common property' acts as a counterpoint to delineate a category of females whose sexual ownership is 'exclusive'.

Women who enter prostitution, then, are not unique in viewing themselves as a commodity and their bodies as 'saleable' (James *et al.* 1975, p.43). As Laws observes, 'the rules for women in courtship delineate an image of woman as commodity. Her power to attract is her "capital" which she should invest frugally to assure an adequate future income' (1979, p.179). The cash nexus of sexuality (for example, dating, the marriage 'bargain', the 'kept woman', the mistress, and so on (Salamon, 1984)) continues to influence a good deal of male-female interaction. At the extreme the prostitute has been seen as the symptom of a much wider 'female sexual slavery' (Barry 1981) inasmuch as she is locked into an inherently exploitative or victimizing role.

More than 89000 persons were arrested for prostitution in the United States in 1978 (US Department of Justice, 1980) 19000 more than in 1976.[5] Although law-makers make no formal distinction between men and women, and although most states prohibit both sides of the transaction, women still comprised 68 per cent of all prostitution arrests (FBI Uniform Crime Reports 1979, p. 197). Another 19 per cent were male prostitutes, and only 10 per cent were customers. More women were arrested for prostitution than for committing any other crime. Almost 71 per cent of all females' first arrests involved prostitution (United States Department of Justice 1979, p. 464).

Enforcement practices discriminate against women of colour and those of lower social strata. Most arrests are of women who work the streets (85 to 90 per cent), rather than those who work as independent 'call girls', or for massage parlours and escort services (Davis and Anderson 1983). While approximately 40 per cent of street prostitutes are women of colour, this group comprises 55 per cent of those who are arrested; and among those who are sentenced to prison, 85 per cent are from minority racial groups (Alexander 1980; Bressler and Leonard 1978).

Child prostitutes are largely drawn from an estimated one million runaways in the United States every year. Approximately 200000 are arrested on runaway charges; another 3000 are arrested on prostitution charges, of whom about 77 per cent are girls (Alexander 1980). Many child prostitutes work intermittently because they are jailed, returned to parents by the police, or seek help in a shelter for runaways. A review of research in the United States indicates that between 31 and 66.7 per cent of young female prostitutes are incest survivors (Weisberg 1985, Chs. 4–5; see also Armstrong 1978). Many children may enter prostitution because they accept the pattern of exploitation from others or because the incest-victim-turned-prostitute now gains control by demanding payment (Herman 1981). The policy of arresting teenage runaways may also contribute to alienation and law-breaking.

Lacking in family and social supports, the estimated half a million juvenile prostitutes are particularly subject to victimization (Alexander 1980; Brown 1979; cf. Boyer and James 1982). They are even more vulnerable than adult prostitutes to being detained for longer periods of time in custody (Sarri 1976), to becoming illicit drug or alcohol dependent, and to becoming the victim of a violent crime (Schur 1984). Regardless of age, street prostitutes report a variety of occupational hazards — physical abuse by customers and pimps, customer rape, forced perversions, non-payment, robbery, client's violation of the prostitution contract, and unfair split of payment with pimps. Such crimes are rarely reported because of self-blame and police indifference (Silbert and Pines 1981, pp.395–399). Prostitutes are more likely than non-prostitutes to be homicide victims because they are highly mobile, have frequent encounters with previously unknown males, and lack strong social ties. Sometimes the killer is a mass murderer, who claims dozens of lives before he is apprehended by police. In Seattle, Washington, the 'Green River' victims include 27 women, most of them prostitutes, street women or hitchhikers. Another 15 women, likely victims, remain on the missing list (*Seattle Post Intelligencer*, 16 October 1984).

Prostitution is intimately connected with a city's entertainment/conference industry, often operates with the connivance of local police, and often has *de facto* legalization in massage parlours, escort services and other third-party-run businesses which must buy licenses. Clients of prostitutes are on the whole 'average' businessmen; they have been characterized as typically middle class, between 35 and 50 years of age, and married with children (Davis 1978, pp. 195–222; Heyl 1974). Financial need serves as an inducement for involving women in the sex trades, including working as models or as live performers in the growing pornography industry, where many drift into full-time prostitution (Alexander 1980; Velarde 1975, pp. 251–63).

Opponents of the current criminalization policy are drawn from both women's groups and legal reformers. Such groups stress that the current laws and enforcement practices against prostitutes are:

1. *Unfair:* they embody one set of moral beliefs, those of social conservatives, vice squad personnel, the 'moral majority' and misogynists, and ignore other, equally important interests — those of women, children, liberals and feminists;
2. *Ineffective*: criminalizing prostitution contributes to the current legal morass in the criminal justice system, in which petty crimes pre-empt court time, and drain the system of resources;
3. *Discriminatory*: police are most likely to arrest minority and disadvantaged street prostitutes;
4. *Costly*: penalizing prostitution costs city governments millions of dollars yearly, and contributes to the 'revolving door' whereby offenders are merely recycled through the system, and out on the street within hours, and then returned;
5. *Counter-productive:* prostitution cannot be eradicated, but only controlled. Enforcement actually seems to spread rather than repress street prostitution (Cohen 1980).

Radical feminists reject legalization of prostitution, which they argue shifts control from the pimp to the state. Legalization also legitimates the exploitation and abuse of women under the guise of standard business practices. Few feminists wish to perpetuate a system in which victimization and degradation play such a large part. From the position of a feminist analysis, until the general status of women rises, and employment and salary opportunities are equal to those of men, prostitution will continue to offer a needed option to low-wage labour for many women, and it should be decriminalized.

The state and women in crisis

Despite the anomalies of state intervention — its coincidental support of patriarchal social structure, and provision of some measure of legal protection and expanded rights for women (Goldstein 1981, pp. 5–28) — most women's groups seek a strong alliance with the state. Their demands involve full participation in society, including expanded job opportunities and equal pay, adequately funded social welfare programmes, expansion of day-care centres, protection from rape and battering, equal justice for women offenders, decriminalization of prostitution, access to abortion and contraception for all women, regardless of social class, race, or age, and paid labour for homemakers and community volunteers.

The current crisis in social control over women revolves around the revocation of state support, and the reconfirmation of the state as women's opponent. The feminist call for equal opportunities and rights has been muted in capitalist societies because women remain segregated by class, race, sex, ethnicity and religion. Further, these divisions have been aided and abetted by dominant market and state institutions. Observe, for example, how the state joins in the symbolic crusade with right-wing groups against the liberation of prostitution and abortion. The compensatory ethic of women's groups arouses a collective awareness among women toward more effective publicizing and politicizing of their common needs.

From the perspective of the state's interests in maintaining hegemonic determinacy of gender roles, the female as deviant is giving way to the female as political threat. New or revived control mechanisms used against women are met by feminist campaigns to increase women's options, and this movement has entered the sphere of the law. One cannot dismiss women who are challenging gender apartheid in the 1980s when their demands for equality are being honoured, at least partially, with legislation enacted by male-dominated governments. Society does not have to reckon with deviants when making decisions; it does, however, have to reckon with oppositions whose votes can affect political careers. Historically, the transinstitutionalization of the female has evolved from the patriarchal male authority of the family to the welfare/punitive state, and to the contemporary legal arena, where precedents for equal rights have been gained on a number of women's issues.

One of the challenges faced by contemporary feminist legal scholars has been to persuade women that whereas the law may be perceived as a major factor in the historical oppression of women, so might the legal process be a means of rectifying those imbalances.[6] As Brophy and Smart suggest, '...it is important to distinguish between the law and legal processes in order to identify the contradictions which allow space for change' (1985, p. 17).

Legal systems have been mystified for women-at-large. They are commonly perceived as automatically discriminating against women, in part, because women historically have been excluded from the creation, interpretation and enforcement of laws. From this perspective, legal processes have subverted women's interests and have served the state as a control agent which helps keep women 'in their place' (Babcock, Friedman, Norton and Ross 1975). As innumerable contemporary litigations have demonstrated, however, there is nothing inherent to the law which effectively rationalizes or inevitably perpetuates this structural injustice. Feminists, including most feminist lawyers, are not suggesting that revolutionary social transformation can best (or only) occur within the parameters of the legal system, but there is clearly an increasing propensity for women to utilize the law in their struggle against the vestigial patriarchal controls over women's lives. Bottomley, for example, defends the use of the law in protecting women's rights in part on the grounds that the law '... is a complex and changing form which gives us some space to struggle within', and, by seeking justice through the legal system '...we are maintaining a public profile and refusing to be privatised, either into the hands of welfare agencies or into the dangers of private ordering' (1985, pp. 184–185).

Perhaps the strongest argument that can be made from a feminist perspective is that a legal judgement on behalf of an individual female litigant or defendant is, in effect, one that portends the defence of *all* women's rights within any given society (Pask, Mahoney and Brown 1985). Unlike traditional informal resolutions of conflict conducted privately (which appear to hold more promise of mediating and conciliating conflicts between individuals), formal adjudication offers the only channel through which the interests of all women can be equally represented. As acknowledged by Smart, even though the law cannot be viewed pragmatically as an altogether objective and neutral medium for obtaining equal rights, the legal system is nevertheless '...a multi-faced system of regulation, containing its own contradictions, and most importantly, capable of change and positive influence rather than just negative restraint' (1984, p. 221). The essential caveat, of course, is that sexist traditions and ideologies are rampant in both the formal and informal spheres of social control.

The inconsistencies in the application of the law relative to women's rights, the public controversy over these developments, and the rise of anti-feminist groups like the Moral Majority and Real Equal Active for Life (REAL) Women, are all historically repetitive indicators of the social confusion and disagreement concerning gender roles, prerogatives and liabilities. The structural weakening of male monopoly in the public sphere results in cognitive conflict, and painful shifts of comprehension. The resolution of that conflict can only be manifested through the reorganization of the social structure, with attendant shifts in gender status.

The experience of the coming decade concerning women's rights to control their own bodies, and to participate fully in the ordering and changing of society, will determine the future of women in the twenty-first century. If a middle-road liberal ideology is reconstructed, women predictably will continue to be discriminated against economically on the basis of age, race and class, but they will not be so severely restricted in terms of sexual proclivity or gender. If the current right-wing upsurge holds its ground, women can expect increasingly punitive and institutionalized controls for what will be commonly labelled 'deviant' behaviours; that is, behaviours which counter the gender roles demanded of females. When this labelling occurs it neutralizes and obfuscates a political phenomenon by defining it as deviant. To institutionalize opposition in the name of health, welfare, treatment, penalty and public safety is to attempt to silence that opposition. Women's reaction to such domination could create a more profound rupture, accelerating a renewed cycle of opposition. Whatever the future, it promises *not* to be serene.

10 Routinizing the discovery of secrets: computers as informants

Gary T. Marx
Nancy Reichman

Police in the United States traditionally have relied heavily on unsolicited information from citizens to direct their efforts (Black 1980; Reiss 1971).[1] In a democratic society there is much to be said for this means of mobilization. It can offer a degree of citizen control over police discretion. This, along with other limitations on the autonomy of police to initiate investigations, is surely a necessary feature of liberty.

The traditional citizen-reporting approach may work well where there are clear victims or observers who are aware that infractions have occurred and who are willing to report what they know. It is less effective when those with information are intimidated or otherwise not forthcoming. When witnesses are not even present, when there is no clear individual victim, when the offence is hidden or highly technical, or where a well-organized conspiracy is present, the traditional approach is irrelevant.

Reliance on citizens for information can have two major drawbacks:

1. The ratio of offences citizens choose to report, relative to those they actually know about, may be too low or may be systematically biased in an undesirable direction;
2. There are many offences of which citizens are unaware.

These drawbacks have become more apparent in recent decades. In response, an important area of criminal justice reform has sought to improve the ability of social control agents to discover offences and offenders systematically.

Reforms intended to improve the discovery process

Systematizing or routinizing discovery has taken two broad forms. One form responds to the problem of underreporting. It seeks to structure the environment so that citizens will be more likely to come forward

This chapter is reprinted (with minor revisions) from *The American Behavioral Scientist*, Vol.27, No.4 (March/April 1984), pp.423–450.

with information. Toll-free hotlines where citizens may anonymously call in tips, televised police appeals for information, neighbourhood crime watches, and citizen patrols seek to make reporting easier and more accessible and to increase the flow of information to police.[2] Protections for those who report have also been enhanced.[3]

The second form of enhancing information discovery involves police taking initiatives to discover infractions on their own, without being dependent on what citizens may choose to report. Undercover work is an example. Police increasingly have sought to discover crimes by becoming a party to them, whether as fellow conspirators, observers, or victims (Marx 1982). Another form of police initiative we have chosen to call 'systematic data-searching.' As illustrated by the discovery of a California woman who fraudulently received welfare aid for 38 non-existent children, systematic data-searching involves gleaning data, usually in computerized form, for direct or indirect evidence of infractions.

While it would be worthwhile to devote equivalent attention to each attempt at enhancing the discovery process, we have chosen instead to explore systematic data-searching in greater detail[4] because of its relative newness, its rapid expansion, and its having received little research attention. Although considerable attention has been devoted to the vast new crime opportunities computers offer (Parker 1976; Whiteside 1978), less attention has been given to the role of computers in *discovering* crimes. Elsewhere (Reichman and Marx 1985) we have considered computers as a form of legal mobilization. Here we focus more directly on the techniques themselves.

Systematic data-searching involves more than mere application of computer technology to existing law enforcement processes.[5] It is in some ways a new tool. It permits the joining of heretofore independent pieces of information in order to expose offences and offenders that would have remained hidden unless such links were drawn. Systematic data-searches do not merely expedite existing discovery processes. They offer an entirely new means of exposing law-breaking. They offer a 'value-added' or inductive method that differs from traditional, deductive methods. Rather than drawing inferences from a 'crime scene' that has natural, seemingly self-evident boundaries, systematic data-searching permits investigators to construct criminal scenarios from disparate data and events. They may also permit a form of statistical surveillance.

This chapter draws on eight interviews with specialists in computer detection and over 100 other interviews carried out in the course of our research on undercover tactics and insurance fraud investigations. Information from these interviews is not presented quantitatively, nor is it used to test hypotheses. It is hoped that our discussion can contribute to the type of systematic research required to answer the questions to be posed.

A more detailed look at systematic data-searching

Systematic data-searching has been facilitated by new computer developments. These developments have occurred concurrently with the increased prominence and attention given to what can be called 'low-visibility' offences. Much white-collar crime, such as price fixing, corruption and trade violations, can be so characterized. The significant expansion of benefits provided by the modern welfare state has also generated new opportunities for fraud. The implications of this for exploitation have rarely been noted.[6]

Inhibitors to discovery go far beyond the physical barriers and the right to privacy that are noted in the literature as factors limiting the detection of offences by routine patrols of public areas (Mawby 1981; Stinchcombe 1963). The impersonal and routine settings in which these offences occur and the very large numbers of potential offences/ offenders mean that, in contrast to more traditional offences, control agents usually cannot rely on prior reputation as a means of suspicion.

Many crimes by or against organizations are deceptively masked as legitimate organizational transactions. Applying for and receiving welfare benefits, for example, is legal unless the fact of employment is concealed. Similarly, filing a property insurance claim is legitimate unless there was no loss. Since the infractions occur in the context of many similar, legitimate transactions, they do not stand out immediately as instances of wrongdoing. Organizational members and routine organizational processes also may shield illegal action from exposure.[7]

The legitimate and routine appearance of the violations in such cases is in sharp contrast to predatory crime, or even 'victimless' crime, where the act is illegal and traces of the activity are instantly obvious. No similar 'on-site' clues alert social control agents that low-visibility offences have occurred. There is no 'smoking gun'.

Beyond their entrenchment in routine organizational processes, low-visibility offences are often difficult to discover because they occur serially, and because information about them is dispersed across institutional settings. The discovery of such offences is mainly enhanced by the pooling of information. Death records are a good example. Although they have major bearing on many federal entitlement programmes, death records are maintained locally. Historically, there has been no systematized way for federal agencies to obtain these records automatically to confirm programme eligibility. In addition, technical advances such as automatic cheque-writing and depositing may further mask discovery. The system grinds along on its own initial momentum, in the absence of an order to decease.

Systematic data-searches appear well suited for the exposure of these types of low-visibility offences. In their simplest form, searches may be applied to a single body of data. Before computerization, records such as applications were checked for internal consistency, errors and missing information. But this was often done superficially, with little cross-checking and in an inconsistent and non-systematic fashion. The individual clerk or auditor usually had vast discretion over whether and what to check.

With computerization, screening can become routinized, broadened, and deepened. Computers permit forms of investigation that previously were impractical. In contrast to traditional techniques that could assess static demographic data, computers permit analysis of more complex transactional data, such as number of visits to a doctor, phone calls to particular individuals, travel patterns, bank deposits, and the timing and interrelations of events (Burnham 1983). A much more textured and dimensional picture is possible.

An internal computer data-search may reveal discrepancies, contradictions, and irregularities that would be missed by a clerk reviewing a single form. Equity may be increased as all forms are checked, not just those that happen to catch the fancy of an auditor. The IRS, for example, now is able to screen the over 90 million tax returns it receives for missing information and mathematical errors. Cross-referencing distinct data bases (as with social security numbers and death records) may expand and qualitatively change the nature of the search. Data analysis may yield profiles of likely offenders. Patterns of offending behaviour may be discovered through aggregation not possible if one follows a 'Sherlock Holmes logic' of deduction and looks at only a few cases. Indicators may be created that suggest a violation has occurred. The investigator may then follow or track these cases over time.

Two increasingly prominent styles of computerized data-searching are *matching* and *profiling*. These certainly do not exhaust all forms of searching, but they are among the most important.[8] Although they may overlap or appear sequentially, the two are analytically distinct and offer a way of organizing our discussion of empirical material.

Matching

Matching involves the comparison of information from two or more distinct data sources. It may be used for cross-checking and verification or for the discovery of inconsistencies and multiple listings which suggest that violations have occurred. According to one estimate, approximately 500 computer matching programmes are being carried out routinely at the state and federal levels in the United States (US

Senate 1982, p. 20). Use of this procedure is likely to increase significantly following implementation of the Deficit Reduction Act of 1984 which requires that state governments implement income and eligibility verification programmes in order to receive federal funds for various assistance programmes.

Among the most dramatic examples of violations that matching techniques discover are those involving impersonation and false representation. For example, a cross-check of social security rolls and Medicare records resulted in the arrest of 29 people who cashed cheques made out to dead friends and relatives. One woman had been forging the name of a deceased friend for 14 years. Officials reported uncovering losses of over $30 million (*New York Times*, 20 May 1983).[9] In another example of third parties exploiting what was once a valid claim, a matching of black lung programme payments with social security records revealed that the programme was continuing to provide compensation to 1200 individuals listed as deceased (United States Department of Health and Human Services 1981, p. 24). In what one prosecutor called 'the most concerted effort yet not simply to respond to complaints but to affirmatively go out and detect fraud', the United States Office of Education has used computer searches to flag suspicious applications in federal student loan programmes. The rate at which fraud has been uncovered as a result has more than tripled (*Boston Globe*, 27 June 1983).

A second type of violation commonly discovered is 'double dipping'. A person may be legitimately entitled to the benefit in question, but through seeking the same benefit in different jurisdictions, or using different names, or (where payment legitimately terminates) by subsequently reapplying, he or she may fraudulently obtain additional benefits. For example, a match of the welfare rolls of 34 jurisdictions involving 5 million records turned up 3500 cases where persons appeared to be receiving public assistance in more than one state (United States Department of Health and Human Services 1981, p. 30). Some welfare systems will automatically cross-check birth records whenever a person claims to have twins, since false claims regarding twins are a well-known means of seeking increased benefits (*New York Times*, 3 August 1982).

Computer matching has also been used to discover false claims that would render an applicant ineligible for the benefit in question. For example, in Massachusetts, computer matching has been used to find welfare recipients with bank deposits in excess of the amount permitted. The welfare department supplied banks with the names and social security numbers of all welfare recipients. Matching these numbers with their customer information, the bank officials gave the state a list of welfare recipients holding cash assets in their banks. The inquiry discovered over 1600 instances in which assets in excess of the $5000 limit appear to have been held (US Senate 1982, p. 240).

Fraudulent claims may involve an event rather than some aspect of a person's biography. A common form of insurance fraud involves purchasing the title certificate for a wrecked car sold as salvage. The car is insured and subsequently reported as stolen. Theft insurance would then be collected on a non-existent car. However, with computer matching this has become more difficult to accomplish. The National Auto Theft Bureau now maintains records of all vehicles sold as salvage and/or reported stolen.[10] By comparing theft reports with salvage records, the computer matching programme permits instantaneous discovery of a type of fraud that previously lay hidden in two rarely connected bodies of data.

Matching may be used to identify persons who fail to meet an obligation. For example, in an effort to discover income tax evasion, particularly by self-employed persons, the IRS is testing a system that matches tax records to estimates of income based on the type of neighbourhood a person lives in, and the type of car he or she drives. The data are to be purchased from private marketing firms that sell computerized lists to direct-mail companies. The IRS is also matching data from county recorders of deeds with tax returns, to find individuals who fail to pay capital gains taxes owed from the sale of real estate (*New York Times*, 29 August 1983).

Matching can also be used in a preventive way, for example, by linking the failure to meet an obligation with a new request. In rules announced by the Office of Management and Budget in 1983, federal agencies are now prohibited from making loans, procurement contracts, or major grants until they have screened applicants through credit bureau inquiries to ensure that they are not delinquent in repaying prior government loans and other overdue obligations (*New York Times*, 24 September 1983).

Profiling

Matching may also be used to construct profiles of violations or violators, although the logic of profiling is more indirect than that of matching. An inductive logic is followed to seek clues that will increase the probability of discovering infractions through random data-searches.

Profiling permits investigators to correlate a number of distinct data items in order to assess how close a person or event comes to a predetermined characterization or model of infraction. The modal characteristics and behaviour patterns of known violations or violators are determined relative to the characteristics of others presumed to be non-violators.[11] Indicators of possible violations are developed from this comparison. Where the behaviour is complex and evolving, a model may be developed of the interrelations among the relevant factors. But most common is a simple laundry list of 'red flag' characteristics. The greater the number of such characteristics present, the more suspect the case in question becomes. A second, more in-depth investigation is then carried out to determine if a case that has been flagged as suspicious actually involves the violation.[12] Profiling is indirect because the indicators used are not direct indices of illegality. However, their joint appearance is thought to be associated with an increased likelihood that a violation has occurred or will occur.

Profiling may be *singular* or *aggregative*. The former consists of a model of distinct attributes. The latter consists of the reappearance of factors that singularly would not trigger suspicion, but where their appearance across cases, such as a single person's being the owner of several inner-city buildings that burn down, signals a need for further investigation.

Singular profiling focuses on discrete characteristics or events. There is nothing illegal or exceptional about being a male, purchasing a one-way airline ticket, paying for it with cash, or obtaining a ticket at the last minute at the airport. But analysis suggests that when these factors occur together, the chances of a hijacking attempt are increased. The same logic applies to a drug courier profile used to stop suspicious persons at airports.

The IRS was an early user of profiles in efforts to identify tax violators. Persons claiming deductions beyond a certain percentage of their income and certain configurations of deductions are likely to trigger more detailed inquiry. One way to get on the IRS's 'tax gap hit list' appears to be to purchase audit insurance (*Wall Street Journal*, 29 June 1983). The logic here is that people who purchase audit insurance are likely to have something to hide and are gambling that it is cheaper to purchase the insurance than to pay the tax.

Profiles also can be used in a preventive way. The development of arson early-warning detection systems in Seattle, Boston, New Haven and other cities illustrates this function (National Legislative Conference on Arson 1982). Computer-based arson prediction models are used to identify buildings thought to be at risk of being burned, opening up the possibility for preventive action. In another form of prevention, the profile may result in interdiction before the act can be carried to completion. Airline hijacking profiles are one example whereby the refusal to issue tickets to passengers matching the profile may prevent the offence (*Time*, 26 July 1976). Interrogations and searches resulting from drug courier profiles are another example.

Profiles developed for identifying welfare fraud can be used to prevent ineligible cases from entering the system. For example, in Sacramento County (California) a profile for identifying suspicious cases has been developed around the number and age of children, health care, and school records. This model is based on an assumption of at least occasional childhood illness and treatment. If a recipient claims children and there are no school records and no medical claims for the children, further investigation occurs (US Senate 1982).

Profiles of auto theft and bodily injury fraud are increasingly used in insurance cases. Profiles are based on factors that often accompany fraud, such as losses occurring close to the inception date of a policy, or where claimants avoid using the United States mail in correspondence regarding the claim. A series of questions, a checklist of responses, and an associated point system have been developed that allow adjusters to quantitatively rate the degree to which a particular claim is consistent with ideal fraud types (Reichman 1987).

The Educational Testing Service uses profiling to help in the discovery of cheating. In 1982 the service sent out about 2000 form letters alleging 'copying' to persons taking a scholastic aptitude test. The letters note that a statistical review 'found close agreement of your answers with those on another answer sheet from the same test center. Such agreement is unusual and suggests that copying occurred'. Students were told that in two weeks their scores would be cancelled and colleges notified, unless they provided 'additional information' to prove they had not cheated. An important factor in the sending of such letters is the 'K-index' which compares incorrect answers among test-takers (*New York Times*, 2 July 1983).

Another form of profiling is based not on the distinctive characteristics of any one case, but on the frequency with which certain factors appear across cases. The *aggregate* profile emerges from the accumulation of similar incidents or configurations. There is an implicit threshold. Once this is reached, red flags appear. Aggregative profiling is often directed against systematic and repetitive violations rather than the one-time infraction.

Such profiling has been used extensively in efforts to find insurance fraud. For example, the State of Florida's Division of Insurance Fraud maintains an index of all bodily injury insurance claims. The index is used to ferret out violations that cut across seemingly unrelated claims. Thus when the same doctor-lawyer combination reappears on a significant number of personal injury claims, investigators have reason to look further for a fake accident ring. This pooling of information may give the analyst reason for suspicion that would not appear to an insurance company office paying a single claim.

Similar logic underlies the Property Insurance Loss Registry (PILR), a not-for-profit discovery organization sponsored by the insurance industry. Among other information, it records the location of fires, insurees, mortgagees and contractors. A current fire prompts a search through the PILR index for other similar fires involving the same persons or organizations. While the discovery of other fires is not directly discrediting, it suggests that further inquiry into the fire loss is appropriate.

Profiling is also used in some parts of the private sector to identify drug users. For example, one drug consultant searches computerized company personnel records looking for employees under 35 who show higher-than-average rates of:

1. Absenteeism;
2. Requests for early dismissal or time off;
3. Lateness;
4. Sick leave;
5. Accidents; and
6. Worker's Compensation claims.

An employee who shows sufficient elements of this profile may be asked to undergo a blood or urine test to determine the presence of drugs (*Newsweek*, 22 August 1983).

Uses of the results

In the language of the data analyst, the results of an initial computer search are referred to as 'raw hits'. Depending on search type, these include indications of direct infractions or a sufficient number of red flags alerting agents to possible violations. A name on both the welfare and city employment rolls, the repetition of an event or characteristic beyond some identifiable threshold (such as four consumer complaints against the same company), or a person or event that matches a profile associated with previous violations, are examples. These raw hits include the total universe of hits. This universe in turn is made up of 'solid hits', 'misses' and 'inconclusives'.

'Solid' or 'true' hits are instances in which conclusive evidence of violation is found.[13] But what happens when additional investigation yields conclusions that negate the initial finding of a hit? In most cases, what appeared to be hits will simply be considered misses and it will be possible to explain away the initial suspicion. Misses appear as a result of errors, situational factors that lead to a different interpretation of the facts, or, in the case of profiling, as an inevitable attribute of probabilistic reasoning.[14] In other cases, while sufficient evidence of an infraction is not available, neither is the conclusion of a miss. No evidence is found to base doubt on the original reasons for suspicion, and evidence to strengthen it may even have been found. The term 'inconclusive' is appropriate here. Where there is reason to think that a violation will eventually appear, one response is to monitor or track a case over time.[15]

The goals of a data-search may change with its repeated use. When a system is first applied to an existing database, its goal is likely to be the discovery of current or past offences. It may seek to detect 'bad apples'. It searches for illegitimate cases. For example, recipients of the black lung benefits are provided with payments for children up to the age of eighteen. When the US Department of Health and Human Services (HHS) screened its records, 3000 offspring were found whose ages exceeded the eligibility standard, although not all of these were continuing to receive payments (United States HHS 1981, p. 25). The statistical technique of discriminant analysis is used by the Farmer's Home Administration to identify problem loans. Based on patterns identified in previous cases of default and foreclosure, the technique permits investigators to screen out current loans which exhibit characteristics associated with a high probability of default (President's Council 1983).

Once a database has been purged of such cases, however, the goal may shift to deterrence and prevention. Preventing fraud and abuse before they occur is in fact the new objective of the President's Council on Integrity and Efficiency (PCIE), which was established in March 1981 to promote and co-ordinate the activities of inspectors general, many of whom pioneered the use of computer matching. Programme administrators hope that publicity about data-searching will in itself deter potential offenders.[16] Public relations efforts may seek to create the impression that the computer's awesome power is all-knowing. This may build upon the mystique surrounding technology in general, and computers in particular. Fear and trembling may be engendered among the naive who impute unrealistic powers to the computer. There is a parallel to the unwarranted power some persons impute to the lie detector. This is reminiscent of Richard Nixon's immortalized words on the Watergate tapes: 'Listen, I don't know anything about polygraphs, and I don't know how accurate they are, but I do know that they'll scare the hell out of people'.

Where such deterrence is not present, applying the search before people are officially entered on the rolls or, in the case of the black lung example above, assuming that they are removed at the appropriate time, may anticipate violations and allow for preventive measures. In a private sector example, major credit card companies may soon be confirming the personal identity of credit card holders through signature verification technology. A technique has been developed for analysing the pressure and direction of a signature as it is being signed. This could then be compared to data stored from previous signatures (*Wall Street Journal*, 9 June 1983).

Some policy and research issues

> I hope you do not assume yourselves infallibilitie of judgment when the most learned of the apostles confesseth that he knew but in parts and saw but darkly through a glass.
>
> Sir Richard Saltonstall

It is clear that data-searching techniques such as matching and profiling can significantly enhance the likelihood of violation discovery. As we noted earlier, systematic data-searching seems particularly well suited to ferreting out certain low-visibility offences that involve organizational processing. As with undercover sting operations, their dramatic results make for high profile media attention. These techniques generally have been positively received. Their use is expanding rapidly. But, as with any tactic, they have a cost. The lunch is never free, whatever other attractions it may have. Two of the most important costs are the consequences of error and the implications for civil liberties.

Errors

Important factors in the assessment of data-searching are the cause, frequency and consequences of various types of error. At least five sources of error can be identified:

1. Erroneously reported or incorrectly entered data;
2. Time lags;
3. Computer hardware and software problems;
4. The decontextualized nature of the decision process; and
5. The probabilistic nature of profiling.

The extent of erroneously reported, or incorrectly entered, data will vary greatly across programmes and data types. We know little about its frequency. A study of the social security numbers of over 2 million food stamp and AFDC (Aid to Families with Dependent Children) recipients found 5100 instances in which non-issued numbers were in use. Approximately one-third of these cases resulted from data input errors — the numbers were transposed by the applicant or by programme officials (US Senate 1982, p. 5). In the first computer run of the Massachusetts bank records match, 24 per cent of the social security numbers used in the matches were incorrect (US Senate 1982, p. 224). A procedure, adopted later, which coupled the first letter of the surname with the social security number, helped reduce errors based on incorrect matches to 7 per cent. Although this is a significant reduction in the error rate, the ease and magnitude of such errors is disturbing.

The process used to create the database must be seen to reflect human judgement and not be seen as a perfect reflection of reality. It must be approached tentatively. Were the data gathered under coercion or periods of great stress? Are data collectors and processors aware of proper data collection procedures and motivated to follow them?[17] Do programme staff have incentives for falsifying data? If matters of judgement are involved, how high is reliability across judges? Even when the agency that initially gathers the data discovers an error, the ease of access to computerized information on the part of other agencies may limit its ability to control the flow of erroneous information. The automatic interfacing of computer systems may mean that the original processors of the data are unaware of the ultimate users and uses of such information.

The time lag between events, the reporting of events, and input into computerized data-banks and analysis offers another source of error. For example, in New York State a match of work records with a list of persons receiving assistance in the last quarter of 1978 revealed that 10 per cent of welfare recipients were actually working. A second review disclosed that at least half these persons were on both lists legitimately. Some recipients had been on welfare during the beginning of the quarter and only subsequently found work. Because the data were not updated in a timely fashion, some innocent individuals were initially suspect (*Boston Globe*, 23 July 1979).

Computer hardware problems may lead to data errors. Among problems that can be caused by faulty hardware is the 'doubling up of records' so that the value of a variable is recorded twice. This can wreak havoc with quantitative eligibility requirements such as a minimum amount in the bank, age, or number of children. Such hardware problems are easy to correct technically once they are located, but this requires vigilance in looking for errors and an incentive to make corrections. In the interim, persons may experience loss of benefits or receive benefits to which they are not entitled.

Another, not uncommon, technical problem lies with software errors. In using large databases, formatting errors can easily occur. If a command has been formatted incorrectly, the wrong variable may be extracted for analysis. For example, when applicants provide income data for several years, a formatting error could abstract a previous year's income for current income.[18]

The error sources considered thus far are largely technical. With sufficient experience, resources, cross-checks, updating, and incentives, they can probably be reduced to an acceptable minimum. But this may not be the case with errors that are related to substituting technical for human judgement, and where profiles are based on samples for which the true parameters are unknown. The most serious questions raised by systematic data-searching lie here.

When a machine recommends a decision, the recommendation is

only as good as the data and programmes that have gone into it. One measure of goodness has been considered above — whether the data are erroneous in some technical sense. But a more subtle meaning involves completeness and sensitivity to unique parameters. When used as a decisive guide, rather than as an aid, systematic data-searching is misused. The machine should not be a substitute for human discretion and judgement.

Errors in interpretation may arise because of the acontextual nature of the data analysis. Only a fraction of reality's richness is abstracted and put into machine-analysable form. There is a bias toward general features characterizing many cases, rather than the atypical, idiosyncratic, or extenuating circumstance.

As we move from the formal and general categories used to develop aggregate patterns basic to the actuarial method, to inferences about particular persons in specific situations, problems may appear. An example of this can be seen in the case of a nursing home resident who lost her Medicaid eligibility as a result of the Massachusetts bank matching programme described above. The data that resulted in her being dropped were technically correct as far as the search programme was concerned. Yet it was a wrong decision. The woman's bank account included a certificate of deposit held in trust for a local funeral director to be used for her funeral expenses. Although federal regulations exempt burial contracts from asset calculation, the trust was included in the determination of her assets and she was excluded from the programme (US Senate 1982, pp. 106–107).

In another case, a Washington DC welfare recipient obtained a job at the Department of Health, Education and Welfare (DHEW). Although she properly notified the welfare department of her changed status, word never reached those responsible for mailing the cheques. The cheques kept coming despite her repeated attempts to inform the welfare department of her new status. She eventually cashed the cheques to pay off doctor bills incurred as the result of a serious illness. Subsequently she was indicted on a felony charge and her name (along with fifteen others) was listed in local newspaper stories describing the results of DHEW's computer matching of its own employee records. Many of the others indicted also had informed the welfare department that they were currently working. When the judge learned the details, a majority of the cases, including that of the woman described above, were dismissed or reduced to misdemeanours. Yet the damage to these people's reputations, and six months of uncertainty before their cases came to trial, cannot be undone.[19]

A final source of error inheres in the very idea of profiling. It stems from statistical reasoning and group comparisons. With aggregative profiling some hits composed of repetitive events will appear as a result of chance. For example, sometimes persons showing roughly equivalent error patterns on a test will represent random factors rather than cheating. Some persons may simply experience the bad luck to have a series of fires on properties they own without arson as the cause.

The database used for constructing a profile may be reasonably accurate as far as it goes, but may simply not be representative of the larger universe of events. Important data may never enter the system. Thus it is sometimes argued that our knowledge of criminals is distorted because it is based primarily on those who get caught and they may be less competent than those who manage to avoid apprehension.

When data-gathering on controversial and confidential topics is separated from data analysis, users may not be in a position to know much about the representativeness of the data they are given. Prosecutors, for example, usually have no choice but to rely on the selectively reported information police bring them on gambling (Reuter and Rubenstein 1978).

Even in the unlikely event that a profile was to be developed that described the characteristics of all true violators, it would also likely characterize many non-violators. For example, in the case of hijacking, the extreme rarity of the offence per airline passenger will result in many more false positives than true hits. This also may be true for airport drug courier profiles that include such criteria as arriving from a city noted as a drug source, casual dress, scanning the concourse, making a telephone call on arrival, and appearing nervous (US v. Harrison, 1982). While the profile turns up solid hits, it may also cause much embarrassment and inconvenience to those wrongly interrogated. Procedures for taking reparative action, to the extent that this is possible, are clearly appropriate.

Whatever the source, errors will occur. In considering their costs, it is useful to separate errors involving false accusations from those involving the failure to identify violations. Type I errors involve false accusations. Like the dolphins who are inadvertently trapped in nets put out for tuna, innocent persons are caught in the net thrown out for offenders. Loss of benefits, defamation of character, alienation, and a more general delegitimation can result from such errors. In the case of false accusation, the state has a moral, and often a legal, obligation to provide a means of review. Although Type I errors have an individualized impact, they may incur high societal costs as they challenge democratic ideals of fair process.

Type II errors reflect an inefficient discovery mechanism (that is, not netting the universe of offenders). Their consequences vary according to whether one seeks to discover infractions that have already occurred or those that are planned. Not identifying a direct violation (for example, that a person is obtaining public assistance while working) may be inefficient, but it does not produce a clear direct cost since the behaviour would have remained hidden irrespective of whether a weak search process was in place. On the other hand, as the case of arson or hijacking suggests, when the goal is prevention, the failure to recognize a set of behaviours or events as consistent with a profile of wrongdoing can have more serious consequences.

Type I errors almost always become manifest because the investigation reveals a miss, or a falsely accused person protests. But whether or not Type II errors are identified varies across offence types. Such errors are likely to be discovered only if a victim reports the offence or if it of necessity becomes public. For example, hijacking offers a great contrast to drug smuggling. With a profile in place, every hijacking attempt represents a Type II error. But completed drug smuggling violations are far more difficult to identify. The extent of Type II errors involving the former can be checked continuously, but with drugs this is almost impossible. Where profiles can be checked they are subject to more frequent revision and, presumably, improvement. Where the size of Type II errors cannot be determined, the profile remains the captive of its assumptions, which must remain invalidated. The IRS, with the power to investigate large samples of taxpayers at random, illustrates one method of assessing the extent of Type II errors that would not otherwise be visible.

The assessment of errors also must consider the rate of error relative to the rate of true hits. If you increase the capacity to get true hits, do you proportionately increase the rate of errors or does the error rate grow exponentially? Or are there instances in which they might even be inversely linked?

In his novel *1984*, Orwell imagined a social control system that was both highly efficient and repressive. Perfect control over information was the key element (whether the ability to discover information or to manage beliefs). While not explicitly mentioned, computer technology was implied. Our review certainly does not question the repressive potential of such technology. But the sources of error we have noted clearly call into question limits on the efficiency and accuracy of computer control technology and illustrate the high cost of mistakes.

Civil liberties

Computer data-searching involves the same civil liberties issues raised by the use of computer files in general.[20] Visions of the central all-knowing computer and Kafkaesque nightmares lurk on the horizon. Important concerns are privacy, constitutional and legislative protections, and due process of law.

Critics argue that these searches are more intrusive than other forms of information surveillance because those subject to them are likely to be unaware that any search is going on. They may have given direct or willing consent for neither the search nor the disclosure of personal information to others. In cases where consent has been given, this may be a result of duress and coercion rather than a real choice, since the individual may believe that a failure to give consent will mean foregoing a badly needed benefit.[21]

Privacy may also be violated by the improper disclosure of data to third parties without the consent of the subject. Or the data may be improperly obtained by them. The sharing of data across agencies heightens the risk of unrestricted or unwarranted access to confidential information. Even without such exchanges, the general inadequacy of security around these kinds of data sets invites abuse.[22]

The use of computerized records for purposes unrelated to their initial collection has also been questioned. At the federal level in the United States, such use is normally prohibited by privacy legislation. However, the US Privacy Act of 1974 exempts computer matching programmes when they are classified as 'routine use' procedures, meaning when they are used for purposes compatible with the reasons for which the data were collected originally.[23] Broad interpretations of 'compatible purpose' have made it possible to include nearly any government initiated venture. The 'routine use' classification can thus be used to circumvent protections against invasions of privacy the legislation was designed to prevent.

The programmes may be questioned in the United States on Fourth and Fifth Amendment grounds. Searches can be viewed as 'fishing expeditions', devoid of any substantial evidence of wrongdoing by the person in question. As such, they may be seen to violate the Fourth Amendment's protection against unreasonable searches and seizures. When data voluntarily given for one purpose are used for another, a person's right to protection against self-incrimination may be violated.

To the extent that one is not provided with proper notice that an individual is subject to a search, timely notice that one is a 'hit', or an opportunity to contest the results of a search, due process questions also emerge.[24]

In contrast to conventional criminal accusations, data-searching may transform the presumption of innocence into an assumption of guilt. It can lead to imperious behaviour as an agency cuts off benefits or cancels test scores without even a hearing. Accusations become equivalent to convictions without a trial. The burden of proof may be on the target of the hit to show that the violation did not occur, rather than on the agency to show that it did. Officials may abdicate responsibility for their accusations to computer programs or models. In such cases suspects effectively lose their rights to face their accusers, at least directly.[25] Challenges may be possible only after punitive action has been taken.

Supporters, however, argue that a balance must be struck between the rights of the individual and the needs of the state, and do not view matching programmes as undue intrusions. Properly conducted computer searches are seen to be less intrusive than other forms of search, such as rummaging through a person's bank records. Data-searches abstract specific variables from records, with total disregard of other variables. In contrast, an individual searcher can scan entire records picking and choosing among items. Further, consent for computer searches is often given, or implied when one voluntarily provides the data. Advocates claim that with proper guidelines and administration, problems are minimal.[26]

Thus far, most of the debate between opponents and supporters has reflected competing values. It also has been at a very general level and has not made distinctions between types of search or error. Disagreements are now based primarily on value positions, with neither side able to examine adequately the empirical premises that bear upon the arguments. Given the absence of adequate data on most of the issues in question, it could hardly be otherwise. We have only minimal data on the extent of falsely accused people and the ratio of hits to misses for various kinds of searches. Little is publicly known about the validity of different profiles. Data on the frequency of the concerns raised by civil libertarians (or the counter-claims regarding the effectiveness of guidelines offered by supporters) are also missing. Nor do we have studies showing whether the discovery benefits continue over time or become neutralized with regular use.[27]

We do not have the detailed case studies of the actual operation of matching and profiling programmes that are requisite for sound policy recommendations. There has been little discussion of how risks can best be minimized and errors corrected, or of how competing values should be weighed. How do matching and profiling differ from each other with respect to the costs of error? What are the relative costs of Type I and Type II errors? Should there be a presumption against using such techniques, or certain forms of them just as there are with the use of weapons or Fourth Amendment searches, except under special circumstances and when no other practical means are available? How does systematic data-searching compare to other means of obtaining information on low-visibility offences such as undercover tactics and efforts to increase citizen reporting?[28]

As in so many other areas of contemporary life, technological developments have outpaced the establishment of ethical and legal standards for their use. The United States Federal Privacy Act of 1974 does not address many of the issues raised by recent computer developments. Less than one-fifth of the states have laws requiring written standards for the collection, maintenance and dissemination of personal information, though this number is growing. Of course, as time passes and problems are identified, the quality of computer use in the areas considered above will no doubt improve. But this is likely to be offset by problems associated with the continuing expansion of computers to new untested areas.

Some theoretical implications

The significance of systematic data-searching goes beyond the public policy questions considered above. It also has implications for understanding society and the nature of social control. The use of computers as informants is but a small part of a broad social process of rationalization.

The recent growth of matching and profiling is part of a more general process of rationalization that began in the nineteenth century. The same broad social forces affecting the economy also touch the criminal justice arena (Reichman 1986; Spitzer 1979). In a rational effort to control the environment, policy has become more systematic and routinized. Social control has sought greater effectiveness, efficiency, certainty and predictability.

Rather than having to rely on what citizens happen to report or police accidentally discover, control agents are taking greater initiative. This may bring greater equity as police seek independence from the biases a citizen-based reporting system may entail. With a sceptical and scientific ethos and a broad database that can be inexpensively screened, it becomes prudent to consider everyone a possible suspect. Analysis rather than tradition becomes the basis for action.

Eliminating the traditional temporal distinction between locating an offence and searching for an offender may yield greater efficiency. Some systematic data-searches collapse these processes as offence and offender are discovered simultaneously.

Yet, just as Mark Twain observed that claims of his death were greatly exaggerated, so too may claims about the efficacy of a rationalized criminal justice system be overly optimistic. In the case of systematic data-searching, for example, if it does not contain within it the seeds of its own destruction, it at least contains an ironic vulnerability to its own neutralization (Marx 1981). In any setting of strategic conflict, efforts at systematization (unless kept secret) can be exploited by skilled adversaries.[29]

The certainty such techniques seem to offer may be illusory. Their advantages may be temporary or may result in a skewed population of apprehended offenders. Routinizing discovery procedures usually involves focusing attention on a limited number of indicators. These may be invested with far more predictive power than they warrant. Focusing attention on specific indicators implicitly diverts attention from others and can result in tunnel vision.[30] The indicators chosen can easily come to be treated in a ritualised way. Enforcement agents may be held accountable for following correct procedures, rather than for the results of following these procedures. Only superficial concern may be given to whether indicators are valid or have been obtained or presented properly.

Although deterring or discovering some offenders, routinization can offer an almost guaranteed means of unauthorized access to others, who gain knowledge of the system and take actions to neutralize it. Altheide (1975) has illustrated how security operations designed to restrict territorial access also can serve as a means for facilitating unofficial entry. The same holds for access to the benefits that systematic data-searching is designed to control.

By learning what prompts a hit or a red flag, knowledgeable violators may take steps to avoid them. Some variables used in matching and profiling can be manipulated or avoided easily. For example, the well-publicized match of welfare and bank records in Massachusetts no doubt led some persons to hide money in banks outside the state, to entrust it to others, or to convert assets to a different form.

Another form of neutralization occurs in the use of false names and identification numbers. Basic to some contemporary matching is discovering the same name, identification number, address, and the like on lists that should be mutually exclusive. This can be avoided through the use of false identification.[31] A record check may attest to the validity of a given document, but it is unlikely to reveal that the record does not legitimately belong to the person presenting it.

Publication of the characteristics used to profile arsonists or hijackers may offer such persons a way to avoid detection. The likelihood of detecting an arson pattern through the Property Insurance Loss Registry described above is reduced when each property is in a different and unrelated name. In response to five hijackings to Cuba in a two-month period, the United States Federal Aviation Administration is considering changing its behaviour profile (*New York Times*, 7 July 1983).

Awareness of this neutralization potential raises questions about who is likely to get caught in a routinized discovery system. Clearly, not all potential offenders have sufficient knowledge or skill to neutralize the system. However, over time, it seems likely that these systems will disproportionately net the marginal, amateur, occasional, or opportunistic violator, rather than those who are more systematic, repetitive, skilled, or professional in their rule-breaking. The latter, ironically, may be granted a kind of license to steal, even while headlines hail the effectiveness of control agents using new techniques.[32] To be sure, where costly violation of the public trust or serious crimes are involved, any apprehension may be desirable. But the routinization of discovery does raise a type of equity issue rarely heard. The question is not the familiar one of how authorities use their discretion in deciding what laws to enforce or whom to go after, but, given the means at their disposal, what kinds of cases they are likely to discover.[33]

Beyond questions of equity, efficiency, and the cyclic and dynamic nature of rule enforcement and violation, there is a broader question about the reach of social control. Observers such as Foucault (1977) view an irreversible continuing historical process of more intensive and extensive social control. The capacity of the modern state to gather information and to punish is seen to extend ever deeper into the social fabric. Control is based on 'observation, surveillance, and inspection' rather than primarily on physical coercion. Conformity is thought to emerge out of fear of a pervasive and omnipresent panoptic eye. The net has widened and the mesh thinned (Cohen 1979; Marx 1985, 1986). While computer matching and profiling may seem to be relatively pale and benign variants of this, variants they are.

How far do we want those in authority to go in their power to discover infraction? In a time of pervasive citizen concern about crime and the increased prevalence of low-visibility offences, there is a great deal to be said for enhancing this ability. The proportion of offences discovered by police relative to those reported by citizens is increasing.

Yet there is another side as well. A different version of the equity problem may appear when there is a gap between the knowledge of violation and the ability to sanction. While ignorance is not bliss, there is a certain wisdom to the inability of the three monkeys to see evil when responsive action is not possible. Powerful new instruments of discovery may overload the system. Authorities may discover far more violations than they can prosecute or process. This overabundance can lead to demoralization and the misuse of discretion. Charges of corruption and favouritism may appear and the system may be perceived as unfair.

If this were all that was at stake, awareness of the potential problems and well-conceived policy for structuring choices might suffice. But there is a more ominous side. Paradoxically, *both* repression and equal law enforcement may be inhibited when authorities lack information. As Selznick observes:

> Do we need or want agencies of control so efficient and so impartial that every actual offence has an equal chance of being known and processed? ... I am concerned that we do not respond too eagerly and too well to the apparent need for more effective mechanisms of social control. In the administration of justice, if anywhere, we need to guard human values and forestall the creation of mindless machines for handling cases according to

> set routines. Here vigilance consists in careful study of actual operations so that we may know what will be lost or gained. (1948, p. 84)

Systematic data-searching, along with the new citizen reporting programmes, undercover policy practices, electronic surveillance, and other technical means, offer compelling and little understood arenas for such study.

PART III
TRANS-INSTITUTIONALIZATION AND THE CARCERAL NETWORK

Introduction

The five essays in Part III of the anthology examine the marriage of exclusive and inclusive modes of social control as the community becomes an extension of the total institution, or as the community is extended into the total institution. The main focus of the section is on the use of inclusive strategies to supplement exclusive measures, particularly in terms of decarceration, deinstitutionalization and transinstitutionalization, and the strategic role of parole as a mechanism for controlling prisoners and regulating the size of prison populations. In terms of inclusive strategies penetrating the prison, the discussion turns to recent attempts to develop private prison industry in the reappearance of what Weiss terms 'the ideal factory'.

The first chapter, Thomas G. Blomberg's 'Criminal justice reform and social control: are we becoming a minimum security society?', reviews some of the recent transitions in criminal justice philosophy, discusses how that philosophy has become manifest in practice, and poses some disturbing questions about what an extrapolation of these realities might imply.

The force of Blomberg's argument lies in the concatenation of two well-documented trends. The first emerges from the plethora of diversion and deinstitutionalization programmes that grew in the 1960s. Designed originally to provide a community *alternative* to incarceration, Blomberg notes that these programmes have instead become a *supplement* to them. Instead of *fewer* individuals going to prison, there are now more than ever. And instead of diverting individuals *out* of the criminal justice system, the new programmes have diverted more people *into* it. Moral issues notwithstanding, one might be able to justify this net-widening process if its effects were demonstrably positive, but Blomberg documents a disturbing rash of negative impacts associated with these interventions. The bottom line, therefore, is that more and more individuals are becoming subject to the scrutiny and surveillance of criminal justice personnel, not because of any discernible positive outcomes, nor because of a proliferation of criminal behaviour, but purely because the organizational character of the criminal justice system and its personnel has pushed the tentacles of justice even further into the community.

The second trend which Blomberg discusses concerns the increasing pervasiveness of surveillance techniques. Instead of the traditional 'report once a week' to a probation officer, the author documents the advent of the *reductio ad absurdum* of non-institutional surveillance. This alternative, currently practised in at least eight states, involves a comprehensive form of supervised custody known variously as 'home confinement', 'intensive supervision', 'community control', or 'house arrest'. Frequently coupled with electronic surveillance, it is hard to imagine a more pervasive way for the institutional discipline of prisons to be transferred to the community.

Taken together, these two trends foretell a disturbing future. As more and more individuals become subjected to increasingly pervasive and efficient community scrutiny, the term 'minimum security society' becomes an apt descriptor of our social world. In what must be perceived as restrained understatement, Blomberg suggests that '... these sorts of practices and their implications mandate a need for careful scrutiny ... that is sensitive to broader social control issues, given the dismal results of previous diversion and community corrections programmes'.

Chapter 12 presents 'The impact of deinstitutionalization on the criminal justice system: implications for understanding changing modes of social control', by Henry J. Steadman and Joseph P. Morrissey. This article, which is simultaneously illuminating and indicative of the obstacles facing empirical research, addresses a number of issues pertaining to the impact of psychiatric deinstitutionalization on the criminal justice system. The argument the authors address permeates both the mental health and criminal justice literatures. Briefly, it asserts that a process of transinstitutionalization has occurred, whereby individuals who formerly would have been treated in mental health facilities are now embraced by the arms of the law.

They cite contributions by themselves and others who argue compellingly that a two-phase deinstitutionalization process did indeed occur within the mental health establishment, although they also note that the phasing and pace of this process varied considerably among states. They also document a sharp increase in the use of state prison systems in the US.

Thus, we know:

1. Mental health populations in state facilities have dropped considerably in number; and
2. Criminal justice populations in state prison systems have risen considerably.

But are these merely two discrete social facts? Or is their coexistence *not* coincidental, but rather an indicator that individuals who *would* have been housed in one system have been shunted to the other? The bottom line for Steadman and Morrissey is that the two elements noted above do *not* provide evidence for transinstitutionalization, although this is not to say that a transinstitutional flow did not occur. Instead, the authors argue that the 'state mental health system' and the 'state prison system' are best construed as extreme ends of a mad-bad continuum, with a myriad of mental health 'buffer groups' (for example, community mental health centres, flop houses) and less monolithic criminal justice agencies (for example, community services, local gaols) lying in between. Thus, to the extent that there are transinstitutional shifts in populations that have occurred in the last two decades, it is unlikely that we will see the acute schizophrenic being shunted into a state prison, and hence looking at transinstitutional shifts from 'state hospital' to 'state prison' is an overly gross and insensitive measure. The more probable manifestation of transinstitutionalization, the authors argue, is that the relatively innocuous mentally ill will more frequently be arrested on relatively minor charges and detained in local gaols, instead of being committed for treatment. Thus, the more sensitive measure and more appropriate focus of the 'transinstitutionalization' process would involve scrutiny of the 'buffer groups' lying between the state hospital and prison systems, as well as longitudinal study of the decisions of 'front-line' personnel such as the police.

The authors deliberately leave questions about the extent of transinstitutionalization unanswered, since the mapping of myriad private, civic, state, and federal agencies — which must be co-ordinated in order to comprehensively assess the process — remains an enormous task still to be completed.

Although Steadman and Morrissey do not discuss it, such research poses a considerable dilemma for those who wish to study social control processes. Does one encourage the more efficient tracking of individuals through the amoebic mad-bad social control system to allow the realization of empirical goals, and thereby exacerbate opportunities for social control? Or does one opt for the minimization of tracking and control mechanisms, but in so doing necessarily thwart opportunities for comprehensive and unambiguous assessment? It is a classic example of how the goals of researchers interested in social theory and the goals of technocrats who wish to maximize the power of the state are served by the same means.

In Chapter 13, Raymond J. Michalowski and Michael A. Pearson present 'Crime, fiscal crisis and decarceration: financing corrections at the state level'. The simplicity of Michalowski and Pearson's title masks considerable complexity in the task they have set for themselves and the data with which they deal, in much the same way as (the authors argue) analysis of national aggregate data may mask considerable variability at the state level. Utilizing data from each of the 50 states for 1970 and 1980, the authors attempt to assess the degree to which decarceration has occurred, and they investigate parallels between this process and changes in rates of crime and state funding for correctional programmes. At the heart of their analysis is a desire to both scrutinize and go beyond the 'fiscal crisis' explanation of decarceration advanced by Scull (1977).

The authors follow a labyrinth of data to reveal that decarceration shows only a meek incarnation, and that the 'fiscal crisis' explanation of carceral trends falters appreciably. In the criminal justice domain, the authors note that although every state held a higher proportion of its population in prison in 1980 than a decade earlier, the rate of increase in all but four states was lower than the rate of growth in crime. Citing this as evidence of 'relative decarceration' (since the devotion of greater amounts of funds to incarcerate greater numbers of prisoners can hardly be called decarceration) Michalowski and Pearson go on to note that at the state level many corrections budgets included substantially greater proportions of funds for non-institutional programmes in 1980 than in 1970. They caution, however, that the impressiveness of these percentage increases was due largely to modest increases from small base levels. In sum, the decarceration thesis receives only weak affirmation from their data.

In the case of the fiscal crisis explanation of decarceration, the most important issue to address is the manner in which 'crisis' is conceptualized. In addition to showing that there was *real* growth in revenues in all 50 states between 1970 and 1980, Michalowski and Pearson also note that the proportion of state revenue devoted to corrections (both institutional and non-institutional) increased in 48 of the states. Despite these increases, however, the proportion of state budgets devoted to corrections in 1981 represented a trivial proportion of overall state expenditures. In the authors' words, '...given the low percentages of revenue involved, corrections cannot be seen as a significant contributor to fiscal crisis within the states. ... To the extent that states did experience a sense of fiscal crisis during the decade from 1970 to 1980, this was a product of changes in the nature of demands on state revenue rather than declines in the revenue base.'

Beyond their contribution to the decarceration and fiscal crisis debate, the authors conclude that there is considerable variability among states in their response to fiscal contingencies, such that future studies would do well to '... include more in-depth analysis of the individual states as well as studies of national aggregates'.

In Chapter 14 ('The reappearance of the "ideal factory": the entrepreneur and social control in the contemporary prison'), Robert P. Weiss comments on the growing trend toward privatization of government services, and discusses its various manifestations within the realm of corrections. Noting that complete privatization engendered political ambivalence in so far as it struck at the heart of the government's *raison d'etre* — the delivery of justice — Weiss describes prison industry as a comfortable reconciliation of state interests and the ideology of privatization. The Reagan administration policy involves contractual agreements between private entrepreneurs and prison administrators. The prison administration supplies the labour power and facilities, the private contractor organizes the labour and receives a profit for so doing. Appealing to conservatives because of the profit potential of cheap, disciplined labour, and to liberals because the institution remains under state control, an essentially utilitarian rationale underlies the development of private prison industry.

In discussing the implications of private prison industry, Weiss draws on historical material from both the United States and Europe (especially France), and adds his own observations of a project in Stillwater, Minnesota. In the US, prison industry appears to have undergone several cycles of legitimacy, from acceptable (in the nineteenth century) to illicit (by the 1920s and 1930s) and back to acceptability again in the 1970s and 1980s.

Taken collectively, the *experience* of prison industry in France and the United States suggests there is real cause for concern in the contemporary incarnation of the prison industry. To conservatives, it would seem to offer an opportunity to satisfy a trilogy of cherished ideals: the diminution of government, an expansion of the repressive apparatus, and profit potential. For liberals, there are prospective rehabilitative benefits coupled with the satisfaction of ostensibly retaining operative and punitive control. And yet Weiss portrays prison industry as a form of exploitation in which economic interests come to dominate policy and practice within the walls of the institution. In this context he discusses the profound impact of private prison industry on class and labour relations both within and outside the prison.

Weiss also suggests that the prison industry phenomenon has profound implications for theories of the state. Since corrections is located squarely within state territory, any intended or inadvertent abdication of state responsibility in this context is of considerable theoretical significance.

Chapter 15, entitled 'Mandatory supervision and the penal economy' (by R. S. Ratner), explores the penal history of Canadian carceral policies from the vantage point of an analysis grounded in political economy. In Canada, as in Britain and the US, recurring government spending deficits have recently been accompanied by the countervailing demand for more extensive and harsher use of imprisonment. Consequently, despite the familiar emergence of punitive policies apparently intent on diversion and deinstitutionalization, the Canadian prison inmate population has continued to grow. Furthermore, stringent parole policies and changes in sentencing legislation (such as the minimum 25-year sentence for first degree murder), accompanied by the abandonment of plans to construct a series of new penitentiaries, have all served to hasten the inevitable problems of a swelling prison population. In his discussion of Mandatory Supervision and penal economy, Ratner examines the utilization of various strategies for conditionally releasing prisoners as a revealing instance of the relationships among fiscal contingencies, demands for punitive severity and mechanisms of social control.

Following the presentation of a short history of the parole concept, Ratner examines the factors leading to the establishment of the Canadian National Parole Board in 1959, and the factors mobilizing subsequent legislative proposals to overhaul the mechanisms of the parole system.

Various changes to the system indicate the continual tension between demands to protect the public, and the desirability of inflicting the least harm on the inmate. Thus the introduction of Mandatory Supervision — the automatic parole of inmates after serving two-thirds of their sentences — reflected desires to limit the discretionary power of the parole board, and at the same time to increase power over inmates during their initial period back on the street. Initially the parole board's jurisdiction was over the inmate after he/she had been released. But fears that Mandatory Supervision might lead to the release of dangerous offenders were assuaged by the introduction of a 'gating' strategy whereby an inmate's parole was suspended immediately upon release.

In 1983 gating was declared to be illegal by the Supreme Court of Canada. At the same time opposition to Mandatory Supervision has been increasing on a variety of fronts fuelled mainly by calls for harsher retributive justice. Ratner argues, however, that because the main function of Mandatory Supervision is to facilitate the control of inmates (both inside and outside prison) rather than their reform, resistance to its abolition is well entrenched. Parole represents an important extension of carceral power. Moreover, since the only way of controlling inmate numbers is to manipulate either their influx or outflow, institutional imperatives favour various parole strategies.

In his final section, Ratner examines the structure of legislative reforms under consideration by the Canadian Federal Government in 1986, showing how the contingencies of prison management together with the principles of retributive justice and rehabilitation interact with the wider exigencies of capitalist political economy to mould penal policy. Taken as a whole, this chapter addresses parole supervision as part of the state's managerial arsenal for handling the dynamics of fiscal crisis via the deployment of social control techniques, as part of its wider role in providing solutions to the problems of surplus labour in a recessionary capitalist economy.

11 Criminal justice reform and social control: are we becoming a minimum security society?[1]

Thomas G. Blomberg

Introduction

In the late 1950s America's criminal justice system began implementation of community-based correctional alternatives for selected adult and juvenile offenders. During the initial stages of the community correctional movement, local institutions, half-way houses, residential centres, group homes and specialized probation services were promoted as alternatives to placing offenders in prisons and reformatories. A second phase of the community correctional movement in the late 1960s involved an explosion of diversion and deinstitutionalization programmes that were promoted as discrete alternatives to the formal criminal justice system. What underlay these transactions was the widely held belief that the criminal justice system had failed. In fact, the system was viewed as having produced more harm than good by stigmatizing offenders and subjecting them to damaging criminal associations, and thereby increasing instead of reducing crime.

Until the 1970s, literature on various community correctional programmes was largely descriptive, theoretical or exhortatory, and without meaningful empirical interests. Evaluations of these programmes (Hylton 1981) reported results that were uneven, contradictory and limited. In effect, evaluation studies of diversion and community correctional programmes were typically focused upon determining the recidivism results associated with these programmes, while other intended or unintended effects on offenders and impacts on the criminal justice system were ignored. These narrow evaluation criteria produced limited results and contributed to an incomplete understanding of the various programmes that comprised the community reform movement.

In the mid-1970s, an expanded approach was taken in a number of evaluation studies of diversion and other community correctional programmes. While the findings from these more recent studies have not been conclusive, several significant trends have emerged. For example, it has been demonstrated (Austin and Krisberg 1981; Hylton

1982) that various reform programmes produce net-widening, by extending instead of simply redistributing the overall population subject to some form of criminal justice control. Further, the programmes have been shown (cf. Cohen 1985a) to produce a number of additional adverse consequences that include increased behaviour difficulties for programme clients, unwanted family intrusions and family dissolutions resulting from several of the programmes' family intervention practices, and accelerated penetration into the formal criminal justice system of those unable to comply with certain mandatory programme requirements.

These important trends suggest several significant questions. Two such questions concern what the American criminal justice system is and what its purposes are. A third question concerns the criteria used to determine when the criminal justice system can legitimately intervene and take control over the lives of citizens and their families. Moreover, and underlying these questions, is a larger issue concerning the changing character of America's criminal justice system, given its expanding jurisdiction and accelerated social control functions. These trends should lead us to question whether we are indeed approaching Orwell's *1984* or what has been referred to by Messinger (1983, personal communication) as the 'coming of a minimum security society' in which ever-increasing state intervention and control can be anticipated. This chapter assesses these trends to demonstrate the pressing need to control an increasingly decentralized and coercive criminal justice network that appears to be in the process of shifting its focus from total institutions into the larger civil community.

Community programmes: widening the client net

The tendency of diversion and other community programmes to widen the control net produces results that are increasing rather than reducing the number of individuals coming into contact with the formal criminal justice system. For example, it has been documented that diversion practices are being applied largely to individuals and families previously not subject to contact with the criminal justice system. The literature assessing the net-widening practices associated with diversion has grown considerably in recent years. Representative of this literature are the studies on juvenile diversion by Blomberg (1977a), the California Department of Youth Authority (1976), Klein (1974, 1975, 1979), Mattingly and Katkin (1975), Sarri (1979), Vorenberg and Vorenberg (1973), and those on adult diversion by Mullen (1975), Petersen (1973), Seitz *et al.* (1978), and Zimring (1974).[2]

The California Youth Authority study evaluated fifteen juvenile diversion projects to determine the extent to which the programmes did divert clients from the juvenile system. The findings indicated that, on average, less than 50 per cent of the programmes' clients were, in fact, diversion clients; that is, those who would have received justice system processing if not for the availability of diversion programmes. The majority of the programmes' clients were termed 'prevention clients'; that is, youth *not* subject to imminent justice system processing, but who were provided diversion services to prevent their *future* delinquency. Similarly, Mullen concluded from a comparative assessment of adult pre-trial diversion programmes that 'in the absence of diversion alternatives, few project participants would have faced jail sentences' (1975, p.24). Further, in a case study of a juvenile diversion programme, Blomberg (1977a) documented a 32 per cent increase in the total number of youth receiving some form of formal justice or diversion service during the programme's first year of operation. This significant numerical increase was attributed to the 'whole-family' treatment focus of the programme which required diverted youth, their siblings, and their parents to participate.

Net-widening reflects, in part, the failure to identify target client populations for community programmes, that is, a specification of the clients who would have been inserted into the criminal justice system prior to the availability of the alternative programmes (Klein 1979). Additionally, the conceptual, definitional and operational ambiguities of diversion and other community programme strategies have facilitated the emergence of their supplemental function — prevention — instead of acting as an alternative. This emergence has been reinforced by the commonly-held belief among various criminal justice personnel that many of the clients who were released prior to the advent of community-based programming were nonetheless in need of treatment or control that was not possible without these additional programmes.

Criminal justice practitioners commonly feel that first or minor offenders should be referred to treatment-control agencies. Early identification and subsequent referral is felt essential for effective crime control. Yet such widely-held notions have *impeded* the implementation of community corrections as envisioned by the logic of diversion, and have contributed to the transformation of various community programmes into prevention programmes which receive the bulk of their clients from parents, schools, and welfare agencies instead of the criminal justice system (Dennison, Humphries and Wilson 1975; McAleenan *et al.* 1977; Statsky 1974). Other researchers have pointed out that, in some areas, diversion programme clients tend to be middle class and without prior records or serious instant offences that would warrant justice system processing. This results in diversion not being available to those of lower-class backgrounds with a prior record and more serious instant offence (Carter 1978a,b; Hackler 1976; Klein 1979; Pitchess 1976).

Adverse effects on clients attributed to community programmes

In the last several years, a number of researchers have reported that clients were adversely affected by their contact with and participation in diversion and other community programmes. These adverse effects have included increased jeopardy for clients and their families, unwanted family intrusions, family dissolutions, accelerated penetration into the criminal justice system, increased behavioural difficulties, and even the imposition of criminal sanctions on parents found unfit. For example, Klein (1975) and Blomberg (1977a) reported that mere contact with diversion programmes can increase individual and family difficulties purely because of increased visibility of clients to programme personnel, rather than because of increased rates of misconduct or family difficulties. A comparative study of adult community corrections by Mullen (1975) revealed that clients who were unable to meet a programme's requirements were likely to be subjected to an informal double jeopardy in which they were returned for prosecution on their original charge, prosecuted vigorously, convicted, and then placed on probation supervision. Mullen argues that most of the clients handled in this manner would not have been subject to formal criminal justice processing if not for the net-widening accompanying the community programme's operations. Similar findings in juvenile programmes have been documented in relation to youth whose families were not amenable to 'whole-family' intervention methods. Specifically, Blomberg found that when families were unable or unwilling to co-operate with diversion personnel in the 'whole-family' intervention process, the children were frequently referred to the juvenile court for out-of-home placement (1977a, pp. 277–280). The family's heightened visibility also resulted in accelerated court penetration of the siblings of clients of diversion programmes who would not have come to the attention of the justice system at all had it not been for the family focus practised in diversion.

The potential of community programmes to create or intensify subsequent behaviour difficulties is supported by Klein's (1975) study of the relationship between rearrest and alternative dispositions for young offenders. Klein shows that diversion of youth who might otherwise have been released outright may well have increased the likelihood of their subsequent rearrest because of their increased visibility to 'treators' and the police rather than because of increased rates of misconduct. Additionally, in a study of an Oregon diversion programme, Polk (1981) documented a case in which an investigation into family background led the programme staff to arrange both the direct placement of a referred youth and several siblings into institutions for delinquent tendencies, and the arrest of the mother and father for moral neglect.

But how is it that a major reform movement has been implemented in ways that directly contradict its stated rationale? This question can be approached from a perspective in which primary concern is given to the *organizational character* of the criminal justice system. Several such characteristics can be identified. These include the system's operation with conflicting treatment and punishment goals, ambiguous technology related to these conflicting goals, ever-present conditions of resource scarcity, and general conditions of operational uncertainty. Operational uncertainty is stimulated and reinforced by frequent upheavals and changes in the wider social, political and economic environment, and results in the criminal justice system assuming an opportunistic character that facilitates a readiness to implement reform programmes for their supplemental power rather than as alternatives. This, in turn, shapes the system's social control capacity.

Given the criminal justice system's organizational character, the transformation of community correctional reform from a liberating concept to a mechanism for accelerated social control has been predictable. Moreover, because of the continuing societal concern about crime and demands for redirecting the criminal justice system's energies, the past experiences with community corrections provide a compelling reason to be concerned about current and future criminal justice reform efforts.

How extensive is net-widening?

The explosion of diversion and community programmes in the United States continues today with an increasing variety of strategies that includes individual counselling, family counselling, chemical abuse therapy, arbitration, restitution, and others. Yet the proliferation of these strategies has not resulted in a decline in the number, capacity, or population of prisons. In contrast, the Bureau of Justice Statistics reported in 1983 that, despite a stable base population in the United States, prisons experienced their largest population increase in the country's history. More than 43000 inmates were added to federal and state prisons. The states of Alabama, Alaska, Utah, Hawaii, Washington, Idaho, North Dakota, Maryland and Indiana increased their prison population by 20 per cent. The number of states under a federal court order to reduce overcrowding rose from 28 to 31, and the number involved in lawsuits concerning prison overcrowding increased from 32 to 37. When consideration is given to the approximately 150000 adults held in local jails and 60000 youths in state and local facilities, the cumulative figure reveals that approximately 2 million are locked up or under official supervision on any given day in the United States.

Current projections of prison populations indicate substantial increases in the very near future. In Texas, for example, the prison population is now 35 000; projections suggest that the figure will jump to 50 000 during the next several years. The current prison population in California is approximately 40 000; projections indicate the figure could increase to 59 000 by 1988 (Bureau of Justice Statistics 1984).

The overall picture of future prison overcrowding becomes even more bleak when consideration is given to the demise of parole and the emergence of mandatory, flat, or determinate sentencing. Historically, according to Berk *et al.* (1983), parole has provided an equilibrating mechanism that has in some measure contributed to the stabilization of prison populations either by checking growth while prison inmate capacities were being enlarged or by permitting growth to take advantage of unused capacity. Determinate sentencing efforts to date have not provided such a regulating influence on prison admissions. As a result, several different responses have emerged in relation to the current prison overcrowding crisis.

One response to overcrowding has been the 'emergency' construction of new prisons across the United States. Past experience demonstrates, however, that the construction of new prisons is succeeded by growth in the number of inmates perceived as suitable for the newly available carceral space. This patterned response has been termed 'the programme magnet phenomenon' and refers to the capacity of newly available prisons to produce a form of institutional net-widening whereby an increased proportion of the population becomes subject to imprisonment. Because of the significant expenditures involved in their construction, however, many states are reluctant to build new prisons.

Another strategy that has emerged in several states (including California, Florida, Georgia, New Jersey, New York, North Carolina, Ohio and Texas) is 'home confinement', otherwise termed intensive supervision, community control or house arrest. Florida's programme is aimed at diverting selected adult offenders from prison by providing intensive supervized custody in the community on a daily basis. This includes evening and weekend surveillance by supervising officers who have a maximum caseload of twenty. The basic conditions prescribed for home confinement (State of Florida, 1983) include the following:

1. Report to a home confinement officer at least four times a week, or, if unemployed full-time, report daily;
2. Perform at least 140 hours of public service work, without pay, as directed by the home confinement officer;
3. Remain confined to residence except for approved employment, public service work, or other special activities specifically approved by the community control officer;
4. Make specific monthly restitution payments for a specified total amount;

5. Submit to, and pay for, urinalysis, breathalyser or blood specimen tests at any time as requested by the home confinement officer or other professional staff to determine possible use of alcohol, drugs or other controlled substances;
6. Maintain an hourly account of all activities on a daily log which, upon request, is submitted to the home confinement officer;
7. Participate in self-improvement programmes as determined by the court or home confinement officer;
8. Promptly and truthfully answer all enquiries of the court or home confinement officer, and allow the officer to visit home and employer;
9. For sex offenders, the court requires, as a special condition of home confinement, the release of treatment information to the home confinement officer or the court.

Four categories of offenders are eligible for home confinement:

1. Probation violators who are charged with either technical or misdemeanour violations;
2. Parole violators charged with technical or misdemeanour violations;
3. Those found guilty of non-forcible felonies; and
4. 'Others' who are deemed by a sentencing judge to be appropriate for the programme.

The 'others' category was included at the request of judges who wished to retain their sentencing discretion.

Following an offender's placement in home confinement, an assessment is conducted to establish a plan with individualized objectives. The plan includes specific sanctions and restraints to be imposed on the offender, target dates for initiating and completing the requirements of the programme, and other ancillary requirements such as participation in self-improvement programmes. The home confinement officer is to provide 'firm guidance' and supervision throughout the implementation of the plan. The plan is to be recorded and signed by the home confinement officer and the client, and kept in the case file.

Home confinement can be terminated by a court order prior to the maximum term of two years that can be spent in the programme. If it is determined that a client has made satisfactory adjustment and completed the requirements of the plan prior to expiration of the court-ordered term, the court can be petitioned to reduce the client to regular probation supervision. Alternatively, in the case of a parole violator on home confinement, the Parole Commission can be petitioned to reduce the client to regular parole supervision. It is also possible to petition the court for early termination of home confinement without further supervision in those cases where it is determined that sufficient adjustment has been made and all programme requirements fulfilled.

While the results of home confinement remain to be determined, several implications can be extrapolated from the experience of previous diversion and related community corrections programmes. Specifically, it appears that home confinement together with various diversion and community corrections programmes may well provide the programmatic means for extending the institutional discipline of prisons into the larger civil community. A number of local jurisdictions and states are now in the process of using electronic technology to monitor home confinement clients in order to increase surveillance effectiveness. This involves placing an electronic device on the arm of the client, which sets off an alarm if the client physically exceeds a prescribed area beyond a telephone monitor located in the residence. Clearly, these sorts of practices and their implications mandate a need for careful scrutiny of home confinement that is sensitive to broader social control issues, given the dismal results of previous diversion and community corrections programmes.

Future criminal justice reforms and social control

In reflecting on recent criminal justice reforms and associated social control trends, Messinger (1983, personal communication) has argued that the United States is experiencing the coming of a 'minimum security society' in which an ever-increasing proportion of the base population will become subject to some form of state control despite a downward trend in the number of serious crimes reported. Indeed, it seems evident that net-widening will accelerate in the future.

While uneven, the history of United States criminal justice reform has reflected a cyclical emphasis upon the initiation of new philosophies and associated policies that were often promoted with untempered optimism and oversold promises. The patterned failure of the policies to fulfil their promises typically led to confusion, cynicism, and subsequent calls for something different based upon still newer reform policies and optimism. Currently, for example, broad liberal support for community corrections has declined, with alternative policies calling for an 'end to the permissive society' now in ascent. These alternative recommendations and policies have included reinstitution of the death penalty, mandatory jail sentences for drunk drivers, longer mandatory prison sentences, restitution, and referral of many youth offenders to adult criminal courts. Parents across the United States are joining various self-help programmes such as 'Toughlove', which emphasize firmness and discipline in dealing with problem children. Many community groups have organized themselves to wage their own war on drugs, crime and other local problems. Underlying these various 'get tough' strategies, to use Boorstin's (1983) term, appears to be a new 'illusion of knowledge' that increased punishment and more penetrating social control policies can check, deter and even eradicate crime. However, as history has documented, simplistic solutions to problems as complex as crime not only fail to fulfil their lofty objectives but often result in a series of unanticipated and unwanted consequences.

While it is of questionable value to speculate about future criminal justice policy, the increasing 'fiscal crisis' and heightened public demand for criminal justice accountability could contribute to a growing receptivity for informed policy change. Consequently, the role of responsible research could become more prominent in informing criminal justice policy. While it should not be anticipated that subsequent criminal justice reforms will be guided by an overriding concern for research results, it seems that such work could become more integral to criminal justice policy-making. Tempered policy — informed by research that specifies the most appropriate measures for alleviating particular social problems and forms of human suffering, while maintaining individual rights and freedoms — is elusive but not beyond grasp.

12 The impact of deinstitutionalization on the criminal justice system: implications for understanding changing modes of social control[1]

Henry J. Steadman
Joseph P. Morrissey

Introduction

The purpose of this chapter is to clarify a number of conceptual and empirical issues concerning the impact of deinstitutionalization on the criminal justice system. Our chapter will be organized into three major parts. *First*, we will review current beliefs and evidence about the criminalization of the mentally ill. This section will review the research on what seems to have become a pervasive theme in both the psychiatric and criminal justice literature that many more mentally ill persons are now found in the criminal justice system as result of reductions in the number of beds available in state mental hospitals. *Second*, we will highlight the structure and timetable of deinstitutionalization as it occurred in the United States. This is essential since, as Morrissey (1982) and Bachrach (1978) have noted, deinstitutionalization was a multifaceted process whose pace varied widely from one state to another. Similar regional variations have occurred in Canada (Richman and Harris 1983) and throughout Western Europe (Goldman, Morrissey and Bachrach 1983; WHO 1980). In focusing on the United States experience, a major facet of our analysis will be an identification of the range of organizations in the mental health and social welfare systems that were involved in deinstitutionalization and how these organizations may have reverberated on the criminal justice system. *Third*, we have some recent data on interactions between mental health and criminal justice systems in six states in the US that were among those most actively involved in deinstitutionalization. These data were gathered for two points in time:

1. Before significant deinstitutionalization had occurred (1968); and
2. Ten years later (1978), after major changes had taken place.

Our basic argument here is that the core process affecting state hospital populations is more aptly described as *trans*institutionalization (patient flow from one institutional setting to another) rather than as *de*institutionalization (patient flow from institutional to noninstitutional settings). As will become clear later in this chapter transinstitutionalization has been a part of the institutional care of the mentally ill for several hundred years. Its rediscovery in the 1970s is not the new phenomenon that many observers would have us believe. Indeed, as will be detailed later, the events of the 1970s can be seen as the reversal of a transinstitutionalization process which began with the demise of the alms-house in the early part of this century. New institutional settings are involved, but the basic processes and outcomes appear to be similar.

The specific question we want to address in this chapter, however, deals with one type of transinstitutionalization, namely the flow of former patients from state mental hospitals to the criminal justice system. This issue is most often framed in terms of the 'criminalization' of the mentally ill, and it is to the research on this topic that we now turn.

Criminalization of the mentally ill

The first major critique of deinstitutionalization in the United States, as it pertained to the criminal justice system, appeared in 1972 with Abramson's observations on events in California, the first state aggressively to deinstitutionalize its public mental hospitals. Abramson argued persuasively that a 'criminalization of mentally disordered behaviour' had occurred. His claim was that relatively minor, nuisance behaviours by ex-mental patients were resulting in criminal charges (disorderly conduct, harassment, and the like) in order to confine persons who were being disruptive as a result of the mental disorder, but for whom no state hospital beds were available.

While Abramson's views were not universally shared (Monahan 1973), they did represent a pervasive belief among both psychiatrists and correctional administrators. These notions were not formulated in macro-concepts such as changing modes of social control, but rather on the convictions that:

1. People in need of public mental health care could not access it; and
2. The job of the correctional administrator had become much more complicated through an influx of mentally ill persons who were highly disruptive in correctional settings (Allodi *et al.* 1977).

The notions articulated by Abramson took on greater currency during the 1970s, despite a dearth of empirical data to support them. Stelovitch (1979), Whitmer (1980), Bonovitz and Bonovitz (1981) and Lamb (1982) among others, agreed that more deviant behaviour was occurring in the community as a result of mentally ill persons being at large, and that the only available community response was arrest and detention in the criminal justice system. This viewpoint was recently espoused in *Psychiatric News*:

> Diminished access to mental hospitals is causing more mentally ill persons to be jailed. The diversion of mentally ill offenders to hospitals is no longer taking place, while one suspects that the diversion of mentally ill persons to jails and prisons is occurring with increasing frequency. (1983, p.7)

Thus, there are perceived to be two primary phenomena leading to the criminalization of the mentally ill. On the one hand, former opportunities for the transfer into state mental hospitals of disruptive, mentally disordered correctional inmates have radically diminished in response to more restrictive admission policies and fewer available beds. On the other hand, human input into the criminal justice system is seen to include more persons who are mentally ill and who formerly would have been detained in state mental hospitals. Thus, the system pressures are increased both from a new clientele coming in and from an old clientele staying.

Despite strong unanimity in the literature, there are no empirical data to support these observations about the impact of state hospital deinstitutionalization on the criminal justice system. In fact, the only published data on changes in the prevalence of mental disorder among inmates is the indirect evidence offered by Steadman and Ribner (1980). Using the proportion of inmates with prior state mental hospitalizations as their measure of mental disorder, they examined records for all persons released from New York State prisons to Albany county in 1968 and 1975, and for all inmates released from the Albany County Jail in the same two years. Among the prison inmates the proportion with state mental histories actually decreased from 19 per cent in 1968 to 13 per cent in 1975. The proportion of local jail inmates increased somewhat from 9 per cent in 1968 to 12 per cent in 1975. In these limited data there was thus little support for the 'criminalization' hypothesis.

Beyond this one study, no research has been reported on the prevalence or incidence of mental disorders in the same correctional facility or same jurisdiction before *and* after deinstitutionalization. This, however, is the only type of research design appropriate for testing the 'criminalization' thesis. In the absence of data it is equally plausible to argue that it is the perceptions of correctional and mental health staff that have changed rather than the composition of their subjects. That is, rates of mentally disordered, disruptive behaviours in correctional settings may have remained stable, but now such conduct may be seen to require intervention by the jail psychologist, rather than the prior, typical response of relegating the inmate to the 'hole'. Clearly issues related to the impact of mental health system changes on the criminal justice system over the past quarter of a century are more problematic than much of the literature on this topic might suggest.

Why this should be a significant issue in the United States is clear from the statistics on the rise of prison populations. From 1955 to 1968, the number of inmates in state and federal prisons remained almost constant with 185780 in 1955 and 187914 in 1968. However, from 1968 to 1981 there was an increase of 90 per cent from 187914 to 353167 inmates. This increase was not just the result of a larger population base. In fact, the rate of incarceration jumped from 94 per 100000 population in 1968 to 153 per 100000 in 1981 (Bureau of Justice Statistics 1982).

In addition to the programmatic and policy perspectives that have been discussed here, there is a second major stream of commentaries on these criminal-justice–mental-health issues. The second approach deals with these concerns from a macro-level sociological stance, and tends to be more systemic, empirical, longitudinal, and reliant on social indicators. But this alternative approach remains poorly developed. The seminal macro-level work on criminal-justice–mental-health interactions is Penrose's (1939) study of relationships between the size of prison and mental health populations. He postulated that, 'as a general rule, if the prison services are extensive, the asylum population is relatively small and the reverse also tends to be true' (1939, p.3). From an analysis based on data from eighteen European countries, supplemented by information from six non-European nations, Penrose concluded that his hypothesis was supported. However, his conclusions are stated in terms of social development patterns whereby:

> ... the services which develop for the control of the socially undesirable members of the community evolve progressively in a certain way. It may be that the first attempt at controlling these people is to provide prisons with a view to punishing them in the hope that they will ultimately be made into good citizens. Thus, the community first evolves a system of jurisdiction supported by prisons; later on, the medico-psychological attitude towards crime develops and the people who, in earlier epochs, would have been confined in prison become subjects for medical investigation and treatment. (Penrose 1939, p.15)

It was not until 1973 that a subsequent analysis of Penrose's thesis was reported. Biles and Mulligan (1973) examined data from six Australian states which produced a zero order correlation of –0.78 between the average 1968 prison census and the number of mental hospital beds. They concluded that:

> ...the data are consistent with the view, also canvassed by Penrose, that the relative use of mental hospitals or prisons for the segregation of deviants

> reflects different styles of administration. In practice, either the police or the courts may make the decision that an offender is mad rather than bad and initiate his admission to a mental health hospital rather than to a prison. And, of course, this decision is facilitated if adequate mental hospital accommodation is available. Thus one way of reducing the numbers of people in prison, though by no means the only way, is to ensure that the mental hospital mode of disposition is clearly seen to be a viable alternative. (Biles and Mulligan 1973, p.279)

The most recent work in this tradition is reported by Grabosky (1980) who analysed United States data from 1930 to 1970. Running bivariate analyses both for total US prisoners and mental patients over time, and for 1967, 1970 and 1973 data for all 50 states, Grabosky found in all time series analyses that there was a *positive* correlation between the sizes of prison and mental hospital populations.

Proceeding to more sophisticated analyses, Grabosky next developed multiple regression models to predict the size of inmate populations in state and local prisons for 1970. Using indicators for minority population, population changes between 1960–1970, crime rate, income, state expenditures, population aged 15–44, and urbanization, he was able to explain 73 per cent of the variance in prison population. The number of mental hospital patients was then forced into this regression equation as the first explanatory variable. The impact of mental hospital population size was negligible. The relative influence of the other independent variables remained unchanged and the explained variance of the equation was not significantly enhanced. Taking this approach to the 1930–1970 time series data produced the same basic result. He concluded, 'Simply stated, the operation of contemporary American penal systems appears generally uninfluenced by the use of custodial alternatives.... [M]uch of the positive covariation can be interpreted as reflecting similar responses to such general factors as budgetary constraint' (Grabosky 1980, pp.69, 65).

Grabosky's approach, using United States social indicators and more sophisticated statistical analyses, produced results quite inconsistent with the earlier work of Penrose, and of Biles and Mulligan. Similarly, it conflicts with the administrative and clinical views that have emerged in the psychiatric and correctional literature in the past decade. While Grabosky's research antedates the major institutional developments of the 1970s and 1980s, it clearly points to the need for empirical research on this subject.

In some ways, Grabosky's finding of co-variation between prison and mental hospital populations, and his attribution of this effect to their mutual sensitivity to fiscal considerations, is consonant with Scull's (1977) conceptualization of decarceration. Scull argues that, as a result of economic practices and ideologies, both the prison and the mental health populations in the United States were steadily decreasing from the 1950s through the early 1970s. While Scull's analysis is much more historically grounded than Grabosky's 'social indicators' approach, their interpretations are quite consistent.

Our attempt to more fully address these same questions involves two distinct approaches. The first is to specify more carefully the actual dynamics of deinstitutionalization in the United States from the mid-1960s through the early 1980s. It will become apparent that inadequate specification of these dynamics has led to much of the ambiguity present in the literature. Second, we will provide some recent data on prison-mental-health populations in six American states from 1968 to 1978.

State mental hospital deinstitutionalization

Although the term 'deinstitutionalization' came into popular use only in the mid-1970s (Bachrach 1976), the phenomenon of shifting the dependent and confined mentally ill from one institutional setting to another has a long history. Perhaps the best known evidence of this process is Foucault's (1965) observation that madmen first came under medical auspices in the sixteenth and seventeenth centuries with the decline of leprosy. The lazar houses or leprosariums which dotted medieval Europe were gradually converted to 'hospitals' for the care of poor vagabonds, criminals and madmen. Another example comes from the mid-nineteenth century when state asylums began to proliferate in the United States. Due to the extensive lobbying efforts of Dorothea Dix and other social reformers, many of the patients admitted to these asylums were insane paupers who had been confined in local jails and workhouses (Grob 1973; Rothman 1971). Hence, direct political activism and a changing economic system shifted the mentally ill from the criminal justice and generic social welfare system into a system of care specifically for them. But perhaps the most dramatic evidence for institutional succession comes from Grob's (1983) recent analyses of the explosive growth in American mental hospitals in the late nineteenth and early twentieth centuries.

Throughout the nineteenth century, chronic or incurable cases and the aged senile in the United States were sent to county and municipal alms-houses; state asylums had concentrated largely on acute cases whose institutionalizations rarely exceeded one year (Grob 1982). Beginning in the 1890s, state authorities began to assume full financial responsibility for the care and confinement of the mentally ill. This policy was designed to remedy the quality of care deficiencies associated with locally-operated asylums and to absolve these governmental units of the maintenance costs of asylum operation.

As Grob points out, local officials soon began to recognize the advantages in redefining insanity to include aged and senile individuals. By transferring such cases from local alms-houses to the state hospitals, fiscal burdens associated with their care were shifted from local to state auspices. The result was a dramatic transformation in the population size and case mix of state mental hospitals. Between 1903 and 1950, the number of patients in state mental hospitals increased by 240 per cent (from 150000 to 512500), a rate of growth nearly twice that of the United States population as a whole. Much of this growth was associated with the admission of senile patients as well as individuals suffering from a variety of diseases and conditions which required custodial care on a lifelong basis rather than treatment by specific psychiatric therapies.

As state hospitals became the general-purpose solution for the social welfare burdens of American society, the alms-houses declined in significance as a public institution and all but disappeared by the mid-twentieth century. As Grob notes, '[W]hat occurred, in effect, was not a deinstitutionalization movement, but rather a transfer of patients between different types of institutions. The shift moreover, was less a function of medical or humanitarian concerns than a consequence of financial considerations' (1982, p. 181).

These events provide an essential historical context for understanding the processes and outcomes of the recent state mental hospital deinstitutionalization movement in the United States. A central thrust of this reform movement was the effort to dismantle and close state mental hospitals and to relocate their clientele in a new network of community-based mental health services (Bachrach 1976, 1978). This dual objective was made plausible by the discovery and widespread use of psychotropic drugs in the mid-1950s, by changes in psychosocial treatment approaches, and by the growing availability of nursing homes and general hospital-based psychiatric services. The near-term accomplishments of this movement seemingly rival the success claims advanced for the early asylums. Between 1955 and 1980, for example, the resident population of state mental hospitals in the United States was reduced by more than 75 per cent, or by approximately 420000 occupied beds; and since the mid-1960s, over 700 community mental health centres (CMHCs), which serve catchment areas representing 50 per cent of the nation's population, have been created with the massive financial support of the federal government.

Upon closer examination, however, there is clear and convincing evidence that the 'bold new approach' embodied in this reform has yet to supplant the state hospitals, and that it may even have created as many problems as it attempted to solve (Bassuk and Gerson 1978; Gruenberg and Archer 1979; Rose 1979). In a number of respects, therefore, the deinstitutionalization movement has followed the cyclical course of earlier mental hospital reforms (Morrissey *et al.* 1980) and its aftermath has set the stage for a new round of planning and programme development in an effort to remedy the failings of public mental health policy during the past decade.

While there are a number of parallels in the processes and outcomes of deinstitutionalization in various parts of the United States, there are substantial differences among states as well. The similarities reside in the two distinct phases of this reform movement: first, its initiation and acceleration by ideological, legal and fiscal interests, and second, the enduring functions of state mental hospitals in the mental health system. The differences between states, in contrast, reside in the *timing and pace of change* in each phase; the *size-composition of the residual populations* still served by these institutions; and the *fiscal-administrative structures* for the delivery of public mental health services in each state. As the evidence for these trends has been described in detail elsewhere (Morrissey 1982), the current discussion will touch upon only the highlights with reference to three states that have been in the forefront of the deinstitutionalization movement in the United States — California, New York, and Massachusetts.

The first consistency is that deinstitutionalization occurred everywhere in two distinct phases. In the first phase, policies governing state mental hospitals were based on a benign form of hospital phase-down that led to the '*opening of the back doors*' of these institutions for the release of long-stay patients and for the early discharge of newly admitted patients. This phase was marked by a gradual census decline, an increased rate of both first and readmissions, and a declining length of stay. As long as 'revolving door' patients could be easily returned to these hospitals (by families, local agencies, or police authorities), deinstitutionalization was not a major political issue. State hospitals provided back-up for the fledgling community mental health programmes which were able, in turn, to concentrate on the development of services for less disabled clients residing in the community.

In the second phase, a newer strategy of '*closing the front doors*' of state hospitals was instituted. Concurrently, the older policy was transformed into a radical programme of rapid census run-downs. This period was marked by dramatic decreases in the resident patient population, a decline in admissions, and brief lengths of stay only for crisis stabilization purposes. The real impacts of these policies, however, were felt in the local communities which were unprepared for the influx of thousands of former patients. Deinstitutionalized patients encountered the hostility and rejection of the general public and the reluctance of community mental health and welfare agencies to assume responsibility for their care. Tens of thousands ended up in rooming houses, foster homes, nursing homes, run-down hotels, and on the streets. The transfer of patients from the 'back wards to the back alleys' (Aviram and Segal 1973) led to widespread concerns that deinstitutionalization was a disaster and that the states had abdicated their responsibilities to the mentally ill (Brown 1979; Gruenberg and Archer 1979; Rose 1979).

Nationally, the demarcation point between these two phases in the United States can be located in the late 1960s. From 1955 (when the state hospital census reached its peak of 558 922 patients) to 1965, the total census reduction amounted to only 15 per cent, or about 1.5 per cent per year. Over the next 15 years (1965–1980) the total census reduction jumped to 71 per cent, or an average decline of about 5 per cent per year. The admissions rate which had been steadily rising since 1955 started a downward trend following 1970. The rate of both census and admission declines began to stabilize in the late 1970s and there now is evidence from several states that state hospital use is on the increase.

These national trends, however, mask important differences in the phasing and pace of deinstitutionalization at the state level (Morrissey 1982). California, for example, moved into the second or radical phase of deinstitutionalization in the early 1960s. It was the first state to reduce sharply its resident patient census. Between 1960 and 1965, while New York and Massachusetts experienced gradual census reductions of 3 to 4 per cent, California reduced its state mental hospital census by 18 per cent. By 1970 the census reduction amounted to 58 per cent, and by 1975 it totalled 82 per cent.

New York did not enter phase two until 1968. In the next 5 years (1968–1973) its patient census was reduced by 39 per cent and by 1975 it was down by 52 per cent. Massachusetts was a latecomer to phase two in 1971, but it quickly outpaced the other two states. By 1975 the state hospital census in Massachusetts was reduced by 63 per cent in just 4 years. By 1980, the national rate of census reduction since 1955 amounted to 75 per cent; in Massachusetts it was 91 per cent, in California 86 per cent, and in New York 73 per cent.

The factors that precipitated the shift from benign to radical phases of deinstitutionalization were common to each state, but they coalesced at different times. The precipitating factors were a combination of civil libertarian reforms in commitment statutes, fiscal incentives for community placement, and administrative policies governing state hospital use. For California, the key events were the initiation of Geriatric Screening Programmes in 1963 to reduce admissions and to locate alternative placements for the senile aged; the creation of a public-assistance programme for the mentally handicapped in 1963 which was considerably expanded with the Medicare and Medicaid amendments to the federal Social Security Act in 1965; and the enactment of the Lanterman-Petris-Short (LPS) legislation which became effective in 1969. The LPS legislation extensively revised the criteria and procedures for involuntary hospitalization and transferred responsibility for all clients in the mental health system to local communities (Bardach 1972; Jacobson 1973).

New York, for example, experienced major civil libertarian reform in commitment laws concurrent with the federal Medicaid-Medicare entitlements in the Social Security Act of 1965 (Morrissey 1982). The real impetus for rapid census decline however did not occur until 1968 when the Department of Mental Hygiene announced a new policy concerning the screening and limitation of geriatric admissions to state mental hospitals. As in California, this policy had the effect of accelerating the pace of census reduction. With more effective control over the 'front door' of state hospitals, departmental authorities began to shift the fiscal burden of care for elderly and long-stay patients from the state to the federal level via federal entitlement programmes. This policy led to the rapid growth of the nursing home and board-and-care industries in New York. Massachusetts followed a similar course with the enactment of revised commitment statutes (which became effective in 1971), restrictive admission policies, and accelerated use of federal entitlements to support discharged patients in nursing homes and alternative community residences.

All of this in no way implies that state mental hospitals have been supplanted in the US mental health service system. Nationally there were approximately 138000 resident patients and 330000 admissions (mostly 'revolving door' patients) in 1980. The enduring functions of state mental hospitals involve custody, social control and treatment for many of the most disturbed and troublesome patients (Morrissey *et al.* 1980). The scope and mix of these residual functions vary considerably across states. Moreover, as of the late 1970s, the large majority of admissions to state hospitals in New York (63 per cent), Massachusetts (68 per cent) and California (78 per cent) consisted of involuntary patients considered 'dangerous' to themselves and/or others.

Throughout the past twenty years, the United States mental health service system has expanded and become much more diversified with the explosive growth of general hospital psychiatric units, CMHCs, and psychiatric out-patient programmes of various sorts. However, most of this expansion has concentrated on newer, formerly unserved, community populations. Thousands of former state hospital patients were largely untouched by these developments. Supported by federal benefit programmes, many now reside in nursing homes, adult homes, community residences, and other institutional settings in the community. These mostly private, profit-making facilities serve the custody and protective service functions once performed almost exclusively by state facilities. The growth of what Warren (1981) has characterized as 'social control entrepreneurialism' has thereby perpetuated the segregation of the chronically mentally ill in a new ecological arrangement in the community.

While comparative state-level data on these alternative placements are not readily available, national data suggest that many former patients now reside in new 'asylums' or institutional settings in the community. In 1974 approximately 85 000 nursing home residents had been transferred directly from mental hospitals. Of the 1.3 million nursing home residents in 1977, approximately 250 000 had a primary psychiatric diagnosis and 100 000 had secondary psychiatric disorders. Another 400 000 residents were found to suffer from senility without psychosis (Goldman *et al.* 1981). Thus, nearly 56 per cent of nursing home residents have conditions that led to state hospital admissions in prior decades. Moreover, it is estimated that between 800 000 and 1 500 000 chronically mentally ill patients now live in private homes or a variety of community residences, including board-and-care homes. These data clearly indicate that, rather than 'deinstitutionalization', a process of *transinstitutionalization* has occurred for many former patients. Indeed, the patient-flow between state hospitals and nursing homes seems to represent the reversal of the flow from alms-houses to state hospitals in the early part of this century.

The highlights of these national and state-level deinstitutionalization trends have several implications for the issues considered in this chapter. First, deinstitutionalization was not a fixed, unilinear process which affected individual states in the same way. Second, a host of alternative institutions were created in the aftermath of state hospital census reductions to absorb and accommodate tens of thousands of former patients. Third, the evidence suggests that *trans*institutionalization was the dominant feature of changes concerning nursing home and adult home placements. Fourth, while these alternative programmes are operated mostly under private auspices public funds still pay for the sustenance and care of these patients. And fifth, state hospitals still serve their historic functions of custody, control and treatment, albeit at a reduced level, and for more targeted populations against which the mental health system's police powers are accentuated.

To this point we have not mentioned the issue of transinstitutionalization between the state hospital and criminal justice systems, primarily because the actual complexities of deinstitutionalization need to be appreciated before its impact on criminal justice can be understood. The extent to which this is the case should become apparent as we proceed to look specifically at how these phenomena may be related to trends in the criminal justice system.

Deinstitutionalization and the criminal justice system

In this section we will be focusing on a study that one of us (Steadman) recently conducted with John Monahan. That project was an attempt to develop a multi-state database before and after deinstitutionalization. Rather than approaching these questions of deinstitutionalization's impacts by simply correlating the size of institutional populations, our goal was to obtain individual level data on the persons coming into the respective systems at two points in time. The impact of deinstitutionalization is pivotally concerned with the accompanying changes in past, and potential, mental health contact among prison admissions. To correlate figures for total institutional populations really says little about whether the clientele of one system has actually been passed on to the other. Individuals need to be tracked between institutions to directly address the core question of whether 'transinstitutionalization' has actually occurred.

The issue of transinstitutionalization from mental hospitals to prisons involves at least two distinct populations. The first includes persons who, prior to deinstitutionalization, were in mental hospitals but who may now be in prisons. The second includes persons who formerly would have gone into mental hospitals but are now going to prison. In other words, some people who may have been retained for inordinately long periods in mental hospitals were 'dumped' out and, not being able to survive in the community, soon ended up in prison. A second group at risk are those who, hypothetically, had no prior mental hospital histories, but would have been admitted after police apprehension had there been both beds available and 'attractive' admissions procedures in place (that is, easy, fast, and medically-based). Instead, police officers are now faced with long waits in general hospital emergency rooms, the prospects of court commitment proceedings, and a small chance of actually getting the person into an available bed. Under these circumstances, the mentally disordered offender is arrested and eventually incarcerated.

To address how many inmates were produced from altered police practices would require data on frontline police actions before and after the era of rapid deinstitutionalization. Such data are totally unavailable. Bittner's (1967) qualitative article relying on anecdotal evidence offers some insights prior to deinstitutionalization, and Teplin's (1984) ongoing work promises empirical data on contemporary police practices *vis à vis* the suspected mentally ill. Returning to the first group of patients who may have been dumped into criminal justice agencies, no quantitative database exists on the comparative characteristics of the admissions to the criminal justice systems before and after deinstitutionalization. Nevertheless, we did discover record systems in several states that were maintained well enough to consider constructing such a database retrospectively. Once these data were assembled, we set out to investigate changes in the careers of mental hospital and prison admissions, and in the corresponding patterns of contact with both institutions, across time and across systems.

Six states were chosen for study. The primary criteria for inclusion were firstly, a reasonably well maintained management information system, and secondly, approved access to said system. The six states selected were California, Arizona, Texas, Iowa, New York and Massachusetts. This set of six states was geographically diverse and accounted for 26 per cent of the United States prison population in both 1968 and 1978. They also contributed 16 per cent of the US state mental hospital population in both years.

The years 1968 and 1978 were selected for study as a reasonable time-span to measure the deinstitutionalization process described earlier in this chapter. More practically, 1968 was about as far back as one could go and still expect to find the quality of records required. This date did not compromise the desired design since major policy initiatives for deinstitutionalization occurred at about this time or within a few years in the six study states. Since the study was initiated in 1978 this was the most recent year for which data were available.

Random samples of approximately 400 males over 18 years old admitted to state prisons and 400 adult males admitted to state mental hospitals for both 1968 and 1978 were selected in New York and California. In the four other states, random samples of approximately 300 adult male admissions to state prisons and 100 adult male admissions to state mental hospitals were drawn for each of the two years. The sample was limited to males since they comprise 96 per cent of the United States prison population (Weis and Henney 1979). The final sample for analysis was 6273 males of whom 3897 were prisoners and 2376 were mental patients.

For each prison or mental hospital admission, data were gathered on the person's history of:

1. Arrests;
2. State imprisonments; and
3. State mental hospitalizations.

Computer and manual file-searches were used to locate the complete history of each individual. In Massachusetts, for example, this required manual card-file-searches in each of seventeen state hospitals for the entire patient and inmate state sample totalling 737 individuals. Assurances of confidentiality were given to officials in each system and institutional research review committees discussed these assurances where required.

The core question on which we focused was: To what extent did the proportion of prison inmates with prior mental hospitalizations change between 1968 and 1978 in each state? If the deinstitutionalization of the state hospitals impacted directly on prisons, then the proportion of inmates coming into the system in 1978 with state hospitalizations should have increased over the 1968 baseline. Before examining those results, it may be useful to consider the patterns of deinstitutionalization and trends in prison populations in the six study states.

The data in Table 12.1 clearly indicate that considerable deinstitutionalization of state mental hospitals occurred in all six study states. The 1968 year-end census of mental hospitals in the six states was 64400. By 1978 this figure had plummeted by 61 per cent to 24731, almost precisely mirroring total United States trends. Only in Iowa was the decrement a moderate one (–15 per cent). The rate of decline in the other states ranged from –38 per cent in Arizona to –77 per cent in Massachusetts. At the same time, the prison census climbed in each state with the exception of California. Across the six states there were 56734 inmates at 1968 year end and 71381 in 1978; that is, a 25 per cent increase.

To adequately understand deinstitutionalization, however, it is essential to examine admission rates as well as census figures. While the *census* of state mental hospitals did fall dramatically between 1968 and 1978, the number of *admissions* declined only slightly. In 1968 there were 66077 male admissions to the six states' mental hospitals, while there were 60161 male admissions in 1978. As compared to the census decline of 61 per cent, the admissions decreased only 9.5 per cent. This discrepancy between a sharply declining hospital census and a relatively stable admission rate is accounted for by drastically reduced lengths of hospital stay. Thus, as discussed above, it is entirely inappropriate to depict deinstitutionalization as a trend that terminated most admissions to state hospitals. On the contrary, almost as many persons were being admitted in the late 1970s as in the mid-1960s. They just did not stay as long.

While the volume of mental hospital admissions was fairly constant between 1968 and 1978, the characteristics of the persons admitted changed substantially. Across the six states studied, the 1968 mean age for hospital admissions of 39 years had decreased to 33 by 1978. The percentage of whites among admitted patients also dropped, from 82 per cent in 1968 to 68 per cent in 1978.

The pronounced trends in mental hospital admissions toward increased numbers of younger persons and non-whites were not paralleled in the prisons. Across the six states, the mean age of prison admissions was 29 years in 1968 and 28 in 1978. Also, the proportion of whites among prison admissions was relatively stable, decreasing from 56 per cent in 1968 to 52 per cent in 1978.

Table 12.1 *State mental hospital and prison male census and admissions in six study states: 1968 and 1978*

State	*Hospital male census*			*Hospital male admissions*			*Prison male census*			*Prison male admissions*		
	1968	*1978*	*% Change*	*1968*	*1978*	*% Change*	*1968*	*1978*	*% Change*	*1968*	*1978*	*% Change*
New York	37877	13271	−65.0	25131	20740	−17.5	12404	19635	+58.3	6124	8572	+40.0
California	10446	5297	−49.3	20132	14206	−29.4	27369	20178	−26.3	11251	11694	+3.9
Arizona	598	368	−38.5	594	776	+30.6	1626	3275	+101.4	894	1774	+98.4
Texas	7088	3364	−52.5	8355	15499	+85.5	11842	23570	+99.0	6075	11948	+96.7
Iowa	843	716	−15.1	3500	4175	+19.3	1700	1985	+16.8	831	919	+10.6
Massachusetts	7548	1715	−77.3	8365	4765	−43.0	1793	2738	+52.7	428	1540	+259.8
TOTAL	64400	24731	−63.6	66077	60161	−9.0	56734	71381	+25.8	25603	36447	+42.4

The state mental hospitals in these six states appear to have begun serving a different clientele in quite different ways. The demographic composition of the state prison inmates, in contrast, remained fairly constant, although there was a substantial increase in their number. This again raises the principal question whether the hospitalization history of the prison inmates changed over this ten year period.

The percentage of prison admissions with a history of at least one mental hospitalization prior to their imprisonment in 1968 and 1978 is presented in Table 12.2. There is little consistency across the six states in the percentage of admissions with such histories in either year, or in the direction of change in these percentages. In New York, Arizona and Massachusetts, the proportion of admissions with prior mental hospitalizations decreased (non-significantly) from 1968 to 1978. California, Texas and Iowa, on the other hand, recorded significant increases. Since the magnitude of the three increases was so much greater than the size of the three decreases, there was a significant overall increment in the percentage of prisoners with a history of prior hospitalization in the six study states from 7.9 per cent in 1968 to 10.4 per cent in 1978.

Among our six study states, Texas had the most dramatic increase in the number of prison admissions with prior hospitalization. In 1968, only 18 previously hospitalized persons were admitted to Texas prisons. Pro-rated according to general increases in the prison admission figures, one would have expected 35 such persons to have been admitted in 1978. In fact, there were 1004 such admissions in 1978. Apparently many persons formerly housed in Texas mental hospitals were by then confined in Texas prisons. Given that Texas prison admissions increased by 5873 persons between 1968 and 1978 and given that there were 969 more prison admissions with prior hospitalizations in 1978 than would have been expected, one could estimate that only 16.5 per cent of the total increase in admissions to Texas state prisons between 1968 and 1978 was attributable to the admissions of prior mental patients.

In sum, the evidence that the rapid growth in state prison populations between 1968 and 1978 was attributable substantially to the shift of persons from state mental hospitals to state prisons is weak. During the period of maximum deinstitutionalization of mental hospitals, the percentage of former patients among the ranks of prison admissions decreased in as many study states as it increased. While the *absolute* number of prison admissions with a history of mental hospitalization universally increased between 1968 and 1978, in three states their *relative* frequency declined when compared to general prison admissions over the course of the decade. There is simply no

Table 12.2 Male prison admissions with prior state mental hospitalizations: 1968 and 1978

	Per cent of admissions with prior hospitalization				Number of admissions with prior hospitalization		
State	*1968*	*1978*	*Test*		*1968*	*1978*	*% Change*
New York	12.1	9.3	Z= 1.28;	NS	741	797	+7.6
California	9.5	15.2	Z= 2.45;	p=.01	1069	1777	+66.2
Arizona	3.9	2.2	Z=−1.17;	NS	35	39	+11.4
Texas	0.3	8.4	Z= 4.86;	p=.001	18	1004	+5477.8
Iowa	7.7	16.7	Z= 3.34;	p=.001	64	153	+139.1
Massachusetts	12.5	9.0	Z=−1.33;	NS	54	139	+157.4
Mean	7.9	10.4	Z 2.70;	p=.01	330	652	+97.3

consistent pattern of major contributions by deinstitutionalized mental patients to the surge in United States prison populations in the 1970s.

Implications

It is important to note that the data just presented are consistent with Grabosky's work discussed earlier in this chapter. Using both US national data from 1930 to 1970 and individual state records at three points in time, Grabosky found no significant relationships between the size of state prison populations and the size of state mental patient populations. Examining aggregated individual level indicators of prior contacts with the mental health system, our results were inconsistent. In no way did they show a stable pattern of state hospital patients finding their way into prison and thereby increasing the size of state penal systems. Nonetheless, as we will elaborate below, such an investigation of empirical relationships between state mental hospital and state prison admissions only marginally addresses broader questions concerning the impact of deinstitutionalization on the criminal justice system.

Throughout this paper we have been purposely somewhat imprecise in what we meant by the term 'criminal justice system'. Being consistent with the literature (Biles and Mulligan 1973; Grabosky 1980; Penrose 1939), our data focused on the state prison system. However, if one reflects carefully on the observations of the frontline clinicians and correctional administrators reviewed in the first section of this chapter, it is clear that most of them are focusing on the *local gaol*, not the state prison. The ready availability of prison statistics notwithstanding, we clearly need to shift the focus of our analyses to the local gaol.

In 44 of the 50 American states the gaol is a locally-financed and locally-operated facility. Its purposes are mainly to serve as the initial holding and booking site for all arrestees, and as a safe pre-trial detention centre for defendants who cannot make or are refused bail. Secondarily, persons convicted of crimes with sentences less than one year (that is, misdemeanours) serve their time in local gaols. Given the current overcrowding of many United States prisons some counties are also detaining convicted felons for which they are reimbursed by the states. The local gaol, then, is the frontline site of carceral confinement through which all detained persons must pass (and many never pass beyond).

The gaol is the focal point for pre-trial detention and for the minor offender. Is it not, therefore, logical if the mentally ill are now entering the criminal justice system rather than the state mental hospital system, that it is the gaol rather than the state prison in which they will be most visible? It is hard to get into United States prisons today. First-time offenders or minor criminals cannot fit. These are the classes into which persons unable to get into mental hospitals as a result of deinstitutionalization would most often fall. While this scenario makes logical sense and is consistent with clinical perceptions, the only longitudinal data available to substantiate these claims are from our very limited study (Steadman and Ribner 1980) on the Albany (New York) County Jail where the proportion of inmates with prior mental hospitalizations increased from 9 per cent to 12 per cent from 1968 to 1975. Beyond these data, nothing exists to measure the impacts of deinstitutionalization on the local gaol. Clearly this research is badly needed. But even if it is conducted, such an approach will not adequately address questions about the changing relationships between the mental health and criminal justice systems.

Research that includes only the state mental hospital and prison as the focal organizations (and even work that incorporates the local gaol as a separate component) is clearly inadequate. In another paper (Steadman *et al.* 1984), we have suggested that to comprehensively analyse the interrelationships of these systems, the idea of 'buffer groups' might be introduced. That is, rather than deinstitutionalized mental patients flowing directly into gaols or prisons, these disordered persons impact on other groups in the community. It is members of these other groups who then may end up in correctional facilities being replaced in the community by the persons who previously would have been in state mental hospitals. Figure 12.1 depicts this conceptualization.

The complexities of Figure 12.1 occur from the introduction into the diagram of the numerous community residential arrangements for the mentally ill. The specific labels of these places vary from state to state and from country to country, but the experiences of the chronically mentally ill in this post-deinstitutionalization era are depressingly similar. Their options range from the streets to shelters to ghetto housing in Single Room Occupancy Hotels (SROs) to various types of board-and-care homes to skilled nursing facilities to, in a very few cases, private homes. If we are interested in assessing changing modes of social control, and the way in which deinstitutionalization impacts on the criminal justice system, this range of residential environments must be considered.

In some instances, such as SROs, these alternative residences are not new creations, but their previous occupants were displaced by residents whose government subsidies were more dependable. In other instances such as adult homes, these facilities emerged as the state offered some fiscal incentives to private operators to develop large residential settings. Under either situation, it is clear that an analysis of how deinstitutionalization has impacted on criminal justice must include a consideration of how these smaller, more often privately-run facilities

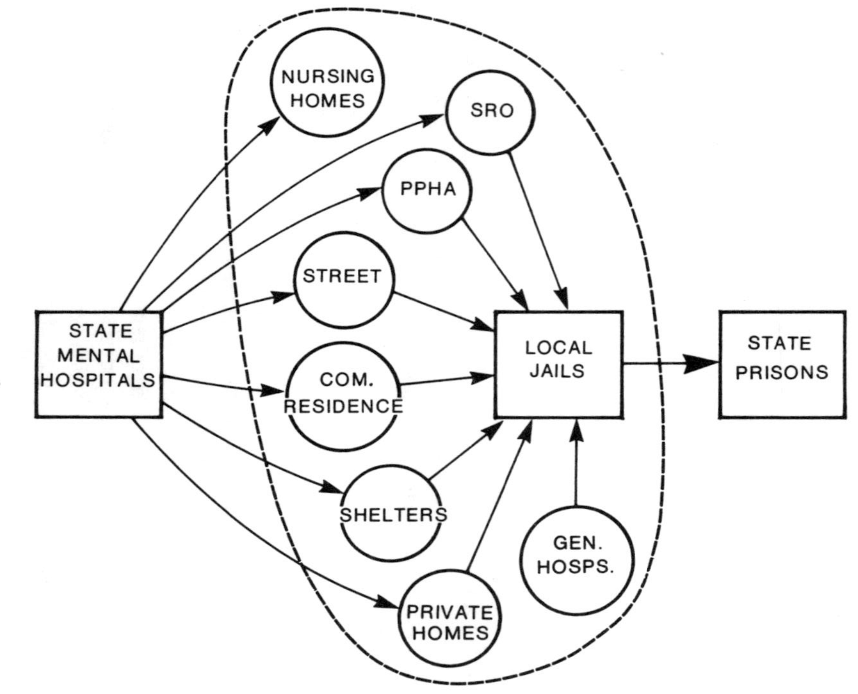

Figure 12.1 The Transinstitutional Network

have affected the community and the latter's responses to deviance. Whether it is these newly-situated mentally ill persons who have been getting arrested, or whether it has been groups who had previously resided in the community but became more active in crime and less tolerated, can only be speculated upon.

One interpretation of these dynamics has been developed by Barbara Duffee of our project staff. In an in-house paper she noted:

> The release of mental patients has increased the level of deviance in the community, but rather than attempting to once again remove the mental patients, the communities re-draw deviance boundaries, forcing an increased prosecution of criminal deviance. Thus, it is not the ex-mental patient in particular that is prosecuted but rather all groups on the fringe of a community.
>
> The basis of this argument can be derived from some of the recent functionalist approaches to deviance.... Erikson's study *Wayward Puritans* suggests that a disruption in solidarity increased repressive justice. Inverarity ... also found support that repressive justice increases during a boundary crisis. Lauderdale, in the same vein, reiterates that 'moral boundaries of a social system move independently of the actual behaviour of individuals defined as "deviant" by the system'.... He concludes that 'evidence from our study supports the contention that deviants, independent of their actions, will be more severely rejected and stigmatised following an external threat to their corporate social system'.... Certainly, it is not difficult to view the increased levels of deviance brought about by the influx of ex-mental patients as both a boundary crisis and an external threat to the social system.

Should this dynamic have occurred, deinstitutionalization's impact on the criminal justice system would not show up as more persons with histories of state mental hospitalization entering gaols and prisons. Rather, the pressure that the more apparent mentally disordered behaviours put on social tolerance levels might have been felt by 'buffer groups' between the mentally disordered and the correctional system. Furthermore, there is a new category of mentally disordered person which is puzzling mental health personnel and for whom the use of hospitalization records would be misleading. These are the 'young chronic' patients. They are predominantly males in their mid- to late-twenties who are severely impaired. Typically, they have had symptoms and serious disabilities since their teens, but have few state hospitalizations. Their disorders are often associated with violent behaviour, often involving illicit drug or alcohol abuse. Undoubtedly, in earlier eras such persons would have been admitted, perhaps involuntarily, to state hospitals. If deinstitutionalization has reduced the opportunities for care in state mental hospitals, this newly recognized population would be entering the criminal justice system without lengthy histories of hospitalization. Thus they are neither those persons 'dumped' into the community, nor those whose histories would allow any empirical conclusions about a shift in social control responsibilities.

The bottom line to this chapter is basically that there is no empirical evidence supporting the spill-over impact of deinstitutionalization on the correctional system. However that is not surprising. First, the empirical research reported here has focused on state prisons where there is the least likely chance for observable effects. Second, there is a complex of mental health related facilities which have grown up in the community over the past fifteen years that serve buffer functions and thereby militate against any direct impacts. These facilities, as they relate to the criminal justice system, have not been examined. Finally, if there have been any impacts on the criminal justice system, they are most likely to appear in the local gaol, the frontline correctional facility which is most directly dependent on community responses to criminal deviance. The modes of social control of the mentally ill in the past twenty years have become decentralized through the use of smaller facilities and through a shift to private operators and county funding streams. Whether and how these, in turn, have impacted on the criminal justice system is entirely unclear. As such, these generic questions have no national boundaries and are germane to virtually all Western countries, provinces and states regardless of the shape or pace of their deinstitutionalization. If we are to understand how the mental health and criminal justice systems relate to one another, research attention must be shifted to these alternate institutions and their interfaces with the local gaol.

13 Crime, fiscal crisis and decarceration: financing corrections at the state level

Raymond J. Michalowski
Michael A. Pearson

Introduction

Since the mid-1970s prison overcrowding has been frequently described as having reached 'crisis' proportions (Carlson 1977; Conrad 1980; Flanagan 1975; Gettinger 1976; Krajik and Gettinger 1982). In response to this crisis, new programmes for returning offenders to some type of community control have become increasingly common.[1] Programmes such as the Overcrowding Emergency Powers Act in Michigan, the expansion of 'administrative good time' in Illinois, increased uses of 'furlough' programmes in Connecticut and South Carolina, the institution of 'intensive probation' to reduce new prison commitments in North Carolina, and sentencing guidelines in Minnesota that use prison capacity as a consideration in determining sentence length (Bureau of Justice Statistics 1983a, p. 1; Mathias and Steelman 1982) indicate that many states are beginning to feel that they have reached the acceptable fiscal limits to prison expansion. That is, state correctional systems may be experiencing the:

> ...structural pressures to curtail sharply costly systems of segregative control...[which are] intensified by the fiscal crisis encountered in varying degrees at different levels of the state apparatus. (Scull 1977, p.152)

It is these pressures that Scull identifies as the driving force behind 'decarceration'. From this perspective, current efforts to expand release mechanisms and other non-institutional corrections reflect efforts by state managers to resolve the tension between 'social investment' and 'social expenditures' that O'Connor (1973) views as underlying the fiscal crisis of the state.

If fiscal pressures are, in fact, the central motivating factor underlying increased usage of non-institutional forms of penal sanctioning, then states which experience the greatest fiscal pressures should show the greatest expansion of non-institutional programmes. This in turn should be correlated with comparatively lower rates of incarceration as more convicted offenders are handled in non-prison settings. Our earlier analysis (Michalowski and Pearson 1983), however, indicated that state revenue per capita as a measure of fiscal strength of states was not a significant predictor of rates of incarceration after controlling for other factors. Nor did changes in per capita state revenue between 1970 and 1980 correlate significantly with changes in rates of incarceration between 1971 and 1981 (one year lag). The two most powerful predictors for both rates of incarceration during a single year, and changes in rates between 1970 and 1980 were, instead, the rate of violent crime and the percentage of black males in the population.

This earlier analysis, however, did not directly address the relationship between the fiscal strength of states and the relative proportion of correctional expenditures devoted to non-institutional correctional programmes. The following discussion examines descriptive data regarding correctional expenditures and their relationship to both crime and fiscal pressures for each of the 50 United States. Studies of correctional practices using data aggregated at the national level, while useful in their ability to derive summary statistics, often mask subtle but significant differences among states. It is our intention here to reintroduce some texture and detail to discussions surrounding current correctional practices at the state level.

Specifically, we are interested in how the individual states have performed in several areas:

1. To what extent have changes in rates of crime and rates of imprisonment been reflected in changes in prison populations, and to what extent do these relationships vary among states?
2. Have changes in expenditure for state correctional systems been consistent with changes in levels of state revenue? If not, to what extent have expenditures for state correctional systems increased or decreased as a proportion of total state revenue?
3. Is there any indication that state correctional systems have shifted larger proportions of their budgets toward non-institutional forms of penal sanctions? To what extent does this shift, if any, reflect fiscal pressures in terms of low revenue growth?
4. To what extent have changes in expenditures paralleled increases in prisoner populations? Have these changes affected prison conditions as measured by the amount of money spent for each prisoner?

The data

Data regarding the Crime Index for the years 1970 and 1980 were obtained from *Crime in the United States* (Federal Bureau of Investigation 1971, 1981). Index crimes include the felony offences of murder, rape, robbery, burglary, larceny, auto theft and arson. Prison populations and rates of imprisonment for 1970 and 1971 were taken from *Prisoners in State and Federal Institutions, 1970–1973* (Bureau of Prisoner Statistics 1974), and for 1980 and 1981 from the same document published by the Bureau of Justice Statistics (1982, 1983b). Prison population and rate of incarceration are based on the number of prisoners held at the year end. While these data regarding prisoner populations do not measure rate of prisoner flow (the total number of prisoners who passed through the prison system), they represent the best measure of the size of a state's prison system. Data regarding state revenues and expenditures were taken from *State Finances* (US Department of Commerce 1971, 1981) for the years 1970 and 1980. Data were gathered regarding:

1. Total state revenue;
2. Total expenditures for corrections;
3. Total *operational* expenditures for corrections; that is, total expenditures less capital expenditures;
4. Operational expenditures for prisons;
5. Operational expenditures for non-institutional corrections; and
6. Expenditures for capital construction.

While the data concerning revenue are, in general, appropriate for the purposes here, several idiosyncratic features of these variables should be recognized. First, in 1981, 19 states held prisoners in local gaols as a result of overcrowding in state prisons (Bureau of Justice Statistics 1982, p. 3).[2] Unfortunately, the available data on correctional expenditures do not indicate whether or not transfer disbursements by state governments to local counties or other jurisdictions for the housing of state prisoners are included. Thus, for a few states the reported total cost of corrections may be slightly lower than in actuality. In most of the states in question, however, the number of prisoners held in local gaols in 1981 was a relatively small proportion of the overall prison population. Ten states had less than 3 per cent of their prisoner populations in local gaols, three had between 3 and 8 per cent, and only Alabama (20 per cent), Mississippi (25 per cent) and New Jersey (12 per cent) held a substantial number of prisoners in local facilities. Thus, we can expect discrepancies in the data due to differential accounting for expenditures to local gaols to be relatively small.

Second, the data regarding revenue and the data regarding expenditures should not be viewed as referring to the same body of funds. The actual revenue collected in 1970 and 1980 does not necessarily comprise the same revenue pool upon which expenditures during those same years were planned. In most states, actual expenditures are the product of revenue projections at the time budgets are drawn and adjustments to those budgets as actual revenues exceed or fall short of projections. This is particularly true in those states that have constitutionally-mandated balanced budgets. Additionally, some states vote biennial budgets and hence plan expenditures based on two-year revenue projections, with subsequently more extensive revisions to expenditure plans as the actual revenue to finance the second year of the budget develops. Because revenue in the year of expenditure does play an important role in determining actual (as opposed to projected) expenditures we chose to examine revenue and expenditures for single years rather than lag revenue behind expenditure. While both lagged and unlagged expenditures relative to revenues have advantages and disadvantages, it is our assessment that comparing expenditures and revenues for a single year provides a better picture of the relationship between fiscal pressures and correctional expenditures.

Third, in cases where financial data refer to changes between 1970 and 1980, all 1980 figures are held to 1970 constant dollars to adjust for inflation.

Fourth, comparisons to determine the effect of changes in crime rates or state revenues on size of prison populations are based on a one-year lag relative to prison populations. That is, data regarding prison populations are for the years 1971 and 1981 while crime data and fiscal data are for 1970 and 1980. This is done for two reasons. One is to account for the lapse time between crime and imprisonment. Lagging crime one year behind imprisonment more accurately reflects the temporal process of arrest, adjudication and sentencing than do data for crime and imprisonment taken from the same year. Similarly, when the concern is whether or not revenues and expenditures influence the size of prison populations, a one-year lag provides for the time it would take to adjust the prison population to available revenue. Where expenditures on a per-prisoner basis are calculated, however, the data are taken from the same year, since it is the money spent in a given year that determines the general conditions of prisoner life *in that year*.

Lastly, there are several states for which the data are problematic. The changes in correctional expenditure and prison populations for Delaware must be viewed in light of the fact that between 1971 and 1981 that state combined its gaols and prisons into a single correctional system. This results in highly inflated rates of change between 1971 and 1981 in reported prison populations. There also appear to be some inaccuracies in the published data for Alaska and Wyoming for 1971, again resulting in possibly inflated rates of change. The data for those states should be viewed with caution.

Changes in crime and imprisonment

Our first questions were (a) to what extent have changes in rates of crime been reflected in changes in prison populations and changes in

Table 13.1 Percent changes in crime rates, prison populations, rates of violent crime and rates of imprisonment: 1970–1981

	(a) % Change in crime rate 1970–1980	(b) % Change in prison population 1971–1981	(c) % Change in violent crime 1970–1980	(d) % Change in rate of imprisonment 1971–1981
Alabama	164.6	94.6	51	69.1
Alaska	130.8	433.5	72	156.2
Arizona	137.2	271.9	75	150.3
Arkansas	137.7	98.0	50	69.2
California	81.9	67.5	86	32.7
Colorado	100.3	41.6	48	8.2
Connecticut	128.4	139.8	142	44.8
Delaware	127.9	822.6	46	544.5
Florida	133.4	140.7	87	63.4
Georgia	153.9	107.0	82	68.3
Hawaii	120.3	373.2	145	128.4
Idaho	167.9	174.6	154	114.8
Illinois	124.8	130.6	5	117.5
Indiana	117.2	84.8	67	66.4
Iowa	230.8	76.2	152	75.3
Kansas	150.9	39.4	92	30.3
Kentucky	78.5	30.5	20	15.9
Louisiana	126.9	126.1	60	92.9
Maine	282.5	90.7	133	44.1
Maryland	98.1	88.6	36	67.3
Massachusetts	102.4	71.5	196	69.7
Michigan	73.6	57.0	11	53.2
Minnesota	134.9	30.3	49	21.8

	(a) % Change in crime rate 1970–1980	(b) % Change in prison population 1970–1981	(c) % Change in violent crime 1970–1980	(d) % Change in rate of imprisonment 1971–1981
Mississippi	295.9	152.1	90	115.2
Missouri	96.5	70.3	36	62.7
Montana	207.0	219.2	99	185.3
Nebraska	183.8	57.0	22	40.3
Nevada	121.6	237.2	129	104.0
New Hampshire	292.3	80.3	221	46.4
New Jersey	133.3	32.0	110	24.1
New Mexico	108.6	137.4	110	74.5
New York	76.2	115.1	52	123.0
North Carolina	149.4	102.6	25	63.4
North Dakota	250.2	133.3	58	73.7
Ohio	128.5	65.1	75	64.1
Oklahoma	159.0	40.7	112	47.9
Oregon	123.9	62.8	90	32.6
Pennsylvania	104.7	76.0	71	74.5
Rhode Island	102.8	154.5	99	77.7
South Carolina	163.1	178.1	131	113.5
South Dakota	181.5	78.6	31	67.8
Tennessee	138.2	128.2	66	98.6
Texas	127.0	97.0	52	51.8
Utah	147.9	93.2	120	38.8
Vermont	239.1	151.9	141	65.6
Virginia	115.0	88.5	18	52.4
Washington	119.1	91.8	109	54.1
West Virginia	166.1	23.4	48	12.4
Wisconsin	217.0	75.6	112	66.8
Wyoming	185.7	112.2	247	33.0

rates of imprisonment, and (b) to what extent do these relationships vary among states? Table 13.1 reports changes in rates of crime, prison populations and rates of imprisonment. As Column A indicates, between 1970 and 1980 every state recorded a substantial increase in the rate of Crime Index offences. The mean increase was 150 per cent with Mississippi logging the greatest increase (296 per cent), and New York the lowest (76.2 per cent). Similarly, every state showed an increase in its prison population. Column B indicates, however, that in 36 states prison populations grew at a slower rate than Crime Index offences. There are several factors that may account for this. First, prison populations are constrained in so far as prison capacity is limited at any point in time and the construction of new facilities may be only reluctantly initiated, and then take years to complete.

Second, the rate of growth in prison populations may be less sensitive to growth in overall rates of crime than to changes in rates of violence, as was indicated by our previous study (Michalowski and Pearson 1983). Imprisonment is a more likely outcome for violent crimes than for property crimes for several reasons. For one thing, crimes of violence result in arrests proportionately more often than do property crimes. In 1981, for example, while 46 per cent of violent crimes led to an arrest, only 16 per cent of property crimes did so (Federal Bureau of Investigation 1982, pp. 153, 154). Also, offenders convicted of violent crimes are generally perceived as more dangerous, and therefore deserving of punishment for longer periods of time and in more cases than property offenders. One recent sentencing study found, for example, that 81 per cent of convictions for armed robbery resulted in a prison sentence, compared to 65 per cent of convictions for residential burglaries. Moreover, sentences for convicted armed robbers averaged 11 years versus 4.4 years for residential burglaries (US Department of Justice 1985).

Between 1970 and 1980 all states experienced an increase in the rate of violent crime. However, this growth was proportionately lower than the growth in the overall rate of crime. That is, while rates for both violent and property crime increased during the decade 1970–1980, the latter grew at a faster pace. Thus, during this period, violent crime declined nationally from approximately 11 per cent of all Index crime to 8 per cent. Between 1970 and 1980 nearly all states registered a decline in the proportion of Index crime accounted for by violent offences. The exceptions were California, Connecticut, Hawaii, Massachusetts, Nevada, New Mexico and Wyoming. The mean decrease in the ratio of violent crime to all crime was approximately 24 per cent. A comparison of Columns B and C in Table 13.1 reveals that in only 18 states did prison populations fail to grow as fast or faster than the rate of violent crime. This is in stark contrast with the 36 states in which the rate of expansion in prison population lagged behind growth in the overall Index crime rate. The failure of prison populations in many states to keep pace with the increase in Index crime may result from the fact that the preponderance of this growth was for those offences which are relatively less likely to result in prison sentences. This possibility, however, must be measured against the fact that while violent offenders are caught and imprisoned more often, those convicted of some other type of offence still constitute the majority of prisoners. In 1981, for instance, 64 per cent of all new admissions to state prisons were for property or public order violations (Greenfeld and Minor-Harper 1984, p. 3).

While the rate of growth in prison populations is a measure of pressures on the institutional apparatus of prisons, these figures are not adjusted for population changes, and growth in the general population will inevitably have some impact on the number of prisoners with whom a state must deal. For example, 10 states — Alaska, Arizona, Hawaii, Idaho, Mississippi, Montana, Nevada, Rhode Island, South Carolina and Vermont — experienced more than 150 per cent growth in their state prison populations between 1971 and 1981 (we are excluding Delaware). Except for Vermont and Rhode Island, all of these states were in the Western and Southern regions that experienced the largest population growth during the decade. Thus, part of the 'crisis' in corrections may be a product of geographic shifts in the population. Prison systems in fast-growing states may be unable to expand swiftly enough to keep pace with growth in the general population and its concomitant in the form of increased numbers of convicted offenders.

Benton and Silberstein (1983) hypothesize the opposite consequence of population growth in their research on the expansion of state prison systems. They postulate that states with high population growth will have increased tax revenues with which to afford new prison construction, and also a growth climate in which 'prison expansion may seem more reasonable and more politically justifiable ...' (pp. 122–123). Part of the difference between their position and ours arises from the fact that Benton and Silberstein are studying the growth of prison systems as measured by new construction, while we are concerned with changes in the actual numbers of prisoners. To some extent, therefore, both conclusions may be correct. States with high population growth may be more able and willing to physically expand their prison systems, and at the same time unable to do so at a pace equivalent to the growth in actual numbers of prisoners. However, during the time period they study — 1975–1980 — population shifts toward sun-belt states were taking place during a period of deep economic crisis that affected the high growth as well as the low growth states. During this time many states sought to minimize 'non-productive' capital expenditure in numerous areas, including prison construction. In particular, many high growth states sought to accelerate their growth through broad tax concessions and infrastructural improvements designed to attract new industry. Thus, fast growing states during the 1970–1980 decade may have been no more inclined to expand prison systems than slow growth states. Benton and Silberstein (1983, p.124) indirectly offer some confirmation of this. The three states that they identify as having high growth in both prisoner populations and prison construction are Delaware, Wyoming and Nevada. Our data show that all three enjoyed above-average growth in tax revenue during the decade in question, and Wyoming and Nevada also were well above average in general population growth. Yet as Benton and Silberstein note, new prison construction in all three states was a consequence of judicial court orders to relieve overcrowding, not domestic willingness to build new prisons.

Column D of Table 13.1 displays percentage increases in the rate of imprisonment per 100 000 population in each state between 1971 and 1981. While this statistic does not focus as sharply on the problem of population pressures on prison facilities as do data regarding actual numbers of prisoners, it provides a better sense of differences among states in punitiveness, in so far as it controls for population size. Every state held a larger proportion of its population in prison in 1981 than in 1971. However, only in Alaska, Arizona, Hawaii and New York (again excepting Delaware) did this rate of growth equal or exceed the rate of growth in crime. In all other states increments in imprisonment rates were outpaced by growth in the rates of Index crime.

Additionally, in 30 states the rate of imprisonment also did not equal the rate of growth in violent crime. While there is some evidence of a trend toward longer sentences (Greenfeld and Minor-Harper 1983b, p.3) the failure of imprisonment rates to keep pace with crime rates raises the possibility that the proportion of convicted offenders going to prison is declining rather than increasing. Longer sentences have had the effect of increasing the number of people in prison on any given day (Bureau of Justice Statistics 1984, p. 1). This, in turn, pushes prison systems to or beyond capacity. The result is that as crime rates rise *proportionately fewer* convicted offenders can be incarcerated. Alternatively, while some may be serving longer sentences, accelerated release mechanisms are applied to other (probably non-violent) offenders as a means of controlling prison populations.

While it is often claimed that punitiveness has intensified in recent years, our figures indicate that in the vast majority of states, crimes generated prisoners proportionately less often in 1981 than in 1971. There are, of course, many possible reasons for this, such as police and

Table 13.2 Changes in total correctional expenditures as part of state revenues*

	(a)	(b)	(c)	(d)	(e)
			State revenues spent on corrections		
	% Change in state revenue**	% Change in Correctional Expenditures	As % of state revenues	% Change in proportion of state revenues	% Change in prison population
	1970–1980	1970–1980	1970	1970–1980	1971–1981
Alabama	55.2	167.5	0.78	72.2	94.6
Alaska	33.5	135.9	0.53	76.7	433.5
Arizona	83.8	323.8	0.88	130.6	271.9
Arkansas	76.5	338.8	0.50	148.6	98.0
California	59.9	50.7	1.44	–5.7	67.5
Colorado	77.8	121.3	1.28	24.4	41.6
Connecticut	41.8	86.4	1.63	31.4	139.8
Delaware	67.0	60.0	2.82	–4.2	822.6
Florida	86.5	223.0	1.44	73.1	140.7
Georgia	60.8	170.0	1.37	67.9	107.0
Hawaii	57.3	109.4	0.68	33.1	373.2
Idaho	77.4	121.3	0.95	24.8	174.6
Illinois	30.9	114.5	1.20	63.8	130.6
Indiana	41.2	133.6	1.04	65.4	84.8
Iowa	49.7	89.4	1.18	26.4	76.2
Kansas	53.7	52.9	1.40	–0.5	39.4
Kentucky	66.6	229.8	0.89	97.9	30.5
Louisiana	64.6	304.3	0.66	145.5	126.1
Maine	64.6	29.2	1.52	–21.5	90.7
Maryland	68.3	84.4	2.52	9.5	88.6
Massachusetts	58.9	68.2	1.50	5.8	71.5
Michigan	51.0	135.5	0.98	55.9	57.0
[illegible]	[illegible]	[illegible]	[illegible]	[illegible]	30.3

Mississippi	55.7	258.1	0.53	129.9	152.1
Missouri	45.3	145.1	0.93	68.7	70.3
Montana	66.2	164.5	1.00	59.1	219.2
Nebraska	56.3	213.0	1.07	100.2	57.0
Nevada	114.1	183.8	1.81	32.5	237.2
New Hampshire	60.5	118.8	0.91	36.3	80.3
New Jersey	69.7	109.2	1.34	23.2	32.0
New Mexico	82.3	266.7	0.80	101.2	137.4
New York	32.7	82.3	1.24	37.3	115.1
North Carolina	61.1	129.6	1.94	42.5	102.6
North Dakota	77.4	84.8	0.59	4.2	133.3
Ohio	58.7	9.0	1.68	−31.3	65.1
Oklahoma	60.8	218.9	0.78	98.3	40.7
Oregon	97.1	110.1	1.35	6.5	62.8
Pennsylvania	43.9	53.6	0.88	6.7	76.0
Rhode Island	60.3	55.0	1.45	−3.3	154.5
South Carolina	89.9	257.1	0.93	88.0	178.1
South Dakota	51.5	67.2	0.86	10.3	78.6
Tennessee	59.8	136.7	1.65	48.0	128.2
Texas	78.9	141.2	0.93	34.7	97.0
Utah	72.6	130.7	0.89	33.6	93.2
Vermont	30.8	33.7	1.66	2.2	151.9
Virginia	61.5	300.0	1.14	147.6	88.5
Washington	63.2	49.2	1.68	−8.6	91.8
West Virginia	57.9	55.1	0.55	−1.7	23.4
Wisconsin	56.0	33.4	1.64	−14.5	75.6
Wyoming	107.5	506.9	0.81	192.4	112.2

* Includes expenditures for correctional institutions, non-institutional corrections and capital expenditures.
** All 1980 revenue figures were computed in 1970 dollars.

judicial overload, prison capacity, or increases in multiple crimes by single offenders. In general, though, the figures do not substantiate the notion that punitive outcomes occurred proportionately more often relative to crime in 1981 than in 1971. Penal system capacity and state reluctance to expand this capacity to keep pace with growing rates of crime appear to have limited the translation of punitive sentiments into punitive systems.

Fiscal crisis and correctional expenditures

Our second questions concern (a) whether changes in expenditures for state correctional systems have been consistent with changes in levels of state revenue, and (b) if not, to what extent have expenditures for state correctional systems increased or decreased as a proportion of total state revenue? Despite the frequent assumption that many states experienced declines in revenues as a result of the recession during the mid-1970s, Column A of Table 13.2 indicates that all states enjoyed a *real* growth in revenue over the course of the decade, after 1980 figures were adjusted for inflation. Thus, to the extent that states did experience a sense of fiscal crisis during the decade from 1970 to 1980, this was a product of changes in the nature of demands on state revenue rather than declines in the revenue base. Specifically, the sense of fiscal crisis may be explained by increased demands on states to commit more money to 'social investments' such as high-tech education, research and industrial parks, and to improve roads and communications to bolster a flagging private sector economy.

Column B of Table 13.2 shows the percentage increase in correctional expenditures between 1970 and 1980 in constant 1970 dollars.[3] All states posted an increase; however, the range was substantial, extending from a mere 9 per cent increase in Ohio to a 338 per cent increase in Arkansas (excluding the suspect 506 per cent figure for Wyoming).

The cost of maintaining correctional systems, particularly their prison component, is frequently thought to consume a substantial proportion of state revenues and to represent a serious burden on taxpayers. However, as Column C indicates, in 48 out of 50 states the total cost of corrections was less than 2 per cent of state revenues, and in 22 states it was under 1 per cent of revenues in 1970. As indicated in Column D, Table 13.2, between 1970 and 1980 correctional expenditures in most states increased as a proportion of state revenue. However, at the end of the decade in 41 out of 50 states correctional expenditures still remained less than 2 percent of revenues (as calculated by increasing the 1970 figure in Column C by the percentage factor in Column D). The fact that the revenue share of corrections did increase in most states indicates that rising prison populations placed some additional strain on state revenues during the decade in question. Nevertheless, given the low percentages of revenue involved, corrections cannot be seen as a significant contributor to fiscal crisis within the states.

Because correctional systems serve politically weak clients, they are easy targets of calls for cost-cutting and 'fiscal responsibility', particularly in states experiencing economic slumps. Moreover, heightened punitiveness among the population may make increased expenditures to improve prison conditions more difficult to obtain. A comparison of Columns B and E in Table 13.2 offers some support for the idea that states experiencing fiscal crisis might display a reduced willingness (or capacity) to fund corrections. In 20 states[4] (excluding Delaware) the prison populations grew faster than correctional budgets. Moreover, all of these states (with the exceptions of California and Hawaii) were from the northern half of the nation, the majority were heavily industrialized states, and none were in the southern 'sunbelt' region that experienced substantial economic and population growth at the expense of the northern industrial tier during the 1970–1980 decade. The correctional apparatus in these states in particular may be feeling the effect of fiscal crisis as state managers seek to shift budgetary priorities to recapture lost economic vigour in the state's private sector.

Table 13.3 reports *operational expenditures*, that is, expenditures to fund the daily operations of the correctional system — excluding costs for new construction. These figures show that all states spent more to operate their correctional systems in 1980 than they did in 1970. Moreover, in 41 states the increase in what states spent to run their correctional systems (Column B) exceeded the increase in state revenue (Column A). Thus, in most states correctional operations increased its share of revenue in 1980 over 1970. But, comparing Columns B and D in Table 13.3 also shows that, similar to Table 13.2, in 21 states[5] the growth in operational expenditures (again excluding Delaware) still did not keep pace with growth in prison populations. This growing gap between prison populations and correctional budgets suggests two possibilities:

1. That more offenders are being handled through non-institutional correctional programmes that require less expenditure per client; and/or
2. That less money is being spent for each prisoner involved.

The following section addresses these possibilities.

Financing deinstitutionalization

The third set of questions posed here are (a) whether there is any

Table 13.3 Changes in expenditures for correctional operations as a share of state revenues by states*

	(a) % Change in state revenues** 1970–1980	(b) % Change in correctional operations expenditures 1970–1980	(c) % Change in operations expenditure state revenues	(d) % Change in prison population 1971–1981
Alabama	55.2	216.0	103.5	94.6
Alaska	33.5	93.6	45.0	433.5
Arizona	83.8	249.0	89.9	271.9
Arkansas	76.5	317.1	136.3	98.0
California	59.9	37.9	-13.7	67.5
Colorado	77.8	98.6	11.6	41.6
Connecticut	41.8	57.9	11.4	139.8
Delaware	67.0	143.0	45.4	822.6
Florida	86.5	243.7	84.2	140.7
Georgia	60.8	136.1	46.8	107.0
Hawaii	57.3	83.6	16.7	373.2
Idaho	77.4	129.5	29.4	174.6
Illinois	30.9	84.5	40.9	130.6
Indiana	41.2	127.5	61.1	84.8
Iowa	49.7	72.5	15.2	76.2
Kansas	53.7	54.8	0.6	39.4
Kentucky	66.6	192.9	75.8	30.5
Louisiana	64.6	306.7	147.0	126.1
Maine	64.6	38.1	-16.1	90.7
Maryland	68.3	60.6	-4.5	88.6
Massachusetts	58.9	79.8	13.1	71.5
Michigan	51.0	140.5	59.2	57.0
[illegible]	[illegible]	[illegible]	1.5	30.3

Mississippi	55.7	195.9	90.0	152.1
Missouri	45.3	89.7	30.6	70.3
Montana	66.2	157.8	55.1	219.2
Nebraska	56.3	111.5	35.2	57.0
Nevada	114.1	119.4	2.4	237.2
New Hampshire	60.5	106.9	28.9	80.3
New Jersey	69.7	73.2	2.0	32.0
New Mexico	82.3	111.3	15.9	137.4
New York	32.7	135.5	77.4	115.1
North Carolina	61.1	117.9	35.2	102.6
North Dakota	77.4	85.5	4.5	133.3
Ohio	58.7	19.3	-24.8	65.1
Oklahoma	60.8	195.7	83.9	40.7
Oregon	97.1	78.3	9.5	62.8
Pennsylvania	43.9	55.3	7.9	76.0
Rhode Island	60.3	59.1	-0.7	154.5
South Carolina	89.9	261.6	90.3	178.1
South Dakota	51.5	53.1	1.0	278.6
Tennessee	59.8	195.3	84.7	128.2
Texas	78.9	120.9	23.4	97.0
Utah	72.6	158.6	49.8	93.2
Vermont	30.8	27.1	-2.8	151.9
Virginia	61.5	256.2	120.5	88.5
Washington	63.2	58.5	-2.8	91.8
West Virginia	57.9	54.7	-1.9	23.4
Wisconsin	56.0	57.3	0.8	75.6
Wyoming	107.5	18997.4	9102.5	112.2

* Includes operational expenditures for institutional and non-institutional corrections, but excludes capital expenditures.
** All revenue figures computed in 1970 constant dollars.

Table 13.4 *Changes in institutional versus non-institutional expenditures for correctional operations*

	(a) % Change in correctional operations expenditures, 1970–1980	(b) % Change in correctional expenditures for institutions, 1970–1980	(c) % Change in non-institutional expenditures, 1970–1980
Alabama	216.0	188.6	230.9
Alaska	93.6	41.6	435.0
Arizona	249.0	206.3	8146.5
Arkansas	317.1	258.7	1529.9
California	37.9	36.8	42.9
Colorado	98.6	57.1	481.8
Connecticut	57.9	25.8	245.6
Delaware	143.0	90.4	3948.7
Florida	243.7	197.5	587.3
Georgia	136.1	107.8	342.9
Hawaii	83.6	82.7	89.8
Idaho	129.5	91.1	563.2
Illinois	84.5	58.1	260.2
Indiana	127.5	105.4	365.8
Iowa	72.5	63.6	224.4
Kansas	54.8	44.7	284.7
Kentucky	192.9	123.7	807.9
Louisiana	306.7	340.1	222.5
Maine	38.1	27.4	146.2
Maryland	60.6	10.1	373.9
Massachusetts	79.8	4.8	411.9
Michigan	140.5	129.6	223.2
Minnesota	57.9	50.3	92.1
Mississippi	195.9	152.2	906.8
Missouri	89.7	57.7	271.4
Montana	157.8	66.9	2387.3
Nebraska	111.5	50.4	1215.0
Nevada	119.4	96.8	332.4
New Hampshire	106.9	106.8	107.5
New Jersey	73.2	52.9	258.5
New Mexico	111.3	105.3	160.3
New York	135.5	134.9	137.8
North Carolina	117.9	95.4	234.9
North Dakota	85.5	85.6	83.1
Ohio	19.3	–0.7	155.6
Oklahoma	195.7	137.2	583.1
Oregon	78.3	31.9	493.7
Pennsylvania	55.3	55.4	54.4
Rhode Island	59.1	38.6	137.7
South Carolina	261.6	251.0	344.4
South Dakota	53.1	57.1	12.9

Tennessee	195.3	185.8	270.8
Texas	120.9	94.7	688.7
Utah	158.6	60.0	996.8
Vermont	27.1	-27.0	437.8
Virginia	256.2	183.8	707.6
Washington	58.5	31.5	218.1
West Virginia	54.7	51.7	78.0
Wisconsin	57.3	28.3	169.0
Wyoming	18997.4	85.6	132.0

indication that state correctional systems have shifted larger proportions of their budgets toward non-institutional forms of penal sanctions, and (b) to what extent does this shift, if any, reflect fiscal pressures in terms of low revenue growth? Table 13.4 reports changes in rates of growth for expenditures on institutional and non-institutional forms of corrections. Column A indicates that all states spent more to operate their correctional systems in 1980 than in 1970. This increase was reflected in heightened expenditures for both prison and non-institutional corrections. As Column B indicates, all states except for Ohio and Vermont also recorded a real growth in the amount of money spent to operate their prisons. A comparison of Columns B and C, however, demonstrates that expenditures for non-institutional programmes grew more rapidly than expenditures for prisons in 46 out of 50 cases (Louisiana, North Dakota, Pennsylvania and South Dakota being the only exceptions).

The substantial rise in non-institutional expenditures, when compared to changes for prisons, might possibly reflect a process of *relative* decarceration. We say 'relative' because it is difficult to characterize the absolute rise in prison populations during the decade of the 1970s as reflecting a process of 'decarceration'. However, the increased share of operations expenditures consumed by probation, parole and other community-based corrections programmes suggests that these activities may be handling a larger proportion of the offender population than in the past. There are two qualifications to this interpretation that should be considered.

The first is that the large proportional growth in expenditures for non-institutional corrections represents a large increase in a small number. As Column A of Table 13.5 shows, prison costs accounted for most of the expenditures for correctional operations in 1970, ranging from 99 per cent in Arizona to a low of 71 per cent in Louisiana. Column B, however, demonstrates that the proportion of operating expenditures devoted to prisons declined in 46 out of 50 states between 1970 and 1980. That is, the vast majority of states experienced a proportional reallocation of correctional dollars away from institutions

Table 13.5 Changes in total correctional expenditures as part of state revenues

	Institutions/ operations 1970	% Change in institutions' share of operations	Dollars per prisoner spent in 1970*	% Change in dollar per prisoner 1970–1980*
Alabama	92.4	–8.7	1801	89.1
Alaska	86.7	–26.8		
Arizona	99.4	–12.2	4840	– 0.5
Arkansas	95.4	–14.0		
California	81.9	–0.8	4720	47.1
Colorado	90.2	–20.9	5074	17.0
Connecticut	85.3	–20.3	10807	–6.7
Delaware	98.6	–21.6	7047	4.3
Florida	84.3	–13.4	2502	35.2
Georgia	87.9	11.9	3290	–11.0
Hawaii	87.3	–0.4	15153	–33.2
Idaho	91.5	–16.7	5425	–3.8
Illinois	86.9	–14.3	6209	–5.9
Indiana	91.5	–9.7	3423	35.2
Iowa	94.5	–5.1	1674	15.8
Kansas	95.8	–6.5	5250	10.3
Kentucky	89.8	–23.6	3091	76.6
Louisiana	71.5	8.2	1760	107.7
Maine	91.0	–7.7	9751	–4.1
Maryland	86.1	–31.4	6539	–26.1
Massachusetts	84.2	–41.6	9507	–7.4
Michigan	88.3	–4.5	3583	37.8
Minnesota	81.8	–4.8	7989	19.0
Mississippi	94.2	–14.7	2358	30.6

Missouri	85.0	–16.8	3207	–2.5
Montana	96.0	–35.2	12257	–41.1
Nebraska	94.7	–28.9	4639	7.2
Nevada	90.4	–10.3	6232	–26.2
New Hampshire	79.6	–0.6	8135	54.7
New Jersey	90.1	–11.7	4261	56.7
New Mexico	89.2	– 2.8	5656	10.3
New York	81.1	–0.2	5580	30.8
North Carolina	83.9	–10.3	4723	–18.5
North Dakota	92.5	0.1	10081	47.5
Ohio	87.2	–16.6	5107	–32.3
Oklahoma	86.8	–19.7	2043	79.5
Oregon	89.9	–26.0	6712	–25.0
Pennsylvania	89.3	0.0	5827	20.5
Rhode Island	79.2	–12.9		
South Carolina	88.7	–2.9	2684	30.8
South Dakota	90.9	2.6	4890	0.8
Tennessee	88.8	–3.2	3234	33.0
Texas	95.5	–11.8	1897	–6.6
Utah	89.4	–38.1	7301	–15.3
Vermont	88.3	–42.5	22722	–65.4
Virginia	86.1	–20.3	3167	53.7
Washington	85.5	–17.0	9005	–14.0
West Virginia	88.5	–1.9	4220	13.2
Wisconsin	79.3	–18.4	7274	–4.1
Wyoming	90.3	–99.0	6891	–19.7

*Blanks indicate unavailable data, making computation impossible.

and towards non-institutional programmes. Nevertheless, it should be kept in mind that percentage changes in expenditures for non-institutional programmes (Column B, Table 13.4) may project an over-inflated sense of growth, since the initial base upon which they are computed is small. Likewise, it is important to recognize that a shift of a few percentage points in the share of correctional budgets spent on prisons can represent a substantial amount of money given the large dollar amounts of initial prison budgets.

A second possible caveat to the interpretation of Table 13.4 is that the proportionally smaller share of correctional revenue expended on prisons, and the correspondingly larger share of the operations budget devoted to non-institutional programmes, may reflect a decrease in allocations per incarcerated offender. This brings us to our final questions: (a) to what extent have changes in expenditures paralleled increases in prisoner populations, and (b) to what extent have these changes affected prison conditions, as measured by the amount of money spent for each prisoner?

Column C of Table 13.5 shows dollar per prisoner expenditures for each of the states in 1970. These figures are based on the amount of money spent for institutions, exclusive of capital construction. While new construction does presumably contribute eventually to the quality of prison life, and while today's prisoners may be enjoying the benefits of past capital expenditures, it is the operations expenditures for institutions which primarily shape the quality of prison life in any given year. Moreover, since capital expenditures fluctuate substantially from one year to the next depending on whether significant new construction is under way, we felt that operational expenditures for prisons provided the best measure of prison conditions in any single year, and also the best basis on which to calculate changes in quality of prison life over time.

The statistics in Column C show substantial variation in per-prisoner expenditures. Iowa recorded the lowest with a figure of $1670 per prisoner in 1970, followed closely by Louisiana ($1760), Alabama ($1800) and Texas ($1900). Top honours for the most costly prisons on a per-convict basis belonged to Vermont at $22700 per prisoner. These extremes, however, must be viewed in light of the relationship between fixed and variable costs of imprisonment. The exceptionally high figure for Vermont (as well as for other states which spent $10000 or more per convict) reflect, at least in part, a high ratio of fixed to variable costs. Each of these states is relatively small, but maintains one or more state prisons. Even though these prisons house relatively few convicts compared to those in the larger states, there is a fixed minimum for maintaining this type of physical plant. While fixed costs for running prisons increase with prison size, economies of scale tend to reduce the costs per prisoner housed. Additionally many of those states with high per-prisoner expenditures are located in the North while many with lower expenditures are situated in the South, such that part of the reason for differences in per-prisoner expenditures may reflect fuel costs. Still, there are several exceptions to this pattern. Arizona, for instance, spends somewhat more per prisoner than Nebraska, and California spends more than Michigan. That is, per-prisoner expenditures are also influenced by factors associated with attitudes toward convicts and political willingness to spend money on prisoners.

The last of our initial questions concerns the changes in expenditures per prisoner as a rough measure of prison conditions. Column D of Table 13.5 presents a mixed picture. Twenty-one states were spending less for each prisoner housed in 1980 than in 1970. The remainder showed either a growth or the same level of per-prisoner expenditure. Many states which showed a decline in per-prisoner expenditures also displayed a relatively high rate of increase in monies devoted to non-institutional corrections. Of those 21 states with a decrease in per-prisoner expenditures, 18 experienced more than 150 per cent growth in non-institutional expenditures. The relationship between non-institutional expenditures and per-prisoner allocations would seem to be further supported by the fact that, with the exception of Hawaii, none of the states which had an increase of less than 100 per cent in its non-institutional budget (Table 13.4, Column C) showed a decline in dollars spent per prisoner (Table 13.5, Column D). This pattern, however, is complicated by the fact that some states (notably Arkansas, Colorado, Idaho, Massachusetts, Nebraska, Oklahoma and Virginia) posted substantial increases in non-institutional expenditures while maintaining or increasing the amount of money spent on a per-prisoner basis. Moreover, we found no statistically significant relationship between size of increase in non-institutional expenditures and whether or not a state experienced a decrease or an increase in dollars spent per prisoner.

While the picture is mixed, it is clear that many states have shifted funds proportionately toward non-institutional corrections. It is difficult to say for certain whether this is a consequence of some overt commitment to the rehabilitative potential of community-based supervision as compared to imprisonment, or the inadvertent by-product of prison overcrowding as states move toward early releases to parole and other community forms of supervision. However, in considering the substantial rise in prison populations, the increasing number of states that are under some form of court order to reduce overcrowding, and those which have adopted some mechanism to 'trigger' releases once a certain level of capacity is reached, it would appear that increased expenditures for non-institutional programmes resulted more from the pressures of fiscal crisis than from some rehabilitative sentiment. That is, we find support for the proposition that states underwent a process of *relative decarceration* in the 1970–1980 period rather then having funded growth in non-institutional correctional programmes to achieve some particular therapeutic goal.

Conclusion

Descriptively, the data here suggest some tentative answers to our initial questions. First, while prison populations grew in all states between 1970 and 1980, their rate of growth was generally less than increases in the rate of crime, although they followed more closely the rate of increase in violent offences. Of particular significance is the *lack* of evidence for the proposition that law-breakers *in general* are more likely to be imprisoned today than in the past. While some may be incarcerated longer, others are either serving shorter sentences or not going to prison at all. If this were not the case the growth in prison populations would have more closely paralleled the rise in crime.

Second, the cost of financing corrections increased more rapidly than the growth in general state revenues in the decade between 1970 and 1980, resulting in a larger share of state revenues being devoted to correctional expenditures. While the proportions of the states' funds spent on corrections remained small (1 to 3 per cent) corrections did command more of state budgets at the end of the decade than at the beginning. Given a general reluctance to spend money on prisoners, even this small increase may have been perceived as an onerous burden. This may have been particularly so as increased demands for social investment, along with increasingly punitive attitudes, made money spent on the 'criminal element' appear wasted.

Third, the rise in correctional expenditures has been disproportionately directed toward non-institutional corrections. Non-institutional expenditures, on average, increased from about 10 per cent of correctional operations budgets in 1970 to about one-third of operations budgets in 1980. With respect to our last question, the picture is mixed. There is no immediately apparent relationship between increases in expenditures for non-institutional corrections and dollars spent per prisoner.

Overall, the figures here suggest both trends and discontinuities in the way state correctional systems have responded to the rise in crime and the dramatic increases in prison populations in the years between 1970 and 1980. While all states spent more on corrections in 1980 than in 1970 some states have maintained or increased the amount spent per prisoner while others have overseen a decline. Similarly, while expenditures for non-institutional corrections have increased in all states, this increase has been much more dramatic in some than in others. The final conclusion to be drawn from these figures is that the patterns and practices of imprisonment, at least in the United States with its 50 different prison systems, vary noticeably from one political jurisdiction to another. Thus, while aggregate national statistics can provide clear and useful summary data, they may obscure important variations among states. For this reason, future prison research should include more in-depth analysis of the individual states as well as studies of national aggregates.

14 The reappearance of 'the ideal factory': The entrepreneur and social control in the contemporary prison[1]

Robert P. Weiss[2]

Since the recession of the mid-1970s and the numerous successful tax-cut propositions that followed, municipal governments across the United States have been shifting public services to the private sector. Fire protection, transportation, electric power, and solid waste collection are among the services whose 'privatization' has been accomplished with little controversy. More recently, privatization of many activities traditionally performed by the state and federal governments has been promoted by intellectuals of the 'neo-conservative' movement. Most disturbing to New Deal liberals, entrepreneurs have been breaking up the welfare state monopoly over health care (Alford 1975), social work, and mental health services. Privatization has converged with the move to 'deinstitutionalize' the aged, the mentally ill, the retarded, and the delinquent.

Neo-conservatives have interpreted the election of Ronald Reagan to the US Presidency in 1980 as a statement that 'government has become too large, too expensive and too intrusive', according to Martin Anderson (Assistant to the President for Policy Development), and that 'it is now time to translate that mandate into pragmatic, sensible actions that bring about responsible change in the boundaries that separate the sovereignty of the individual and private institutions from the sovereignty of government' (Anderson 1982).

In contrast to liberals and traditional conservatives alike, 'neo-conservatives do not adhere to the philosophical separation between government and business', according to David Stoesz (1981), in his analysis of the neo-conservative challenge to social welfare; 'as an ideological movement, neo-conservatism weds the entrepreneurial ethic with pragmatism', favouring 'utilitarian solutions to societal problems (1981, pp.2,3). Neo-conservatives do not deny the existence of social problems, and they acknowledge the need for social welfare provision, but 'it does not follow that the state is the only, or the most effective, or the cheapest, or the most sensitive social agency' (Novak 1982, p.12). 'Totalitarian' tendencies of government can be avoided by diverting some of its traditional responsibilities to other social structures. Neo-conservatives are outspoken promoters of the participation of community groups, voluntary associations, and churches in social welfare activities. Although non-profit organizations help perpetuate traditional (conservative) values, neo-conservatives fault them for being unresponsive to 'market forces' (Stoesz 1981). The real focus of neo-conservative social policy, liberal and radical critics argue, is *privatization as commercialization.* In a complete reversal of conservative position on policy, government programmes that were once considered a drain on business (because the tax funds could have been better used for capital investment) are now valued as a new market, where entrepreneurs can turn administrative costs into potentially large profits. They argue that the private sector is not only less expensive, but more effective in service delivery. This same argument is currently being applied to criminal justice.

Incarceration is a governmental activity that has remained largely unexploited in this century by the private sector. Yet, incarceration could be big business. It has an enormous potential for profit-making: in 1984, federal, state, and local governments spent over $10 billion to confine nearly 650000 persons (Becker and Stanley 1984). The supply of jail space cannot keep abreast of demand. Harsh sentencing practices, combined with taxpayer unwillingness to finance adequate prison space, has created serious overcrowding. Not surprisingly, the privatization of jails, prisons, and detention centres increasingly is being proposed as a partial solution to this problem. About two dozen institutions in the US, including detention centres for illegal aliens, maximum-security juvenile institutions, and medium-security prisons for adult offenders, are now run by private firms. The marketing of corrections promises to attract new providers; private *financing* for prison construction and private *facility ownership* are alternative ways out of the dilemma of expanding prisoner population and shrinking revenues (Mullen 1985). Privatization allows the simultaneous achievement of two cherished neo-conservative ideals which would ordinarily be contradictory: *diminution* of government and *expansion* of the repressive apparatus.

Because imprisonment deals directly with the issue of sovereignty, the private operation of prisons raises especially disturbing questions concerning the role and meaning of the state. Liberal critics argue that the administration of justice is the *raison d'être* of government — a function that cannot be delegated.[3] Citing Locke, they contend that the right to punish is the essence of political power. Other critics (Schoen 1985; Tolchin 1985a,b,c) point to the possible effects of special interests on public policy. 'Will private providers use their political power to lobby for the development or continuation of programmes that may not be in the public interest?' (Mullen 1985, p.5). Defenders of privately run prisons, including James K. Stewart, Director of the National Institute of Justice, argue that, taken separately, there is nothing that has not been done by the private sector before, including the use of force in the form of private security.[4]

Whilst the private operation of penal facilities may be objectionable to most liberals, the notion of private industry within state-operated prisons appeals to those of most political persuasions. For example, Kenneth F. Schoen (1985), a leading critic of private prisons, was instrumental in instituting private industrial operations in Minnesota's state prisons as Commissioner of Corrections. Those concerned with the abuse of power in privately operated facilities see private employment as less threatening; control, they say, would remain in the hands of government officials. And everyone would seem to benefit. With a 400 per cent increase in expenditure of public funds on prisons in the last fifteen years (Sexton *et al.* 1985, p.1), all advocates of private penal industry point to fiscal concerns as a rationale; privatization may be a way to help defray the costs of incarceration (Auerbach 1979; Hawkins 1983; Logan and Rausch 1985; Miller and Jensen 1974; Poole 1983; Schaller 1981). Proposals centre on paying prisoners a wage, from which would be subtracted costs for room and board, taxes, and mandatory deductions for savings, victim restitution, and family support. Additional savings to taxpayers would accrue in the form of higher quality goods at a reduced cost to taxpayers (Auerbach *et al.* 1979, p.11). Moreover, the fiscal saving leaves more resources for job training and the reduction of idleness.

The concept of 'penal industry' draws advocates from across the entire political spectrum, and liberals find a strange bedfellow in the former Chief Justice of the United States, Warren E. Burger, who is an outspoken proponent of 'factories with fences' rather than 'warehouses with walls', as he put the matter in a recent speech. Burger frequently points to the fiscal benefits of room and board and taxes paid by prisoners in the five states that have private employers in prison industries (Reske 1985).

After a brief history of private involvement in penal industry, I examine several rationales for the re-emergence of private employment in prisons. This is followed by discussion of a joint state-federal prison industries programme, focusing on one such programme at a Minnesota facility. Particular attention in this case study will be given to the power of the entrepreneur to influence penal operations and the effect of convict labour on the free-world labour market. This essay represents only an introduction to the analysis of the privatization of corrections, and deals mainly with the class and labour implications of private prisons and private prison industries. Another area that must subsequently be investigated more completely concerns the implications of such developments for theories of the state.

Factories with fences

The notion of productive penal labour is not new; most of today's rationales were first expressed more than a century ago. Prison reformers of the nineteenth century spoke of the 'work ethic' as the key to salvation for criminals, and prison wardens talked about the value of economically self-supporting institutions. In the United States, private productive arrangements took several discrete forms. In the South, the 'convict lease' was popular. With this arrangement, private companies took charge of the labour and welfare of the entire prisoner population. Prisoners in the Northern states were either leased to entrepreneurs who set up shop in the prison ('contract' system), leaving the welfare and security of the prisoners to state officials, or they simply provided raw materials for prison shops ('piece-price' system). The convict lease system, of course, was slavery (there is provision for penal slavery in the Thirteenth Amendment of the US Constitution); under the other two systems prisoners were paid little or nothing.[5] Not surprisingly, penal labour was very profitable for private employers and state governments; the contract system alone produced $17 million worth of merchandise nationwide in 1885 (US House of Representatives 1887). Forces external to the prison, however, militated against the continuation of a profit system in penal labour.

As early as 1801, small manufacturers opposed the unfair competition presented by the exploitation of convict labour; sometimes they were 'successful in effecting the passage of restrictive legislation aimed at reducing competition from the prisons' (Lewis 1967, p.48). In 1886, the Knights of Labour began a campaign to restrict convict labour, and Chicago area manufacturers of shoes, wagons, stoves, and furniture organized the National Anti-Convict-Contract Association (Mohler 1925, pp.569–70). These efforts succeeded, and by 1895 the total value of goods produced in prisons decreased to less than half of the 1885 value. Several states, including Illinois, New York, and Massachusetts, abolished the contract system altogether. To break up large operations, other states passed legislation diversifying prison work, limiting the percentage of inmates working in particular industries, or restricting the use of particular technologies in prison work (for example, power machinery). It was not until the 1920s and 1930s, however, that powerful state and federal legislation effectively ended large-scale prison production for profit, most notably in the provisions of the Hawes-Cooper Act of 1929 and the Ashurst-Sumners Act of 1935 — federal laws that prohibited interstate commerce in prison-made goods.

Many states retreated to 'state-use' systems exclusively, producing such articles as licence plates and office furniture for government departments and agencies. Some states made legal provisions that authorized exceptions whereby certain goods could be sold into open competition within the boundaries of their respective states. For example, twelve states authorized the open sale of farm machinery whilst at least three did the same for cordage products (Jensen 1974). Some of these prison industries still operate and continue to turn a profit. Nevertheless, with one respite, interstate commerce remained illegal. President Roosevelt temporarily revived industrial production for interstate commerce when he issued a decree in 1942 that permitted the federal government to procure from federal, state, or territorial prisons any goods needed for the war effort. President Truman rescinded the order in 1947, and American prisons headed into an extended period of low production and idleness. Charges of unfair business competition and the opposition of organized labour constrained penal industry. But many penologists were pleased to see the exploitative character of prison labour disappear (Sutherland and Cressey 1960, p.527).

The post-war years were the heyday of rehabilitation penology, a period in which the 'treatment' approach exercised considerable influence, if not on actual prison structure and operations, certainly in correctional rhetoric. Auerbach *et al.* (1979) contend that the rehabilitation model of the time had deleterious effects on prison industries, with 'over-assignment, lack of accountability, inattention to quality control standards, and overall "make-work" nature common to most prison work programmes . . .', combining to 'strip the work itself and the prisoner of any sense of dignity and self-worth. Work became a vehicle rather than an end in itself' (1979, p.9). And these were the fortunate prisoners; more than one-half of the state prison population languished in idleness.

Should penologists welcome the return of the entrepreneur to the prison workplace? Advocates of private penal industry deny that this will be the same old exploitation. What is different about their proposals for private sector involvement and those of the nineteenth century is the extent to which prison industries would resemble their free-world counterparts. Wages are to be paid to 'prisoner employees' at the minimum wage rate or at rates that prevail for similar work in the locality in which it is performed (Auerbach *et al.* 1979, p.11). In some formulations, 'fringe benefits' are proposed, including 'vacations with pay, sick leave, workers' compensation, unemployment compensation, special housing, improved food ration, liberalised visiting opportunities, special workers' recreation area, special clothing, and special workers' canteen' (Auerbach, *et al.* 1979, p. 21).[6] This is not mollycoddling the prisoner, Auerbach *et al.* hasten to add: the primary purpose of prison industries 'is to replicate as closely as possible conditions in the free world and this means rewards as well as performance expectations' (1979, p.22).

The theoretical basis for providing a 'realistic' work setting lies in the principles of the 'justice-as-fairness' model (Fogel and Hudson 1981). Proponents of this perspective (Hawkins 1983; Schaller 1981) distance themselves from the rehabilitative rationale which — because of critiques concerning programme efficacy (Martinson 1974) and moral legitimacy (Morris 1974; Rothman 1973) — is largely discredited as a purpose of punishment. The 'justice perspective' is said to be based on utilitarian principles and not the therapeutic ideal: 'Correctional agencies should engage prisoners as the law otherwise dictates; as responsible, volitional, and aspiring human beings, and not conceive of them as patients' (Schauer quoted in Fogel and Hudson 1981, p.viii). Prisoners can improve themselves if given the 'responsibility' that work requires, and one of the best opportunities to exercise 'free will' is in prison-based manufacturing operations (Schaller 1981, p.223) that resemble as closely as possible their free-world referents. In this way, the *work ethic* would be enhanced by such privatization (Auerbach *et al.* 1979, p.9; Hawkins 1983, p.117; Miller and Jensen 1974, p.22; Schaller 1981, p.222). The 'drudgery' typical of the 'state-use' system would be replaced with 'meaningful' work in the private sector; prisoners' self-respect and 'dignity' as workers would be enhanced (Auerbach *et al.* 1979, p.3; Schaller 1981, p.22) as their stake in society is increased through participation in free enterprise penal industry.

Other private sector advocates present a *moral argument* which asserts that, on humanitarian grounds, convicts should be released from their 'prison of unemployment' and idleness. Hawkins (1983, p.116) goes further to argue that under the United Nations' 1948 Universal Declaration of Human Rights, prisoners have a 'right to work'. Denmark, Sweden, Norway, and Mexico are cited as explicit adherents. Now, some might ask, why should convicts enjoy a right that is not accorded to free-world workers? And given the contemporary rates of unemployment, would this not violate the principle of 'less eligibility' — the centuries-old social policy which holds that the living condition of those incarcerated in poorhouses and prisons should be less desirable than the living condition of those occupying the lowest stratum of wage labour? Can one expect the cooperation of prison guards, who are major carriers into prison of the 'less eligibility' principle? Hawkins (1983, p.86) sees 'less eligibility' as misguided and anachronistic — 'the greatest obstacle to the rational organisation of prison industry'. Following Braithwaite's line of reasoning on the subject, Hawkins (1983, p.197) argues that 'a principle of *greater* rather than *lesser* eligibility should be applied to the prison population' as a matter of simple justice and equity. 'Compulsory unemployment in addition to the deprivation of liberty' constitutes a 'gratuitous excess of cruelty', Hawkins continues

(1983, p.116). Most states have adopted incapacitation as a major emphasis in penal theory and practice, and because the incapacitative policy is based on 'judgments about future behaviour that will in many cases be mistaken', Hawkins claims we have a 'moral obligation' to expand rehabilitative opportunities, although, once again, he reminds the reader that the rehabilitative ideal is not the principal justification for prisoner employment.

Bowditch and Everett (1985) point out, however, that there are certain impediments external and internal to the prison, including business and labour union opposition and the prison regime, that must be considered in attempts to implement free enterprise in the prison workshop. Hawkins (1983) and Auerbach *et al.* (1979) claim that business and labour objections are obsolete: 'In today's market the small private manufacturer, the "mom and pop" type of operation that served as the principal competition for prisoners in the last century, has been replaced by the giant corporation and the industrial conglomerate' which have no reason to fear competition (Auerbach *et al.* 1979, p.4). And to sceptics who ask about union objections, Hawkins answers that union 'views and tolerance of prison labour have softened over time' (1983, p.108). Whatever the validity of these assertions, there are still some internal impediments to the introduction of private industry.

The present organizational structure and operational routine of a typical modern American prison does not easily accommodate cost-efficient, profit-orientated industrial enterprises. Normal security concerns mean such day-to-day activities as head counts and lock-downs, and there are administrative and medical appointments, as well as educational programmes scheduled during business hours. Much time is absorbed shuttling prisoners back and forth to meals. All of this means lost time on the production line, lower efficiency, and inevitably less profit. While acknowledging that 'security will always remain the paramount concern of any prison', Auerbach *et al.* (1979) point out that the 'successful operation of a business-like industry project inside a prison requires that legitimate security concerns be balanced with equally legitimate business concerns'.

Free Venture prison industries programme

The first steps toward a 'rational solution to the prison labour problem' (Hawkins 1983, p.103) came in 1974 when the Law Enforcement Assistance Administration (LEAA) of the US Department of Justice requested proposals for an in-depth study of the 'economic and rehabilitative aspects of prison industries'. LEAA chose from a pool of over sixty applicants, supposedly the largest number of bidders for one contract in the history of the agency. In early 1975 the contract was given to ECON Inc., a consulting firm which in turn subcontracted the work to the American Foundation Inc. of Philadelphia. The Foundation, which had maintained an 'Institute of Corrections' since 1960, set technicians to work surveying state correctional systems and prison industry operations. Initially, these technicians were to select suitable testing sites for 'new concepts' developed by Foundation staff, and to implement selective testing by providing technical assistance to industries staff. LEAA promised 'start-up' funding to participating states.[7] The American Foundation published its research in six volumes, together entitled, *A Guide to Effective Prison Industries* (Auerbach *et al.* 1979). The first volume, entitled *Creating Free Venture Prison Industries: Programme Considerations*, provides a programme overview and rationale, with succeeding volumes devoted to the more technical aspects of programme implementation such as product selection, marketing, management and organization, and engineering principles.

A Guide to Effective Prison Industries called for a radical restructuring of prison industries, and consequently demanded a significant shift in policy and attitude on the part of industries and security staff alike. As presented in this volume, the basic components of Free Venture are:

1. A full working day for prisoners;
2. A wage based on production;
3. Productivity standards comparable to those of 'outside' industry;
4. Management control over hiring and firing of industry workers;
5. Self-sufficient to profitable shop operations within a reasonable period of time after start-up; and
6. An attempt to place released prisoners in jobs relevant to their work experience.

These proposals for 'normalization' of the internal environment of prison industry were followed by efforts to amend laws governing prison labour. The most important of these to date is the *Percy Amendment* to Public Law 96–157 (27 December 1979). In essence it amends 1930s federal legislation that prohibited interstate commerce in prison-made goods. It authorizes the administrator of LEAA to 'certify' state correctional industries to engage in interstate commerce, providing they meet certain Free Venture inspired guidelines. These guidelines incorporate the *Percy Amendment* provisions that 'inmate employment will not result in the displacement of employed workers, or be applied in skills, crafts, or trades in which there is a surplus of available gainful labour in the locality, or impair existing contracts for services'. As of 1985, over 20 states have legislated changes that authorize some form of contracting between industries and private companies. By January 1985, according to Sexton *et al.* (1985, p.6), the private sector had invested more than $2 million in 26 industries which together employed nearly 1000 prisoners at wages ranging from $0.25 to $7.75 per hour. Between 1976 and 1984, prisoners were paid $4.4 million in wages, and they, in turn, paid more than $775 000 in taxes and $470 000 in room and board charges. These figures have been cited by Warren Burger (Reske 1985) in support of his 'factories with fences' campaign.

Individual state correctional systems implementing Free Venture have altered the plan in relation to their unique conditions and needs. Some, like Minnesota, have been innovators in their own right. For over ninety years, Minnesota Correctional Industries (MCI) has been selling its products to both government agencies and private businesses within Minnesota. In 1907, the State Legislature authorized the manufacture of farm machinery which would be sold on the open market. By the 1920s, Minnesota was the most successful state in open market production. The net profits from the sale of binding twine and agricultural implements in 1920–21 was in excess of $500 000, after having paid convicts a 'decent wage' (Barnes 1969, p.284). Subcontracting small-scale industrial work from private industry was authorized in Minnesota as early as 1959, anticipating Free Venture recommendations by twenty years. In 1973, with the urging of Corrections Commissioners David Fogel and Kenneth Schoen, the State Legislature authorized the presence of private industry shops on the grounds of correctional facilities.

We will turn next to a case study of private operations in a state prison in Stillwater, Minnesota. A state long known for its liberal politics and private sector involvement in progressive social experiments, Minnesota provides us with a fair example of the application of the 'justice perspective'.[8] Private operations at Stillwater allow us to examine the promise of private sector advocates such as Auerbach *et al.*, who maintain that, under private arrangements:

> ... the prisoner ceases to be the object of constant surveillance and is accepted as a worker where his/her ability to produce quality items is what is important. Here the coercive, manipulative relations which are a natural outgrowth of the 'keepers vs. kept' syndrome are temporarily replaced each day by an atmosphere which focuses on real world concerns. In short, the 'normal' world of work imposes itself upon the prison for at least eight hours each day.... (1979, p.9)

Minnesota state industries: the factory in the prison or the prison in the factory?

In the nineteenth-century maximum-security Minnesota Correctional Facility at Stillwater, Cell Hall 'D' is unlike any other cell hall. In this area between the four-tiered steel cell block and the windowed cell house wall facing it, prisoners have made a 'student lounge'. Freshly painted and carpeted, the lounge contains tables, plants, a magazine carousel, study lamps, and a small library. Quiet and relaxed, this is the living and studying area for 44 students enrolled in a special college programme, a programme that is funded and directed by the prisoners themselves. Insight Inc., their business organization, generates revenues through a telemarketing business and a contract with Control Data Corporation to train homebound people in computer programming; its profits pay college tuition for all programme participants (Benidt 1985). Participants have special privileges, such as discretion in locking their cells, a quiet environment, and late hours.

The ground tier of cells in Block D houses the offices and workrooms of Insight. Several of the cells are occupied by solitary prisoners busy selling tyres and inner tubes by phone to retailers. An advertising brochure for Insight's telemarketing services points to the exceptional discipline of its telemarketers: a claim supported in part by Insight's 1985 profit report of $500 000 for its various businesses (Benidt 1985). This experiment in penal capitalism has met the approval of Warren Burger himself, who was impressed enough to attend one of Insight's baccalaureate commencements.

Insight workers are part of Stillwater's larger profit-oriented industrial system, the various divisions of which are collectively called Minnesota State Industries (MSI). Many prisoners are attracted to MSI by the promise of an enhanced wage and special privileges, but our examination of the wage structure and disciplinary regime of MSI reveals the seamy side of free enterprise in penal industry.[9] In November of 1983, MSI converted its wage-scale to an incentive plan based on the requirements of the American Correctional Association Standard 1.4.8, which specifies that workers are to be paid on a scale reflecting skill level and the quality and quantity of their work. With hourly wages ranging from $1.50 to $4.55, prisoners work for one of three employers:

1. Control Data Corporation, manufacturers of Magnetic Peripherals (disk drive units),[10]
2. School Bus and Auto/Truck Repair (auto mechanics), a state-owned business, and
3. Transcontinental Telemarketing Corporation.

The most desirable employer, Control Data, had between 82 and 140 men assigned to its assembly line in 1984, and paid its workers between $3.35 and $4.00 per hour.[11] School Bus had a manpower quota of 28 that year, and paid less than the minimum wage. Transcontinental paid its 20 workers $1.50 per hour and a 2½ per cent commission *when* group sales exceeded $300 000 in any given month.

In contrast to Minnesota's Free Venture participants, offenders employed within 'state industries' of other midwestern prisons average between $2.00 and $3.50 *per day* in wages. When MSI received Interstate Certification from the US Department of Labour Office of Economic Security, however, inmate workers were subtly advised that their wages might be subject to numerous deductions (up to 80 per cent) as required by the *Percy Amendment* to Public law 96–157, and Minnesota Statutes (Chapter 243.23, subdivision 2 and 3). These deductions include:

1. Withholding taxes (Federal, state, and possibly, local);
2. 'Reasonable' charges for room and board as determined by regulations which shall be issued by the Commissioner of Corrections (Minnesota has not deducted this as of 1985);
3. Allocations for support of family, pursuant to state statutes, court order, or agreement by the offender;
4. Contributions to any fund established by law to compensate the victims of crime.

Industry workers were further advised that state law authorizes the Commissioner of Corrections to set aside a portion of the inmate's wages and to disburse these funds to the prisoner upon release or in case of extreme family emergency. This policy, called Mandatory Savings, is presently in effect. In response to critics who would argue that, when considering these deductions, the 'normalized' wage represents a sleight of hand, Hawkins (1983, pp.111–112) points out that after taxes and necessary expenses, 'the vast majority of wage earners on the outside world' retains only a small balance of their pay-cheque for free spending.

When one turns to shop discipline, the 'normalized' world of work in Free Venture is even less appealing. The terms of the standard 'Inmate Employee Contract' would have pleased Henry Ford. The contract provides for the following:

1. A probationary period of six months. Failure to meet performance standards results in dismissal without the right of appeal;
2. Progression through the pay-scale in any shop is entirely at the discretion of the shop foreman (a civilian) and Industry management. Published pay rises on a time scale are to be used as guidelines, but poor attendance or work performance may result in a reduction of pay rises or no rise at all;
3. Inmates must not allow their unauthorized out-hours to exceed seven hours in any one calendar month. Out-hours that result from shop injuries, administrative idleness, or authorized medical lay-ins will not be included in the seven hour limit. If at any time, this

seven out-hour limit is exceeded, dismissal from Industries will occur, with no appeal. If there is reason to believe a worker is abusing the medical lay-in privilege, his or her attendance record will be reviewed by a committee composed of the Plant Manager, the Production Manager, the Personnel Specialist, and the Shop Foreman, and action will be taken if warranted;[12]

4. In the case of reduced production in any shop, employees may be temporarily assigned to another job or shop, as needed, or be subject to temporary lay-off, a decision made by the foreman;
5. No pay will be granted for hours not worked. This applies whenever a shop is shut down for any period of time due to administrative decisions, adverse weather, lack of work, or other similar causes;
6. After two warnings, violations of Industry Rules, as published, will result in disciplinary action up to and including dismissal;[13]
7. Employees are subject to dismissal at any time if the quality and quantity of work under their control falls below a standard established by industry management.[14]

The final provision states that a condition of employment 'shall be the willingness to move to a designated living area, as job and/or probationary status dictates'.

How do Stillwater inmate-employees view these 'realistic' conditions of employment? The observations of one prisoner at Stillwater, the Personnel Accounting Clerk, are worth quoting at length:

> As can be easily determined by reviewing the foregoing 'Do's' and 'Do Not's' contained within the foregoing quasi-legal bullshit, a whole lot of time is wasted threatening the inmate's job assignment, which would have a detrimental effect upon any man's job performance and attitude, if the entire environment was not itself already detrimental. (Chartier 1985, p.10)

And what about the enhancement of worker dignity and reinforcement of the work ethic private sector advocates claim? The Stillwater employee continues:

> Personally, it is my observation that people work for the money, and not out of diligent habits. As such, the private labour force working for all divisions of Industry is a success. It is far better to have some significant savings upon leaving one of these garbage cans after 'X' number of months and/or years than only a few hundred based upon a $2.00 a day economy. Slavery is still slavery by any other name, but some compensation has its benefits.

What enables employers to wield so much power over their labour force? How is the mandated behaviour enforced? Workers' awareness of the large pool of prisoners eligible and eager to work at the limited number of private sector jobs makes threats of dismissal an effective disciplinary tool. In limiting the number of private sector jobs, Free

Venture not only ensures compliance with its disciplinary demands, it promotes the identification of a prisoner-employee elite. In other words, by reconstituting penal labour into wage labour, by turning members of the nation's relative surplus population[15] into a proletariat, Free Venture partially recreates the class structure within prison walls, making prison more closely parallel the larger society. The involuntarily idle, many of those working in (low paid) state-use industries and maintenance jobs, laid-off workers (who are disqualified from unemployment compensation by the *Percy Amendment*), those who are dismissed for violation of minor rules, and the temporarily incapacitated become members of the *floating surplus population* in relation to the Free Venture labour market. Other potential members of this segment are those to whom the higher pay of private projects is not a significant incentive because they receive 'supplements to the low wage of state-run projects through such mechanisms as veterans' benefits' (Sexton *et al.* 1985, p.7), and are unwilling to face the higher performance standards demanded by the private sector.

Finally, Auerbach *et al.* (1979, p.9) describe a third stratum in these terms: 'The Free Venture Programme may hold little attraction, for example, to the offender who has coldly and rationally decided that he/she can always make an easier, better living as a pimp or a drug pusher than as a working person'. Those able, but unwilling, to co-operate with private initiatives, along with the *lumpenproletariat* become in effect the *stagnant surplus population* of the prison social structure. They enter a new category of deviance, doubly stigmatized. The dull-witted, the infirm, and the physically handicapped form the bottom 'sediment'. As in the operation of the labour market in the free world, those who refuse to work must clearly be 'less eligible' than those occupying the lowest stratum of the working class. Recognizing this, Schaller comments:

> Many institutions provide to all prisoners, or in some instances all prisoners involved in institutional programmes, a weekly support payment sufficient to allow the purchase of basic personal necessities. Industrial wages should not be linked with this institutional 'welfare' payment in the sense that such a payment *becomes* the wage. As in the free world, the minimum industrial wage should be set at a level above this welfare payment, to insure that it does in fact constitute a legitimate incentive to work. (1981, p.227)

The reintroduction of capitalist enterprise into prisons is influencing the prison regime and inmate social structure in ways many liberal proponents may not have anticipated. And if private enterprise reaches a large enough scale nationwide, it will probably have an impact on the operation of the free labour market as well. In the next section I consider some additional social control effects of private enterprise within the prison and then discuss probable external consequences.

Prisoners as workers

A wage-based industrial system existed in France from the beginning of the penitentiary system, and there may be lessons in French history for the contemporary period. Patricia O'Brien, in her seminal study of the nineteenth century French prison, observes:

> The control of the entrepreneur extended into every facet of prison life as a result of his control over the work process. Work was crucial for the disciplinary system and the entrepreneur was the single most important person in determining the structure of work. The entrepreneurs and work bosses were external agents in the system; they were, nevertheless, fundamentally important for daily surveillance and discipline. (1982, p.163)

We have seen that in the case of Stillwater, Free Venture prisoner-employees *qua* workers are held accountable for 'any institutional infraction' — as a consequence, the employer and his agents, who have no direct right of punishment over the prisoner, exert not only *direct* control of prisoner behaviour in the shop, but *indirect* control of inmate behaviour at other times.

The Free Venture proposal would not only influence work organization but overall prison structure and operation as well. Architects of Free Venture stress that the demands of industrial operations must take priority over traditional institutional concerns. Suggestions for lengthening the hours of production have included bag lunches for workers and rescheduling other institutional services to avoid interruptions in production. With the goals of productivity, not rehabilitation, in mind, Schaller (1981, pp.225, 230) even goes so far as to endorse the practice in Connecticut where 'social workers service the prison labour force in the shops rather than in individual offices'.

In addition to restructuring the institutional regime, the re-introduction of capitalist industry will impinge on the social relations of prisoners. The entrepreneur influences the social organization of the prison through the system of special privileges it accords workers. Miller and Jensen (1974, pp.23–24) point out that a wage system may disrupt the conventional power structure based on inmate subcultures. Traditionally, prison leaders help maintain control in exchange for custodial largesse 'in the form of immunities from enforcement of prison rules, rewards and special treatment.... Private bargains between correctional authorities and inmate leaders determine the actual allocation of punishment within the confines of the prison walls.' Miller and Jensen see a likelihood that this system of private bargains may be undermined by payment of wages to prisoners, thus reducing 'an individual prisoner's reliance upon disbursement of custodial largesse by prison leaders, and it is hoped eliminating many of the arbitrary punishments which characterise today's prisons'. Overlooked by the authors is the possibility of a black market of goods and services controlled by the new class of prisoner-workers, a possibility made more likely by the market orientation of the prison as a whole. Nevertheless, others would argue, the new work system is giving an improved meaning and order to interactions between prisoners and the administration, as well as to the relations of prisoners with each other.

But, would not the special privileges and income disparities among prisoners lead to friction? Might the wage-rate differences among workers within the same industry create conflict? Hawkins (1983) believes not. The principle of 'absolute fairness' between prisoners is in practice already subject to many variations. Moreover, he argues:

> Inequity, inequality, and anomaly are inherent in all punishment. Imprisonment as a punishment does not fall equally on all subjected to it. The degree to which any particular conditions of confinement are afflictive varies inevitably within the personality and prior experience of each prisoner. (1983, p.112)

Expressing the free-enterprise advocate's assumption about human nature and inequality, Hawkins concludes: 'And even if it were possible to transform penal institutions into enclaves of absolute isonomy, that intrinsic inequity would not diminish; it would, for many prisoners, be reinforced'.[16]

Although the creation of a new prisoner worker class threatens to transform the entire social structure of the prison, the greatest social impact of private penal enterprise may be felt outside the walls — by the free world labour-force. Capitalist penal industry is a potential threat to free-world workers in two ways:

1. It prepares a part of the 'reserve army of the unemployed' for duty in the free world, creating a more effective lever to drive down wages, and
2. Its manufacturers are at times in direct competition with domestic companies and, hence, jobs.

The use of incarceration as part of an attempt to instill 'the habits of industry' in a surplus population whose members were resistant to capitalism was behind the origin of the English 'houses of correction' in the seventeenth and eighteenth centuries, according to Ignatieff (1978, p.11). Paraphrasing the polemicists of nineteenth-century France to help shed light on the function attributed to penal labour (especially the debate concerning the subject of wages), Foucault observes:

> The labour by which the convict contributes to his own needs turns the thief into a docile worker. This is the utility of remuneration for penal labour; it imposes on the convict the 'moral' form of wages as the condition of his existence. Wages inculcate the 'love and habit' of work... (1979, p.273).

After thirty years of the rehabilitative rationale, the prison may be re-emerging as a workplace and a viable method of 'controlling marginalised populations while facilitating entry, or re-entry, of cheap labour to meet new investment needs' (Jankovic 1980). With a modest expenditure, industries that do not require capital investment in heavy equipment can exploit a labour-force possessing great flexibility and discipline. The burgeoning service sector, including telecommunications and computer operations, is a good prospect because of its minimum wage and minimal skill requirements. In 'electronic out-work' the rural isolation of most state prisons is not a problem; in fact, the isolation is helpful in that the conditions of the *Percy Amendment* concerning a wage rate 'which is not less than that paid for work of a similar nature in the locality in which the work was performed' can be met more easily. The major industries in areas where most state prisons are concentrated are agriculture and the prisons business itself. Like the telecommunication businesses that located inside Stillwater, the Phoenix headquarters of Best Western International, needing reservation agents willing to work holidays and weekends, established a telephone reservation centre inside the nearby Arizona Correctional Institute for Women in Phoenix. According to Sexton *et al.* a similar industry, 'operated by Howard Johnson's, Inc., is located inside a women's prison in Oklahoma' (Sexton *et al.* 1985, p.3).

Bettina Berch, in her article 'The resurrection of out-work' (1985), notes with interest:

> ... that changes in the regulation of convict labour have moved in parallel fashion to changes in the regulation of industrial out-work. In 1940 Congress banned interstate commerce in prison-made goods for private profit.... But in 1979 the Republicans pushed through legislation enabling [the Free Venture Programme]. (1985, p.43)

Home knitting was banned in 1942, and Republicans are now attempting to repeal prohibitions against 'household manufacturing'. Free Venture proponents (Hawkins 1983, p.108) claim, however, that this development does not constitute unfair competition because these jobs would be going to the Third World. Auerbach *et al.* (1979) argue:

> For many years now labour intensive industrial operations have been fleeing the United States in search of cheaper, third world labour.... some manufacturers have identified the American prisons as an attractive alternative to the sometimes expensive move to foreign based production.... It is not at all unrealistic to assert that, in the future, prison manufacturing operations will pose a greater threat to Hong Kong and Seoul than they do to Detroit or Pittsburgh. Jeremy Bentham's principle of 'lesser eligibility' has thus been turned inside out, with American prison labour's status enhanced at the expense of the foreign worker. (1979, p.4)

Nowhere else in the United States can capital get away with paying the minimum wage, or with providing no unemployment compensation or health insurance, while enjoying free use of facility space, political stability, and the efforts of a disciplined labour-force. If prisons prove competitive with the 'offshore office', 'runaway shops' may return to the United States in the form of 'internal colonialism', to borrow a concept from Alvin Gouldner (1977–78) applied to another context. Will these changes in social control provoke changes in class relations? The questions that O'Brien (1982, pp.163–164) asked of the nineteenth century French prison again become relevant. Will convicts develop a consciousness as workers? In what way will prisoners as workers correspond to and identify with workers outside of prison? How will free workers regard their criminal counterparts? Will prisoner-workers attempt to organize? And what about strikes?

Summary and conclusion

Whilst the United States prison population has reached record levels over the past decade, there has also been a trend to reduce the size, scope, and cost of government. These conflicting trends have posed major dilemmas for policy-makers, and the privatization of prisons has been offered by some as a solution. The idea of private prisons has been especially popular among neo-conservative academics and policy advisors. They have promoted privatization with the help of technical experts and intellectuals in residence at such conservative 'think-tanks' as The Reason Foundation, The Heritage Foundation, and The American Foundation Inc. Privatization is not only a cheaper and more efficient way of incarcerating people, but the private sector possesses a greater flexibility and speed in relation to construction contracts, enhancing the ability of prison capacity to respond to 'the laws of supply and demand' (Logan and Rausch 1985). In effect, by taking government out of penal administration we can achieve more state control.

Liberal critics have questioned the propriety of delegating the power to punish to corporations. Private industry within government-operated prisons, however, has received support from those of nearly all political persuasions. Fogel and Hudson (1981), Schaller (1981), and Hawkins (1983) view private employment of prisoners as a less threatening form of privatization, and advocate private work arrangements as an alternative to the enforced therapy and idleness that prevailed as punishments during the post-war 'rehabilitation' era of penal history. They stress the 'voluntary' nature of the Free Venture programme: 'Coerced participation in prison work activities paves the way for worker exploitation and its attendant by-products as mentioned earlier: sabotage, diminished production, disruptive behaviour, and work stoppages' (Schaller 1981, p.223). Moreover, 'normalization' would enhance the dignity of work (Fogel 1981, p.vii). In the most optimistic versions of Free Venture (Auerbach *et al.* 1979), prisons would appear as 'exclusive' institutions, much like the New Army, where members of the underclass could come to experience 'meaningful' work.

In our case study of the work programme at Stillwater we saw that the presence of capital was not as benign as many liberals would have us believe. The prison regime was determined largely by profit considerations, rather than security, rehabilitation, or other traditional administrative concerns. And entrepreneurs exercised a measure of control over their prisoner-employees — both on and off the shop-floor — that most industrial managers can only dream of possessing. With nearly a half million persons willing to work for the minimum wage (minus deductions), penal labour threatens free-world workers. While some union leaders point to prisoner exploitation, others point out that convicts are eligible for a welfare benefit greater than that provided for free citizens. Unlike free-world workers, prisoners are assured housing, medical care, and a subsistence diet. Free Venture threatens to undermine the bargaining position of free labour, and this prospect may further reinforce traditional worker animosity toward convicts.

A new development is on the penal horizon. The *conjunction* of private prisons and private penal industry has profound implications for both convicts and their keepers, and guards *vis-à-vis* administrators. The privatization of prisons entails a shift in power among the structural interests of corrections. The typical 'corporate warden' is a well-paid pensioned state or federal service retiree, who is recruited by companies funded by 'venture-capital' firms (Becker and Stanley 1985, p.729; Krajick 1984, p.11). Examples include veteran correctional officials such as T. Don Hutto, former Commissioner of Corrections in Arkansas and Virginia, who is now president of Corrections Corporation of America, and Charles Fenton, who was warden of three major federal prisons, and is now President of Buckingham Security. These former government functionaries lend experience and enhance the legitimacy of the enterprise. The occupational prospects for those lower on the professional ladder are not so bright, however. Whilst penal facility administrators and departmental bureaucrats from the public sector have an opportunity to enter the managerial ranks of private prison corporations, rank-and-file security personnel become 'proletarianized'. Wages, fringe benefits, and working conditions will be affected by the desire for profit.

The issue of prisoners as workers acquires a new dimension in an entirely privatized setting, and the prospect of guard-workers disciplining a class of prisoner-employees suggests a whole new set of issues. Will guard-workers in the commercial prison relate to convicts as fellow workers? Will traditional inmate complaints about exploitation assume a new meaning to guards who themselves feel exploited, perhaps by the same employer?

Free market criminal justice advocates often employ the language and reasoning of classical liberalism. Because prison 'supply, especially at current prices, is unable to meet demand' (Logan and Rausch 1985, p.303), commercial prisons would open a bottleneck denounced by neo-conservatives. This 'new source of supply', more attuned to market forces, would possess a 'flexibility' (to expand) that promises not only to save money but enhance justice as well, at least from the viewpoint of the 'just deserts' model: 'prison flow should respond to crime rates, which are largely beyond state control':

> At least at the margins, then, the prison system must be able to expand and contract as the shifting demands of justice require. (Logan and Rausch 1983, p.115)

The rational market model ignores *political* influence. Instead of responding to the changing demands of criminal justice, would prison capacity and sentence length mainly be constrained by economic concerns and the political influence of penal entrepreneurs? And prison capacity need not be influenced by the number of convicts that entrepreneurs could profitably employ. The idle prisoner would not be a liability in a system where prisoners are not only a source of surplus value in the workshop but are commodities *qua* idle prisoners as well. Capitalists not only know how to shift the support of the surplus population on to the shoulders of the working-class taxpayer, but they may have found a way to profit directly from them as well.

15 Mandatory Supervision and the penal economy
R.S. Ratner

Introduction

The economic hardships of the 1980s appear connected to demands for greater harshness in the Canadian criminal justice system. Canada has always had a comparatively large proportion of its population in prison[1] (Waller and Chan 1974). Even in the past decade, with control policies purportedly bent on deinstitutionalization and diversion, inmate populations have continued to grow (Chan and Ericson 1981; Culhane 1985; MacLean 1986). Between 1978–1979 and 1982–1983, for example, the official average daily adult prison population in Canada (federal and provincial institutions combined) increased 22 per cent from 21 963 to 26 924, and the population on probation and parole increased 31 per cent from 61 738 to 80 912 (*Juristat* 1984). During 1982–1983, provincial institutions, on average, functioned at 97 per cent of operational capacity and 90 per cent of total available capacity; the corresponding rates in federal penitentiaries were 93 and 88 per cent respectively (*Juristat* 1984). Obviously, the system was approaching its holding capacity. Further, more stringent parole policies, and new sentencing legislation (including the minimum 25-year life sentence for first degree murder instituted in 1976) served to hasten the inevitable crunch. Earlier plans to build 26 new penitentiaries were jettisoned, forcing authorities to resort to the practice of 'double-bunking' in order to absorb the influx of new prisoners.[2] Growing tensions, attributable in part to the effects of double-bunking, flared up into major prison disturbances, particularly in the maximum security institutions of Kent (British Columbia), Stony Mountain (Manitoba), and Archambault (Quebec).[3] Yet in the absence of new prison construction,[4] administrators were reduced to the sole option of raising the number of prisoners conditionally released (Solicitor General Canada 1984, pp. 23, 72). Since public apprehension over Parole Board leniency had already instigated a more conservative parole-granting policy (Solicitor General Canada 1981a, Table A18), the main release mechanism has been 'Mandatory Supervision' (MS). This allows penitentiary inmates who are not released on parole to accumulate time by statutory or earned remission, and to serve that time under supervision in the community. Remission, or 'time off for good behaviour', can comprise as much as one-third of an inmate's sentence, so most Mandatory Supervision releasees leave prison *automatically* at the two-thirds mark of their sentence, even if they have been assessed as poor candidates for parole. This statutory release of prisoners under Mandatory Supervision has come under heavy criticism recently, particularly following media accounts of the violent offences committed by prisoners who have been released into the community on MS. Demands for swift revocation of MS violators, and calls for the abolition of earned remission, have led to new legislation, partly in order to assuage public anxieties while salvaging MS as a viable conditional release option.

The manner in which the authorities have attempted to confront serious budgetary and legitimation problems through this new legislation illustrates the important role performed by 'criminal justice' in response to the pressures of a faltering economy. Bills C–67 and C–68 (described below) which address the problems of conditional release, and which are expected to become law by mid-1986, deserve scrutiny, therefore, as a revealing instance of the relationship between fiscal crisis and mechanisms of social control.

A short history of parole[5]

The idea of 'parole' can be traced to an order of the English Privy Council in 1617, which made it a policy of the government to transport convicts overseas when it was found necessary to reduce the increasing prison population. After the American Revolutionary War, English convicts were sent to New South Wales in Australia where the Governor was given the power of conditional pardon, which later developed into the ticket-of-leave system introduced by Captain Alexander Maconochie, Governor of Norfolk Island, a penal colony east of Australia. Maconochie's 'good time' principle (leading to the ticket-of-leave) was elaborated on and improved in Ireland and in the United States, demonstrating that a system of conditional liberation was workable for both the protection of society and the rehabilitation of the criminal.

Parole began in Canada with the passage of the Ticket-of-Leave Act in 1899 by the Federal Parliament. Prior to 1899, prisoners were released from custody by Order of the Governor General upon the advice of a Minister of the Crown as an expression of the Royal Prerogative of Mercy. These releases were, in most cases, unconditional as there was no one to enforce any condition. Between 1899 and 1905, the number of tickets-of-leave, or 'licences' as they were called, increased markedly, and by the end of World War I, this experimental parole system had become an established institution.

Since Canada was a vast and sparsely settled country, the task of developing a system of close parole supervision was not an easy one.[6] As a result, the parole policy was fairly conservative and much reliance was placed on a provision in the Ticket-of-Leave Act for monthly reporting by the parolee to the local police. Even so, criticism that parole had been granted too liberally was part of the aftermath of social unrest following World War I (epitomized by the Winnipeg General Strike of 1919), which precipitated a demand for more severity in the criminal justice system. This led to a reorganization of the Remission Branch, a section of the Department of Justice responsible for the administration of the Ticket-of-Leave Act. Soon afterwards, the granting of tickets-of-leave was again liberalized to counter the increase in prison population during the Depression years, and then to allow prisoners to join the Armed Forces or to accept employment in war industry. Considerable expansion in social services took place during the post-war years, and a voluntary aftercare movement spread (including the Salvation Army and the John Howard and Elizabeth Fry Societies) which assisted in community investigations and parole supervision.

In 1953, the Minister of Justice appointed a Committee, under the chairmanship of Mr Justice Gerald Fauteux, to enquire into the ticket-of-leave system. The Fauteux Committee reported in 1956 that while it was 'astonished' that 'such antiquated legislation' could provide 'such satisfactory results' (1956, p.55), it felt the parole authority should become organizationally independent from the penal service (1956, p.80). The *Fauteux* Committee endorsed some period of supervision in the community prior to the expiration of sentence, and recommended the implementation of a statutory parole period for all prison releasees. The suggestion was that this supervision period should correspond to the time earned by way of statutory remission.

The recommendations of the Fauteux Report were implemented in 1959 with the proclamation of the Parole Act and the creation of a National Parole Board. The new legislation transferred the authority to grant conditional release to a board with members appointed by the Governor-in-Council. The concepts of reform and rehabilitation were incorporated into the law as statutory considerations in the granting of parole, with parole envisioned as a logical step between confinement and freedom. In order to implement this latter function, a National Parole Service was established to prepare cases for Board consideration and to supervise parolees in the community.[7]

Partly in response to the civil rights movements in the late 1960s (which once again called the criminal justice system into question), the Government created the Canadian Committee on Corrections in 1969, under the direction of Quebec Superior Court Judge Roger Ouimet. The Committee undertook its study on the premise that society should receive the maximum protection from criminals that is consistent with the freedom of the people to be protected, at the same time inflicting no more harm on the offender than is necessary. The Report of the Committee (Ouimet 1969) contained recommendations for extensive changes to the criminal justice system, including restrictions on the discretionary authority of the National Parole Board, and the establishment of a period of statutory supervision. The Committee expressed concern that the most dangerous offenders were being released without any of the controls or benefits of supervision which were accorded to the better risk parolees. The Committee's recommendation for a 'statutory conditional release' programme based on the statutory remission period was meant to extend supervision to those who were being released directly into the community. This recommendation resulted in amendments to the Parole Act of 1969 requiring that an inmate released as a result of remission be supervised in the community, under a programme known as 'Mandatory Supervision', for the remainder of the sentence. Release under Mandatory Supervision could be suspended if the offender violated specified conditions, and could be revoked by the Parole Board if an investigation confirmed that the suspension was warranted.

At first, the Board's jurisdiction was deemed to be relevant only to an offender's behaviour *after* he/she had been released. As the number of violent crimes committed by individuals released on Mandatory Supervision appeared to be increasing, Section 16 of the Parole Act, relating to the suspension of release 'to protect society', was re-examined. One interpretation concluded that the Board had the authority to *suspend, immediately upon release*, an individual who is obviously dangerous at the designated time of his or her Mandatory Supervision, in order to prevent further harm to the public. Thus, the practice of 'gating' was initiated.

Between September 1982 and May 1983, 11 MS releasees were gated (out of 1737 releases over that period). All 11 had histories of violence or serious sexual offences, or both. A number of those gated placed the matter before the courts on the grounds:

1. That the gating policy was an unreasonable reading of those sections of the Parole Act used to justify it; and
2. That the practice violated Section 9 of the Canadian Charter of Rights and Freedoms, which prohibits arbitrary detention or imprisonment.

In May 1983, the Supreme Court of Canada declared gating to be illegal, and all gated individuals who were still incarcerated were released on MS. In the meantime, the Solicitor General of Canada had placed before the Senate an amendment to Bill S–32 which would have legalized gating. A revised version, Bill C–35, was introduced in the House of Commons, but died on the Order Paper. The 1983–1984 Annual Report of the Solicitor General comments on these developments:

> The Board continues to place the highest priority on minimising the risk to society when making its decisions to grant conditional release. The Board and the Correctional Service of Canada are making every effort to ensure the early identification and effective handling of potentially dangerous offenders prior to release on Mandatory Supervision. Under current law, the Board has no authority to deny release, into the community, of inmates who have earned remission time and yet may be deemed a danger to society.... Bill S–32 and subsequently, Bill C–35, were introduced with the objective of amending the Mandatory Supervision regulation to give the Board discretionary authority in such cases. The legislation was not passed at the dissolution of Parliament, but it is expected to be re-introduced in 1984–85. (Solicitor General Canada 1984, p.49)

Accordingly, Bills C-67 and C-68 were introduced to Parliament in 1985, and (at the time of writing this chapter) the National Parole Service is operating on the assumption that these bills will clear their third and final reading before May 1986.

The criticisms of Mandatory Supervision are rife. Inmates feel that they are unfairly subject to supervision on the remission time that was lawfully earned. Indeed, ever since 1868, prisoners in Canada have been released, without obligation, at the two-thirds mark of their sentence for good behaviour. Only since 1970 have inmates so released been placed under Mandatory Supervision.

Various citizens' groups (especially those belonging to the crime victims' movement), under the impression that criminal violence is on the increase in Canada despite evidence to the contrary (Solicitor General 1984, p.6)[8] have called for the abolition of Mandatory Supervision, the end of the National Parole Board, and more stringent parole conditions for violent criminals. The police, too, are opposed to the mandatory release aspect of Mandatory Supervision, and the Canadian Association of Chiefs of Police has urged that earned remission be abolished, and that inmates serve the whole of their sentence in prison, subject only to the possibility of parole (Canadian Association of Chiefs of Police 1977).

Parole officers, while generally supportive of the extension of services to MS releasees, dislike having to supervise uncooperative clients. Penitentiary authorities regret the disciplinary problems represented by those MS releasees who are returned to custody, although they favour the earned remission concept since it provides a strong incentive for 'good behaviour', thus contributing to the safety of prison staff.

Advocates of parole have also questioned Mandatory Supervision on the grounds that such a release mechanism reduces the opportunities for genuine parole, thereby accounting for the declining number of full paroles granted in recent years (Nuffield 1982, p.69). Civil libertarians complain of the arbitrary nature of many MS revocations, the oppressive nature of supervision practices, the undermining of benefits that accrue from earned remission, and, more recently, the explicit violations of the Canadian Charter of Rights and Freedoms arising out of MS regulations.

The proposed legislation to modify the Mandatory Supervision programme has been criticized by task forces of the Canadian Bar Association since 1983 on the grounds that the amendments are piecemeal and will only exacerbate already dangerous levels of prison overcrowding.[9]

Earlier expressions of dissatisfaction with Mandatory Supervision led to the creation of two further commissions of inquiry into the Canadian parole system: the Hugessen Committee, which reported in 1973, and the Goldenberg Committee of the Senate, which presented its recommendations in 1974. Both committees strongly endorsed some period of supervision prior to the expiration of a prisoner's sentence. Subsequently, the Law Reform Commission's report 'Studies on imprisonment' (1976) recommended the abolition of both statutory and earned remission, but advocated a period of transition for all inmates that would provide assistance and supervision for the last one-third of the sentence. In 1977, the 'Report to Parliament' by the Parliamentary Sub-committee on the Penitentiary System in Canada commented on the 'arbitrary aspects' of both parole and MS, but it included no specific recommendations for modifying the current system, other than to suggest that it be reviewed in an effort to remedy some of its problematic features.

In 1981, after examining the sundry and conflicting proposals regarding Mandatory Supervision, the Solicitor General's Joint Committee ended their deliberations on this indecisive note:

> The available options for Mandatory Supervision would appear to be either ineffective or at odds with each other in responding to all concerns; or would entail unreasonably high costs (in various areas including financial) in comparison with the expected benefit; or would simply be organisationally or politically impossible. Moreover, some of the concerns are literally insoluble, a by-product of criminal justice. (Solicitor General 1981)

But the more retributive mood of the 1980's ushered in the mislabelled 'justice model' of corrections,[10] which, along with the media notoriety given to the sporadic crimes of violence committed by offenders who had been released on MS, climaxed in the 'gating' of several MS releasees and the subsequent legislation contained in Bills

C-67 and C-68. Although independent research has shown that predictions regarding 'dangerousness' cannot as yet effectively identify individuals who are likely to commit violent offences (Hackler and Gauld 1981), and that a conservative parole-granting policy is sacrificing the rehabilitative and financial benefits that a more liberal parole policy would provide (Shewan 1985), the proposed amendments to the Parole Act, permitting greater control over MS releasees, have been strongly endorsed by the Parole Board (*Liaison* 1985, pp.6–7).

Functions of Mandatory Supervision

Before considering the specific effects of key provisions in the new legislation, we need to identify basic institutional imperatives and show how these relate to structural contradictions emerging in Canadian society — those which engender the size of the prison population and corresponding policies of social control. The habitual reluctance to take analysis of correctional issues to this more abstract level has obscured the reasons for the perpetuation of vain 'rehabilitative' attempts. As MacLean notes:

> ... prisons still operate despite their failure.... This observation may lead one to conclude that there exist other objectives of the penal system that are as yet latent and undetected.... Perhaps this line of inquiry may prove fruitful in explaining the continued maintenance of Canada's penal system when so much evidence indicates that it is failing. (1983, p.408)

Justice researchers and administrators in the United States have been more candid than their Canadian counterparts about their perception and implementation of correctional policy as a method of *controlling prison populations* (Mathias and Steelman 1982; Zedlewski 1984). Canadian policy analysts and officials have deprecated this outlook, as typified by the remarks of John Konrad, Chairman of the British Columbia Board of Parole, delivered at a recent Canadian Congress on Criminal Justice:

> In Canada, unlike evidently the US, parole has never (at least not officially) been intended to serve as a mechanism to control prison population. Many of the US states have been quite candid about this and have, in fact, enacted legislation to further the objective of controlling prison population by means of parole.... It should be obvious to any casual observer that parole has an effect on prison population (in more ways than numerically); however, I would submit that if the control of prison population becomes the objective (as opposed to the result) of parole, we will see a serious deterioration of its value in relation to the historical functions of parole, such as the protection of the public and the rehabilitation and re-integration of the offender. (Solicitor General Canada 1983, p.18)

Such demurrals notwithstanding, there is no denying that the penitentiary inmate population *is* a function of the balance between the number of admissions and the number of releases (see for example, Solicitor General of Canada 1984, pp.25–29 and 72–6; Canadian Centre for Justice Statistics 1985, pp.119–37), and that the population growth rate is, therefore, subject to policy controls.

At this point, it is possible to identify four institutional-level imperatives relevant to the debate on Mandatory Supervision:

1. *Decarceration*: the need to allow for a level of deinstitutionalization that would contain the costs of prison construction.

   At present, there are over 12000 federal prisoners at an average annual cost of $40000 per inmate. The cost of supervising an offender on parole or MS is approximately $4000 per annum. The average daily number of offenders on Mandatory Supervision within the Correctional Service of Canada (CSC) is 1800. Approximately 3000 new prisoners are released annually on MS and 1200 are recommitted for new offences or violations of technical restrictions imposed by the Parole Board (Correctional Services of Canada 1984). Total federal expenditures (including both CSC and NPB) on adult corrections in 1983–1984 amounted to $666 million (Canadian Centre for Justice Statistics 1985, pp.108–9). There is little question that if Mandatory Supervision were abolished, prison populations would increase, and at a time when Canada's detention facilities are running at, or near, full occupancy and when construction of new ones is prohibitively expensive.[11] In this respect, the policy of Mandatory Supervision enables the prison to absorb new offenders within existing facilities by releasing a significant percentage of the penitentiary population (close to 25 per cent annually) into the community. This alleviates institutional overcrowding and stimulates the development of less costly community-based services.[12]
2. *Recarceration*: contrarily, the need to assure a new level of reinstitutionalization that would foster organizational expansion.

   Mandatory Supervision has effectively lengthened the control of the state over penitentiary inmates by up to 50 per cent of their non-remitted sentence term, and approximately 500 inmates per year are returned to prison (see Table 15.1 and Figure 15.1) on technical revocations, without any statistical evidence available to suggest that this action has resulted in the prevention of criminal acts.[13] In this respect, Mandatory Supervision augments the carceral power of the National Parole Board, enabling it to maintain and expand correctional resources, power, and autonomy. Unsurprisingly, budgetary expenditures and personnel for both the CSC and the NPB have increased regularly since their formation.[14] Moreover,

*Table 15.1 Outcome (to June 1980) of MS releases from 1970 to 1979**

Year of release	Total releases on MS	Revoked without new offence	Revoked with new offence	Offence after successful completion**	Successful completion, and no subsequent readmissions	Still under supervision
		Number (and releases) of MS releases				
1970	3	0 (0.0)	1 (33.3)	1 (33.3)	1 (33.3)	0 (0.0)
1971	30	8 (10.0)	25 (31.3)	10 (12.5)	37 (46.2)	0 (0.2)
1972	871	103 (11.8)	227 (26.1)	131 (15.0)	410 (47.0)	0 (0.0)
1973	1,780	234 (13.1)	415 (25.0)	248 (13.9)	852 (47.8)	1 (0.1)
1974	2,382	251 (10.5)	616 (23.9)	297 (12.5)	1,209 (50.7)	9 (0.3)
1975	2,431	329 (13.5)	623 (25.6)	278 (11.4)	1,199 (49.3)	2 (0.1)
1976	2,555	520 (20.4)	594 (23.2)	218 (8.5)	1,219 (47.7)	4 (0.1)
1977	2,822	578 (20.5)	547 (19.4)	278 (9.9)	1,408 (49.8)	11 (0.3)
1978	2,913	551 (18.9)	454 (15.6)	271 (9.3)	1,513 (51.9)	124 (4.2)
1979***	2,524	465 (18.4)	369 (14.6)	59 (2.3)	985 (39.0)	646 (25.6)

* Table A-25 of the *Solicitor General's Study of Conditional Release*, Report of the Working Group, Department of the Solicitor General, Canada, March, 1981.

** These cases successfully completed their Mandatory Supervision period, but were subsequently readmitted to penitentiary for a new offence after the completion of the MS period.

*** It should be noted that many of the persons released in this year were still under supervision as of June 1980, and revocation rates for this release year must therefore not be taken as definitive.

the uninterrupted pattern of increase in crime control expenditures and agency employment rates, even in the face of growing government deficits, suggests that criminal justice expenditures represent a form of state spending that transfers purchasing power to a wide range of persons who might otherwise be unable to act as consumers in the general economy (MacLean 1986; Quinney 1979). By increasing employment in this manner, and thus facilitating the realization of surplus value, economic and political crises are to some degree averted, at least in the short term.

3. *Control*: the need to extend surveillance in order to monitor 'trouble' and widen the involvement of agencies of 'criminal justice'.

   In this respect, the interest in deterrence and prevention is largely feigned since control authorities recognize that, barring major structural changes (which they seldom wish to initiate), it is not possible to prevent crime (*ergo*, the 'justice model' of sentencing and corrections). The 'realistic' aim of criminal justice in a deteriorating capitalist economy such as now exists in Canada, becomes that of identifying and isolating those sectors of the population which must be subjected to unrelenting control, since their relative vulnerability to economic crisis constitutes them as the core of potential dissent. Mandatory Supervision, which places one such cluster of individuals under permanent scrutiny (through 'supervisory' powers that often result in a return to custody), can neutralize dissidence both within and beyond prison walls.

4. *Legitimation*: the need to legitimate the above functions through claims of protecting the public and providing humanitarian services to the fallen.

   The rhetoric of 'reintegration' is bruited, though public safety is accorded priority over inmate rehabilitation, thus polarizing the two objectives. In this respect, the comparatively meagre resources allotted to community-based treatment[15] attest to the hollowness of reintegration schema. Legitimation strategies net greater political dividends when they are invoked on behalf of greater coercive control, such as when public remonstrations over the sensationalized violations of MS releasees are used to justify more repressive policies. Any such escalation of control, however, must be careful not to overtax fiscal capacity nor 'expose' the motive of organizational expansion.

Changes in the penal economy

Turning now to the ways in which the Mandatory Supervision programme is likely to be affected by the new legislation, four key provisions in Bill C-67 are expected to have considerable impact in the context of the above institutional imperatives.[16] They are as follows:

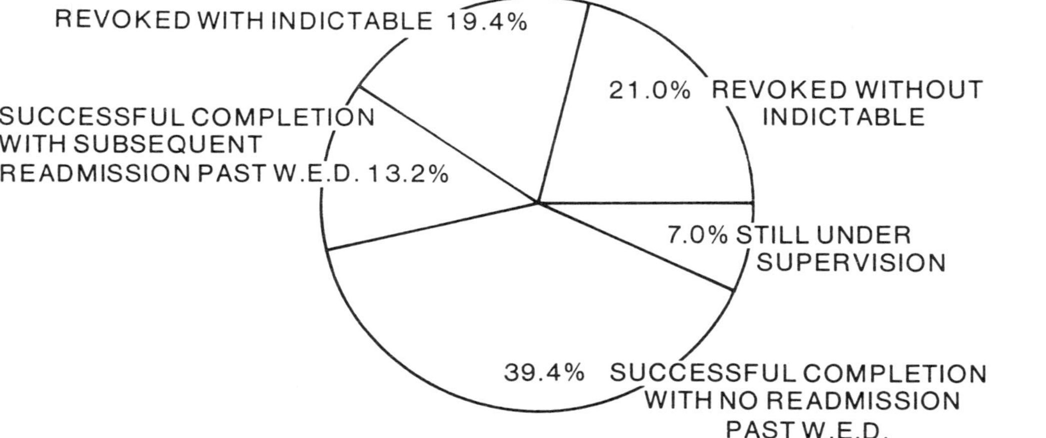

Data supplied by the Pacific Regional Office, Abbotsford, B.C.

Figure 15.1 *Follow-up of all Mandatory Supervision releases (25660 in Canada 1957/76 through to 1984/85 and their outcome to June 1985*

1. Prevention of automatic release.
2. Earlier assessment of parole eligibility.
3. Prescribed residency requirements.
4. One-shot revocation.

These provisions are considered sequentially, and then in their interrelation. The discussion of each provision is prefaced by the section of Bill C-67 ('An Act to Amend the Parole Act and the Penitentiary Act' — First Reading, 27 June 1985) that gives the relevant amendment.

Prevention of automatic release: Section 15.4(4)

> On completion of the hearing and review of the case of an inmate pursuant to this section, the Board may, if it is satisfied that the inmate is likely to commit, prior to the expiration according to law of the sentence he is then serving, an offence causing the death of or serious harm to another person, by order,
>
> (a) direct that the inmate shall not be released from imprisonment prior to the expiration according to law of the sentence he is serving at the time the order is made.

The intent of the above subsection is to build in some procedures for the Parole Board to refuse Mandatory Supervision to those individuals who are due to be released at the two-thirds mark of their sentence, since they are deemed to be 'dangerous' and likely to commit a serious offence even before warrant expiry. Parole Board officials do not expect that this provision will significantly alter the numbers of those in custody, nor worsen conditions of overcrowding in the penitentiaries.[17] It is thought that only a few dozen prisoners a year would be identified for detention, enough to abate the rising tide of hostility toward MS and parole, and take the pressure off the much larger group of non-dangerous prisoners scheduled for release. Some CSC officials acknowledge that the provision is a 'legitimation technique', although it is feared that the anticipated effect may backfire when detained inmates are eventually released at warrant expiry.[18] Identifying those requiring detention is also regarded as a difficult matter, given that predictions of dangerousness are currently so imprecise (Hackler and Gauld 1981). Moreover, since much violence is situationally generated, and therefore impossible to predict in many instances, a small number of undetained releasees will inevitably commit violent offences, so the detention procedure cannot completely quell public anxieties. Ironically, the Board may be perceived as more liable than before for errant releasees since it has now installed a formal procedure for detention hearings.

In sum, legitimation benefits may be reaped through this provision (although there are potential complications), perhaps justifying further extensions of the Board's authority. Fiscal implications are relatively minor, except for the additional workload for those who must build a case for or against detention. This could lead to some increase of CSC personnel and promote a not unwelcome spurt of organizational expansion.

Assessment of parole eligibility: Section 8.(1,2)

> The Board shall review the case of every inmate who is sentenced to imprisonment in or transferred to a penitentiary for two years or more at the times prescribed by the regulations *but not later than the day* on which an inmate has served the portion of the term of imprisonment, as prescribed by the regulations, that must be served before day parole may be granted.

This amendment, which may well be the major change wrought by Bill C-67, requires that the Board review all inmate cases no later than the day-parole eligibility date — the one-sixth mark of the sentence — with a view to releasing all inmates as early as possible in order that they might serve most of their sentence in the community rather than in prison.[19] It is believed that public safety would be enhanced, in the long run, by acclimatizing prisoners to the community on a more sustained basis than is now afforded by such measures as temporary absences.[20] More importantly, it is predicted that the one-sixth review will compensate for any further growth in the prison population attributable to 'detentions' of those scheduled for release on Mandatory Supervision. Earlier and compulsory parole eligibility reviews, calling for direct panelling rather than paper-assessment of inmates, would likely identify more potential releasees and prevent institutional overcrowding — a crucial objective given the Treasury Board edict to scrap the earlier government plans for extensive prison construction.[21] Correctional authorities do, of course, anticipate an initial crush of case preparation and increased screening as more day-paroles are granted at the one-sixth mark.[22] Accordingly, the new legislation provides for ten extra full-time country-wide Board members, raising the number to thirty-six. Increased hiring of CSC personnel (for case preparation and parole supervision) seems inevitable. Thus, some institutional expansion will be one likely outcome of this feature of the new legislation.

The most problematic aspect of this particular amendment concerns the availability of community resources. At present, there are too few beds available in half-way houses, and the existing array of educational, therapeutic, and lifestyle programmes is inadequate to absorb any significant increase in the number of offenders on parole.[23] While the legislation could lead to public demands for more resources, it is not at all clear that community residents welcome the prospect of more offenders circulating in their neighbourhoods, particularly when they continue to conceive of parole as non-punishment, rather than as serving jail time in the community. Public anxieties, therefore, will be difficult to trivialize, especially when parolee transgressions are accorded media notoriety.[24] Consequently, the legitimation procured via detention of MS releasees could be lost through alarm caused by apparent failures in the early release system.

Prescribed residency requirements: Section 15.4 (4)

> On completion of the hearing and review of the case of an inmate pursuant to this section, the Board may, if it is satisfied that the inmate is likely to commit, prior to the expiration according to law of the sentence he is then serving, an offence causing the death or serious harm to another person, by order,
>
> (b) Impose, subject to subsection (5), as one of the conditions of release on mandatory supervision of the inmate, residence in a community-based residential facility.

Subsection (b) legitimates and reinforces the imposition of 'technical conditions' (or restrictions), including the ordering of MS releasees into private care or CSC residential facilities as a special condition of release.[25] Prior to this amendment, the Parole Service could only place inmates in a private community residence such as a John Howard Society facility, and only with the inmate's consent. If MS releasees now refuse to reside in a correctional residential centre, their Mandatory Supervision status can be revoked.

While such residency (and other) special conditions are clearly intended for control purposes, Parole Service officials reason that the conditions assist in managing the sentence in the most effective way, that is by re-establishing the releasee in the community while affording an added measure of protection to the public. MS releasees who are 'turfed out' of maximum security institutions need 'help', particularly in the first six months when many are returned to custody; yet they are unlikely to seek help on a voluntary basis. While the technical conditions probably do assist some MS releasees in avoiding a return to custody, most are embittered by compulsory residence requirements, arguing that their earned remission entitles them to release without being answerable to anyone.

In sum, increased supervisory control is the trade-off for more liberal release rates. The stumbling-block is the availability of community resources and the attitude of community residents towards the heightened emphasis on community-based corrections. Parole authorities are currently scrambling to make do with a hodgepodge of CSC half-way houses, private care agencies, and provincial parole facilities.

There are concerns that a serious commitment to community corrections is lacking at the executive levels of government, perhaps owing to fears of public disapproval and voter recriminations.

One-shot revocation: Section 24.22 (1)

> Where an inmate was released subject to mandatory supervision in respect of a sentence imposed for an offence mentioned in the Schedule to the Parole Act and the mandatory supervision is revoked, the inmate
>
> (a) Shall, except in respect of a consecutive sentence or portion thereof imposed after his release on mandatory supervision and served prior to the revocation of the mandatory supervision, forfeit all statutory and earned remission standing to his credit, whether accrued before or after the coming into force of this section; and (b) is not entitled to be released from imprisonment, solely as a result of remission, prior to the expiration according to law of the sentence, as determined in accordance with section 14 of the Parole Act, that he was serving on the date of his release.

This amendment provides that, subject to certain exceptions, upon revocation of Mandatory Supervision, an inmate convicted of an offence mentioned in the Schedule to the Parole Act forfeits all remission then standing to his or her credit and is not entitled to be released from imprisonment until the sentence has been served. In practice, however, only those Mandatory Supervision releasees who had originally met some of the criteria for detention, but who were released nonetheless, would be slated for one-shot revocation. In some cases, parole officers will have the option of ordering a troublesome MS releasee to a half-way house run by CSC, rather than order a suspension. Moreover, the MS releasee who is revoked may subsequently apply for parole, however slim his chance of regaining a conditional release status. These 'loopholes' are intended to prevent a massive return of MS releasees to the prisons.

On the negative side, the one-shot revocations that do occur are likely to spark increased litigation. Parole authorities, constrained by the 'duty to act fairly', will need to treat revocations as though they were preparing a court case, resulting in added pressures on overburdened personnel.[26] Another problem will be the potentially explosive situation confronting prison authorities as more and more MS revokees serve 'dead time' in the institution. Those serving out their sentence to warrant expiry, along with the growing number of 'lifers' in Canadian penitentiaries,[27] make the inmate population crunch a certainty, so long as there are no substantial funds for constructing new custodial facilities. Parole Board officials estimate that about 200 extra prisoners per year will be returned to custody on one-shot revocation. Clearly, the revocation provision would need to be used sparingly in order to avoid contributing to prison unrest, yet widespread public apprehension will pressure authorities to invoke it more often than institutional circumstances can allow.

It seems probable that the combined numbers of detentions and revocations will inflate prison populations to some degree and create more complex managerial problems. Parole Board authorities, normally operating under a *release* philosophy, will be reluctant to detain and revoke, but if these new powers are used hesitantly, the public may withdraw its already wavering support for community-based corrections. At the same time, early release mechanisms and technical conditions imposing residency requirements on MS releasees will undergird a new commodification of inmate 'merchandise', and will also deflate institutional pressures caused by overcrowding. But they also pose dangers of a legitimation backlash, a likely consequence of insufficient government support for residential accommodation and programmes.

The official position of the National Parole Board and Correctional Service of Canada is reflected in the testimony of the Chairman of the Parole Board and the Commissioner of Correctional Services in their appearance before the House of Commons Legislative Committee on Bills C-67 and C-68.[28] Questioned about the *net* effect of the various provisions, they estimated that 100 to 200 prisoners per year scheduled for automatic release would be detained, that approximately the same number of conditionally released prisoners would be revoked with forfeiture of all remission credits, and that 400–500 additional prisoners annually would obtain early release on day parole following the one-sixth review, yielding, in the balance, a slight reduction of the prison population. Pacific Regional Parole Service staff interviewed about this legislation, however, situated as they are on the frontlines, are sceptical. They see the legislation as a dubious compromise between early release and watered-down gating provisions and worry that the provisions will mislead and frustrate the public, eventually stirring demands for the abolition of MS. There are concerns that the detention and revocation provisions will be overly restrictive in cases requiring a greater exercise of discretion. Board members anticipate lawsuits and Charter-based legal challenges resulting in added paperwork that will limit the possibilities for constructive interventions.

So while Bills C-67 and C-68 are readily characterized by correctional authorities as a 'government con job', both NPB and CSC officials recognize the need to reallocate resources away from capital construction. One anxious undercurrent, however, is that the government's ulterior motive in promoting community-based corrections may be to privatize the parole service. CSC regional planners foresee the possibility of irresponsible management and abuse should the state lose control of the administration of the sentence.

At this time, the difficulties posed by the new legislation dampen optimism. A 'worst scenario' is eminently possible. The prevention of automatic release will anger prisoners who, as a result, may be more likely to commit further offences once they finally obtain release at warrant expiry. Their new offences will instigate counter-pressures to detain more potential releasees, which in turn will aggravate the overcrowding/double-bunking problems within the institutions. The compensatory release of more prisoners through the one-sixth review may be discontinued after an initial trial period, should community-based corrections fail to gain public confidence, given the absence of generous government support. Underfunded correctional resources will become preoccupied with security considerations and turn into small gaols, prompting community fears which could then be more easily mobilized in the service of a 'law and order' crackdown, which would then justify a widening of the carceral net. MS releasees who are returned to custody with no further opportunity for earned remission will form institutional nuclei of discontent, igniting prison disturbances. Released at warrant expiry, they will commit retaliatory offences rationalizing a new wave of lock-ups and repression.

At worst, then, Bills C-67 and C-68 can bring a new regime of terror to the penitentiaries and a Machiavellian control of public fears. Fortunately, the new legislation includes a provision for parliamentary review three years after enactment. It is to be hoped that by that time, prisons and communities will not yet have become a mutual recruitment base.

Conclusions

We have seen that the issue of Mandatory Supervision offers a specific institutional entry point for grasping the connections between the dynamics of fiscal crisis and the functions of social control. The problem is only one of the multiple areas in which the state is faced with the task of devising managerial solutions to the problem of surplus labour in a recessionary capitalist economy. Thought of in this way, Mandatory Supervision, and the legislative efforts to sustain its viability, figure as an example of the quasi-normalization of 'deviant' populations (Spitzer 1975b), a palatably repressive solution which allows for the extension of surveillance along with a flexible strategy of decarceration/recarceration according to fiscal capacity and ideological need. While the principal intent of this mode of 'adjustment' is to preserve the stability of bourgeois rule (Mandel 1985), mounting contradictions suggest that the equilibrating effects of such policies are no longer able to reconcile the structural imperatives of accumulation, legitimation, and control. If Mandatory Supervision once served as an homeostatic device regulating the flow of surplus labour through the penitentiaries, this seems less possible amid the increasing economic and fiscal turbulence of the current period. The administrative *ad hoc*ery packed into Bills C-67 and C-68 strives to maintain Mandatory Supervision as part of the instrumentation of the state in the manufacture of the 'seamless web' of social control in late capitalist society, but the strategy of accommodating to the fiscal crises of advanced capitalist society through a 'widening net' of social control (Austin and Krisberg 1981; Matthews 1979) seems to be nearing its limits. Austerity in penal discipline (Platt 1982) ultimately controverts the declared principles of democratic society,[29] and overproduces deviance in the search for more parsimonious means of social control.

PART IV
DECARCERATION, DECENTRALIZATION AND THE EXTENSION OF CONTROL SYSTEMS

Introduction

The three chapters in this final section of the book, by Andrew Scull, Roger Matthews, and Stanley Cohen, take stock of the revisionist literature on social control. Scull presents a number of reflections concerning his seminal work on deinstitutionalization, Matthews considers several problematic trends in the revisionist literature, and Cohen examines the theoretical and political implications of the 'destructuring' and 'abolitionist' movements that have characterized the neoprogressive period.

Chapter 16, 'Decarceration reconsidered', originally appeared as the 'Afterword' to the second edition of *Decarceration* by Andrew T. Scull, and is reprinted here by permission of the author and Basil Blackwell. In this essay, which was published six years after the first edition of the book, Scull discusses the implications of carceral trends in the intervening period, and reflects on criticisms of his explanation of the decarceration phenomenon.

He argues that the effects of 'community care' in the realm of mental health documented in *Decarceration* have become increasingly obvious in the late 1970s and early 1980s. The lack of constructive or well-conceived programmes for patients in community settings indicates that deinstitutionalization has simply created an alternative form of warehousing the 'mentally disabled' and, in so doing, has extended the philosophy of various forms of state or state sponsored custodialism into the community.

In sharpening his analysis of decarceration to account for different trends in Western capitalist nations, Scull suggests that the much greater rate of decline in the number of mental hospital in-patients in the United States (as compared to Britain) can be attributed to the structure of state expenditure in the US — such that individual states have been able to transfer costs to the Federal Government by displacing costs for mental health (a state responsibility) to various kinds of welfare and income assistance (areas of federal responsibility).

In answer to suggestions that his dismissal of the importance of the role of psychoactive drugs in the deinstitutionalization of mental patients was based on an inadequate reading of the evidence, Scull marshals findings from a variety of newer studies to indicate that the final nail in the coffin of 'medical explanations' appears to have been driven home. Indeed, incentives to reduce the rising cost of mental institutions existed long before the 'discovery' of fiscal crisis.

While Scull argues that his reflections on trends in mental health practices since the appearance of *Decarceration* in 1977 require little revision, the same cannot be said of the 'community corrections' movement. In offering an autocritique of his earlier position, Scull now maintains that prisons and asylums cannot be analysed as a unitary phenomenon. Prison populations have grown substantially in the US (and to a lesser extent in Britain) since the early 1970s, reflecting the growth of a strong ideological backlash against criminals — part of the political ascendancy of the new right in both countries.

To explain the discrepancy between trends in criminal justice and mental health Scull notes that the notion of radical non-intervention found little appeal among criminal justice policy-makers, and that ideological factors resulting in increased control have typified recent developments in the realm of criminal justice. Diversion has served to widen the control net by diverting people into the system rather than out of it, during a period when recorded crime rates have expanded dramatically. But despite the qualification admitting a degree of singularity to the operation of criminal justice and mental health, Scull still maintains that the impetus to decarceration in both systems can be traced to a single origin — the fiscal crisis of the capitalist state.

In Chapter 17, ('Decarceration and social control: fantasies and realities') Roger Matthews repeats his earlier critique (1979) of what he terms the functionalism and economism underlying Scull's fiscal crisis thesis. Matthews suggests that three further characteristics of the revisionist social control literature serve as impediments to the clarification and understanding of control processes — namely, *globalism*, *empiricism*, and *impossibilism*.

By 'globalism' Matthews means the tendency of theorists to overgeneralize from particular situations or circumstances by:

1. Ignoring or blurring significant sociopolitical boundaries;
2. Generalizing from idiosyncratic or unrepresentative samples;
3. Generalizing from one nation to others; and
4. Using 'metatheoretical futuristic scenarios' (as exemplified by the characterization of the net widening effect of diversion and kindred programmes as an 'Orwellian nightmare').

Matthews suggests that the 'empiricist' tendency of much contemporary social control theory, because it fails to problematize appearances, creates a twin mystification. First, the expansion of community corrections and incarceration are invoked to explain each other. The idea that other independent variables (such as the volume of crime) effect the level of control activity is rarely considered. Second, community corrections are usually evaluated in terms of crude measures of recidivism. There is little consideration of the relative degree of effectiveness of various programmes (or, indeed, what relative effectiveness might entail); and exogenous influences on reoffence patterns — such as contextual and social structural factors — are generally ignored.

'Impossibilism' — the view that 'nothing works' — permeates the spectrum of political alliances in the social control literature to the point, Matthews argues, that an impasse has been reached. All social movements, no matter how progressive or benevolent they seem, are variously seen to make matters worse, to reinforce capitalist domination, or both. There is little room left for the possibility of reform, and the contradictory nature of capitalist social relations, especially those embodied in the state, is ignored altogether.

Matthews emerges as a vigorous critic of the two themes which delineate the impossibilist dilemma. He rejects both the vision of social control as an all-engulfing movement, and the advocacy of minimal statism as the logical resistance to it. In their place he recommends a perspective that would conceptualize recent trends as indicating a fundamental reconstruction of social control processes. Such a reformulation might have the potential to produce new strategies and new techniques, focusing on different targets and driven by new social and economic imperatives.

The final chapter in this book is Stanley Cohen's 'Taking decentralization seriously: values, visions and policies'. This paper brings us full circle to the central problems and paradigms that have informed much of the material in this book. In reflecting on developments in the social control literature over recent years, Cohen leads us through a 'Pilgrim's Progress', charting the dramatic transformations of images and policies about crime and deviance, punishment and social control over the past two decades. He guides us through the heady years of 'inspiration', where the 'destructuring package' burst forth from the 'deviant imagination' (Pearson 1975), with the attendant recognition that social control theory and practice were unremittingly political phenomena, that radical alternatives needed to be located and applied. Destructuration/abolitionism was in fact a complex aggregate of ideas and activities, varying according to degrees of commitment, intensity of tone, and targets of application. While the visions arose in many forms — decarceration, diversion, decategorization, delegalization, deprofessionalization — there was a common adhesive in their shared commitment to strategies of 'decentralized community control', to visions of inclusion rather than exclusion.

But something went wrong during the pilgrimage. In the 1970s, the visions were 'confronted with reality', and the assessment of new ideals and practices became a bleak and cynical business. Disillusioned autocritique emerged from former converts, and paved the way for the neo-conservative renaissance of the 'new realists'. Radical critiques of the destructuring package gained momentum, as various dangers were exposed to view. Cohen categorizes a range of arguments that were summoned to account for such failure, and to condemn community control as a sinister supplement to state power. Various theories were offered to explain the demise, involving variously: good theory transformed into bad policy, the sabotage wrought by self-interested professionals, the paramountcy of convenience over conscience, and the inevitable erosion of liberal reform in the broad sweep of historical process.

Critical criminologists, the parents and guardians of the destructuring visions, were left with the awful task of presiding over and theorizing the downfall of their own offspring. They often dealt with the contradictions by retreating to a radical 'impossibilism' (see Matthews, this volume) where 'nothing is do-able', 'no one is changeable', 'all revisionism is swallowed up and spit out as centralized state control'. As well, many came to spurn the romanticism of earlier times, erecting a 'Left Realism', grounded in the grim reality of crime and social control, that was to use the old system to advantage (in criminalizing the predators and the powerful) and preserve the 'soft' parts of the system (welfare, mental health) against neo-conservative campaigns in the 1980s. Characterized by Cohen as a form of 'radical regression', left realism assumes a defensive posture, operates from the justifiable assumption that things are bad all over. It searches for solutions in pragmatic terms and available structures, instead of in visionary politics and radical destructuring movements. Realists of the left confront the neo-conservatives on their own turf — the stark experience of crime and centralized control — in so doing they are inevitably caught up in 'self-denunciation', a restriction of possibilities (the alternatives, in any event, are largely shaped by others) — in Bunyan's terms, a 'slough of despond'.

Cohen suggests that there are two ways out. A political alternative would involve 'a cautious reaffirmation of the original values behind the destructuring/abolitionist/inclusionary visions'. That is, the old ideals still apply; as Cohen writes, 'it still makes sense to look for more humane, just and workable alternatives to the criminal justice system's mechanisms of apprehension, judgement and punishment'. Second, an analytic alternative amounts to a more optimistic reading of the social control literature of the past two decades. Cohen argues for an appreciation of success (even if partial and fleeting) in such areas as informal justice (cf. Cain 1986), and for an 'experimental and inductive attitude' — one that will permit optimism, activism and the exploration of workable alternatives. He further advocates a balance between the *naiveté* of visionaries and the cynicism of demystifiers, and a reassessment of social control theory through the lens of legal pluralism (addressing the relationship between local norms and wider structures) and Foucaultian analysis (considering the localized microphysics of power as incidental to the 'workings of capital'). Cohen provides an inventory of various 'semi-autonomous fields' that provide a potential locus for future exploration of decentralized community control. These include:

1. Experiments in community control and informal justice;
2. Self-help and mutal-aid organizations;
3. Systems of private and workplace justice;
4. Organizations possessing internal justice mechanisms;
5. Communes and other 'utopian' social collectivities;
6. 'Spontaneous' forms of living and working communally; and
7. Entire non-centralized, acephalous societies.

As Cohen asserts, to 'take decentralization seriously' it may be necessary to move away from the realm and discourse of criminal justice ('the awful clutches of criminology'), and toward these alternative fields. The vision of abolitionism *must* survive intact, and can only do so outside of the centralist statist system of law and control. Classic abolitionist projects — finding alternatives to criminal law, locating and developing structural contexts supporting community control — are central to decentralization strategies. Cohen maintains that all of this is still possible, but cautions that *attrition* rather than abolition is the preferred (and 'realist') directive for engagement, that is, 'a gradual wearing away of the criminal law by a process of benign neglect'). Advocates of decentralization must tread warily through a minefield of contradictions, unintended consequences, and new forms of non-statist control.

Finally, such steps need to be taken in the context of a 'wider theory of power'. Cohen enlists Foucault as a source of optimism, as theoretical support for decentralized strategies based in a localization of power. A serious analysis of micro-systems of power is a prerequisite, says Cohen, for any alternative intended to balance visionary and pragmatic possibilities. As he concludes, 'taking decentralization seriously implies not just a particular value preference but a more complicated theory than we admitted about the exercise of power in the modern state'.

16 Decarceration reconsidered
Andrew T. Scull

I

When I completed the first edition of *Decarceration*, towards the end of 1975, the advocates of deinstitutionalization clearly dominated public debate in the United States about the proper approach to the mad and the bad. Indeed, even in Europe where — outside the sphere of mental health — the idea of abolishing or creating alternatives to incarceration had been much slower to take hold, such notions had begun to circulate freely. Opposition, if not silent, was fragmented and muted, and often could simply be dismissed as self-interested. Among the public at large, it took the form of protest by residents of particular communities against the placement of ex-inmates of any kind in *their* neighbourhood. Sometimes this caused harassment, threats of vigilante action, even arson, but in the politically more sophisticated and better organized communities, the favourite tactic was exclusionary zoning (Coates and Miller 1973, p.67; Greenberg 1975, p.28; Segal 1974, p. 143). Such particularistic activities were simply designed to protect the parochial concerns of residents, who clearly wished to minimize contact with the very deviants whom they should be eagerly embracing, according to the decarceration ideology. Limited opposition of this sort, by its very nature, was not likely to coalesce into a more broadly based attack on the policy *tout court*. Provided the burden could be shifted elsewhere, to other less vociferous, less powerful populations, the discontent could readily be diffused without serious modification of the underlying programme. These complaints just reinforced other pressures to deposit the decarcerated in the poorest, most deteriorated, and least desirable of urban locations.

Attempts to stimulate a general repudiation of the movement were largely the work of state employee unions (for example, California State Employee's Association (CSEA) 1972; American Federation of State, County and Municipal Employees (AFSCME) 1975). They sought to create moral panics (Cohen 1972) among the general population by skilled manipulation of 'exemplary tales' concerning the squalor of conditions in which ex-inmates were living and the violence to which

This chapter is reprinted from the 'Afterword' to *Decarceration* (2nd edition), by Andrew T. Scull, by permission of Basil Blackwell, Cambridge, England.

they were prone, and the deleterious effects of these on both property values and public order. But although such efforts were not without their successes (Scull 1983, Ch. 4) they were vulnerable to the accusation that they expressed no more than the vested interest of those with direct responsibility for the shortcomings of the institutional alternative.

Within the past few years, of course, the situation has changed rather markedly. Concentrating for the moment on the mentally ill, the main focus of my earlier analysis, one notable feature has been the recognition, even in 'the heart of darkness', that community care is not all sweetness and light. Though there is an understandable reluctance in many quarters to acknowledge the full extent of 'the demise of state responsibility for the seriously mentally ill and the current crisis of abandonment' (Gruenberg and Archer 1979, p.498)[1] even government officials and leading figures within the psychiatric establishment now concede that there is a profound disjuncture between the myth and the reality of 'community care'. The failures of contemporary policy have become the occasion for scathing critiques by politicians (Senate Special Committee on Aging 1976) and government bureaucrats (General Accounting Office 1977), not to mention a Maudsley lecture to the Royal College of Psychiatrists (Jones 1982). They have prompted denunciations in the *New England Journal of Medicine* (Borus 1981; Mollica 1983) and complaints about 'the wholesale neglect of the mentally ill, especially the chronic patient and the deinstitutionalised' from the President of the American Psychiatric Association (Langsley 1980). Three journals concerned with the analysis of social policy have devoted entire issues to the topic (*American Behavioural Scientist* 1981; *Journal of Social Issues* 1981; *Milbank Memorial Fund Quarterly* 1979).

One or two of my early critics (see Kaplan 1978)[2] argue that my portrait of the failures of contemporary policy was overdrawn. Such claims seem implausible now. Studies of deinstutionalized patients show that 'few live with biological or social relatives' (Estroff 1981, p. 120),[3] and that even in this minority of cases, families grow restive under the serious and cumulative burden they represent, ultimately spurning and rejecting them (cf. Davis, Dinitz and Pasamanick 1974).[4] In the United States, in particular, board-and-care homes and nursing homes have increasingly become 'the dominant force in the residential care system [of the mentally ill]' (Emerson, Rochford and Shaw 1981, p.772).[5]

One important consequence of this massive relocation programme is that 'the return of the patients to the community has, in many ways, extended the philosophy of custodialism into the community rather than ending it at the gates of the state hospital' (Kirk and Thierren 1975, p.212). State and federal payments to the burgeoning entrepreneurial class 'servicing' the chronically mentally ill are scarcely munificent, after all, and, at best, would purchase only the most basic forms of custodial care. Data from a number of studies suggest that survival level subsistence is indeed the best for which discharged patients can hope. In the words of a recent Oregon study, 'a typical day for a mentally ill person in a nursing home was sleeping, eating, watching television, smoking cigarettes, sitting in groups in the largest room, or looking out the window; there was no evidence of an organised plan to meet their needs' (General Accounting Office 1977, pp.15–16).

On a nationwide basis, the United States National Institute of Mental Health (NIMH) has reported that 'as the level of provided service declines — from nursing care homes to personal care homes — the admissions from mental hospitals as a percentage of total admissions to these homes increases' (NIMH 1975, p.6). Meanwhile, trends within the boarding home industry also suggest a declining quality of care. A shift is underway towards larger, more heavily capitalized units, and away from small, family-run homes, 'which are marginal economic operations, providing many relatively low-income people with an additional source of money. The larger homes, in contrast, are clear-cut business enterprises requiring substantial amounts of capital investment, and are highly concerned with costs and profits' (Emerson *et al.* 1981, p.772). This development is unlikely to meet with serious resistance from the states, since these larger 'board and care homes require fewer [state] support services in order to function, a critical advantage in an era of cutbacks in state funding and direct services' (Emerson *et al.* 1981, p.774; see also Lerman 1982, p. 11).

Under the conditions that currently prevail, market failure is structurally guaranteed. A large number of atomized, uninformed consumers, whose mental condition renders them all but incapable of initiative or of exercising meaningful choice, have been discharged into a hostile community and left to cope as best they can — in the virtual absence of state supported aftercare or follow-up services.[6] As I suggested in the first edition of *Decarceration*, their plight has created a fertile ground for a new trade in lunacy, an entrepreneurial industry resembling the private madhouses of eighteenth-century England (Parry-Jones 1972) which remains almost wholly unregulated by the state. Indeed, in a double sense, the state can hardly *afford* to regulate this industry in anything but a purely cosmetic fashion. First, of course, a serious effort to provide regulation would demand the commitment of substantial resources, and even then I would remain sceptical of its effectiveness.[7] Second, if the state attempted to insist on adequate standards of care, in all probability, given current levels of reimbursement, it would simply dry up the supply of beds. Thus, the

United States Senate's finding that only three states make a serious attempt to supervise board-and-care homes is wholly unsurprising (cf. Lerman 1982, p.9).[8] The income of those speculating in this species of human misery is almost wholly inelastic (being fixed by the welfare payments that are their 'clients'' principal source of income), so that profits are strictly dependent on successfully paring costs. Since the volume of profit is inversely proportional to the amount expended on inmates, the logic of the market-place ensures that the operators have every incentive to warehouse their charges as cheaply as possible.[9]

The mere size of the community facilities within which many of the mentally disabled are housed provides *prima facie* evidence that they have simply been transferred from public to private warehouses. As Lerman notes, 'public discussions and modern technology often refer to a 200-bed home for the aged or a 100-bed residential treatment centre for disturbed youth as a "community" not an "institutional" residential facility' (Lerman 1982, p.3) — a verbal sleight of hand designed to obfuscate the fact that, according to the National Centre for Health Statistics, more than 50 per cent of those placed in nursing homes were in facilities with more than 100 beds, and a further 15 per cent were in facilities housing more than 200 at a time. In the course of its investigations in Michigan, the General Accounting Office found one such home that specialized in 'the mentally disabled had 440 beds while another had 330' (General Accounting Office 1977, p.16). In Massachusetts, investigators were informed that it was standard state practice 'to place formerly institutionalised persons in those nursing homes where the quality of care was poorer and safety standards not complied with as rigidly as in other nursing homes ... Generally speaking, the more ex-mental patients there were in a facility, the worse the conditions' (General Accounting Office 1977, pp.13–14). Similarly, in New York, there have been repeated media exposés of the massive concentrations of ex-inmates in the squalid single-room occupancy hotels on the Upper West Side of Manhattan, and in homes run by former hospital employees in the Long Island communities surrounding Pilgrim and Central Islip State Hospitals (see Hynes 1977; Mesnikoff 1978).[10]

Such developments have not occurred without explicit and implicit state sponsorship and encouragement. In New York State, the scandals over the connections between the board-and-care industry and the political establishment eventually forced a full-scale official enquiry and subsequent prosecutions (Hynes 1977). Hawaii faced a massive shortage of beds in licensed boarding homes when it adopted a policy of accelerated discharge. The problem was resolved, with unusual bureaucratic flexibility, through 'the proliferation, with the explicit encouragement of the state mental health division, of unlicensed boarding homes for the placement of ex-hospitalised patients' (Kirk and Thierren 1975, p.211). Nebraska at first shied away from such a *laissez-faire* approach, deciding apparently that some form of state oversight was called for. Accordingly, in a splendidly original variation on the ancient practice of treating the mad like cattle, the state placed the licensing and inspection of board and care homes in the hands of its state Department of Agriculture. Subsequent citizens' complaints about the resultant conditions led to second thoughts about the desirability of taking official notice of board-and-care operators' practises, so the state withdrew the licences, *but not the patients*, 'from an estimated 320 of these homes, leaving them without state supervision or regulation' (General Accounting Office 1977, p.19). Missouri simply noted the existence of some '775 unlicensed facilities in [the] State housing more than 10 000 patients' (Senate Committee on Aging 1976, p.724) and continued to dispense the state funds on which their operators depended. Still other states, like Maryland and Oregon, opted for perhaps the safest course of all — no follow-up of those they released, and hence a blissful official ignorance about their subsequent fate (General Accounting Office 1977, p.95).

Intended as a cheap alternative to the state hospital, these board-and-care homes have instead become a poor alternative to living. They constitute perhaps the most extreme example of 'the failure of deinstitutionalisation policies to provide even minimally adequate aftercare and community support services anywhere in the nation' (Rose 1979, p.440; see also Bassuk and Gerson 1978; Van Putten and Spar 1979). Given this 'almost unanimous abdication from the task of proposing and securing any provision for a humane and continuous form of care for those mental patients who need something rather more than short-term therapy for an acute phase of their illness' (Sedgwick 1982, p.38) it should come as no surprise to learn that decarceration 'has not succeeded in ameliorating precisely those alleged results of institutionalisation that [supposedly] led to it: the sociocultural and interpersonal isolation, degeneration and stigmatisation of these patients; the assymetrical [sic] dependency and vast power differences between patients and non-patients; the encouragement of chronicity contained in the treatment system and related social policies' (Estroff 1981, pp.116–117).

In view of the depths of misery and maltreatment associated with recent American mental health policy, Kathleen Jones's claim that 'so far the United States has made a much better job of the business of deinstitutionalisation' (Jones 1979a, p.567) would, if accurate, constitute an even more damning indictment of British practice than she perhaps intended. Apparently, what led her to make this unfortunate assertion was the combination of a relatively intimate knowledge of the failures of British policies with a rather naive acceptance at face value of the claims made by American advocates of deinstitutionalization (cf. Jones 1979b; Mollica 1980). Certainly, at the level of rhetoric, Americans have by and large been more active and shameless. Practically, however, the British experience has not (yet?) been quite so awful.

In part, this is simply because deinstitutionalization has not been as rapid or far-reaching in Britain. This discrepancy was evident even by 1970 (Scull 1983, pp.68, 70) but it has become still more marked over the past decade. The population of English mental hospitals has continued to decline by a relatively modest average of just over 3 per cent a year (see Table 16.1). As Tables 16.2 and 16.3 reveal, however, during the late 1960s the decline in the American mental hospital census was consistently larger than this, and the discrepancy only widened during the 1970s. Overall, while the inpatient census of English mental hospitals has declined by approximately one-half since the mid-1950s, the American mental hospital population has fallen to less than a quarter of what it was then.

Table 16.1 Average daily number of inpatients in mental hospitals in England, and annual decrease in patient population, 1970–1980.

Year	Number	% Decrease	Year	Number	% Decrease
1970	106,000		1976	83,800	3.68
1971	103,000	2.83	1977	80,800	3.58
1972	100,000	2.91	1978	78,200	3.22
1973	94,000	6.00	1979	76,500	2.17
1974	90,000	4.44	1980	75,200	1.70
1975	87,000	3.33			

Source: Department of Health and Social Security: Health and Personal Social Services Statistics for England. London: Her Majesty's Stationery Office. All figures rounded.

Table 16.2 Rate of decline of United States mental hospital populations, selected periods, 1955–1976.

Period	% Decline per year	Period	% Decline per year
1955–1960	0.8	1972–1974	10.8
1960–1964	2.1	1974–1976	10.2
1964–1972	5.5		

Source: National Institute of Mental Health, Bethesda, Maryland.

Table 16.3 United States state and county mental hospitals, resident patients on December 31, and annual decrease in patient population, 1970–1980

Year	Number	% Decrease	Year	Number	% Decrease
1970	339,000		1976	171,500	10.40
1971	309,000	8.85	1977	159,523	7.00
1972	276,000	10.68	1978	153,544	3.77
1973	255,000	7.61	1979	140,355	8.53
1974	215,600	15.45	1980	132,164	5.84
1975	191,400	11.22			

Source: National Institute of Mental Health, Bethseda, Maryland.

The pattern of events during the 1970s amply confirms my suggestion, in the first edition of *Decarceration*, that the major source of the more rapid decline in United States mental hospital populations was the fragmentation of the American political structure, and the opportunities decarceration opened up for states to transfer costs to the federal level. As Lerman (1982, p.91) has noted, just as the accelerated discharge of the elderly in the late 1960s was brought about by the advent of Medicare and Medicaid (together with Old Age Assistance, Aid to the Permanently and Totally Disabled, and Old Age and Survivor Insurance), so the further accleration in 1972 and thereafter reflected the 'availability of new welfare resources', in this case the passage of new legislation authorizing the new Supplemental Security Income Programme. Of utmost importance, the new programme offered 'the unprecedented opportunity to transfer traditional state costs on to a 100 per cent federal funding source. None of the earlier federal programmes had offered this type of long-term incentive' (Lerman 1982, p.104; see also Witkin 1976), accounting for the rapidity and enthusiasm with which states seized the opportunity to implement further cutbacks in inpatient populations. In Britain, however, in the absence of this additional incentive, the rush to empty mental hospitals has been understandably less headlong.

Ex-patients in Britain have also been, for the most part, spared the excesses associated with the 'new trade in lunacy' (cf. Scull 1981). The chains of private board-and-care homes and the dilapidated 'welfare hotels' (which we have seen are now so large a part of American mental health 'services') have few precise British equivalents. In part, this probably reflects the somewhat lower numbers of chronic patients discharged. Undoubtedly, too, it mirrors the more entrepreneurial character of American capitalism, and the greater legitimacy accorded to the process of privatization of state and welfare services (Spitzer and

Scull 1977) in a society still ideologically dominated by the myth of the benevolent 'invisible hand'.

Notwithstanding all of these qualifications, the British experience with community care remains dismal enough in all conscience. As Peter Sedgwick points out:

> In Britain no less than in the United States, 'community care' and 'the replacement of the mental hospital' were slogans which masked the growing depletion of real services for the mentally ill; the accumulating numbers of impaired, retarded and demented males in the prisons and common lodging houses; the scarcity not only of local authority residential provisions for the mentally disabled, but of day-care centres and skilled social work resources; the jettisoning of mental patients in their thousands into the isolated, helpless environment of their families of origin, who appealed in vain for hospital admission (even for a temporary period of respite), for counselling or support, and even for basic information and advice ... (1982, pp.193–194; see also Ebringer and Christie-Brown 1980; Korer 1978; Rollin 1970).

Jones is herself not unaware of these catastrophic failures masquerading under the official guise of a 'revolution' in psychiatric care. It is her awareness of the failures that prompts her bitter comparison of British policy with an idealized, indeed mythological, portrait of American practices.[11] For her, much of the blame can be apportioned to administrative lapses. In particular, the reorganization of the British National Health Service in 1973, which eliminated any distinctive organization for the mental health service, left 'no administrative focus, no forum for policy debate, and no impetus to personal development. The result is that the British services are now fragmented and to a large extent the personnel are demoralised' (Jones 1979a, pp.565–566; see also Jones 1982; Scull 1983).

But while low morale and administrative chaos have certainly contributed to worsening the situation, they are scarcely the major sources of current difficulties. More centrally important is the absence of the necessary infrastructure of services and financial supports without which talk about community care is simply a sham. During 1973–1974, for example, while 300 million pounds was spent on the mentally ill still receiving institutional treatment, a mere 6.5 million was spent on residential and day-care services for those 'in the community'. Local authority spending on residential facilities for the mentally ill was a derisory 0.04 per cent of their total expenditures (Sedgwick 1982, p.251).[12] Three years later, 116 out of 170 local authorities still provided not a single residential place for the elderly mentally infirm (*The Guardian*, 13 January 1976)[13] and since then, the intensifying fiscal crisis of the Thatcher-Reaganite years has simply reinforced the existing conservative hostility to social welfare services, and made the prospect of providing even minimal levels of support services still more remote.[14]

II

It seems fair to say, then, that developments in the mental health sector over the past eight or nine years have involved the extension and intensification of the trends already visible in the mid-1970s, rather than any substantial modifications or changes of direction. To that extent, the descriptive account I provided in the first edition of *Decarceration* has held up quite well. It remains the case that 'evidence of benefits to [deinstitutionalised] psychiatric patients, especially those hospitalised over long periods, is not to be found anywhere in the professional literature' (Rose 1979, p.431) and the priority of fiscal over therapeutic concerns has become even more apparent in the same period. Still, some re-examination of the specifics of the *explanation* I offered of deinstitutionalization seems in order.

One of the most controversial claims made in the first edition of this book was that the role of psychoactive drugs in bringing about decarceration had been grossly exaggerated. Given the coincidence between the downturn in mental hospital populations and the introduction of phenothiazines, one can readily understand why many simply assumed, and continue to assume (for a recent example, see Davis 1981, p.257), that deinstitutionalization was no more than a reflex response to another technical breakthrough of modern medicine. But, as I showed, the attempts to provide detailed empirical support for this proposition are scientifically shoddy and largely fail to accomplish their purpose. I suggested then that, rather than being the primary reasons for the changes we have observed, the drugs played only a secondary role, helping to persuade physicians of the feasibility of community treatment, and easing the management of patients by reducing florid symptomology. I further suggested that unless other pressures and incentives to deinstitutionalize had existed, the new technology would probably have been employed simply to ease internal management problems (very much as electroshock had previously been used), and not to precipitate mass discharges of elderly and chronic patients.[15]

A number of more recent, detailed case studies have provided further support for these contentions.[16] Lerman's review of deinstitutionalization in California shows that the process did not get under way until several years after the use of ataraxic drugs had become widespread in the state hospital system, and concludes that 'California required the hiring and promotion of new state hospital leaders (committed to deinstitutionalization) in order to utilize the new technology on behalf of pro-release, rather than institutional maintenance policies' (Lerman 1982, p.209). Likewise, Aviram and Segal's review of California data leads them to discount any major role for the phenothiazines: 'It is our opinion that the provision of financial support through public assistance programmes was primarily responsible for the mass emigration from state hospitals that began in California in 1962' (1978, p.37; see also Aviram, Syme and Cohen 1976, p.574).[17] Noting the marked interstate variations in the speed with which deinstitutionalization took place, and the geographically variable patterns of rapidly accelerating discharges over time, the authors of a comparative epidemiological review of hospitalization rates in New York, Illinois, Texas, Virginia, and California pointedly remark, 'it would be naive to claim that psychoactive drugs suddenly became more effective'. Instead, they conclude that decarceration is indeed 'best explained by the creation and implementation of specific programmes aimed at reducing the number of hospitalised patients, either by control of admissions or by change of release policies or both' (Aviram *et al.* 1976, p.574).[18]

Perhaps the final nail in the coffin of the 'medical' explanation of deinstitutionalization was provided by Peter Sedgwick's review of international data on the timing of the run-down of institutional populations in Western Europe. Were the switch to community treatment simply a response to the advent of effective anti-psychotic medications, one would expect to see close similarities in the discharge patterns. Actually, the reverse is true: there are marked variations from one society to another in both the timing and the extent of the decline in mental hospital populations. Most damaging of all for:

> ... the view that these new medications constitute a collective miracle drug which eradicates the worst psychotic symptoms and enables large-scale discharges into the community to take place as a direct result of their chemical action ... [is] the relatively late point (1970) at which the in-patient numbers in French mental hospitals began to dip, following a post-war population explosion in the asylums which continued throughout the very period of the fifties and sixties that had been marked by a firm de-hospitalisation in British and American psychiatry. It should be noted that chlorpromazine (Largactil), the most prominent of the new tranquillisers, had actually been first synthesised in France as early as December 1950, by the pharmaceuticals firm Rhone Polenc. It is not to be supposed that this lag of 20 years between the availability of the chemical First Cause and its effects on hospital practice was due to inactivity on the part of the merchandisers of Largactil in France. (Sedgwick 1982, p.198)

But the fact that the mental hospital populations in France, West Germany, Italy, Spain, and elsewhere continued to grow into the 1960s and sometimes beyond, has serious implications not just for the proponents of the 'magic bullet' explanation of decarceration, but also for my own account. As a number of my critics have rightly pointed out (Goldstein 1982; Matthews 1979; Sedgwick 1982; Warner 1985), my original argument presents the relationship between the adoption of a policy of deinstitutionalization on the one hand, and the advent of welfare capitalism and the growing fiscal crisis of the state apparatus on the other, as a necessary and essentially deterministic one. A larger comparative perspective unquestionably demonstrates that such a claim is an oversimplification. The existence of a well-developed system of social welfare services, and the intensifying fiscal crisis of the last decade and a half, certainly created powerful structural *pressures* to adopt a policy of deinstitutionalization and, as a growing body of research documents, they have profoundly shaped the implementation of 'community care'. But the Western European experience demonstrates that the connections are by no means as automatic and inevitable as I previously implied.[19]

In the long run, then, any fully adequate explanation of deinstitutionalization in the mental health sector must allow us to understand, not just its rapid and 'successful' implementation in Britain and North America, but also its much more erratic and halting progress in Western Europe. Unfortunately, we remain a long way from possessing such a unified account. Richard Warner's invocation of the conditions in the labour market (Warner 1985), while suggesting a possible explanation for some of the fluctuations over time in rehabilitation efforts and the recovery rates of schizophrenics, and for some of the variations in the outcomes for 'schizophrenia' between industrial nations and non-wage-labour societies in the developing world (cf. World Health Organization 1979), gives us no adequate means of accounting for the differences between (for example) France, Italy, and England. No more persuasive is Peter Sedgwick's attempt to link variations in the 'de-hospitalizing' movement to the development of a liberal social psychiatry, whose intellectual ancestry he traces back to 'the progressive anti-fascist mobilisations of the forties' (Sedgwick 1982, pp.205–213).

Gaining an adequate understanding of these cross-societal variations must surely be a major goal of future research in this area. I remain convinced, however, that a crucial part of the answer is to be found in the factors I previously identified. As I suggested in both *Museums of Madness* (Scull 1979) and in the first edition of *Decarceration*, the operations of different general systems of public assistance form the essential structural and political preconditions for the particular forms taken by the mental health systems of each epoch. In my earlier work, I identified two major factors prompting a shift away from a segregative 'solution' to the problems posed by the chronically crazy. The first of these was the existence of welfare payments, which guaranteed at least a minimal maintenance to the poor living outside the institutions. The second major factor was the subsequent development, from the mid-to-late 1960s onwards, of an intensifying fiscal crisis of the state apparatus — a crisis which has continued to worsen over the ensuing decade and a half.

To begin with, and indeed on a continuing basis, the construction of the infrastructure of a modern welfare state was the *necessary*, if not always a sufficient condition for the adoption of a policy of deinstitutionalization. Such programmes not only made large-scale discharges possible, they also sharply raised the opportunity cost of not adopting a policy of this sort. As the research I have cited earlier in this chapter shows, the linkage between the extension of welfare programmes and the contraction of state hospital populations has remained persistently close, particularly in the United States. Even in the halcyon days of the late 1950s, in the never-had-it-so-good heyday of post-war capitalist expansion, and long before, as Peter Sedgwick reminds us, the 'fiscal crisis of the state had been discovered by any economic researcher' (1982, p.202), there were powerful economic incentives to slow, and if possible, reverse the upward spiral in mental health populations. Admissions were already rising sharply, in both Britain and the United States, as they continued to do throughout the 1960s (in both countries, they more than doubled between 1955 and 1970).[20] Without a major decline in the average length of stay, an extraordinary expansion of the mental hospital system would have been required to house this influx. To make matters worse, the Victorian barracks inherited from the nineteenth century were in a terminal state of decay and dilapidation. As a British government spokeswoman concluded at the time, replacement of this 'appalling legacy' was 'not a question of a few million pounds ... [but] a question of thousands of millions over many years' (Patricia Hornsby Smith, Parliamentary Secretary to the Minister of Health, in *Hansard*, 19 February 1954, vol. 523, col. 2371). Finally, unionization of state workers meant that they shared in the increase in wage rates after World War II, and contributed to the very sharp increases in the running costs of the existing hospitals. The subsequent fiscal crisis merely added to these pressures and made them far more intense and urgent, a situation I held primarily responsible for the rapid acceleration in discharge rates then observable.

The issue of whether (and to what extent) the decarceration of the mentally ill has produced cost savings has provoked considerable debate, though there has been widespread recognition that 'the pivotal political assumption that appears to have motivated deinstitutionalisation is that state tax dollars would be saved ...' (Borus 1981, p.340). A variety of academic and governmental researchers have concluded that major savings have resulted (cf. General Accounting Office 1977; Murphy and Datel 1976; Sheehan and Atkinson 1974). Rose, for example, estimates 'cost savings to the states in the ten-year period from 1965 to 1974 would be approximately $5.4 billion ... without regard to accelerated admissions rates and added capital construction costs' (1979, p.448). Others, however, have been more sceptical, pointing to continuing rises in state mental health budgets and alleging that apparent cost savings in one sector have been at least partly offset by increased expenditures elsewhere (see Borus 1981; Lerman 1982, Ch. 6; Matthews 1979).

The methodological difficulties in this area are formidable. As the General Accounting Office recently acknowledged, 'the state of the art of determining the costs in alternative long-term care settings is still in the early stages of development' (1977, p.6) — with the result that elementary mistakes continue to be made. Rose (1979), for example, appears to base his calculations of cost savings on the *average* cost rather than the marginal cost of hospitalization. If so, he seriously overstates the savings which have resulted, since, in the short run at least, many of the costs of a mental hospital system are fixed and unchangeable, regardless of the number of inmates who occupy it.

On the other hand, those who are sceptical of the cost savings produced by decarceration are prone to errors that even more seriously *underestimate* the magnitude of the sums involved. In noting the continuous rise in mental health budgets, they often fail to allow for the effects of inflation and, much more significantly, they do not incorporate into their analysis a whole series of factors which, in the absence of decarceration, would most certainly have produced a veritable explosion in expenditures on the mentally ill. I have already pointed out some of these, notably rapidly rising admission rates, and the decay of the physical infrastructure of the hospital system.[21] To these must be added the substantial increase in the general population over the past three decades, and the growing number of the aged, a substantial proportion of whom were traditionally warehoused in public mental hospitals.[22] In assessing the savings resulting from decarceration, it simply will not do, therefore, to compare *actual* expenditure levels over time and to conclude that if they rise, cost savings have not resulted. Instead, the calculations must be based on the relevant counterfactual: what would be the approximate level of state expenditures on the mental health services had governments persisted with traditional segregative approaches to the problem, rather than adopting a programme of massively accelerated deinstitutionalization and diversion?

While precise estimates are obviously unattainable, the basic financial impact of the new policies is surely not in doubt.[23] Nor can there be much doubt about the social impact of the new approach. Bitter experience ought by now to have taught us to scorn millenial claims that the adoption or rejection of the asylum will substantially ameliorate the mental patient's situation. We must recognize instead that neither institutional treatment nor community care is in any sense a panacea, and that both, if inadequately funded, provide ample opportunity for, and many examples of, squalor, neglect, abuse and inhumanity. Deinstitutionalization of the mentally ill, while securing the negative right to be free of organized interference in one's life, has all too often meant the denial of the positive right to care and attention. As a result, for the majority of those affected with chronic mental illness, what has changed is the packaging rather than the reality of their misery.

III

If developments in the mental health sector since I wrote the first edition of *Decarceration* have involved no fundamental departures from the patterns I originally described and analysed, the same can hardly be said of the so-called community corrections movement. On the ideological level, the 1970s witnessed a strong conservative backlash against anything smacking of leniency towards crime and criminals. The law and order issue was a favourite weapon of politicians on the right, and their electoral success with this tactic soon persuaded most of their opposition to fall into line. In the academic world, orthodox criminologists scurried to provide a mantle of scholarly respectability for such tactics as mandatory fixed sentences and longer terms of imprisonment (Fogel 1975; Wilson 1975, 1981), with even liberals rediscovering the virtues of swiftness and certainty in punishment (Martinson 1974; see generally Greenberg and Humphries 1979).

Moreover, so far from matching the remorseless and, for much of the period, accelerating decline in mental hospital populations, our prison and gaol populations have once again increased (to record levels). Overcrowding is rife, and old and discarded buildings are being reopened and crammed with prisoners (Flynn 1978, pp.131–132). California has even resorted to housing its overflowing population of convicts in tents. As Table 16.4 reveals, the British population changed somewhat erratically, but generally declined between 1970 and 1974. Thereafter, however, it rose by just over 17 per cent over the next 7 years. Similarly, the populations of state and federal prisons in the United States levelled off at just over 190000 in the late 1960s, and remained essentially static in the first years of the 1970s. Indeed, allowing for population change, the rate of imprisonment continued to fall every year until 1972. 1974 however, marked the first of a series of sharp increases in both the absolute numbers imprisoned and the rate of imprisonment per 100000 people. Here the percentage increase in numbers imprisoned was very much steeper than in England — an extraordinary 80.1 per cent in the years from 1972 to 1981 (see Table 16.5).

Table 16.4 Average daily prison and borstal population in England and Wales

Year	Number	Rate/100000	Year	Number	Rate/100000
1970	39028	80.2	1976	41443	84.3
1971	39708	81.3	1977	41570	84.6
1972	38328	78.2	1978	41796	85.1
1973	36774	74.8	1979	42220	85.9
1974	36867	75.0	1980	42264	85.8
1975	39820	81.0	1981	43311	87.8

Source: *Annual Abstract of Statistics* 1983, p.82. London: Her Majesty's Stationery Office

Table 16.5 United States: federal and state prisoners on 31 December

Year	Number	Rate/100000	Year	Number	Rate/100000
1970	196429	96.7	1976	263291	123.1
1971	198061	96.4	1977	285456	132.4
1972	196183	94.6	1978	294396	135.4
1973	204211	97.8	1979	301470	137.3
1974	218466	103.6	1980	314272	139.0
1975	240593	113.3	1981	353167	153.0

Source: United States Bureau of Justice Statistics

We need to bear in mind, of course, that long, continued, secular increases in crime rates have generated a much larger population eligible for the attentions of the criminal justice system. To an extent, therefore, one might reasonably argue that diversionary programmes have enabled the authorities to avoid some of the expenditures for prison accommodation they would otherwise have incurred.[24] But obviously one can push this argument only so far, and in the United States in particular, the sheer size of the increase in prison populations, which has occurred alongside and despite a dramatic rise in the use of probation and other non-institutional forms of punishment, suggests the need for a fundamental reassessment of the significance of recent 'reforms'.

To begin with, my earlier conclusion that 'community corrections meant a further erosion of the sanctions imposed on criminals' conduct now seems much too crude to capture the complexities which the introduction of the new programmes has entailed. With hindsight, one could argue that I fell victim to exactly the danger I warned of — that of taking reformist rhetoric at face value and, as a result, assuming that the *language* of radical non-intervention closely coincided with everyday practice.[25] Taking self-criticism a step further, notwithstanding my own criticisms of the 'total institutions' literature (Scull 1983, Ch. 6) it is now apparent that when I wrote the first edition of *Decarceration* I remained 'imprisoned' within one of the central assumptions of that research: that it made sense (and presented no analytic difficulties) to study prisons and asylums as a unitary phenomenon (Kaplan 1978, pp.205–206 correctly takes me to task for this). While I would still contend that such assimilation is sometimes theoretically and empirically justified, and that similar imperatives do explain the *origins* of the drive to decarcerate prisoners and patients, I also recognize how important it is to remain sensitive to crucial differences between the two groups, and to the ways in which these serve to modify policy outcomes over time.

In the light of the developments that have taken place over the past decade, the central question seems to be why, granted that governments were bent on finding 'cheaper alternatives to incarceration ... decarceration has not turned out to be a cheaper form of punishment. If anything, it seems to have been accompanied by a substantial growth of the criminal control apparatus' (Chan and Ericson 1981, pp. 39,47). This in turn has entailed a marked rise in expenditures on police and prisons, as well as other, less visible parts of the criminal justice apparatus.

Following the line of analysis adopted by Rothman (1980) in his discussion of Progressive Era reforms, Chan and Ericson (1981) have suggested that to explain these patterns, we must look to the ways in which the organizational interests of the professions running the criminal justice system have ensured the transmogrification of yet another generation of 'reforms' in the directions dictated by administrative convenience and bureaucratic aggrandizement. Plausible as this explanation is, however, it is clearly incomplete and insufficient as it stands.[26] As James Jacobs (1983b) has recently argued, the suggestion that correctional bureaucrats have an insatiable appetite for organizational growth ignores the fact that, 'historically, prison officials have been more concerned with the issue of "control" than with capacity; prestige in the profession has gone to those who could run a "tight ship" rather than to those who presided over the largest number of prisoners'. To comprehend why, on this occasion, they have moved in an expansionist direction, and have secured a substantial amount of public and political support for 'widening the net' (Cohen 1979), we must surely incorporate other elements into the equation.

Of quite central importance, I think, has been the accelerating volume of crime over the past quarter of a century. Whether that increase reflects shifts in society's age structure (Greenberg 1977a), the dislocations and social atomization characteristic of contemporary capitalism (Hall, Critchley, Jefferson, Clarke and Roberts 1978; see also Bottoms 1983, pp. 193–194), or, more doubtfully, the artificial by-product of a 'control wave' (Ditton 1979), its existence provides powerful ammunition for those seeking a larger commitment of resources to crime control. Indeed, there is substantial evidence that the 'fear of crime' has become an issue capable of mobilizing powerful if somewhat confused pressures for 'action' among an otherwise fractured and fragmented public. It is an issue which transcends standard ideological divisions to provide 'strong support for a fundamental change in punishment policy — one that pushes toward greater severity and more frequent use of incarceration'.[27] The radical non-interventionism which had a powerful appeal for the professoriate in the sixties and early seventies (and which initially — although for different reasons — found some support among the policy-makers as well), turns out to possess little attraction for the proletariat or bourgeoisie, for whom the most vital question remains, 'What is to be done?'

As this suggests, in comprehending why decarceration for the criminal has meant heightened control rather than neglect, we need to attend carefully to the character of the population to be controlled. The importance of this factor is readily seen if we compare the criminal and the mentally ill. It is one of the many ironies with which the sociology of social control abounds, that the casual dumping of the disorientated and senile has been made easier by the fact that the measures designed to dispose of them are ostensibly undertaken from a benevolent and humanitarian concern for their welfare. However great the discrepancy between the ideology and the reality of asylum existence — indeed, precisely *because* of that discrepancy (Deutsch 1973; Orlans 1948; Rawls 1980) — enormous energy and substantial resources have been devoted for more than a century and a half to elaborating, disseminating, and perpetuating what has all too often been the illusion of concern with the inmate's welfare.[28] As someone who is sick and therefore cannot be held responsible for his condition or situation, the mental patient is the recipient of treatment 'for his own good'. If it is concluded that traditional approaches are destructive and anti-therapeutic, then non-intervention, dressed up as community treatment and promoted in the name of the very virtues once attributed to the asylum, can be advocated on the grounds of its advantages to the client. But prisoners are not clients, and pain, privation, and suffering are seen by many as their just desserts. Because they 'chose' to offend, retribution is in order. The humanity of community corrections is thus its Achilles heel, precisely the feature most likely to alienate (fiscal) conservatives and indeed the public at large, who might otherwise be attracted by the idea. Criminals recidivate because of an innate or acquired depravity, and if prisons are unpleasant places, that is exactly what they should be.[29]

Beyond striking increases in prison populations, evidence is now accumulating that the development of so-called 'diversionary programmes' leads to a 'more voracious processing of deviant populations, albeit in new settings and by professionals with different names' (Cohen 1979, p. 350; see also Blomberg 1977a; Downs 1978; Lerman 1975; Klein 1976b; Messinger 1976; Rutherford and Bengur 1976; Warren 1981). Thus, unlike the situation with the mentally ill, the decarceration of the criminal has, over time, meant the widening of the network of social control. Here, as Chan and Ericson put it, 'people are not diverted *from*, but *into* and within the system' (1981, p.55).[30] Most subtly, this process has involved a more or less deliberate 'blurring of the boundaries' of the network of social control (Cohen 1979). Finding one's way through the maze of supervised release schemes, half-way houses, community correctional centres, group homes, foster homes, pre-trial release centres, deferred sentencing agencies and the like, requires a nice ability to make (increasingly meaningless) conceptual distinctions. At the extreme, 'it becomes difficult to distinguish a very "open" prison — with liberal provisions for work release, home release, outside educational programmes — from a very "closed" halfway house'. The 'administrative surrealism' extends further, incorporating a systematic obfuscation of the issue of guilt and innocence as it stretches to incorporate 'preventive, diagnostic or screening enterprises aimed at potential, pre-delinquent, or high-risk populations', and allowing programme failure, the violation of agency norms rather than statutes, to become the basis of future punishment (Cohen 1979).

Greenberg provides a striking example of how this can transform programmes to 'deinstitutionalize' status offenders, through:

> ... the imposition of special conditions on probationers to facilitate revocation. Thus prostitutes [for example] will be forbidden for a two-year period from being 'parked in a motor vehicle with lone male motorists', cannot 'approach male pedestrians or motorists or engage them in conversation upon a public street or in a public place' and must agree to 'submit [her] person, vehicle, and place of residence to search and seizure at any time of the day or night, with or without a search warrant, whenever

> requested to do so by a peace officer. [The administrators of the penal system are thereby granted powerful new resources with which to coerce their 'clients', since] probationers who are accused of involvement in a new crime but who refuse to plead guilty can still be imprisoned even if not convicted of a new offence in a criminal trial [through the simple administrative device of] a probation violation hearing in which the relevant standard is 'preponderance of the evidence', a weaker requirement than the 'reasonable doubt' standard required in a criminal trial. (1975, pp. 10–11)[31]

As with the implementation of an earlier generation of reforms in the first quarter of the twentieth century (Rothman 1980; Scull 1981), the outcome of changes ostensibly aimed at decreasing state intervention has all too often been the development of programmes which expand the reach of social control agencies and expose new populations to their (generally unwelcome) attentions. In practice, 'the meaning of "diversion" has been shifted from diversion from to "referral to" [with a consequent extension of] the costs, caseload, and system purview even further than had previously been the case' (Klein 1976a, p. 10). Cressey and McDermott neatly capture the discrepancy between rhetoric and reality. Examining a whole series of 'diversionary' schemes, they note:

> If 'true' diversion occurs, the juvenile is safely out of the official realm of the juvenile justice system and he is immune from incurring the delinquent label or any of its variations — pre-delinquent, delinquent tendencies, bad guy, hard core, unreachable. Further, when he walks out of the door from the person diverting him, he is technically free to tell the diverter to go to hell. We found very little 'true' diversion in the communities studied. (1974, pp.3–4)

This tendency is hardly surprising, for neglect has clear disadvantages as a social control strategy, at least when dealing with criminals and some delinquents. Although the advocates of diversion consistently ignore or play down the importance of the deterrent and retributive functions of punishment, to the extent that crime represents a 'rational' form of activity, the erosion of sanctions threatens to elicit more of it. The crazy and senile can, by and large, be contained and isolated while being neglected. Even were we to grant the attractions of unpoliced ghettos, however, the same result cannot be secured by releasing criminals. The targets they victimize are insufficiently selective and not adequately geographically concentrated or controllable. Moreover, a strategy of this sort creates serious ideological problems. To allow criminals to violate the law, with something approaching impunity, significantly weakens the incentives to conform while simultaneously provoking public outrage. It is likely to trigger vigilante responses, thus threatening the state's monopoly of legal violence. In the process, it exhibits an insidious yet powerful tendency to undermine the legitimacy of a social and political order that permits such developments.

We must appreciate, therefore, the advantages possessed by the crime control bureaucracies as they have sought to protect and extend their empires. By playing upon the fears and mobilizing the disquiet of the public, the correctional staff can readily justify a substantial expansion of the amount and intensity of professional involvement and activity. Thus one may anticipate that Lerman's (1975) findings on the way the California Community Treatment Project has been manipulated by and in the interests of the correctional establishment will turn out to be applicable more generally.

This leaves unresolved, however, the issue of why the criminal justice bureaucracy has been so protective of its state supported activities, whereas most mental health professionals have cheerfully abandoned their concern with the chronically crazy.[32] I suggest that this paradox disappears when we bear in mind the structural constraints and opportunities facing these two groups of controllers. The advent of community psychiatry and the growing willingness of insurance carriers to provide some coverage for mental disorders (together with the existing private psychiatric sector) mean that the higher status mental health professionals have ample alternative markets for their skills. Furthermore, those markets offer significant advantages. Though often heavily subsidized by tax money, they are free of the stigma of publicly provided care. Rather than the hopeless, impoverished and often senile patients characteristic of public psychiatry, they attract the less disturbed and more readily treatable, and the social status of the new clients is often higher (Chu and Trotter 1974). In terms of prestige, income and closer assimilation to the patterns of conventional medical practice, these fields are clearly preferable to the meagre awards associated with institutional psychiatry. Once the more articulate and politically influential professionals have been bought off in this fashion, whatever opposition is generated by hospital run-downs naturally comes primarily from low-status workers with little credibility.[33]

On the other hand, notwithstanding all their efforts to 'professionalize', police and prison officers have few transferable skills and operate in a severely restricted market. The careers of even the senior ranks remain inextricably bound up with servicing a lower class clientele. Even in the context of a burgeoning private security industry (Shearing and Stenning 1981; Spitzer and Scull 1977), their collective interests remain inseparably linked to the fortunes of the public sector, to a degree that simply does not hold for such groups as psychiatrists. Hence the vigour with which those running the system have sought to exploit their natural advantages to transform decarceration into a policy of more pervasive intervention and control.

The convergence created by the special problems involved in controlling crime — 'the occupational interests of correctional and prison employees and administrators [and] public demands, partly instrumental and partly symbolic, for sterner measures to stop increasing crime' (Greenberg 1975, p.16) — merely reinforces the tendency towards greater intervention already signalled in the pervasive and uncritical stress on rehabilitation so deeply entrenched in the community corrections literature and practice. Battered by assaults on its constitutionality, effectiveness, and moral justification (American Friends Service Committee 1972; Gaylin 1974; Kittrie 1972; Leifer 1969), the therapeutic ethic now appears to be giving ground in institutional settings (see Allen 1981).[34] From both right and left, there are renewed calls for fixed sentencing based upon deterrent and retributive considerations rather than rehabilitation (Fogel 1975; Van den Haag 1975; Von Hirsch 1976; Wilson 1975). What seems to be happening, however, is that the self-same therapeutic rationalizations and practices are being reinvoked as the basis for the new community programmes.[35] In substantial measure, it has been by exploiting the opportunities decarceration offers for blurring the boundaries between guilt and innocence, accentuating discretion, and promulgating an aggressive ideology of treatment and prevention, that the crime control bureaucracy has transformed something that promised to curtail their operations into the basis for further expansion of their activities.

The discretionary decision-making that forms an integral part of any programme of coercive 'rehabilitation' is a crucial feature of community corrections at all levels of its operation. It is most obvious in decisions about who is eligible for community dispositions in lieu of the harsher sanction of imprisonment. The very sense that the former is less punitive (or non-punitive), and can actually *prevent* more crime, diminishes concern with whether the 'client' has actually committed the offence that nominally brought him to the attention of the authorities. Instead of an adjudication focused on prior conduct there is an assessment of whether the accused can benefit from the services offered by the programme, a decision which often entails intentional avoidance of due process and of the issue of guilt and innocence. The whole approach thus brings with it the danger 'of highly intrusive intervention concerning matters of personal choice that have no direct bearing on criminal activity' (Greenberg 1975, p.6). To the extent that these features generate further perceptions of injustice or unfairness, the long-run tendency must be for them to undermine further the legitimacy of a criminal justice system already widely regarded as inequitable and arbitrary.

This outcome is in no sense an aberration. On the contrary, in 'corrections' as in other social control systems, the more control comes to be legitimated in terms of diagnosis and treatment rather than rules, responsibility and punishment, the more likely it is to intrude into the emotions, thought, and behaviour of the individual and to be concerned with generalized behavioural problems rather than specific acts. The threat thus looms of a massive extension of official intervention into the lives of those who had previously escaped notice or attention — all under the guise of 'helping' them. In fact, 'the more benign, attractive, and successful the programme is defined [as being] ... the more it will be used and the wider it will cast its net' (Cohen 1979, p.348).[36]

17 Decarceration and social control: fantasies and realities

Roger Matthews

Decarceration, it would seem, has had a short and not very illustrious history. When Andrew Scull 'discovered' decarceration in the mid-1970s and warned of its potential dangers, he claimed to have shown that 'decarceration has been taking place on an increasing scale and has been adopted as the most desirable way of dealing with deviance in both England and America' (Scull 1977, p.121).

Yet less than a decade later, Barbara Hudson pronounced, with some relief, that 'the decarceration era — both symbolically and in practice — is truly over' (1984, p.58). She even suggests that decarceration may never actually have occurred in practice other than at the level of official discourse. The re-expansion of the prison during the so called 'decarceration era' is, she argues, evidence enough that 'decarceration' was something of a misnomer. Thus it would seem that if the decarceration era occurred it was a tragedy; but there is no certainty that it ever occurred at all.

This paradoxical situation — which is symptomatic of the widespread uncertainty associated with decarceration, the expansion of community corrections, and the search for alternatives to incarceration — is the outcome, in part, of a certain conceptual ambiguity contained in Scull's original text. He initially defined the key term 'decarceration' as a 'state sponsored policy of *closing down* institutions'. Within the penal sphere, however, as Hudson and others have pointed out, there is little evidence of penal institutions actually being closed down. Apart from a few notable exceptions such as the 'Massachusetts Experiment', there are precious few examples in either Britain or North America that fall within this definition. But such a definition is unnecessarily narrow, and Scull's original presentation would certainly have been less influential and impressive if he had restricted himself to that usage.

In the course of the book Scull comes increasingly to use the term in a wider and more dynamic way, referring to 'the transformation of traditional mechanisms so as to promote the return to the outside world of so many who previously would have been incarcerated' (1977, p.45).

A version of this chapter appears in Volume 15, Issue 1 of the International Journal of the Sociology of Law (February 1987).

Thus, 'decarceration' comes to include not only the closing of institutions — what might be termed 'pure' decarceration — but also the deinstitutionalization and diversion of 'offenders' who previously would have been 'eligible' populations for incarceration.

If we use the term decarceration in this wide and more dynamic sense, then it follows that it must be conceived of as a *process* which cannot be grasped in phenomenalist terms (for example, the number of institutional closures or number of inmates.). Two analytic problems are raised by a phenomenalist perspective. Firstly, since no criteria have been specified by which to recognize populations eligible for decarceration, it is difficult to assess who would have been incarcerated under 'normal' conditions. Secondly, if the process of decarceration incorporates the processes of deinstitutionalization and diversion — for example, community absorption, screening, pre-trial diversion and the development of various alternatives to prison — then 'decarceration' effectively comes to encompass almost all those processes through which penal populations are selected at any given time. In this form the term loses its historical specificity, and much of its heuristic value.

The net result of these two analytic problems is that we are in imminent danger of losing sight of the role and overall impact of the pervasive anti-institutional ethos which surfaced throughout the sixties and seventies and fuelled the (so-called) 'decarceration' movement. This movement found continued expression in a wide range of penal and legislative policies that are now generally falling into disfavour.

The growing disillusionment and scepticism that surrounds the decarceration movement is, however, not based on a clear understanding or assessment of these processes. Rather, it seems to be inspired by a general feeling of uncertainty and confusion which characterizes much of the recent social control literature. The most perplexing aspect of this literature is the way in which most of the key terms, such as deinstitutionalization and diversion, seem at odds with the processes that they are supposed to identify. On closer examination, they often turn out to express the opposite of the processes they designate. As Stan Cohen has pointed out, these forms of conceptual ambiguity and uncertainty have helped to create a kind of *Alice in Wonderland* world in which:

> 'Informal' means created and sustained by the formal state apparatus; 'decentralised' means centrally controlled; 'accessibility' means rendering justice more inaccessible; 'non-coercive' means disguised coercion; 'community' means nothing; 'informalism' means undermining non-state models of informal control; 'benevolent' is beginning to mean "malign". (Cohen 1984, p.87)

These confusing and misleading inversions are in part a function of the complex and contradictory nature of the object itself. But they are also a product of the dominant approaches employed in the literature and the associated forms of empirical investigation. Some of the more glaring and persistent theoretical obstacles to the clarification of these issues — most notably functionalism and economism — have been addressed previously (cf. Ignatieff 1983; Matthews 1979; Stedman-Jones 1977). It has been argued that the process of decarceration, in particular, cannot be adequately understood either as an organic or logical development which follows the 'needs' of capitalism, or as a phenomenon which can be directly 'read off' or immediately grasped as a 'reflection' of underlying economic conditions. Apart from these two, unfortunately, much too prevalent tendencies, there have been three other major obstacles to the clarification of social control processes in general, and decarceration in particular — globalism, empiricism and impossibilism.

Globalism

Globalism refers to the tendency to overgeneralize from the particular, to dissolve or ignore recognized boundaries, and/or to move directly to an unmediated level of conceptualization. This tendency, not at all unknown within sociology, has recently become extremely prevalent in the social control literature. One of the main attractions of this approach is the attempt to identify major social trends and movements. Social control analysis is at its most impressive where it can identify social movements which transcend local and even national boundaries, particular political configurations, and conventional social divisions.In an important sense, then, the appeal of social control analysis derives from its generality, its universality, its globalism. However, this appeal may also become a major source of weakness — an Achilles heel.

Globalism can occur at a number of different levels, but in relation to the decarceration debate it takes four major forms:

1. Ignoring or blurring significant boundaries and divisions.
2. Generalizing from unrepresentative or idiosyncratic samples.
3. Universalizing from one nation.
4. Adopting meta-theoretical futuristic scenarios.

Ignoring or blurring significant boundaries and divisions

The most noticeable point of overgeneralization in the decarceration literature has been the tendency, initially employed by Scull, to generalize directly from the experience of asylums to prisons and juvenile institutions. Although there appeared to be some indication of a parallel movement in the 1960s, it became increasingly clear towards the mid-1970s that the constraints on the penal system were substantially different from those on asylums. Scull (1983, reprinted in this volume), in a reconsideration of his original thesis and in light of the changing imperatives within penal policy, modified his position:

> Let me confess at the outset that [there are] serious limitations to studying prisons and asylums as a unitary phenomenon. It is not that such assimilation is never theoretically or empirically justified, or that I feel that I was completely wrong in invoking similar imperatives to explain the drive to decarcerate prisoners and patients. But I now recognise how important it is to remain sensitive to crucial differences that modify policy outcomes. (Scull 1983, p.158)

But the problem of globalism in this form goes far beyond the unwarranted shift from patients to prisoners. The significance of the decarceration process itself may be substantially different for different subgroups, and a level of analysis is required which can grasp more complex and detailed divisions than those among the 'mad, the bad and the sad'. Nor is the decarceration process likely to have the same impact upon all social categories or types of offender. Anyone seriously interested in 'policy outcomes' or further developing deinstitutionalization strategies could not effectively operate with such broad divisions. Overgeneralization in this form will tend to encourage unrealistic and unworkable policies in which important differences are either obscured or dismissed, or alternatively, seen as a deviation from the norm.

The blurring of the categories of analysis and lumping together of diverse groups into an undifferentiated whole carries a further important consequence in its train. It tends to involve, or at least encourage, a unidimensional analysis in which fiscal crisis, unemployment or advances in technology are variously presented as the primary or sole determinant. The complex interplay of social forces and their impact upon different populations is jettisoned in favour of a monocausal analysis. The dynamic processes of decarceration, deinstitutionalization and diversion continually defy this linear mode of analysis.

Generalizing from unrepresentative and idiosyncratic samples

There is always a tendency in the social control literature to generalize from small unrepresentative samples and to inflate their significance — particularly when they lend support to the argument. This is as much a problem in the analysis of decarceration as elsewhere. Often the original cautions and qualifications are forgotten and the results are presented as authoritative. But this type of obstacle can be relatively easily overcome and poses less of a problem within the decarceration debate than the continued over-reliance on idiosyncratic and decontextualized studies.

Two of the central points of reference in the literature are drawn from the experience in Massachusetts and California. These comprise the well known 'Massachusetts Experiment', which managed to close down the juvenile reformatories virtually 'overnight', and the California Treatment Programme, which attempted to deinstitutionalize youngsters into the 'community' (cf. Klein 1979; Lerman 1975; Scull 1977). Both experiments have served as influential examples of the possibilities and pitfalls associated with decarceration and deinstitutionalization. Massachusetts in particular is offered as a prime example of how a radical 'deep end' strategy can be effectively implemented. But as a general example of how a policy of decarceration might be effectively pursued elsewhere, the Massachusetts experience is extremely limited. In addition to the unique problems of the state prior to the implementation of juvenile decarceration, Massachusetts enjoys a level of political and administrative autonomy which is exceptional, and would be extremely difficult to replicate elsewhere.

Just as it was a peculiar localism and political fragmentation that allowed Jerry Miller's entrepreneurship to flourish in Massachusetts, so too did these elements serve to obstruct efforts to effect a policy of decarceration in California (see Bakal and Polsky 1978). It is not surprising that the experiences of Massachusetts and California have not been replicated and that Miller is now in 'exile' and apparently 'waits in vain for the call to return to the crusade' (Rutherford 1986, p. 106).

Apart from these two (now rather dated) points of reference, many other available studies of control practices appear to the student of decarceration as peculiarly decontextualized. This is in large part due to the prominence of 'top down' explanations which depict changes in control practices as the product of well-orchestrated decision-making processes, managed and manipulated by the 'ruling class' or the 'powerful'. But changing modes of control may also reflect demands from below, forged through social and class struggles, or they may reflect institutional tensions and contradictions (cf. Cain 1985). Also, as Paul Lerman discovered:

> Part of the problem of responding to the deinstitutionalization policy is that it is not a coherent fully formulated policy carefully orchestrated through a clear policy initiative. Instead it is an emergent, partial strategy meshed in with other processes and strategies. (Lerman 1982, p.14)

These piecemeal and defensive strategies are often responses to specific sets of conditions, and we must therefore remain sensitive to the contexts in which policies are implemented. It is not just that there is a shortage in Britain and North America of good representative and comparative studies of the decarceration process, but those which *have* been produced are often analytically divorced from the economic and political contexts out of which they have emerged.

Universalizing from one nation

Much of the debate around decarceration has been dominated by the American experience. Although some studies have been invaluable, there has been a tendency to present them in such a way as to suggest that America *leads* the decarceration movement. Developments in other advanced capitalist countries which are dissimiliar to the American examples are described as 'lagging behind' or are seen as deviating from the appropriate path (see Scull 1977, p.56). In terms of penal strategies, however, America, like Britain, may be described more realistically as 'backward'.

If we are looking for good examples of decarceration and deinstitutionalization, it is not to America or Britain that we should look. More instructive examples of the deinstitutionalization of penal populations have occurred in Europe, Australia and Japan. Holland, for example, has been identified as a consummate example of decarceration. Like the Australians, the Dutch have managed to substantially reduce their custodial population at a time when the serious crime rate has continued to increase (cf. Biles 1983; Morrison 1985; Tulkens 1979). Indeed, the reduction of the Netherlands penal population was realized during a period of 'exceptional' conditions. As David Downes points out:

> By Scull's definition, the Netherlands is a classic example of decarceration, particularly in the penal sphere. It does not appear, however, to conform to his theory of fiscal crisis. The major reduction in prison population, both in terms of average daily populations, and its relation to the rise in crime rates, came in the late 1950s and 1960s, precisely when the Netherlands was experiencing an unprecedented growth in prosperity and a relative absence of fiscal crisis. (1982, p.336).

In France, too, there has been a substantial reduction in the juvenile custodial population in the recent past, while in Italy the prison population has halved in the last forty years and the numbers of those now 'serving time' has been reduced to a few thousand (see Ferrajoli and Zolo 1985; King 1983).

What is remarkable in the current period, and what should command our attention, is not the *universality* of decarceration, but rather its *differentiation*, even within neighbouring states. This also underlines the point that shifts in decarceration cannot simply be read off from economic development. There is, it would seem, a growing recognition of the need for specificity. Indicative of this need, a group of Australian criminologists, concerned with developing strategies of crime control, recently stated that:

> Methodologically, we reject the universalistic notion present in much American criminology that American problems, analysis and solutions are readily transferable to other social formations. (Boehringer *et al.* 1983, p.2).

Adopting meta-theoretical futuristic scenarios

The very term 'social control' usually triggers a whole range of powerful images and fantasies of future utopias, dystopias, or heterotopias as popularly portrayed in the writings of Orwell, Burroughs, Huxley and the like.[1] Although one might expect that a central task of social control analysis would be to demystify and evaluate these scenarios, it often seems that the reverse is the case.[2] That is, it is often explicitly or implicitly from the standpoint of these popular scenarios that current practices are assessed.

If we take, for example, the often reported consequence of developing 'alternatives' to incarceration — net-widening, which refers to the inadvertent expansion of the 'social control network' and the inclusion of new populations who would previously not have been subject to control — we can see the manifestation of this tendency. In the bulk of the literature, 'net-widening' is seen as a negative phenomenon reflecting the unnecessary and unwanted encroachment of the state into private life. Thus, the expansion of state intervention *in itself* is seen as a problem generating images of the growing authoritarian state enmeshing and constraining a society of presumably free and equal men and women. Thus:

> 'Widening the net' describes the nightmare of the benevolent state gone haywire. This horror has already been vividly portrayed in Orwell's *1984*, Solzhenitsyn's *Cancer Ward*, Kesey's *One Flew Over the Cuckoo's Nest* and Burgess' *Clockwork Orange*. Social scientists and criminologists have just caught up with the humanists. (Austin and Krisberg 1981, pp.188–89)

The preoccupation with the 'spectre' of 'net-widening' as an essentially negative entity also reflects, on the one hand, the liberalism which underscores much of the analysis, and, on the other hand, glosses the differential nature of much of this intervention (cf. Bayer 1981). Much of what parades under the heading of 'net-widening' may be constructive and progressive. Social workers, community workers, youth workers and the like are not simply 'agents of social control', nor are they just 'clearing up after capitalism' or 'papering over the cracks', for if nothing else these agents have undoubtedly brought much needed resources into deprived areas (Cohen 1985a). It is hardly surprising, during a period in which sociologists and criminologists have been bemoaning the demise of informal control systems, that new, more formal, modes of intervention should arise (Mathiesen 1983). In opposition to the liberal assumption, however, formal control is often *less* intrusive than the unrelenting surveillance of informal controls. It is also invariably less effective and framed to focus on particular 'targets', with the result that certain populations tend to 'slip through the cracks' and appear to be 'beyond' control (Durnford 1977). A growing population is left to fester in the inner cities — it was here that Orwell was probably at his most prophetic — and is subject to a minimal degree of formal intervention (Roper 1983).

Whatever sense one makes of the growing public participation in crime control, the spread of vigilantism, the expansion of private police and prisons, the abject failure of the police to reduce crime despite massive technological investment, the growing concerns about public order and riots, these developments do not imply that 'social control' is necessarily becoming either more effective or pervasive (Kinsey, Lea and Young 1986; Michalowski 1983; Shearing and Stenning 1981).

An interesting example of how social control theorists have been directed by visions of *1984* and the like can be seen in the appropriation of Foucault's influential (but extremely ambiguous) text *Discipline and Punish*. Virtually all of Foucault's many followers have stressed the vision of an all-encompassing totalitarian society organized through an increasingly integrated carceral system which constitutes a 'deep' strategy for organizing populations into disciplined, individualized and manageable entities. The text undoubtedly 'allows' such a reading, but it can, and arguably should, be read very differently. Thus:

> *Discipline and Punish* may be read as a critical analysis of at least one source of the very idea of a social whole. The theme of the book is not (as is sometimes assumed) that we all live in a totally administered society — one big Panopticon. A utopian image of a totally administered rational society can be found easily enough in Bentham, and in the more or less explicitly utilitarian reform projects Foucault analyses. But the point of analysing its occurence there is precisely to dispel the realist or objective illusion that our societies *are* administered wholes. Conversely, Foucault propounds no global analysis of society of his own. His book is thus a 'dispersed' analysis of one kind of preoccupation with society as a whole. (Rajchman 1983/4, p. 11)

Thus rather than stressing the fragmentary, pluralistic, and relativist elements in his analysis, Foucault has mainly been read in line with the Orwellian fantasy of the totally administered society. Not surprisingly, therefore, there has been a widespread adoption of the so-called 'dispersal of discipline' thesis, describing an apparent shift from the 'concentration to the dispersal of social control', and from systems of corporal punishment to 'infinite discipline' (cf. Christie 1978; Cohen 1979; Mathiesen 1983).

In a recent challenge to this thesis, Bottoms (1983) has attempted to redress the imbalance by stressing that current social control analysis has tended to overlook some important recent developments within penal policy, such as the fine, community service orders, suspended sentences and victim compensation. These do not involve an extension of discipline, he argues, for they are 'non-disciplinary' forms of punishment. This again raises questions over the 'correct' reading of Foucault (cf. Santos 1985; Waltzer 1983). But Bottoms, although he makes a valuable contribution by identifying these 'neglected' features of policy, does not seem fully to appreciate the ways in which these apparently 'non-disciplinary' elements are linked to and are ultimately dependent upon the prison.[3] As such, they do not constitute a break with this pivotal disciplinary mechanism, and thus they must serve to extend and enhance its power. There are, however, a number of important recent developments in control which *could* conceivably be characterized as 'non-disciplinary', such as mass unemployment, ghettoization, selective privatization, and the adoption of various strategies such as 'true' diversion and deinstitutionalization, which have returned 'problem populations' back to the regulation of the market, and informal social networks.

The important point regarding 'net-widening' and the 'dispersal of discipline' thesis is to recognize that there are inherent dangers to the unwanted and unintended expansion of the penal system, and that 'alternatives' can too easily become 'extensions' and 'additions'. Nonetheless, as Bottoms suggests, 'some attention needs to be given, in any full discussion of contemporary punishment, to which cases are deemed to require disciplinary punishment and which not: to the *differentiation* of discipline' (Bottoms 1983, p. 196).

Empiricism

A second major obstacle to the clarification of decarceration and social control processes is the widespread adoption of a methodology which relies upon generalizations gleaned from collections of untheorized 'facts': namely empiricism. Colin Sumner has pointed out how such an approach is commonly employed:

> What seems to happen is that when a phenomenon is observed spontaneously, the observer associates its aetiology with the circumstances in which it appears. For example, in orthodox criminology, research of an empiricist kind has observed the coexistence of poverty, criminal behaviour, broken family ties and delinquent juvenile gangs within working class neighbourhoods. From this sighting criminological researchers have gone on to correlate crime with poverty, broken homes, working class values etc. Rather than seeing all these circumstances (including crime) as normal exigencies of life for a class for a specific position within a particular social structure (and thus comprehending the connections between social structure and class conditions) the theory-less researchers took the appearances and attempted to make them explain each other. (Sumner 1979, p.180)

Relying on the selection of an apparently random collection of 'facts', empiricism remains trapped at the level of appearances. Rather than attempting to decipher underlying relations, the empiricist attempts to gather as many 'factors' together as possible which might have some bearing on the problem to be explained. But since there is no way of deciding whether all of the relevant factors are present in the analysis it is never certain whether the relevant factors have been identified. As such, empiricism tends to offer a relatively contingent and indeterminate mode of enquiry.

In terms of decarceration the commitment to empiricism constructs a twin mystification. On one side it observes the simultaneous expansion of community corrections and incarceration and uses one to explain the other. On the other hand it employs similar techniques to 'demonstrate' that the various diversion and deinstitutionalization strategies are not working effectively by evaluating them primarily in terms of their associated rates of recidivism.

These are important considerations, for in concert they have inspired much of the disillusionment currently surrounding the decarceration movement. These empiricist studies have been used to 'show' that decarceration has been either ineffective or counter-productive.

To be sure, there have been a number of attempts to explain the simultaneous expansion of community corrections and prisons in terms of 'net-widening' and 'thinning the mesh' by which larger populations are drawn into the control network — a predictable percentage of whom will eventually work their way up the tariff and into prison. But it has already been suggested that these effects may be less pervasive than is often imagined, and that deinstitutionalization and diversion can be effective under certain conditions in deflecting 'offenders' from institutions (Musheno 1982; Quay and Love 1977). The erroneous notion that any form of contact with the criminal justice system will invariably propel petty offenders into the mainstream of the system is an unfortunate and misleading legacy of labelling theory (Wellford 1975).

The empiricist may readily admit that there might be other significant factors affecting the levels of both incarceration and community corrections. One obvious, but rarely incorporated example, is the growth of serious crime. If we try to comprehend decarceration as a process, and to accommodate eligible populations within our analysis, then it is crucial that we take into account the changing incidence and distribution of crime. But it is not just a question of 'adding' the variable of crime or running correlations of crime with other variables in the analysis, but of theorizing the relations among them and of comprehending decarceration as a dynamic process. Thus it is not the absolute size of the prison population which should be our primary point of reference but the *relationship* between the imprisonment rate, the crime rate and the growth of community corrections (Box and Hale 1986). For although in England and Wales and America the absolute level of incarceration has increased, there has been a significant proportional decline in the use of prison for certain categories of convicted defendants in both contexts (see Figure 17.1; also Bottoms 1983; Scull 1977).

Moreover it is extremely misleading to characterize community-based corrections and traditional forms of segregative control as mutually self-regulating systems. Although it may appear in the current period that both systems are mutually reinforcing, an historical investigation reveals that they have a distinct aetiology, that they draw on different populations, have a different social focus, and distinct modalities of intervention (see Garland 1981; Lerman 1983). Thus the size, shape, and capacity of both community-based corrections and segregative systems will be conditioned by a range of determinants apart from each other.

Similar difficulties arise in relation to recidivism. It was one of the unfortunate, but probably necessary conditions for the establishment and expansion of many community-based projects, that they claimed the ability to reduce recidivism and by implication the rate of crime. In certain projects and particular cases this may well have been a reality, but it soon became apparent that the rate of recidivism was not better or worse in the apparently more humane and progressive community-based agencies than in the old segregative institutions (Greenberg 1977). This finding was readily seen by the critics of decarceration as a serious failure. Moreover the continued increase in serious crime in many Western countries served as a further indictment (Hylton 1982).

But recidivism is an extremely unreliable measure. As James Q. Wilson has pointed out, although there is continual reference to recidivist 'rates', most studies are not dealing with rates at all but with the 'percentage' of offenders who commit another crime within a certain period of time after release — normally two years. But it may well be the case that the reoffence involves a *lesser* or *different* crime than the original. Also the narrow preoccupation with recidivism tends to obscure the *frequency* with which offences were committed after release (Wilson 1980).

Assessing the percentage or even frequency of reoffending may tell us little or nothing about the benefits for the recipient of one type of correctional system over another since this type of research usually proceeds on the assumption 'that the poor and the oppressed have no psychic lives at all' (Cohen 1985a). Also, the focus on recidivism tends to ignore the social and structural pressures towards reoffending which may, in themselves — irrespective of the relative merits of the different correctional facilities — affect the rate of recidivism. Thus:

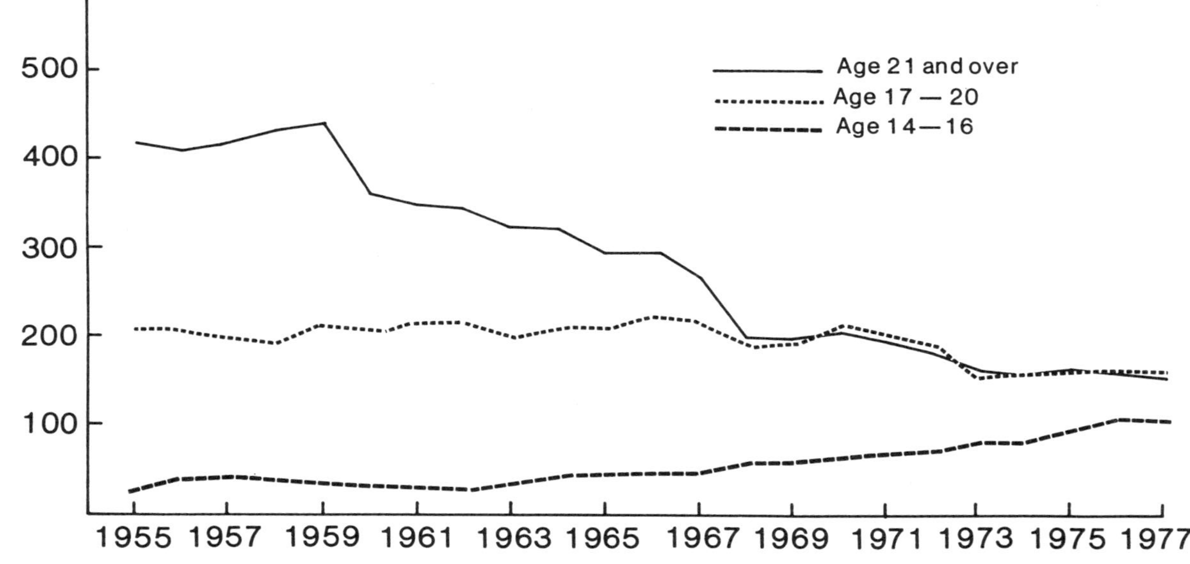

From: Inquiry into U.K.Prison Services (May Committee Report) Vol. 1. HMSO. 1979

Figure 17.1 Receptions into custody per 1000 found guilty of indictable offences – males 1955–77

> . . . to the extent that criminal activity represents a rational response to the absence of opportunities realistically available, community corrections may be largely irrelevant because it is in a position to generate few new opportunities. (Greenberg 1975, p. 5)

But the overriding problem with the endless studies on recidivism is their generality. In his now famous study, Martinson found that the extant research indicated there was no one option which worked for *all* offenders. In these terms 'success' becomes an all or nothing proposition. Martinson provided no effective measure of the *degree* of effectiveness, and since no particular mode of intervention could be shown to work across the board for all offenders he concluded that none of them could be described as a 'success' (Martinson 1974). Palmer, however, reworking the same data, showed that important differences could be detected. He suggested that:

> Rather than ask 'What works — for offenders as a whole?' we must increasingly ask which methods work best for which type of offenders and under what conditions or in what types of setting. (Palmer 1975, p. 150)

Although Palmer is correct that a realistic policy analysis must engage with the specificity of the phenomenon, he does seem to appreciate that Martinson's conclusion was not simply an error or a problem of interpretation but resulted directly from his empiricist mode of enquiry and his reliance upon inductive generalizations. By the same token, it is not enough to argue, as Wilson (1980) does, that some studies of recidivism show positive results.

The problem lies not only in adopting better 'indicators', disaggregating the 'facts', or searching for more positive results, but in the development of a mode of enquiry which can grasp the relevant processes as dynamic events. This requires the elaboration of a contextualized theoretical and conceptual analysis. As opposed to the claim of 'systematic empiricism' that our concepts must be limited to observable categories, we need to go behind the immediately observable and develop a scientific analysis which can distinguish essences from appearances and comprehend the relations between them. To paraphrase Marx, if the world could be adequately understood at the level of appearances then (social) science would be redundant. What is required is the development of an adequate level of abstraction. This does not involve the same process as developing generalizations. Indeed, in an important sense, it represents the opposite of the cumulative generalizations characteristic of empiricism.

> Abstraction in science moves from the observational level to the theoretical and back to the observational level. Thus there is a continual abstractive process which forms a dialectic through which theoretical statements may be

> modified or expanded to sharpen their explanatory power and increase their scope of application. Generalisations, however, are either true or false and must be either rejected if a contrary case is found, or stated as a probability, which has the drawback that it is incapable of explaining particular cases. (Willer and Willer 1973, p. 23)

Thus in terms of explanation and prediction empiricism is extremely weak, and although it is currently enjoying something of a renaissance, it tends to inhibit understanding rather than encourage it. Ultimately, this empiricist epistemology acts as a brake upon theoretical development. It offers a preoccupation with the technology of statistical manipulation — the numbers game — or, alternatively, encourages the endless search for potentially related variables. And since the researcher can never be sure that the existing combination of factors is sufficient, research invariably remains inconclusive and equivocal. As a result a large proportion of this type of research, as in the case of Martinson, has a strong affinity with pessimism, or impossibilism.

Impossibilism

Impossibilism in its hard form claims that 'nothing works', and in its softer versions claims that 'nothing works — very well'. This thoroughgoing pessimism, which has permeated and deeply affected a wide range of recent debates, draws support from right across the political spectrum. The right, for example, argue that deinstitutionalization and diversion have failed to provide the kind of moral economies which they initially promised. Alternatively, the liberals have focused on what is seen as the unnecessary and undesirable expansion of state control; while the left see decarceration either as a thinly disguised fiscal strategy masquerading as a humane intervention, or as a policy which when inserted into a fundamentally unjust and inequitable criminal justice system, will eventually be undermined by an all too absorbent state apparatus (Mathiesen 1980). Reflecting on recent developments associated with the decarceration movement, Scull concludes:

> Only a confirmed Pangloss can view the realities of a traditional penal system with equanimity, but what I have learned about the community corrections movement simply reinforces my conviction that tinkering around with the criminal justice system in a radically unjust society is unlikely to advance us very far toward justice, equity or (come to that) efficacy. Perhaps the best I can do is to persuade others to share my sense of discomfort. (Scull 1983, p. 165)

This is the impossibilist impasse in a nutshell. Prisons are a disaster, community corrections are invariably worse, realistic reform cannot be achieved without a fundamental transformation of the social structure, which is unlikely to occur in the forseeable future, so there is nothing that can be done. Like many commentators Scull's sense of impossibilism stems from his commitment to a functionalist metaphysic, in which all social movements, no matter how progressive or benevolent in intent, can be guaranteed either to make matters worse, or to reinforce capitalist domination, or both (Young 1986). However, if by some chance decarceration or diversion actually do show some signs of working then this can only be 'allowed' because it serves to reduce pressure on the criminal justice system.

From this perspective there is little sense of the role of progressive reforms or of the contradictory nature of capitalist social relations and the capitalist state (Offe 1984). To reject the possibility or desirability of penal reform is not to adopt a position of neutrality. It is rather to give support — albeit by default — to those interests which see 'alternatives' as too soft and which 'reluctantly' urge the re-expansion of the prison as the only viable strategy — given the impossibility of doing anything else.

Apart from functionalism, impossibilism draws heavily on the interactionist tradition. From this perspective any interventionist policy always has to contend with a set of diverse and often antagonistic interests, such that by the time it is implemented it may bear little relation to its original formulation. Given this predictable gap between conceptualization and implementation, deinstitutionalization and diversion can be said to have never been 'properly' implemented or assessed, and must therefore be considered a failure in terms of the original formulation (Klein 1979). Also, because, in practice, policies are likely to be affected by proximate contingencies they will invariably be subject to modification and adaption. As there will always be a gap between intentions and outcomes, theory and practice, words and deeds, and rhetoric and reality, an adequate level of 'failure' or distortion can be predicted in advance; and since 'programme integrity' cannot be guaranteed, intervention is always in danger of turning sour. The pressing need, however, is to reduce the gap between intentions and outcomes and to develop more effective and sensitive policies. But the preferred solution to this dilemma is non-interventionism, minimalism and the attempt to do less harm rather than more good (Gaylin *et al.* 1978). Paradoxically, it was in this vein in Britain during the 1970s that rationales to reduce the level of care for juveniles in the name of 'individual freedom' were developed, while an expansionist penal programme under the banner of 'just desserts' and 'determinate sentencing' was sustained (see Cohen 1985a; Pitts 1986; Thorpe *et al.* 1980).

The experience of the apparent impossibility of either living with the state or realistically living without it has served to reinforce liberal pessimism, such that it has increasingly come to resemble the conservative perspective against which it had set itself in the post-war period (Bayer 1981; Wolfe 1981). One of the most thoroughgoing statements of this brand of pessimism was presented by Rothman, who argued for the adoption of the 'failure' model.

> Heretofore, at the heart of the penal system or of parole and probation was a 'success' model, we could reform the deviant. As an alternative, I believe we may accomplish more by frankly adopting a failure model by recognising our inability to achieve such heady and grandiose goals as eliminating crime and remaking offenders. Let us accept failure and pursue its implications. (1974, p.657)

Impossibilism in this context is sustained by an over-inflation of goals. No one seriously believes we can 'eliminate' crime or 'remake' offenders, but there is nothing unrealistic about reducing crime or offering offenders a less damaging and less dehabilitating alternative to the traditional prison.

At the heart of the impossibilist dilemma is an increasingly conflicting set of assessments concerning the characteristic nature of state intervention in the current period. As de Sousa Santos points out:

> While some authors have shown the tendency for the state to intervene and penetrate more and more in the civil society and to do so in an increasingly authoritarian way — what has been described as the 'regulatory state', 'authoritarian statism', 'surveilled democracy', 'liberal corporatism', or 'friendly fascism' or 'fascism with a human face' — other authors (and even the same authors) have converged in the idea seemingly inconsistent with the previous one, that the state is increasingly inept to perform the variety of tasks — facilitative and repressive, legitimation oriented and accumulation oriented — expected from it by an economic and social structure dominated by monopoly capital. According to this idea the state lacks either the financial resources (the argument of fiscal crisis), or the institutional capacity (the argument of the inadequacy of the state bureaucracy to adapt to a fast-changing economic environment) or still that it lacks the mechanisms that in civil society steer the action and account for efficiency (the argument of the lack of market signals). The state emerges in these analyses as both an all-engulfing leviathan and as a failing structure (to the point that a theory of the failure of the state is already being called for). (Santos 1985, p. 301)

This tension at the heart of social control analysis suggests that current control movements are far more contradictory and uneven than is normally indicated, and that the 'state's' response is massively differentiated. Thus it is highly misleading to present current movements exclusively as an all-engulfing global expansion of social control on the one hand, or as a movement towards minimal statism on the other. Rather, what appears to have occurred in the recent past is a fundamental *reconstruction* of the control process producing new strategies, new techniques, focusing on different targets, and directed by new social and economic imperatives. Any comprehensive theory of social control must take these tensions and contradictions as its point of departure (Offe 1984; Spitzer 1982).

Decarceration and the reconstruction of the penal population

If we look at the custodial population in England and Wales in the post-war period, what is most remarkable, apart from its size, is its changing composition. It has become increasingly young and black, and includes a rising percentage of females. The growing youthfulness of the custodial population has become increasingly recognized and identified as a point of concern:

> This reduction in the average age of prisoners has not been due to a fall in the numbers of older men entering the system but to an enormous rise in the number of young men received. Between 1957 and 1977 receptions of those aged 21 and over under sentence of immediate imprisonment varied relatively little over the period from an annual total of 27 838 to 29 564. Over the same years reception of young men and boys aged under 21 rose from 4901 to a startling 22 169, that is from 16 per cent of male receptions to 43 per cent. (Baldock 1980, p. 150)

Baldock describes this shift as nothing short of a revolution in the composition of the penal population with over half the custodial population in England and Wales being under 24 years old. Moreover, as Hudson notes: 'If Scull's original thesis had been correct (namely that decarceration in Britain lagged behind the USA but could be expected to become a similarly established tendency) then more recent years should show a fall in the number of young people detained' (Hudson 1984, p. 51).

The custodial population in England and Wales has also become noticeably blacker. The available evidence indicates that the black male population in prison averages around 20 per cent, while the proportion in borstals and in youth custody centres can be as high as 60 per cent (Gordon 1983; Kettle 1982; Home Office 1986). The number and percentage of women in custody has also been increasing substantially. Between 1970 and 1980 the average daily population of women in custody almost doubled from around 800 to 1500. Although the figures remain relatively small, this marks a considerable increase in numbers and also a slight increase in the proportion of female offenders in custody (*Criminal Statistics* 1981). This figure is particularly noteworthy in light of the well publicized intentions of the Home Office to phase out female incarceration by the end of the century.

The movements of the American custodial population, however, follow a distinctly different trajectory. In that country the number of juveniles incarcerated in public institutions has declined. In long-term facilities in particular, the number of youths under 18, after increasing from 38353 in 1960 to 57691 in 1970, has dropped dramatically — down to 30948 in 1979. Over the same period the number of juveniles in private institutions has gone up from approximately 8000 to 28000 (Lerman 1984). Although the idea is strongly supported by most commentators, it is far from certain that the substantial increase in the private sector is a direct result of the decrease in the public sector. This 'obvious' correlation has yet to be demonstrated (Krisberg and Schwartz 1983). However, the recent development of what Lerman refers to as a 'youth-in-trouble' complex involving the juvenile justice, private, medical and welfare systems impedes calculation of the number of juveniles in custody. But the evidence does suggest that the number of American juveniles in penal facilities, particularly following the Juvenile Justice and Delinquency Act (1974), has decreased significantly. Also, according to the Bureau of Justice figures for 1980 the largest group of inmates is drawn from the 18–29 age group who account for some 63 per cent of the population (Bureau of Justice 1980). This gives the American correctional system a distinctly different *shape* than the British system; whereas the age structure of the British system assumes the familiar pyramidal configuration, the American system is more elliptical.

In terms of ethnic distribution, however, the movements in America appear to resemble those in England and Wales. Christianson suggests that:

> Many people may be unaware . . . that not only has the prison system gotten bigger, but it has also gotten blacker. Analysis of national prison statistics for 1973 and 1979 reveals that the number of blacks in state correctional institutions increased from about 83000 to about 132000 and that the black share of the state prison population rose from about 46.4 per cent to 47.8 per cent. Considering that blacks account for a minority of the total United States population — an estimated 11.5 per cent in 1976 — this overrepresentation is very striking indeed. Whereas the incarceration rates for whites increased from about 46.3 per 100000 to 65.1 per cent from 1973 to 1979, the black incarceration rate rose from 368 to 544.1 per 100000 during that period. (Christianson 1981, p.366)

The incarceration rate of black males is the highest of any race/sex group in US prisons — more than six times that for white males. It should be noted, however, that Christianson's figures related only to state institutions and that the rate of blacks incarcerated in federal institutions is considerably lower (47 per cent versus 34 per cent). Also the racial distribution in US prisons remained roughly stable between 1978 and 1982 (Bureau of Justice 1982, p.7). Thus although the American black prison population has increased, the rate of increase is nowhere near as dramatic as it is for England and Wales. Indicatively, although the black population in America is an estimated 11.5 per cent of the total, they constitute approximately 47 per cent of the prison population. The black (Afro-Caribbean) population in England and Wales is around 1–2 per cent while the estimated prison rate for this group is about 8 per cent. If we consider the age distribution of the black population in each country these differences become more pronounced.

If it is the case that juvenile and black populations in the United States have followed a different course or have risen less dramatically than their British counterparts, then it appears in the case of females that the American movements have been similar although more emphatic. Between 1970 and 1982 there has been a rapid growth in the number of female prisoners in state and federal institutions, increasing from approximately 6000 in 1970 to 16000 in 1982. The proportion of women in the total prison population has gone up from 3.5 per cent in 1974 to 4.3 per cent in 1982. Significantly, the largest increase among female prisoners has been in the group sentenced to more than one year (Bureau of Justice 1983).

Thus we see that if we move away from global comparisons and empiricist correlations, and focus instead on the composition of what appear to be similar penal developments, profound differences are evident. These comparisons, of course, would stand further interrogation and are only presented here as indicative of the substantial qualitative differences between two ostensibly similar systems. It is from an appreciation of these differential movements that the specificity of the decarceration movement and other social control processes needs to be assessed. Such an analysis suggests that strategies such as decarceration and deinstitutionalization, rather than being 'failures', have impacted upon different populations in significantly different ways, and have been associated with a fundamental reorganization and reconstruction of the penal population.

Conclusions

Making sense of these complex processes will require a more sophisticated theoretical approach than is realizable through overgeneralizations, directionless statistical manipulation, and the kind of relentless pessimism which characterizes much of the literature. Where these prominent approaches — globalism, empiricism and impossibilism — come into combination they tend to reinforce each other. Their combined effect is to render policy assessment, theoretical development and the search for progressive policy alternatives virtually redundant. Since the overriding expectation is that the policy will fail, atheoretical empiricism can be readily adopted to provide the confirmation. Thus, if globalism and impossibilism help to formulate the questions, empiricism can be relied upon to provide the answers.

Alternatively, empiricism can encourage and sustain a commitment to pessimism, particularly where 'success' is presented in all-or-nothing terms. Furthermore, the open-ended and often ambiguous conclusions which undifferentiated generalizations help to produce, lend themselves readily to pessimism and uncertainty. The combination of globalism and empiricism can also impart a peculiar oscillation between grand generalizations on the one hand, and an assortment of unrelated particulars on the other. The tendency is for the underlying relations to remain submerged and for theoretical analysis to be displaced. This space, however, can rapidly be filled by a relatively painless injection of impossibilism.

The danger of the impossibilist ethos, especially when sustained by an empiricist epistemology and a globalist perspective, is not only that it provides a disincentive to the formulation of realistic and progressive policies, but also that it can similarly lead to the premature abandonment of a search for alternatives to incarceration. It is arguably the persistent pessimism which surrounds deinstitutionalization and diversion strategies in Britain and North America that has inadvertently lent support to the movement toward a re-expansion of the prison system. By reducing the decarceration process to an epiphenomenon, or by condemning it to a premature burial despite continued and widespread evidence of its 'success', many theorists have discouraged debate and ignored the gains which have been made during the 'decarceration era'. Dismissing the potential of these movements, encouraging a belief that everything is getting worse, that *1984* is just around the corner — even if a little late — and suggesting that the only thing which might be worse than living with prisons is living without them, is to exchange the possibility of realistic and progressive interventions for dystopian fantasies.

18 Taking decentralization seriously: values, visions and policies

Stanley Cohen

The decentralization of social control must be understood as part of a complex package of ideologies, theories and social movements which captured liberal and radical thinking about social control over the past two decades. My subject in this paper is not the social origins of this package, nor the actual (or alleged) changes which have been caused by (or accompanied) it. I have given such an account elsewhere (Cohen 1985a), setting out the two intellectual strategies which have been used to understand shifts in social control theory and policy. The first is to locate specific changes (in rhetoric or in practice) in terms of overall master patterns which are conceived in sociological, historical or archaeological terms (progress, rationalization, extension of discipline, legitimation crisis, epistemological breaks — or whatever). The second is to conceive these changes as the product of particular reform movements (such as diversion, anti-psychiatry or decriminalization) and then to use the tools of social policy analysis to examine such matters as implementation, consequences and evaluation.

These remain the most important subjects on the sociological agenda. We are still some way from knowing why the old system was challenged so radically, what the meaning was of these challenges, what changes (if any) have taken place, and how to account for the apparent gap between intentions and results.

This chapter, however, is less an addition to this analytic literature than a slightly distant reflection on it. In particular, I will be concerned with the stated or implied preferences — values, visions and policies — to which this literature has been heading. My method will be to trace a Pilgrim's Progress: from inspiration, then disillusionment through to cautious reaffirmation.

Inspired by alternatives ...

There was something genuinely creative in the impulse which, some twenty years ago in North America and Western Europe, took hold of much liberal and radical thinking about crime and punishment, deviance and social control. Of course there were antecedents (labelling theory could be traced back to Durkheim, decentralization is the base of the classical anarchist tradition), and of course there were elements of confusion, romanticism and downright silliness. But the creative edge of the 'deviant imagination' (Pearson 1975) was its sense that matters of deviance and social control were integral to the constitution of the good society. That is, the theory and practice of social control could not be resolved in technicist and positivist terms; these were political issues.

This impulse expressed itself in many diverse ways: in the formation of movements aimed to weaken, bypass or even abolish conventional structures of legality, punishment control and treatment; in the advocacy and actual setting up of innovative and radical alternatives to the conventional system; in the struggles of various deviant, criminal and other stigmatized groups against the institutions and ways of thinking which had imprisoned them; in the adaptation of various sociological theories and political ideologies (labelling, Marxist, libertarian and others) to rationalize these movements; and in the development within criminology, law, social work and psychiatry of various 'radical', 'critical' or 'counter' cultures: intellectuals and activists dedicated to reconstituting their disciplines and professions.

These diverse streams of thought and practice can be classified in a number of different ways. First, they varied in terms of their commitment to what I have called 'destructuring' and what in Western Europe is known as 'abolitionism'. Sometimes the negative, destructive tone was muted ('look, why don't you at least try this as an alternative to the old system'); sometimes it was moderately utopian ('abolish first, then let's talk about alternatives'); sometimes, abolitionism was proclaimed proudly as a value for its own sake. Second, they ranged from liberal, reformist movements which were continuous with Progressivist, Fabian and other such middle-range accommodative tendencies, to more genuinely radical and theoretically informed visions — glimpses of an alternative social order and not just different 'methods of control'. The one edge was pragmatic, the other visionary.

And third, there was a different emphasis about just *what* should be abolished or destructured. Some stressed physical apparatus and visible practices (prisons, criminal justice agencies, mental hospitals), others wanted to get rid of accepted thought processes and cognitive categories (positivist criminology, the very concept of crime, the medical model of mental illness). This corresponds, more or less, to Foucault's distinction between non-discursive and discursive practices.

Such variations — how abolitionist, how radical and how idealist — appear in each of the various components of the destructuring package. These components are easily identified in the negative terminology of 'de', 'anti-' and 'non-':

1. *Decarceration* (or deinstitutionalization, prison abolition): to close

down or phase out the traditional closed institutions (prisons, asylums) and to locate control, treatment and care in the open community;

2. *Diversion*: to deflect various offenders from being processed by the official criminal justice apparatus, and to direct them instead into innovative community-based agencies, which are not a formal part of the official system;
3 *Decategorization* (also delabelling, destigmatization): to break down the various discourses and cognitive systems which create categories of deviance. Thus, decriminalization tries to reduce the scope of the state's power to declare certain behaviour criminal; abolitionism wants to dispense altogether with the concept of crime; anti-psychiatry questions the whole status of mental illness as an illness;
4. *Delegalization* (and deformalization, informal justice, private justice): to find new and to cultivate traditional forms of justice, dispute resolution and conflict management outside the formal criminal justice system;
5. *Deprofessionalization*: in place of the structures of professional monopoly and power (in criminal justice, social work or psychiatry), to set up networks of citizen contol, public participation, self and mutual help and informal care.

The common core of these overlapping (and sometimes incongruent) strategies lies in some notion of *decentralized community control*. In its less ambitious versions, this is a project of traditional liberal reformism within the interstices of the social democratic state. In its more ambitious versions, the very hegemonic systems of power and knowledge identified with the centralized state were to be broken up and returned to the people. Ideally — for pragmatists and visionaries alike — all this should take place at each of the three fateful stages through which deviants (notably delinquents and criminals) are processed, that is: identification (categorization, labelling, detection); adjudication (justice, sentencing, diagnosis, allocation); and disposal (deployment, punishment, treatment).

The inspiration behind the prosaic phrase 'decentralized community control' can be understood in another way: a vision of *inclusion* rather than *exclusion* as the preferred mode of social control (Cohen 1985a). The traditional exclusionary mode was the product of the original projects of rationalization associated with the birth of the modern state: centralization, criminalization, classification, segregation and professionalization. These projects created the great structures of knowledge and power which are known as the 'criminal justice' and other systems. Exclusion means physical separation — segregation, isolation and incarceration behind walls — and also social separation: the allocation of individuals to categories of deviance via the process of what Foucault (1977) calls 'normalization'.

The destructuring/abolitionist movements, on the other hand, represent the moment when the inclusionary impulse dominated social control rhetoric. The structures of knowledge and power which allow for exclusion are now to be weakened, bypassed or eliminated altogether. Inclusion means: incorporation, integration and assimilation. Deviants are to be retained physically as long as possible within the boundaries of conventional institutions (family, school, neighbourhood, workplace) and conceptually within the bounds of ordinary knowledge. This is 'normalization' not in Foucault's definition (distribution according to the certified metrics of normality), but in Lemert's (1964) exactly opposite definition of the same term: accommodation to rule-breaking before setting in motion the rituals of exclusion.

These, then, are some ways of visualizing the inspirations and alternatives of the sixties: reform movements, abolitionist attacks, destructuring ideologies, the vision of inclusion. The analytical task, as I have said, still remains: looking for historical roots, background assumptions, theoretical genealogies and political strategies.

But the sociological pilgrim who moves straight from this visit into the past to contemplating the present 'state of the art' about social control will encounter some rather strange problems. In the discourse of conventional criminology, it looks as if nothing at all has changed. True, there are new courses and textbooks on 'Community Corrections' and true, they tell of new agencies, professions and methods. But there is no sense of any visionary transformation. The reforms have been absorbed and integrated. Here, at the centre of the discourse, it is business as usual.

But in the critical literature on law, social control, justice and the state — the literature that doesn't even like to call itself criminology (Pepinsky 1986) — all is not well.

... Confronted with reality

If the last half of the 1960s was the moment of the counter-culture, the dawning of the Age of Aquarius — walls to be torn down, chains to be removed, the experts defrocked, the possibilities of another world revealed — so a decade later came the Age of Realism. Taking stock in the seventies became a bleak business, and also a sophisticated business: demystification not just of the old fossilized structures — always easy targets for criticism — but of the very alternatives and visions which radicals had themselves offered in the good years.

Conservative ideologists did not have to do very much of this hard work. Liberals, civil libertarians and empirical social scientists had unintentionally helped them by showing that: good intentions lead to bad consequences, benevolent treatment ends up as coercion, less harm is better than more good, everything costs too much, and, anyway, nothing works. The 'new realists of crime control' (Platt and Takagi 1977) had little trouble establishing their hegemony.

The radical discourse took longer to find its consensus — radicals have never been strong on 'evaluation' of their own intentions — but eventually a disturbing pattern of conclusions revealed itself. A new orthodoxy emerged. In the wider left-intellectual culture this took the form of a distancing from and discrediting of erstwhile mentors and their theories. So Marcuse, Laing, Illich, and Fanon were dismissed for their idealism, utopianism and romantic excesses. 'New Left' became a term of contempt. A harder, grimmer and more realistic form of theory and praxis was found — for example, in the structural Marxism of Althusser and (from an opposite direction but equally antagonistic to the new left visionary politics) the stern histories of E.P. Thompson.

In the much narrower world of social control theory and 'critical criminology', the disenchantment did not immediately take quite this portentious form. Still, echoes of the same themes began to emerge in critical thinking about decarceration and community control (Cohen 1979; Scull 1977); delegalization and informal justice (Abel 1982a); and (most explicitly) anti-psychiatry (Sedgwick 1982). Cain's recent (1985) summary of the radical critique of informal justice can be transposed to any one part or to the whole of the destructuring package:

1. It is *unnecessary* — an elaborate new infrastructure of agencies has been set up to deal with conflicts which would have been handled and solved informally anyway (if only by 'lumping it');
2. It is a *failure in its own terms* — informal justice is not always cheap; it doesn't work like its supposed prototypes (moots, village courts); it deals with the wrong cases (only the trivial); it becomes a subsidiary rather than substitute form of justice; its practitioners and practices are not those of the 'real' local community; it becomes professionalized, co-opted and dependent on the official system for referrals. In short, it becomes reformalized;
3. It is *sinister* — it solves the state's problems of legitimacy by deflecting potential criticism and opposition; it neutralizes and individualizes conflict; it disguises coercion; it extends the net of state social control;
4. It is *impossible anyway* — the project of transferring models from one society or period to another is hopelessly idealist; justice is a state organized, centralized system and so the notion of informal justice is a contradiction in terms.

Cain's list could be reproduced almost identically from the late 1970s evaluations of decarceration, community control and diversion. Thus:

1. Reforms and alternatives are supported for the wrong reasons (fiscal crises, legitimation crises, or whatever);
2. The old structures (prison, juvenile institutions, professional monopolies) still remain and are even becoming stronger. Despite 'community control', rates of incarceration increase, despite 'decentralization', the reach of the centralized state widens;
3. Alternatives are co-opted and absorbed. These reforms turn out to be not (in Mathiesen's (1974) terms) 'abolitionist reforms' but 'legitimating reforms': the old regime is strengthened rather than weakened.
4. The new structures are neither cheaper, nor more humane, nor more effective;
5. All sorts of previously unimagined problems and dangers (Cain's 'sinister' results) have now been created: the net of social control intensified and widened and coercion disguised.

And here is yet another way of classifying the dismal message of the new evaluators — by looking at the supposed objects of social control:

1. The weak, pathetic and sick — they are subject to too little 'control'. Neglected and deprived of help, treatment and services (under the libertarian, non-interventionist banners of decarceration and anti-psychiatry), they are left to suffer silently or to be exploited by commercial interests. They should be looked after.
2. The petty or 'potential' delinquents — they are subject to more intrusive and disguised control (net widening) in the name of diversion or prevention. They could be left alone — as they were before all the new alternatives came along.
3. The parties to minor conflicts and disputes — they, too, find themselves subject to new and ineffectual forms of intervention and conflict resolution which merely neutralize real social conflicts. They should be left to solve their problems naturally (as they always did) or alternatively be given proper access to the full power of the formal legal system.
4. The hard core, serious criminals — they are subject to further degradation. As the soft end of the system appears more and more benign, so the hard core (chronics, recidivists) appear more hopeless and become easy targets for such policies as selective incapacitation.
5. The powerful — they are still left free to carry out their depradations. Their actions should be criminalized and subject to the full weight of the formal punishment system.
6. The ordinary population — they are subjected to further and more subtle involvement in the business of social control. Everyday life

becomes 'controllized' by Crime Prevention Through Environmental Design, secret agents and informers, new systems of surveillance of public space, and data-banks. Whole populations are made the object of preventive social control before any deviant act can take place.

A final way of summarizing the conclusions of the new evaluations would be to say that reforms motivated by the inclusionary impulse are misguided. They fail precisely because they lead to further forms of exclusion. Thus, the decision of whom to include calls for an act of formal classification, and this means further separation; inclusionary agencies are dependent for their space and clientele on the state's exclusionary apparatus, which then absorbs them; inclusionary alternatives still remain staffed by state accredited professionals; the dispersal of control through decentralization ends up drawing in new (that is, previously included) populations; even inclusion by tolerance leads to forms of ecological separation and the ghettoization of deviant populations.

These are all different ways of arriving at the same set of dismal conclusions. Things have not turned out in the way they were supposed to; unintended consequences are always bad; things are worse than they seem; and they are getting even worse.

Now of course this is a caricature. The new reflective literature is by no means uniform in its tone or direction. There is, especially, a great deal of difference between critics who feel that the original inspirations were misguided and those who still retain at least some of the vision and do not regard failure as inevitable. And the literature is full of internal inconsistencies. At times, the emerging patterns are 'sinister' because they are new and incomprehensible, at other times because they are merely a replication of the same old story. Alternatives are simultaneously denounced for their proliferation and for the fact that they are not actually being implemented. Abel, for example, after showing that informalism extends state control, neutralizes conflict, redistributes state resources to the privileged, advances professional interests and legitimates state and capital, then notes: 'Despite the current surge of enthusiasm for informalism, there are relatively few programmes and these are underfunded and little used' (1982a, p. 305). Particular 'success stories' — rape crisis centres, the gay movement — are lavishly praised, but then ignored in the overall evaluations.

To be charitable to those of us who took part in this debunking, it must be said that the confusion was in the world and not just the observers' theories. The results of the destructuring movements were indeed complicated, ambiguous, contradictory — and dialectical. But it was only the dark side of the dialectic that was exposed. To travel from the radical social control literature of the mid-sixties to its equivalent in the mid-eighties is to sense not just confusion (which would be fine) but a different sense of the possible.

... Stranded by demystification

Various theories have been proposed — of different levels of sophistication and persuasion — to explain how this sad state of affairs came about. They can be divided into four main groups:

1. The original values, visions and preferences are still to be commended (or at least not denounced) but there was a policy problem. The programmes were simply not implemented in the way they should have been. Things go wrong. You feed good ideas into organizations — but the plan gets fouled up because of misunderstandings, the wrong allocation of resources, or political obstructionism.
2. A more sophisticated version of the first theory also leaves the original values unquestioned, but places the blame for failure in the hands of the professional establishment. Acting (as ever) out of relentless self-interest and the imperative to expand at all costs, professionals will distort and blunt any radical impulse by exploiting it for their own ends. Thus the police take over diversion programmes; experts organize dispute settlements; professional therapists initiate self-help groups.
3. In yet another version of the first two theories (associated with David Rothman's (1971, 1980) well known histories) there is a recurrent historical tension between 'conscience' and 'convenience'. Again there is process of undermining and co-option: organizations and professionals absorb good ideas but transform them to meet managerial imperatives and wider functional needs. Moreover, the ideas themselves — conscience, doing good, humanitarian reform — are open to some suspicion. There are limits to benevolence.
4. The final group of theories rests on a built-in omniscience about all liberal social reform. Armed with the right conceptual apparatus, it should have been clear from the beginning that nothing good could have come from the original reform visions. It is obvious that these ideas have undeclared purposes and it is equally obvious that they will 'fail' because there are underlying historical processes (an extension of discipline, rationalization, or whatever) which unfold despite, and independent of, the intentions and proclamations of reformers.

Each of these theories makes good sense in its own way. But I am less interested here in the adequacy of the causal explanation, than in the political preference which is derived from the analysis. What we find here is that the models which are analytically the weakest — those which insist on the naive distinction between theory (knowledge) and practice (power) — are also those which allow for the most transparent reading of values. If you say that a good idea was badly implemented, the idea remains good. But if you say that all good intentions end up badly, or (in the more sophisticated and radical of the theories) that good intentions do not matter too much anyway, then it is not too clear what you think about the values behind those intentions.

Why does all this matter? Simply because the proponents of the original destructuring/abolitionist ideas were not always 'them'; that is, the people whom the theories were criticizing: the managers, bureaucrats, technicist criminologists, the powerful. They were us. *We* were the ones who wanted to abolish prisons, to weaken professional monopolies, to find forms of justice and conflict resolution outside the official system, to undermine the power of the centralized state, to create possibilities for real community and social justice. Critical scholarship has well exposed the problems of this original agenda — but the very effectiveness of this demystification job is a little embarrassing. You have to distance yourself from those original ideas and reforms, dismiss your enthusiastic support for them as matters of false consciousness or perhaps a product of over-enthusiastic youthful exuberance. Life seems more complicated as you get older; about that early love you say 'well, yes, I wasn't really in love at the time, I only thought I was'.

This distancing takes two forms. The first is to assert the role of the intellectual as outsider and simply to resume the task of radical demystification. Critical theory continues exposing flaws, debunking and showing that things are not what they seem and, of course, are never *better* than they seem. At its extreme, this leads to a variety of radical impossibilism which asserts that all reforms are doomed and which despairs of the prospect of any real changes short of a total transformation of the social order. Thus *radical pessimism* joins the old conservative pessimism of the 'realists of crime control' (people and society are beyond change, stay with the old remedies however partial) and the newer neo-liberal pessimism (benevolence invariably goes wrong, avoid harm rather than do good, settle for restricted goals).

This is an altogether familiar stance: pessimism combined with the dread of reformism. The second form of distancing, however, is rather strange: an actual reversal of earlier positions. Confronted, on the one hand by the apparent failures of the radical visions of the 1960s, and on the other by the hegemony of conservative ideology, an influential group of radical criminologists in Britain and North America has begun a massive stocktaking of their earlier theoretical and political perspective. The result has been the emergence of what has been called the *left realist*, *socialist realist*, or *radical realist* position.[1] By some irony, the term 'realist' — used less than a decade ago to denounce the bleak, unimaginative policies of conservatives and neo-liberals — is now proudly asserted as a value.

This is not the place for even a summary, let alone a full evaluation of this important new paradigm nor its many implications for theoretical criminology. On the more limited question of what happened to the destructuring vision, two strands in the left realist position emerged. The first, at the meta-theoretical level, draws directly on the changes in the wider left intellectual culture. The theories of the sixties — labelling, the early phase of the 'new criminology' — are denounced as the product of 'New Left excesses': they are 'romantic', 'petty bourgeois', 'Fanonist'. Above all, the new theories were guilty of the thought-crime of 'left idealism': they had been constructed merely by inverting the paradigms of positivism and correctionalism. But this idealist project simply did not reflect social reality. Crime is not a myth but a real threat to the powerless (working class, women, minority groups); traditional positivist questions of causation still remain on the agenda; the point is not to abandon law and order, but to construct a socialist version of law and order. The fight should be on the conservative's own terrain — the reality of crime — and not on some promised land of the future.

This leads to the second strand in the left realist paradigm: a renewed appreciation of certain elements in the old system. The criminal law model — criminalization and punishment — must be retained for street crime, and expanded to cover the crimes of the powerful;[2] the police must be democratized and socialized rather than attacked as oppressors; prisons have to remain; the weak must be given the full protection of the rule of law. The soft parts of the system — welfare, social work, treatment, rehabilitation — instead of being attacked as disguised forms of social control, should be defended in the face of the conservative onslaught on the welfare state.

We are witnessing, then, a form of *radical regression* or what Cain (1985) calls 'defensive formalism'. Aware of the failures of the original vision (but too sophisticated to blame these on technical problems of implementation); contemplating a system which is still oppressive, unjust and ineffective (but for which the inclusionary vision presents no immediate solution); confronted by vocal and organized victims (such as women who suffer from male violence) who want real protection (but by the full force of the state and not some mythical 'community'); dissatisfied with mere debunking (and willing to suggest reforms which are part of a long-term political programme), the left realists have arrived at a clear theoretical milestone.

All of this is clear and convincing. Faced with the realities of social control in those societies which witnessed the destructuring impulse twenty years ago, demystification, pessimism, defensive formalism and regression are all perfectly understandable responses. By any possible criterion — the safety and security of ordinary citizens, the welfare of the individual offender, the needs of the victim, a general sense of justice — things are bad.

My doubt is whether self-denunciation is the only way out of this slough of despond.

... Enlightened by memory

These are two alternative ways out. The first is political: a cautious reaffirmation of the original values behind the destructuring/abolitionist/inclusionary visions. The other is analytical: a slightly different reading of the literature on social control. These solutions express what Cain (1985) nicely calls a 'squeak of hope'. As she notes, even the chorus of radical pessimism about informal justice (the despairing sense that the devil we knew, formal justice, may have been better), '. . .is occasionally punctuated by an attenuated left wing squeak of hope that by some dialectical feat a "genuinely" human and popular form of justice may emerge' (Cain 1985, p. 335).

By 'cautious reaffirmation' I mean simply the recognition that the values by which we judge the current system to be defective, are much the same as those which informed the original vision. That is, the inclusionary ideals which looked appealing then, are just as appealing now. It still makes sense to look for more humane, just and workable alternatives to the criminal justice system's mechanisms of apprehension, judgement and punishment. It still makes sense to say that mutual aid, good neighbourliness and real community are preferable to the solutions of bureaucracies, professionals and the centralized state (and that this prospect touches genuine psychic and social needs, and is not just a trick to divert attention from real social conflict). Criticisms of the inhumanity and irrationality of the prison are as valid today as twenty years ago. It should not be impossible to imagine a way of stopping the relentless categorization of deviants ... and so on.

In fact, even in some of the harshest of revisionist criticisms, those original values are not completely negated. Abel, for example, after an effective demolition of what passes as 'informal justice' recognizes that:

> It is advocated by reformers and embraced by disputants precisely because it expresses values that deservedly elicit broad allegiance: the preference of harmony over conflict, for mechanisms that offer equal access to the many rather than unequal privilege to the few, that operate quickly and cheaply, that permit all citizens to participate in decision making rather than limiting authority to 'professionals', that are familiar rather than esoteric and that

> strive for and achieve substantive justice rather than frustrating it in the name of form. (Abel 1982a, p.310)

Accompanied by the memory of such values, it should now be possible to approach the revisionist evaluations (and the rest of the literature on social control) in a somewhat different way. This requires a conscious suspension of the all-purpose assumptions that today's ideas are necessarily more radical (and more realistic!) than those of the past and that capitalist social democracies should be suspected precisely when they pretend to benevolence. Both these assumptions are often combined in what Foucault calls '... a widespread facile tendency, which one should combat, to designate that which has just occurred as the primary enemy, as if this were always the principal form of oppression from which one had to liberate onself' (1984, p. 248).

With such assumptions out of the way, we might instead cultivate: first, a sensitivity to success (however ambivalent), and second, an experimental and inductive attitude.

First, what will happen if we look for success rather than expect failure — or at least formulate some pragmatic criteria for what counts as relative success? This is the strategy which Cain (1985) follows in her re-evaluation of the informal justice literature. She acknowledges a particular set of values, looks what the agencies are actually doing and then extrapolates successes — however short-lived, unstable and vulnerable — from the fleeting histories of 'pre-figurative institutions' as they emerge and before they are co-opted. These are the type of defining characteristics of success which she finds in the history of informal justice: class identification is open and explicit; the client is constituted as a collective subject; so, too, is the opposition seen in collective, class terms; there is a long-term 'prophylactic' solution (for example, education and politicization) and not just a resolution of the individual case; the agency operates beyond the courtroom (for example, picketing, striking); agency workers are accountable to the collectivity for whom they work (and not the individual client, employer, profession or the state); the internal organization of the agency is democratic and non-specialist. Cain then goes on to note the absence of these features in other forms of justice: professional, populist and incorporated.

This is a commendable strategy for making the 'squeak of hope' a little louder — although I altogether disagree with the particular value system which Cain uses; that is, what is good from a 'class standpoint' or for 'working-class interests'. I would prefer a different set of criteria and one which is not dependent on the Marxist (or any other) intellectual's notion of what is another group's objective interests. And such criteria must allow for an ambivalent sense of what constitutes success or failure. For example: decentralization and inclusion can be said to have failed by leading to a greater (rather than, as intended, lesser) involvement in the business of deviancy control. But to the extent that this involvement comes from ordinary people and not licensed functionaries of the central state, this is just the type of success which should be encouraged.

Second, and more concretely, the inductive attitude does not begin by listing abstract criteria or programmatic intentions which would have to be fulfilled in particular cases, but rather starts with the cases themselves. We cannot speak in advance of fixed forms (autonomy, informality, self-help) which will always be 'right' or political alliances which will always be 'wrong'. The policy arena becomes, rather, a site on which preferred values can be clarified.

We have to cultivate, in other words, a pragmatic and experimental attitude. Experience and research should be used to identify models that nearly work (in the sense of approximating desired values) and those that clearly fail (by undermining desired values). This means examining value preferences to see what policies they imply — what would decentralized community control look like? — but it does not mean judging results only in terms of their concordance with the original aims. The question is 'what is happening?' and not just 'is what is happening what was intended to happen?'. This is a useful stance not only for the pragmatist of social policy, but also for the analyst who is so trapped in the rhetoric of intended versus unintended consequences, that he/she misses those determinants of social policy which are external to the original value system.

The next question is *where* to look for success (however limited and ambivalent) and for opportunities to be inductive. And then, having located these sites, what is their relationship to the wider social order? These questions have, of course, been posed in the social control literature — but the answers have been one sided. The simple advocates of community and decentralization have been wrong to imagine that their projects can be kept apart from the wider power structure, while the demystifiers and critics are wrong to think that these projects will be totally contaminated by the outside world and can never offer glimpses of a different social order.

This debate only makes sense in terms of polarities which are as old as sociology itself: micro- versus macro-, reform versus revolution, autonomy versus dependence. In social control theory, the most interesting versions of these debates come from: first, legal pluralism — with its theory of how to conceptualize the relationship between local normative orders and the wider social structure; and second, Foucault — with his theory of micro-systems of power whose logic is not reducible to the workings of capital.

I will return later to Foucault's theory of local power but let me adapt from the legal pluralist literature the notion of 'semi-autonomous fields' (Moore 1978). These are social units which can generate rules, customs and symbols internally and which have the means to induse compliance — but which are vulnerable to rules and decisions from the outside world. Here are some fields in which the vision of decentralized community control can be examined; this is merely a list and obviously not a survey of each subject.

The first and most obvious place to look is the actual record of experimentation with decentralized forms of community control and informal justice. This is the literature which I have already addressed, and I just want to quote one altogether random example of how such fields may be used for value clarification.

This is the experience of Community Boards and Citizens Panels in cities such as San Francisco.[3] On the one hand, the disputes which appear before the Board are often trivial, the weaker participants might benefit more from formal legal settlements, and social conflict might be prematurely neutralized. On the other hand: there is little sign of direct state control; the whole process is voluntary; the participants 'donate' their conflict to the Board rather than to the state; disputes are resolved before they become actual 'crimes'; the parties are encouraged to take full responsibility for their action; there is no cost or professional lawyers; and there is the possibility for a solution mutually acceptable to both parties.

At the level of the wider social order, the criticisms remain. But the field itself generates values and experiences which have their own autonomy.

The second field is to be found in the network of self-help, mutual-aid and similar organizations which were set up by various victims' and deviants' movements over the past two decades. The mode of self- and mutual-help — once confined to urban ethnic groups[4] — has taken many diverse forms: the 'Anonymous Deviant' format (gamblers, addicts, alcoholics, overeaters) in which organizations are sponsored, staffed and controlled by deviants or ex-deviants; co-operative and non-professional forms of treatment and care such as alternative health clinics, shelters for women who are victims of rape or domestic abuse and communal homes for runaway teenagers.

This model has received surprisingly little attention in the literature as a form of social control. In one notable exception, Davis and Anderson (1983) usefully distinguish self- and mutual-help as a separate mode of control alongside custodial control and community care. They divide this mode in turn into forms with different degrees of pervasiveness over clients' (or 'members'') lives — a continuum which ranges from various sect or cult-like organizations (religious, mystical, anti-drug) characterized by total and authoritarian control over members' lives, to 'transformative' groups (such as feminist health collectives) through to specific self-help groups (such as Weight Watchers).

The features of this model — as described by Davis and Anderson and other sympathetic observers — are quite similar to Cain's approved criteria of informal justice. These include: ideological commitment; politicization of the language of incompetence, dependence and stigma; means are chosen not in terms of pragmatic, bureaucratic or professional criteria of efficiency, but because they serve to express and dramatize the world view of the members; an explicit anti-professionalism (demystification of professional expertise, pooling of resources and knowledge); advocacy of wider social change (or, in some instances, secession from the dominant order); democratic internal organization (no formal hierarchy or division of labour, authority lies in the collective, minimal formal rules); a tendency for social control to be personalistic, moralistic and based on holistic notions of change and commitment (self criticism, thought reform, the use of dramatic myths such as 'total abstinence over alcohol', 'woman's absolute control over her body'); financial self-sufficiency, independence from the state ... and decentralization.

This is not the place to consider the many intrinsic objections to these modes of control (such as the dangers of the authoritarian irrationality which led to Jonestown) or their potential for co-optation into the state apparatus. Enough to note again that these are indeed models in practice of the vision of decentralized community control. If we take this vision seriously, these are just the places where its promise must be examined.

A third field consists of systems of private and workplace justice. These include the type of formal systems such as workers' courts, workers' councils, and trade union assemblies which are well documented in the standard literature on industrial self-management as well as the intricate informal systems of private justice studied in the more recent literatures on the hidden economy, workplace crime and organizational deviance.

As with self and mutual help, this field offers extraordinarily rich possibilities to the student and/or advocate of decentralized control. There is now a wealth of factual material. There are also well-developed debates, for example, between those who argue for perpetuating the ingenious, spontaneous normative controls used by participants in the hidden economy, and those who see dangers in formalizing self control, thereby asking workers to police the very forms of resistance left open to them, and to provide management with a convenient disciplinary tool removed from the protection of the rule of law.[5] This is a literature also sensitive to the question of the relationship between semi-autonomous fields and the wider social order (cf. Henry 1985, and Chapter 3 this volume).

Fourth, there is an allied body of research and theory — best covered by the legal pluralists themselves in their search for autonomous fields — dealing with organizations which generate their own internal mechanisms of justice, regulation and discipline. The best documented examples include the army, professional associations, and educational institutions such as universities.

A fifth body of literature, which is developed in its own terms but hopelessly neglected by students of crime control, deals with planned or actual communes, collectives and other forms of utopian social orders. In the long historical record on these alternative forms of living and the intensive study of experiments such as the Israeli kibbutz, there is a wealth of material on the regulation and control of deviance. Questions of autonomy, dependence and cooptation; the importance of the ideological commitment to the whole person rather than the isolated act; when do internal controls take on the character of law; when do exclusionary controls (such as expulsion) take over from the dominant inclusionary mode ... these are all well traversed subjects.

A sixth and related set of experiences is not at all defined and hardly exists as a separate 'semi-autonomous field'. It consists of the network of more-or-less spontaneous forms of communal living and working which developed out of the post-1960s movements: feminist, anti-nuclear, environmental. To the extent that these draw on the classic utopian and anarchist traditions, they are close to my previous category but they are much less organized, encompassing and coherent than, say, a commune or kibbutz. Steinert — who sees all this as a promising development for abolitionists — refers to the 're-emergence' in European countries over the last twenty or so years of '... a sub-culture with its own infra-structure of meeting places, units of production and distribution, cultural activities, media and a distinct way of living ...' (Steinert 1986).

Seventh, and finally, there lies the possibility of studying not any one particular type of semi-autonomous field but contemplating whole societies which are characterized by non-statist, non-centralized forms of social control (such as the traditional acephalous society) or which allow such forms of control to flourish. There are encouraging, if belated, signs of criminological interest in the anthropological literature,[6] and an increasing interest in China allows for the study of historical swings from the decentralized, non-bureaucratic, non-statist mode to an approximation of the Western model.

In this context, whole societies which claim a socialist legality are also of interest. It must be said, though, that the lessons here have hardly been encouraging for the advocate of decentralized community control: guilt by association; the principle of equivalence; the privatization of the public domain (citizens using the official system to settle personal grudges) and opening of private life to state scrutiny; the tendency towards pure instrumentality.

To anyone who is serious about the vision of decentralized community control, my suggestion is to contemplate these seven 'fields' together in order to arrive at some general conclusions. In particular: what are the conditions for attaining success (as measured by our memory of those original values) and what are the limits which prevent it from being attained? The point of this exercise is not to be morally uplifting (the sociological role no more requires optimism than pessimism) but to do justice to the complexities of social reality.

My own provisional conclusion is rather simple and predictable: the further away we move from the discourse of criminal justice, the more likely are we to find the conditions for realizing those values. Moreover, this type of success is achieved in those fields where social control is not viewed as a separate function.

The only way to extract this type of generalization (and its policy limitations) is to avoid the terrible clutches of criminology. Foucault is right that this is not wholly possible — that we can never emerge from our own discourses — but even within the confines of criminology, my sort of conclusion would be 'acknowledged knowledge'. On the first page of every textbook on deviance and crime is the truth which only the abolitionist movement has taken seriously: that the criminal justice system is not the only form of social control. The left realists are correct in attacking the early phase of the critical paradigm for its idealist inversion of the assumptions of positivist/correctionalist criminology. But to return to the terrain of the traditional criminal justice model — however justified this might be on other theoretical and political grounds (Young 1986, 1987) — is not just to abandon the vision of decentralized community control but to renounce a major weapon for creating an alternative criminology.

You cannot, that is, have it both ways: statist criminal law *and* decentralization. To be realistic about law and order must mean to be unrealistic (that is, imaginative) about the possibilities of order without law. To take decentralization seriously means that you must be an abolitionist.

This is not simply because those values are so difficult to realize within the interstices of the criminal justice system, but because the very nature of the system *must* undermine them. The realist/pessimist evaluations are, again, quite correct. Let us remind ourselves of those original values which, in the idealism of the sixties, were seen even as basic human desires, frustrated by the culture. Thus:

1. The desire for *community*: the wish to live in trust and fraternal co-operation with one's fellows in a total and visible collective entity.
2. The desire for *engagement* — the wish to come directly to grips with social and interpersonal problems ...
3. The desire for *dependence* — the wish to share responsibility for the control of one's impulses and the direction of one's life' (Slater 1970, p.5).

These seem to me unlikely candidates for 'basic human desires' and there are even good reasons for rejecting them as absolute values. But there is no doubt that they cannot be fulfilled by the criminal justice system — even when it tries, and especially when it tries. The criminal law is correctly characterized by the abolitionists as a state run organization which maintains the monopoly on defining certain behaviour as criminal and then organizing the punishment of such behaviour by the deliberate infliction of pain. If we want to limit this monopoly — and decentralization is surely one way of doing so — then the last thing we should be doing is allowing the system to busy itself with community. We must take away, not give.

To express this another way: in 'real' decentralized community control, we find not just those features revealed by a comparative survey of those 'fields' (strong ties to parent social movements such as feminism, a strategy of political education, internal democracy, and so on) but the overriding criterion of an independent critical relationship to the state criminal law system. Left realists believe that this independent critical status can eventually be attained by fighting the system on its own terrain. But the essence of state power is not just the particular way it deploys its forces of criminalization and punishment, but its initial normalizing power — that is, its radical monopoly to define what is right. As long as this exists, it is not enough to call for community control over the police or even citizen community patrols.

Thus 'taking decentralization seriously' implies undertaking something like the two classic abolitionist projects. The first is to find alternatives to the criminal law in the civil law, tort and other forms of dispute and conflict resolution. The second is to specify and then achieve the type of structural conditions under which real community control can take place.[7]

Abolitionists are criticized precisely because they are romantic, naive or disingenuous enough to actually take these projects seriously. And in truth, much of this criticism is justified — although I doubt whether abolitionists such as Christie or Hulsman mind being called romantics, nor are they much impressed by the standard arguments in favour of the criminal law. My own position lies somewhere between the realist and abolitionist position. I would recommend a cautious reaffirmation of the values behind decentralized community control — 'cautious' for these do not seem to me absolute values which cancel out all others. And instead of abolition — which *is* unrealistic — I would advocate *attrition*: a gradual wearing away of the criminal law, by a process of benign neglect, until it is only used when there is genuinely no alternative.

This caution derives from a number of ancient problems which are almost too obvious to itemize. They are all variations on the fallacy of extrapolating from the small homogenous social unit to the large, hierarchical total society. Thus:

1. There are forms of harm, loss and injustice inflicted by organizations, corporations, the state and the powerful which are difficult to think of in terms other than 'crime' and for which there are few effective substitutes to the criminal law model.
2. Non-statist, informal modes of control will not only leave the powerful untouched but — as the realists point out — leave the powerless and minority groups least protected (the abolitionists reply that they are not much protected now, but this hardly proves the case for informalism).
3. The ideology of the whole person, which tends to govern successful forms of community control, is not always desirable. We have only to look at the type of holistic judgements made — in their different ways — by religious cults, positivist criminology and totalitarian political systems. Instead, we might prefer the more limited focus of the 'back to justice' model. Neo-classicism, as Christie correctly points out, makes the act too important, but some acts are too trivial to have to bother about the person.
4. Contrary to what abolitionists claim, not all acts designated as crime are actually forms of conflict, dispute or trouble. Except by stretching these words beyond all recognition, we cannot translate crime control into these terms. The armed robber does not have a conflict with the security guard, the corporation dumping poisonous waste is not in dispute with the community, the violator of traffic regulations does not have any trouble.
5. In a society in which the power to control is invested not just in the state but in the commercial market, and in particular in the hands of large corporate interests, non-statist forms of decentralization cannot be valued in themselves. Nowhere is this better illustrated than in the growing critical literature on private security. At first sight, what could be better: autonomy from state control,

decentralization, no positivist notion of disciplinary measures aimed at the individual soul, control embedded in a structure which appears consensual. But put this into practice, under the sole force of commercialism, and we have all the horrors that Shearing and Stenning describe in their nice analysis of Disneyworld: social control which is '... embedded, preventative, subtle, co-operative and apparently non-coercive and consensual' (1985, p. 347).

Of course the problem with Disneyworld (and the similar examples of shopping complexes, condominium estates and the other 'feudal like domains' which students of private security have investigated) is that they represent only a part of the community package. They require no knowledge of the individual, they are authoritarian, and they are not informed by any progressive ideology. These points are obvious — we all understand why Disneyworld is different from a kibbutz — but to be fair to the community vision, we have to take the whole package together and not judge the results of the component parts.

In any event, these are some of the standard objections to the abolitionist claims and aspirations. To the extent that such objections are correct, so does full realization of the vision of decentralized social control become impossible, undesirable or both.

But this again is to leave the debate within the discourse of criminology. In the same way as the pragmatic search for value-realization had to extend beyond what is called social control, so too does the theory of decentralization. My cautious reaffirmation of those sixties values and the sense in which they are unrealizable without full abolition (which in turn is an unlikely project) need grounding in a wider theory of power. This is something which neither conventional criminologists nor even radical social control theorists have undertaken.

Take the very notion of decentralization itself. This derives from a master metaphor which sees political power in terms of centre and periphery. We are asked to imagine such things as deviants being drawn away from the centre, or the periphery being awarded the power that belonged to the centre. But this metaphor rests on a largely unexamined view of state power, which at times leans towards the most extreme form of elitist centralism, at other times towards the most amorphous form of pluralism.

This produces some curious results in the social control literature. For example, most of the sceptical students of decarceration, community control and informalism (including myself) have relied heavily on Foucault to bolster our pessimism. The ritual quotes from Foucault were pulled out to prove that nothing could escape the awesome power of the state. Legal and disciplinary powers somehow 'escape' from the centre, filter out and disperse themselves, and then colonize the furthest extremities ('capillaries') of the social order. The dominant image is the panopticon: a central vantage point which permits full surveillance of every peripheral point.

But this was surely a one-sided reading of a theory whose main thrust was to *deny* the privileged position given to the central state apparatus. Foucault is explicitly setting himself against both Hobbes's Leviathan, and Leninist theory, in which the seizure of centralized state power is the whole point of politics.[8] For Foucault, the king's head has long been cut off; power is not wielded by a single subject, there is no central source of command, no practical centre to political life. As Waltzer (1983) and Taylor (1984) both suggest, the images of micro-systems of power not reducible to the workings of state or capital, of cross-cutting alliances, strategies and effects, all allow a reading of Foucault as being close to the old pluralism of American political science — with this difference: 'Foucault is concerned not with the dispersion of power to the extremities of the political system but with its exercise in the extremities. For the Americans, power was dispersed to individuals and groups and then recentralised, that is, brought to bear again at the focal point of sovereignty. For Foucault there is no focal point but an endless network of power relations' (Waltzer 1983, p. 483).

No doubt the theory permits some contradictory readings here. But to wheel in Foucault to support a simple theory of a concentrated and centralized state power which infiltrates all other local forms of social control, is hardly justified. Nor do Foucault's politics come near to traditional revolutionary centralism: there is no discernible sovereign state to take over or ruling class to replace. The same micro-physics of power can and will reproduce itself in quite different political systems. In this sense, Foucault is a reformist: each micro-system is not quite autonomous but it is 'particular' and has to be challenged on its own terms.[9] And in his apparent preference for the acephalous, androgynous, precategorical world which existed before the knowledge/power system of the modern state, he is certainly more of an abolitionist than a realist.[10] So instead of invoking Foucault to give theoretical dignity to demystification and realism, he could just as well be used to help celebrate the only successes which are possible: short-lived victories on limited terrain.

Be that as it may, my point here is that 'taking decentralization seriously' implies not just a particular value preference but a more complicated theory than we admitted about the exercise of power in the modern state.

Summary

Let me retrace my steps through the 'critical' literature on social control of the last two decades. My route was a somewhat tortuous one, full of diversions and dead-ends. This is the result of my own lack of commitment to any master plan (such as liberalism, left realism or abolitionism) — a failing, I would like to think, not of my own psyche but of the social world's refusal to correspond to any one theory.

In the 1960s, most of the accepted systems and ideologies for the social control of deviants became the object of radical attacks under such organizing frameworks as destructuring, abolition and inclusion. The desired alternatives came together in the vision of decentralized community control. Soon — with varying degrees of enthusiasm, commitment and faithfulness to the original vision — experiments and reforms in this direction were carried out. When, a decade later, the results of these attempts were scrutinized, the situation was invariably found to be disappointing. The reforms had not been properly implemented, they failed in their own terms, they had even made matters worse.

In a general atmosphere of scepticism and retrenchment, radical critics arrived at their own version of the 'realism' which had come to dominate conservative and neo-liberal rhetoric of crime control. This radical realism took two forms: the first was to continue debunking, exposing and demystifying the pretensions of counter-cultural reformism, the second was to develop a new theory of political strategy more attuned to the current realities of crime. This took the shape of 'regression' and 'defensive formalism' — less an enthusiasm to create alternatives to the prevailing systems of knowledge and power (such as the criminal law) than an attempt to exploit them for social justice and for working-class interests.

The price of realism is a certain loss of imagination. Before dismissing the prospect of decentralized community control as a hopeless detour, and returning instead to the realist path, I suggested a serious examination of the various fields of social control in which the values behind the alternative vision may be realized. This led me to a cautious reaffirmation rather than denunciation of those values, but at the same time to the reluctant conclusion that they cannot be achieved within the interstices of the statist criminal law model. I say 'reluctant' because, however appealing might be the prospect of abolition, it offers no realistic solution to all problems of crime control.

While theory might help, the old choice still remains — between visionary politics and *realpolitik*.

Endnotes

Introduction

1. Although, in contrast to Spitzer (this volume), we interpret Foucault as providing a non-state-centred perspective on power and social control, Spitzer's problematization of the state control focus of much revisionist theory is entirely appropriate.

Chapter 1

1. This chapter would have been impossible without Tamotsu Shibutani's Santa Barbara seminars on pragmatism and the Chicago school and the continuous exchange of ideas with, and the editorial skills of, Donald R. Cressey. This does not mean, of course, that my responsibility for the chapter's contents should be shared with anybody (my debt to Kenneth Burke (1950), in the title, is via C. Wright Mills).
2. This chapter is part of a much broader research project on the state and social control (Melossi, in press).
3. See Melossi (1985a) for all the qualifications which are required and also for a discussion of other factors affecting punishment 'in action'.

Chapter 2

1. The growth of private security is documented in *The Hallcrest Report* (1985, p.112) which concludes that 'private protection resources (sic) significantly outnumber combined local, state and federal sworn law enforcement personnel and guards by a ratio of nearly 2 to 1'.
2. Early forms of 'thief-taking' and other varieties of 'putting-out' security served as precursors to the development of publicly organized and supported systems of policing. For a full account of this process in the areas of both policing and imprisonment see Spitzer and Scull (1977a/b).
3. A fascinating glimpse into the developing conception of the security commodity can be found in *Man's Quest for Security* (1966). In the foreword to that volume, based on a symposium sponsored by an insurance company, William Haber (pp.v–vi) observes that 'All of life — and business activity is no exception — is surrounded with a substantial degree of insecurity. Every institution in our society whose object is to provide protection against insecurity, whether to corporate institutions or families and individuals, against the vicissitudes of change, against the uncertainties of tomorrow, performs an indisposable function in society'.
4. The effort to discover the essence of capitalist institutions and legal arrangements within the commodity form has had a long and less than distinguished history. The limitations of this approach to the investigation of law are discussed in Redhead (1982) and Spitzer (1983b).
5. It is instructive here to consider the contrast between the portrait of state control presented by Orwell in *1984* and that which could readily be drawn from the study of control in contemporary capitalist societies. This is especially the case, in so far as a number of recent commentators on social control refer to elements of the Orwellian vision as a starting point for their understanding of the relationship between markets, states and the ordering of social life (cf. Cohen 1985a; Cohen and Scull 1983; Marx 1984). In Orwell's portrayal (1949) of state-directed political control — with all the attendant horrors of propaganda, identification, conditioning, and the systematic villification of internal and external enemies — the most

assiduous application of these controls occurs in the case of party members —those who are fully participating in and shaping the movement of the system. The *proles*, on the other hand, are essentially left to rule themselves with occasional assistance from the bread, circuses and pornography dutifully produced by the Ministry of Truth. In contrast to this vision stands the fact that 'mass consumption' democracies have bifurcated their control systems in a very different way. Instead of coercing and intimidating the 'middle classes', these classes are bound to the social order through the symbols and rituals of acquisition, while the more direct political controls are focused on the 'proles', who in the contemporary context are far more likely to be managed through constraint than absorption. We must be careful, however, not to overstate the significance of coercion for the 'lower classes' who are tied to different, although no less powerful, forms of commodity identification.

Chapter 3

1. This chapter is an abbreviated version of the author's essay *Seer-sam-funnet* ('The Viewer Society'), which has appeared in Norwegian, Danish and Swedish with the Norwegian Universities Press (1984), Social- og Sundhedspolitisk Gruppe (1985) and Korpen Publishers (1985) respectively. An English translation of the whole essay exists in typed form and may be obtained through communication with the author.

Chapter 4

1. Thanks for comments on an earlier draft go to Monika Platek and to members of the ongoing colloquium of the Workshop on Political Theory and Policy Analysis at Indiana University.
2. Newman's major point, typically overlooked, is that the imprisonment Von Hirsch advocates is far more painful and gratuitously violent than the corporal punishment Newman prefers. Newman is outraged by the excessive use of prisons; he nonetheless presumes punishment necessary to justice.
3. If exclusivity of channels of information becomes institutionalized, a material manifestation is class stratification, with attendant inequities and violence.

Chapter 5

1. A version of this paper was presented at the 37th Annual Meeting of the American Society of Criminology in San Diego, 14 November 1985. This chapter is the outcome of exchanges with a number of scholars, most notably, Peter Fitzpatrick and Elizabeth Morrissey. In guiding the analysis I am particularly indebted to Dr Morrissey whose paper 'Power and control through discourse: The case of drinking and driving problems among women' (1985) plus our discussions on the issues of constructionism and deconstruction, have had considerable influence on my thinking. The research material drawn on here is taken from a study of private justice, more fully reported in Henry (1983). I thank the British Economic and Social Research Council for supporting that study with Grant No. HR 5907/2.
2. Description is difficult since this is just another constructive process begging its representations to be construed as having a close correspondence to that which they represent. As such any discussion about the constitution of social forms or their interrelationship itself engages in their production and invests in particular versions of their appearance.
3. The term dialectic has a number of uses in sociology. In the classic Marxist formulation it refers to materialist societal change by way of emergent contradictions from the social organization of an era, which become seeds for a transcendent era. The transcendent form contains its own, albeit different, emergent contradictions repeating the cycle of change. Of course in both Hegel's earlier usage and Sartre's later philosophy, ideas are the moving dialectical force. In both uses dialectic means constant movement and tension.

Another use is to see dialectics as a method of analysis whereby components of a totality are analysed in relationship to the totality of which they are constituent. I am accepting some of the implications of this use taking dialectics as descriptive of the nature of the relationship between parts and wholes, and am going on to suggest that the reason for the tensions between them is in the nature of the way these are ongoingly produced by human agents' discursive practices. The result, as John Lowman (personal communication) has pointed out, is that I end up in an idealist rather than materialist position (though I see this as a socially constructed dichotomy). While I acknowledge that other human agents produce forms that I have not produced, their productions are not once but continuously produced. The only way that such reproduction can be sustained and rendered as an object to me, is to validate the forms others produce by investing in them and further reproducing them. That I choose not to do this holds the only promise for my ability to change them, since the only influence I can have is over the forms I produce for myself. For useful discussions on dialectics see Ball (1979), Friedrichs (1972), Schneider (1971), and Swingewood (1975).

Chapter 7

1. Unfortunately I only came to read Stan Cohen's wide-ranging *Visions of Social Control* (1985a) after the completion of this chapter. Readers who are interested in matters discussed here are advised to turn to Cohen's book, in particular Chapter 6, 'Visions of order'.
2. For a fuller review and critical discussion of approaches to crime prevention in the community, see Weiss (1987).
3. Of course, the unwelcome features of private and vigilante-style bodies in the eighteenth, nineteenth and indeed the twentieth centuries should not be forgotten (cf. South 1986). Einstadter (1984) raises pertinent issues with regard to the prevention- or control-orientations and potentials of citizen patrols. Despite being seen by some as 'manifestations of popular justice', Einstadter argues that neighbourhood patrols must be viewed in a 'broader context' and suggests that, in fact, 'they add to and often are extensions of existing systems of state control, and as of now they neither *replace* that control nor promise to do so in the near future' (1984, p. 204). Perhaps Einstadter is being a little too negative here, but I have some sympathy with his view that we live in the 'era of the watched society' and would display sufficient caution of my own as to suggest that we do need to be watchful in our turn about developments like 'neighbourhood patrols', and so on.

   This is not, it should be added, only a phenomenon of concern in the United States. In the United Kingdom, the National Association of Probation Officers, to take one example, has declared its strong reservations about crime prevention strategies which 'carry the implication that the fault lies with the careless citizen who allows the burglar easy access. This approach can encourage a narrow response which encourages a siege mentality. . . .' (NAPO 1985, p. 17). The NAPO report sees similar dangers in the planning of neighbourhood watch schemes which risk:

   > . . . intrusive and unwarranted scrutiny of 'suspicious' behaviour by over-zealous street wardens. At worst this may heighten rather than allay feelings of insecurity, produce rather than reduce conflicts within communities and tip over into policing by self-appointed vigilantes'. (NAPO, 1985, p. 17)

Chapter 8

1. Our research in this area has taught us that the exploitation of weaknesses in an opponent's position is not always confined to the opponent's institutional weaknesses. Discovery and exploitation of personal vulnerabilities among individual members of a bargaining team, although it may be considered unethical by some, is apparently not an uncommon strategy adopted by parties in collective bargaining.

2. The Pacific Western Airlines strike in early 1986 provides a recent example of the adoption of such strategies. The discovery of illegal wiretapping of the union team's hotel room caused some embarrassment for the employer (see 'Security firm dismissed after wiretap charge', *Toronto Globe and Mail*, 23 January 1986). A spokesperson for the struck employer stated that the security company had been instructed only 'to protect our employees and company property. We recognize this type of activity ... is illegal, and [it] has been done without the company's knowledge.'
3. The most relevant cases in the Ontario jurisdiction have been: *Radio Shack* [1979] OLRB Reports 1220; *Re Robin Hood Multi Foods Inc.* [1981] OLRB Reports July 972; *Skyline Hotel* [1980] OLRB Reports December 1811; and *K-Mart Canada (Peterborough)* [1981] OLRB Reports January 60. By contrast, the most recent United States National Labour Relations Board decision on union infiltration by an employer was in 1964 (*Re Wallace Press Inc.* 56 LRRM 1037 (1964)).
4. On the first day of the strike, a document entitled 'Lawful Picketing: Guidelines for Organised Labour' was circulated among picketers by the Metropolitan officers. In part it read:

> It is the policy of the Metropolitan Police Force to refrain, as far as possible from stationing uniformed officers at strike scenes.
>
> This policy has been established with the co-operation of your District Labour Council, and the Building and Trades Construction Council, on the understanding that your union executive members and picket captains accept the responsibility of policing strike scenes; advise you of the laws pertaining to picketing; accept responsibility for your conduct while at the strike scene.
>
> On occasions when it has become necessary to assign uniformed officers, our findings were that the conduct of pickets which necessitated police intervention has resulted from picketers not being familiar with what is acceptable and what is not acceptable conduct according to the law regarding picketing.
>
> The following are guidelines to assist you in preventing breaches of the peace, based on court decisions involving conduct by pickets, conduct which is not acceptable and does not fall within the meaning of lawful picketing i.e. *picketing limited to obtaining or communicating information* (emphasis in original).

In addition to outlining the parameters of what the police consider to be lawful picketing, the document also contains excerpts from the *Criminal Code*, detailing the offences of intimidation (s.381), mischief (s.387), and assault (ss. 244 and 245). A shorter document entitled 'Strike guidelines for management' was also given to a senior management employee.

5. The 'article about K-Mart' was a newspaper account of the *K-Mart* conspiracy case discussed above.
6. The Registrar of Private Investigators and Security Guards, under the *Ontario Private Investigators and Security Guards Act* RSO 1980, c.390, is a member of the Ontario Provincial Police Force, and the licensing of contract security agencies and personnel is effectively administered by that police force.
7. One member of the three-member panel of the Ontario Labour Relations Board which heard this case dissented from the majority ruling of the two other members on this point (OLRB Decision, p.66).
8. The Board ordered the Security Company to pay only half of these estimated costs, because it concluded that the mere fact that the complaint against the automotive Company had been withdrawn did not mean that it should not be considered equally responsible, with the Security Company, for the losses suffered by the Union as a result of the Investigator's activities.
9. The Board simply said that it found 'no merit' in this submission by the Security Company (OLRB Decision, p.60).

Chapter 9

1. All demographic data referred to in this chapter are in the American context.
2. These vocabularies of motive are presented as ideal-typifications rather than being determined quantitatively.
3. An alternative interpretation (Lowman, personal communication) is that men *do* perceive rape as an unacceptable social behaviour given social expectations about male desirability and sexual performance; men are expected to be 'successful' in attracting women without using force (or without having to purchase sexual services, a sure sign of macho 'failure'). This does not make a rapist's denial of rape any the more palatable, but it does suggest that care must be taken in describing just what social expectations about sexual behaviour consist of.
4. In most parts of Canada, girls have not been brought to court for status offences at a significant rate (cf. Hatch and Faith 1985). The Young Offenders Act, in operation since April 1984, legislates that girls will not be treated differentially by the criminal justice system. Overall, incarceration for either youth or adult offences is less frequent in Canada than in the United States. In 1985 there were approximately 250 women in Canada serving sentences of two years or more, whereas in the state of California, whose population is equivalent to that of Canada, over 1500 women were serving sentences of approximately two years or more.
5. In Canada, arrests of prostitutes declined by 82 per cent between 1974 and 1982, while government bodies have sought new remedies. A 1985 national study sponsored by the Department of Justice (see Special Committee on Pornography and Prostitution 1985) concluded that prostitution should be decriminalized. In contrast, law enforcement agencies have accelerated harassment against street prostitutes, and a return to formal sanctions against the presence of street prostitutes was enacted in December 1985.
6. Optimism about the use of the legal system as a vehicle toward social equity has been buttressed in Canada by the implementation in April 1985 of the Canadian Charter of Rights and Freedoms, of which section 15(1) states:

   > Every individual is equal before and under the law and has the right to the equal protection and equal benefit of the law without discrimination and, in particular, without discrimination based on race, national or ethnic origin, colour, religion, sex, age or mental or physical disability.

Chapter 10

1. We are defining 'police' very broadly. By 'police' we refer to those charged with the policing function, regardless of what the formal title is. All persons who enforce rules must confront issues around the discovery of their violation.
2. Such programmes do generate information. For example, a Baltimore call-in radio programme, 'Report a Pusher', led to 91 arrests on drug charges. During the four-hour programme, police appealed to citizens for information on drug trafficking. Off the air, detectives took calls and recorded names, licence numbers, and other information about persons callers suspected of being involved in narcotics transactions (*New York Times*, 7 November 1982). In Michigan, $1000 is offered for information leading to the arrest and conviction of arsonists. From the inception of this reward system in 1975 to 1981, 26 payments were made (*Arson News* 1981). What is not usually considered is how much of the information provided would have been forthcoming even in the absence of such programmes.
3. Thus federal and, in many places, state legislation and judicial decisions have offered new protections for whistle-blowers. The Federal Witness Protection Programme provides relocation and a new identity to informants (see Montanino 1984). Legislation has also introduced negative sanctions for *not* reporting things such as child abuse and certain hazardous working or environmental conditions.
4. The methods are not mutually exclusive. For example, a lead generated by a hotline or a computer search may lead to an undercover operation. Computers, of course,

are part of a broader family of rapidly developing technological means, including electronic surveillance and forensic science, also used to enhance discovery.

5. For example, it contrasts with a New York City programme called 'CATCH' (computer-assisted terminal criminal hunt) designed to streamline the identification of suspects. CATCH is a computerized 'mug book' permitting quick retrieval of names of suspects who fit the description fed into the system. Computers have simply improved upon a traditional tactic (*Computerworld*, 7 April 1980).

   In focusing on the discovery of offences we are also referring to something beyond merely checking a second data base to find a person's address (such as the Selective Service's use of IRS data to locate people suspected of failing to register for the draft) or using that database for sanctioning purposes, as with the state's garnishment of income tax refunds due to fathers who default on child support payments.
6. In 1959 entitlement programmes accounted for 15 per cent of the federal budget; in 1970 such expenditures had increased to one-third of the $62 billion budget; by 1981 they were $300 billion — almost half the budget.
7. See Katz (1978), Vaughan (1980) and Altheide and Johnson (1980) for discussions of the ways task differentiation and bureaucratic organization can shield deviance and neutralize control.
8. Matching across databases, which is one of our concerns here, shares much with the more traditional and common searching of a single database. At an abstract level the correlation of distinct information involves the same logic of inquiry. But the former raises questions of privacy and compatibility (which may have implications for errors and misinterpretations) not found when a single data source belonging to the agency in question is used. Profiling, the second technique we consider, may draw upon single or multiple data sources.

   While similar privacy issues are raised, matching is distinct from simply looking at another agency's data for cases. For example, Skolnick and Woodworth (1967) have noted how police in Westville located cases of statutory rape from the files of other public agencies. In a British example, Mawby (1981) reports on police identifying drug users by monitoring hospital emergency room activities for drug overdoses.
9. It is well to note that all accounts of the dramatic success of such programmes have come from advocates who carried them out. Whether an external audit and a careful figuring of costs and benefits would yield equivalent support is another matter. For example, the New York Civil Liberties Union (1982) argues that the unreported costs of New York State's wage-reporting system, a match of public assistance, unemployment records, and reported earnings, may add up to three or four times those officially stated, while savings may be far less than assumed.
10. This is a not-for-profit clearing-house supported by insurance companies to provide information and assistance to the insurance industry and law enforcement.
11. Of course the profile is only as good as this assumption. Some in this group are undiscovered violators, though designers of profiles usually assume that this constitutes a small proportion.
12. Depending on whether the data offer direct or only indirect evidence of violation, matching may also trigger a more in-depth investigation. But the more in-depth investigation is always found with profiling.
13. The discovery of infractions, of course, is only the first stage in the enforcement process. How the information is used, and whether it is even used at all, are distinct questions that we will not consider here. Among actions that may result from discovery are prosecution, restitution, denial of a claim or benefit, public relations, blackmail or bribery, and entering into some form of exchange relationship with the violator, such as turning the person into an informer or witness. An overabundance of cases, and disinterest or bias on the part of the enforcement agent, may result in no action being taken. Or, in Silbey and Bittner's (1982) term, the 'reservoir of unenforced law' may be directed toward enforcement ends far from those intended by drafters of the original legislation.

14. Raw hits are less meaningful for profiling than for matching on average. Since profiles are based on statistical reasoning rather than the often binary and mutually exclusive categories (at least with respect to an agency's rules) of matching, far fewer solid hits are to be expected.

    Efforts to make insurance rates and benefits 'gender blind' involve some equivalent issues. While perhaps rational and fair in the aggregate, for any given case the prediction on which they are based can be wrong and unfair. A controversial Rand study (Greenwood 1982), for example, proposed that courts use a profile of the career criminal in deciding the length of sentencing for convicted criminals. A person is presumed to be a high risk for a career in crime if he or she shows at least four of seven variables (for example, in gaol for more than half of the preceding two years, previous conviction for the same crime, a record before the age of 16, or unemployed for more than half of the preceding two years).
15. Interesting civil liberties and policy questions are raised about the intensity and duration of such monitoring. The monitoring of a targeted person because of an inconclusive search can be separated from the routine monitoring that may occur when computers are part of the system being searched/monitored, rather than merely an instrument of the search. Discovery may be built into the work process. For example, an economic forecaster was arrested after it was discovered that he illegally tapped into a Federal Reserve computer in an attempt to obtain secret information about money supply. The computer recognized the tapping. The man was identified through a trace on his phone line (*New York Times*, 5 January 1983).

    Social security field offices use a specialized 'intelligence terminal' that records the author of all computer entries. This is used to monitor the work performance of data entry clerks, and can also be used as an audit trail (*Wall Street Journal*, 7 July 1982).

    The completed input of records and the time they take to process can be logged, as can things such as the number of keystrokes for a given worker. In Massachusetts Blue Cross/Blue Shield claims offices a computer keeps track of worker productivity. Wages are adjusted every two months to reflect the output of data clerks (Kuttner 1983).

    The monitoring of a targeted person is also separate from the use of 'computer software time bombs' that may automatically go off when a particular data configuration appears. For example, where personal biography intersects organizational rules in a predictable way, computers can be programmed to respond to changes in a person's status that affect eligibility for a benefit. Changes in age are a clear example.
16. For example, former Inspector General of the Department of Agriculture, Thomas McBride, who was instrumental in establishing federal matching programmes, reports that the publicity generated about a food stamp matching programme resulted in a number of persons asking to be dropped from the programme (United States Senate 1982, p. 20). Whether all of these persons were ineligible or would have been discovered from the match is another question.
17. Criminal records, for example, offer an area where data quality leaves much to be desired. Laudon's analysis of the FBI's automated criminal industry file (1986) found that 54 per cent of the records disseminated had data quality problems.
18. In a slightly different context, computer programme errors may lead to erroneous medical diagnoses. The General Accounting Office reported that improperly programmed medical instruments have led to wrong diagnoses and at least one death (*New York Times*, 22 August 1983).
19. The failure to cut off a cheque once a recipient has reported a change in status represents a type of government-sponsored random integrity test of citizens (although this is not intended). This shows some parallel to indiscriminately applied undercover temptations. In both cases, according to the letter of the law, persons may be guilty technically. But it is not clear that any broad social purpose is served by offering very attractive temptations to persons who may be weak and vulnerable,

in the absence of indications of prior wrongdoing on their part.

Advances in banking technology may unintentionally make it morally and technically easier for such fraud to occur. For example, Louise Van Vooren died in 1976. The government continued to send her social security cheques directly to her bank for automatic deposit until 1981. During this time her daughter drew on the money that was regularly deposited in her deceased mother's account. This seems to involve a lesser degree of moral turpitude than cases where the deceased's signature is forged directly on the social security cheque. As with the above welfare cases, should such unwitting government encouragement in a violation be treated in the same fashion as more autonomous violations?

20. See, for example, Westin and Baker (1972), Rule *et al.* (1980), and Perrolle (1983) for treatments of privacy and computers.
21. For example, in 1983 a federal judge in the District of Columbia ruled that a form mailed to 4 million social security recipients 'makes a mockery of the consent requirement'. The crippled, blind and disabled recipients of supplemental security income were led to believe that their assistance might be denied if they refused to authorize access to their otherwise confidential tax returns.
22. For example, United States Department of Health and Human Services auditors found that the Social Security Administration's system for transferring large volumes of data between centralized computers and local offices could be improperly accessed rather easily. This was also the case for access to Social Security Administration terminals (US Department of Health and Human Services 1981, p. 11).
23. For a discussion of the politics of conferring 'routine use' status, see Kirchner (1981).
24. For example, Office of Management and Budget guidelines for federal matching programmes require that information concerning 'routine use' matches be published in the *Federal Register* in reasonable proximity to their implementation. Technically, those subject to data-searching are given notice in this way. However, such publication requirements may have little meaning, since those subject to data searching are unlikely to read the *Federal Register*. Furthermore, the 'reasonable proximity' requirement does not assure publication before the search is implemented. For example, a match conducted on federal student loans in August 1982 was not published in the *Federal Register* until December 1982 (United States Senate 1982, p. 182).
25. The often incomprehensible and hidden nature of the process for determining guilt may show some parallel to the use of witches, trials by ordeal and related magical means in other contexts.
26. For example, see United States Senate (1982, pp. 4–40).
27. One difficulty in assessing impact is whether or not the rates of infraction stay the same. For example, 1981–1983 saw a significant increase in the use of systematic data-searching and a concomitant rise in the discovery of fraud. But it is difficult to know how much of this is due to better discovery and how much to a worsened economy that may have resulted in increased rates of fraud.
28. Undercover means, for example, are expensive, restricted in scope, intrusive, and may 'discover' crimes that would not have occurred were it not for the instigative activity of the investigation. Yet they can make discoveries not possible with other means. The investigator can exercise considerable initiative over the process. In contrast, efforts to increase citizen reporting are still relatively passive and dependent on whether, and with what, citizens choose to come forward. Undercover means are inexpensive and can cover a broad range of persons and areas. Anonymous means such as hotlines can encourage responsible as well as irresponsible accusations. Systematic data-searching can be broad in scope and relatively inexpensive, and can avoid problems such as generating crime or maliciously inspired accusations, but, as noted, it has other costs.
29. Of course, keeping it a secret may work against the goal of deterrence. An implicit

choice may be made between minimizing neutralization and maximizing deterrence. One solution is to hint at the powerful means of discovery being used without being specific. But leaks and the experience of apprehended persons work against this.

30. Lipsky (1980, p.122), for example, finds that the routinization of bureaucratic functions reduces the chance to discover unique circumstances requiring flexible responses. The problem is compounded when a computer rather than a human agent is involved. Reliance on the computer (or any other machine) as a surrogate for human decision-making may permit violations that deviate from the average to go undetected.
31. For example, in using a social security number other than one's own the unsophisticated person may simply make up a number and run the risk of being detected because he or she has chosen a number that was never issued. But sophisticated offenders will simply take a genuine number belonging to someone else and use that. Their chance of being discovered via a match of claimed to real social security numbers is slight. On the frequency and ease with which false identification is used, see the *Report of the Federal Advisory Committee* (1976).
32. This depends on the relative distribution of offender types. There is likely to be significant variation across offences.
33. Beyond pushing toward discovery of a particular type of offender within an offence category, the computer may subtly influence the type of offences to which police devote their energies. For example, a former chief of the Kansas City Police Department believes that computerization has led to an undue focus on minor offences (unregistered cars, parking scoff laws) that can be dealt with very efficiently at the expense of other more important and difficult to solve crime problems (cited in Goldman 1983). The effectiveness of the means becomes an important, and often barely recognized, factor in deciding what ends will be pursued. To revise a familiar expression, 'where there is a way there is a will'.

Chapter 11

1. I am grateful to Stanley Cohen and Sheldon L. Messinger for their critical comments and suggestions on an earlier draft of this chapter.
2. For a discussion of net-widening in the case of adults, see Blomberg (1980).

Chapter 12

1. We have used the term 'social control' in the title of this chapter to make it consistent with the theme of this volume. It is, however, something of a misnomer. What this chapter deals with is society's wielding of its police powers in the form of coercive control. As Janowitz (1975) and Meier (1982) have thoroughly documented, only since World War II has the term 'social control' become commonly misused to cover the range of social institutions which obtain socially desired behaviour through the use of force and coercion. Historically, this concept referred to the use of persuasion, socialization, and subtle forms of influencing value preferences to obtain desired behaviours. Such influences are not present in or are secondary to most of the forms of societal control with which we are dealing here. These involve little social control and considerable coercive control.

Chapter 13

1. In recent years the private, for-profit prison has emerged as another alternative to state prisons. However, during the years under consideration here the private prison had not yet developed as a significant alternative to more traditional forms of state-run penal programmes.
2. These were Alabama, California, Florida, Kentucky, Louisana, Maine, Maryland, Massachusetts, Michigan, Mississippi, Montana, New Jersey, New Mexico, Oklahoma, South Carolina, Tennessee, Utah, Virginia and Washington.
3. Figures in Table 13.2 include expenditures for capital construction.

4. These were the states of Alabama, California, Colorado, Florida, Kentucky, Louisana, Maine, Maryland, Massachusetts, Michigan, Mississippi, Montana, New Jersey, New Mexico, Oklahoma, South Carolina, Tennessee, Utah, Virginia and Washington.
5. These were the states of Alaska, Arizona, California, Connecticut, Hawaii, Idaho, Illinois, Iowa, Maine, Maryland, Montana, Nevada, New Mexico, North Dakota, Ohio, Pennsylvania, Rhode Island, South Dakota, Vermont, Washington and Wisconsin.

Chapter 14

1. '... The "house of terror" for the needy, which was still a dream for capital's soul in 1770 rose very few years later as a gigantic "workhouse" for the industrial worker: it is called the factory. And this time the ideal paled beside reality' (from Karl Marx, *Capital*, Vol. I, quoted in Melossi 1980, p. 74). Melossi (1980, p. 75) theorizes: 'After the factory had been recognised as an ideal workhouse, then prisons became ideal factories; punishment finally acquired the double characteristic of a tangible representation of the dominant social ideology. It was merely its extreme and radical expression, and simultaneously, it was the place for repression and re-education.'
2. The author wishes to acknowledge, in several critical discussions, the assistance of Christopher J. Perl in helping me develop ideas for this chapter. Of course, I assume responsibility for the text. I would also like to thank Anne Rowland for her editorial assistance.
3. However questionable as an issue in political philosophy, the privatization of corrections has been supported in Federal law and in court decisions. For a review of the legal issues, see Robbins (1985).
4. And one might note, with some apprehension, private police organizations entering the prison business: 'A significant development is the entry into the field of Wackenhut Corp., the nation's largest independent private security company. Wackenhut has submitted two proposals for the construction and operation of INS (Immigration and Naturalization Service) facilities. It is also working with several states on the possible operation of adult medium-security facilities — with Wackenhut to finance, design, construct and operate them' (Fixler 1984).
5. But the Bridewell in England (by 1579) and the 'rasphouses' of Holland had numerous paid occupations (Rusche and Kirchheimer 1968, pp. 41–43), as did the penitentiary in nineteenth-century France (O'Brien 1982).
6. Braithwaite (quoted in Hawkins 1983, p. 111), perhaps beside himself over the prospects of private prison industry, remarks: '[I]t is likely that most union opposition to prison industry would evaporate if prisoners were paid award wages and joined the appropriate union'. See also Singer (1973).
7. In 1976, LEAA selected and funded three states (Connecticut, Minnesota, and Illinois) for implementation of the Free Venture plan. In 1978, four additional states (Colorado, Iowa, South Carolina, and Washington) were added to the programme, but this time LEAA required a percentage in matching funds. Not long afterwards, the American Institute for Criminal Justice in Washington DC took over responsibility for the co-ordination of Free Venture.
8. The industrial operations in the state prison at Stillwater were Minnesota's first to convert to free enterprise. The prison facilities at medium-security Lino Lakes, however, were designed especially to accommodate free enterprise industrial operations, and now host a diversity of industries staffed by selectively assigned prisoners. Therefore, Lino Lakes might offer the researcher a better model of Free Venture.
9. Data concerning Minnesota State Industries have been collected from the Personnel Accounting Department's 'Annual research and analyses report for the period January through December, 1984', which includes a monthly production efficiency report for December 1984.

10. Faced with a drastically declining market for its computers, Control Data terminated production of its very productive Still water facility in early 1986.
11. According to *The New York Times* (Gargon 1983), the 'median wage for an electronic assembler, someone who assembles electronic components, in Minnesota is $6.50 an hour. In Minneapolis, the median wage is even higher at $7.20 an hour.' Union representatives have not been completely indifferent to the disparity between wages at Stillwater and those that prevail at nearby Minneapolis. According to *Business Week* (1984): 'John Zalusky, an economist for the AFL-CIO, says that this project penalises union members. He also contends that inmates are not being paid fair wages and have no way of complaining if working conditions are unacceptable. He says the federation will oppose a congressional plan to expand the experiment to 20 sites. "We tread a pretty thin line when we have this plan but protest slave labour in the Soviet Union," he remarks.'
12. According to the 'Annual research and analysis report for 1984', seven of the twenty-five dismissals from Control Data were for unauthorized out-hours.
13. The 'Inmate Employee Industry Rules' at Minnesota lists 31 behaviours, including the following: 'any institution rule infraction will be cause for dismissal'; 'an inmate's employment shall be terminated at the point he registers his second unauthorised lay-in in any one calendar month'; 'in cases where an inmate fails to perform in a satisfactory manner in terms of behaviour and production performance, he will be subject to dismissal'; 'being habitually tardy or absent without authorisation will be cause for termination'; 'threatening, intimidating, coercing, or interfering with fellow inmates (sic) employees will be cause for termination'; 'causing loss of material or parts due to carelessness will be cause for termination'; 'engaging in sabotage or espionage will be cause for termination; 'misusing, destroying or damaging any industry or institution property will be cause for termination'; 'deliberately restricting output will be cause for immediate termination'; 'falsifying industry records will be cause for immediate termination'. In addition to the 'Industry Rules', there are 15 'Shop Safety Rules'.
14. Of the 25 dismissals from control Data assembly in 1984, 17 were for violations of this rule.
15. Surplus populations are those members of capitalist society who are economically redundant and marginal to the productive relations of capitalism, and who function as a lever to drive down wages. These people are essential to supply and demand of the market, and so also function to discipline labour:

    > This relative surplus population, the industrial reserve army, takes a variety of forms in modern society, including the unemployed; the sporadically employed; the part-time employed; the mass of women who, as houseworkers, form a reserve for the 'female occupations'; the armies of migrant labour, both agricultural and industrial; the black population with its extraordinary high rates of unemployment; and the foreign reserve of labour.
    >
    > Marx distinguished three forms of the reserve army of labour, or relative surplus population: the floating, the latent, and the stagnant. The *floating* is found in centres of industry and employment, in the form of workers who move from job to job, attracted and repelled (that is to say, hired and discarded) by the movements of technology and capital, and suffering a certain amount of unemployment in the course of this motion ... Marx speaks of the *stagnant* relative surplus population, whose employment is irregular, casual, marginal, and which merges with the 'sediment' as Marx calls it, of relative surplus population which dwells in the world of pauperism. ... (Braverman 1974, p.386).

    Correspondence of the class structure in the prison with that of the free world is only approximate, of course. For example, we apply the term 'floating' to those who are actively seeking work and who have a good prospect of being 'called up'. This retains the essential feature of the concept.
16. For the results of a study of the effects of 'LEAA Free Venture prison industry

programmes on the behaviour and attitudes of inmate participants, non-participating inmates, the host institution, and civilian staff', see Grissom (1981).

Chapter 15

1. The rate of imprisonment in Canada was 150 per adult 100000 population in 1982 (Correctional Services Canada 1984).
2. By March 1983, there were 526 inmates double-bunked in 13 institutions and by August 1984, about 970 in 17 institutions. In October 1984, federal prisons in Canada were said to have 7 per cent more inmates than cells (McKenzie 1985, p. 5).
3. Cf. *Globe and Mail*, 16–18 July 1984.
4. Prison construction has not been entirely shelved since 1982. Existing facilities are being expanded, and two new super-maximum security units are now under construction at Renous, New Brunswick and Port Cartier, Quebec. But this is still a significant reduction as compared with other plans (cf. *Let's Talk*, vol. 10, no. 10, 30 May 1985, p. 7).
5. This historical account is culled mainly from section 101-1 of the *Policy and Procedures Manual* (Government of Canada, 1986); Solicitor General Canada (1981b, Section 11); Nuffield (1982, Ch. 1) and *Backgrounder Documents* issued by the National Parole Board.
6. The Salvation Army was the dominant player in the supervision and guidance of paroled offenders, through its special Prison Gates Programme.
7. The Parole Service was under the auspices of the Chairman of the Parole Board until 1973, then became the responsibility of the Commissioner of Corrections in 1979. This marked the legal integration of the formally separate Parole and Penitentiary Services under the auspices of the Correctional Services of Canada (CSC). The Parole Board is now an agency within the Department of the Solicitor General, which also includes Correctional Services Canada, the Royal Canadian Mounted Police (RCMP), the Canadian Security Intelligence Service (CSIS), and the Ministry Secretariat.
8. See also *Vancouver Sun*, 21 September 1985. In contrast, see Nairn (1985).
9. Cf. *Vancouver Sun*, 4 March 1983; *Globe and Mail*, 22 August 1985; and *Globe and Mail*, 7 November 1985.
10. See, for example, the remarks of John Konrad, the Chairman of the B.C. Parole Board, in *Liaison* (1981, pp. 10–13). See also, the ambivalence toward the advent of the justice model in corrections reflected in recent conference papers by the Chairman of the National Parole Board, William Outerbridge (1984, 1985).
11. This is true even though federal inmates released to Mandatory Supervision represent only about 2 per cent of the total non-custodial annual caseload (approximately 80000). Almost 90 per cent of the total are offenders sentenced to probation under provincial community supervision (*Juristat* 1984, p. 5).
12. A listed principle guiding the relationship of the National Parole Board to non-governmental organizations involved in the supervision of conditional releases reads as follows: '... ensuring that the referral rate of conditional release cases to non-governmental organizations offering these services is adequate and that NGO resources are well utilized so as to enable them to operate with stability' (Consultation Centre, Solicitor General Canada, undated).
13. Approximately 40 per cent of all federal prison admissions annually are returned to custody from parole and MS, and half of that number are returned for technical reasons. The cost is roughly $100 million per year.
14. During fiscal year 1984–1985, the Service employed 10727 person-years, a 4.8 per cent increase over 1983–1984. Budgetary expenditures for the year were $739.9 million, an increase of 13.5 per cent from the previous year, of which $132.5 million was directed to capital costs (Solicitor General Canada 1985, pp. 55, 58).
15. In 1983–1984, custody centres had an operating budget of $420 million in contrast to community supervision at approximately $28 million (Canadian Centre for Justice Statistics, pp. 112–113).

16. This discussion is based primarily on interviews with National Parole Board and National Parole Service officials (Pacific Region), interviews with full parole, day parole, and Mandatory Supervision releasees, interviews with prison activists, lawyers, correctional administrators, and official government documents.
17. Parole Board officials estimate that only 2 per cent to 3 per cent of MS releases would be detained. This is a somewhat anomalous figure, however, given that of the 1600 inmates in the Pacific Region, about 600 are at the 5 and 6 levels of maximum security. This suggests a fairly large pool of potential detainees.
18. Unless the inmate can be declared certifiable, and placed indefinitely in a Regional Psychiatric Hospital.
19. This excludes those who are serving life sentences, or who are on indeterminate sentences. Parole reviews are currently undertaken at the one-third mark of the sentence or after seven years, whichever comes first.
20. This assumption is fortified by the recent United States experience with flat-time sentencing, where correctional authorities are now reverting back to review mechanisms.
21. Parole Service officials estimate 50 per cent double-bunking in the Pacific region by 1990, given current trends.
22. Even if a release is not granted at this point, the inmate becomes familiar with the screening process and a new hearing is held within one year.
23. This problem will only be aggravated if the Parole Board succeeds in getting permission to switch full parole violators to the more supervised status of day parole, thus avoiding a return to custody.
24. As one Parole Service supervisor put it, 'The reality is that you only need one spectacular incident a year (that is, MS failure) to keep thousands locked up inside. Society is demanding vengeance, not the "rule of law"'.
25. Various technical conditions are already applied to MS releases in the province of British Columbia, though they are not typically used in other provinces, particularly in the Maritimes.
26. Bill C-68 clarifies the Parole Board's exclusive jurisdiction to grant, refuse, terminate, or revoke certain forms of conditional release, including Mandatory Supervision. Procedures for doing so are specified, with the added qualification that terms and conditions imposed must be 'reasonable' rather than 'desirable'; likewise reasonableness rather than desirableness would be the test for suspension and apprehension of paroled inmates.
27. Presently there are 1800 prisoners serving a life sentence in Canada; over 1500 of these are serving life minimum sentences, with only about 350 of them out on parole (Cf. 'Lifers', *Backgrounder Documents*, National Parole Board, Government of Canada undated).
28. Cf. remarks of William Outerbridge and Real LeBlanc, House of Commons, Issue No. 2, 'Minutes of proceedings and evidence of the legislative committee on Bill C-67 and Bill C-68', Thursday 24 October 1985.
29. The recourse to blatantly unjust disciplinary controls in prisons (for example, involuntary transfers, administrative segregation, solitary confinement, 'gating', and so on) has precipitated court actions invoking the 'cruel and unusual punishment' doctrine (cf. Jackson 1983) and litigation referring to the Charter of Rights and Freedoms (cf. vol. 10, 1985, of the *Queen's Law Review*).

Chapter 16

1. The reluctance is comprehensible since, after all, those now recognizing some of the defects of community care were often among the main cheerleaders of deinstitutionalization, and in some instances, at least, bear personal responsibility for the implementation of the new policy.
2. Kaplan claims that part of the difficulty arises from my 'middle class bias', which leads me to recoil from the conditions of existence in the ghetto.

Apparently, what I perceive to be 'truly horrible', is in fact a life 'rich in social interaction and communal feeling', indeed, one often preferable to the 'serialized' existence of the American middle class (pp. 193–194). I leave it to the reader to judge the merits of these claims.

3. Talbott (1980, pp. 44–45) reports that in the 1950s, 65 per cent of deinstitutionalized patients returned to their families, compared with only 23 per cent now, a figure which drops off sharply within a year or two of discharge. Based on NIMH data, Goldman, Gattozzi and Taube (1981) have recently estimated the number of chronically and seriously mentally disturbed people in the United States at 1.7 million. Of these, 150 000 were in state, county, and Veterans' Administration psychiatric hospitals, and approximately 1.15 million were in nursing homes and board and care homes (750 000 and 400 000 respectively). Thus, all other community settings, ranging from welfare hotels to families of origin, housed about 400 000 of the chronically mentally disabled.
4. Cf. Davis *et al.* (1974): 'Our data show that the majority of patients do not hold jobs nor do they function very well in their domestic roles; most patients ultimately alienate their families and are divorced or rejected by their primary groups'. See also Arnhoff (1975), and Wing (1978).
5. NIMH estimates are that by the mid-1970s, nursing homes had become 'the largest single place of care for the mentally ill', absorbing some $4.3 billion, or 29.3 per cent of the direct care costs associated with mental illness (cited in General Accounting Office 1977, p. 11).
6. As Borus points out, 'The state hospital took responsibility not only for mental health care, but also for the patient's housing, food, finances, medical care, medications, work activities, and social relations. The deinstitutionalized patient's limited ability to cope is often overwhelmed when he or she is forced to seek these types of care from multiple, uncoordinated community agencies. ... The wishful notion that these patients will require such supportive services only for a transitional period is not supported by the data, which show that the mentally ill need ongoing care to maintain a reasonable level of function' (1981, p. 340). See also Davis *et. al.* (1974); Stein and Test (1980); Test (1981). Since such continuing care is routinely absent in all but a handful of well-publicized but wholly unrepresentative demonstration projects, it is obvious why misery, morbidity, steady deterioration and loss of basic social capacities are so widespread. Note that even in the well-funded demonstration project studied by Soloman, Baird and Evestine (1980), with the attention of a special team, half the discharged patients were doing very little or nothing at all eighteen months after discharge.
7. There is, of course, a long history of regulatory bodies being captured by the interest groups they are supposed to regulate (for the classic approach to this problem, see Breyer 1982; Levine 1981; Peltzman 1976; Posner 1974; Stigler 1971), and the previous attempt to control the excesses of a profit-oriented mad business through official inspection — in nineteenth century England — does not inspire confidence. It was in part the inability of inspection to counter the structural imperatives of the marketplace that led an earlier generation of reformers to urge the construction of the public asylum system (cf. Jones 1955; Scull 1979). I see no reason to believe that episodic visits by regulators will somehow suffice to protect the vulnerable from a situation in which the structure of economic incentives systematically rewards exploitation and neglect.
8. We shall examine the consequences of this situation at more length below.
9. For the effects of this on daily operations, see Kielhofner (1980) and Emerson *et al.* (1981).
10. For similar findings for New Jersey, see New Jersey State Commission (1978).
11. Particularly notable in this regard is her endorsement of American Community Mental Health Centres as the solution to the problems of delivering care to chronic mental patients, a suggestion that reflects a lack of acquaintance with the dismal role actually played by these facilities. Community Mental Health Centres have quite

self-consciously selected 'less troubled patients', including very substantial numbers diagnosed as 'not mentally ill' but merely 'maladjusted' (Langsley 1980, p. 817), and have deliberately avoided serving 'the needs of those who have traditionally resided in state psychiatric institutions' (Kirk and Thierren 1975, p. 210).

12. Commenting on some of the results of this situation, Minto (1983, p. 169) rightly notes that: 'There can be few states more pathetic than the withdrawn, hallucinated, neglected, and sometimes starving schizophrenic, barely capable of existence let alone a decent quality of life, who is left to "enjoy" his miserable state in the wholly spurious name of individual freedom'.
13. By way of comparison, in New York State in 1974, the average proportion of mental health budgets allocated to aftercare was 6.5 per cent; for Pilgrim State Hospital, the largest state facility, the figure was 1.1 per cent (General Accounting Office 1977, pp. 207–208).
14. For the United States, note Mollica's pessimistic conclusion that 'the financial pragmatism of the states appears to preclude any possibility of a unified mental health policy and to undermine public psychiatry's ability to guarantee adequate and effective treatment' (1983, p. 369).
15. For a very similar assessment of the quite limited role of drug therapy (linked in this case with a much more optimistic evaluation of community care), see Minto (1983, esp. p. 167).
16. There is also growing recognition of another problem connected with drug treatment, to which I had earlier drawn attention: the immense amount of neurological damage we are busy doing to substantial segments of the population via long-term administration of neuroleptics. Ominously, questions are now being raised in the psychiatric literature about whether 'the cure is worse than the disease' (Gardos and Cole 1976; Jeste and Wyatt 1979; Teppe and Hass 1979). In the words of an eminent British psychiatrist, 'the side effects occasioned by these drugs may be pretty intolerable. ... There is a danger, as I see it, that the injudicious use (or abuse) of psychotropic or tranquillizing drugs ... may be edging [us] back to the era of bromides and paraldehyde from which we escaped nearly half a century ago' (Rollin 1979, p. 1775).
17. 'The fact that the rate of decline in California accelerated significantly after 1963, almost a decade after the introduction of psychoactive drugs, and that the greatest decrease was in age groups and diagnostic categories which are usually less amenable to these drugs, clearly suggest that we should look for other factors besides chemotherapy as the ones responsible for this change.'
18. For a more extended review demonstrating that 'the trend to community care is largely independent of drug therapy ... [and that] recovery rates and levels of functioning in schizophrenia have not improved overall since the introduction of these drugs', see Warner (1985, Ch. 11).
19. Note, however, that Odegard's study suggests that the later advent of deinstitutionalization in Norway is intimately bound up with the development of a 'new and improved pension system for persons incapacitated by illness, which was introduced in 1960 and which includes psychotic invalids. ... This has made possible the discharge of many psychotic individuals and is probably the main reason why the rates of discharge as "not cured" did not show any great increase until after 1960' (Odegard 1967).
20. Cf. p. 67 and Table 8, and p. 145 in the second edition of *Decarceration*.
21. The potential impact of the latter problem in the United States has been greatly exacerbated by two further developments: the rash of lawsuits (most famously Wyatt v. Stickney, 344, Fed. Supp. 373 [Northern District, Alabama, 1972]), over the so-called right to treatment, which have led the courts to attempt to define a required 'minimum quality of care' associated with much higher staff-patient ratios, the provision of a 'more humane psychological environment', and generally higher expenditure per patient; and the requirement to upgrade hospital facilities in order to meet the standards of the Joint Commission on the Accreditation of Hospitals, an

essential step in order to be eligible for major non-state funding of the hospital system.

22. See Grob (1983). Note that the rise in mental hospital admission rates occurred despite this development as an act of deliberate state policy of screening programmes designed to cut down on geriatric admissions to the state hospital system (Senate Special Committee on Aging, November 1971, pp. 61–75); and, in later years, explicit changes in commitment laws aimed at excluding the 'senile' from state hospitals altogether (cf. Scull 1981a, pp. 745–746).
23. Lerman's (1982) discussion of the origins of deinstitutionalization in California is in general one of the more sophisticated attempts to grapple with these issues, and does at least begin to recognize the existence of 'hidden' savings and their impact on public policy; but having identified some of the underlying factors that enter into the equation, he shies away from recognizing their fundamental significance. He does, however, suggest a plausible reason for the marked interstate discrepancies in the speed with which decarceration was implemented, the differential sophistication of the state mental health bureaucracies. He argues that short-run costs generally increased in the early stages of deinstitutionalization, since states had to supply matching funds in order to capture federal subsidies. In consequence, 'States whose leaders exhibited entrepreneurial skills, and were supported by executives and legislators willing to risk increased spending in order to gain long-term fiscal benefits via deferred construction and maintenance of facilities, displayed marked population reductions by 1969. Laggard states waited until Supplementary Security Income [allowing 100 per cent federal financing of the decarcerated] was introduced in 1972' (Lerman 1982, p. 209).
24. I emphasized this point in the first edition of *Decarceration*, and Anthony Bottoms (1983, pp. 166–167, 182–184) has also recently deplored the tendency to focus only on prison numbers and rates per 100 000 which has the unfortunate corollary that 'data on the *proportion* of convicted offenders given imprisonment or probation are given little or no attention', and the sharp decline in the proportion of convicted defendants given imprisonment is simply overlooked.
25. In mitigation, I would plead that in 1975 the contradictions between social control talk and action (Cohen 1979, 1983) were far less blatant in this area than they have now become.
26. For a related critique of Rothman's original argument, see Scull (1981b).
27. Compare, in this regard, Jacobs (1983a, pp. 115–132), who analyses the defeat of a recent New York prison bond by the electorate. Notwithstanding the fact that 'The prison bond's opponents were traditionally liberal organisations, predominantly based in New York City,' Jacobs notes the 'powerful irony ... [that] New York City voters, traditionally the most liberal in the state, strongly *supported* prison expansion', and the voices defeating the bond issue came from conservative, Republican, law-and-order voters of upstate New York. Partly, this may have reflected unwillingness to 'pay to lock up New York City's problems'. More centrally, the crucial determinant of voting patterns seems to have been the degree of fear and concern about crime, itself a quite direct reflection of the local crime rate.
28. That many of those employed to run such places are not hypocrites but true believers does not detract from the falsity of these beliefs. The benefits of such mythologies accrue largely to those who perpetuate them, not to their alleged beneficiaries. Inmates are generally all too aware of the emperor's missing clothes, save where sharing the illusion makes their lives more bearable. Arnold Hauser has pointed out that this is not atypical of ideological constructs:

    > What most sharply distinguishes a propagandistic from an ideological presentation and interpretation of the facts is ... that its falsification and mystification of the truth is always conscious and intentional. Ideology, on the other hand, is mere deception — in essence self-deception — never simply lies and deceit. It obscures truth in order not so much to mislead others as to maintain and increase the self-confidence of those who express and benefit from such deceptions. (quoted in Muraskin 1976, p. 559)

29. Compare California Governor Deukmejian's claim to be 'delighted' by overcrowded prisons 'because it keeps criminals out of the way of the law-abiding public'; and an anonymous legislator's claim that voters would like to see convicts 'locked up sixteen to a cell' (*Los Angeles Times*, 8 September, Section 2, p. 14). And note the studious avoidance of the question of the welfare of prisoners by proponents of the recent New York prison bond. As James Jacobs notes in this connection, 'humanitarianism apparently had little political appeal' (Jacobs 1983a, p. 118).
30. For extensive documentation of this point, see Austin and Krisberg (1981, 1982), Blomberg (1980), Hylton (1981, 1982), and for a trenchant overview of the whole net-widening phenomenon, see Cohen (1985a, Ch. 2).
31. For a description of a program of this sort, see Wold and Mendes (1974).
32. In Minto's words (1983, pp. 168–169), 'The mental hospital scene has been one of steady and increasing resistance to the provision of psychiatric treatment and long-term support to a group of sick people who do not respond to current treatment. . . . It is almost as though the patient's inability to be cured has become a personal insult to his treaters, who respond to his continuing disability as if it were a specific act of non-cooperation in the treatment process, rather than a distressingly constant malady over which the patient has little control.' We are witnessing, then, 'the disowning of the chronic schizophrenic patient by the psychiatric services . . . more and more psychiatric resources have been applied to patient groups least needing medical care, while the serious neglect of an overtly ill group of patients continues to exist'.
33. Moreover, many even of these workers have found an alternative source of income, as operators of the board and care homes to which mental patients have now been discharged.
34. This applies of course, to institutional settings in general, including those, such as mental hospitals, whose nominal justification is self-consciously therapeutic. The growing willingness of courts to intervene to secure 'patients' rights' has necessarily involved considerable legalistic circumspection of the behaviour and judgements of therapeutic staff. By thus limiting professional autonomy (Freidson 1970), 'legalization' has made institutional psychiatry even less attractive to professionals.
35. This transfer of the therapeutic rationalization from the sphere of formal incarceration to that of community corrections obviously deserves more extended treatment than I can give it here. One of the most critical questions it raises, of course, is why this flip-flop is occuring. Richard Abel (personal communication) has suggested one plausible explanation — that community dispositions are both less visible and, because they are less imbued with state action, less subject to constitutional scrutiny. Elsewhere, he has made an analogous point about the relationship between the distribution of bias in the criminal justice system and the visibility of that bias in favour of official agents. See Abel (1978).
36. For a more extended critique of recent development in community corrections than I have had space for here, see Scull (1983).

Chapter 17

1. Foucault has made some interesting observations on the difference between utopias and heterotopias:

> Utopias afford consolation; although they have no real locality, there is nevertheless a fantastic untroubled region in which they are able to unfold; they open up cities with vast avenues, superbly planted gardens, countries where life is easy, even though the road to them is chimerical. Heterotopias are disturbing, probably because they secretly undermine language, because they make it impossible to name this and that, because they destroy syntax in advance, and not only the syntax with which we construct sentences but also the less apparent syntax which causes words and things (next to and also opposite one another) to hold together. That is why utopias permit fables and discourse: they run with the very grain of language and are part of the fundamental dimension of the *fabula*; heterotopias

> (such as those to be found in Borges) dessicate speech, stop words in their tracks, contest the very possibility of grammar at its source; they dissolve our myths and sterilize the lyricism of our sentences' (Foucault 1970, p. xviii).

2. This is to take issue with Stan Cohen's contention that:

> Our private terrain is inhabited by premonitions of *1984*, *A Clockwork Orange*, and *Brave New World*, by fears of the increasing intrusion of the state into private lives and by a general unease that more and more of our actions and thoughts are under surveillance and subject to record. Our professional formulations about social control though, reveal little of such nightmares and science fiction projections (Cohen 1979, p. 339).

3. What remains extremely unclear in Foucault's writings is the *relation* between different types of power in any epoch. It is far from clear in Foucault's work, for example, whether juridical power facilitates, masks, supercedes, complements, or comes into conflict with disciplinary power. Also there are various interpretations of the exact meaning of disciplinary power; de Sousa Santos, for example, interprets disciplinary power in the following terms:

> [In contrast] disciplinary power has no centre, it is exercised throughout society, it is fragmented and capilliary: it is exercised from the bottom up, constituting its own targets as vehicles of its exercise; it is based upon a scientific discourse of normalisation and standardisation produced by the human sciences. (1985, p. 325)

Chapter 18

1. For statements of this position, see the journal *Crime and Social Justice* over the last three or four years (for example Platt (1982) and Taylor, (1981)), Lea and Young (1984) and — most comprehensively — Young (1986, 1987).
2. I deal elsewhere (Cohen 1985b) with how criminalization appears in the new critical paradigm.
3. I draw here on information provided by Raymond Schonholz at the International Conference on Prison Abolition, Amsterdam, June 1985.
4. Auerbach (1983) traces the continuities between the organic systems of justice and self-help developed by urban ethnic minorities in the United States and later, more conscious experiments in 'justice without law'.
5. For a review — from the point of view of the latter side of this debate — see Scraton and South (1984).
6. Note particularly Michalowski's current textbook (1985) — the only one I know which makes a serious comparison betwen 'order and trouble in simple societies' and the nature of state law.
7. These, for example, are Christie's conditions for a 'low level of pain delivery': close personal knowledge; no group has any monopoly over power; those who pass judgements are vulnerable and accountable to their subjects; members of the group are mutually interdependent on each other; members share beliefs such as 'each human body contains a sacred soul' (Christie 1981, pp. 81–91).
8. This is the reading of Foucault suggested recently by two eminent political philosophers — Waltzer (1983) and Taylor (1984).
9. For Taylor and Waltzer, the problem in Foucault's political theory is not the absence of a central subject or the presence of local power. It is rather that his explanation of the microphysics of power invokes some notion of an overall logic, fit or 'intelligibility'. This ends up as a form of functionalism.
10. On Foucault as an abolitionist, see de Folter (1986).

References

A Brief Collection of Some Part of Executions, Extortions and Excesses, London 1620

Abel, R. L., 'From the Editor', *Law and Society Review*, 1978, vol. 12, pp. 333–340

Abel, R. L., 'Conservative Conflict and the Reproduction of Capitalism: The Role of Informal Justice', *International Journal of the Sociology of Law*, 1981, vol. 9, no. 3, pp. 245–267

Abel, R. L., 'The Contradictions of Informal Justice' in R. L. Abel (ed.), *The Politics of Informal Justice*, vol. 1, pp. 267–320, Academic Press, New York 1982a

Abel, R. L. (ed.), *The Politics of Informal Justice*, 2 volumes, Academic Press, London 1982b

Abramsom, M. F., 'The Criminalisation of Mentally Disordered Behaviour: Possible Side Effect of a New Mental Health Law', *Hospital and Community Psychiatry*, 1972, vol. 23, April, pp. 101–105

AFSCME, *Out of Their Beds and Into the Streets*, American Federation of State, County, and Municipal Employees, Washington DC 1975

Agnew, J-C., 'The Consuming Vision of Henry James' in R. W. Fox and T. J. J. Lears (eds), *The Culture of Consumption*, Pantheon, New York 1983

Alexander, P., *A Look at Prostitution*, National Task Force on Prostitution, San Francisco 1980

Alford, R. R., *Health Care Politics*, The University of Chicago Press, Chicago 1975

Allen, F. A., *The Decline of the Rehabilitative Ideal: Penal Policy and Social Purpose*, Yale University Press, New Haven 1981

Allodi, F. A., H. B. Kedward, and M. Robertson, 'Insane But Guilty: Psychiatric Patients in Jail', *Canada's Mental Health*, 1977, vol. 25, June, pp. 3–7

Altheide, D. L., 'The Irony of Security', *Urban Life*, 1975, vol. 4, no. 2, pp. 179–195

Altheide, D. L., and J. M. Johnson, *Bureaucratic Propaganda*, Allen and Bacon, London 1980

American Behavioural Scientist, 'Special Issue on New Forms of Social Control: The Myth of Deinstitutionalisation', 1981, vol. 24, no. 6

American Friends Service Committee, *Struggle for Justice*, Hill and

Wang, New York 1972

Anderson, M., 'Forward' to E.S. Savas, *Privatising the Public Sector: How to Shrink Government*, Chatham House Publishers, Chatham, NJ 1982

Anderson, N., *The Hobo*, The University of Chicago Press, Chicago 1923

Anderson, P., *Lineages of the Absolutist State*, New Left Books, London 1974

Armitage, G. (ed.), *The History of the Bow Street Runners*, Wisehart and Company, London 1932

Armstrong, L., *Kiss Daddy Goodnight*, Hawthorn Books, New York 1978

Arnaud, J., and T. Mack, 'The Deinstitutionalisation of Status Offenders in Massachusetts: The Role of the Private Sector' in J. Handler and J. Zatz (eds.), *Neither Angels Nor Thieves: Studies in Deinstitutinalisation of Status Offenders*, National Academy Press, Washington DC 1982

Arnhoff, F., 'Social Consequences of Policy Toward Mental Illness', *Science*, 1975, vol.188, June, pp.1277–1281

'Arson Control Has Most Successful Year', *Arson News*, 1981, January

Auerbach, B., R.H. Lawson, J. Luftig, B. New, J. Schaller, G.E. Sexton, P. Smith, *A Guide to Effective Prison Industries, Volume 1, Creating Free Venture Prison Industries: Programme Considerations*, The American Foundation, Philadelphia 1979

Auerbach, J.S., *Justice Without Law?*, Oxford University Press, New York 1983

Austin, J., and B. Krisberg, 'Wider, Stronger and Different Nets: The Dialectics of Criminal Justice Reform', *Journal of Research in Crime and Delinquency*, 1981, vol.18, January, pp.165–196

Austin, J., and B. Krisberg, 'The Unmet Promise of Alternatives to Incarceration', *Crime and Delinquency*, 1982, vol.28, no.3, July, pp.374–409

Aviram, U., and S. Segal, 'Exclusion of the Mentally Ill: Reflections on an Old Problem in a New Context', *Archives of General Psychiatry*, 1973, vol.29, pp.126–131

Aviram, U., S.L. Syme, and J.B. Cohen, 'The Effects of Policies and Programmes on Reduction of Mental Hospitalisation', *Social Science and Medicine*, 1976, vol.10, no.11–12, pp.571–577

Babcock, B., A. Friedman, E. Norton, and S. Ross, *Sex Discrimination and the Law: Causes and Remedies*, Little, Brown and Company, Boston 1975

Bachrach, L., *Deinstitutionalisation: An Analytical Review and Sociological Perspective*, National Institute of Mental Health, Rockville MD 1976

Bachrach, L., 'A Conceptual Approach to Deinstitutionalisation', *Hospital and Community Psychiatry*, 1978, vol. 29, September, pp. 573–578

Bakal, Y., and H. Polsky, *Reforming Correctional Institutions for Juvenile Offenders*, D.C. Heath, Lexington MA 1978

Baldock, J.C., 'Why the Prison Population Has Grown Larger and Younger', *Howard Journal*, 1980, vol. 19, no. 3, pp. 142–155

Ball, R.A., 'The Dialectical Method: Its Application to Social Theory', *Social Forces*, 1979, vol. 57, no. 3, March, pp. 785–798

Balvig, F., 'Om Aeldre Kvinders Angst for Kriminalitet' ('On Older Women's Anxiety Over Criminality') in *Rapport fra Kontaktseminaren*, Sundvolden (Report from the Symposium, Sundvolden, Scandinavian Research Council for Criminology), Oslo 1979

Bant, P., *Stopping Rape: Successful Survival Strategies*, Pergamon Press, New York 1985

Bardach, E., *The Skill Factor in Politics: Repealing the Mental Commitment Laws in California*, University of California Press, California 1972

Barnes, H.E., *The Repression of Crime: Studies in Historical Penology*, Patterson Smith, Montclair, NJ 1926

Barrett, N.S., 'Women in the Job Market: Unemployment and Work Schedules' in R.E. Smith (ed.), *The Subtle Revolution: Women at Work*, Urban Institute, Washington DC 1979

Barry, K., *Female Sexual Slavery*, Avon Books, New York 1981

Bart, P., *Stopping Rape: Successful Survival Strategies*, Pergamon Press, New York 1985

Bassuk, E., and J. Gerson, 'Deinstitutionalisation and Mental Health Services', *Scientific American*, 1978, vol. 238, pp. 46–53

Baudrillard, J., *The Mirror of Production*, Telos Press, St. Louis 1975

Bayer, R., 'Crime, Punishment, and the Decline of Liberal Optimism', *Crime and Delinquency*, 1981, vol. 27, no. 2, pp. 169–190

Beck, B., 'The Politics of Speaking in the Name of Society', Presidential Address, Society for the Study of Social Problems, reprinted in *Social Problems*, 1977, vol. 25, no. 4, April, pp. 353–360

Becker, C. and D. Stanley, 'The Downside of Private Prisons', *The Nation*, 15 June 1984, pp. 728–730

Belle, D. (ed.), *Lives in Stress: Women and Depression*, Sage Publications, Beverly Hills 1982

Bendix, R., *Max Weber: An Intellectual Portrait*, Doubleday, Garden City, NY, 1960.

Benidt, B., 'Prisoner-run Programme Gives Inmates Education and Hope', *Minneapolis Star and Tribune*, 16 June 1985, p. 1A

Bennett, J. W., *Hutterite Brethren: The Agricultural Economy and Social Organization of a Communal People*, Stanford University Press Palo Alto, CA, 1967

Bentham, J., *Works IV*, Bowring, London 1843

Bentley, A. F., *The Process of Government*, Harvard University Press, Cambridge MA 1908

Benton, F. W., and J. Silberstein, 'State Prison Expansion: An Explanatory Model', *Journal of Criminal Justice*, 1983, vol. 11, no. 2, pp. 121–128

Berch, B. 'The Resurrection of Out-of-Work', *Monthly Review*, 1985, vol. 67, no. 6, pp. 37–46

Beresford, M. W., 'The Common Informer, The Penal Status and Economic Regulation', *Economic History Review*, 1957–1958, vol. 10, 2nd Series, pp. 221–238

Berger, P., and S. Pullberg, 'Reification and the Sociological Critique of Consciousness', *History and Theory*, 1966, vol. 4, pp. 196–211

Berk, R. A., S. Messinger, D. Raama, and R. Berrochecia, 'Prisons as Self-Regulating System: A Comparison of Historical Patterns in California for Male and Female Offenders', *Law and Society Review*, 1983, vol. 17, no. 4, pp. 547–586

Berle, A. A., and G. C. Means, *The Modern Corporation and Private Property*, Macmillan, New York 1983

Berman, M., *All That is Solid Melts Into Air*, Simon and Schuster, New York 1982

Bernard, J. S., *The Female World*, The Free Press, New York 1981

Biles, D., 'Crime and Imprisonment: A Two Decade Comparison Between England and Wales and Australia', *British Journal of Criminology*, 1983, vol. 23, no. 2, April, pp. 167–172

Biles, D., and G. Mulligan, 'Mad or Bad? — the Enduring Dilemma', *British Journal of Criminology*, 1973, vol. 13, no. 3, July, pp. 275–279

Bing, J., 'Diktning og data' (Fiction Writing and Data), *Dagbladet*, 1983, April

Bing, J., 'Mulighetenes skjerm. Om videospill og hjemmedatamaskiner', (The Screen of Possibilities. On Video Games and Home Computers), in Hilde Andresen (ed.), *Hva skjer foran skjermen*, Cappelen 1984

Birnbaum, N., *The Crisis of Industrial Society*, Oxford University Press, New York 1969

Bittner, E., 'Police Discretion in Emergency Apprehension of Mentally Ill Persons', *Social Problems*, 1967, vol. 14, pp. 278–292

Bittner, E., 'The Police on Skid Row: A Study of Peace Keeping', *American Sociological Review*, 1967, vol. 32, no. 5, pp. 699–715

Black, D. J., *The Manners and Customs of Police*, Academic Press, New

York 1980

Black, D.J. (ed.), *Toward A General Theory of Social Control*, vol. I, Academic Press, New York 1984a

Black, D.J. (ed.), *Toward a General Theory of Social Control*, vol. II, Academic Press, New York 1984b

Blake, J., 'The Changing Status of Women in Developed Countries', *Scientific American*, 1974, vol. 231, September, pp. 136–147

Blomberg, T.G., 'Diversion and Accelerated Social Control', *Journal of Criminal Law and Criminology*, 1977a, vol. 68, no. 2, pp. 274–282

Blomberg, T.G., 'The Juvenile Court as an Organisation and Decision-Making System,' *International Journal of Comparative and Applied Criminal Justice*, 1977b, vol. 1, no. 2, pp. 135–145

Blomberg, T.G., *Social Control and the Proliferation of Juvenile Court Services*, R and E Research Associates, Inc., San Francisco 1978a

Blomberg, T.G., 'Diversion From Juvenile Court: A Review of the Evidence' in F. Faust and P.J. Brantingham (eds), *Juvenile Justice Philosophy*, West, St. Paul, MN 1978b

Blomberg, T.G., 'Widening the Net: An Anomaly in the Evaluation of Diversion Programmes' in M. Klein and K. Teilmann (eds.), *Handbook of Criminal Justice Evaluation*, Sage, Beverly Hills 1980

Blomberg, T.G., 'Diversion's Disparate Results and Unresolved Questions: An Integrative Evaluation Perspective', *Journal of Research in Crime and Delinquency*, 1983, vol. 20, no. 1, pp. 24–38

Blomberg, T.G., 'An Assessment of Community Control in Florida', Florida Department of Corrections, 1984

Boehringer, G., *et al.*, 'Law and Order For Progressives? An Australian Response', *Crime and Social Justice*, 1983, vol. 19, Summer, pp. 2–12

Bonovitz, J.C., and J.S. Bonovitz, 'Diversion of the Mentally Ill Into the Criminal Justice System: The Police Intervention Perspective', *American Journal of Psychiatry*, 1981, vol. 138, July, pp. 973–976

Boorstin, D.J., *The Americans: The Democratic Experience*, Random House, New York 1973

Boorstin, D.J. *The Discoverers: A History of Man's Search to Know His World and Himself*, Random House, New York 1983

Borus, J.F., 'Deinstitutionalisation of the Chronically Mentally Ill', *New England Journal of Medicine*, 1981, vol. 305, no. 6, pp. 339–342

Boston Globe, 28 July 1979

Bottomley, A., 'What is Happening to Family Law? A Feminist Critique of Conciliation.' In J. Brophy and C. Smart (eds), *Women in Law: Explorations in Law, Family and Sexuality*, Routledge and Kegan Paul, London, 1985

Bottoms, A. E., 'Neglected Features of Contemporary Penal Systems' in D. Garland and P. Young (eds), *The Power to Punish*, pp. 166–202, Heinemann, London, Humanities Press, New York 1983

Boulding, E., *The Underside of History: A View of Women Through Time*, Westview Press, Boulder Colorado 1976

Bowditch, C., and R. S. Everett, 'Private Prisons: Problems Within the Solution', Paper Presented at the 37th Annual Meeting of the American Society of Criminology, San Diego 1985

Box, S., and C. Hale, 'Unemployment, Crime and Imprisonment and the Enduring Problem of Prison Overcrowding' in R. Matthews and J. Young (eds), *Confronting Crime*, Sage, London 1986

Boyer, D. and J. James, *Intervention with Female Prostitutes*, University of Washington, Department of Psychiatry and Behavioural Sciences, 1982

Boynton, L., *The Elizabethan Militia*, Routledge and Kegan Paul, London 1967

Brady, J. P., 'Sorting Out the Exile Confusion: Or a Dialogue on Popular Justice', *Contemporary Crises*, 1981, vol. 5, pp. 31–38

Braithwaite, J., *Prisons, Education and Work*, Australian Institute of Criminology and University of Queensland Press, A.C.T., Australia 1980

Bråten, S., *Dialogens vilkår i datasamfunnet* (The Conditions of Dialogue in Data Society), Universitetsforlaget, Oslo 1983

Braverman, H., *Labour and Monopoly Capital*, Monthly Review Press, New York 1974

Bressler, L., and D. Leonard, *Women's Jail: Pretrial and Post-Conviction Alternatives*, available from UUSN, 1251 Second Avenue, San Francisco CA 94122, 1978

Brett-James, N. G., *The Growth of Stuart London*, Allen and Unwin, London 1935

Breyer, S. G., *Regulation and its Reform*, Harvard University Press, Cambridge, Massachussetts 1982

Bridenbaugh, C., *Vexed and Troubled Englishmen 1590–1642*, Oxford University Press, Oxford 1968

Brogden, M., *The Police: Autonomy and Consent*, Academic Press, London 1982

Brophy, J. and C. Smart, *Women in Law: Explorations in Law, Family and Sexuality*, Routledge and Kegan Paul, London, 1985

Brown, P., 'Social Implications of Deinstitutionalisation', *Journal of Community Psychology*, 1979, vol. 8, pp. 314–322

Brownmiller, S., *Against Our Will: Men, Women and Rape*, Simon and Schuster, New York, 1975

Brozan, N., 'Jurors in Rape Trials Studied', *New York Times*, 17 June 1985

Bureau of Justice Statistics, *Prisoners 1925–1981*, US Department of Justice, Washington DC 1980

Bureau of Justice Statistics, *Prisoners in State and Federal Institutions, 1980*, US Government Printing Office, Washington DC 1982

Bureau of Justice Statistics, *Setting Prison Terms*, US Government Printing Office, Washington DC 1983a

Bureau of Justice Statistics, *Prisoners in State and Federal Institutions*, US Government Printing Office, Washington DC 1983b

Bureau of Prisoner Statistics, *Prisoners in State and Federal Institutions, 1970–1973*, US Government Printing Office, Washington DC 1974

Burnham, D., *The Rise of the Computer State*, Random House, New York 1983

Burton, C., *Subordination: Feminism and Social Theory*, George Allen and Unwin, Sydney 1985

Business Week, 'Convict Labour Has the Unions Worried', 16 April 1984, p.51

Cain, M., 'Beyond Informal Justice', *Contemporary Crises: Crime, Law and Social Policy*, 1985, vol. 9, no. 4, pp. 335–373

California Department of Youth Authority, *The Evaluation of Juvenile Diversion Programmes: Survey of Diversion Programmes*, Sacramento, California 1975a

California Department of Youth Authority, *The Evaluation of Juvenile Diversion Programmes: First Annual Report*, Sacramento, California 1975b

California Department of Youth Authority, *The Evaluation of Juvenile Diversion Programs: Second Annual Report*, Sacramento, California, 1976

CSEA, *Where Have All the Patients Gone?*, California State Employees Association, Sacramento 1972

Canadian Association of Chiefs of Police, 'Resolutions Adopted at the 72nd Annual Conference, August 26, 1977', *Canadian Police Chief*, 1977, vol. 66, no. 4, p. 72

Canadian Centre for Justice Statistics, *Adult Correctional Services in Canada, 1983–1984*, Statistics Canada, Ottawa 1983

Carlen, P., *Women's Imprisonment: A Study in Social Control*, Routledge and Kegan Paul, London 1983

Carlson, N. A., 'Toward a More Balanced Correction Philosophy', *Law Enforcement Bulletin*, 1977, vol. 46, no. 1, pp. 22–25

Carter, R. M., 'The Diversion of Offenders' in G. G. Killinger and P. F. Cromwell Jr (eds), *Corrections in the Community: Alternatives to Prison: Selected Readings*, West, St Paul, Minn. 1978a

Carter, R. M., *Evaluation of the Deinstitutionalisation of Status Offenders, Project Through the System Rates Methodology*, Social

Science Research Institute, University of Southern California 1978b

Carter R.M., and M.W. Klein, *Back on the Street: The Diversion of Juvenile Offenders*, Prentice-Hall, Englewood Cliffs NJ 1976

Chan, J.B.L., and R.V. Ericson, *Decarceration and the Economy of Penal Reform*, Research Report, University of Toronto Centre of Criminology, Toronto 1981

Changing Work, 'Special Theme: Economic Conversion', 1985, no.2, Winter, pp.20–49

Chartier, G. 'Contemporary Penal Labour: Concepts and Misconceptions', 1985, Mimeo

Chesler, P., *Women and Madness*, Avon, New York 1972.

Chesney-Lind, M., 'Judicial Paternalism and the Female Status Offender', *Crime and Delinquency*, 1977, vol.23, no.2, pp.121–130

Christianson, S., 'Our Black Prisons', *Crime and Delinquency*, 1981, vol.27, no.3, pp.364–375

Christie, N., 'Conflicts as Property', *British Journal of Criminology*, 1977, vol.17, January, pp.1–19

Christie, N., 'Prisons in Society; Or Society as a Prison: A Conceptual Analysis' in J. Freeman (ed.), *Prisons Past and Future*, Heinemann, London 1978

Christie, N., *Limits to Pain*, Martin Robertson, Oxford 1981

Christie, N., *Hyor Tett et Samfunn*? (How Tight a Society), Universiteforlaget (University Press), Oslo 1982

Chu, F., and S. Trotter, *The Madness Establishment*, Grossman, New York 1974

Cicourel, A.V., *Method and Measurement in Sociology*, Free Press, New York 1964

Cicourel, A.V., *The Social Organisation of Juvenile Justice*, Wiley, New York 1968

Cicourel, A.V., 'Notes on the Integration of Micro- and Macro- Levels of Analysis' in K. Knorr-Cetina and A.V. Cicourel (eds), *Advances in Social Theory and Methodology: Toward an Integration of Micro- and Macro-Sociologies*, Routledge and Kegan Paul, London 1981

Clark, J.M., *Social Control of Business*, Whittlesey House, New York 1926

Clark, L.N.G., and D.J. Lewis, *Rape: The Price of Coercive Sexuality*, Women's Press, Toronto 1977

Clark, P., and P. Slack, *English Towns in Transition 1500–1700*, Oxford University Press, Oxford 1978

Coates, R., and A. Miller, 'Neutralisation of Community Resistance to Group Homes' in Y. Bakal (ed.), *Closing Correctional Institutions*, Lexington Books, Lexington, Massachussetts 1973

Cockburn, J. S. (ed.), *The History of English Assizes From 1558 To 1714*, Cambridge University Press, Cambridge 1972

Cockburn, J. S., 'The Incidence and Nature of Crime 1558–1625'. In J. S. Cockburn (ed.) *Crime in England 1550–1800*, Methuen, London 1977

Cohen, B., *Deviant Street Networks: Prostitution in New York City*, D. C. Heath, Lexington MA. 1980

Cohen, S. (ed.), *Images of Deviance*, Penguin, Harmondsworth UK 1971

Cohen, S., *Folk Devils and Moral Panics: The Creation of the Mods and Rockers*, MacGibbon and Kee, London 1972

Cohen, S., 'The Punitive City: Notes on the Dispersal of Social Control', *Contemporary Crises: Crime, Law and Social Policy*, 1979, vol. 3, pp. 339–363

Cohen, S., 'Social Control Talk: Telling Stories about Correctional Change' in D. Garland and P. Young (eds), *The Power to Punish: Contemporary Penality and Social Analysis*, Heinemann, London 1983

Cohen, S., 'The Deeper Structures of Law, or "Beware the Rulers Bearing Justice": A Review Essay', *Contemporary Crises*, 1984, vol. 8, pp. 83–93

Cohen, S., *Visions of Social Control: Crime, Punishment and Classification*, Polity Press, Cambridge 1985a

Cohen, S., 'The Object of Criminology: Reflections on the New Criminalization', Paper given at Annual Meeting of the American Society of Criminology, San Diego 1985b

Cohen, S., and A. T. Scull (eds), *Social Control and the State*, Martin Robertson, Oxford 1983

Cohen, S., and J. Young (eds), *The Manufacture of News: Deviance, Social Problems and the Mass Media*, London, Constable 1973

Colker, R., 'Pornography and Privacy', *Law and Inequality: A Journal of Theory and Practice*, 1983, vol. 1, no. 2, November, pp. 191–237

Collins, R., 'A Conflict Theory of Sexual Stratification', *Social Problems*, 1971, vol. 19, Summer, pp. 3–19

Computerworld, 7 April 1980

Conrad, J. P., 'There Has to be a Better Way', *Crime and Delinquency*, 1980, vol. 26, no. 1, January, pp. 83–90

Conrad, J. P. 'The Society of Lifers', *The Prison Journal*, 1983, vol. 63, no. 1, pp. 125–133

Cornwall, J., 'Evidence of Population Mobility in the Seventeenth Century', *Bulletin of the Institute of Historical Research*, 1967, vol. 11, no. 102

The Corporation of the City of London, Guildhall Records Office, 'An Act of Common Council for the Better Ordering of the Night

Watch within ye City of London and the Liberties Thereof', *Journal of Common Council*, 1663, 10 October

The Corporation of the City of London, Guildhall Library, *Kings Proclamations*, 17 February 1628, 17 September 1630, 12 February 1634, 25 November 1642

The Corporation of the City of London, Guildhall Records Office, *Lord Mayor's Proclamations*, 1603, 30 September, vol. 10, no. 48, vol. 10, no. 49, vol. 10, no. 73, vol. 16, no. 71

The Corporation of the City of London, Guildhall Library, 'Instructions to be Observed by the Several Justices of the Peace in the Several Counties within the Commonwealth for the Better Prevention of Robberies, Burglaries and Other Outrages', *Miscellaneous Proclamations*, London 1649

The Corporation of the City of London, Guildhall Library, 'Two Orders of Parliament: The One, Appointing the Giving of Ten Pounds to Every One who shall bring in a High-way-man. The Other: Referring to the Council of State to give Reprieves to Persons Guilty of Robberies, if they Shall Discover any of their Accomplices', *Miscellaneous Proclamations*, 1649, 8 November

The Corporation of the City of London, Guildhall Library, 'Two Orders of Parliament Concerning the Apprehending of Thieves', *Miscellaneous Proclamations*, 1650, 10 January

The Corporation of the City of London, Guildhall Records Office, *Repertories of the Court of Aldermen*, vol. 23, no. 548, vol. 26, no. 1979, vol. 34, nos 125 and 183

The Corporation of the City of London, *The Corporation of London, Its Origins, Constitutional Powers and Duties*, Oxford University Press, London 1967

The Corporation of the City of London, Guildhall Records Office, 'The Humble Petition of Robert Wilkins about Miscarriages of Watching', *Watch and Ward Miscellaneous Manuscripts*, Box 245

Correctional Services Canada, *Some Basic Facts About Corrections in Canada*, Department of Supply and Services, Ottawa 1984

Corrigan, P., and V. Gillespie, *Class Struggle, Social Literacy, and Idle Time*, Studies in Labour History, Brighton 1978

Coser, L. A., *Functions of Social Conflict*, Free Press, New York 1956

Coward, R. *Patriarch Precedents: Sexuality and Social Relations*, Routledge and Kegan Paul, London 1983

Cressey, D., 'Occupation, Migration and Literacy in East London 1580–1640', *Local Population Studies*, 1970, no. 5, pp.53–60

Cressey, D. R., and R. A. McDermott, *Diversion from the Juvenile Justice System*, National Institute of Law Enforcement and Criminal Justice, Washington DC 1974

Crime and Delinquency, 'Diversion in the Juvenile Justice System',

1976, vol. 22, no. 4

Cruickshank, C. G., *Elizabeth's Army*, Oxford University Press, Oxford 1966

Culhane, C., *Still Barred From Prison: Social Injustice in Canada*, Black Rose Books, Montreal, Quebec 1985

Cunningham, W., and T. Taylor, 'Doing More With Less: Private Security Options for Decreasing Police Workload', *The Police Chief*, 1985, no. 15, May, pp. 62–63

Curran, J., 'Communications, Power, and Social Order' in M. Gurevitch *et. al.* (eds), *Culture, Society and the Media*, Methuen, London 1982

Dahl, H. F., 'Når grensene krysses. Enintroduksjon til massekommunikasjonen', (When the Borders are Crossed. An Introduction to Mass Communication), in H. F. Dahl (ed.), *Massekommunikasjon*, Gyldendal 1973

Daly, M., *Gyn/Ecology: The Meta Ethics of Radical Feminism*, Beacon Press, Boston, 1978

D'Amico, R. 'Desire and the Commodity Form', *Telos*, 1978, vol. 35, Spring, pp. 88–122

Danzinger, S., R. Haveman, and R. Plotnick, 'Income Transfer Programmes in the United States', *Federal Finance: The Pursuit of American Goals*, 1980, vol. 6, US Government Printing Office, Washington DC

Datesman, S. K., and F. Scarpitti, *Women, Crime, and Justice*, Oxford University Press, New York 1980

Davies, M. G., *The Enforcement of English Apprenticeship 1563–1642*, Harvard University Press, Cambridge 1956

Davis, A., S. Dinitz, and B. Pasamanick, *Schizophrenics in the New Custodial Community*, Ohio State University, Columbus 1974

Davis, J. M., 'Organic Therapies' in H. I. Kaplan, A. M. Freedman, and B. J. Sadock (eds), *Comprehensive Textbook of Psychiatry*, vol. 3, Williams and Wilkins, Baltimore 1981

Davis, K., 'The Sociology of Prostitution', *American Sociology Review*, 1937, vol. 2, pp. 746–755

Davis, N. J., 'Feminism, Deviance and Social Change', in E. Sagarin (ed.), *Deviance and Social Change*, Sage Publications, Beverly Hills 1977

Davis, N. J., 'Prostitution: Identity, Career and Legal-Economic Enterprise' in J. M. Henslin and E. Sagarin (eds), *The Sociology of Sex*, Schocken Books, New York 1978

Davis, N. J., *Sociological Constructions of Deviance: Perspectives and Issues in the Field*, W. C. Brown Publishers, Dubuque, Iowa 1980

Davis, N. J., and B. Anderson, 'Gender, Crime and the Sociology of Knowledge: Uncovering Ideological Biases in an Academic

Tradition' in R.B. Smith and P.K. Manning (eds), *An Introduction to Social Research: Handbook of Social Science Methods*, vol. 1, Ballinger Publishing Company, New York 1982

Davis, N.J., and B. Anderson, *Social Control: The Production of Deviance in the Modern State*, Irvington Publishers, New York 1983

Davis, N.J., and J. Keith, *Women and Deviance: Issues in Social Conflict and Change: An Annotated Bibliography*, Garland Press, New York 1984

Defleur, M., and S. Ball-Rokeach, *Theories of Mass Communication*, 4th edition, Longman, New York 1982

De Folter, R., 'On the Methodological Foundation of the Abolitionist Approach to the Criminal Justice System: A Comparison of the Ideas of Hulsman, Mathiesen and Foucault', *Contemporary Crises: Crime, Law and Social Policy*, 1986, vol. 1, no. 1

Dennison, L., L. Humphreys, and D Wilson, 'A Comparison: Organisation and Impact in Two Diversion Projects', Paper Presented at the Annual Meeting of the Pacific Sociological Association, Victoria, BC, Canada 1975

Department of Health and Human Services, Office of the Inspector-General, *Annual Report*, United States Government Printing Office, Washington DC 1981

Deutsch, A., *The Shame of the States*, Arno, New York 1973

Dewey, J., *The Public and Its Problems*, Alan Swallow, Denver 1927

Diamond, I., 'Pornography and Repression: A Reconsideration', *Signs*, 1980, vol. 5, no. 4, pp. 686–701

Dinnerstein, D., *The Mermaid and The Minotaur: Sexual Arrangements and Human Malaise*, Harper and Row, New York 1977

Ditton, J., *Controlology*, Macmillan, London 1979

Dobash, R.E., and R.P. Dobash, *Violence Against Wives: A Case Against the Patriarchy*, Free Press, New York 1979

Dobash, R.P. and R.E. Dobash, 'Community Response to Violence Against Wives', *Social Problems*, 1981, vol. 28, June, pp. 563–581

Dobb, C., 'Life and Conditions in London Prisons 1553–1643, With Special Reference to Contemporary Literature', Oxford B. Litt. Dissertation, Bodelian Library, Oxford 1953

Donnerstein, E., 'Aggressive Erotica and Violence Against Women', *Journal of Personality and Social Psychology*, 1980, vol. 39, no. 2, pp. 269–277

Donzelot, J. *The Policing of Families*, Pantheon, New York 1979

Downes, D. and P. Mitchell, 'The Origins and Consequences of Dutch Penal Policy Since 1945', *British Journal of Criminology*, 1982, vol. 22, no. 4, pp. 325–362

Downs, G.W., *Bureaucracy, Innovation, and Social Policy*, Lexington

Books, Lexington MA 1978
Dugdale, W., *The History of St. Paul's Cathedral*, London 1658
Dunford, F.W., 'Police Diversion: An Illusion?', *Criminology*, 1977, vol. 15, no. 3, pp. 335–352
Durkheim, E., *Rules of Sociological Method*, Macmillan, New York 1982 (originally published in 1895 in French)
Durnford, F.W., 'Police Diversion: An Illusion?', *Criminology*, 1977, vol. 15, no. 3, pp. 335–352
Ebringer, L., and J.R.W. Christie-Brown, 'Social Deprivation Among Short Stay Psychiatric Patients', *British Journal of Psychiatry*, 1980, vol. 136, January, pp. 46–52
Edelman, M., 'Space and Social Order', *Journal of Architectural Education*, 1978, vol. 32, no. 2, November, pp. 2–7 (reprinted as Reprint #328, Institute for Research on Poverty, University of Wisconsin, Madison 1979)
Edwards, S.M., *Women on Trial*, Manchester Press, Manchester 1984
Ehrlich, E., *Fundamental Principles of Sociology of Law*, Harvard University Press, Cambridge 1912
Einstadter, W., 'Citizen Patrols: Prevention or Control?', *Crime and Social Justice*, 1984, vol. 21, no. 2, pp. 200–212
Ellis, E.M., B.M. Atkeson, and K.S. Calhoun, 'An Assessment of Long-Term Reaction to Rape', *Journal of Abnormal Psychology*, 1981, vol. 90, pp. 263–266
Elton, G.R., 'Informing for Profit' in G.R. Elton (ed.), *Star Chamber Stories*, Methuen, London 1958
Emerson, R.M., E.B. Rochford, and L.L. Shaw, 'Economics and Enterprise in Board and Care Homes for the Mentally Ill', *American Behavioral Scientist*, 1981, vol. 24, pp. 771–785
Estroff, S.E., 'Psychiatric Deinstitutionalisation: A Socio-Cultural Analysis', *Journal of Social Issues*, 1981, vol. 37, no. 3, pp. 116–132
Everitt, A., 'Social Mobility in Early Modern England', *Past and Present*, 1966, vol. 13, November, p. 56
Ewen, S., 'Advertising as a Way of Life', *Liberation*, 1975, January, pp. 17–34
Ewen, S., and E. Ewen, *Channels of Desire*, McGraw-Hill, New York 1982
Falandysz, L., 'Victimology in the Radical Perspective' in H.J. Schneider (ed.), *The Victim in International Perspective*, De Gruyter, Berlin 1982
Faulkner, E.J. (ed.), *Man's Quest for Security*, University of Nebraska Press, Lincoln 1966
Fauteux, C. (Chairman), *Report of the Committee Appointed to Inquire Into the Principles and Procedures Followed in the Remission Service of the Department of Justice, Canada*, Queen's Printer, Ottawa 1936

Federal Bureau of Investigation, *Crime in the United States, 1970*, US Government Printing Office, Washington DC 1971

Federal Bureau of Investigation, *Crime in the United States, 1980*, US Government Printing Office, Washington DC 1981

Felstiner, W.L.F., 'Influence of Social Organisation on Dispute Processing', *Law and Society Review*, 1974, vol.9, Autumn, pp.63–94

Ferrajoli, L., and D. Zolo, 'Marxism and the Criminal Question', *Law and Philosophy*, 1985, vol.4, no.1, pp.71–99

Fisher, F.J., 'London as an "Engine of Economic Growth"' in P. Clark (ed.), *The Early Modern Town*, Longman's, London 1976

Fisher, F.J., 'The Development of London as a Centre of Conspicuous Consumption in the Sixteenth and Seventeenth Centuries' in C. Wilson (ed.), *Essays in Economic History*, vol.2, Edward Arnold, London 1962

Fishman, R., *Criminal Recidivism in New York: An Evaluation of the Impact of Rehabilitation and Diversion Services*, Praeger, New York, 1977

Fitzpatrick, P., 'Law, Plurality and Underdevelopment' in D. Sugarman (ed.), *Legality, Ideology and the State*, Academic Press, London 1983a

Fitzpatrick, P., 'Marxism and Legal Pluralism', *Australian Journal of Law and Society*, 1983b, vol.1, pp.45–59

Fitzpatrick, P., 'Law and Societies', *Osgoode Hall Law Journal*, 1984, vol.22, pp.115–138

Fixler, P.E., 'Behind Bars We Find an Enterprise Zone', *The Wall Street Journal*, 29 November 1984, p.34

Flanagan, J., 'Imminent Crisis in Prison Populations', *American Journal of Correction*, 1975, November–December

Flynn, E.E., 'Classification for Risk and Supervision: A Preliminary Conceptualisation' in J. Freeman (ed.), *Prisons Past and Future*, Heinemann, London 1978

Fogel, D., *We Are the Living Proof: The Justice Model for Corrections*, Anderson, Cincinnatti OH 1975

Fogel, D., and J. Hudson (eds.), *Justice as Fairness: Perspectives on the Justice Model*, Anderson Publishing, Cincinnatti, OH 1981

Foucault, M., *Madness and Civilisation*, Random House, New York 1965

Foucault, M., *The Order of Things*, Tavistock, London 1970

Foucault, M., *The Birth of the Clinic*, Pantheon, New York 1973

Foucault, M., *Discipline and Punish, The Birth of the Prison*, Pantheon, New York 1977

Foucault, M., *Power/Knowledge*, Pantheon Books, New York 1981

Foucault, M., 'Space, Knowledge and Power', Interview in Skyline,

March 1982, Reprinted in P. Rabinow (ed.), *The Foucault Reader*, pp.239–256, Pantheon Books, New York 1984

Fowler, R., 'Power', *Handbook of Discourse Analysis*, 1985, vol.4, pp.61–82

Fowler, R., R Hodge, G.R. Kress, and T. Trew, *Language and Control*, Routledge and Kegan Paul, London 1979

Fox, M.F., and Hesse-Biber, *Women at Work*, Mayfield Publishing, Palo Alto, California 1984

Fox, R.W., and T.J.J. Lears (eds), *The Culture of Consumption*, Pantheon Books, New York 1983

Fraser Committee on Pornography and Prostitution (in Canada), *Report of the Special Committee on Pornography and Prostitution*, vol.1 and 2, Ministry of Supply and Services, Canada, Ottawa 1985

Freidson, E., *Profession of Medicine*, Dodd, New York 1970

Freire, P., *Pedagogy of the Oppressed*, Penguin Books, New York 1972

French, A.H., 'The Population of Stepney in the Early Seventeenth Century', *Local Population Studies*, 1969, no.3

French, R., and A. Beliveau, *The RCMP and the Management of National Security*, Institute for Research on Public Policy, Montreal 1979

Freud, S., 'New Introductory Lectures On Psychoanalysis' in *The Standard Edition*, vol.22, pp.1–22, Hogarth, London 1933

Friedenberg, E.Z., *The Disposal of Liberty and Other Industrial Wastes*, Doubleday, New York 1977

Friedman, M., *Capitalism and Freedom*, University of Chicago Press, Chicago 1962

Friedrichs, R.W., 'Dialectical Sociology: Toward a Resolution of the Current "Crises in Western Sociology"', *British Journal of Sociology*, 1972, vol.23, no.3, pp.263–275

Fuller, R.B., *Synergetics: Explorations in the Geometry of Thinking*, 2 vols, Macmillan, New York 1975 and 1979

Galanter, M., 'Justice in Many Rooms: Courts, Private Ordering and Indigenous Law', *Journal of Legal Pluralism*, 1981, vol.19, pp.1–47

Galtung, J., 'Violence, Peace and Peace Research', *Journal of Peace Research*, 1969, vol.6, July, pp.167–191

Gardos, G., and J. Cole, 'Maintenance Antipsychotic Therapy: Is the Cure Worse Than the Disease?', *American Journal of Psychiatry*, 1976, vol.133, pp.32–36

Gargan, E.A., 'The Nation's Prisoners Join the Labour Force', *The New Times*, 28 August 1983

Garland, D., 'The Birth of the Welfare Sanction', *British Journal of Law and Society*, 1981, vol.8, no.1, Summer, pp.29–45

Garland, D., *Punishment and Welfare*, Gower, Aldershot UK 1985

Garland, D., and P. Young, *The Power to Punish*, Heinemann, London 1983

Gaylin, W., *Partial Justice*, Knopf, New York 1974

Gaylin W., *et al.*, *Doing Good: The Limits of Benevolence*, Pantheon Books, New York 1978

General Accounting Office, *The Mentally Ill in the Community: Government Needs to Do More*, Government Printing Office, Washington DC 1977

General Accounting Office, *IRS Can Do More to Identify Tax Return Processing Problems and Reduce Processing Costs*, Government Printing Office, Washington DC 1982

Gettinger, S., 'US Prison Population Hits All-time High', *Corrections Magazine*, 1976, vol. 2, no. 3, pp. 9–20

Gibbons, D. C., 'Forcible Rape and Sexual Violence', *Journal of Research in Crime and Delinquency*, 1984, vol. 21, no. 3, pp. 251–269

Gibbons, D. C., *Gender Advertisements*, Harper Colophon Books, New York 1979

Gibbs, J. P., 'Laws as a Means of Social Control', in J. P. Gibbs (ed.), *Social Control*, Sage, Beverly Hills 1982

Giddens, A., *The Constitution of Society*, Polity Press, Cambridge 1984

Giddens, A., *The Nation-State and Violence*, University of California Press, Berkeley 1985

Gierke, O., *Political Theories of the Middle Age*, Cambridge University Press, Cambridge 1958

Goffman, E., *The Presentation of Self in Everyday Life*, Doubleday Anchor Books, Garden City NY 1959

Goldman, D., 'The Electronic Rorschach', *Psychology Today*, 1983, vol. 17, February, pp. 36–43

Goldman, H. H., N. Adams, and C. Taube, 'Deinstitutionalisation: The Data Demythologised', *Hospital and Community Psychiatry*, 1983, vol. 34, no. 2, February, pp. 129–134

Goldman, H. H., A. A. Gattozzi, and C. A. Taube, 'Defining and Counting the Chronically Mentally Ill', *Hospital and Community Psychiatry*, 1981, vol. 32, January, pp. 21–27

Goldman, H. H., J. P. Morrissey, and L. Bachrach, 'Deinstitutionalisation in International Perspective: Variations on a Theme', *International Journal of Mental Health*, 1983, vol. 11, Winter, pp. 153–165

Goldstein, L. F., 'The Constitutional Status of Women: The Burger Court and the Sexual Revolution in American Law', *Law and Policy Quarterly*, 1981, vol. 3, no. 1, pp. 5–23

Goldstein, M., 'Review of Andrew Scull's Decarceration', *Con-*

temporary Sociology, 1982, vol. 11

Gordon, P., *White Law: Racism in the Police, Courts and Prisons*, Pluto Press, London 1983

Gorz, A., 'Security: Against What? For What? With What?', *Telos*, 1984, vol. 58, Winter, pp. 158–167

Gouldner, A. W., 'Stalinism: A Study of Internal Colonialism', *Telos*, 1977–1978, 34, Winter, pp. 5–48

Government of Canada, National Parole Board, *Policy and Procedures Manual*, Ottawa 1986

Grabosky, P. N., 'Rates of Imprisonment and Psychiatric Hospitalisation in the United States', *Social Indicators Research*, 1980, vol. 7, January, pp. 63–70

Gramsci, A., *Quaderni del Carcere*, Einaudi, Torino 1975

Great Britain, Public Record Office, *Acts of the Privy Council, Elizabeth (1)*, vol. XXII (1591–2), vol. XXIII (1593–4), vol. XXIV (1594–5), vol. XXV (1595), vol. XXVI (1596–7), vol. XXVII (1597–8), vol. XXVIII (1597–8), vol. XXIX (1598–9)

Great Britain, King's Proclamation (25 May 1627), 'A Proclamation for the Better Execution of the Office of his Majesties Exchanger, and Reformation of Sundry Abuses and Frauds Practices upon His Majesties Coins'

Greenberg, D. F., 'Problems in Community Corrections', *Issues in Criminology*, 1975, vol. 10, no. 1, Spring, pp. 1–34

Greenberg, D. F., 'Delinquency and the Age Structure of Society', *Contemporary Crises*, 1977a, vol. 1, no. 2, pp. 189–223

Greenberg, D. F., 'The Correctional Effects of Corrections' in D. Greenberg (ed.), *Corrections and Punishment*, Sage, Beverly Hills CA 1977b

Greenberg, D. F., 'The Dynamics of Oscillatory Punishment Processes', *The Journal of Criminal Law and Criminology*, 1977c, vol. 68, pp. 643–51

Greenberg, D. F., and D. Humphries, 'The Cooptation of Fixed Sentencing Reform', *Crime and Delinquency*, 1979, vol. 26, pp. 206–225

Greenfeld, L., and S. Minor-Harper, 'Prison Admissions and Releases 1981', US Department of Justice, *Bureau of Justice Statistics*, Washington, DC 1984

Greenwood, P. W., *Selective Incapacitation*, Rand, Santa Monica, California 1982

Greenwood, V., and J. Young (eds), National Deviancy Conference, *Permissiveness and Control: The Fate of the Sixties Legislation*, Macmillan, London 1980

Griffin, S., *Pornography and Silence: Culture's Revenge Against Nature*, Harper and Row, New York 1981

Griffiths, J., 'What is Legal Pluralism?', Mimeo, paper presented to the Annual Meeting of the Law and Society Association, Amherst, 12–14 June 1981

Grissom, G.R., *Impact of Free Venture Prison Industries Upon Correctional Institutions*, US Department of Justice, Washington DC 1981

Grob, G.N., *Mental Institutions in America: Social Policy to 1875*, Macmillan, New York 1973

Grob, G.N., *Mental Illness and American Society, 1875–1940*, Princeton University Press, Princeton NJ 1983

Gross, J.T., 'Social Control under Totalitarianism' in D.J. Black (ed.), *Toward a General Theory of Social Control*, vol.2, Academic Press, New York 1984, pp.59–77

Gruenberg, E., and J. Archer, 'Abandonment of Responsibility for the Seriously Mentally Ill', *Milbank Memorial Fund Quarterly/Health and Society*, 1979, vol.57, no.4, pp.485–506

Gurvitch, G., *The Sociology of Law*, Routledge and Kegan Paul, London 1947

Gutierrez–Johnson, A., 'The Mondragon Model of Cooperative Enterprise: Conditions Concerning its Success and Transferability.' *Changing Work*, 1984, vol.1 (Autumn), pp.35–41

Habermas, J., *Legitimation Crisis*, Beacon Press, Boston 1975

Hacker, A. (ed.), *U.S.: A Statistical Portrait of the American People*, The Viking Press, New York 1983

Hackler, J., 'Logical Reasoning Versus Unanticipated Consequences: Diversion Programmes as an Illustration', *Ottawa Law Review*, 1976, vol.8, no.2, pp.285–289

Hackler, J., and L. Gauld, 'Parole and the Violent Offender', *Canadian Journal of Criminology*, 1981, vol.23, no.4, pp.407–413

Hale, J., 'War and Public Opinion in the Fifteenth and Sixteenth Centuries', *Past and Present*, 1962, vol.22, no.4, July, p.18

Hall, S.M., C. Critchley, A. Jefferson, S. Clarke, and B. Roberts, *Policing the Crisis: Mugging, the State, Law and Order*, Macmillan, London 1978

Hallcrest Systems, *The Hallcrest Report: Private Security and Police in America*, Chancellor Press, Portland, Oregon 1985

Hamilton, G.G., and J.R. Sutton, 'The Problem of Control in the Weak State: Domination in the US, 1880–1920', Unpublished paper, 1984

Handler, J.F., and J. Zatz (eds.), *Neither Angels Nor Thieves: Studies in Deinstitutionalisation of Status Offenders*, National Academy Press, Washington DC 1982

Hartmann, H., 'Capitalism, Patriarchy and Job Segregation by Sex', *Signs*, 1976, vol.1, no.3, part 2, Spring, pp.137–169

Hatch, A. J., and K. Faith, 'The Female Offender in Canada', presented at the American Society of Criminology, San Diego, November 1985

Hawkins, G., 'Prison Labour and Prison Industries', *Crime and Justice: An Annual Review of Research*, 1983, vol. 5, pp. 85–127

Hayter, L., 'Introduction — Security and Society' in N. Currer-Briggs (ed.), *Security, Attitudes and Techniques for Management*, Hutchinson, London 1968

Heckewelder, J. G. E., *History, Manners and Customs of the Indian Nations Who Once Inhabited Pennsylvania and the Neighbouring States*, Crown Publishers, New York 1971 (originally 1819)

Henck, T., and Logan, C., *Mondragon: An Economic Analysis*, George Allen and Unwin, London/Boston 1982

Henningsen, G., *Heksenes advokat - historiens største hekseproces* (The Witches' Advocate. History's Greatest Witch Hunt), Delta 1981

Herman, J. L., *Father-Daughter Incest*, Oxford University Press, London 1981

Henry, S., *Private Justice: Towards Integrated Theorising in the Sociology of Law*, Routledge and Kegan Paul, London 1983

Henry, S., 'Community Justice, Capitalist Society and Human Agency: The Dialectics of Collective Law in the Co-operative', *Law and Society Review*, 1985, vol. 19, no. 2, pp. 301–325

Henry, S., 'Private Justice and the Policing of Labour: The Dialectics of Industrial Discipline' in C. D. Shearing and P. Stenning (eds), *Private Policing*, Sage, Beverly Hills 1986

Heyl, B. S., 'Prostitution: An Extreme Case of Sex Stratification' in F. Alder and R. J. Simon (eds), *The Criminality of Deviant Women*, Houghton Mifflin, Boston 1979

Hill, C., *Reformation to Industrial Revolution*, Pelican Books, Middlesex 1969

Hill, C., *The World Turned Upside Down: Radical Ideas During the English Revolution*, Pelican Books, Middlesex 1972

Hobsbawm, E. J., 'The Crises of the Seventeenth Century' in T. Ashton (ed.), *Crises in Europe 1550–1660*, Doubleday Company, New York 1967

Holmstrom, L. L., and A. W. Burgess, *The Victim of Rape: Institutional Reactions*, John Wiley and Sons, New York 1978

Home Office, 'Crime Prevention; Circular 8/84', Home Office (Issued in connection with the Department of Education and Science, Department of the Environment, Department of Health and Social Security, Welsh Office), London 1984

Home Office, 'The Ethnic Origin of Prisoners', *Statistical Bulletin*, Issues No. 17, 1986

Howson, G., *Thief-Taker General*, Hutchinson, London 1970

Hudson, B., 'The Rising Use of Imprisonment: The Impact of Decarceration Policies', *Critical Social Policy*, 1984, No. 11, Winter

Hurstfield, J., *Freedom, Corruption and Government in Elizabethan England*, Jonathan Cape, London 1973

Hussein, A., 'Extended Review of "Discipline and Punish" by Michel Foucault', *Sociological Review*, 1978, vol. 26, no. 4, November, pp. 932–939

Hutter, B., and G. Williams (eds.), *Controlling Women: The Normal and the Deviant*, Croom Helm, London 1981

Hylton, J. H., 'The Growth of Punishment: Imprisonment and Community Corrections in Canada', *Crime and Social Justice*, 1981, vol. 15, pp. 18–28

Hylton, J. H., 'Rhetoric and Reality: A Critical Appraisal of Community Correctional Programmes', *Crime and Delinquency*, 1982, vol. 28, no. 3, July, pp. 341–373

Hynes, C., 'Private Proprietary Homes for Adults: Their Administration, Management, Control, Operation, Supervision, Funding and Quality', Deputy Attorney General's Office, New York 1977

Ignatieff, M., *A Just Measure of Pain: The Penitentiary in Industrial Europe*, Macmillan, London 1978

Ignatieff, M., 'State, Civil Society and Total Institutions' in S. Cohen and A. Scull (eds), *Social Control and the State*, Martin Robertson, London 1983

Immarigeon, R., 'Victim-Offender Reconciliation Programmes and the Criminal Justice System: Confusion and Challenge', *VORP Network News*, 1984, vol. 3, Autumn

Innis, H. A., *Empire and Communication*, Oxford University Press, Oxford 1950

Jackson, M., *Prisoners of Isolation*, University of Toronto Press, Toronto 1983

Jacobs, J., *The Death and Life of Great American Cities*, Vintage Books Random House, New York 1961

Jacobs, J. B., *New Perspectives on Prisons and Imprisonment*, Cornell University Press, Ithaca 1983

Jacobs, J. B., 'The Politics of Prison Construction', *Review of Law and Social Change*, 1983

Jacobsen, D., 'Scale and Social Control' in F. Barth (ed.), *Scale and Social Organisation*, Universitesforlaget (University Press), Oslo 1978

Jacobson, D., 'From Protective Custody to Treatment in a Hurry', *Social Work*, 1973, vol. 18, no. 2, March, pp. 55–64

James, J., J. Withers, M. Haft, and S. Theiss, *The Politics of*

Prostitution, Social Research Associates, Seattle 1975

James, M., *Social Problems and Social Policy During the Puritan Revolt 1640–1660*, Barnes and Noble, London 1967

Jankovic, I., 'Labour Market and Imprisonment', *Crime and Social Justice*, 1977, vol. 9, pp. 17–31

Janowitz, M., 'Sociological Theory and Social Control', *American Journal of Sociology*, 1975, vol. 81, July, pp. 82–108

Jeffrey, C. R., *Crime Prevention Through Environmental Design*, Sage, Beverly Hills 1971

Jeste, D. V., and R. J. Wyatt, 'In Search of Treatment for Tardive Dyskenesia: A Review of the Literature', *Schizophrenia Bulletin*, 1979, vol. 5, no. 2, pp. 251–293

Joas, H., 'System Integration and Social Integration from the Perspective of Symbolic Interactionism', unpublished paper, 1983

Joas, H., *G. H. Mead: A Contemporary Re-examination of His Thought*, Polity Press, Cambridge 1985

Johansen, T., 'Kulissenes regi' (The Staging of Human Action) in K. Andenæs, T. Johansen, and T. Mathiesen (eds), *Maktens ansikter*, Gylendal 1981

Jones, K., *Lunacy, Law and Conscience, 1744–1845*, Routledge and Kegan Paul, London 1955

Jones, K., 'Deinstitutionalisation in Context', *Milbank Memorial Fund Quarterly*, 1979, vol. 57, pp. 552–569

Jones, K., 'Integration or Disintegration in the Mental Health Services', *Journal of the Royal Society of Medicine*, 1979, vol. 72, pp. 640–648

Jones, K., 'Scull's Dilemma', *British Journal of Psychiatry*, 1982, vol. 141, September, pp. 221–226

Jordan, W. K., *The Charities of London 1480–1660*, Allen and Unwin, London 1960

Journal of Social Issues, Special Issue on Institutions and Alternatives, 1981, vol. 37, no. 3

Judges, A. V. (ed.)., *The Elizabethan Underworld*, Routledge and Sons, London 1930

Juristat, vol. 4, no. 5, Statistics Canada, Canadian Centre for Justice Statistics, Ottawa 1984

Kahn-Hut, R., A. K. Daniels, and R. Colvard (eds), *Women and Work: Problems and Perspectives*, Oxford University Press, New York 1982

Kamen, H. A. F., *The Iron Century: Social Change in Europe 1550–1660*, Cardinal, London 1980

Kaplan. L., 'State Control of Deviant Behaviour: A Critical Essay on Scull's Critique of Community Treatment and Deinstitutionalisation', *Arizona Law Review*, 1978, vol.20, no.1, pp.189–232

Katz, J., 'Concerted Ignorance: The Social Construction of Cover-Up', *Urban Life*, 1979–80, vol.8, no.3, pp.295–316

Kelsen, H., *General Theory of Law and State*, Russell and Russell, New York 1961 (original translation, 1945)

Kempe, A.J., *Historical Notices of the Collegiate Church on Royal Free Chapel and Sanctuary of St. Martin le Grand*, Longmans, London 1825

Kettle, M., 'The Racial Numbers Game in Our Prisons', *New Society*, 1982, vol.61, 30 September, pp.535–537

Kielhofner, G., 'Evaluating Deinstitutionalisation: an Ethnographic Study of Social Policy', PhD Dissertation, School of Public Health, University of California, Los Angeles 1980

King, M., 'Children's Justice: French Style', *Social Work Today*, 1983, December

Kinsey, R., J. Lea, and J. Young, *Losing the Fight Against Crime*, Basil Blackwell, Oxford 1986

Kircher, J., 'A History of Computer Matching in Federal Government Programmes', *Computerworld*, 14 December 1981

Kirk, S., and M. Thierren, 'Community Mental Health Myths and the Fate of Former Hospitalised Patients', *Psychiatry*, 1975, vol.38, pp.209–217

Kitson, F., *Low-Intensity Operations: Subversion, Insurgency and Peace-keeping*, Faber and Faber, London 1971

Kittrie, N.N., *The Right to be Different*, Penguin, Baltimore 1972

Klapmuts, N., *Diversion From the Juvenile Justice System*, National Council on Crime and Delinquency, Washington, DC 1974

Klare, K.E., 'Judicial Deradicalisation of the Wagner Act and the Origins of Modern Legal Consciousness', *Minnesota Law Review*, 1978, vol.62, pp.265–339

Klare, M.T., 'Rent-a-Cop: The Boom in Private Police', *The Nation*, 1975, vol.221, pp.486–491

Klein, D., 'The Etiology of Female Crime: A Review of the Literature', *Issues in Criminology*, 1973, vol.8, Autumn, pp.3–30

Klein, M.W., 'Labeling, Deterrence, and Recidivism: A Study of Police Disposition of Juvenile Offenders', *Social Problems*, 1974, vol.22, no.2, pp.292–303

Klein, M.W., *Alternative Dispositions for Juvenile Offenders*, University of Southern California, Los Angeles 1975

Klein, M.W., 'On the Front End of the Juvenile Justice System' in R.M. Carter and M.W. Klein (eds), *Back on the Street: The Diversion of Juvenile Offenders*, Prentice-Hall, Englewood Cliffs NJ 1976a

Klein, M.W., 'Issues and Realities in Police Diversion Programmes', *Crime and Delinquency*, 1976b, vol.22, no.4, pp.421–427

Klein, M.W., *The Juvenile Justice System*, Sage, Beverly Hills, California 1976c

Klein, M.W., 'Deinstitutionalisation and Diversion of Juvenile Offenders: A Litany of Impediments' in N. Morris and N. Tonry (eds), *Crime and Justice: An Annual Review of Research, vol. 1*, University of Chicago Press, Chicago 1979

Klein, M.W., and K.S. Teilman, *Pivotal Ingredients of Police Juvenile Diversion Programmes*, National Institute for Juvenile Justice and Delinquency Prevention, Washington DC 1976

Klein, M.W., and S. Kutchins, *Pretrial Diversionary Programmes: New Expansions of Law Enforcement Activity Camouflaged as Rehabilitation*, Paper Presented at the Annual Meetings of the Pacific Sociological Society, Hawaii 1975

Knorr-Cetina, K., *The Manufacture of Knowledge: An Essay on the Constructivist and Contextual Nature of Science*, Pergamon Press, Oxford 1981a

Knorr-Cetina, K., 'Introduction: The Micro Sociological Challenge of Macro-sociology: Towards a Reconstruction of Social Theory and Methodology' in K. Knorr-Cetina and A.V. Cicourel (eds), *Advances in Social Theory: Towards an Integration of Micro- and Macro-Sociologies*, Routledge and Kegan Paul, London 1981b

Kobrin, S., and M.W. Klein, *Community Treatment of Juvenile Offenders: The DSO Experiments*, Sage, Beverly Hills CA 1983

Korer, J., 'Not the Same as You: The Social Situation of 190 Schizophrenics Living in the Community', Psychiatric Rehabilitation Association, London 1978

Krajick, K., and S. Gettinger, 'Overcrowded Time: Why Prisons Are Overcrowded and What Can be Done', Edna McConnel Clark Foundation, New York 1982

Krajick, K., 'Prisons for Profit: the Private Alternative', *State Legislatures*, April 1984, pp.9–14

Krisberg, B., and I. Schwartz, 'Rethinking Juvenile Justice', *Crime and Delinquency*, 1983, vol.29, July, pp.333–364

Kuperstock, K., *Worried About Crime?*, Herald Press, Scottdale PA 1985

Kuttner, B., 'The Declining Middle', *Atlantic*, 1983, July, pp.60–72

Lamb, R.H., 'The Mentally Ill in an Urban County Jail', *Archives of General Psychiatry*, 1982, vol.39, January, pp.17–22

Lamo de Espinosa, E., 'Social and Legal Order in Sociological Functionalism', *Contemporary Crises: Crime, Law and the State*, 1980, vol.4, pp.43–76

Langsley, D.G., 'The Community Mental Health Centre: Does It

Treat Patients?', *Hospital and Community Psychiatry*, 1980, vol. 31, pp. 815–819

Laudon, K. C., 'Data Quality and Due Process in Large Record Systems: Criminal Record Systems', *Communications of the Association for Computing Machinery*, Forthcoming

Law Reform Commission of Canada, *Studies on Imprisonment*, Supply and Services Canada, Ottowa 1976

Laws, J. L., *The Second X: Sex Role and Social Role*, Elsevier, New York 1979

Lea, J., and J. Young, *What Is To Be Done About Law and Order?*, Penguin, Harmondsworth 1984

Lears, T. J. J., *No Place of Grace: Antimodernism and the Transformation of American Culture, 1880–1920*, Pantheon Books, New York 1981

Lederer, L. (ed.), *Take Back the Night: Women on Pornography*, William Morrow, New York 1980

Leem, M. W. L., *A History of Police in England*, Methuen, London 1901

Leifer, R., *In the Name of Mental Health*, Aronson, New York 1969

Leiss, W., *The Limits to Satisfaction*, University of Toronto Press, Toronto 1976

Lemert, E. M., *Social Pathology*, McGraw Hill, New York 1951

Lemert, E. M., *Human Deviance, Social Problems and Social Control*, Prentice-Hall, Englewood Cliffs NJ 1967

Lengermann, P. M., 'The Founding of the American Sociological Review', *The American Sociological Review*, 1979, vol. 44, pp. 185–194

Le Bon, G., *Psychologie des Foules*, Alcan, Paris 1892

Lerman, P., *Community Treatment and Social Control*, University of Chicago Press, Chicago 1975

Lerman, P., 'Trends and Issues in the Deinstitutionalisation of Youth in Trouble', *Crime and Delinquency*, 1980, vol. 26, no. 3, July, pp. 281–298

Lerman, P., *Deinstitutionalisation and the Welfare State*, Rutgers University Press, New Brunswick NJ 1982

Lerman, P., 'Child Welfare, the Private Sector, and Community-Based Corrections', *Crime and Delinquency*, 1984, vol. 30, no. 1, January, pp. 5–38

Let's Talk, 30 May 1985, vol. 10, no. 10, p. 7

Levi-Strauss, C., *The Elementary Structures of Kinship*, Beacon Press, Boston 1949

Levine, M., 'Revisionism Revisited? Airline De-regulation and the Public Interest', *Journal of Law and Contemporary Problems*, 1981, vol. 44

Lewis, O. F., *The Development of American Prison Customs, 1776–1845*, Patterson Smith, Montclair NJ 1967 (originally published 1922)

Lewontin, R., S. Rose, and L. Kamin, *Not in Our Genes: Biology, Ideology and Human Nature*, Pantheon, New York 1984

Liaison, 1981, vol. 7, no. 3, pp. 10–13

Liaison, 1983, vol. 11, no. 9, pp. 6–7

Lincoln, S. B., 'Juvenile Referrals and Recidivism' in R. M. Carter and M. W. Klein (eds), *Back on the Street: The Diversion of Juvenile Offenders*, Prentice-Hall, Englewood Cliffs, NJ 1976

Lincoln, S. B., et. al. 'Recidivism Rates of Diverted Juvenile Offenders', Paper Presented at the National Conference on Criminal Justice Evaluation, Washington, DC 1977

Lindblom, C. E., *Politics and Markets*, Basic Books, New York 1977

Lipsky, M., *Street Level Bureaucrats*, Russell Sage, New York 1980

Lipson, M., *On Guard: The Business of Private Security*, Quadrangle/New York Times Book Company, New York 1975

Logan, C. H., and S. P. Rausch, 'Punish and Profit: The Emergence of Private Enterprise Prisons', *Justice Quarterly*, 1985, vol. 2, no. 3, pp. 303–318

Lowman, J., 'Crime, Criminal Justice Policy and the Urban Environment' in D. Herbert, and R. J. Johnston (eds.), *Geography and the Urban Environment: Progress in Research and Applications*, vol. 5, pp. 307–341, Wiley and Sons, New York 1982

Lowman, J., and R. J. Menzies, '"Out of the Fiscal Shadow": Carceral Trends in Canada and the United States', *Crime and Social Justice*, 1987, vol. 26, pp. 95–115

Lukacs, G., *History and Class Consciousness*, MIT Press, Cambridge MA 1971

Lupton, D., *London and the Country Carbonated and Quartered into Several Characters*, N. Oakes, London 1932

MacCaffrey, W. T., 'Place and Patronage in Elizabethan Politics' in S. T. Rindoff (ed.), *Elizabethan Government and Society*, Athlone Press, London 1969

MacLean, B., 'Contradictions in Canadian Prisons: Some Aspects of Social Control Mechanisms' in T. E. Fleming and L. A. Visano (eds), *Deviant Designations: Crime, Law, and Deviance in Canada*, Butterworths, Toronto 1983

MacLean, B., 'State Expenditures on Canadian Criminal Justice' in B. MacLean (ed.), *The Political Economy of Crime: Readings for a Critical Criminology*, Prentice-Hall, Scarborough, Ontario 1986

Mahoney, E. R., *Human Sexuality*, McGraw-Hill Book Company, New York 1983

Mandel, M., 'Democracy, Class and the National Parole Board', *The Criminal Law Quarterly*, 1985, vol. 27, no. 2, pp. 159–181

Marcuse, H., *One-Dimensional Man*, Beacon Press, Boston 1964

Martinson, R., 'What Works? Questions and Answers About Prison

Reform', *The Public Interest*, 1974, vol. 35, Spring, pp. 22–54

Marx, G. T., 'Thoughts on a Neglected Category of Social Movement Participant: The Agent Provocateur and the Informant', *American Journal of Sociology*, 1974, vol. 80, no. 2, pp. 402–442

Marx, G. T., 'The New Police Undercover Work', *Urban Life*, 1980, vol. 8, no. 4, pp. 399–446

Marx, G. T., 'Ironies of Social Control: Authorities as Contributors to Deviance Through Escalation, Nonenforcement and Covert Facilitation', *Social Problems*, 1981, vol. 28, no. 3, pp. 221–246

Marx, G. T., 'Who Really Gets Stung: Some Questions Regarding the New Police Undercover Work', *Crime and Delinquency*, 1982, vol. 28, no. 2, April, pp. 165–193

Marx, G. T., 'Notes on the Discovery, Collection and Assessment of Hidden and Dirty Data' in J. Kitsuse and J. Schneider (eds), *Studies in the Sociology of Social Problems*, Ablex, Norwood, New Jersey 1983

Marx, G. T., 'I'll Be Watching You: The New Surveillance', *Dissent*, 1985, Winter, pp. 26–34

Marx, G. T., 'The Iron Fist and the Velvet Glove: Totalitarian Potentials Within Democratic Structures' in J. Short (ed.), *The Social Fabric*, Sage, Beverly Hills CA, 1986

Marx, K., *Writings of the Young Marx on Philosophy and Society*, L. D. Easton and K. H. Guddat (eds), Anchor Books, New York 1967

Marx, K., *Theories of Surplus-Value*, Pt. I, Progress Publishers, Moscow 1969

Marx, K., *Grundrisse*, Penguin Books, London 1973

Marx, K., *Capital*, vol. I, Lawrence & Wishart 1974

Marx, K., and F. Engels, *The Communist Manifesto*, Penguin, Harmondsworth, England 1967

Mathias, R., and D. Steelman, *Controlling Prison Populations: An Assessment of Current Mechanisms*, National Council on Crime and Delinquency, Ft. Lee 1982

Mathiesen, T., *The Politics of Abolition*, Macmillan, London 1974

Mathiesen, T., *Law, Society and Political Action*, Academic Press, London 1980

Mathiesen, T., 'The Future of Control Systems — The Case of Norway' in D. Garland and P. Young (eds), *The Power to Punish*, Heinemann, London 1983

Mathiesen, T., *Seer - samfunnet* (The Viewer Society), The Norwegian Universities Press 1984, Korpen Publishers, Oslo 1985

Matthews, R., 'Decarceration and the Fiscal Crisis' in B. Fine, R. Kinsey, J. Lea, S. Picciotto, and J. Young (eds), *Capitalism and the Rule off Law*, Hutchinson, London 1979

Mattingly, J. and D. Katkin, *The Youth Service Bureau: A Reinvented*

Wheel?, Paper Presented at the Annual Meeting of the Society for the Study of Social Problems, San Francisco 1975

Mawby, R. I., 'Overcoming the Barriers of Privacy', *Criminology*, 1981, vol. 18, no. 4, pp. 501–521

May Committee Report, *Inquiry into UK Prison Services, Vol. 1*, HMSO, London 1979

Maynard, D. W., *Inside Plea-Bargaining: The Language of Negotiation*, Plenum, New York 1984

Mayo, E., *The Human Problems of an Industrial Civilisation*, Viking, New York 1960

McAleenan, M. *et al.*, *Final Evaluation Report. The West San Gabriel Juvenile Diversion Project*, Occidental College, Los Angeles 1977

McDermott, J., 'Rape Victimisation in 26 American Cities', US Department of Justice, Law Enforcement and Assistance Administration, Washington DC 1979

McGuffin, J., *The Guinea Pigs*, Penguin, London 1974

McIntosh, M., 'Thieves and Fences: Market and Power in Professional Crime', *British Journal of Criminology*, 1976, vol. 16, no. 3, July, pp. 257–266

McKenzie, H., 'Overcrowding in Federal Prisons', Current Issue Review 84–25 E, Political and Social Affairs Division, Research Branch, Library of Parliament, Ottawa 1985

McMullan, J. L., *The Canting Crew: London's Criminal Underworld 1550–1700*, Rutgers University Press, New Brunswick NJ 1984

Mead, G. H., 'Natural Rights and the Theory of the Political Institution', in *Selected Writings*, Bobbs-Merrill, Indianapolis 1964a (originally 1915), pp. 150–170

Mead, G. H., 'The Psychology of Punitive Justice' in *Selected Writings*, Bobbs-Merrill, Indianapolis 1964b (originally 1918), pp. 212–239

Mead, G. H., 'The Genesis of the Self and Social Control', in *Selected Writings*, Bobbs-Merrill, Indianapolis 1964c (originally 1925), pp. 267–93

Mead, G. H., *Mind, Self and Society*, The University of Chicago Press, Chicago 1934

Meier, R. F., 'Perspectives on the Concept of Social Control', *Annual Review of Sociology*, 1982, vol. 8, pp. 35–55

Melossi, D., 'The Penal Question in *Capital*' in A. Platt and P. Takagi (eds), *Punishment and Penal Discipline*, Crime and Social Justice Associates, Berkeley CA 1980

Melossi, D., 'A Politics Without a State: The Concepts of "State" and "Social Control" From European to American Social Science', *Research in Law, Deviance and Social Control*, 1983, vol. 5, pp. 205–222

Melossi, D., 'Punishment and Social Action: Changing Vocabularies of

Punitive Motive within A Political Business Cycle', *Current Perspectives in Social Theory*, 1985a, vol. 6, pp. 169–197

Melossi, D., 'Overcoming the Crisis in Critical Criminology: Toward a Grounded Labelling Theory', *Criminology*, 1985b, vol. 23, no. 2, pp. 193–208

Melossi, D., *The State of Social Control*, Polity Press, Cambridge UK, in press

Melossi, D., and M. Pavarini, *The Prison and the Factory: Origins of the Penitentiary System*, Macmillan, London 1981

Menzies, R. J., 'Doing Violence: Psychiatric Discretion and the Prediction of Dangerousness', PhD Dissertation, University of Toronto Department of Sociology, 1985

Merry, S. E., *Urban Danger*, Temple University Press, Philadelphia 1981

Mesnikoff, A. M., 'Barriers to the Delivery of Mental Health Services: The New York City Experience', *Hospital and Community Psychiatry*, 1978, vol. 29, no. 6, pp. 373–378

Messinger, S. L., 'Confinement in the Community', *Journal of Research in Crime and Delinquency*, 1976, vol. 13, pp. 82–92

Messinger, S. L., 'The Future of Punishment', in J. Skolnick, M. Forst and J. Schreiber (eds) *Crime and Justice in America*, Publishers Inc., Del Mar CA 1977

Messinger, S. L., Personal Correspondence, 1983

Metropolitan Police, 'Commissioner Opens International Security Exhibition', Press Release, Metropolitan Police Press Bureau, 15 April, London 1985

Michalowski, R. J., 'Crime Control in the 1980s: A Progressive Agenda', *Crime and Social Justice*, 1983, Summer, pp. 13–23

Michalowski, R. J., *Order, Law and Crime: An Introduction to Criminology*, Random House, New York 1985

Michalowski, R. J., and M. A. Pearson, 'The Structural Correlates of Imprisonment', Unpublished paper presented at the Annual Meeting of the American Society of Criminology, November, 1983

Milbank Memorial Fund Quarterly, 'Special Issue on Deciphering Deinstitutionalisation', 1979, vol. 57

Milgram, S., 'Some Conditions for Obedience and Disobedience to Authority', *Human Relations*, 1965, vol. 18, January, pp. 57–75

Miller, M. B., 'At Hard Labour: Rediscovering the 19th Century Prison', in A. Platt and P. Takagi (eds), *Punishment and Penal Discipline*, Crime and Social Justice Associates, Berkeley, Cal. 1980

Miller, N., and W. Jensen, 'Reform of Federal Prison Industries: New Opportunities for Public Offenders', *Justice System Journal*, 1974, vol. 1, pp. 1–27

Millman, M., 'She Did It All for Love: A Feminist View of the Sociology of Deviance' in M. Millman and R. M. Kanter (eds), *Another Voice*, Doubleday Anchor Books, New York 1975

Mills, C. W., 'Language, Logic and Culture' in *Power, Politics and People*, Oxford University Press, New York 1963, pp. 423–438

Mills, C. W., 'Situated Actions and Vocabularies of Motive' in *Power, Politics and People*, Oxford University Press, New York 1963, pp. 439–452

Mills, C. W., *Sociology and Pragmatism*, Oxford University Press, New York 1966

Minnesota Correctional Facility, 'Inmate Employee Industry Rules' in *Industry Employee Manual: Minnesota Correctional Facility – Stillwater*, November 1984

Minto, A., 'Changing Clinical Practice, 1950–1980' in P. Bean (ed.), *Mental Illness: Changes and Trends*, John Wiley, Chichester 1983

Mnookin, R., and L. Kornhauser, 'Bargaining in the Shadow of the Law: The Case of Divorce', *Yale Law Journal*, 1979, vol. 88, pp. 950–997

Mohler, H. C., 'Convict Labour Policies', *Journal of Criminal Law and Criminology*, 1925, vol. 15, pp. 530–97

Mollica, R., 'Community in Mental Health Centres: An American Response to Kathleen Jones', *Journal of the Royal Society of Medicine*, 1980, vol. 73, pp. 863–870

Mollica, R., 'From Asylum to Community: The Threatened Disintegration of Public Psychiatry', *New England Journal of Medicine*, 1983, vol. 308, no. 7, pp. 367–373

Monahan, J., 'The Psychiatrisation of Criminal Behaviour: A Reply', *Hospital and Community Psychiatry*, 1973, vol. 24, no. 2, February, pp. 105–107

Moore, S. F., *Law As Process*, Routledge and Kegan Paul, London 1978

Morris, N., *The Future of Imprisonment*, University of Chicago Press, Chicago 1974

Morrison, G., 'Small is Beautiful? Observations on the Dutch Penal Scene', *Prison Service Journal*, 1985, no. 59, July, pp. 2–7

Morrissey, E. R., 'Power and Control Through Discourse: The Case of Drinking and Drinking Problems Among Women', Working Paper no. 9, Department of Sociology and Criminal Justice, Old Dominion University, Norfolk 1985

Morrissey, J. P., 'Deinstitutionalising the Mentally Ill: Process, Outcome, and New Directions' in W. Gove (ed.), *Deviance and Mental Illness*, Sage, Beverly Hills, California 1982, pp. 147–176

Morrissey, J. P., H. Goldman, and L. Klerman, *The Enduring Asylum: Cycles of Institutional Reform at Worcester State Hospital*, Grune and Stratton, New York 1980

Mullen, J., *The Dilemma of Diversion: Resource Materials on Adult Pretrial Diversion Intervention Programmes*, Government Printing Office, Washington DC 1975

Mullen, J., 'Corrections and the Private Sector', *Research in Brief*, March 1985, National Institute of Justice

Murray, C., 'The Physical Environment and the Community Control of Crime' in J.Q. Wilson (ed.), *Crime and Public Policy*, ICS Press, San Francisco 1983, pp.107–124

Murray, C., T. Motoyama, W. Rouse, and H. Rubenstein, *The Link Between Crime and the Built Environment: The Current State of Knowledge*, vol.1, American Institute for Research, Washington 1980

Muraskin, W.A., 'The Social Control Theory of History', *Journal of Social History*, 1976, vol.9, no.4, pp.559–556

Murphy, J., and W. Datel, 'A Cost Benefit Analysis of Community Versus Institutional Living', *Hospital and Community Psychiatry*, 1976, vol.25, pp.165–170

Musheno, M.C., 'Criminal Diversion and Social Control', *Social Science Quarterly*, 1982, vol.63, no.2, June, pp.280–292

Myren, R.A., 'Justiciology: An Idea Whose Time Has Come', *Justice Reporter*, 1980, vol.1, April, pp.1–7

Myklebust, D., 'Statens bygninger' (The State's Buildings), Samitiden, 1984

Nairn, D.A., 'A Victim's Father's Perspective on Inmate Releases', *Contact*, 1985, vol.4, no.1, pp.2, 4

National Association of Probation Officers, 'Criminal Justice — An Alternative Strategy', National Association of Probation Officers, London 1985

National Institute of Mental Health, *Statistical Notes*, NIMH, Rockville MD 1975

National Legislative Conference on Arson, *Anti-Arson Manual*, Columbus OH 1982

Neumann, F., *The Democratic and the Authoritarian State*, Free Press, New York 1957

New Jersey State Commission of Investigation, *Abuses and Irregularities in New Jersey's Boarding Home Industry*, State Commission of Investigation, New Jersey 1978

Newman, G., *The Punishment Response*, Lippincott, Philadelphia 1978

Newman, O., *Defensible Space*, Macmillan, New York 1972

Newman, O., *Architectural Design for Crime Prevention*, US Government Printing Office, Washington DC 1973

Newman, O., and K. Franck, 'Stability in Urban Housing Developments — Complete Report', Institute for Community

Design Analysis, Washington DC 1980

New York Civil Liberties Union, *An Evaluation of New York State's Wage Reporting System: The Real Cost of Computer Matching*, New York 1982

New York Times, 21 December 1980, 3 August 1982, 7 November 1982, 20 May 1983

Novak, M., 'Mediating Institutions: The Communitarian Individual in America', *The Public Interest*, 1982, no. 68, pp. 3–20

Nozick, R., *Anarchy, State and Utopia*, Basic Books, New York 1974

Nuffield, J., *Parole Decision-Making in Canada*, Solicitor General, Ottawa, Canada 1982

Oakeshott, R., *The Case for Worker's Co-ops*, Routledge and Kegan Paul, London 1978

Oakley, A., *Woman's Work*, Vintage Books, New York 1976

O'Brien, P., *The Promise of Punishment: Prisons in Nineteenth Century France*, Princeton University Press, Princeton 1982

O'Connor, J. R., *The Fiscal Crisis of the State*, St. Martin's Press, New York 1973

Odegard, O., 'Changes in the Prognosis of Functional Psychosis Since the Days of Kraepelin'. *British Journal of Psychiatry*, 1967, vol. 113, pp. 813–822

Offe, C., *Contradictions in the Welfare State*, Hutchinson, London 1984

Olsen, J. P., and H. Sætren, 'Massemedier, eliter og menigmann' (Mass Media, Elites and Laymen) in J. P. Olsen (ed.), *Meninger om makt*, Universiteforlaget, Oslo 1980

Orlans, W., 'An American Death Camp'. *Politics* 1948, vol. 5, pp. 162–8

Orwell, G., *1984*, Harcourt Brace, New York 1949

Osterberg, D., *Makt og materiell* (Power and Material), Pax 1971

Ouimet, R., (Chairman, Committee on Corrections), *Toward Unity: Criminal Justice and Corrections*, Queen's Printer, Ottawa 1969

Outerbridge, W., 'The Unfulfilled Promise of the Justice Mode'. Paper presented at the Ninth Annual Conference of the American Probation and Parole Association, Boston, Mass., 26 August 1984

Outerbridge, W., 'Abolish Parole: Why Ask the Wrong Question?' Paper presented at the School of Criminology, University of Montreal, 3 October 1985

Palmer, T., 'Martinson Revisited', *Journal of Research in Crime and Delinquency*, 1975, vol. 12, no. 2, July, pp. 133–152

Park, R. E., 'Symbiosis and Socialisation: A Frame of Reference for the Study of Society', *American Journal of Sociology*, 1939, vol. 45, pp. 1–25

Park, R. E., *The Immigrant Press and Its Control*, Greenwood, Westport CT 1970

Park, R. E., *The Crowd and the Public*, The University of Chicago Press,

Chicago 1972

Park, R. E., and E. W. Burgess, *Introduction to the Science of Sociology*, The University of Chicago Press, Chicago 1969

Parker, D., *Crime By Computer*, Scribner and Sons, New York 1976

Parker, E. B., 'Technological Change and the Mass Media' in I. di Sola Pool and W. Schramm (eds), *Handbook of Communication*, Rand McNally, Chicago 1973

Parkes, J., *Travel in England in the Seventeenth Century*, Oxford University Press, London 1925

Parry-Jones, W., *The Trade in Lunacy*, Routledge and Kegan Paul, London 1972

Parsons, T., *The Structure of Social Action*, McGraw-Hill, New York 1937

Parsons, T., *The Social System*, Free Press, New York 1951

Parsons, T., 'On Building Social System Theory: A Personal History' in *Social Systems and the Evolution of Action Theory*, pp. 22–76, Free Press, New York 1977

Pask, E. D., K. E. Mahoney, and C. A. Brown, *Women, the Law and the Economy*, Butterworths, Toronto 1985

Pearson, G., *The Deviant Imagination: Psychiatry, Social Work and Social Change*, Macmillan, London 1975

Peltzman, S., 'Toward a More General Theory of Regulation', *Journal of Law and Economics*, 1976, vol. 14

Penrose, L. S., 'Mental Disease and Crime: Outline of a Comparative Study of European Statistics', *British Journal of Medical Psychology*, 1939, vol. 18, pp. 1–15

Pepinsky, H. E., 'A Radical Alternative to "Radical" Criminology' in J. A. Inciardi (ed.), *Radical Criminology: The Coming Crisis*, Sage, Beverly Hills, California 1980

Pepinsky, H. E., 'A Season of Disenchantment: Trends in Chinese Justice Reconsidered', *International Journal of the Sociology of Law*, 1982, vol. 10, no. 3, August, pp. 277–285

Pepinsky, H. E., 'Better Living through Police Discretion', *Law and Contemporary Problems*, 1984, vol. 47, no. 4, Autumn, pp. 249–267

Pepinsky, H. E., 'The Sociology of Justice', *Annual Review of Sociology*, 1986, vol. 12, pp. 93–108

Pepinsky, H. E., and P. Jesilow, *Myths That Cause Crime*, 2nd ed., Seven Locks Press, Cabin John MD 1985

Perrolle, J., 'Computer Generated Social Problems', Paper Delivered at the Society for the Study of Social Problems Meeting, Detroit 1983

Peterson, T. K., 'The Dade County Pretrial Intervention Project: Formalisation of the Diversion Function and its Impact on the Criminal Justice System', *University of Miami Law Review*, 1973, vol. 28, pp. 86–114

Pitchess, P., 'Law Enforcement Screening for Diversion' in R. Carter and M. W. Klein (eds), *Back on the Street: The Diversion of Juvenile Offenders*, Prentice-Hall, Englewood Cliffs NJ 1976, pp. 221–233

Pitts, J., 'Thinking About Intermediate Treatment', *Youth and Policy*, 1987, (forthcoming)

Platt, T., 'Crime and Punishment in the United States: Immediate and Long Term Reforms from a Marxist Perspective', *Crime and Social Justice*, 1982, vol. 18, pp. 38–45

Platt, T., 'Managing the Crisis: Austerity and the Penal System' in *World Capitalist Crisis and the Rise of the Right*, Synthesis Publications, San Francisco 1982

Platt, T., and P. Takagi, 'Intellectuals For Law and Order: A Critique of the New "Realists"', *Crime and Social Justice*, 1977, vol. 8, pp. 1–6

Poggi, G., *The Development of the Modern State*, Hutchinson, London 1978

Polk, K., 'Delinquency Prevention and the Youth Service Bureau', *Criminal Law Bulletin*, 1971, vol. 7, pp. 490–529

Polk, K., 'Youth Service Bureaus: The Records and Prospects', Mimeo, University of Oregon, Eugene 1981

Poole, R. W. Jr, 'Objections to Privatisation', *Policy Review*, 1983, vol. 24, pp. 105–119

Posner, R., 'Theories of Economic Regulation', *Beu Journal of Economics and Management Science*, 1976, vol. 14

Pospisil, L., *Anthropology of Law*, Harper and Row, New York 1971

Poster, M., *Marxism and History: Mode of Production versus Mode of Information*, Polity Press, Cambridge 1984

Pound, J., *Poverty and Vagrancy in Tudor England*, Longman, London 1971

President's Council on Integrity and Efficiency, *A Summary Report of Inspector General's Activities*, Washington DC 1983

President's Commission on Law Enforcement and the Administration of Justice, *The Challenge of Crime in a Free Society: Juvenile Delinquency*, US Government Printing Office, Washington DC 1967

Prestwich, M., *Cranfield: Politics and Profits Under the Early Stuarts, The Career of Lionel Cranfield, Earl of Middlesex*, Clarendon Press, Oxford 1966

Pringle, P., *Hue and Cry: The Birth of the British Police*, Methuen Press, London 1955

Psychiatric News, 'More and More Mentally Ill Being Held Behind Prison Bars, Psychiatrist Reports', *Psychiatric News*, 1983, vol. 7, no. 7, October, p. 12

Quay, H.C., and C.T. Love, 'The Effect of Juvenile Diversion Programmes on Rearrests', *Criminal Justice and Behaviour*, 1977, vol. 4, no. 4, December, pp. 377–396

Quinney, R., *Criminology* Second Edition, Little Brown, Boston 1979

Rabkin, J.G., 'Epidemiology of Forcible Rape', *American Journal of Orthopsychiatry*, 1979, vol. 49, no. 4, pp. 634–647

Rajchman, J., 'The Story of Foucault's History', *Social Text*, 1983/84, No. 8, Winter

Rawls, J., *A Theory of Justice*, Harvard University Press, Cambridge, Massachusetts 1971

Rawls, W., *Cold Storage*, Simon and Schuster, New York 1980

Raynor, J.L. and G.T. Crook, (eds), *The Complete Newgate Calendar*, Navarre Society, London 1926

Redhead, S., 'Marxist Theory, the Rule of Law and Socialism', in P. Beirne and R. Quinney (eds), *Marxism and Law*, Wiley, New York 1982, pp. 328–342

Reich, W., *The Mass Psychology of Fascism*, Farrar, Straus & Giroux, New York 1970

Reichman, N., 'Ferretting Out Fraud: The Manufacture and Control of Fraudulent Insurance Claims', PhD Dissertation, Massachusetts Institute of Technology, 1983

Reichman, N., 'Managing Crime Risks: Towards an Insurance Based Model of Social Control' in S. Spitzer and A. Scull (eds.), *Research in Law, Deviance and Social Control* vol. 8, JAI Press, Greenwich CT 1986

Reichman, N., 'The Widening Webs of Surveillance: An Examination of Private Police Unravelling Deceptive Claims' in C.D. Shearing and P.C. Stenning (eds), *Private Police: Crime and Justice Annual* vol. 21, Sage Publications, Beverly Hills, CA 1987

Reiman, J.H., *The Rich Get Richer and the Poor Get Prison*, 2nd Ed., John Wiley, New York 1984

Reiss, A.J., *The Police and the Public*, Yale University Press, New Haven CT 1971

Reiss, A.J., 'The Legitimacy of Intrusions into Private Space' in C.D. Shearing and P.C. Stenning (eds), *Private Police: Crime and Justice Annual*, vol. 21, Sage, Beverly Hills CA 1987

Reker, G.T., *et al.*, 'Juvenile Diversion: Conceptual Issues and Programme Effectiveness', *Canadian Journal of Criminology*, 1980, vol. 22, pp. 36–50

Report of the Federal Advisory Committee on False Identification, *The Criminal use of False Identification*, US Government Printing Office, Washington DC 1976

Reppetto, T.A., 'Crime Prevention and the Displacement Phenomenon', *Crime and Delinquency*, 1976, vol.22, April, pp.166–177

Reske, H.J., 'Burger Wants Bench Vacancies Filled', *Plattsburgh Press Republican*, 30 December 1985, p.77

Reuter, P., and J.B. Rubenstein, 'Fact, Fancy and Organised Crime', *Public Interest*, 1978, vol.53, Autumn, pp.45–67

Richman, A., and P. Harris, 'Mental Hospital Deinstitutionalisation in Canada', *International Journal of Mental Health*, 1983, vol.11, Winter, pp.64–83

Robbins, I.P., 'Statement of Ira P. Robbins Before the Subcommittee on Courts, Civil Liberties and the Administration of Justice of the House Committee on the Judiciary Concerning *Privatisation of Corrections*, 13 November 1985

Roberts, M., *The Military Revolutions 1560–1660*, University of Belfast Press, Belfast 1956

Rollin, H., 'From Patients into Vagrants', *New Society*, 15 January 1970, pp.90–93

Roper, C., 'Taming the Universal Machine' in C. Aubrey and P. Chilton (eds), *Nineteen Eighty Four: Autonomy, Control and Communication*, Comedia Publishing, London 1983

Rorty, R., *Consequences of Pragmatism*, University of Minneapolis, Minneapolis 1982

Rose, S.M., 'Deciphering Deinstitutionalisation: Complexities in Policy and Programme Analysis', *Milbank Memorial Fund Quarterly/Health and Society*, 1979, vol.57, no.4, Autumn, pp.429–460

Ross, E.A., *Social Control: A Survey of the Foundations of Order*, Macmillan, New York 1901

Ross, E.A., 'Social Control' in *Social Control and the Foundations of Society*, Beacon, Boston 1959

Ross, H.L., and V. Sawhill, 'Time of Transition: The Growth of Families Headed by Women', Urban Institute, Washington DC 1975

Roth, R.T., and J. Lerner, 'Sex-Based Discrimination in the Mental Institutionalisation of Women', in D.K. Weisberg, *Women and the Law*, Schenkman Publishing Company Inc., Cambridge MA 1982, pp.107–140

Rothman, D.J., *The Discovery of the Asylum*, Little, Brown, Boston 1971

Rothman, D.J., 'Decarcerating Prisoners and Patients', *Civil Liberties Review*, 1973, no.1, pp.8–30

Rothman, D.J., 'Prisons and the Failure Model', *Nation*, 1974, vol.219, December, pp.656–659

Rothman, D.J., *Conscience and Convenience: The Asylum and its Alternatives in Progressive America*, Little, Brown, Boston 1980

Rothschild-Whitt, J., 'The Collective Organisation: An Alternate to Rational Bureaucratic Models', *American Sociological Review*, 1979, vol. 44, no. 4, pp. 509–527

Rule, J., *et al.*, *The Politics of Privacy*, New American Library, New York 1980

Rule, J., D. McAdam, L. Stearns and D. Uglow, 'Documentary Identification and Mass Surveillance in the United States', *Social Problems*, 1981, vol. 31, no. 2, pp. 222–234

Rumbelow, D., *I Spy Blue: The Police and Crime in the City of London from Elizabeth I to Victoria*, Macmillan Press, London 1971

Rusche, G., and O. Kirchheimer, *Punishment and Social Structure*, Russell and Russell, New York 1968 (originally published 1939)

Russel, D. E. H., *The Politics of Rape*, Stein and Day, New York 1975

Rutherford, A., *Growing Out of Crime*, Penguin, Harmondsworth 1986

Rutherford, A., and O. Bengur, *Community Based Alternatives to Juvenile Incarceration*, US Government Printing Office, Washington DC 1976

Rutherford, A., and R. McDermott, *Juvenile Diversion*, US Government Printing Office, Washington DC 1976

Ryan, W., *Blaming the Victim*, Vintage Books, New York 1972

Salamon, E., *The Kept Woman: Mistresses in the '80s*, Orbis Publishing Ltd, London 1984

Salgado, G., *The Elizabethan Underworld*, Methuen, London 1977

Salisbury-Jones, G. T., *Street Life in Medieval England*, Pen-In-Hand Publishing Company, Oxford 1938

Samaha, J., *Law and Order in Historical Perspective: The Case of Elizabethan Essex*, Academic Press, London 1974

Sanday, P. R., 'The Socio-Cultural Context of Rape: A Cross Cultural Study', *Journal of Social Issues*, 1981, vol. 37, no. 4, pp. 5–27

Santos, B. S., 'Law and Community: The Changing Nature of State Power in Late Capitalism', *International Journal of the Sociology of Law*, 1980, vol. 8, no. 4, pp. 379–397

Santos, B. S., 'On Modes of Production of Social Power and Law', Working Paper, The Institute of Legal Studies of the University of Wisconsin, Madison 1984

Santos, B. S., 'On Modes of Production of Law and Social Power', *International Journal of the Sociology of Law*, 1985, vol. 13, no. 4, pp. 299–336

Sapir, E., 'Communication', *Encyclopedia of Social Science*, 1933, vol. 3–4, pp. 78–80

Sarri, R., 'Juvenile Law: How It Penalises Females', in L. Crites (ed.), *The Female Offender*, D. C. Heath, Lexington MA 1976

Sarri, R., 'Juvenile Aid Panels: An Alternative to Juvenile Court Processing', in P. L. Brantingham and T. Blomberg (eds), *Courts and Diversion: Policy and Operation Studies*, Sage, Beverly Hills CA 1979

Savas, E. S., *Privatising the Public Sector*, Chatham House Publishers, Chatham, NJ 1982

Schaller, J., 'Normalising the Prison Work Environment' in D. Fogel and J. Hudson (eds), *Justice as Fairness: Perspectives on the Justice Model*, Anderson Publishing, Cincinatti OH 1981

Scheff, T. J., 'Toward a Sociological Model of Consensus', *American Sociological Review*, 1967, vol. 32, pp. 32–46

Schneider, L., 'Dialectic in Sociology', *American Sociological Review*, 1971, vol. 36, pp. 667–678

Schoen, K. F., 'Private Prison Operators', *The New York Times*, 28 March 1985, p. A31

Schur, E. M., *Labelling Women Deviant: Gender, Stigma, and Social Control*, Random House, New York 1984

Schwartz, R. D., 'Social Factors in the Development of Legal Control: A Case Study of Two Israeli Settlements', *Yale Law Journal*, 1954, vol. 63 (February), pp. 471–91

Schwartz, T., *The Responsive Chord*, Anchor, New York 1974

Schwendinger, H., and J. Schwendinger, 'Defenders of Order or Guardians of Human Rights?', *Issues in Criminology*, 1970, vol. 5, no. 2, pp. 123–157

Schwendinger, J., and H. Schwendinger, 'Rape and Inequality and Levels of Violence', *Crime and Social Justice*, 1981, vol. 16, Winter, pp. 3–31

Scott, T. M. and M. McPherson, 'The Development of the Private Sector of the Criminal Justice System', *Law and Society Review*, 1971, vol. 6, no. 2, pp. 267–288

Scraton, P., and N. South, 'The Ideological Construction of the Hidden Economy: Private Justice and Work Related Crime', *Contemporary Crises: Crime, Law and Social Policy*, 1984, vol. 8, no. 1, pp. 1–18

Scull, A., *Decarceration: Community Treatment and the Deviant: A Radical View*, Prentice-Hall, Englewood Cliffs NJ 1977 (2nd Edition, Polity Press, Cambridge 1984)

Scull, A., *Museums of Madness*, St Martin's Press, New York 1979

Scull, A., 'A New Trade in Lunacy: The Recommodification of the Mental Patient', *American Behavioral Scientist*, 1981, vol. 24, pp. 741–54

Scull, A., 'Community Corrections: Panacea, Progress or Pretense?' in D. Garland and P. Young (eds), *The Power to Punish*, Heinemann, London 1983

Scully, D., and J. Marolla, 'Rape and Psychiatric Vocabularies of Motive: Alternative Perspectives', in A. W. Burgess (ed.),

Handbook on Rape and Sexual Assault, Garland Publishing, New York 1984

Seaver, D.O., and A. Wainhouse, *The Marquis de Sade*, Grove Press Inc, New York 1966

Sedgwick, P., *Psychopolitics*, Pluto Press, London 1982

Segal, S.P., 'Life in Board and Care: Its Political and Social Context', in *Where is My Home?*, NTIS, Scottsdale AR 1974

Seitz, S., W. Rhodes, and T. Blomberg, 'The Demoines Exemplary Project', Final Report Submitted to the Law Enforcement and Assistance Administration, 1978

Selznick, J., 'Foundations of the Theory of Organisation', *American Sociological Review*, 1948, vol.13, pp.25–35

Sexton, G.E., F.C. Farrow, C. Franklin, and B.J. Auerbach, 'The Private Sector and Prison Industries', *Research in Brief*, August 1985, US National Institute of Justice

Shakespeare, W., *The Tragedy of Macbeth*, Yale University Press, New Haven 1954

Shearing, C.D., *Dial-a-Cop: A Study of Police Mobilisation*, University of Toronto Centre of Criminology, Toronto 1984

Shearing, C.D., M.B. Farnell, and P.C. Stenning, *Contract Security in Ontario*, University of Toronto Centre of Criminology, Toronto 1980

Shearing, C.D., and P.C. Stenning, 'Modern Private Security: Its Growth and Implications' in M. Tonry and N. Morris (eds), *Crime and Justice: An Annual Review of Research, vol.3*, University of Chicago Press, Chicago 1981, pp.193–245

Shearing, C.D., and P.C. Stenning, 'Private Security: Implications for Social Control', *Social Problems*, 1983, vol.30, no.5, June, pp.493–506

Shearing, C.D., and P.C. Stenning, 'From the Panopticon to Disney World: The Development of Discipline' in A.N. Doob and E.L. Greenspan (eds), *Perspectives in Criminal Law – Essays in Honour of John Ll.J. Edwards*, Canada Law Book Company, Aurora, Canada 1985, pp.335–349

Sheehan, D.N. and J. Atkinson, 'Comparative Cost of State Hospitals and Community Based Inpatient Care in Texas', *Hospital and Community Psychiatry*, 1974, vol.25, pp.242–4

Shewan, I., 'The Decision to Parole: Balancing the Rehabilitation of the Offender with the Protection of the Public', *Canadian Journal of Criminology*, 1985, vol.27, no.3, pp.327–339

Shibutani, T., 'Reference Groups and Social Control' in A.M. Rose (ed.), *Human Behaviour and Social Processes*, Houghton Mifflin, Boston 1962, pp.128–147

Sighele, S., *La Folla Delinquente*, Bocca, Torino 1894

Silbert, M.H., and A.M. Pines, 'Occupational Hazards of Street Prostitutes', *Criminal Justice and Behaviour*, 1981, vol.8, no.4, pp.395–399

Silbey, S., and E. Bittner, 'The Availability of Law', *Law and Policy Quarterly*, 1982, vol.4, no.4, pp.399–434

Singer, N.M., 'Incentives and the Use of Prison Labour', *Crime and Delinquency*, 1973, vol.19, pp.200–211

Singlemann, J., 'The Sectoral Transformation of the Labour Force in Seven Industrialised countries, 1920–1970', *American Journal of Sociology*, 1978, vol.83, pp.1224–1234

Sklare, M.J., 'On the Proletarian Revolution and the End of Political-Economic Society', *Radical America*, 1969, vol.3, pp.1–41

Skocpol, T., 'Political Response to Capitalist Crisis: Neo-Marxist Theories of the State and the Case of the New Deal', *Politics and Society*, 1980, vol.10, no.2, pp.155–201

Skolnick, J., and J. Woodworth, 'Bureaucracy, Information and Social Control: A Study of a Morals Detail', in D. Bordua (ed.), *The Police*, Wiley and Sons, New York 1967, pp.99–136

Skowronek, S., *Building a New American State*, Cambridge University Press, Cambridge 1982

Slack, P.A., 'Poverty and Politics in Salisbury 1597–1666', in *Crises and Order in English Towns 1500–1700*, Routledge and Kegan Paul, London 1972

Slack, P.A., 'Vagrants and Vagrancy in England 1598–1664', *Economic History Review*, 1974, vol.27, 2nd series, pp.360–379

Slater, P., *The Pursuit of Loneliness*, Beacon Press, Boston 1970

Smart, C., *Women, Crime and Criminology: A Feminist Critique*, Routledge and Kegan Paul, London 1977

Smart, C., *The Ties That Bind: Law, Marriage and the Reproduction of Patriarchal Relations*, Routledge and Kegan Paul, London 1984

Smith, D.E., and S.J. David (eds), *Women Look at Psychiatry*, Press Gang Publishers, Vancouver 1975

Smith, T.V., 'The Social Philosophy of George Herbert Mead', *The American Journal of Sociology*, 1931, vol.37, p.369

Snitow, A., C. Stansell, and S. Thompson (eds), *Powers of Desire: The Politics of Sexuality*, Monthly Review Press, New York 1983

Solicitor General Canada, *Study of Conditional Release*, Report of the Working Group, Ministry of Supply and Services Canada, Ottawa 1981a

Solicitor General Canada, *Mandatory Supervision: A Discussion Paper*, Ministry of Supply and Services Canada, Ottawa, 1981b

Solicitor General Canada, 'Correctional Law Review: First Consultation Paper', *Mimeo*, Ottawa 1983

Solicitor General Canada, *Selected Trends in Canadian Criminal Justice*,

Ministry of Supply and Services Canada, Ottawa 1984
Solicitor General Canada, *Solicitor General Annual Report 1983–1984*, Ministry of Supply and Services, Ottawa 1984
Solicitor General Canada, *Solicitor General Annual Report 1984–1985*, Ministry of Supply and Services, Ottawa 1985
Soloman, E.B., R. Baird and L. Everstire, 'Assessing the Community Care of Chronic Psychotic Patients', *Hospital and Community Psychiatry*, 1980, vol.31, pp.113–16
South, N., 'Private Security, the Division of Policing Labour and the Commercial Compromise of the State' in S. Spitzer and A. Scull (eds), *Research in Law, Deviance and Social Control*, vol.6, JAI Press, Greenwich CT 1984, pp.171–198
South, N., 'Private Security and Social Control: The Private Security in the United Kingdom, its Commercial Functions and Public Accountability', PhD Thesis, Centre for Occupational and Community Research, Middlesex Polytechnic, London 1985
South, N., 'Law, Profit and "Private Persons": Some Aspects of Private and Public Arrangements for Policing and Social Control in 17th and 18th Century England' in C.D. Shearing and P.C. Stenning (eds.), *Private Policing: Crime and Justice Systems Annual*, vol.21, Sage, Beverly Hills 1986
Spergel, A.I., *et. al.*, 'Response of Organisations and Community to a Deinstitutionalisation Strategy', *Crime and Delinquency*, 1982, vol.28, no.3, pp.426–449
Spitzer, S., 'Punishment and Social Organization: A Study of Durkheim's Theory of Penal Evolution', *Law and Society Review*, 1975a, vol.9, no.4, Summer, pp.613–637
Spitzer, S., 'Towards a Marxian Theory of Deviance', *Social Problems*, 1975b, vol.22, no.5, pp.638–651
Spitzer, S., 'The Rationalisation of Crime Control in Capitalist Society', *Contemporary Crises*, 1979, vol.3, no.2, pp.187–206
Spitzer, S., 'The Dialectics of Formal and Informal Control' in R. Abel (ed.), *The Politics of Informal Justice*, vol. 1, Academic Press, New York 1982
Spitzer, S., 'The Rationalisation of Crime Control in Capitalist Society', in S. Cohen and A.T. Scull, *Social Control and the State*, Martin Robertson, Oxford 1983a, pp.312–333
Spitzer, S., 'Marxist Perspectives in the Sociology of Law', in R.H. Turner and J.F. Short, *Annual Review of Sociology*, vol.9, 1983b, pp.103–124
Spitzer, S. and A.T. Scull, 'Privatisation and Capitalist Development: The Case of Private Police', *Social Problems*, 1977, vol.25, no.1, pp.18–29
Spitzer, S., and A.T. Scull, 'Social Control in Historical Perspective:

From Private to Public Responses to Crime' in D. Greenberg (ed.), *Corrections and Punishment*, Sage, Beverly Hills 1980

Stang Dahl T. and A. Snare, 'The Coercion of Privacy: A Feminist Perspective' in C. Smart and B. Smart (eds), *Women, Sexuality and Social Control*, Routledge and Kegan Paul, London 1978

Staples, W.C., and C.A.B. Warren, 'Social Junk as Human Commodities: A Historical Perspective on the Privatisation and Profitisation of Social Control', Paper Presented at the Annual Meetings of the Pacific Sociological Association, San Jose 1983

State of Florida, *An Implementation Manual for Community Control*, Florida Department of Corrections, Tallahassee, Florida 1983

Statsky, W.P., 'Juvenile Courts: Decentralising Juvenile Jurisprudence', *Capital University Law Review*, 1974, vol.3, no.1, pp.1–31

Steadman, H.J., 'Decentralisation of Social Control', Presentation at Symposium, School of Criminology, Simon Fraser University, Burnaby, British Columbia, 4–5 April 1984

Steadman, H.J., J. Monahan, B. Duffee, E. Hartstone, and P.C. Robbins, 'The Impact of State Mental Hospital Deinstitutionalisation on the United States Prison Population, 1968–1978', *Journal of Criminal Law and Criminology*, 1984, vol.75, no.2, Summer, pp.474–490

Steadman, H.J., and S.A. Ribner, 'Changing Perceptions of the Mental Health Needs of Inmates in Local Jails', *American Journal of Psychiatry*, 1980, vol.137, no.9, September, pp.1115–1116

Stedman-Jones, G., 'Class Expression Versus Social Control', *History Workshop Journal*, 1977, vol.4, pp.162–170

Steffensmeier, D.J., 'Sex Differences in Patterns of Adult Crime, 1965–1977: A Review and Assessment', *Social Forces*, 1980, vol.58, no.4, June, pp.1080–1108

Stein, L.J. and M.A. Test, 'Alternatives to Mental Hospital Treatment'. *Archive of General Psychiatry*, 1980, vol.37, pp.392–7

Steinert, H., 'Beyond Crime and Punishment', *Contemporary Crises: Crime, Law and Social Control*, 1986, vol.10, no.1, pp.21–38

Stelovitch, S., 'From the Hospital to the Prison: A Step Forward in Deinstitutionalisation?' *Hospital and Community Psychiatry*, 1979, vol.30, September, pp.118–120

Stenning, P.C., and M.F. Cornish, *The Legal Regulation and Control of Private Policing in Canada*, University of Toronto Centre of Criminology, Toronto 1975

Stenning, P.C., and C.D. Shearing, 'The Quiet Revolution: The Nature, Development and General Legal Implications of Private Security in Canada', *Criminal Law Quarterly*, 1980, vol.22, pp.220–248

Stigler, G., 'The Theory of Economic Regulation', *Bell Journal of Economics and Management Science*, 1971, vol.2

Stinchcombe, A.L., 'Institutions of Privacy in the Determination of Police Administrative Practice', *American Journal of Sociology*, 1963, vol.69, no.2, pp.150–160

Stockard, J., and M.M. Johnson, *Sex Roles: Sex Inequality and Sex Role Development*, Prentice-Hall Inc, Englewood Cliffs, New Jersey 1980

Stoesz, D., 'A Wake for the Welfare State: Social Welfare and the Neoconservative Challenge', 1981, Mimeo

Stone, L., *The Crisis of Aristocracy 1553–1641*, Clarendon Press, Oxford 1965

Stone, L., 'The Fruits of Office: The Case of Robert Cecil, First Earle of Salisbury, 1596–1612' in F.J. Fisher (ed.), *Essays in the Economic and Social History of Tudor and Stuart England*, Cambridge University Press, Cambridge 1961

Stow, J., *The Survey of London*, Everyman Library Edition, J.M. Dent and Sons Limited, London 1958

Streib, V.L., 'Expanding a Traditional Criminal Justice Curriculum Into a Social Control Curriculum', *Journal of Criminal Justice*, 1977, vol.5, Summer, 1977 pp.165–169

Sudnow, D., 'Normal Crimes', *Social Problems*, 1965, vol.12, no.3, pp.255–276

Sumner, C., *Reading Ideologies: An Investigation into a Marxist Theory of Ideology and Law*, Academic Press, London 1979

Sutherland, E.H., 'White-Collar Criminality', *American Sociological Review*, 1940, vol.5, February, pp.1–12

Sutherland, E.H., 'Is "White-Collar Crime" Crime?', *American Sociological Review*, 1945, vol.10, April, pp.132–139

Sutherland, E.H., and D.R. Cressey, *Principles of Criminology* 6th Edition, J.B. Lippincott, Philadelphia PA 1960

Swart, K., *The Sale of Offices in the Seventeenth Century*, Martinus Nijhoff, The Hague 1949

Swingewood, A., *Marx and Modern Social Theory*, Macmillan, London 1975

Szasz, T.S., *The Manufacture of Madness*, Harper, New York 1970

Talbott, J.A., 'Toward a Public Policy on the Chronic Mental Patient', *American Journal of Orthopsychiatry*, 1980, vol.50, pp.43–53

Tappan, P.W., 'Who is the Criminal?', *American Sociological Review*, 1947, vol.12, February, pp.96–102

Tawney, R.H., *The Agrarian Problem in the Sixteenth Century*, Longman and Green, London 1912

Taylor, C., 'Foucault on Freedom and Truth', *Political Theory*, 1984, vol.12, no.2, pp.152–183

Taylor, I., *Law and Order: Arguments for Socialism*, Macmillan, London 1981

Teplin, L. A., 'Criminalising Mental Disorders: The Comparative Arrest Rate of the Mentally Ill', *American Psychologist*, 1984, vol. 39, no. 7, July, pp. 794–803

Teppe, S. J., and J. F. Haas, 'Prevalence of Tardive Dyskinesia', *Journal of Clinical Psychiatry*, 1979, vol. 40, pp. 508–16

Test, M. A., 'Effective Community Treatment of the Chronically Mentally Ill: What is Necessary?' *Journal of Social Issues*, 1981, vol. 37, pp. 71–86

The Life and Death of Mary Frith Commonly Called Moll Cutpurse, London 1612

Thomas, W. I., and F. Znaniecki, *The Polish Peasant in Europe and America*, The University of Chicago Press, Chicago 1927

Thornley, I. D., 'The Destruction of Santuary' in R. W. Seton-Watson (ed.), *Tudor Studies*, Longmans, London 1924

Thorpe, D., *et al.*, *Out of Care*, Allen and Unwin, London 1980

Tittle, C. R., 'Book Review of R. Fishman (1977) Criminal Recidivism in New York City: An Evaluation of the Impact of Rehabilitation and Diversion Services', *Contemporary Sociology*, 1979

Tolchin, M., 'Jails Run by Private Concern Force it to Face Questions of Accountability' *The New York Times*, 19 February, 1985a, p. A15

Tolchin, M., 'Experts Foresee Adverse Effects From Private Control of Prisons' *The New York Times*, 17 September, 1985b, p. A17

Tolchin, M., 'Prospects of Privately Run Prisons Divide Pennsylvania Legislators', *The New York Times*, 15 December, 1985c, p. 78

Tolchin, M., 'Bar Group Urges Halt to Privately Run Jails', *The New York Times*, 12 February 1986, p. A28

Travis, C., and C. Wade, *The Longest War: Sex Differences in Perspective*, Harcourt, Brace Jovanovich Publishers, New York 1984

Trubek, D., 'Critical Legal Studies and Empiricism', *Stanford Law Review*, 1984, vol. 36, no. 1–2, pp. 575–622

Tulkens, H., *Some Developments in Penal Policy and Practice in Holland*, Barry Rose, NACRO, London 1979

Turk, A. T., 'Law as a Weapon in Social Conflict', *Social Problems*, 1976, vol. 23, no. 3, pp. 276–291

Turner, J. H., and J. Starnes, *American Society: Problems of Structure*, 2nd edn, Harper and Row, New York 1976

Unger, R. M., *Law in Modern Society*, The Free Press, New York 1976

United States Bureau of Justice, *Prisons and Prisoners*, US Government Printing Office, Washington DC 1980

United States Bureau of Justice, *Prisoners in State and Federal*

Institutions on December 31, 1982, NCJ 93311 12/84, Washington DC 1983

United States Department of Commerce, '*State Finances, 1970*, US Government Printing Office, Washington DC 1971

United States Department of Commerce, '*State Finances, 1980*, US Government Printing Office, Washington DC 1981

United States Department of Justice, *Sourcebook of Criminal Justice Statistics*, Washington DC, 1979

United States Department of Justice, *Sourcebook of Criminal Justice Statistics*, Washington DC, 1980

United States House of Representatives, 'Report of the United States Commissioner of Labour', 1887 House Executive Documents, 49th Congress, Second Session, no. 1, Part 5, pp. 269–339

United States Senate Committee on Governmental Affairs, Subcommittee on Oversight of Government Management, *Oversight of Computer Matching to Detect Fraud and Mismanagement in Government Programmes*, US Government Printing Office, Washington DC 1982

United State v. Harrison, 1982, 667 F2d 1158 Fourth Circuit Court of Appeals

Vaage, O., *Krittik av Journalistikk Hovedrapport* (Critique of Journalism: Main Report), Norsk Journalisthogskole, Oslo 1985

Van den Haag, E., *Punishing Criminals: Concerning a Very Old and Painful Question*, Basic Books, New York 1975

Van Putten, T. and J. E. Spar, 'The Board and Care Home: Does it Deserve a Bad Press?' *Hospital and Community Psychiatry*, 1979, vol. 30, pp. 461–4

Vaughn, D., 'Crime Between Organisations: Implications for Victimology' in G. Geis and E. Stotland (eds), *White Collar Crime: Theory and Research*, Sage Publications, Beverly Hills CA 1980, pp. 77–97

Velarde, A. J., 'Becoming Prostituted: The Decline of the Massage Parlor Profession and the Masseuse', *British Journal of Criminology*, 1975, vol. 15, no. 3, pp. 251–263

Vintner, R. D., G. Downs and J. Hall, *Juvenile Corrections in the States: Residential Programs and Deinstitutionalisation, A Preliminary Report*, National Assessment of Juvenile Corrections, University of Michigan 1975

Von Hirsch, A., *Doing Justice: The Choice of Punishment*, Hill and Wang, New York 1976

Vorenberg, E. W., and J. Vorenberg, 'Early Diversion For the Criminal Justice System: Practice in Search of a Theory', in L. E. Ohlin (ed.), *Prisoners in America*, Prentice-Hall, Englewood Cliffs NJ 1973

Wade, J., *A Treatise on the Police and Crimes of the Metropolis*, reprinted edition, Patterson Smith, Montclair, New Jersey 1972 (originally 1829)

Wall Street Journal, 7 July 1982

Waller, I., and J.B.L. Chan, 'Prison Use: A Canadian and International Comparison', *Criminal Law Quarterly*, 1974, vol. 17, pp. 47–71

Waltzer, M., 'The Politics of Michel Foucault', *Dissent*, 1983, vol. 30, pp. 481–490

Warner, R., *Recovery From Schizophrenia: Psychiatry and Political Economy*, Routledge and Kegan Paul, London 1985

Warren, C.A.B., 'New Forms of Social Control: The Myth of Deinstitutionalisation', *American Behavioural Scientist*, 1981, vol. 24, no. 6, July/August, pp. 724–740

Weber, M., *The Protestant Ethic and the Spirit of Capitalism*, Unwin Paperbacks, London 1985 (originally 1904 in German)

Weis, J., and J. Henney, 'Crime and Criminals in the United States', in S.L. Messinger and E. Bittner (eds), *Criminology Review Yearbook*, Sage, Beverly Hills, California 1979

Weiss, R. 'The Community and Prevention' in E. Johnson (ed.), *Handbook on Crime and Deliquency Prevention*, forthcoming

Weiss, R., 'The Emergence and Transformation of Private Detective Industrial Policing in the United States, 1850–1940', *Crime and Social Justice*, 1978, vol. 9, Spring-Summer, pp. 35–48

Weiss, R., 'The Community and Prevention' in E. Johnson (ed.), *Handbook on Crime and Delinquency Prevention*, Greenwood Press, Westport Connecticut 1987

Weisberg, D.K., *Children of the Night: A Study of Adolescent Prostitution*, D.C. Heath, Lexington 1985

Weitz, S., *Sex Roles: Biological, Psychological and Social Foundations*, Oxford University Press, New York 1977

Wellford, C., 'Labelling Theory and Criminology: An Assessment', *Social Problems*, 1975, vol. 22, no. 3, pp. 332–345

Western, J., *The English Militia in the Eighteenth Century*, Routledge Kegan Paul, London 1965

Westin, A., and M. Baker, *Databanks in a Free Society: Computers, Record-Keeping and Privacy*, Quadrangle, New York 1972

'When Computers Track Criminals', *Technology Review*, 1983, vol. 86, no. 3, April, pp. 75–76

White, M.G., *Social Thought in America: The Revolt Against Formalism*, Beacon, Boston 1947

Whiteside, T., *Computer Capers*, New American Library, New York 1978

Whitmer, G., 'From Hospitals to Jails: The Fate of California's

Deinstitutionalised Mentally Ill', *American Journal of Orthopsychiatry*, 1980, vol. 50, January, pp. 65–75

Wilkins, L.T., *Consumerist Criminology*, Heinemann, London, 1982

Willer, D., and J. Willer, *Systematic Empiricism: Critique of Pseudo Science*, Prentice-Hall, Englewood Cliffs NJ 1973

Williams, P., 'The Northern Borderland Under the Early Stuarts' in H.F. Bell and R.L. Ollards (eds), *Historical Essays 1600–1750*, Adam and Charles Black, London 1963

Williams, R., 'Advertising: The Magic System' in R. Williams (ed.), *Culture and Society*, Oxford University Press, New York 1958, pp. 170–212

Wilson, J.Q., *Thinking About Crime*, Basic Books, New York 1975

Wilson, J.Q., 'What Works? Revisited', *Public Interest*, 1980, no. 61, Autumn, pp. 3–17

Witty, C.J., *Mediation and Society: Conflict Management in Lebanon*, Academic Press, New York 1980

Wolfe, A., *The Limits of Legitimacy*, Free Press, New York 1977

Wolfe, A., 'Sociology, Liberalism and The New Right', *New Left Review*, 1981, no. 128, July/August, pp. 3–27

World Health Organisation, *Changing Patterns in Mental Health Care*, World Health Organisation Regional Office for Europe, Copenhagen 1980

Wrigley, E.A., A Sample Model of London's Importance in Changing English Society and Economy', *Past and Present*, 1967, vol. 37, July, pp. 44–70

Young, J., *Realist Criminology*, Gower, Aldershot 1987

Young, J., 'The Failure of Criminology: The Need for Radical Realism' in R. Matthews and J. Young (eds), *Confronting Crime*, Sage, London 1986

Zedlewski, E., 'The Economics of Disincarceration', UNIJ Reports no. 185, US Department of Justice, Washington DC 1984, pp. 4–7

Zimring, F.E., 'Measuring the Impact of Pretrial Diversion From the Criminal Justice System', *University of Chicago Law Review*, 1974, vol. 41, pp. 224–241

Zinn, H., *A People's History of the United States*, Harper Colophon, New York 1980

Name index

Subject index